1991

TEACHING READING IN TODAY'S ELEMENTARY SCHOOLS

Fourth Edition

TEACHING READING IN TODAY'S ELEMENTARY SCHOOLS

Paul C. Burns

late of University of Tennessee at Knoxville

Betty D. Roe

Tennessee Technological University

Elinor P. Ross

Tennessee Technological University

HOUGHTON MIFFLIN COMPANY   BOSTON
Dallas   Geneva, Illinois
Palo Alto   Princeton, New Jersey

*Dedicated to Michael H. Roe
and James R. Ross*

Cover illustration by Lance Hidy, © 1982.

Chapter opener photo credits:
Chapter 1: © Elizabeth Crews • Chapter 2: © Carol Palmer • Chapter 3: © Elizabeth Crews • Chapter 4: © Susan Lapides • Chapter 5: © Elizabeth Crews • Chapter 6: © Cary Wolinsky/Stock, Boston • Chapter 7: © Elizabeth Hamlin/Stock, Boston • Chapter 8: © Michal Heron/Woodfin Camp • Chapter 9: © Ulrike Welsch • Chapter 10: © Jim Cronk/Lightwave • Chapter 11: © Jean-Claude Lejeune • Chapter 12: © Paul Conklin • Line drawing on page 43 rerendered from an original by Michelle R. Banks, Memphis State University.

Text credits:
Excerpt on p. 18 from Charles R. Cooper and Anthony R. Petrosky, "A Psycholinguistic View of the Fluent Reading Process," in *Journal of Reading*, December 1976. Reprinted with permission of Cooper and Petrosky and the International Reading Association.
Excerpt on pp. 18–19 from Charles R. Cooper and Anthony R. Petrosky, "A Psycholinguistic View of the Fluent Reading Process," in *Journal of Reading*, December 1976. Reprinted with permission of Cooper and Petrosky and the International Reading Association.

Printed in the U.S.A.

Library of Congress Catalog Number: 87-80577

ISBN: 0-395-35757-8

ABCDEFGHIJ-RM-9543210-8987

Contents

Eclectic Approaches 338

Classroom Example 339

7 READING/STUDY SKILLS 348

Study Methods 350

SQ3R 350 • SQRQCQ 351 • Other Techniques to Improve Retention 352 • Test-taking Skills 353

Flexibility of Reading Habits 355

Adjustment of Approach 355 • Adjustment of Rate 355 • ReFlex Action 357

Locating Information 358

Books 358 • Reference Books 361 • Libraries 371

Organizational Skills 373

Note-taking 373 • Outlining 375 • Summarizing 378

Metacognition 380

Graphic Aids 381

Maps 382 • Graphs 384 • Tables 387 • Illustrations 387

8 READING IN THE CONTENT AREAS 392

Content Texts Compared to Basal Readers 394

Readability 395

Cloze Tests 396 • Readability Formulas 399

General Techniques for Content Area Reading 401

Directed Reading-Thinking Activity (DRTA) 401 • Directed Inquiry Activity (DIA) 402 • Guided Reading Procedure 402 • The SAVOR Procedure 404 • Oral Reading Strategy 405 • Question-Only Strategy 405 • Learning Text Structure 405 • Language Experience Approach (LEA) and Other Writing Techniques 406 • Feature Analysis Plus Writing 407 • Webs Plus Writing 408 • Concept-Text-Application (CTA) Approach 409 • K-W-L Teaching Model 409 • Study Guides 409 • Manipulative Materials 411 • Integrating Approaches 412

Specific Content Areas 412

Language Arts 413 • Social Studies 417 • Mathematics 424 • Science and Health 428

Preface

Audience and Purpose

This book has been written primarily for the preservice elementary school classroom teacher. It is intended for a first course in reading methods. Inservice classroom teachers and teachers preparing to become reading specialists may also use the book as part of an introductory reading education course. Although primarily oriented to teachers, the book is also suitable for administrators, because the text contains much information helpful in the administration and direction of a school's reading program.

This book is designed to familiarize teachers with all the important aspects of elementary reading instruction. It presents much practical information about the process of teaching reading. Theoretical background and the research base behind suggestions have also been included to give the teacher or prospective teacher a balanced perspective.

The primary aim of the book is to prepare teachers for developing fluent reading in their students and for fostering the enjoyment of reading in their classrooms. The large amount of the school day spent on reading instruction in the primary grades makes this content especially important to the primary grade teacher. In the intermediate grades students must handle reading assignments in the content areas as well as in reading periods. Our book—in particular the chapters on content area reading and study skills—also contains much information that can help teachers teach the skills appropriate for content area reading tasks.

Revisions in This Edition

This book has been extensively revised. New understandings about the reading process have been included throughout the book, and the research base for these understandings has been fully updated. A number of topics of recent concern, such as metacognition and the reading-writing connection, are each addressed in several chapters. Teacher modeling of reading skills during instruction is described and recommended, and sample "think alouds" are offered. Example facsimiles of elementary school reading materials and exemplary activities continue to be plentiful; they have been revised and updated throughout.

There is a new chapter devoted entirely to meaning vocabulary in this edition. Concept development and a multitude of vocabulary development techniques, such as semantic maps and word webs, semantic feature analysis, and computer techniques, receive attention.

Other chapters have undergone thorough revision. Among the most significantly revised is the comprehension chapter, which has been expanded to include new or fuller treatment of schema theory; anaphora; interpretation of figurative language; prereading, during reading, and postreading activities; and questioning techniques. The introductory chapter now contains a discussion of interactive reading theories and additional principles of teaching reading. The prereading chapter has been expanded to include discussions of metalinguistic awareness; emergent literacy; phonemic segmentation; and timely recommendations related to pre-first-grade reading instruction.

The chapter on major approaches to reading instruction offers expanded treatment of the basal reader approach; the language experience approach, including discussion of computer applications and implementation ideas for intermediate grades; and computer approaches. Information on test-taking skills, fuller treatment of summarizing and reading rate, and many general techniques for content area reading have been added to the chapters on study skills and on content area reading.

The literary appreciation chapter presents a strengthened and up-to-date discussion of the integration of reading and the language arts program. In the chapter on assessment, treatment of process-oriented assessment has been added, and test listings have been updated and expanded. Teacher effectiveness is now thoroughly discussed in the chapter on classroom management, as is managing computer-assisted instruction. Expanded coverage of children who have English as a second language is included in the chapter on readers with special needs; many materials to be used with exceptional children are cited.

Coverage and Features

The first chapter discusses the components of the reading act, theories related to reading, and principles of teaching reading. Chapter 2 presents information on reading readiness and a multitude of activities useful in developing readiness. The next three chapters are devoted to techniques of teaching word recognition, meaning vocabulary, and comprehension skills; major approaches to reading instruction are described in Chapter 6. Chapter 7 discusses methods of teaching reading/study skills, and Chapter 8 tells how to present the reading skills necessary for reading in individual content areas. Chapter 9 deals with literary appreciation and recreational reading. Assessment of pupil progress is discussed in Chapter 10, and classroom management and organization are treated in Chapter 11. Chapter 12 covers the teaching of reading to exceptional students. The Appendix contains answers to Test Yourself quizzes.

This text provides an abundance of practical activities and strategies for improving students' reading performance. Illustrative lesson plans, learning-center ideas, worksheets, independent task or activity cards, and instructional games are all presented in this text. Thus, it should continue to be a valuable reference for inservice teachers.

In order to make this text easy to study, we have included the following features:

Introductions to each chapter help readers develop a mental set for reading the chapter and give them a framework into which they can fit the ideas they will read about.

Setting Objectives, part of the opening material in each chapter, provides objectives to be met as the chapter is read.

Key Vocabulary, a list of important terms with which readers should be familiar, is included to help students focus on key chapter concepts.

Self-Checks are keyed to the objectives and are located at strategic points *throughout* each chapter to help readers check whether they have grasped the ideas presented.

Test Yourself, a section at the end of each chapter, includes questions that check retention of the material in the chapter as a whole; these questions may also serve as a basis for discussion.

Self-Improvement Opportunities are activities in which the readers can participate in order to further their understanding of the ideas and methods presented in the chapter.

A *Glossary* contains meanings of specialized terms used in this book.

Acknowledgments

We are indebted to many people for their assistance in the preparation of this text. In particular, we would like to recognize the contribution that Paul C. Burns made to the first and second editions of this book. Some of his ideas and much of his organization have been incorporated in this text. His death in the summer of 1983 was a loss to us as his colleagues and friends and a loss to the field of reading as well. As a prolific writer and an outstanding teacher, his contributions to reading education were exceptional.

Although we would like to acknowledge the many teachers and students whose inspiration was instrumental in the development of this book, we cannot name all of them. We offer grateful recognition to the following reviewers, whose constructive advice and criticism helped greatly in the writing and revision of the manuscript:

Dr. Jack Bagford
University of Iowa

Dr. Norman E. Koch
Western Oregon State College

Dr. J. O. Miller
Central Missouri State

Dr. Lawrence L. Smith
State University, College of Buffalo

Dr. Virginia B. Stanley
Clemson University (South Carolina)

Dr. Anne E. Wolf
Baruch College (New York)

In addition, appreciation is expressed to those who have granted permission to use sample materials or citations from their respective works. Credit for these contributions has been given in the footnotes.

Betty D. Roe
Elinor P. Ross

Chapter 1

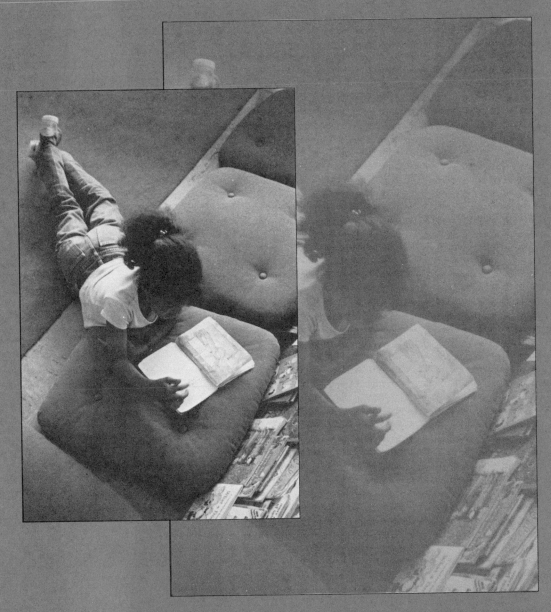

The Reading Act

Introduction

Attempts to define reading have been numerous. This is partly because of the complexity of the reading act, which includes two major components—a process and a product—each of which is complicated. Teachers need to be aware of these components and of their different aspects in order to respond effectively to reading needs. In addition, they will find that familiarity with some theories related to the reading process and with important principles of teaching reading can be helpful in planning reading activities.

This chapter analyzes the components of the reading act and discusses the reading product and process. It describes three theories about the reading process and presents some sound principles for reading instruction, with explanatory comments.

Setting Objectives

When you finish reading this chapter, you should be able to

1. Discuss the reading product.
2. Describe the reading process.
3. Explain three types of theories of the reading process: subskill, psycholinguistic, and interactive.
4. Name some principles upon which effective reading instruction is based.

Key Vocabulary

Pay close attention to these terms when they appear in the chapter.

affective	modality	schemata
auditory acuity	motivation	self-concept
auditory discrimination	paired-associate	semantic cues
bottom-up models	learning	subskill theories
fixations	perception	syntax
grapheme	phoneme	tactile
interactive theories	psycholinguistic	top-down models
kinesthetic	theories	vicarious experience
metacognitive	regressions	visual acuity
strategies	reinforcement	visual discrimination

COMPONENTS OF THE READING ACT

The reading act is composed of two parts: the reading process and the reading product. By *process* we mean a method, a movement toward an end that is

accomplished by going through all the necessary steps. Eight aspects of the
reading process combine to produce the reading product. When they blend and interact harmoniously, good communication between the writer and reader results. But the sequences involved in the reading process are not always exactly the same, and they are not always performed in the same way by different readers. Example 1.1 is a diagram of the reading act, listing the various aspects of the process that lead to the product.

A *product* is the consequence of utilizing certain aspects of a process in an appropriate sequence. The product of reading is the communication of thoughts and emotions by the writer to the reader. Because your main goal as a teacher of reading is to help students achieve the reading product, we will discuss the reading product first.

The Reading Product

As we have pointed out, the product of the reading act is communication, the reader's understanding of ideas that have been put in print by the writer. A wealth of knowledge is available to people living today because we are able to read material that others wrote in the past. Americans can read of events and accomplishments that occur in other parts of the globe. Knowledge of great discoveries does not have to be laboriously passed from person to person by word of mouth; such knowledge is available to all who can read.

As well as being a means of communicating generally, reading is a means of communicating specifically with friends and acquaintances who are nearby. A note may tell a child that Mother has gone to town, or it can inform a babysitter about where to call in case of an emergency. A memo from a person's employer can specify which work must be done.

Reading can be a way of sharing another person's insights, joys, sorrows, or creative endeavors. Being able to read can make it possible for a person to find places he or she has never visited before (through maps, directional signs), to take advantage of bargains (through advertisements), or to avert

▶ **EXAMPLE 1.1:** The Reading Act

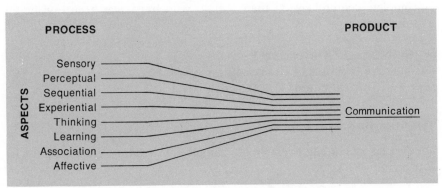

disaster (through warning signs). What would life be like without this vital means of communication?

Communication is dependent upon comprehension, which is affected by all aspects of the reading process. Word recognition skills, the associational aspect of the reading process, are essential, but comprehension involves much more than decoding symbols into sounds; the reader must derive meaning from the printed page. Some people have mistakenly considered reading to be a single skill, exemplified by pronouncing words, rather than a combination of many skills that lead to deriving meaning. Thinking of reading in this way may have fostered the unfortunate educational practice of using a reading period for extended drill on word calling, in which the teacher asks each child to "read" aloud while classmates follow in their books. When a child cannot pronounce a word, the teacher may supply the pronunciation or ask another child to do so. When a child miscalls, or mispronounces, a word, the teacher usually corrects the mistake. Some pupils may be good pronouncers in such a situation, but are they readers? They may be able to pronounce words beautifully and still not understand anything they have read. Although pronunciation is important, reading involves much more.

Teachers who realize that all aspects of the reading process have an effect on comprehension of written material will be better able to diagnose children's reading difficulties and as a result offer sound instructional programs based on children's needs. Faulty performance related to any of the aspects of the reading process may result in an inferior product or in no product at all. Three examples of this condition follow.

1. If a child does not clearly see the graphic symbols on a page, he or she may be unable to recognize them.
2. If a child has developed an incorrect association between a grapheme (written symbol) and a phoneme (sound), incorrect word recognition will result and will hamper comprehension.
3. If a child does not have much experience in the area written about, he or she will comprehend the passage less completely than one who has a rich background. For example, a child who has lived on or visited a farm will understand a passage concerning farm life with greater ease and more complete comprehension than a child who has never been outside an urban area.

✔ **Self-Check: Objective 1**
Discuss the product of the reading process.
(See Self-Improvement Opportunities 1 and 2.)

The Reading Process

The process of reading is extremely complex. In reading, children must be able to

1. perceive the symbols set before them (sensory aspect);
2. interpret what they see as symbols or words (perceptual aspect);
3. follow the linear, logical, and grammatical patterns of the written words (sequential aspect);
4. relate words back to direct experiences to give the words meaning (experiential aspect);
5. make inferences from and evaluate the material (thinking aspect);
6. remember what they learned in the past and incorporate new ideas and facts (learning aspect);
7. recognize the connections between symbols and sounds, between words and what they represent (associational aspect);
8. deal with personal interests and attitudes that affect the task of reading (affective aspect).

Reading seems to fit into the category of behavior called a skill, which has been defined by Frederick McDonald as an act that "demands complex sets of responses—some of them cognitive, some attitudinal, and some manipulative" (Downing, 1982, p. 535). Understanding, rather than simple motor behavior, is essential. The key element in skill development is *integration* of the processes involved, which "is learned through practice. Practice in integration is only supplied by performing the whole skill or as much as is a part of the learner's 'preliminary fix.' . . . one learns to read by reading" (Downing, 1982, p. 537). This idea is supported by a great deal of current opinion. Whereas reading can be broken down into subskills, reading takes place only when these subskills are put together into an integrated whole. Performing subskills individually is not reading (Anderson et al., 1985).

Not only is the reading process complex, but each aspect of the process is complex as well. The whole process, as shown in Example 1.2, could be likened to a series of books, with each aspect represented by a hefty volume. A student would have to understand the information in every volume to have a complete grasp of the subject. Therefore, the student would have to integrate information from *all* of the volumes in order to perform effectively in the area of study. The *series* would be more important than any individual volume.

Sensory Aspects of Reading

The reading process begins with a sensory impression, either visual or tactile. A normal reader perceives the printed symbol visually; a blind reader uses the tactile sense. (Discussion of the blind reader is beyond the scope of this text, although the visually handicapped reader is discussed in Chapter 12, "Readers with Special Needs.") The auditory sense is also very important, since a beginning stage in reading is the association of printed symbols with spoken language. A person with poor auditory discrimination may find some reading skills, especially those involved with phonics, difficult to master.

6 ▶ **EXAMPLE 1.2:** Aspects of the Reading Process

Teaching
Reading in
Today's
Elementary
Schools

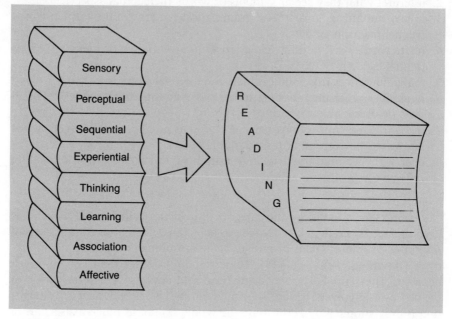

Vision   Many visual demands are imposed upon children by the reading act. They must be able to focus their eyes on a page of print that is generally fourteen to twenty inches away from them, as well as on various signs and visual displays that may be twenty or more feet away. In addition to having visual acuity (or sharpness of vision), children must learn to discriminate visually among the graphic symbols (letters or words) that are used to represent spoken language. Reading is impossible for a person who cannot differentiate between two unlike graphic symbols. Because of these demands, teachers should be aware of how a child's sight develops and of the physical problems that can handicap reading.

Babies are farsighted at birth and gradually become less farsighted as they mature. By the time they are five or six years old, most children have attained 20/20 vision; however, some do not reach this point until later. Several authorities feel that the eyes of many children are not ready for the demands of reading until the children are eight years old. To complicate matters, visual deterioration begins almost as soon as 20/20 vision is attained. Some research indicates that approximately 30 percent of people who once had 20/20 vision no longer have it in both eyes by age seventeen (Leverett, 1957).

Farsighted first graders may learn reading skills more easily by working on charts and chalkboards than by using workbooks and textbooks. Teachers should avoid requiring farsighted children to do a great deal of uninterrupted reading, and they should also use large print for class handouts (Biehler and

Although nearsighted children may do well when working with books, they are often unable to see well enough to respond to directions or exercises written on charts or chalkboards.

Some children may have an eye disorder called astigmatism, which results in blurred vision. This problem, as well as the problems of nearsightedness and farsightedness, can generally be corrected by glasses.

If a child's eyes do not work well together, he or she may see two images instead of one. Sometimes when this occurs the child manages to suppress the image from one eye. If suppression continues over a period of time, he or she may lose sight in that eye entirely. If suppression occurs for only short periods, the child may be likely to lose the appropriate place on the page when reading and become confused and frustrated.

Eye movement during reading appears to the casual observer as a smooth sweep across a line of print. Actually, a person makes numerous stops, or *fixations,* when reading in order to take in the words and phrases and react to them. A high proportion of total reading time is spent on fixations; therefore, fixation time is closely related to speed of reading. Both the time and the frequency of fixations will vary according to the difficulty of the material. Easy material involves fewer and briefer fixations.

Eye movements back to a previously read word or phrase in order to reread are called *regressions.* Although they can become an undesirable habit, regressions are useful if the reader performs them to correct false first impressions.

It takes time for children to learn to move their eyes across a page in a left-to-right progression and to execute a return sweep from the end of one line to the beginning of the next line. This is a difficult maneuver. Those who have not yet mastered the process will find themselves rereading and skipping lines. Both of these activities hamper comprehension. Although teachers often attempt to correct faulty eye movements, such movements are more often *symptoms* of other problems (for example, poor muscle coordination or poor vocabulary) than *causes* of problems. When the other problems are removed, these symptoms usually disappear.

Hearing If a child cannot discriminate among the different sounds (phonemes) represented by graphic symbols, he or she will be unable to make the sound-symbol associations necessary for decoding unfamiliar words. Of course, before a child can discriminate among sounds, he or she must be able to hear them; that is, auditory acuity must be adequate. Deaf and hearing impaired children are deprived of some methods of word identification because of their disabilities. (See Chapter 12 for more information.)

Perceptual Aspects of Reading

Perception involves interpretation of the sensory impressions that reach the brain. Each person processes and reorganizes the sensory data according to his or her background of experiences. When a person is reading, the brain receives a visual sensation of words and phrases from the printed page. It recognizes and gives meaning to these words and phrases as it associates them with the reader's previous experience with the objects, ideas, or emotions represented. For this reason, a single text may be interpreted differently by readers with different backgrounds of experience (Anderson et al., 1985).

For example, the printed words *apple pie* have no meaning for a person until that person associates them with the object they represent. Perception of the term *apple pie* can result not only in a visual image of a pie but also in a recollection of its smell and taste. Of course, prior experience with the thing named by the word(s) is necessary for the person to make these associations.

Since different people have had different experiences with apple pies, and apple pies can smell, taste, and look many ways, people will attach different meanings to the words *apple pie*. Therefore, individuals will have slightly different perceptions when they encounter these or any other words. The clusters of information that people develop about things (such as apple pies), places (such as restaurants or airports), or ideas (such as justice or democracy) are sometimes referred to as *schemata*. Every person has many of these schemata. Recent theories describe reading comprehension as the act of relating textual information to existing schemata (Pearson et al., 1979). More information about this relationship is located in Chapter 5.

Visual Perception Visual perception involves identification and interpretation of size, shape, and relative position of letters and words. *Visual discrimination,* the ability to see likenesses and differences in visual forms, is an important part of visual perception because many letters and words are very similar in form but very different in pronunciation and meaning. Accurate identification and interpretation of words results from detecting the small variations in form. A child might have good visual acuity and not be able to discriminate well visually. Teachers can help children develop this skill through carefully planned activities (discussed in Chapter 2).

Auditory Perception Auditory perception involves *auditory discrimination*, detecting the likenesses and differences in speech sounds. Children must be able consciously to separate a phoneme (sound) from one spoken word and compare it with another phoneme separated from another word. Since many children have not developed the ability to do this well by the age of five or six years, a phonics-oriented beginning reading program can be very demanding (Pearson et al., 1979). As is true of visual discrimination, a child can have good auditory acuity and not be able to discriminate well auditorily. The skill can be taught, however. (Instructional activities for auditory discrimination are also discussed in Chapter 2.)

Sequential Aspects of Reading

Printed material that is written in English generally appears on a page in a left-to-right, top-to-bottom sequence. A person's eyes must follow this sequence in order to read. We pointed out earlier that readers occasionally regress, or look back to earlier words and phrases, as they read. While these regressions momentarily interrupt the reading process as the reader checks the accuracy of initial impressions, the reader eventually returns to the left-to-right, top-to-bottom sequence. This sequence is discussed in more detail in Chapter 2, as a part of prereading activities.

Reading is also a sequential process because oral language is strung together in a sequential pattern of grammar and logic. Since written language is a way of representing speech, it is expressed in the same manner. The reader must be able to follow the grammatical and logical patterns of spoken language in order to understand written language.

Experiential Background and Reading

As indicated in the section on perceptual aspects, meaning derived from reading is based upon the reader's experiential background. Children with rich background experiences have had more chances to develop understanding of the vocabulary and concepts they encounter in reading than have children with meager experiences. For example, a child who has actually been in an airport is more likely to be able to attach appropriate meaning to the word *airport* when he or she encounters it in a reading selection than a child who has not been to an airport. Direct experience with places, things, and processes described in reading materials makes understanding of the materials much more likely.

Vicarious (indirect) experiences are also helpful in conceptual development, although they are probably less effective than concrete experiences. Hearing other people tell of or read about a subject; seeing photos or a movie of a place, event, or activity; and reading about a topic are examples of vicarious experiences that can build concept development. Since vicarious experiences do not involve as many of the senses as do direct, concrete experiences, the concepts gained from them may be developed less fully.

Some parents converse freely with their children, read to them, tell them stories, show them pictures, and take them to movies and on trips. These parents are providing rich experiences. Other parents, for a variety of reasons, do not offer these experiences to their children. A child's experiential background may be affected by parental rejection, indifference, or overprotection, by frequent illness, by the use of a nonstandard dialect in the home, or by any number of other reasons. Consider an example of how overprotection can limit a child's experiences: a first-grade boy enters school unable to use scissors, to color, or to play games effectively. At home he has been denied the use of scissors so he will not hurt himself, the use of crayons so the house will not be marred, and permission to play outside or on the floor so he will not get dirty. This child's teacher will need to give him a great deal of help in order to build up his experiential background.

Teachers can help to broaden children's concrete experiences through field trips, displays of objects, and class demonstrations. They can also help by providing rich vicarious experiences, such as photographs, filmstrips, movies, records and tape recordings, many classroom discussions, and storytelling and story-reading sessions.

If reading materials contain vocabulary, concepts, and sentence structures that are unfamiliar to children, their teachers must help them develop the background necessary to understand the materials. Because the children's experiential backgrounds will differ, some will need more preparation for a particular selection than others will.

Teachers can help children learn the standard English found in most books by telling and reading stories, encouraging show-and-tell activities, leading or encouraging class discussions, utilizing language experience stories (accounts developed cooperatively by teacher and class members about interesting happenings), and encouraging dramatic play (enactment of roles or imitations of people or things). The new words encountered during field trips and demonstrations will also help.

Good readers can skillfully integrate information in the text with prior knowledge about the topic, but poor readers may either overemphasize the symbols in the text or rely too much on their prior knowledge of the topic. Poor readers who focus primarily on the text may produce nonsense words that look like the ones in the text. This occurs because such readers are not attempting to connect what they are reading to their experiences or to demand sense from reading. Poor readers who depend too much on prior knowledge may not make enough use of clues in the text to come close to the intended message (Anderson et al., 1985).

The Relationship Between Reading and Thinking

Reading is a thinking process. The act of recognizing words requires interpretation of graphic symbols. In order to comprehend a reading selection thoroughly, a person must be able to use the information to make inferences and read critically and creatively—to understand the figurative language, determine the author's purpose, evaluate the ideas presented, and apply the ideas to actual situations. All of these skills involve thinking processes.

Chambers and Lowry point out that

reading is more than merely recognizing the words for which certain combinations of letters bring about a correct recall. It includes the whole gamut of thinking responses: feeling and defining some need, identifying a solution for meeting the need, selecting from alternative means, experimenting with choices, rejecting or retaining the chosen route, and devising some means of evaluating the results. (1975, p. 114)

Teachers can guide students' thinking by asking appropriate questions. Students will be more likely to evaluate the material they are reading if they have been directed to do so. *How* and *why* questions are particularly good. However, questions can also limit thinking: if children are asked only to locate isolated facts, they will probably not be very concerned about main ideas in a passage or the purpose of the author. Test questions also affect the way students read assignments: if the usual test questions ask for evaluation or application of ideas, children will be apt to read the material more thoughtfully than if they are asked to recall isolated facts.

The Relationship of Reading to Learning

Reading is a complex act that must be learned. It is also a means by which further learning takes place. In other words, a person learns to read and reads to learn.

Learning to read depends upon motivation, practice, and reinforcement. Teachers must show children that being able to read is rewarding in many ways—that it increases success in school, helps in coping with everyday situations outside of school, bestows status, and provides recreation. Children are motivated by the expectation that they will receive these rewards, which then provide reinforcement to continue reading. Reinforcement encourages them to continue to make associations between printed words and the things to which they refer and to practice the skills they need for reading.

After children have developed some facility in reading, it becomes a means through which they learn other things. They read to learn about science, mathematics, social studies, literature, and all other subjects—a topic treated in depth in Chapter 8.

Reading as an Associational Process

Learning to read depends upon a number of types of associations. First, children learn to associate objects and ideas with spoken words. Next they are asked to build up associations between spoken words and written words. In some cases—for instance, when a child is presented with an unfamiliar written word paired with a picture of a familiar object—the child makes a direct association between the object or event and the written word, without an intermediate connection with the spoken word. In teaching phonics, teachers set up associations between graphic symbols (graphemes) and sounds (phonemes).

This type of learning is called *paired-associate learning.* In order to learn through association, a child must be presented with the written stimulus (for example, a printed letter or word) along with the response that the teacher expects it to elicit (the spoken sound or word). The child must pay attention during this process to both the stimulus and the expected response. Mediation takes place at this point.

Gagné defines mediation in this way: "Most investigators agree that the efficient learning of a two-element verbal association requires the use of an *intervening link,* having the function of *mediation* or coding. . . . Such links are usually implicit ones, that is, they occur inside the learner and do not appear as overt behavior" (1965, p. 99). The more such links a person has available, the faster he or she will be likely to learn.

The child should practice the association, even to the extent of "overlearning," and he or she should respond actively. Immediate reinforcement of correct answers and correction of wrong ones can help to establish the association. The sooner the teacher provides the reinforcement after the child makes the response, the more effective the reinforcement is likely to be. For example, the teacher might show a child the word *time* and tell him or her that this printed word is "time." Then the teacher would show the word again and ask the child to respond with the word "time." The teacher may drill the child in a variety of situations, requiring the child to respond with "time" each time that word is presented.

Practice in and of itself, however, is not always enough to set up lasting associations. The more meaningful an association is to a child, the more rapidly he or she will learn it. Children can learn the words after only a single exposure if the words have vital meaning for them (Ashton-Warner, 1963).

Affective Aspects of the Reading Process

Interests, attitudes, and self-concepts are three affective aspects of the reading process. These aspects influence how hard children will work at the reading task. For example, children who are interested in the materials presented to them will put forth much more effort in the reading process than will children who have no interest in the available reading materials.

In the same manner, children with positive attitudes toward reading will expend more effort on the reading process than children with negative attitudes will. Positive attitudes are nurtured in homes where the parents read for themselves and to their children and where reading materials are provided for children's use. In the classroom, teachers who enjoy reading, who seize every opportunity to provide pleasurable reading experiences for the children in their classes, and who allow time for recreational reading during school hours are encouraging positive attitudes. Reading aloud to the children regularly can also help accomplish this objective. Also, if a child's peers view reading as a positive activity, that child is likely to view reading in the same way.

Negative attitudes toward reading may be developed in a home environment where parents, for a variety of reasons, do not read. Children from such homes may be told that "reading is for sissies." They may bring such ideas to the classroom and spread them among children who have not previously been exposed to such attitudes. The "reading is for sissies" attitude affects everyone in the classroom negatively, regardless of gender.

Attitudes, or the affective domain, can be classified in five main levels (Krathwohl, Bloom, and Masia, 1964.) The first three, presented here with descriptions of how to recognize them in reading behavior, are most appropriate for the elementary school years.

Reading is not a single skill but a combination of many skills and processes in which a reader interacts with print to derive both meaning and pleasure from the written word.   (© Elizabeth Crews)

1. Receiving (attending): Students are at least willing to hear or study the information, as indicated by
   a. perceiving the reading concepts.
   b. reading on occasion, particularly on a topic of interest.
   c. identifying what they do not understand in reading.
2. Responding: Students will respond to the material being studied through
   a. completing reading assignments
   b. making an effort to figure out words and to understand what they read.
   c. seeking out reading opportunities.
3. Valuing: Students have a commitment to what they are learning and believe it has worth, as suggested by
   a. voluntarily working to improve their skills through wide reading.
   b. choosing reading when other activities are available.
   c. reading in their spare time.

Children with poor opinions of themselves may be afraid to attempt a reading task because they are sure that they will fail. They find it easier to avoid the task altogether and to develop "don't care" attitudes than to risk looking "dumb." Children with good self-concepts, on the other hand, are generally not afraid to attack a reading task, since they feel that they are going to be successful.

There are several ways to help children build positive self-concepts. First, in every possible way, the teacher should help the children feel accepted. A definite relationship exists between a teacher's attitude toward a child, as perceived by the child, and the child's self-concept. One of the best ways to make children feel accepted is for the teacher to share their interests, utilizing those interests in planning for reading instruction. The teacher should also accept children's contributions to reading activities even if they are not clearly stated.

Second, the teacher can help children feel successful by providing activities that are simple enough to guarantee satisfactory completion. For poorer readers, we recommend the language experience approach (see Chapter 6), as well as appropriate materials such as high-interest, low-vocabulary books.

Third, the teacher should avoid comparing a child with other pupils. Instead, children's reading progress should be compared with their own previous work. Private records of books read, skills mastered, or words learned are much better than public records in which one child consistently compares unfavorably with others.

Fourth, the teacher should minimize the focus that is put on the differences between reading groups to avoid giving children the idea that unless they are members of the top group they are not worthy people. Comparisons and competition among groups should be avoided, and the bases on which groups are formed should be varied.

↙ Self-Check: Objective 2

List the eight aspects of the reading process presented in this section and explain each one briefly. Reread the section to check your explanations.
(See Self-Improvement Opportunity 1.)

The Reading Process: Selected Theories

A theory is a set of assumptions or principles designed to explain phenomena. Research findings have resulted in many theories related to the reading process, but as R. J. Smith et al. have pointed out, no current theory adequately explains "all of the mysteries of reading" (1978, p. 19). Theories that are based on good research and practical observations can be helpful when you are planning reading instruction, but do not lose sight of the fact that current theories do not account for all aspects of this complex process. In addition, theories grow out of hypotheses—educated guesses. New information may be discovered that proves part or all of a theory invalid.

It would not be practical to try to present all of the theories related to reading in the introductory chapter of a survey textbook. Therefore, we have chosen to discuss three theoretical approaches, subskill, psycholinguistic, and interactive theories, to give you a feeling for the complexities inherent in choosing a theoretical stance. The choices that teachers make about types of instruction and emphases in instructional programs are affected by their theoretical positions concerning the reading process.

Subskill Theories

Some educators see reading as a set of subskills that children must master and integrate. They believe that, although good readers have learned and integrated these subskills so well that they use them automatically, beginning readers have not learned them all and may not integrate well those that they have learned. This situation results in slow, choppy reading for beginners and perhaps also in reduced comprehension, because the separate skills of word recognition take so much concentration. Teaching these skills until they become automatic and smoothly integrated is thus the approach that these educators take to reading instruction (Weaver and Shonhoff, 1984).

R. J. Smith et al. (1978) point out that teachers need to teach specific skills in order to focus instruction. Otherwise, instruction in reading would be reduced to assisted practice—a long, laborious trial-and-error approach. Weaver and Shonhoff suggest that

although some research suggests that *skilled* reading is a single, holistic process, there is no research to suggest that children can learn to read and develop reading skill if they are taught using a method that treats reading as if it were a single process. Therefore, for instructional purposes, it is probably best to think of reading as a set of interrelated subskills. (1984, p. 36)

Similarly, LaBerge and Samuels (1985) believe that a teacher watching a bright student learning to read may observe that the student is attaining one skill (reading) slowly. On the other hand, the same teacher watching a slow learner attempting to learn to read may observe that the student is slowly learning many skills (phonics, etc.). "This comes about because the child often must be given extensive training on each of a variety of tasks, such as letter discrimination, letter-sound training, blending, etc. In this manner a teacher becomes aware of the fact that letter recognition can be considered a skill itself" (p. 713).

Since fluent readers have mastered each of the subskills to the point where they are automatic and have made their integration automatic, they do not clearly see the dividing lines among these skills during their daily reading. "One of the hallmarks of the reader who learned the subskills rapidly is that he was least aware of them at the time, and therefore now has little memory of them as separate subskills" (LaBerge and Samuels, p. 714).

Proponents of the subskill theory are not, however, in agreement as to what subskills are involved. Most would present one list for decoding subskills (for example, knowledge of letter-sound correspondences and recognition of prefixes and suffixes) and another list for comprehension subskills (for example, identifying details and making inferences), but their sets of lists are rarely identical. In this textbook, we have identified the word recognition (Chapter 3) and comprehension (Chapters 4 and 5) subskills that we feel are most important.

A body of research supports the subskill theory. For example, Guthrie (1973) found that reading subskills correlated highly with each other for students who were good readers. These students seemed to have integrated the skills to produce a good reading product. The correlations among reading subskills for poor readers were low. These students seemed to be operating at a level of separate rather than integrated skills. Guthrie's findings led to the conclusion that "lack of subskill mastery and lack of integration of these skills into higher order units" were sources of disability among poor readers (Samuels and Schachter, 1984, p. 39).

LaBerge and Samuels's hierarchical model of perceptual learning suggests that

the sequence of learning is from distinctive features, to letters, to letter clusters, and to words. In the process of learning to recognize a letter, the student must first identify the features that comprise it. For the lower case letters *b*, *d*, *p*, and *q*, the features are a vertical line and a circle in a particular relationship to each other; that is, the circle may be high or low and to the left or right side of the vertical line. Having identified the parts and after an extended series of exposure to the letters, the learner sees it as a unit; that is, the parts are perceptually unitized. (Samuels and Schachter, 1984, p. 40)

This model illustrates the process by which students master smaller units before larger ones and integrate them into larger units after mastery. Many lists of decoding subskills include the ones mentioned here.

Samuels and Schachter (1984) report a supportive study in which Donald Shankweiler and Isabelle Liberman tried to determine how well a child's fluency in oral reading of paragraph material could be predicted from his or her ability to read selected words in tests. They found that "roughly 50 percent of the variability in oral reading of connected words is associated with how well one can read these words in isolation" (p. 40). In other words, a child's oral reading of connected discourse tended to be only as good as his or her oral reading of individual words. Recognition of words in isolation (sight words) is one decoding subskill. Since some research on perception and reading indicates that people do master smaller units before larger ones, teaching subskills (smaller units) rather than expecting students to learn to read without such instruction is supported.

Harry Silberman found that an experimental skill-based program for teaching beginning reading was not at first successful with all of the children in the program; although the brighter children acquired the reading skill, less bright children could not apply their knowledge to words that had not specifically been taught. Evaluators found that an important subskill had been omitted, and after the subskill was added to the program, all the children managed to master the transfer to words not specifically taught (Samuels and Schachter, 1984).

Singer (1985) identified systems that he felt were basic to the power of reading. These systems are "graphophonemics (matching word sounds); semantics (vocabulary); morphemics (suffixes); and reasoning ability, which includes conceptualization ability (mental age)" (p. 645). He also identified systems basic to speed of reading. They are "speed and span of perception (phrase perception discrimination), semantics (vocabulary), and reasoning (mental age). Each system is composed of a sequence of substrata factors" (p. 645). For example, Word Recognition in Context and Word Perception Discrimination underlie Phrase Perception Discrimination. Teachers using Singer's model would focus on the instructionally modifiable subskills represented in the model, such as matching word sounds, vocabulary, and suffixes.

Those who teach a set of subskills as a means of instructing children in reading generally do recognize the importance of practicing the subskills in the context of actual reading in order to ensure integration. But some teachers overlook this vital phase and erroneously focus only upon the subskills, overlooking the fact that they are the means to an end and not an end in themselves.

Psycholinguistic Theories

Psycholinguistic theories, as the name implies, are based on the disciplines of psychology and linguistics. Kenneth Goodman, a noted psycholinguist, describes reading as a psycholinguistic guessing game in which readers "select the fewest, most productive cues necessary to produce guesses which are right the first time." He points out the importance of the reader's ability to anticipate the material that he or she has not yet seen (Goodman, 1973, p. 31). He also points out that readers bring to their reading all of their accumulated experience, language development, and thought in order to anticipate meanings in the printed material (p. 34).

The contrast between subskill and psycholinguistic theories is apparent in this statement, which describes a psycholinguistic view:

Learning to read does not require memorization of letter names, or phonic rules, or large lists of words, all of which are in fact taken care of in the course of learning to read, and little of which will make sense to a child without some experience of reading. Nor is learning to read a matter of application to all manner of exercises and drills, which can only distract and perhaps even discourage a child from the business of learning to read. And finally learning to read is not a matter of a child relying upon instruction, because the essential skills of reading—namely the uses of nonvisual information—cannot be taught. (F. Smith, 1978, p. 179)

F. Smith, like other psycholinguists, believes that children learn to read as they learn to speak, by generating and testing hypotheses about the reading material and getting appropriate feedback. In addition, he believes that although reading cannot be taught, children can be given opportunities to learn. First they need to have people read to them, and then they need the chance to read for themselves, with help. The contrast between this position and the subskills approach is striking. Teaching a sequential set of subskills to be integrated into the reading process is vastly different from merely establishing conditions that will allow students to learn to read.

Psycholinguists point out that, although the ability to combine letters to form words is related to learning to read, it has little to do with the process of fluent reading. When a person reads for meaning, he or she does not always need to identify individual words. A person can comprehend a passage without having identified all of the words in it. The more experience a reader has had with language and the concepts presented, the fewer clues from visual configurations he or she will need to determine the meaning of the material. Fluent readers make frequent use of semantic (meaning) and syntactic (word-order) clues within the material as well. They engage in the following activities as they process print:

1. The reader discovers the distinctive features in letters, words, and meaning.
2. The reader takes chances—risks errors—in order to learn about printed text and to predict meaning.
3. The reader reads to identify meaning rather than to identify letters or words.
4. The reader guesses from context at unfamiliar words, or else just skips them.
5. The reader takes an active role, bringing to bear his or her knowledge of the world and of the particular topic in the text.
6. The reader reads as though he or she expects the text to make sense.
7. The reader makes use of redundancies—orthographic, syntactic, and semantic—to reduce uncertainty about meaning.
8. The reader maintains enough speed to overcome the limitations of the visual processing and memory systems.
9. The reader shifts approaches for special materials.
10. The reader shifts approaches depending on the purpose. (Cooper and Petrosky, 1976, pp. 191–95)

The reading process is described in the following way by psycholinguistic theorists:

the brain directs the eye to pick up visual information from the configurations on the page; once the information starts coming into the brain, the brain processes it for meaning using its prior knowledge of language (syntactical rules that lend themselves to prediction) and content. The initial incoming information, if we conceive of this model working in slow motion, resides in the visual configurations on the page. The bridge between the visual configurations (surface structure) and meaning (deep structure) is syntax, and the frame of reference for this entire process is the knowledge and experience already stored in the brain in memory. The final outcome of the process is the identification of meaning. Psycholinguistics, then, combines cognitive psychology and linguistics in order to analyze and understand the language and thinking process, including reading, as it occurs in humans. (Cooper and Petrosky, 1976, p. 185)

Psycholinguists point out the importance of syntax (word order in sentences) in decoding written material. In the English language certain syntactic or word-order clues are predictable. These clues are listed below.

1. adjective/noun sequence (happy children, tall buildings, intelligent woman)
2. verb/adverb sequence (walked slowly, talks rapidly, works quietly)
3. adverb/verb sequence (cheerfully gave, truthfully spoke, lovingly cared)
4. article/noun sequence (the toy, a top, an egg)
5. article/adjective/noun sequence (the friendly cow, the clever girl, the beautiful mountains)
6. verb/complement sequence (weighed ten pounds, served six years, had many friends)
7. preposition/article/noun sequence (into the woods, over the hill, inside the tent)
8. qualifier/adjective or adverb sequence (very tall, rather well, quite late)
9. possessive noun/noun sequence (dog's tail, Seward's folly, child's toy)

The following sentence patterns are common.

1. noun/verb (The boy ran.)
2. noun/verb/noun or noun/verb/adverb (Mary drove the tractor. Mary walked rapidly.)
3. noun/verb/noun/noun (Bill gave Bev a watch.)
4. noun/linking verb/noun or -/adjective or -/adverb (My boss is a tyrant. The apples were sweet. Ms. Jones was out.)

These basic sentence structures are commonly transformed in the following ways:

Negative: Terry is here. → Terry is not here.
Question: She is singing. → Is she singing?
Use of *there:* A pencil is in the desk. → There is a pencil in the desk.
Command: You rake the leaves. → Rake the leaves.
Passive: A baseball broke the window. → The window was broken by a baseball.
Possessive: Pat owns that dog. → That is Pat's dog.

The four common sentence patterns and six transformations cited above are a part of the speaking repertoire of most children; therefore, most children are prepared for encountering them in reading instructional materials. Other language structures that are not a part of children's speaking repertoires may appear in their reading materials. In the following cases, the teacher needs to be alert for possible difficulties in understanding:

Appositives: Mary, my aunt, came in.
Infinitives as sentence subjects: To exercise is healthy.
Conjunctive adverbs: Since it's raining, take your umbrella.
Paired conjunctions: Either he leaves or I do.
Clauses as sentence subjects: What you do is your business.
Absolute constructions: The meeting over, she left.

Children usually enjoy putting sets of words together to make sentences. In the beginning years of school, teachers can teach sentence patterns by showing examples rather than by attempting linguistic descriptions. Later they can ask children to identify sets of sentences or to build fragments into sentences according to some particular patterns. They can develop exercises in which sentences of varying patterns are compared; ask students to examine articles and stories for evidence of sentence patterns; and use excerpts from a child's own writing to provide examples of sentence patterns. For ideas on how to emphasize semantic cues, see the section on context clues in Chapter 4.

Canady (1980) has described some good classroom practices based upon a psycholinguistic view of the reading process.

1. Allow children to read an entire meaningful story without providing assistance. Encourage logical guesses, regressions to self-correct, and skipping words if necessary. After students have finished reading, have them tell what they remember.
2. Use the language experience approach.
3. Help children become aware that they are reading when they read labels, signs, or advertisements.
4. Let children learn reading skills as they read meaningful materials. Focus on reading as comprehension.

Weaver (1980) also recommends the language experience approach (see Chapter 6). In addition, she suggests using sustained silent reading and sharing and experiencing reading (both discussed in Chapter 9), as well as reading for a specific purpose (stressed throughout this book).

Interactive Theories

An interactive theoretical model of the reading process depicts reading as a combination of two types of processing—top-down (reader-based) and bottom-up (text-based)—in continuous interaction. In top-down processing, reading begins with the generation of hypotheses or predictions about the material by the reader, with the visual cues in the material being used to test these hypotheses as necessary (Walberg, Hare, and Pulliam, 1981). For instance, the reader of a folktale that begins with the words "Once upon a time there was a man who had three sons . . ." will form hypotheses about what will happen next. He or she may predict that there will be a task to perform or a beautiful princess to win over and that the oldest two sons will fail but the youngest will attain his goal. Because of these expectations, the reader may read the material fairly quickly, giving attention primarily to words that confirm the expectations. Close reading will occur only if the hypothesis formed is not confirmed and an atypical plot unfolds. Otherwise, the reader can skip many words while skimming for key words that move the story along.

Processing of print obviously cannot be totally top-down, because a reader has to begin by focusing on the print (Gove, 1983). Frank Smith's position, as described in the section on psycholinguistic theories, appears to fit well into the top-down camp. As was also pointed out in the section on psycholinguistic theories, Kenneth Goodman sees the reader as possessing a store of knowledge about the world, about language, and about print. He believes that the reader uses this knowledge to predict what the printed page contains and to confirm or refute the predictions. According to Goodman, reading the exact words on the page is less important than understanding the message (Otto, 1982). Although many people identify Goodman's theoretical position as top-down, Goodman claims that his model is interactive (Harris and Sipay, 1985).

In bottom-up processing, reading is initiated by examining the printed symbols and requires little input from the reader (Walberg, Hare, and Pulliam, 1981). As Gove says, "Bottom-up models assume that the translation process begins with print, i.e., letter or word identification, and proceeds to progressively larger linguistic units, phrases, sentences, etc., ending in meaning" (1983, p. 262). A reader using bottom-up processing might first sound out a word letter-by-letter and then pronounce it, consider its meaning in relationship to the phrase in which it is found, and so on. A reading teacher embracing this approach would expect a child to reproduce orally the exact words printed on the page. In Samuels's automaticity model, decoding is seen as a bottom-up process, whereas comprehension allows for top-down processing (Otto, 1982). Samuels believes that beginning readers must be able to decode automatically, without consciously giving attention to decoding, before attention is available for comprehension. Although many people classify Samuels's original model as a bottom-up model, Samuels does not do so himself. His modified model actually contains elements of both top-down and bottom-up processing, qualifying it as interactive (Harris and Sipay, 1985). Often, in fact, theoretical models have aspects of *both* bottom-up and top-down perspectives. Classification is based upon degree of emphasis on one position over another.

An interactive model assumes parallel processing of information from print and information from background knowledge. Recognition and comprehension of printed words and ideas are the result of using both types of information (Gove, 1983). However, not all interactive models agree about the degree of influence of each type of processing, about the kind of processing that initiates the reading process, or about whether or not the two types of processing occur simultaneously (Harris and Sipay, 1985).

Rumelhart's "early model postulated that, at least for skilled readers, top-down and bottom-up processing occur simultaneously. . . . Because comprehension depends on both graphic information and the information in the reader's mind, it may be obstructed when a critical skill or a piece of information is missing" (Harris and Sipay, 1985, p. 10). For example, a reader who is unable to use context clues may fail to grasp the meaning of an unfamiliar word that is central to understanding the passage; similarly, a reader who has no background knowledge about the topic may be unable to reconstruct the ideas that the author is trying to convey.

✔ Self-Check: Objective 3

Compare and contrast subskill, psycholinguistic, and interactive theories of the reading process.
(See Self-Improvement Opportunity 1.)

FOURTEEN PRINCIPLES OF TEACHING READING

Principles of teaching reading are generalizations about reading instruction based on research in the field of reading and observation of reading practices. The principles listed here are not all-inclusive; many other useful generalizations about teaching reading have been made in the past and will continue to be made in the future. However, the principles listed here are ones that we believe are most useful in guiding teachers in planning reading instruction.

Principle 1   Reading is a complex act with many factors that must be considered.

The discussion earlier in this chapter of the eight aspects of the reading process makes this principle clear. The teacher must understand all parts of the reading process if he or she is to plan reading instruction wisely.

Principle 2   Reading is the interpretation of the meaning of printed symbols.

If a person does not derive meaning from a passage, he or she has not been reading, even if the person has pronounced every word correctly. Chapters 4 and 5 focus upon obtaining meaning from reading materials.

Principle 3   Reading involves constructing the meaning of a written passage.

"In addition to obtaining information from the letters and words in a text, reading involves selecting and using knowledge about people, places, and things, and knowledge about texts and their organization. A text is not so much a vessel containing meaning as it is a source of partial information that enables the reader to use already-possessed knowledge to determine the intended meaning" (Anderson et al., 1985, p. 8).

Readers construct the meanings of passages they read by using both the information conveyed by the text and their prior knowledge, which is based upon their past experiences. The way different readers construct meaning will obviously vary somewhat as their backgrounds of experience vary. Some readers will not have enough background knowledge to understand a text, and others may fail to make good use of the knowledge they have (Anderson et al., 1985). For example, a text may mention the importance of mountains in isolating a group of people living in them. Students familiar with mountainous areas will picture steep grades and rough terrain, which make road building difficult, and will understand the source of the isolation, although it is never mentioned in the text.

Principle 4   There is no one correct way to teach reading.

Some methods of teaching reading work better for some children than for others. Each child is an individual who learns in his or her own way. Some are visual learners; some are auditory learners; some are kinesthetic learners. Some need to be instructed through a combination of modalities, or avenues of perception, in order to learn. The teacher should differentiate instruction to fit the diverse needs of children in the class. Of course, some methods also work better for some teachers than they do for others. Teachers need to be acquainted with a variety of methods so they can help all of their pupils. Chapter 6 covers a number of approaches to reading instruction.

Principle 5   Learning to read is a continuing process.

Children learn to read over a long period of time, acquiring more advanced reading skills after they master prerequisite skills. Even after they have been introduced to all reading skills, refinement continues. No matter how old people are, or how long they have been out of school, they can continue to refine their reading skills. Reading skills require practice. If people do not practice, the skills deteriorate; if they practice, their skills continue to develop.

Principle 6   Students should be taught word recognition skills that will allow them to unlock the pronunciations and meanings of unfamiliar words independently.

Children cannot memorize all the words they will meet in print. Therefore, they need to learn techniques of figuring out unfamiliar words so that they can read when the assistance of a teacher, parent, or friend is not available. Chapter 3 focuses on word recognition skills that children need.

Principle 7   The teacher should diagnose each student's reading ability and use the diagnosis as a basis for planning instruction.

Teaching all children the same reading lessons and hoping to deal at one time or another with all of the different pupils' difficulties is a shotgun approach and should be avoided. Such an approach wastes the time of those children who have attained the skills that are currently being emphasized and may not ever meet some of the desperate needs of other children. Teachers can avoid this approach by using standardized and teacher-made tests to pinpoint the strengths and weaknesses of each individual in the classroom. Then they can divide the children into needs groups and teach them what will really be of help to them, or give each of them an individual course of instruction. Chapter 10 describes many useful tests.

Principle 8   Reading and the other language arts are closely interrelated.

Reading—the interaction between a reader and written language, through which the reader tries to reconstruct the writer's message—is closely related to all other major language arts (listening, speaking, and writing). Learning to read should be treated as an extension of the process of learning spoken language, a process that generally takes place in the home with little failure if children are given normal language input and feedback on their efforts to use language. Extensive input of natural language, opportunities to respond to this language, and feedback on appropriateness of responses provide children with a good learning environment (Hart, 1983).

A special relationship exists between listening and reading, which are *receptive* phases of language, as opposed to the *expressive* phases of speaking and writing. Mastering listening skills is important in learning to read, for direct association of sound, meaning, and word form must be established from the start. The ability to identify sounds heard at the beginning, middle, or end of a word and the ability to discriminate among sounds are essential to the successful phonetic analysis of words. Listening skills also contribute to interpretation of reading material.

Students' listening comprehension is generally superior to their reading comprehension in the elementary school years, particularly with easy materials. Listening and reading become more equal in both word recognition rate and in word-per-minute rate later on. Not until the latter part of the sixth or the seventh grade does reading proficiency reach the stage where students prefer reading to listening in many learning situations. This implies that it is profitable to present instruction orally in the elementary school. Generally, more advanced children prefer to learn by reading; slower ones prefer to learn by listening, particularly when the concepts and vocabulary are especially difficult. While reading and listening are not identical and each has its own advantages, there are many ways in which they are alike. Teachers must be aware of these similarities so they can provide efficient instruction.

One of the most important principles of reading instruction stresses the interrelationship of reading and the other language arts, including the receptive language skill of listening comprehension.   (© Jim Cronk/Lightwave)

People learn to speak before they learn to read and write. Through experience with their environments, they begin to associate oral symbols or words with certain people, places, things, and ideas. Children's reading vocabularies are generally composed largely of words in their speaking vocabularies. These are words for which they have previously developed concepts and words that they can comprehend.

The connection between reading and writing is particularly strong. Both reading and writing are basically constructive processes. Readers must construct or attempt to reconstruct the message behind written text. Their purposes for reading will affect the result of the reading activity, as will their knowledge about the world and about written language. Because of their differing purposes and backgrounds of experience, not all readers will interpret the same passage in the same way. Evaluation of the accuracy of the message construction takes place as readers monitor their reading processes. Revision of the constructed meaning may take place if the need is apparent.

Starting with purposes for writing that affect the choice of ideas and the way these ideas are expressed, writers work to create written messages for others to read. In completing the writing task, they draw upon their past experiences and their knowledge of writing conventions. As they work, they tend to read and review their material in order to evaluate its effectiveness and to revise it, if necessary.

One means of relating early writing experiences to reading experiences, the language experience approach, is described in Chapter 6. Writing is also sometimes used as a follow-up or enrichment activity in basal reading lessons.

The skills needed for all four language arts are interrelated. For example, the need to develop and expand concepts and vocabulary, essential to reading, is evident in the entire language arts curriculum. Concepts and vocabulary terms to express these concepts are basic to listening, speaking, and writing, as well as to reading activities. Spoken and written messages are organized around main ideas and supporting details, and people listen and read in order to identify the main ideas and supporting details conveyed in the material. Chapter 5, "Comprehension," contains many examples of reading skills that have parallel listening skills and related writing and speaking skills.

Principle 9   Reading is an integral part of all content area instruction within the educational program.

Teachers must consider the relationship of reading to other subjects within the curriculum of the elementary school. Other curricular areas frequently provide applications for the skills taught in the reading period. Textbooks in the various content areas are often the main means of conveying content concepts to students. Supplementary reading in library materials, magazines, and newspapers is also frequently used. Inability to read these materials with comprehension can mean failure to master important ideas in science, mathematics, social studies, and other areas of the curriculum. Students who have poor reading skills may therefore face failure in other areas of study because of the large amount of reading that these areas often require. In addition, the need to write reports in social studies, science, health, or other areas can involve many reading and study skills: locating information (using the alphabet and the dictionary); organizing information (outlining, note-taking, and preparing bibliographies); and using the library (using the card catalog, call numbers, classification systems, and references such as encyclopedias and atlases).

The teacher who gives reading instruction only within a reading period and who treats reading as separate from the rest of the curriculum will probably achieve teacher frustration rather than pupil change and growth. While a definitely scheduled period specifically for reading instruction may be recommended, this does not mean that teachers should ignore reading when teaching content subjects. The ideal situation at any level is not "reading" for an hour's period, followed by "study" of social science or science for the next period. Instead, although the emphasis will shift, both reading and studying should be integrated during all periods at all levels.

Elaboration of these points may be found in Chapter 7, "Reading/Study Skills," and in Chapter 8, "Reading in the Content Areas," but we should clarify one further idea at this time. Teachers sometimes assume the existence of a dichotomy—that children learn to read in the primary grades and read to learn in the intermediate and upper grades. While it may be true that teachers devote less attention to the actual process of learning to read at the intermediate level, there is still need for attention to the primary reading skills as well as to higher-level skills.

Principle 10   The student needs to see why reading is important.

Children who cannot see any advantage in learning to read will not be motivated to learn this skill. Learning to read takes effort, and children who see the value of reading in their personal activities will be more likely to work hard than those who fail to see the benefits. Teachers should have little trouble demonstrating to youngsters that reading is important: it helps people to travel from place to place, to make needed purchases, to keep informed about current conditions, and so on. In addition to emphasizing the children's future needs for reading, teachers should attempt to show the children immediate, personal values of reading in the classroom each day. They can help the children see the value of reading in school activities by labeling cabinets and drawers where supplies are stored, by writing individual student responsibilities and privileges on the board each day, and by listing classroom rules on a prominently displayed chart. They can show children that reading is a good recreational pursuit by describing the pleasure that they derive from reading in their spare time.

Principle 11   Enjoyment of reading should be considered of prime importance.

It is possible for our schools to produce capable readers who do not read; in fact, today it is a common occurrence. Reading can be entertaining as well as informative. Teachers can help students realize this fact by reading stories and poems to the children daily and setting aside a regular time for pleasure reading, during which many good books of appropriate difficulty levels for the students and on many different interest areas are readily available. Children will also see that reading conveys pleasure if they observe their teachers doing recreational reading. When the children read recreationally, the teacher should do this also, thereby modeling desired behavior. Pressures of tests and reports should not be a part of recreational reading times. Chapter 9 provides some guidance for teachers in this area.

Principle 12   Readiness for reading should be considered at all levels of instruction.

Not only when reading instruction begins, but whenever instruction in any reading skill takes place, at all grade levels, teachers should consider the readiness of the child for the instructional activity. A teacher should ask, "Does the child have the prerequisite skills necessary for learning this new skill?" If the answer is no, then the prerequisite skills should be thoroughly developed before the teacher presents the planned activity.

Principle 13   Reading should be taught in a way that allows each child to experience success.

Asking children to try to learn to read from materials that are too difficult for them is ensuring failure for a large number. Teachers should give children instruction at their own levels of achievement, regardless of grade placement. Success generates success. If children are given a reading task at which they can succeed, they gain the confidence to attack in a positive way other reading tasks that are presented to them. This makes the likelihood of their success at these later tasks much greater. In addition, some studies have shown that if a teacher *expects* his or her students to be successful readers, they will in fact *be* successful.

Teachers tend to place poor readers in materials that are too hard for them more frequently than they place good readers in such materials. Children who are given difficult material to read use active, comprehension-seeking behaviors less than do children who are reading instructional-level material (material they can understand with a teacher's assistance). If the placement of poor readers on levels that are too high is standard, inefficient reading strategies that emerge when material is too difficult will be reinforced, and it is less likely that more efficient strategies will be developed. Poor readers give up on reading tasks more quickly than do good readers. Although they do not have high expectations of success under any circumstances, their expectations of success decrease more after failure than do those of good readers (Bristow, 1985).

Teachers should place poor readers in material that they can read without undue focus on word recognition. This will allow poor readers to focus on comprehending the message of the text. Also, because they may not have had the idea that reading should make sense, urging poor readers to make sense of written messages can be helpful. Poor readers' comprehension skills can be improved if teachers help them develop appropriate background for reading selections and help them develop such metacognitive (self-monitoring) strategies as rereading, self-questioning, purpose-setting, and predicting. Finally, poor readers must be convinced that they will be capable of greater understanding if they apply specific strategies that have been taught. Success must be within reach (Bristow, 1985).

Hart (1983) states that threat of failure (especially public failure) may cause students to "downshift" to a less sophisticated part of the brain that does not have the pattern detection capabilities and program-storing capabilities of the cerebrum, which is the locus of language functions. Therefore, threat of failure can induce failure.

Principle 14   Encouragement of self-direction and self-monitoring of reading is important.

Good readers direct their own reading, making decisions about how to approach particular passages, what reading speed is appropriate, and *why* they are reading the passages. They are able to decide when they are having difficulties with understanding and can take steps to remedy their misunderstandings (Anderson et al., 1985). When they do this, they are using metacognitive strategies. More information on the way good readers read flexibly and monitor their reading is found in Chapters 5 and 7.

No matter what teaching approaches are used in a school or what patterns of organization predominate, these principles of teaching reading should apply. Each teacher should consider carefully his or her compliance or lack of compliance with such principles.

✔ Self-Check: Objective 4
We have discussed fourteen principles related to teaching reading. Explain how knowledge of each principle should affect your teaching of reading.
(See Self-Improvement Opportunity 3.)

Summary

The reading act is composed of two major parts—the reading process and the reading product. The reading process has eight aspects—sensory, perceptual, sequential, experiential, thinking, learning, association, and affective—that combine to produce the reading product, communication.

Three of the many types of theories of the reading process are subskill theories, psycholinguistic theories, and interactive theories. Subskill theories depict reading as a series of subskills that children must master so that they become automatic and smoothly integrated. Proponents of subskill theories are not in agreement as to which subskills are needed. Psycholinguistic theories, which are based on psychology and linguistics, depict reading as a process in which readers select the least number of cues necessary to predict the meaning of the text. The readers generate and test hypotheses about the reading material and get feedback from the material. Psycholinguists such as Frank Smith believe that reading cannot be taught but that conditions can be arranged that will allow students to learn. Interactive theories depict reading as the interaction of two types of processing—top-down and bottom-up. Both types of processing are used to recognize and comprehend words. According to the bottom-up view, reading is initiated by the printed symbols (letters and words), and proceeds to larger linguistic units until the reader discovers meaning. According to the top-down view, reading begins with the reader's generation of hypotheses or predictions about the material, with the visual cues in the material being used to test these hypotheses as necessary. Therefore, according to interactive theories, both the print and the reader's background are important in the reading process.

Some principles related to reading instruction that may be helpful to teachers include the following:

1. Reading is a complex act with many factors that must be considered.
2. Reading is the interpretation of the *meaning* of printed symbols.
3. Reading involves *constructing* the meaning of a written passage.
4. There is no one correct way to teach reading.
5. Learning to read is a continuing process.
6. Students should be taught word recognition skills that will allow them to unlock the pronunciations and meanings of unfamiliar words independently.
7. The teacher should diagnose each student's reading ability and use the diagnosis as a basis for planning instruction.
8. Reading and the other language arts are closely interrelated.
9. Reading is an integral part of all content area instruction within the educational program.
10. The student needs to see why reading is important.
11. Enjoyment of reading should be considered of prime importance.
12. Readiness for reading should be considered at all levels of instruction.
13. Reading should be taught in a way that allows each child to experience success.
14. Encouragement of self-direction and self-monitoring of reading is important.

Test Yourself

True or False

_____ 1. Over a period of time a single, clear-cut definition of reading has emerged.
_____ 2. Reading is a complex of many skills.
_____ 3. Youngsters entering first grade are often farsighted.
_____ 4. When children read, their eyes move smoothly over the page from left to right.
_____ 5. Faulty eye movements usually cause serious reading problems.
_____ 6. Regressions are always undesirable.
_____ 7. Perception involves interpretation of sensation.
_____ 8. Questions can affect the way students think while reading.
_____ 9. The more meaningful learning is to a child, the more rapidly associative learning takes place.
_____ 10. Word calling and reading are synonymous.
_____ 11. Teachers go to school so that they can learn the one way to teach reading.
_____ 12. People can continue to refine their reading skills as long as they live.

_____ 13. Diagnosis of reading problems for every child in a class is a waste of a teacher's valuable time.

_____ 14. Diagnosis can help a teacher plan appropriate instruction for all of his or her pupils.

_____ 15. Reading and the other language arts are closely interrelated.

_____ 16. Content area instruction should not have to be interrupted for teaching of reading skills; reading instruction should remain strictly within a special reading period.

_____ 17. Understanding the importance of reading is unimportant to the reading progress of a child.

_____ 18. Teachers should stress reading for enjoyment as well as for information.

_____ 19. Readiness for reading is a concept that applies only to beginning reading instruction.

_____ 20. One of the early sentence transformations used by many children is the passive transformation.

_____ 21. Reading seems to fit in the "skill" category of behavior.

_____ 22. Current theories about reading account for all aspects of the reading process.

_____ 23. No research supports the view that reading is a set of subskills that must be mastered and integrated.

_____ 24. LaBerge and Samuels's model of perceptual learning indicates that the sequence of learning is from distinctive features, to letters, to letter clusters, to words.

_____ 25. Psycholinguistic theory, as explained by Frank Smith, indicates that the essential skills of reading cannot be taught.

_____ 26. A bottom-up model of the reading process assumes that reading is initiated by the printed symbols, with little input required from the reader.

_____ 27. Frank Smith's theoretical position seems to fit a top-down model.

_____ 28. With an interactive model, parallel processing of information from print and from background knowledge takes place.

_____ 29. Reading involves constructing the meaning of a written passage.

_____ 30. Reading and writing are both constructive processes.

_____ 31. Teachers give good readers materials that are too hard for them more often than they give poor readers such materials.

_____ 32. Metacognitive processes are self-monitoring processes.

Self-Improvement Opportunities

1. Study the following definitions of reading, which have been suggested by well-known authorities. Decide which aspect or combination of aspects of the reading process has been emphasized most in each definition.

a. "Reading may be defined as the attaining of meaning as a result of the interplay between perceptions of graphic symbols that represent language, and the memory traces of the reader's past verbal and nonverbal experiences." (Albert J. Harris and Edward R. Sipay, *How to Teach Reading: A Competency-Based Program*. New York: Longman, 1979, p. 27.)

b. "Reading is a sampling, selecting, predicting, comparing and confirming activity in which the reader selects a sample of useful graphic cues based on what he sees and what he expects to see." (Kenneth Goodman, quoted in Theodore L. Harris and Richard E. Hodges, eds., *A Dictionary of Reading and Related Terms*. Newark, Del.: International Reading Association, 1981, p. 265.)

c. "Reading means getting meaning from certain combinations of letters. Teach the child what each letter stands for and he can read." (Rudolph Flesch, *Why Johnny Can't Read and What You Can Do About It*. New York: Harper & Row, 1955, pp. 2–3.)

d. "Reading is a process of looking at written language symbols, converting them into overt or covert speech symbols, and then manipulating them so that both the direct (overt) and implied (covert) ideas intended by the author may be understood." (Lawrence E. Hafner and Hayden B. Jolly, *Teaching Reading to Children*. 2nd ed. New York: Macmillan, 1982, p. 4.)

e. "Reading is thinking . . . reconstructing the ideas of others." (Robert Karlin, *Teaching Elementary Reading: Principles and Strategies*. 3rd ed. New York: Harcourt Brace Jovanovich, 1980, p. 7.)

f. "Reading involves the identification and recognition of printed or written symbols which serve as stimuli for the recall of meanings built up through past experience, and further the construction of new meanings through the reader's manipulation of relevant concepts already in his possession. The resulting meanings are organized into thought processes according to the purposes that are operating in the reader." (Miles A. Tinker and Constance M. McCullough, *Teaching Elementary Reading*. 4th ed. Englewood Cliffs, N.J.: Prentice-Hall, 1975, p. 9.)

g. "Reading involves nothing more than the correlation of a sound image with its corresponding visual image, that is, the spelling." (Leonard Bloomfield and Clarence L. Barnhart, *Let's Read: A Linguistic Approach*. Detroit: Wayne State University Press, 1961, dustjacket.)

h. "Reading typically is the bringing of meaning *to* rather than the gaining of meaning *from* the printed page." (Henry P. Smith and Emerald V. Dechant, *Psychology in Teaching Reading*. Englewood Cliffs, N.J.: Prentice-Hall, 1961, p. 22.)

2. Note the points of agreement in the various definitions given above.

3. After studying the principles of reading instruction given in this chapter, see if you can formulate other principles based upon your reading in other sources.

4. Study a story presented in a basal reader for a grade level of your choice. Giving illustrative sentences, list the kinds of sentence patterns and transformed sentences presented in the story.

5. To help in your further study of elementary school reading, participate in the activities of organizations such as the International Reading Association. The meetings, publications (particularly *The Reading Teacher*), and projects sponsored by the organization provide some of the best ways to keep informed about new ideas on teaching reading. Other periodicals dealing with timely ideas on reading instruction include:

Elementary School Journal—University of Chicago Press, 5835 Kimbark Avenue, Chicago, IL 60637

Exceptional Children—Council for Exceptional Children, 1141 South Jefferson Davis Highway, Jefferson Plaza, Suite 900, Arlington, VA 22202

Horn Book Magazine—Horn Book, Inc., 585 Boylston Street, Boston, MA 02116

Instructor—Instructor Publications, Inc., P.O. Box 6099, Duluth, MN 55806

Journal of Reading Behavior—National Reading Conference, 1070 Sibley Tower, Rochester, NY 14604

Language Arts—National Council of Teachers of English, 1111 Kenyon Road, Urbana, IL 61801

Perceptual and Motor Skills—Perceptual and Motor Skills, Box 9229, Missoula, MT 59807

Reading Research and Instruction—College Reading Association, Box 872, University Plaza, Atlanta, GA 30303

Reading Research Quarterly—International Reading Association, Inc., 800 Barksdale Road, Newark, DE 19711

6. Read the "Research Views" sections of *The Reading Teacher*, beginning with the October 1985 issue and continuing with other issues in which Peter Mosenthal has dealt with defining reading and examining reading theories (see the bibliography for this chapter). Decide what the place of reading theory should be in relationship to classroom instruction, using the ideas in these sections and other articles you locate for yourself.

7. Compare critically the suggestions made in this and the following chapters with those in other professional references, to achieve a more intensive study of the subject.

Bibliography

Anderson, Richard C., Elfrieda H. Hiebert, Judith A. Scott, and Ian A. G. Wilkinson. *Becoming a Nation of Readers*. Washington, D.C.: National Institute of Education, 1985.

Anderson, Richard C., and P. David Pearson. "A Schema-Theoretic View of Basic Processes in Reading." In *Handbook of Reading Research*, P. David Pearson, ed. New York: Longman, 1984, pp. 255–91.

Ashton-Warner, Sylvia. *Teacher*. New York: Simon and Schuster, 1963.

Biehler, Robert F., and Jack Snowman. *Psychology Applied to Teaching*. 5th ed. Boston: Houghton Mifflin, 1986.

Bristow, Page Simpson. "Are Poor Readers Passive Readers? Some Evidence, Possible Explanations, and Potential Solutions." *The Reading Teacher* 39 (December 1985): 318–25.

Burmeister, Lou E. *Foundations and Strategies for Teaching Children to Read*. Reading, Mass.: Addison-Wesley, 1983.

Canady, Robert J. "Psycholinguistics in a Real-Life Classroom." *The Reading Teacher* 34 (November 1980): 156–59.

Chambers, Dewey, and Heath Lowry. *The Language Arts: A Pragmatic Approach*. Dubuque, Iowa: William C. Brown, 1975.

Cooper, Charles R., and Anthony R. Petrosky. "A Psycholinguistic View of the Fluent Reading Process." *Journal of Reading* 20 (December 1976): 184–207.

Downing, John. "Reading—Skill or Skills?" *The Reading Teacher* 35 (February 1982): 534–37.

Gagné, Robert M. *The Conditions of Learning*. New York: Holt, Rinehart and Winston, 1965, pp. 98–107.

Goodman, Kenneth S. "Reading: A Psycholinguistic Guessing Game." In *Perspectives on Elementary Reading*, Robert Karlin, ed. New York: Harcourt Brace Jovanovich, 1973, pp. 30–41.

Gove, Mary. "Clarifying Teachers' Beliefs About Reading." *The Reading Teacher* 37 (December 1983): 261–68.

Guthrie, John T. "Models of Reading and Reading Disability." *Journal of Educational Psychology* 65 (1973): 9–18.

Harris, Albert J., and Edward R. Sipay. *How to Increase Reading Ability*. 8th ed. New York: Longman, 1985.

Harris, Albert J., and Edward R. Sipay. *How to Teach Reading: A Competency-Based Program*. New York: Longman, 1979.

Harris Theodore L., and Richard E. Hodges, eds. *A Dictionary of Reading and Related Terms*. Newark, Del.: International Reading Association, 1981.

Hart, Leslie A. "Programs, Patterns and Downshifting in Learning to Read." *The Reading Teacher* 37 (October 1983): 5–11.

Johnson, Peter H. *Reading Comprehension Assessment: A Cognitive Basis*. Newark, Del.: International Reading Association, 1983.

Krathwohl, David, B. Bloom, and B. Masia. *Taxonomy of Educational Objectives: The Classification of Educational Goals, Handbook 2: The Affective Domain*. New York: McKay, 1964, Appendix A, pp. 176–85.

LaBerge, David, and S. Jay Samuels. "Toward a Theory of Automatic Information Processing in Reading." In *Theoretical Models and Processes of Reading*, Harry Singer and Robert B. Ruddell, eds. 3rd ed. Newark, Del.: International Reading Association, 1985, pp. 689–718.

Leverett, Hollis M. "Vision Test Performance of School Children." *American Journal of Ophthalmology* 44 (October 1957): 508–19.

May, Frank B. *Reading as Communication.* 2nd ed. Columbus, Ohio: Charles E. Merrill, 1986, Chapter 1.

Mosenthal, Peter B. "Defining Reading: Freedom of Choice but Not Freedom from Choice." *The Reading Teacher* 39 (October 1985): 110–12.

Mosenthal, Peter B. "Defining Reading: Taxonomies and Stray Definitions." *The Reading Teacher* 39 (November 1985): 238–40.

Mosenthal, Peter B. "Defining Reading: Operational Definitions and Other Oracles." *The Reading Teacher* 39 (December 1985): 362–64.

Mosenthal, Peter B. "Defining Reading: Translating Definitions of Reading in Research into Practice." *The Reading Teacher* 39 (January 1986): 476–79.

Mosenthal, Peter B. "The Pyramid as a Taxonomic Organizer of Reading." *The Reading Teacher* 39 (February 1986): 606–608.

Mosenthal, Peter B. "From Pyramid Taxonomy to Reading Theories: The Complexity of Simplification." *The Reading Teacher* 39 (March 1986): 732–34.

Mosenthal, Peter B. "Defining Good and Poor Reading—The Problem of Artifactual Lamp Posts." *The Reading Teacher* 39 (April 1986): 858–61.

Mosenthal, Peter B., "The Geometries of Reading." *The Reading Teacher* 39 (May 1986): 968–71.

Mosenthal, Peter B. "Improving Reading Practice with Reading Theory: The Procrustean Approach." *The Reading Teacher* 40 (October 1986): 108–11.

Mosenthal, Peter B. "Defining Progress in Reading Research and Practice: The Theorists' Approach." *The Reading Teacher* 40 (November 1986): 230–33.

Mosenthal, Peter B. "Defining Progress in Reading Research and Practice: The Synthesizers' Approach." *The Reading Teacher* 40 (December 1986): 360–63.

Mosenthal, Peter B. "Defining Progress in Reading Research and Practice: Communities of Common Causes." *The Reading Teacher* 40 (January 1987): 472–75.

Mosenthal, Peter B. "Rational and Irrational Approaches to Understanding Reading." *The Reading Teacher* 40 (February 1987): 570–72.

Otto, Jean. "The New Debate in Reading." *The Reading Teacher* 36 (October 1982); 14–18.

Pearson, P. David, et al. *The Effect of Background Knowledge on Young Children's Comprehension of Explicit and Implicit Information.* Urbana: University of Illinois, Center for the Study of Reading, 1979.

Rumelhart, David. *Toward an Interactive Model of Reading.* Technical Report 56. San Diego, Calif.: Center for Human Information Processing, March 1976.

Rumelhart, David E. "Schemata: The Building Blocks of Cognition." In *Comprehension and Teaching: Research Reviews,* John T. Guthrie, ed. Newark, Del.: International Reading Association, 1981, pp. 3–26.

Samuels, S. Jay, and Sumner W. Schachter. "Controversial Issues in Beginning Reading Instruction: Meaning Versus Subskill Emphasis." In *Readings on Reading Instruction*, Albert J. Harris and Edward R. Sipay, eds. New York: Longman, 1984, pp. 37–44.

Singer, Harry. "The Substrata-Factor Theory of Reading." In *Theoretical Models and Processes of Reading*, Harry Singer and Robert B. Ruddell, eds. 3rd ed. Newark, Del.: International Reading Association, 1985, pp. 630–60.

Smith, Frank. *Understanding Reading*. 2nd ed. New York: Holt, Rinehart and Winston, 1978.

Smith, Richard J., et al. *The School Reading Program*. Boston: Houghton Mifflin, 1978.

Walberg, Herbert J., Victoria Chou Hare, and Cynthia A. Pulliam. "Social-Psychological Perceptions and Reading Comprehension." In *Comprehension and Teaching: Research Reviews*, John T. Guthrie, ed. Newark, Del.: International Reading Association, 1981, pp. 140–59.

Weaver, Constance. *Psycholinguistics and Reading: From Process to Practice*. Cambridge, Mass.: Winthrop, 1980, pp. 251–91.

Weaver, Phyllis, and Fredi Shonhoff. "Subskill and Holistic Approaches to Reading Instruction." In *Readings on Reading Instruction*, Albert J. Harris and Edward R. Sipay, eds. New York: Longman, 1984, pp. 34–36.

Chapter 2

Prereading Experiences
for Children

Introduction

This chapter begins with a discussion of the important concept of readiness and of five major factors to be considered in a readiness program: experiential background, cognitive development and language learning, interest in reading, social and emotional development, and physical development. In developing a prereading program, teachers must base decisions about their approaches on the needs of their students; the program may be activity-based, structured, discovery-oriented, organized around published materials, or a combination of these. It is important to remember that the readiness period does not end when reading begins but continues as the child moves on into reading. Teachers must develop readiness for each new reading task a child attempts.

Setting Objectives

When you finish reading this chapter you should be able to

1. Identify some strategies for helping young children develop concepts and vocabulary.
2. Discuss the value of group and individually dictated story experiences.
3. Understand interrelationships among cognitive development, metalinguistic awareness, and language learning.
4. Explain reasons for the importance of storytelling and story reading and describe how to present a story to a class.
5. Discuss how visual and auditory skills can be developed.
6. List some strategies for helping young children to recognize letters and words.
7. Explain the connections between beginning reading and writing.
8. Identify some issues related to pre–first-grade reading.

Key Vocabulary

Pay close attention to these terms when they appear in the chapter.

auditory discrimination	experiential	phonemic
auditory perception	background	segmentation
cognitive development	invented spellings	predictable books
concrete-operational	kinesthetic-tactile	preoperational period
period	learning	reading readiness
directionality	metalinguistic	vicarious experience
emergent literacy	awareness	visual discrimination
experience chart story		visual perception

The prereading period extends from birth to the time when a child is taught to recognize and read words. During this period, the child learns to understand and speak words, to follow directions, to follow the cumulative development of a story, to study and interpret pictures, to perceive small sight and sound differences, to handle school materials, and to acquire an interest in printed words. These and many other interests and abilities grow gradually until the child reaches a stage of "readiness" for beginning reading instruction.

The modern concept holds that readiness is made up of various factors. It is neither physical nor intellectual maturation alone, although both are involved (since they affect the physical structure of the eye, degree of interest, and level of knowledge). Nor do modern educators believe that readiness is something to wait for passively; they believe that it is a stage into which the child may be guided.

While this chapter focuses upon beginning reading readiness, readiness is important at all reading levels. Even if readers are ready for one level of reading instruction, they will not necessarily be adequately prepared at a higher level. Developing readiness for any reading experience at any level is an important task for teachers.

The concept of readiness has significant implications for designing formal or systematic reading experiences. When a child is not prepared to succeed at a reading task, his or her frustration can produce negative and detrimental effects. If repeated over a period of time, the frustration can become more intense.

Three conditions that a teacher cannot change are likely to affect a child's readiness for reading: gender, home environment, and participation in preschool programs. Teachers should be aware of these in order to understand the possible reasons for certain behaviors or lack of progress; however, they must also guard against developing preconceived ideas about children based on these conditions.

Research studies in North America have revealed that girls surpass boys in reading performance, especially in the lower grades, possibly because of cultural factors (Lehr, 1982). Home environment, including socioeconomic level, family size, type of neighborhood, educational level of the parents, and verbal interaction among family members, also affects children's success in reading. Coleman (1972) reported a positive relationship between socioeconomic level and reading achievement, and Loban (1976) found that children from homes of a higher socioeconomic level had superior verbal ability. Wigfield and Asher stated, however, that a "growing set of findings supports the point that particular environmental measures correlate more strongly with children's academic performance than do SES [socioeconomic status] measures" (1984, p. 431). Environmental measures include the types of disciplinary techniques used in the home, the responsiveness of parents, the arrangement of the physical environment, the degree of parental involvement, and the availability of suitable play materials.

Teachers have observed that children who have participated in some sort of preschool program usually make an easier transition into the reading program than other children do. Most likely, such children have already developed many of the social, communication, and other skills that are basic to beginning reading. Both black and white children who attended preschool educational programs scored higher than non-preschool attenders in achievement and readiness to learn (Knox and Glover, 1978).

From 1970 to 1983 enrollment in preschools increased by 33 percent, despite a 5 percent decline in the total number of children from ages three to five. The trend toward greater preprimary enrollment is attributed to increasing employment of mothers with preschoolers, a recognition of the importance of early education, and wider availability of preschool classes. The U.S. Department of Education predicts further growth only in three- and four-year-old enrollments, since participation of five-year-olds is nearing 100 percent (Plisko and Stern, 1985).

Children who enter first grade vary widely in many ways, such as rate of growth and attitude toward learning. In the following section we present five major factors in which children exhibit differing degrees of readiness and suggest some activities for developing each factor. Additional activities are listed in Appendix A of this chapter.

At times it may be appropriate to view these activities in isolation, but most of the time they become more meaningful when coordinated around units of related experiences. For example, a unit or project may evolve around a central theme, such as "different kinds of weather." Activities for a unit on weather could include listening to stories or poems about weather, interpreting weather pictures, and planning a trip to a weather station. Children could then dictate a class story about the trip, drawing pictures about it and telling their classmates about their illustrations. Such a coordinated experience provides a wealth of opportunities for oral expression, writing practice, artistic expression, and practice of social manners. Some unit themes with many possibilities are

Our School and School Helpers
What Makes a Home a Home
People Who Help Us
Seasons
Celebrations
Growing Things
Transportation
Places We Buy Things in the Community
Our Five Senses

Teachers should clearly delineate goals, activities, helpful materials, and methods of evaluation in planning units of work.

Five important readiness factors—experiential background, cognitive development and language learning, interest in reading, social and emotional development, and physical development—are discussed in this section.

Experiential Background

Providing an adequate background of experience is an integral part of the reading readiness program. The school can supply some of this background; the rest must come from the home. Because the child who is intellectually curious reaps the most from his or her experiences, those who are associated with children should try to stimulate their curiosity about new or unknown things.

A broad experiential background is essential for success in reading because children must be familiar with the concepts and vocabulary they will see in written form in order to gain meaning from them. Experiences are the foundation for building concepts, and concepts are the foundation for building vocabulary. Through their experiences children gain an understanding of ideas and concepts, and they learn words, or labels, for them. Later they will understand more of what they read because they can relate their experiences to the symbols on the printed page. As children encounter a variety of experiences, they modify and refine their perceptions until they get a clear picture of each concept they have acquired. A child may need many experiences to attain a well-rounded impression of a single idea. *School,* for example, is a concept that children will not completely understand until they have experienced it in different ways.

Teachers may help children build broad backgrounds of experience in a variety of ways. The important things to keep in mind are the needs of the children and the available resources. As teachers observe and talk with their students, they can perceive gaps in experience and find ways to fill them. They can provide experiences for the children by inviting guests or by taking them on a field trip, if the expense and distance are not too great and transportation and supervisory personnel are available. Children learn basic concepts through activities such as constructing mobiles and collages, cooking, playing with puzzles, following directions in playing finger games, and so on. Particularly useful are activities that involve the senses: those like the following ones provide opportunities for using words to describe sensations.

1. taking *sight* walks
2. making *sound* mobiles (from pieces of wood, bells, buttons, tin cans, aluminum foil)
3. using a *feel* box or bag for guessing objects by touch
4. holding a *tasting* party (tasting salt, sugar, vinegar)
5. playing a *smelling* game (identifying aromatic objects tied in small, thin cloth bags, such as pieces of banana, fresh orange peels, onions, apples)

Having a news period can be useful. From the reported news, the teacher can make a chart, including items like "We had a fire drill today" or "We talked about the farm." Students can help compile the week's news, decide on headlines, and make illustrations for some items.

Since young children enjoy games, playing them is a good way to stimulate vocabulary development. The children can play a game with prepositions by trying to identify the various positions of an object that is placed *in, on,* or *over* a box. They can learn about adverbs by responding to directions that ask them to walk *quickly, slowly, sadly, quietly, noisily,* or *happily.* They can also play with adjectives by pretending to be *big, little, brave,* or *happy.*

It is important to make use of both planned and unplanned experiences to develop concepts and language. Teachers should use correct vocabulary and specific terms such as *printing press, homogenized,* and *card catalog* in class discussions. They should elicit descriptive words from the children or introduce such words as they ask the children to recall sensory impressions of experiences. Both before and after experiences, teachers should involve children in related language activities. In this way the children increase their verbal ability; that is, their vocabularies and concepts expand as they use new words to talk about their ideas.

Experiences may be either direct or vicarious. Children generally remember direct experiences with actual physical involvement best, but it may not always be feasible to provide direct experiences. Good vicarious experiences, such as listening to stories and watching films, provide opportunities to expand concepts and vocabulary indirectly. Some appropriate experiences of both types are

field trips	films, filmstrips, slides, tapes
resource people	selected television programs
story reading	photographs, pictures, posters
demonstrations	neighborhood walks
exhibits	class holiday celebrations

A class project like the one described below can promote growth in vocabulary and concept development.

● **MODEL ACTIVITY:** *Direct Experience*

Start by saying to the children: "Tomorrow we will make some vegetable soup. Try to remember to bring a vegetable to put in the soup. Now we will write a chart story about the ingredients we will need for our soup." The next morning say: "Tell us about your vegetable. What is it called? What color is it? How does it feel? How does it smell?" Give each child a chance to handle and talk about the vegetables. Then ask: "What do we need to do first to make the soup? What must we do to the vegetables before we put them in the pot? What else should we add?" (Answers include getting and heating the water, washing and cutting up the vegetables, and adding spices and alphabet noodles.)

When the soup is ready to eat, give each child a cupful. As the children eat, ask: "How does your soup taste? Are the colors of the vegetables the same as when we put them into the soup? How have the alphabet noodles changed? Can you name some of the letters that are in your soup?" After they have finished eating, let the children dictate another chart story about the sequence of making the soup and/or their reactions to eating it.

Some of the concepts you can help children acquire from this experience and related discussions are (1) soup is made from firm, fresh, brightly colored vegetables; (2) after they are cooked, the vegetables change in texture and appearance; (3) the noodles get larger from absorbing the water; (4) it takes time to heat water and cook soup; (5) the water absorbs flavor and color from the vegetables and spices; (6) cold water becomes hot when it is placed on a heated surface; (7) certain foods are classified as vegetables. As a result of the experience, children's vocabularies might now include the words *boil, simmer, dissolve, melt, ingredients, squash, celery, turnips, slice, chop, shred, dice, liquid,* and *flavor.* A bonus comes from letting the children manipulate the alphabet letters—identifying them, matching them, and finding the first letters of their names. ●

Looking at pictures is one type of vicarious experience. Pictures are extremely fruitful sources of new ideas and experiences and are useful in developing vocabulary and concepts. Good pictures to use for building experiences are those that tell a story. In order to help children interpret pictures fully, teachers should ask them questions like those in Model Activity: Vicarious Experience.

● **MODEL ACTIVITY:** *Vicarious Experience*

1. Where is the little boy? How do you know?
2. What kinds of things usually happen at the veterinarian's office?
3. Why do you think he took his cat there?
4. Why are the other people there?
5. Who is at the door? How do you know?
6. Why is the boy there without his father or mother?
7. What is the boy doing?
8. What do you think will happen soon? ●

Story writing is a logical extension of either direct or vicarious experiences. It may occur as an introduction to or as an outcome of an experience. If a class writes a story following a field trip, the students should first discuss the trip. By asking carefully selected questions, the teacher can encourage them to form valid concepts and use appropriate vocabulary words. The students then dictate sentences for the teacher to write on a chart like that in Example 2.1. Dictated story experiences provide an excellent opportunity to introduce the coordinated language experience approach discussed in Chapter 6.

Stories about an experience may be dictated by a whole class, a group, or an individual. When individual children tell stories, parents, aides, older

▶ **EXAMPLE 2.1:** Experience Chart Story

Our Trip to the Zoo

We rode in the school bus.
Mr. Spring was the bus driver.
The bus took us to the zoo.
We saw many animals.
We ate popcorn and peanuts.
We thanked Mr. Spring.
Our trip was fun.

children, classroom volunteers, or the teacher can act as scribes. These stories should be about things that are important to the children, such as their families, their pets, or their favorite activities. The children may illustrate them and combine them into booklets that are then shared around the library table and eventually taken home by the authors. Some appropriate experiences for story writing are listed below.

taking a field trip	observing an animal
watching an experiment	popping corn
visiting a science or book fair	experimenting with paints
tasting unusual foods	planting seeds or bulbs
entertaining a visitor	building a pretend space ship

✔ Self-Check: Objective 1

Several ways in which experience can help build concepts and vocabulary have been presented. Name as many as you can. Can you think of some others?
(See Self-Improvement Opportunities 3 and 5.)

Perhaps the most important reason for story writing is that children begin to realize that writing is recorded speech. This awareness occurs as the teacher reads the story back to the children in the words they have just dictated. After repeated readings by the teacher, the children may also be able to "read" the story. The teacher may make copies of the story for all of the children to take home and share with their families. As a result of involvement with the story, children may learn to recognize some high-interest words and words that are used more than once (such as *we* and *bus* in the experience chart story).

Many reading readiness skills are learned through story writing. Children watch as the teacher forms letters that make up words; they notice that language consists of separate words which are combined into sentences. They see the teacher begin at the left side and move to the right and go from top to bottom; they become aware that dictated stories have titles in which the first letter of each important word is capitalized; they realize that sentences begin with capital letters and end with punctuation marks. In addition to becoming familiar with mechanical writing skills, children develop their thinking skills. The teacher's questions are useful in helping them develop skill in organizing and summarizing. As the children retell events in the order of their occurrence, they begin to understand sequence. As they recall the *important* ideas, they begin to form a concept of a main idea.

✔ Self-Check: Objective 2

State why it is important to include group and individually dictated stories in the prereading program.
(See Self-Improvement Opportunity 6.)

Cognitive Development and Language Learning

In recent years the study of language development in isolation has shifted to the study of language learning in relation to cognitive development (Finn, 1985). This means that there is a connection between the way children learn to use language and the way that they grow in the ability to know and understand concepts or ideas. Thinking skills and language skills are closely related; language is a vehicle for understanding and communicating thoughts. Because of the interrelatedness of cognitive development and language learning, we will consider them together.

A child's intelligence is vital in learning to read. At one time people considered a mental age of six and one-half years to be the factor that determined when a child could learn to read. In recent years, however, educators have realized that many other factors also affect readiness for reading, including the child's experiential background and level of language development.

A child's early attempts at language are intuitive; that is, the child uses language reasonably well but lacks *metalinguistic awareness*, which is the ability to think about language and manipulate it objectively. For instance, a youngster may say, "I want some candy," but not be able to tell how many words were spoken or that this group of words is called a sentence. There is a discrepancy between the use of language and an awareness of the meanings of terms, such as *word, sentence,* and *letter,* that refer to language (Hare, 1984). The ability to use language adequately for purposes of communication precedes the ability to understand or explain rules that govern the use of language (Bewell and Straw, 1981).

As with reading, metalinguistic awareness does not occur all at once but advances through stages or levels. Reading often begins with the recognition of familiar sight words, proceeds to the association of sounds with the letters that represent them, and so forth. Metalinguistic awareness usually develops first at the phonological level (awareness of the sounds of language), then at the syntactic level (awareness of grammar), and finally at the semantic level (awareness of the distinction between words as symbols and what they symbolize). The child gradually develops a sensitivity to the elements of language that make reading and writing possible. There is a series of levels of metalinguistic awareness, and students continue to reach higher levels of metalinguistic knowledge as they gain new concepts of language (Bewell and Straw, 1981).

Jean Piaget, a Swiss psychologist highly respected for his theory of cognitive development, asserted that thought comes before language and that language is a way of representing thought. As a child's cognitive capacity matures, thought becomes "inner speech," and in time this inner speech becomes audible (Finn, 1985). Piaget divided cognitive development into four stages: sensorimotor, preoperational, concrete-operational, and formal-operational. A child's developing sense of metalinguistic awareness appears to correspond to the first three of these stages in particular (Bewell and Straw, 1981).

The *sensorimotor period* extends from birth to approximately two years of

age. During this period children learn about objects and form ideas about the world around them through physical manipulation. These ideas are quite simple, of course, and nonverbal. According to Piaget, manipulation of a wide variety of objects seems to be most important for the child's intellectual development at this point. Metalinguistic awareness begins to develop at the phonological level as the child experiments with the sounds (phonemes) of language by babbling (Bewell and Straw, 1981).

The *preoperational period* is divided into two stages, the *preconceptual stage* from age two to four and the *intuitive stage* from age four to six or seven (Burmeister, 1983). During the preconceptual stage children begin to engage in symbolic thought by representing ideas and events with words and sentences, drawings, and dramatic play. As they begin to use symbols to stand for spoken words, they realize that writing represents meaning, a concept that is basic to reading comprehension (Waller, 1977).

At the intuitive stage children are rapidly developing concepts but are limited in their ability to use adult logic. They are egocentric; that is, they consider things only from their own point of view. This characteristic prevents children from thinking clearly about the events in a story, except from their own limited perspectives. Most children who are at this stage demonstrate syntactic or grammatical awareness in their speech, but they are unable to state the rules governing syntax. They have not yet acquired the level of metalinguistic awareness necessary for thinking about language objectively. For instance, they cannot identify individual words in a stream of speech and talk about them as units of language (McDonell and Osburn, 1984). A teacher who wishes to develop the children's skill in recognizing words as basic elements of speech might use the following activity.

● **MODEL ACTIVITY:** *Recognition of the Concept of* Word

Make two copies of a chart story based on an experience the children have shared. Run your fingers under the first sentence on one of the charts as you say to the children: "Read this sentence with me." Then use your hands to block off individual words as you say to them: "Look at the groups of letters between the spaces. We call each group of letters a word." Ask them: "How many words are in this sentence?" Do the same thing with the other sentences on the chart. Then cut the sentences into strips and ask different children to cut the strips into words. Give each child a word. Say to the children: "Can you find your word on our other chart? If you can, put your word with the word on the chart." ●

It is important to realize that an understanding of the concept of *word* develops gradually through many experiences. Also, children are at various levels of readiness for acquiring this concept, so that for some the lesson will verify what they were already beginning to realize and for others, who are less ready, the lesson will have little or no meaning. Another activity to reinforce the concept of *word* and to help children begin to develop a concept for *sentence* is given below.

● **MODEL ACTIVITY:** *Recognition of the Concept of* Sentence

Say to the children: "Today we are going to put some sentences on the board. A sentence is a group of words. Who can tell me a sentence about what day it is?" Mike: "Tuesday." Then say: "You're right, Mike; it is Tuesday. Can you put the word *Tuesday* in a sentence with some other words?" Mike: "Today is Tuesday." Say: "That's right" and write the sentence on the board. Then say: "Now look at the sentence I've written and tell me how many words are in it. Remember to look for the spaces between the groups of letters." Mike: "Three." Then say: "Good. Can someone tell me a sentence about the weather today?" Tina: "It's cloudy outside." Say: "That's a good sentence, Tina" and write the sentence on the board. Say: "Look at Tina's sentence and tell me how many words there are." (You may continue by asking other questions for the children to answer in sentences and then follow the same procedure.) ●

As many children enter school and begin formal reading instruction, they are in a critical stage of cognitive development. Most of them are experiencing "cognitive confusion" regarding the components of language as a result of increased exposure to print. In one study, children up to the age of six and a half confused nonverbal sounds, phrases, and sentences with words, although older children showed increased understanding of the concept of *word* (Downing and Oliver, 1973–74). Until they find themselves in school-like situations, children generally have no need to isolate words from the continuous flow of speech (Hare, 1984). Reading and writing, however, require children to consider language from a different point of view, and in order for them to be successful at these tasks, they need to use the thinking skills associated with Piaget's next stage of cognitive development.

Piaget's third phase of cognitive development is the *concrete-operational period,* which extends approximately from age seven to eleven. During this period children begin to understand *conservation of substance,* the theory that something remains the same regardless of changes in its shape or division. In relation to reading, this means that they can understand that words and letters written in varied scripts, cases, and typefaces represent the same thing. Children acquire the concept of *decentration,* the ability to consider more than one aspect of a situation at a time, at about the same time. For example, reading requires children to deal with words both as linear patterns to be remembered and as representations of meaning to be understood.

Children at this level also acquire the concept of *reversibility,* or the realization that an object can return to its original shape after its form has been changed. In reading, children must convert printed symbols (graphemes) into spoken sounds (phonemes) and then check the results by reversing the process. Another reading-related concept that children learn during this stage is *classification,* or the understanding that something can be a member of two or more classes at the same time. They realize, for example, that a banana can belong to the class of fruit and also to the class of things that are yellow. The relationships between sounds and symbols in the English language are inconsistent and hard to classify; for instance, the letter *a* can represent many different sounds. Therefore, children must have reached the concrete-operational stage of cognitive development before they can benefit from a beginning reading program based on phonics generalizations.

Children who have not yet reached this concrete-operational stage lack many of the cognitive and metalinguistic concepts necessary for reading. Teachers may wish to use the following activity to check a child's stage of cognitive development before beginning formal reading instruction.

● **MODEL ACTIVITY:** *Classification*

Cut out pictures of objects that might be found in a large discount store (furniture, shoes, appliances, toys, and so on). Put the collection of pictures on a table along with several small, empty boxes. Say to a child: "Let's pretend that we are in a large store. Each box is a different part of the store. Can you put all the things together that belong in each part?" The child places the items. Then, in order to understand the child's reasoning, ask questions such as "Why did you put the bicycle with the television set? Why is the toy box with the furniture? Why did you put the tennis shoes with the toys?" ●

Metalinguistic awareness develops rapidly during the concrete-operational period as children learn to read and write. Reading requires children to analyze the structure of language, and writing allows children to reconstruct relationships between sounds and letters in a concrete way (Templeton, 1986). Children work with vowels and consonants, with sounds and letters, and with phrases and sentences. As they refine their abilities to conserve, reverse, classify, and decenter, they begin to perceive many linguistic concepts, including how to add prefixes and suffixes to words to change their meanings and how to make sentence transformations.

The *formal-operational period* occurs between the ages of eleven and fifteen. In this period students are able to reason about ideas that do not relate to direct experiences. They can evaluate, hypothesize, analyze, and think abstractly.

✔ **Self-Check: Objective 3**
Several interrelationships between cognitive development and language learning have been given. Name some of them.
(See Self-Improvement Opportunity 7.)

It is important to note that teachers should not expect children to work successfully at tasks for which they have not yet acquired the necessary cognitive skills. Thought processes differ at various periods of life, and children should not be expected to think like adults. According to Piaget, children need many opportunities for thinking and building concepts through self-directed discovery and manipulation of concrete objects before they are ready for formal instruction in reading and writing (Evans, 1975). Interpreting Piaget's theory for education, Furth (1970) says that teachers should encourage but never impose reading, and that a delay in learning to read will have no negative effect on a child's eventual level of reading achievement. This implies that teachers should wait until children have reached adequate levels of cognitive and linguistic competence before providing formal reading instruction. Because children need time to discover relationships between objects and ideas and between causes and outcomes, reading readiness and beginning reading programs should move gradually from concrete examples to more abstract material, from literal reading skills to higher-level reading skills.

Teachers should also realize that many children fail to understand linguistic terminology, such as *letter, word,* and *sentence,* and therefore cannot make sense out of instruction based on these terms. Isolated drills and memorization of rules without comprehension of their meanings are unlikely to help children learn to read. Beginning reading instruction for children lacking metalinguistic awareness should be based on language experiences and predictable or repetitive stories rather than on phonics and structural analysis. The use of the language experience approach to reading (see Chapter 6) enables children to understand the function of reading and writing in a way that is relevant for them (Downing, 1976).

During their early years, children can benefit from opportunities to practice using language and to further their enjoyment of and sensitivity to language. Many positive experiences with language, including storytelling and story reading, listening comprehension activities, and opportunities for oral expression, provide a sound basis for learning language. These experiences will serve children well, both as they develop increasing metalinguistic awareness and as they begin to read.

Because language is part of the curriculum at all levels, a good foundation in speaking and listening skills is necessary for academic progress. Throughout their learning, children should be encouraged to see the relationships among all the language components.

Storytelling and Story Reading

Reading aloud to children should be a daily occurrence. This story-sharing time creates far-reaching benefits for the listener. Some reasons for reading aloud are given below. (See *The Read-Aloud Handbook* by Jim Trelease for more ideas on storytelling and story reading.)

A teacher's daily reading aloud to children can not only help them to develop an awareness of story structure, but it can also acquaint them with new words and foster their interest in reading. (© Jean-Claude Lejeune)

Children develop awareness of story structure by listening to stories and discussing them.

Books extend experiences by telling about other cultures and lifestyles.

Classics introduce children to fine literature.

Children can develop good comprehension and thinking skills as they listen to stories.

Story time creates a warm feeling and a sense of rapport.

Some stories help children solve their problems and be more tolerant of others.

Stories acquaint children with new words and concepts.

Well-chosen stories can be the basis for creative expression, such as drama, music, and art.

Hearing stories read aloud brings about an interest in reading and a desire to learn to read.

Good readers encourage children to become attentive listeners.

Story time is a time to relax, enjoy, and share a laugh or a tear.

To decide which stories to tell or read ask yourself: Is the story interesting and entertaining to you? Does the story fit your personality, style, and talents? Will it appeal to the interests of the children for whom it is intended? Is the story appropriate to the age and ability level of the children? Is there ample dialogue and action in the story? Are there few lengthy descriptive passages, and can they be easily condensed? Will the story be relatively easy to prepare? Will it add variety and contrast to your repertoire of stories? Is it a story that would be better told than read aloud (Coody, 1979, pp. 25–37)?

There are several guidelines for a teacher who is preparing a story to tell. Read the story carefully. Reread it to get the incidents clearly in mind and to get a clear picture of the details. Tape yourself as you practice telling the story. Use cue cards—of opening lines, main points, climaxes, and closing lines—if they will help you. Memorize essential parts that provide atmosphere or imagery (for example, "'Who's that tripping over my bridge?' roared the troll," or "In the high and far-off times, O best beloved"). Retape your story, concentrating upon improving pitch, range, and voice quality. Make sure you are enunciating clearly and that you are making good use of pauses. Continue to practice telling the story. Use gestures sparingly; do not be overly dramatic. Young children enjoy listening to a story if it stimulates their imaginations and depicts experiences that are understandable, and if they are listening to a good storyteller or reader.

● *MODEL ACTIVITY: Storytelling*

Say to the children: "This morning I'm going to tell you a story that you may already know. It is called 'The Three Little Pigs.' How many of you know it? This story is about three little pigs and a mean old wolf who tries to blow down their houses. I want you to help me tell the story. When the wolf says, 'I'll huff and I'll puff and I'll blow your house in,' I want you to say it along with me. Let's try it now, all together." The children practice saying this line with you. Then tell the story and signal to the children when it is the right time for them to say the line. The same ideas may be used with other stories that have repeated lines, such as "The Three Billy Goats Gruff" and "The Gingerbread Man." ●

Real vs. Imaginary Stories As stories are read and told to them, children learn to differentiate between the real and the imaginary ones. This learning experience can be helped through asking a series of questions such as

1. Could this story really happen? Why do you say so?
2. What is there in the story that shows that it could not happen in real life?
3. How is the character _____ like someone you have known?
4. How could anything like _____ (event) ever happen to you?
5. What in the story is like something in modern life?

6. Where have you ever been or what have you heard about that is like the place described in the story?

Very young children can learn to detect the difference between fantasy and events that might have happened. Children enjoy changing a factual presentation to a fantasy by incorporating talking animals, magical events, or other imaginary elements. The purpose of differentiating between real and imaginary stories is neither to discount fantasy nor to dismiss a story as unworthy because it is untrue; the distinction is part of the foundation necessary for later reading of fiction, particularly of tall tales and humorous stories. Learning to make the distinction may be one of the first critical reading skills developed by young children.

Story Sequence   Understanding the concept of story sequence is difficult for many youngsters. The teacher should begin with just two or three ideas for the children to arrange in order and gradually increase the number of ideas as children show mastery of this skill.

● *MODEL ACTIVITY:* *Story Sequence*

Find three identical copies of books from a discarded basal reader series. Then cut three or four pictures from a story out of two of the books, mount the pictures, and cover them with clear plastic. Say to the children: "This morning I am going to read you a story about a big black bear. As I read, I am going to show you pictures of the story. I want you to listen and look carefully to see what happens first in the story, then what happens next, and finally what happens at the end of the story. When I am finished reading, I will ask you to put these pictures in the same order that you saw them as I read the story." After the story, let the children take turns arranging the cutout pictures in the correct sequence.   ●

Creative Responses   The ability to make predictions is an important reading skill that children can begin to develop during the readiness period. One purpose of reading stories to children is to encourage them to begin to make predictions about what will happen next.

As children learn to anticipate story endings, they should be urged to be creative and to develop their own endings. You can use the following books in a situation where you ask the pupils to complete an unfinished story.

Katy and the Big Snow by Virginia L. Burton. Boston: Houghton Mifflin, 1943.
   Read up to the point where it says "Slowly and steadily Katy started to plow out the city." Ask, "What do you think Katy did?"
Harry by the Sea by Gene Zion. New York: Harper & Row, 1965. Read up to
   the point where Harry was jumping with joy at the hot dog stand. Stop after

"He jumped so much that suddenly . . . " Ask, "What happened when he jumped? What did Harry do then?"

Story of the Three Bears by Eleanor Mure. New York: H. Z. Walck, 1967. Read up to the point where the bears reenter the house. Ask, "What happened then?"

The Three Little Pigs by Paul Galdone. New York: Seabury Press, 1970. Read up to the point where the wolf visits the first little pig's house. Ask, "What happened next?"

✔ Self-Check: Objective 4

What are some reasons for storytelling and story reading? How would you present a story to a group of children? (See Self-Improvement Opportunities 2 and 5.)

Listening Comprehension

The ability to listen is a language skill that is highly important for learning to read and for doing other schoolwork. Instruction in listening may lead to improved reading skills, especially in first grade (Sippola, 1985), and proficiency in listening comprehension in kindergarten and first grade is a fairly good predictor of reading comprehension in the third grade (Anderson et al., 1985). In teaching children to listen, teachers should choose subjects that interest the children, that are related to their own experiences, and that make use of words and concepts they understand. In order to become good listeners, children need to learn to concentrate, to develop their attention spans, and to be good members of an audience. Children must listen attentively to follow directions and must be familiar with many directional terms, such as *row, top of the page,* and *under.* A teacher may find many ways during the day to help children develop the ability to follow directions well. The next activity develops skill in listening and following directions; it also allows the teacher to check a child's understanding of colors and shapes.

● **MODEL ACTIVITY:** *Following Directions*

See that each child has a large piece of unlined paper and a box of crayons. Give this series of directions: "Make a big red *X* in the middle of your paper. Draw a blue circle around the outside of the *X.* Put a yellow line across the middle of the *X.* Put green dots inside the circle."   ●

A teacher can help children improve their listening comprehension by reading informational books to them. When reading these books to the class, the teacher should relate the children's experiences to the content of the books. For example, *Your First Pet and How to Care for It* (Carla Stevens. New York: Macmillan, 1978) is a good book to use when there is a pet in the classroom. Relevant books should be read and made available to children before and after visiting various places on field trips. In other words, books should be an integral part of many classroom activities and experiences. Some general guidelines for use of factual books are

1. Do not read aloud only the part of the book that answers a specified question. Lead students to decide for themselves when an answer has been supplied.
2. Read more than one book on the topic being taught, and ask students to specify what new information was in the second or third book. Also ask them to find the "conflicts" in the sources.
3. Reread parts of a book to emphasize information, and read from several books that provide the same information.
4. Teach locational skills. "In what part of the book did we find that information?"

The following activity shows the possible use of books in a lesson on plants in a kindergarten room.

● **MODEL ACTIVITY:** *Listening for Information*

Set up a science center with books and displays about plants. Say to the children: "Today we are going to talk about plants. First, I am going to read you a book about plants. Listen to see if you can find out how plants grow. Then we will plant something for our room." Read the book and ask questions such as those listed below.

Questions

Where do seeds come from?

What do plants need to make them grow?

How are seeds planted?

How do we take care of plants?

If we want to plant something, what will we need?

Sources for Center

Eat the Fruit, Plant the Seed by Millicent Selsam and Jerome Wexler. New York: Morrow, 1980.

Science Experiences for Young Children: Seeds by Rosemary Althouse and Cecil Main. New York: Teachers College Press, 1975.

Plant Fun: Ten Easy Plants to Grow Indoors by Anita Holmes. New York: Four Winds, 1974.

Projects with Plants by Seymour Simon. New York: Watts, 1973.

How Plants Travel by Joan E. Rahn. New York: Atheneum, 1973.

Vegetables from Stems and Leaves by Millicent Selsam. New York: Morrow, 1972. ●

Oral Expression

Experience in using oral language is especially important for those children who come from home environments where Standard English is not commonly used (Anderson et al., 1985). Children learn to use language through informal conversations with other children and with the teacher. These conversations may be carried on while the children work quietly together at centers or on projects. The schoolroom environment provides many subjects and opportunities for descriptive talk. Children can compare different building blocks and note their relationships—size, weight, color; they can observe several kinds of animals and consider differences in their feet, skin covering, and size; they can compare a variety of fabrics for texture, weight, and purpose.

One means of helping children with description is for the teacher to describe a prominent object in the room. The children listen to the description and take turns identifying what they think the teacher has described. Later, children should describe objects while other children guess what has been described.

Retelling stories gives children opportunities for oral expression and also improves their understanding of literature. Morrow (1985) conducted three related research studies with kindergartners to discover the benefits of story retellings. She found that both retellings and guided discussions led to significant gains for the experimental group over the control group in developing comprehension, providing a sense of story structure, and improving oral complexity in the use of language.

Such uses of language develop the ability to communicate orally with reasonable fluency—to articulate common sounds clearly, to choose words, and to use a variety of sentence structures. In all of their communication with children, teachers should model good speech. They should encourage the children's efforts to use new words and speak in correctly formed sentences.

On certain occasions children may speak to a group or to the entire class, explaining their artwork or telling how to do something. One popular sharing activity is often referred to as show-and-tell. Children share something interesting with the class by telling about it and sometimes by showing it. Show-and-tell can be an effective way of developing oral language, but it can also be a waste of time if it is mishandled.

● **MODEL ACTIVITY:** *Oral Expression (Show-and-Tell)*

Say to the children: "This morning we are going to have show-and-tell. Let's review the rules before we start. I will call on one of you to begin and that one will be the leader for today. After the first time, the leader will call on the other children. Remember that you are to share something important. Don't just tell about a television show or what you had for dinner last night. Think about what you want to say before you raise your hand. The rest of you will be the audience. You should be good listeners. Who would like to start?" ●

Opportunities for oral expression occur frequently during the day. Teachers

should encourage children to use these opportunities to develop their skills in oral communication. Some good ideas for class activities that develop oral expression are

making the daily schedule
choosing a current event to record on the chalkboard
planning projects, activities, or experiences
discussing a new bulletin-board display
interpreting pictures
discussing what to include in an experience story
brainstorming ideas from "What if . . ." situations (Example: "What if we had
    four arms instead of two arms?")
acting out stories
carrying on pretend telephone conversations with play telephones
reviewing the day's events
engaging in dramatic play

Interest in Reading

Since readiness for an activity requires an interest in that activity, one of the first and most important tasks of a reading readiness program is building an interest in reading. Children's attitudes may range from disinclination to indifference to anticipation, exhibited in such behavior as showing interest in signs, enjoying listening to stories, being able to tell stories and recite poems or rhymes, enjoying looking at pictures in books, being able to attend to a sequential picture book, making up stories about a picture, and asking to take books home. In order to develop interest in learning to read, children need to be exposed to language and literature. They need to experience the delight that comes from listening and responding to stories, to handle books and examine pictures, and to see reasons for reading in their daily activities.

Wordless Picture Books

Picture books without words serve three major purposes in the reading readiness program. They develop positive attitudes toward reading because most children enjoy "reading" them. Any reasonable interpretation is acceptable, so children are unlikely to fail in their storytelling. Children also develop oral language skills as they tell their impressions of what is happening, using correct sentence structure and appropriate vocabulary. Finally, they begin working with comprehension skills that they will use later in reading: identifying details, becoming aware of sequence, making inferences, predicting what will happen next, seeing cause-and-effect relationships, and drawing conclusions.

When using wordless picture books, a teacher can help students gain the greatest benefit from the experience by observing a few guidelines. He or she should select books with illustrations that are clear and easy to understand and with story lines that are readily discernible. The teacher should instruct children to look all the way through a book to get an overall perspective before trying to tell the story. (Otherwise, they may interpret each page individually.) He or she should ask questions to develop comprehension (for example, "What is this called?" for vocabulary; "Why does Jack look angry?" for inference).

There are different types of wordless picture books. Most tell stories (Raymond Briggs's *The Snowman*); some develop concepts (Tana Hoban's *Is It Red? Is It Yellow? Is It Blue?*); and others give information (Iela and Enzo Mari's *The Apple and the Moth*). Mercer Mayer's humorous books about a boy and his frog are well liked (*Frog, Where are You?, Frog Goes to Dinner*). John Goodall has written several wordless picture books that use half-page inserts to change the illustrations (*Ballooning Adventures of Paddy Pork*). A good wordless picture storybook is *Changes, Changes* by Pat Hutchins. This book captivates children with its fast-moving sequence of events; two brightly colored wooden dolls rearrange wooden building blocks to create whatever is needed. Children can see cause and effect, perceive logical sequence, and predict what will happen next.

Poetry

Nothing better acquaints children with the melody, rhythm, and flow of language than poetry. By repeating favorite verses, children can develop an appreciation and love of language and experiment with sounds and rhythmic phrases. They may like poetry for its humor, its vivid and sometimes ridiculous images, its quick action, and its delightfully expressive words. The alliteration and rhyming words are not only fun to use, they help in developing phonics skills.

Having the right poem on hand for the occasion, such as Lillian Moore's "Wind Song" on a windy day, is a good way to introduce children to the rich possibilities of poetry. An anthology for young children or a personal card file of children's favorite poems, classified so that the teacher can quickly find the right poem, is a useful resource. Some possible classifications for a poetry file are holidays, seasons, animals, humorous verse, and fantasy. Occasionally, teachers may wish to use records, tapes, or filmstrips with sound effects during poetry time. One possible card for a poetry file is shown in Example 2.2.

Hearing poetry read by a teacher should be a pleasant experience for children. When reading to the class, the teacher should select poems that have variety and include such qualities as worthwhile ideas, honesty, uniqueness, imagery, musical quality, and mood and emotional appeal. Poems should stimulate the children's imaginations and foster their enjoyment. A few excellent poems to read aloud at the prereading level are

"Galoshes" by Rhoda W. Bacmeister (rhythm and sound)
"The Monkeys and the Crocodile" by Laura E. Richards (story, humor)
"Eletelephony" by Laura E. Richards (humor)
"Snow" by Dorothy Aldis (imagery)
"Hiding" by Dorothy Aldis (story, humor)
"Who Has Seen the Wind?" by Christina Rossetti (mood)
"Mice" by Rose Fyleman (humor)
"The Owl and the Pussy-Cat" by Edward Lear (story, humor)
"Every Time I Climb a Tree" by David McCord (mood)
"The Swing" by Robert Louis Stevenson (action, mood)
"Indian" by Rosemary and Stephen Vincent Benét (action)
"Stocking Fairy" by Winifred Welles (fantasy)
"Hello and Goodbye" by Mary A. Haberman (mood)
"The King's Breakfast" by A. A. Milne (story)
"Doorbells" by Rachel Field (characterization)
"The Coin" by Sara Teasdale (wisdom)

Other poets whose work is appropriate for this age group include Harry Behn, Myra C. Livingston, and Walter de la Mare. Mother Goose is still popular with children because of its language patterns, story quality, characterization, and possibilities for active involvement.

▶ **EXAMPLE 2.2:** A Poem for a Poetry Card File

Poetry Card
"Once I Caught a Fish"
Ages 4–6
    1st Half Class: 1, 2, 3, 4, 5
    2nd Half Class: Once I caught a fish alive,
    1st Half Class: 6, 7, 8, 9, 10,
    2nd Half Class: I let it go again.
    1st Half Class: Why did you let it go?
    2nd Half Class: Because it bit my fingers so.
    1st Half Class: Which finger did it bite?
    2nd Half Class: The little finger on the right.
                                     Anon.

Suitability: Choral reading (antiphonal)
Type: Humorous

● *MODEL ACTIVITY: Poetry*

Say to the children: "Boys and girls, we have been reading Mother Goose rhymes and you can say many of them by yourselves now. Let's say some of our favorites together." The children recite rhymes that you suggest. Then say to them: "I have written some of these rhymes on paper. I would like you to make pictures for them. Then we will put these papers together and make pages for a book. I will give each one of you a different rhyme. When you get your rhyme, I will tell you which one you have. Then think about what kind of picture to draw to go with the rhyme. When you are finished, we will have a new book for our library table." ●

Children enjoy participation poems and finger plays in which they can move their bodies or their fingers along with the poem. When listening to "Jump or Jiggle" by Evelyn Beyer, different children can be "lions stalking," "snakes sliding," or "sea gulls gliding." An example of a finger play is "Little Brown Rabbit," for which children can use their fingers to act as rabbits.

Informal Drama

Informal dramatic activities create interest in language and stories. Informal drama is spontaneous and unrehearsed, as opposed to formal drama, in which people memorize lines and wear costumes, and settings may be elaborate. Children assume the roles of characters, either from real life or from stories they have heard. They think, feel, move, react, and speak in accordance with their interpretation of the characters.

Informal drama may take one of many forms. It may begin with simple rhythmic movements or actions in response to poems or songs. Later, children may pantomime stories or actions as the teacher reads. Dramatic play occurs when children simulate real experiences, such as cooking dinner or being a cashier.

In an activity such as the one presented below, children are able to practice language skills as they play the roles of customer, cashier, food preparer, and order taker. They learn to follow directions, fill out forms, and recognize the words for menu items. They also develop mathematical skills as they use play money to pay for their orders and make change.

● *MODEL ACTIVITY: Dramatic Play*

After the children have been discussing their experiences at various fast-food restaurants, say to them: "How could we make a pretend fast-food restaurant in our own classroom? Where could we put it? What are some things we would need? How could we get these things?" Have the children come up with answers and develop a plan. Ask some children to bring in cups, napkins, bags, and plastic containers from a fast-food restaurant and have others paint a sign. One child can bring in a toy cash register. Make an illustrated price list to place above an improvised counter and copies of order forms for the children to use. Help the children learn to read the food words and the prices by asking: "What is the first item on the list? How much does it cost? Can you find it on the order form?" Keep the list simple at first and add new items later. When the fast-food center is ready, different children can assume the roles of customers and workers.[1] ●

Acting out stories spontaneously, or creative dramatics, builds interest in reading because children love to hear stories and then act them out. As the teacher reads a story, the children need to pay close attention to the sequence of events, the personalities of the characters, the dialogue, and the mood. Before acting out the story, the class reviews what happened and identifies the characters. As they act, the children must use appropriate vocabulary, enunciate distinctly, speak audibly, and express themselves clearly. Children will want to dramatize some stories several times, with different youngsters playing the characters each time. The rest of the class forms the audience and must listen carefully.

Use simple stories or selected parts of longer stories with young children who are engaging in creative dramatics. Some good stories are the following:

One Fine Day by Nonny Hogrogian. New York: Macmillan, 1971.
Ask Mr. Bear by Marjorie Flack. New York: Macmillan, 1932.
Caps for Sale by Esphyr Slobodkina. New York: William R. Scott, 1947.
The Three Billy Goats Gruff by Peter Asbjornsen and Jorgan Moe. New York: Harcourt Brace Jovanovich, 1957.
The Ox-Cart Man by Barbara Cooney. New York: Viking, 1979.
Where the Wild Things Are by Maurice Sendak. New York: Harper & Row, 1963.

Puppets are also useful in creative dramatics. Some shy children who are unwilling to speak as themselves are willing to talk through puppets. Children develop good language skills as they plan puppet shows and spontaneously speak their lines (see Model Activity: Puppets).

If teachers want to encourage children to participate in dramatic play, they should have the following kinds of supplies on hand:

costume box
strips of old tickets
order forms and pencils
cash register
old cardboard boxes
old clock with movable hands
calendars, pamphlets, and
    postcards
oak tag strips with felt-tip pens
empty food containers

beauty shop equipment and
    supplies
housekeeping materials
catalogues and seed packets
fast-food paper products
shopping bags
play money
building blocks
tools and kitchen utensils
library cards

[1] For a detailed account of setting up a McDonald's center, see Gaye McNutt and Nancy Bukofzer, "Teaching Early Reading at McDonald's," *The Reading Teacher* 35 (April 1982): 841–42.

● *MODEL ACTIVITY:* *Puppets*

Provide a simple puppet theater and a box of puppets that may be used to represent different characters. The puppet theater can be an old appliance carton with the back cut off and a hole cut near the top of the front.

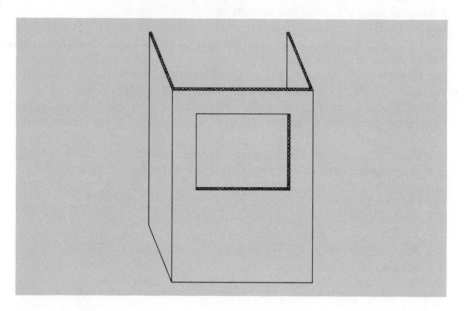

Here are some of the kinds of puppets that the children may use, along with directions for making them:

1. *Finger puppets.* Use fabric or construction paper to make a snug tube that fits over a finger. Decorate it to make it resemble a character.
2. *Paper-bag puppets.* Use paper lunch bags and apply facial features with scraps of fabric or construction paper. The mouth opening should fall on the fold of the bag.
3. *Sock puppets.* Using a child's sock that can fit over a hand, apply buttons, yarn, and bits of felt to make a character's head.
4. *Stick puppets.* Cut out characters that have been colored from coloring books. Mount them on the ends of rulers or sticks. ●

Dramatic play has many benefits. Because children need to carry on conversations, they must use good language skills. By interacting with others, they are developing social and emotional readiness. Frequently children use printed words in their play, which later become sight words. These words may be found on package labels, order forms, street signs, or ticket booths. Children discover the need to read when they must recognize words in order to play the situation. Seeing this need stimulates interest in learning to read.

Social and Emotional Development

Individual and group communication and participation are important factors in social and emotional development. Many children have had little or no experience with a group as large as that found in an ordinary classroom. Each child must learn to work independently and to follow certain patterns in order not to disrupt the learning situation for others. However, many group activities in the classroom call for cooperation and sharing among students and help children develop from self-centered individuals into social beings. Language is the most important basis of cooperation. Both the social patterns within the class and the authority of the teacher are established through language. Communication experiences should be structured so that children feel adequate and secure and can develop desirable attitudes toward themselves and others. Every effort must be made in the classroom to avoid threatening a child's security and disrupting the learning experience of the others in the group. Emotionally, every child has a need for love, attention, and acceptance. If these needs are denied, a child will react with behavior that hinders achievement of his or her goals or those of the school. Aggressive, hostile, and withdrawn children pose problems that are potentially detrimental to the learning process.

A child's social and emotional development can affect his or her success in learning to read. Certain activities can help a child reach maturity. Following are the characteristics of socially and emotionally mature children, along with ideas for promoting the development of each characteristic.

Carrying on sensible conversations; interacting well with other children. Give children opportunities to participate in small group discussions and work on projects with other children. Form groups for various purposes. Encourage children to generate ideas, reach decisions, take turns talking, and complete tasks cooperatively.

Controlling temper; accepting disappointments. Praise children who control their tempers and who accept disappointments gracefully. Ignore inappropriate behavior whenever possible.

Following directions. Encourage children to follow directions, by using exercises such as those described under "Following Directions" in Appendix A to this chapter. Establish routines so that children will know what to expect.

Sharing and taking turns. Show children how to share and take turns by role-playing proper behavior. Stress the need to be patient, to consider the feelings of others, and to take care of property.

Being self-reliant; completing tasks. Give children simple tasks that they can complete independently. Gradually increase the complexity of the tasks. Praise children who are self-reliant.

Having good attention spans. Plan short, high-interest activities. Work with children on an individual basis if necessary. Reward children who maintain their attention with privileges.

Having a positive attitude toward school; seeming eager to learn. Make school an interesting and happy place to be. Allow each child to be successful at something every day. Create a cheerful environment.

Handling school materials competently. Demonstrate the use of scissors, crayons, paste, and paint. Allow children the privilege of using them when they can handle them correctly and put them away as instructed.

Knowing what to do in different situations. Role-play what to do if the teacher must leave the room, if a guest comes, if a child gets sick, if something is lost, and so on. Explain fire drills and routine procedures. Show children what choices they have when they have completed their work.

Working independently at centers. In small groups, show children how to work at centers. Stress how important it is for each child to do his or her own work without interfering with other children. Allow children to work in centers only when they observe the rules.

Putting away and cleaning up. Give children a five-minute warning when free time is nearly over. Have a place for everything, with labels to indicate where things belong. Be sure that paper towels and other supplies required for cleaning up are readily available.

Finding resources independently. Familiarize children with the resources in the classroom. Keep things in their proper places. Allow children to be responsible for using and returning materials.

An activity such as that shown in Model Activity: Duty Chart can help children foster mature social and emotional attitudes.

● **MODEL ACTIVITY:** *Duty Chart*

Say to the children: "In our classroom we need many helpers. What kinds of helpers do we need?" The children suggest answers. Then say: "We will need different boys and girls to help us each week. I have made a duty chart to help us remember whose turn it is to help. Each week we will change the names beside the jobs. Let's read the chart together. We will see who has a job this week."

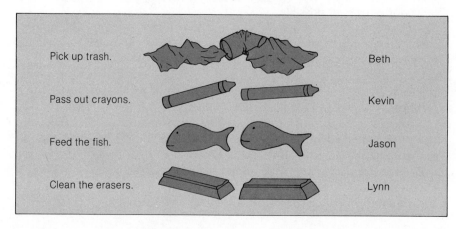

Physical Development

Other than general good health, good vision and hearing are most essential for learning to read. Good visual acuity, at near and far distances, and eye coordination are important for adequate visual functioning in reading. The child's need to make fine visual discriminations (to see likenesses and differences) is obvious; it suggests the usefulness of early activities that involve forms and shapes (such as picture puzzles) and later activities that involve letter recognition (words beginning or ending alike, and so on). Auditory acuity is also important in learning to read. Phonics is based on the ability to hear sounds and discriminate among them. Activities that emphasize beginning sounds and rhyming words are especially useful in developing auditory skills.

Children must also develop some motor coordination skill in order to read successfully—for example, they must be able to hold books the correct distance from the eyes and to turn pages one at a time. There is little relationship between such physical activities as hopping, skipping, and cutting with scissors, however, and learning to read (Anderson et al., 1985). In this section motor coordination is considered only as it relates to directionality and to the use of kinesthetic-tactile learning as an alternative for the auditory-visual approach to reading.

A teacher can use many types of physical activities to prepare children for working with letters and words. The activities that follow are divided into three major categories: visual skills, auditory skills, and motor skills.

Visual Skills

Visual perception, visual memory, and visual discrimination are necessary for reading, in addition to good visual acuity. Perception refers to the brain's processing and understanding of visual stimuli; memory, to a child's ability to recall what he or she has seen; and discrimination, to the ability to distinguish between likenesses and differences. In order to achieve this last skill, the child must first understand the concepts of *like* and *different*.

Activities requiring children to discriminate among letter and word forms promote reading readiness more effectively than activities requiring them to identify similarities and differences in geometric forms (Sippola, 1985). Unless children need practice in developing the concepts of *like* and *different*, it is pointless to have them make distinctions in shapes and forms. Instead, they need practice with simultaneous and successive visual discrimination of letters and words. Simultaneous discrimination occurs when children match printed symbols that are alike while they can see both symbols. In successive discrimination children must find a duplicate symbol after a stimulus card is no longer visible.

The visual perception, visual memory, and visual discrimination activities in this section should be helpful in developing each of these skills. Appendix A to this chapter presents additional visual activities.

● *MODEL ACTIVITY:* *Visual Perception*

Say to the children: "I am going to put a word on the board. The word is *car.* Now I am going to draw a box around it. Karen, come up and trace over the box." ⬚car⬚ "I will put another word on the board. The word has some tall letters in it. The word is *call.* I will draw a box around it, too. Andy, will you trace over this box?" ⬚call⬚ "Let's try another word. In this word one letter goes up and one letter goes down. The word is *dog.* Look at the box I am drawing around *dog.* Trace over this box for us, Skip." ⬚dog⬚ Repeat this process with several other short words with different shapes (ride, said, go, hide). Then give each child a sheet of paper with some large printed words on it. Say to the children: "Look at the words on your paper. I want you to look at each word carefully. Then I want you to make a box around it with your crayon." ●

● *MODEL ACTIVITY:* *Visual Memory*

Write a series of letters on the board, such as *f, o, t, s, m,* and *k.* Say to the children: "I have written some letters on the board." Then say: "Look carefully at the letters that are on the board. I am going to ask you to close your eyes while I erase one of them. When you open your eyes, see if you can tell me which letter I erased." ●

● *MODEL ACTIVITY:* *Visual Discrimination*

Write on the board some letters that are similar in appearance (*b, d, g, p,* and *d*) and also some similarly shaped or identical words (*hot, pat, top, pat, ton*). Say to the children: "Let's look at these letters. Are any of them alike? Which ones are the same? How are the first two letters different? What is different about the other letters?" Ask the same questions about the words. Some children may draw boxes around the letters and words or trace them. Then say to them: "Now I am going to give you a piece of paper with some letters and words on it. Look at the first group of letters. Do you see the letter above the blocks of letters? Can you find a block with a letter in it that is exactly like the letter on top of the blocks? If you can, I want you to color that block red." Repeat the activity with a sample set of words. Then say: "Does everyone understand what to do? Go ahead and color the blocks that have the same letters or words as the ones on top."

b			bad	
g	d		dad	bat
p	b		bad	bed

Auditory Skills

As is true of visual skills, auditory skills necessary for reading include acuity, perception, memory, and discrimination. Auditory perception is the way the brain comprehends information it receives by sound. Many auditory perception activities can help children develop an awareness of their environment, as well as help them with reading.

● *MODEL ACTIVITY:* *Auditory Perception*

Most of the children in this class can recognize the letters of the alphabet. Say to them: "We are going to play a game. I want you to close your eyes and listen while I write a letter on the board. Then I want you to tell me what letter I wrote without looking. First I will write an *s* or a *t* on the board. Think how you make these letters. Then close your eyes and listen while I make either an *s* or a *t*." Make a *t*. Then say: "Which letter did I make?" Most of the children answer "*t*." Say: "Open your eyes and see if you are right. How did you know it was *t* and not *s*? That's right. You heard me crossing the *t*." Other pairs of letters to use are *i* and *l*, *j* and *n*, *x* and *o*, and *f* and *c*. ●

Auditory memory refers to a child's ability to recall information or stimuli that he or she has heard. Several activities will promote the development of auditory memory. Although there is some overlap, they fall into three major categories: echo activities, remembering connected speech, and following directions. Here is one possible echo activity.

● *MODEL ACTIVITY:* *Auditory Memory*

Play the following game with a small group of children. Say to them: "We are going to pretend to go to the store and buy some food. Each one of us will remember what everyone else has bought. Then we will buy one more thing. Let's try it. I will begin. 'I went to the store and bought some bread.' Now Mark must say, 'I went to the store and bought some bread and something else.' " If Mark says, "I went to the store and bought some bread and butter," tell him, "That's the right idea. Now, Sandra, it's your turn." Sandra says: "I went to the store and bought some bread and butter and popsicles." The children continue around the circle, each adding a new item. ●

Auditory discrimination, or the ability to hear likenesses and differences in sounds, is a prerequisite for phonics instruction and is therefore an important skill in the readiness program. As with visual discrimination, attention to general sounds in the environment has value only in teaching concepts of *like* and *different* (Sippola, 1985). Beginning readers need to focus their attention primarily on observing similarities and differences in the beginning sounds and rhyming sounds of words.

Introducing children to simple rhymes is a good way to sensitize them to likenesses and differences in verbal sounds. Ask children to pick out the words that rhyme and to supply words to rhyme with a given word. This ability is fundamental to the construction of "word families." Children should also be able to hear similarities and differences in word endings and in middle vowels; for example, they should be able to tell whether *rub* and *rob*, or *hill* and *pit*, have the same middle sound. Finally, they should be able to listen to the pronunciation of a word sound by sound and mentally fuse or blend the sounds to recognize the intended word. The two activities presented below should help develop such auditory discrimination abilities.

● **MODEL ACTIVITY:** *Auditory Discrimination (Beginning Sounds)*

Name several puppets with double names to stress initial consonant sounds (Molly Mouse, Freddie Frog, Dolly Duck, and Bennie Bear). While holding a puppet, say: "I'd like you to meet Molly Mouse. Molly Mouse only likes things that begin the same way that her name begins. Molly Mouse likes milk, but she doesn't like water. I am going to name some things that Molly Mouse likes or doesn't like. You must listen closely to the way the word begins. Raise your hand if I say something that Molly Mouse likes. Keep your hand down if I say something that Molly Mouse doesn't like. Let's begin. Molly Mouse likes meat." The children should raise their hands. If they don't seem to understand why she likes meat, talk about the beginning sound and give additional examples. Then say: "Molly Mouse likes cheese." The children should keep their hands down. ●

● **MODEL ACTIVITY:** *Auditory Discrimination (Whole Word)*

Give each child in the group or class two cards that are identical except that one has *S* written on it and one has *D* written on it. Say to the children: "Each of you has two cards. Hold up the one that has *S* on it." Demonstrate which card has the *S* by holding it up. Then follow the same procedure with the *D* card. Continue by saying: "I am going to say two words. If the two words sound exactly the same, hold up the card with *S* on it. If the two words do not sound exactly the same, hold up the card with *D* on it. The *S* card means *same*. The *D* card means *different*. The first two words are *boy* and *horse*. All of you should be holding up the *D* card because these two words sound different. The next two words are *funny* and *funny*. Now everyone should be holding up the *S* card because these two words sound the same." Continue with other examples. ●

Additional activities to develop each of these skills are presented in Appendix A to this chapter.

Motor Activities

Most children learn to read readily through an auditory-visual approach, but kinesthetic-tactile activities are also useful for teaching letter and word shapes. These activities utilize the sense of touch and whole body movements for learning letter forms. Some educators believe that children who use body movements to work with letters pay closer attention to the shapes. The kinesthetic-tactile approach is good reinforcement for the average learner and an alternate way to teach the special learner.

● *MODEL ACTIVITY: Kinesthetic-Tactile Learning*

Give each child in the group a card with the word *down* printed on it. Say to the children: "Today we are going to learn to read and write a new word. This word is *down*. Look at your card and say the word with me. Listen to a sentence that has the word *down* in it. 'Put this book down.' Will you do this for me, Jenny? Now I want all of you to start with the tall letter *d* and move your finger under the word as we say it together. Let's do that three times. This time I want you to trace each letter with your finger as we say the word again. Remember to start with the tall letter *d*. Now look at your card and use your finger to write the word *down* in giant letters in the air. See if you can do it this time without looking at your card. Look at your card again and see if you did it right. Turn your card over and try writing the word *down* with your finger on the back of the card. Check to see if you did it right." ●

Children need to establish directionality in reading and writing; that is, they must learn to read from left to right and from top to bottom. Some children can write their names as easily from right to left as from left to right. Such directional errors are common for beginners; they will usually disappear as a child moves along in reading.

● *MODEL ACTIVITY: Directionality*

The children are sitting facing you. Say to them: "How many hands do you have? That's right. You have two hands. One hand is your left hand. The other hand is your right hand." Show the children which hand is left and which is right. Then say: "Raise your left hand up high. Your other hand is your right hand. Now raise your right hand up high." Repeat this process with arms, legs, and feet. Then say; "I want you to listen carefully and do exactly what I say. Hold up your right hand. Stamp your right foot. Put your left hand on your left leg." Give directions slowly and pause long enough to make sure everyone is following directions. ●

Appendix A to this chapter includes additional motor activities.

✔ **Self-Check: Objective 5**

List some activities that you would like to try for developing visual
and auditory skills. (Refer to Appendix A for additional ideas.)
(See Self-Improvement Opportunities 4 and 10.)

MOVING INTO READING AND WRITING

A current view of beginning reading supports the position that during early
childhood youngsters are going through a period of "emergent literacy," or a
developing awareness of the interrelatedness of oral and written language
(Teale and Sulzby, 1986). This is a time of natural growth in language learning
that occurs in the home and community as children see print and understand
its function in their environment. They learn about literacy from adult models,
particularly their parents, and their knowledge of reading and writing develops
concurrently. Before they understand letter-sound associations, they scribble
messages or draw letterlike forms which have meaning for them, and then
"read" their messages to others.

Researchers have found that many kindergarten children already understand many concepts about language, including the following (Mavrogenes,
1986):

1. They make sense out of the writing in their environment by relating words
   (such as *McDonald's*) to corresponding places (a restaurant).
2. They expect print to be meaningful and to communicate ideas.
3. They understand some characteristics of written language, such as directionality, spacing, sequencing, and form.
4. They have some knowledge of letter names, auditory and visual discrimination, and correspondence between written and spoken words.

The concept of emergent literacy differs in some respects from traditional
reading readiness programs, which produce discontinuities in language development, according to Clay (1979). In other words, these programs require
children to find different ways of responding to language situations from the
ways they used during their preschool years. Children do not always see the
connection between some formal skills instruction in reading readiness and
the process of reading and writing. For instance, they may perceive little
transfer from circling different geometric shapes on skills sheets to reading and
writing.

Tasks that are closely related to reading and writing are more valuable for
beginning readers than are general cognitive and motor tasks. Whereas it was
once assumed that teachers prepared children for reading by having them hop
and skip, distinguish colors and shapes, and identify environmental sounds,
research now indicates that specific experiences with language are more

effective preparation (Anderson et al., 1985; Mason, 1984). The following activities are recommended (Mason, 1984).

1. performing tasks that require use of specific vocabulary and complete sentences to name objects and events and to communicate ideas
2. listening to stories
3. writing ideas that have been expressed orally
4. following oral directions

Teachers should use children's interests as a basis for choosing specific materials, activities, and procedures. Predictable books—those that use repetition, rhythmic language patterns, and familiar concepts—are excellent resources for introducing children to the pleasure and ease of reading. Even during a first reading by the teacher, children join in on the repetitive lines or familiar chants. Stories such as Bill Martin's *Brown Bear, Brown Bear* (New York: Holt, Rinehart and Winston, 1970) and the folktale "The Old Woman and Her Pig" (Paul Galdone; New York: McGraw-Hill, 1960) contain familiar sequences. Children are soon reading these books for themselves if the teacher has reread them and pointed out the corresponding words (Rhodes, 1981).

Teachers can use predictable books as modified cloze exercises in which children fill in words that the reader omits. For instance, when the teacher reads, "And the little red hen said—," the children respond, "I'll do it myself!" This procedure enables a child to "confirm the predictability of written language" (Wiseman, 1984, p. 343). Appendix B to this chapter contains a list of predictable or repetitive books.

Teaching Sounds, Letters, and Words

As children learn to read and write, they need to be able to separate the sounds in words, a process referred to as *phonemic segmentation* (Vacca, Vacca, and Gove, 1987). The beginning stages of phonemic segmentation are auditory; children listen for the sounds in a word and tell how many they hear. The teacher might say a familiar word slowly and deliberately, ask the child to repeat it in the same way, and then have the child tap on a table or put down a marker for each sound that is heard. Later the teacher should help the child associate letters with the sounds, perhaps by first making a series of small squares and then writing the corresponding letter or letters in the appropriate square as the child identifies each sound. See Example 2.3 for an illustration of a way in which the letters for the sounds in the word *meat* can be recorded.

Questions that cause the child to think about the sounds heard at the beginning, middle, and end of a word are often helpful in strengthening phonemic segmentation. Although preschoolers generally do not perform well on tasks of phonemic segmentation, some children seem to have acquired an implicit awareness of sounds in words from their own observations about

▶ **EXAMPLE 2.3:** Phonemic Segmentation

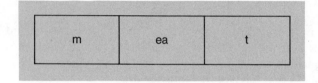

language. After a year of phonics instruction and reading practice, however, most children show significant gains in their ability to separate words into phonemes (Mason, 1984). A child who can segment phonemes, or do the reverse by blending sounds together to form words, is demonstrating metalinguistic awareness on a phonological level.

Once children have some knowledge of the letters that represent the sounds in words, they can write by using "invented spellings." Richgels (1987, p. 523) defines invented spelling as "beginning writers' ability to write words by attending to their sound units and associating letters with them in a systematic, though unconventional, way." Teachers can center phonics instruction on children's experimentation with written language as an alternative to teaching isolated elements in a sequence of phonics skills. Writing with invented spellings enables children to apply their knowledge of letter-sound relationships in purposeful, enjoyable ways. Purposes for writing include writing invitations, thank-you notes, captions for artwork, lists, reports of experiences, daily entries in journals, and stories in story booklets. Example 2.4 shows how a kindergartner reacted to a unit on dinosaurs by drawing a picture and writing a story with invented spellings, and Example 2.5 shows a first grader's use of invented spellings in a message to a friend.

✔ Self-Check: Objective 6
What are some good ways to teach letter and word recognition? (See Self-Improvement Opportunities 8, 11, and 12.)

Teachers need to keep several points in mind while teaching letters and words to beginning readers. Letter names should be taught early so that the teacher and the class have a common referent—for example, understanding when the teacher talks about the letter *f* or the letter *n* (Farr and Roser, 1979, p. 105). Knowledge of letter *names* is important for talking about similarities and differences in printed words, but knowledge of letter *sounds* is more useful in decoding words (Hafner and Jolly, 1982, p. 26). Children who learn both the names and sounds of letters can read better than children who learn only letter names (Anderson et al., 1985). Research points to a high correlation between knowledge of letter names and knowledge of phonics, so teaching of letter names is justifiable if done along with phonics instruction (Groff, 1984).

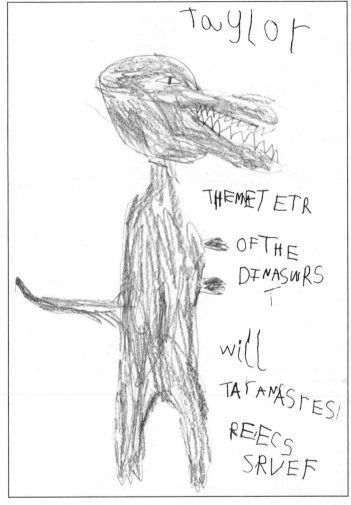

This story reads as follows: The meat eater of the dinosaurs. Will Tyrannosaurus Rex survive?

Source: Taylor Bennett, Capshaw Elementary School, Cookeville, Tennessee, 1987. Used with permission. ◀

It is more difficult to discriminate between some letters (such as *d* and *b* or *p* and *q*) than others, and the teacher should not teach similar letters or letters that are reversals of each other at the same time. Beginning readers have no reason to memorize the letters of the alphabet in order. An activity such as the following can be used in early teaching of letters. Additional activities are presented in Appendix A to this chapter.

▶ **EXAMPLE 2.5:** First Grader's Use of Invented Spellings

This story reads as follows: Roses are red. Violets are blue. These golden flowers remind me of you. Dedicated to Janet.

Source: Trudy Walker, Sycamore Elementary School, Cookeville, Tennessee, 1987. Used with permission. ◀

● **MODEL ACTIVITY:** *Letter Recognition*

Print the letters *E* and *e* on the chalkboard. Point to each letter and ask: "What letter is this?" The children should identify the letters as the capital and lower-case *e*. Then say: "I am going to give each of you a page from the newspaper. Some of these letters will be in the newspaper. Each time you find one, cut it out. Then paste your letters on a piece of paper. Some of the letters may be very big and some may be small." ●

Children who are beginning to recognize letters are also rapidly acquiring sight words, especially names, color and number words, and environmental words. Using bold, colorful logos identified with product advertisements in the real world helps youngsters discover the meaning of print. An experiment with preschoolers revealed that children taught with logo books could identify printed words both with and without the logo context better than children who did not learn logos (Wepner, 1985). Children quickly learn to recognize words or symbols associated with fast-food restaurants, cereal boxes, billboards, T-shirts, or toys. They can learn to recognize these familiar words before they learn all the letters, but their knowledge of environmental words may be imperfect. They may rely more on the context of the word than on the word itself for identification (Anderson et al., 1985). Early reading of environmental words helps children realize that print conveys information, but skill in recognizing these words may not transfer to skills necessary for achievement in school reading classes (Goodall, 1984).

● **MODEL ACTIVITY:** *Sight Word Recognition*

Make a color chart like the one pictured below. On one side of the chart print a list of color words in their corresponding colors. On the other side make some color splotches that match the words, but arrange them in a different sequence from the words. Attach colored yarn tipped with tape or glue to the appropriate color words. Punch a hole beside each splotch of color on the right side of the chart. While working with a small group of children, say: "Here are some colors that you know. Let's name the colors together." Say the colors with the children. "Now let's read these color words together." Read the color words with the children. "Frank, I would like you to read us one of the color words. Then put the piece of yarn from that word through the hole that is beside the same color as the word." Continue in the same way with the other children.

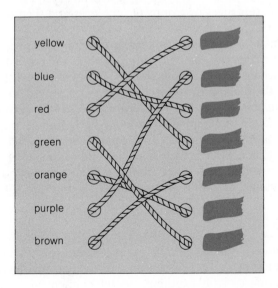

✔ **Self-Check: Objective 7**

**Name some ways that young children can learn to read by writing
and learn to write by reading.**

(See Self-Improvement Opportunity 13.)

Beginning Reading Programs

Many prereading programs for teaching beginning reading and writing skills
use reading readiness workbooks that serve as the first level of a basal reading
series (Paradis and Peterson, 1975). These workbooks introduce the children
gradually and sequentially to such skills as visual discrimination, letter sounds,
and left-to-right directionality. The accompanying teacher's manual gives
detailed directions for using the workbook and suggests a wealth of ideas for
supplementary enrichment activities. A sample lesson from a teacher's guide,
including the student's workbook page and explanation for the teacher, is
shown in Example 2.6.

Collins (1986) has identified several types of preschool reading programs
currently used in private and public schools in the United States. Some of these
center on the use of predictable books or preprimers in basal reading series,
and others use commercial packages with specific instructions for teaching
strategies. Two types of interactive programs are used. The first is a form of
language experience (see Chapter 6), based on stories that are read to students,
and the second is discovery word play, in which children experiment with
words as they play. A cognitive development program is based on Piaget's
developmental theories described earlier in this chapter, and a parental involvement program, used by many private preschools, begins with reading
instruction in the home. Some programs use a holistic approach; children first
consider whole sentences or groups of sentences and then look for patterns
and meanings.

Research shows that children's success in reading depends more on the
teacher's commitment to the curriculum than on the type of program used.
Therefore, teachers should choose the type of program that they believe will
work best for them (Collins, 1986).

The Commission on Reading (Anderson et al., 1985) recommends a balanced kindergarten program that includes both formal and informal approaches in reading and language. This recommendation is based on evidence
that children do benefit from early language and reading instruction. Instruction should be systematic but free from undue stress; preschools should not
become "academic bootcamps" (Anderson et al., 1985, p. 30).

Assessment of Readiness

Assessment of each child's level of reading readiness is a critical element in
the total readiness program. Teachers must not assign children reading-related
tasks that are too difficult for them, nor place them in structured reading

we, can, not

Introducing High-Frequency Words

Purpose	To develop instant recognition of the words *we, can,* and *not;* to practice reading these words in sentences; and to review the words *to, a,* and *go.*

Materials	Getting Ready to Read: page 106
	Getting Ready to Read, Big Book: page 106
	Resource Kit
	  Word Cards: We, we, Can, can, Not, not, go, to, a
	  Picture Card: pool
	  Punctuation Cards: period (.), question mark (?)
	Pocket Chart

Instruction

Place the word card *we* in the pocket chart and ask children to name the letter at the beginning of the word. Then say ● **This word begins with the sound for w, the sound you hear at the beginning of *worm*. I'm going to read a sentence and leave out this word. Think of a word that makes sense and begins with the sound for w.** Point to *we* when you come to the blank in the sentence.

Listen: He won't see us if _____ hide behind the chair.

Ask ● **Who will name this word?** . . . *(we)* **The word is *we*.**
Listen: He won't see us if *we* hide behind the chair.
Place *We* next to *we* in the pocket chart and ask ● **Who will name this word?** . . . *(We)* **Both words are *we*.** Point to each word as you say ● **This word begins with small w. This word begins with capital W.**

In the pocket chart, set up the sentence *We go to a (pool).* Have children name *pool*, then ask ● **Who will read this sentence?** . . . *(We go to a pool.)* Remove the cards from the pocket chart.

Place the word *can* in the pocket chart and ask children to name the letter at the beginning of the word. Then say ● **This word begins with the sound for c, the sound you hear at the beginning of *cat*. I'm going to read a sentence and leave out this word. Think of a word that makes sense and begins with the sound for c.** Point to *can* when you come to the blank in the sentence.

Listen: Now that Marlene is six years old, she _____ tie her own shoes.

Ask ● **What is this word?** . . . *(can)* **The word is *can*.** . . .
Listen: Now that Marlene is six years old, she *can* tie her own shoes.
Place *Can* next to *can* in the pocket chart and ask ● **Who will name this word?** . . . *(Can)* **Both words are *can*.** Point to each word as you say ● **This word begins with small c. This word begins with capital C.**

In the pocket chart, set up the sentence *Can we go?* Point to the question mark and say ● **This is called a question mark. The question mark tells you to read this sentence as you would ask a question. Who will read this question?** . . . *(Can we go?)* Set up the sentence *We can go.* **This sentence is an answer to the question. Who will read this sentence?** . . . *(We can go.)*

Use the same procedure to introduce the word *not*. First, have children name the letter *n* and remind them that *nest* begins with the sound for *n*. Then have them decode the word *not* in spoken context. Next, have them read the word in both its capital and lower-case forms. Finally, have children practice reading the word in a practice sentence.

Word: *not, Not*
Context: They went roller skating, but we could _____ go with them.
Practice Sentence: We can not go.

Guided Practice

Help children to find page 106 in *Getting Ready to Read*. Allow time for children to look at and talk about the page.

Point to the words at the top of the page and say ● **These are the words you were reading in the pocket chart.** Have children read the words as you point to them from left to right. **The children in the story will say these words.**

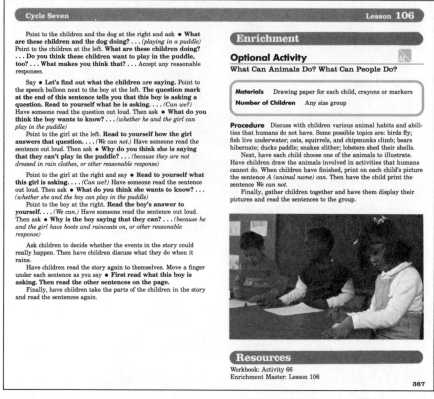

Source: GETTING READY TO READ, by William K. Durr and Robert L. Hillerich, Lesson 106. Copyright © 1986 by Houghton Mifflin Company. Used by permission. ◀

programs until they have the necessary coping skills. The danger that children will develop lasting negative or indifferent attitudes toward reading is great when they are frustrated. If a teacher is in doubt about a child's readiness for formal reading instruction, he or she should wait and be sure, rather than take a chance on starting the child too soon.

On an informal basis, the teacher makes assessments daily as he or she observes how a child reacts to situations, participates in activities, and communicates with others. Rate of learning is not steady, and the teacher will need to be sensitive to variations in growth rates. When a child's curiosity surges ahead, the teacher must find new ways to challenge him or her. If, on the other hand, a child indicates that he or she doesn't really understand a skill or concept, the teacher may need to backtrack and repeat a lesson. A teacher chooses strategies by assessing the needs, interests, and abilities of the students. See Chapter 10 for a more complete discussion of assessment at the readiness level.

Durkin's research (1966) showed that children can learn to read prior to formal school instruction and that early readers tend to maintain their high performance in reading, even after six years of schooling. Currently, a trend exists toward pre–first-grade instruction in reading and writing (Zirkelbach, 1984), but educators caution that children should be encouraged, not forced, to read and write. Youngsters who are pressured to read before they are ready may develop feelings of anxiety and depression (Werner and Strother, 1987). Readiness for reading is basically an individual matter. Some children come to school knowing how to read, and they should continue to read in keeping with their levels of achievement. Other children may indicate readiness for learning to read, and they should be given many opportunities for developing interest and skill in reading. Still others, however, may not be ready for reading until the end of first grade or even later, and these children need activities that will support language learning.

Many researchers question Piaget's contention that cognitive development depends on maturation and cannot be accelerated by instruction. In fact, many preschool children learn about how to read by listening to stories, learning letters and words, and experimenting with writing. This early awareness is positively related to later reading achievement and should be encouraged in preschool programs (Mason, 1984).

A number of professional organizations have identified concerns and made recommendations related to present practices in pre–first-grade reading instruction.[2] Some of the concerns expressed in the documents are listed below.

1. Many programs for pre–first-grade children are too rigid and formal and have inappropriate expectations for the children's levels of development.
2. Children often feel so much pressure from accelerated programs that they are afraid to take risks as they experiment with language.
3. Some programs focus on isolated skill development or abstract reading skills instead of the integration of oral language, writing, and listening with reading.
4. Children often fail to see the pleasure in reading because pre–first-grade programs emphasize skill building instead of reading for enjoyment.
5. Some programs stress high achievement on standardized tests rather than social, intellectual, and emotional development. Children in these programs do not have opportunities to satisfy their curiosity, think critically, and express themselves creatively.

[2] Association for Supervision and Curriculum Development, International Reading Association, National Association for the Education of Young Children, National Association of Elementary School Principals, and National Council of Teachers of English, "Joint Statement on Literacy Development and Pre–First Grade," *The Reading Teacher* 39 (April 1986): 819–21. Also, Board of Directors of the International Reading Association, "IRA Position Statement on Reading and Writing in Early Childhood," *The Reading Teacher* 39 (April 1986): 822–24.

An older sibling's or a parent's reading to a young child is one important way of building readiness for reading.   (© Judith D. Sedwick/The Picture Cube)

The following strategies for improving early reading instruction have been recommended by professional societies.

1. Use the children's experiences and knowledge of oral and written language as the basis for instruction instead of isolated skills.
2. Show respect for the children's own language and make it the base for language activities.
3. Allow all children to experience success with language.
4. Let reading be part of the total communication process, which includes speaking, listening, writing, art, math, and music.
5. Let children's early attempts at writing occur without regard for handwriting skills and correct spelling.
6. Encourage children to take risks with first attempts at reading and writing, and consider any errors to be part of their natural growth patterns.
7. Use familiar stories and materials for instruction in order to give the child a feeling of control and confidence.
8. Be a good model of language usage for children by speaking and listening to them and participating with them in reading and writing activities.
9. Read to them frequently from a wide variety of literary genres.

10. Provide regular periods of time for children to read and write independently.
11. Allow children to share what they think, know, and feel, in order to provide for their affective and cognitive development.
12. Choose testing procedures that are suitable for the child's developmental level and cultural background. Choose tests that are directly related to instructional objectives.
13. Help parents interpret standardized test scores by making them aware of the limitations of formal testing.
14. Communicate with parents about the total language program at school, and provide them with ideas for activities to use at home.
15. Provide opportunities for children to participate actively in the learning process by experimenting with language.

   In a recent position statement (Board of Directors, 1986), the International Reading Association concluded that young children learn about reading and writing through three general types of experiences: (1) interaction with adults through speaking, listening, reading, and writing; (2) independent experiments with print by first scribbling and pretending to read and later by using invented spellings for written communications and rereading familiar stories; and (3) adult models of appropriate language usage.

✔ **Self-Check: Objective 8**
Relate your own experiences in beginning reading to the issues concerning pre–first-grade reading. What are some concerns you might have about teaching reading in kindergarten?
(See Self-Improvement Opportunities 11, 12, 13, and 14.)

Summary

Children begin acquiring knowledge of language at an early age as they listen and learn to speak. Gender, home environment, and participation in preschool programs affect readiness for reading. Teachers can help prepare children for formal reading instruction by engaging them in a variety of activities, which are most meaningful when centered on units of related experiences.

   Five factors are important in determining a child's readiness for reading. *Experiential background* relates to the types and variety of experiences a child has gained during early childhood. If a child's experiences appear to be inadequate, the teacher can fill in gaps by providing such direct and vicarious experiences as taking field trips, inviting resource people to the classroom, using audiovisual aids, and discussing pictures. *Cognitive development, metalinguistic awareness,* and *language learning* are interrelated and important for learning to read. Cognitive development and metalinguistic awareness occur in stages, and language learning takes place through storytelling and story reading, listening comprehension activities, and opportunities for oral expression. *Interest readiness* refers to the importance of developing positive attitudes toward reading through such activities as looking at books, working with poetry, and participating in informal drama. Another factor is *social and emotional development,* which occurs as children learn how to participate in group activities and work independently. The fifth factor, *physical development,* includes those visual and auditory abilities that are essential for learning to read.

Children go through a period of "emergent literacy" as they learn to listen and speak and then to read and write. They learn letter names and sounds, acquire knowledge of sight words, and begin to write with the use of invented spellings. Early reading programs take many forms, including formal skills programs, holistic language and cognitive approaches, and programs centered on basal reading materials. Many educators advocate providing pre–first-grade reading instruction through a balance of formal and informal approaches.

Test Yourself

True or False

_____ 1. Reading readiness is an important consideration only at the initial reading instruction stage.

_____ 2. Boys are usually better readers than girls, especially in the lower grades.

_____ 3. Speaking and listening skills are closely related to learning to read and write.

_____ 4. Children in first grade are too young to understand informational books.

_____ 5. Some environmental measures correlate better with students' academic performance than do socioeconomic measures.

_____ 6. Preschool enrollment is decreasing.

_____ 7. One way to develop social and emotional readiness is to help children learn how to share and take turns.

_____ 8. A close relationship exists between cognitive development and the development of metalinguistic awareness.

_____ 9. Following directions is one way for children to develop auditory memory.

_____ 10. Teachers should read aloud to children about once a week.

_____ 11. Picture reading is an example of a *direct* experience through which a child can learn concepts and vocabulary.

_____ 12. Jean Piaget developed a kinesthetic-tactile approach to reading.

_____ 13. Piaget's theory supports formal reading instruction at the preschool level.

_____ 14. According to Piaget, language comes before thought.

_____ 15. The concrete-operational period of cognitive development generally occurs between the ages of two and seven.

_____ 16. If a child is egocentric, he or she sees things only from a personal point of view.

_____ 17. If you are not sure whether a child is ready for formal reading instruction, you should go ahead and start anyway.

_____ 18. Knowledge of letter names is a good predictor of success in beginning reading.

_____ 19. Prereading experiences are more meaningful when incorporated into units of related experiences.

_____ 20. The term _emergent literacy_ refers to a child's language development during the early years.

_____ 21. Formal instruction in reading is the most important function of the kindergarten.

_____ 22. There is a trend toward pre–first-grade reading instruction.

_____ 23. Children use invented spellings to express themselves in terms of the way they perceive letter-sound associations.

_____ 24. Instruction in listening appears to contribute to reading achievement.

_____ 25. Isolated drills and memorization of rules is better than language experiences for children who are deficient in metalinguistic awareness.

_____ 26. Activities requiring children to discriminate among geometric shapes are as valuable for promoting reading readiness as tasks that require them to discriminate among letter and word forms.

_____ 27. Early reading of environmental words enables children to realize that print represents meaning.

_____ 28. Professional societies recommend that preschools stress skill building and high achievement on formal tests.

Self-Improvement Opportunities

1. Interview two kindergarten children. Write a report on their readiness for initial instruction in terms of the major readiness factors.
2. Start a file of read-aloud books and stories for kindergarten and/or first-grade children.
3. Ask a child to interpret a picture. Report your findings and start your own picture file.
4. Start a collection of rhymes, riddles, and poems that you can use to promote auditory discrimination skills.
5. Use a trade book to help develop the concepts and vocabularies of a small group of children. Report your results.
6. Elicit an individual story from a young child. Write or type it and share it with your peers.

7. Try a classification activity with a child of five or six. What can you say about the child's level of cognitive development?
8. To focus on names with a group of young children, use an activity like one of those described for recognizing names, words, and letters of the alphabet.
9. Study a set of commercially available reading readiness materials. Discuss its strengths and weaknesses.
10. Prepare mini-lessons for one to three children or peers on such topics as visual discrimination, auditory discrimination, or names of colors or numbers.
11. Visit a preschool. How much direct or indirect reading instruction is part of the program?
12. Find some common logos from food package labels and ask a young child to read them. Then see if the child can read words from the logos when the words are printed in black on white cards. On the basis of your observations, write your conclusions about the effects of the background color and design on a child's ability to recognize environmental words by sight.
13. Ask a preschool or first-grade child to write a story. Do not help with spelling. Evaluate the child's knowledge of letter-sound relationships from use of invented spellings.
14. Based on your observations and your reading, make a list of arguments for and against pre–first-grade reading. Then write a summary paragraph explaining what you believe about it.

Bibliography

Almy, Millie, E. Chittenden, and Paula Miller. *Young Children's Thinking: Studies of Some Aspects of Piaget's Theory.* New York: Teachers College Press, 1966.

Anderson, Richard C., Elfrieda H. Hiebert, Judith A. Scott, and Ian A. G. Wilkinson. *Becoming a Nation of Readers.* Washington, D.C.: National Institute of Education, 1985.

Bewell, Diane V., and Stanley B. Straw. "Metalinguistic Awareness, Cognitive Development, and Language Learning." In *Research in the Language Arts,* Victor Froese and Stanley B. Straw, eds. Baltimore: University Park Press, 1981, pp. 105–21.

Board of Directors of the International Reading Association. "IRA Position Statement on Reading and Writing in Early Childhood." *The Reading Teacher* 39 (April 1986): 822–24.

Burmeister, Lou E. *Foundations and Strategies for Teaching Children to Read.* Reading, Mass.: Addison-Wesley, 1983, Chapter 2.

Clay, Marie. *Reading: The Patterning of Complex Behavior,* 2nd ed. Auckland, New Zealand: Heinemann, 1979.

Coleman, John S. "The Evaluation of Equality of Educational Opportunity." In *On Equality of Educational Opportunity*, F. Mosteller and D. P. Moynihan, eds. New York: Random House, 1972.

Collins, Cathy. "Is the Cart Before the Horse? Effects of Preschool Reading Instruction on 4 Year Olds." *The Reading Teacher* 40 (December 1986): 332–39.

Coody, Betty. *Using Literature with Young Children.* 2nd ed. Dubuque, Iowa: William C. Brown, 1979, pp. 25–37.

Cox, Mary B. "The Effect of Conservation Ability on Reading Competency." *The Reading Teacher* 30 (December 1976): 251–58.

Davis, Hazel Grubbs. "Reading Pressures in the Kindergarten." *Childhood Education* (November/December 1980): 76–79.

Di Lorenzo, L. S., and R. Salter. "An Evaluative Study of Prekindergarten Programs for Educationally Disadvantaged Children: Follow-up and Replication." *Exceptional Children* 35 (October 1968): 111–19.

Downing, John. "Reading Instruction Register." *Language Arts* 53 (October 1976): 762–66, 780.

Downing, John, and Peter Oliver. "The Child's Conception of 'a Word.'" *Reading Research Quarterly* 9 (1973–74): 568–82.

Durkin, Dolores. *Children Who Read Early.* New York: Teachers College Press, 1966.

Ellis, DiAnn Waskul, and Fannie Wiley Preston. "Enhancing Beginning Reading Using Wordless Picture Books in a Cross-Age Tutoring Program." *The Reading Teacher* 37 (April 1984): 692–98.

Evans, Ellis D. *Contemporary Influences in Early Childhood Education.* 2nd ed. New York: Holt, Rinehart and Winston, 1975.

Farr, Roger, and Nancy Roser. *Teaching a Child to Read.* New York: Harcourt Brace Jovanovich, 1979.

Finn, Patrick. *Helping Children Learn to Read.* New York; Random House, 1985, Chapter 1.

Furth, Hans G. *Piaget for Teachers.* Englewood Cliffs, N.J.: Prentice-Hall, 1970, Letter 13.

Goodall, Marilyn. "Can Four Year Olds 'Read' Words in the Environment?" *The Reading Teacher* 37 (February 1984): 478–82.

Groff, Patrick J. "Resolving the Letter Name Controversy." *The Reading Teacher* 37 (January 1984): 384–88.

Guthrie, John T. "Preschool Literacy Learning." *The Reading Teacher* 37 (December 1983): 318–20.

Hafner, Lawrence E., and Hayden B. Jolly. *Teaching Reading to Children.* 2nd ed. New York: Macmillan, 1982.

Hare, Victoria Chou. "What's in a Word? A Review of Young Children's Difficulties with the Construct 'Word.'" *The Reading Teacher* 37 (January 1984): 360–64.

Hillerich, Robert L. "An Interpretation of Research in Reading Readiness." *Elementary English* 43 (April 1966): 359–64, 372.

Karnes, M. B., et al. "Evaluation of Two Preschool Programs for Disadvantaged Children: A Traditional and a Highly Structured Experimental Preschool." *Exceptional Children* 34 (May 1968): 667–76.

Kirkland, Eleanor R. "A Piagetian Interpretation of Beginning Reading Instruction." *The Reading Teacher* 31 (February 1978): pp. 497–503.

Knox, Bobbie J., and John A. Glover. "A Note on Preschool Experience Effects on Achievement, Readiness, and Creativity." *The Journal of Genetic Psychology* 132 (March, 1978): 151–52.

Lehr, Fran. "Cultural Influences and Sex Differences in Reading." *The Reading Teacher* 32 (March, 1982): 744–46.

Lesiak, Judi. "Reading in Kindergarten: What the Research Doesn't Tell Us." *The Reading Teacher* 32 (November 1978): 135–38.

Loban, Walter D. *Language Development: Kindergarten Through Grade Twelve.* Research Report No. 18. Urbana, Ill.: National Council of Teachers of English, 1976.

Mason, Jana M. "Early Reading from a Developmental Perspective." In *Reading Research Handbook,* P. David Pearson et al., eds. New York: Longman, 1984, pp. 505–43.

Mavrogenes, Nancy A. "What Every Reading Teacher Should Know About Emergent Literacy." *The Reading Teacher* 40 (November 1986): 174–78.

McDonell, Gloria M., and E. Bess Osburn. "New Thoughts About Reading Readiness." In *Readings on Reading Instruction,* Albert J. Harris and Edward R. Sipay, eds. New York: Longman, 1984, pp. 112–15.

NcNutt, Gaye, and Nancy Bukofzer. "Teaching Early Reading at McDonald's." *The Reading Teacher* 35 (April 1982): 841–42.

Morrow, Lesley Mandel. "Reading and Retelling Stories: Strategies for Emergent Readers." *The Reading Teacher* 38 (May 1985): 870–75.

Nevius, John R., Jr. "Teaching for Logical Thinking Is a Prereading Activity." *The Reading Teacher* 30 (March 1977): 641–43.

O'Donnell, Holly. "What Do We Know About Preschool Reading?" *The Reading Teacher* 33 (November 1979): 248–52.

Paradis, Edward, and Joseph Peterson. "Readiness Training Implications from Research." *The Reading Teacher* 30 (February 1975): 445–48.

Plisko, Valena White, and Joyce D. Stern, eds. "The Condition of Education." Washington D.C.: U.S. Department of Education, 1985, p. 4.

Rhodes, Lynn K. "I Can Read! Predictable Books as Resources for Reading and Writing Instruction." *The Reading Teacher* 34 (February 1981): 511–18.

Richgels, Donald. "Experimental Reading with Invented Spelling (ERIS): A Preschool and Kindergarten Method." *The Reading Teacher* 40 (February 1987): 522–29.

Sippola, Arne E. "What to Teach for Reading Readiness—A Research Review and Materials Inventory." *The Reading Teacher* 39 (November 1985): 162–67.

Teale, William H., and Elizabeth Sulzby. *Emergent Literacy: Writing and Reading.* Norwood, N.J.: Ablex, 1986.

Templeton, Shane. "Literacy, Readiness, and Basals." *The Reading Teacher* 39 (January 1986): 403–409.

Vacca, Jo Anne L., Richard T. Vacca, and Mary K. Gove. *Reading and Learning to Read.* Boston: Little Brown, 1987.

Waller, T. Gary. *Think First, Read Later! Piagetian Prerequisites for Reading.* Newark, Del.: International Reading Association, 1977.

Wepner, Shelley B. "Linking Logos with Print for Beginning Reading Success." *The Reading Teacher* 38 (March 1985): 633–39.

Werner, Patrice Holden, and JoAnna Strother. "Early Readers: Important Emotional Considerations." *The Reading Teacher* 40 (February 1987): 538–43.

Wigfield, Allan, and Steven R. Asher. "Social and Motivational Influences on Reading." In *Handbook of Reading Research.* P. David Pearson, ed. New York: Longman, 1984, pp. 423–52.

Wilson, Susan I. *A Content Analysis of Kindergarten Reading Curricula in Thirteen Large American Cities.* New Brunswick, N.J.: Rutgers University, 1976. [ED 128 760]

Wiseman, Donna L. "Helping Children Take Early Steps Toward Reading and Writing." *The Reading Teacher* 37 (January 1984): 340–44.

Zirkelbach, Thelma. "A Personal View of Early Reading." *The Reading Teacher* 37 (February 1984): 468–71.

CHAPTER APPENDIX A: ACTIVITIES

I. LANGUAGE ACTIVITIES

   A. Metalinguistic Awareness
     1. Give each child a card with different forms of the same letter on it (for instance *g*, *G*, and **g**). Then give each one a newpaper advertisement along with instructions to find letters that are like the ones on the card.
     2. Print in large letters a copy of a recent chart story and make copies of it on a copying machine. Give the children individual copies and ask them to use crayons to trace the letters, using a different color for each word. Remind them that a word has spaces on each side of it.
     3. Let children create words by using movable letters to match the letters on word cards or labels.
     4. Cut a recent chart story into sentence strips, mix up the strips, and then have the children arrange them in the correct sequence.

   B. Storytelling
     1. Cut out scenes and/or characters from an inexpensive storybook of a familiar tale (*Little Red Riding Hood*). Fasten adhesive to the backs of the cutouts and use them for a flannel-board presentation. You may put the pictures up the first time or two, but then let the children place the pictures as you tell the story.

2. Use a puppet to help with a story presentation, either by actually telling the story or by being a character who says its part in a different voice.
3. Type the text of a picture storybook on one or two sheets of paper and mark the places where the pages are to be turned. Then tape these papers to the outside cover of the book. Hold the book so that the children can look at the pictures in the book while you read the story which is taped to the outside cover.
4. Before reading the story, tell the children that they will later dramatize it. After the reading, they either pantomime it as you reread or act out parts of the story independently.
5. Record some favorite stories on tapes. Make a sound (a bell or a clicking sound) when the pages are to be turned. Send children to a listening station to hear a tape and appoint one child to hold the book and turn the pages.
6. To enhance the story, use visual aids, such as having a pair of goggles for the children to try on after they listen to Ezra Jack Keats's *Goggles* (New York: Macmillan, 1969).

C. *Story Sequence*
1. Let children dramatize a story that you have read to them. Tell them before you read to listen carefully to what happens first, next, and last.
2. Place felt pictures from a familiar story randomly on a flannel board. Children arrange the pictures in the correct sequence, moving from left to right.
3. Give children a strip of paper about four inches wide and sixteen inches long, which they fold into fourths so that there are four squares. The children draw one picture in each square to retell the story in the proper order.
4. Have one child retell the major events of a story in the correct order. Let other children listen to see if they agree.

D. *Following Directions*
1. Have the children play Simon Says.
2. Give a three-step direction ("Clap your hands twice, stamp your foot, cross your arms") and then call on a child to carry it out. The class judges whether or not the child performs the actions correctly and in sequence. If the child is right, he or she gives the next series of directions and calls on a classmate.
3. Hand each child a piece of paper and give directions for making an airplane, a hat, a snowflake, or something else.
4. To check a child's understanding of directional terms, ask him or her to come to the front of the room and put the eraser *on* the table, hold it *beside* the table, or place it *under* the table. If the child does everything correctly, he or she may select the next child.

5. Have the children form a circle on the playground or in the gym. Give directions, such as "Turn to your right, march like soldiers, hop on your left foot, clap your hands above your head, swing your arms."
6. Explain a new game to the class. The children must follow the directions in order to play.

E. *Listening Comprehension Activities*
1. Have the children find the silly word in a sentence that you say. Example: "Bill had a *noffelhumper* for supper" (noffelhumper).
2. Name three or four items that are related and ask the children to name the category. Example: dogs, cats, sheep, cows (animals).
3. Name three things that are related and one that is not. The children must select the one that does not belong. Example: books, paper, ice cream, pencils (ice cream).
4. Ask the children to answer riddles. Example: "I am big. I have four wheels. Many people can ride on me. I take children to school. What am I?" (bus)
5. Show a picture to the class. Say several sentences that may or may not refer to the picture. If the sentence is about the picture, the children raise their hands. If the sentence has nothing to do with the picture, the children keep their hands down.
6. Slowly read sentences with selected vocabulary words. Have the children dramatize the meanings of the sentences. Example: "The king *slouched* on his *throne* and *frowned* at his *subjects.*"
7. Tell the children that you are going to pretend to be different people; from what you say they must guess who you are. Use statements like the following: "There's Goldilocks and she's sleeping in my bed" (Baby Bear) or "I want to help boys and girls cross the street safely" (safety patrol or police officer).

II. INTEREST ACTIVITIES

A. *Poetry*
1. Choose poems for choral speaking. Have the class say some poems in unison so that children can imitate good phrasing and intonation. Do other poems "a line a child," with different children saying different lines. An example of this type is "One, two, buckle my shoe."
2. Select some poems for singing, such as "Twinkle, Twinkle, Little Star," "Over in the Meadow," and "London Bridge Is Falling Down." Poetry set to music brings out the phrasing and melodic patterns of language.
3. Read a poem that children can respond to with art. Choose media that are in keeping with the tone of the poem. Crayon resists are good for spooky poems ("Hallowe'en" by Harry Behn); finger painting works well for poems with motion ("The Swing" by Robert Louis Stevenson); and chalk is appropriate for soft, quiet poems ("Pussy Willows" by Aileen Fisher).

4. Choose poems with wonderfully descriptive words. Talk about the sounds of the words and how they make you feel. A good example is "Skins" by Aileen Fisher.

5. Act out nursery rhymes, such as "Jack Be Nimble" and "Little Miss Muffet." This is a good way to check children's understanding of the verses.

6. Have a collection of popular Mother Goose characters for your flannel board. Try using characters from "Jack Spratt Could Eat No Fat," "Mary Had a Little Lamb," "Simple Simon Met a Pie Man," and "The Old Woman Who Lived in a Shoe." Let the children put up the characters and say the corresponding rhymes.

7. Make a bulletin board for poetry. Select a poem that the children enjoy, copy it on a large poster, and let the children make illustrations and put their work on the bulletin board. Change poems as children lose interest.

III. PHYSICAL DEVELOPMENT ACTIVITIES

A. *Visual Perception*

1. Get a set of beginning basal readers that use a lot of repetition. Show the children a word, such as *jump;* then ask them to see how many times that word appears on a certain page.

2. Print each child's name on an envelope. Then print the letters of the child's name on an index card, cut the card apart between the letters, and put these letters in the envelope. Let the child take the letters out and arrange them in the right order. (The same activity may be done with word cards.)

3. Let children supply missing letters. Example: Print the word *play* on each child's paper. Then print portions of the word (pl___y, p___ay p___a___) on the paper for the child to complete.

B. *Visual Memory*

1. Show a card with the word *dog* written on it, but only long enough for the children to study it (about five seconds). Then place it out of sight. From four cards on each child's desk (the *dog* card and cards with the words *man, boy,* and *bus*), ask the children to select the word they were shown.

2. Play a simple version of Concentration with letter or word cards. Mix several pairs of cards and place them face down on a table. Let a child turn over one card, look at the letter or word, and then turn over another card to find a match for the first one. If a match is made, the child keeps the pair of cards and continues until no match is made. If there is no match, replace the two cards and let another child take a turn.

3. Assume that your classroom contains many written words—as labels, on chart stories, for directions, and so on. Show a card with a word on it that is the same as a word already visible in the room. Ask the children to think of a word that they have already seen in the room that is the same as the one you are holding. Let a volunteer take your word card and match it with the appropriate word in the room.

C. Visual Discrimination

1. Print similar letters on the board and help students discover how they are alike and how they are different. Example: *d b, p q, m n.*
2. From a series of letters or words, have the children find the one that is different. Example: *on on no on.*
3. Let the children fill in the missing letters. Example: *j p q g   j __ q g   j __ q __   j __ __ __   __ __ __ __*
4. Ask the children to circle the letter that is different in a series of letters. Example: *s s z   m n m   o c o   d b b*

D. Auditory Perception

1. Say polysyllabic words and have the children clap, tap, or hit a drum for each syllable.
2. Give a letter sound. Then give a word and ask the students if the letter occurs at the beginning, middle, or end of the word. Example: *m, summer, middle.*
3. Tell students a word that begins with a certain sound (*bell*). Then say a sentence that contains the sound several times. Ask the children to raise their hands when they hear the sound. Example: *Betty bounces the ball in the back yard.*

E. Auditory Memory

1. Tap on a table or a desk. Ask the children to repeat the rhythm.
2. Have each child repeat two nonsense words after hearing them once. Example: *soo-sye, bloop-bleep.*
3. Let the children pretend to be in a cave and echo the sounds or words made by the leader of their "expedition."
4. Teach children jingles and rhymes such as nursery rhymes, which focus on rhyming sounds. Example: "Jack be nimble, Jack be quick, Jack jump over the candlestick."
5. Give each child crayons. Name three colors and have the children make dots or lines on their papers in sequence. Example: red dot, blue line, green dot, red line, blue dot, green dot.

F. Auditory Discrimination (beginning sounds)

1. Say a group of words and ask the children to indicate, by raising their hands, which one starts with a different sound. Begin with vastly different sounds and move to similar sounds. Example: *hat, head, mask, home.*
2. Make a chart featuring a letter sound. Write the name of the letter at the top of the chart in both upper and lower case (*B, b*). Ask the children to find pictures of a ball, baby, book, etc., to glue on the chart.
3. Play a guessing game. Ask if there is anyone in the room whose name starts with the same sound as the beginning of the word *top*. The child whose name starts with this sound may give the next clue.
4. Find poems that repeat certain sounds. Examples: "Wee Willie Winkie," "Lucy Locket," "Bye-Baby Bunting," and "Deedle, Deedle Dumpling."

G. *Auditory Discrimination (medial and final sounds, whole word)*
1. Use pictures and ask questions. Example: "Is this a *pat* or a *pet*?"
2. Use riddles to relate sounds to words. For example, ask each child to guess what word, illustrated by the following riddle, begins with the same sound as *pig.*

> I am good to eat.
> I rhyme with teach.
> I am a fruit.
> What am I?

3. Let the children supply the missing rhyming word in a familiar verse.
4. Give an example of rhyming word pairs; then ask the children to tell you which word pairs rhyme. Example; *boy, toy; toy, head.*
5. Ask the children to supply the second line of a rhyming couplet. Example: I saw Sam (eat a ham). I saw Mabel (set the table).

H. *Kinesthetic-Tactile Learning*
1. Mount sandpaper, cardboard, or linoleum letters on a piece of smooth cardboard. Let the children trace the letters and feel their shapes. They may close their eyes and move their fingers lightly over the letters. Then have them reproduce each letter with their pencils.
2. Prepare different kinds of surfaces for writing with the finger in various textures. Use finger paint, shaving cream, or a thin layer of salt or sand on the bottom of a large baking pan.
3. Let children make numbers and letters with their bodies, working with partners.
4. Have children walk out letter shapes that you have placed on the floor with tape, chalk, or string.
5. Let the children tear letter and number shapes out of old newspapers.
6. Make a large letter on a sheet of paper. Tell the children they can make rainbows by tracing over the letter with five or six different colors.
7. Let the children take sticks and make letters in clay or damp sand. Then they can trace the forms with their fingers.
8. Let children write on the chalkboard and magic slates (where the letters disappear when you raise the clear acetate cover).

I. *Directionality*
1. Stress moving from left to right in reading. Move your arm from left to right along a line of print on a chalkboard or on an overhead transparency.
2. Play games that require a knowledge of left and right. Examples: Looby Loo, Hokey Pokey, Simon Says.
3. Put an arrow pointing to the right across the top of a page or put an *X* at the top left corner of a child's paper to remind him or her where to start.
4. Have children arrange sequential pictures from left to right.

5. When children are trying to match word cards, stress the importance of looking at the left letter first and moving on through the word from left to right.

IV. BEGINNING READING AND WRITING ACTIVITIES

  A. *Letter Recognition*
    1. Let children match cards that are coded on the back by color. For instance, when children find *r* to go with *R,* they can turn the cards over to see if they have a match.
    2. Teach alphabet songs to the class. You may want to point to the letters on a chart as you sing them.
    3. Show alphabet picture books and talk about the letters.
    4. Provide movable cardboard or wooden letters for children to manipulate. Also let children place felt letters on a flannel board and magnetic letters on a metal surface. Encourage them to name the letters and copy words.
    5. Play bingo with the children by saying letter names and having the children cover the corresponding letters on their cards. Beginning players should cover all of the letters in order to win. Later, when children understand the concepts for vertical, diagonal, and horizontal rows, they may win by completing one of these patterns.

k	s	r
b	o	t
a	l	p

    6. Let children form letters by bending pipe cleaners, writing a letter with glue and covering it with glitter, or shaping it from clay or dough.

  B. *Sight Word Recognition*
    1. Tape children's names to their desks so that they may see them and copy them frequently.
    2. Label objects in the room with oak-tag strips. Use words or short sentences. For example, one label might read *chalkboard,* and another might say *This is our piano.*
    3. Put on the board daily schedules of things that you plan to do, and read them with the class.

C. Writing
1. Let children use word-processing programs to create simple stories on computers.
2. Have children write daily journal entries and illustrate them.
3. Encourage children to send messages to their friends.
4. Give opportunities for purposeful writing, including invitations and thank-you notes.

CHAPTER APPENDIX B: RESOURCES

For Teachers

Adamson, Pamela. *The First Book of Number Rhymes.* New York: Franklin Watts, 1970.

Briggs, Nancy E., and Joseph A. Wagner. *Children's Literature Through Storytelling and Drama.* 2nd ed. Dubuque, Iowa: William C. Brown, 1979.

Brown, Carl F., and Mac Henry Brown. *Handbook of Reading Activities.* Atlanta: Humanics, 1983.

Christman-Rothlein, Liz, and Jane Caballero. *Back to Basics in Reading Made Fun.* Atlanta: Humanics, 1981.

Coody, Betty. *Using Literature with Young Children.* 2nd ed. Dubuque, Iowa: William C. Brown, 1979.

Delamar, Gloria T. *Children's Counting-Out Rhymes, Fingerplays, Jump-Rope and Bounce-Ball Chants, and Other Rhythms.* Jefferson, N.C.: McFarland, 1983.

Hillert, Margaret. *Action Verse for Early Childhood.* Minneapolis: T. S. Denison, 1982.

Hopkins, Lee Bennett. *Pass the Poetry, Please!* New York: Citation Press, 1972.

Huck, Charlotte S., Susan Hepler, and Janet Hickman. *Children's Literature in the Elementary School.* 4th ed. New York: Holt, Rinehart and Winston, 1987.

Livingston, Myra Cohn, ed. *Listen, Children, Listen.* New York: Atheneum, 1972.

Matterson, Elizabeth. *Games for the Very Young.* New York: American Heritage, 1971.

Mayesky, Mary, Donald Neuman, and Raymond J. Wlodkowski. *Creative Activities for Young Children,* 2nd ed. Albany, N.Y.: Delmar, 1980.

Raphael, Elaine, ed. *Something Special.* Nashville, Tenn.: Incentive Publications, 1982.

Sutherland, Zena, and May Hill Arbuthnot. *Children & Books.* 7th ed. Glenview, Ill.: Scott, Foresman, 1986.

Wallace, Daisy, ed. *Fairy Poems.* New York: Holiday, 1980.

Alphabet Picture Books

Anno, Mitsumasa. *Anno's Alphabet: An Adventure in Imagination.* New York: Thomas Crowell, 1975.

Bayer, Jane. *A, My Name Is Alice.* New York: Dial, 1984.

Brown, Marcia. *All Butterflies: An ABC.* New York: Scribner's, 1974.

Burningham, John. *John Burningham's ABC.* Indianapolis: Bobbs-Merrill, 1967.

Duke, Kate. *The Guinea Pig ABC.* New York: E. P. Dutton, 1983.

Eichenberg, Fritz. *Ape in a Cape.* New York: Harcourt, Brace, 1952.

Feelings, Muriel. *Jambo Means Hello: Swahili Alphabet Book.* New York: Dial, 1974.

Kitchen, Bert. *Animal Alphabet.* New York: Dial, 1984.

Musgrove, Margaret. *Ashanti to Zulu.* New York: Dial, 1976.

Wildsmith, Brian. *Brian Wildsmith's ABC.* New York: Franklin Watts, 1963.

Informational/Concept/Vocabulary Books

Borten, Helen. *Do You Go Where I Go?* New York: Abelard-Schuman, 1972.

Brown, Marcia. *Walk With Your Eyes.* New York: Franklin Watts, 1979.

Cole, Joanna. *A Chick Hatches.* New York: William Morrow, 1976.

Crews, Donald. *Light.* New York: Greenwillow, 1981.

Eugene, Toni. *Strange Animals of Australia.* Washington, D.C.: National Geographic, 1981.

Hoban, Tana. *I Read Symbols.* New York: Greenwillow, 1983.

Hoban, Tana. *Over, Under and Through.* New York: Macmillan, 1973.

Hoban, Tana. *Push-Pull, Empty-Full.* New York: Macmillan, 1972.

McMillan, Bruce. *Here a Chick, There a Chick.* New York: Lothrop, 1983.

Ruben, Patricia. *What Is New? What Is Missing? What is Different?* New York: J. B. Lippincott, 1978.

Spier, Peter. *Gobble, Growl, Grunt.* New York: Doubleday, 1971.

Tarrant, Graham. *Rabbits: A Natural Pop-ups Book.* New York: Putnam, 1984.

Tresselt, Alvin. *It's Time Now!* New York: Lothrop, 1969.

Udry, Janice May. *A Tree Is Nice.* New York: Harper & Row, 1966.

White, Paul. *Janet at School.* New York: Thomas Crowell, 1979.

Predictable/Repetitive Books

Adams, Pam. *This Old Man.* New York: Grosset and Dunlap, 1974.

Aliki. *Go Tell Aunt Rhody.* New York: Macmillan, 1974.

Allen, Roach Van. *I Love Ladybugs.* Allen, Tex.: DLM Teaching Resources, 1985.

Bonne, Rose, and Alan Mills. *I Know an Old Lady.* New York: Rand McNally, 1961.

Carle, Eric. *The Very Hungry Caterpillar.* Cleveland: Collins World, 1969.

Langstaff, John. *Oh, A-Hunting We Will Go.* New York: Atheneum, 1974.

Martin, Bill, Jr. *Brown Bear, Brown Bear.* New York: Holt, Rinehart and Winston, 1970.

Martin, Bill, Jr. *Fire! Fire! Said Mrs. McGuire.* New York: Holt, Rinehart and Winston, 1970.

Peppe, Rodney. *The House That Jack Built.* New York: Delacorte, 1970.

Shaw, Charles B. *It Looked Like Spilt Milk.* New York: Harper & Row, 1947.

Tolstoy, Alexei. *The Great Big Enormous Turnip.* New York: Franklin Watts, 1968.

Wager, Justin (illustrator). *The Bus Ride.* New York: Scott, Foresman, 1971.

Wordless Picture Books[3]

Briggs, Raymond. *The Snowman.* New York: Random House, 1978.

Burton, Marilee R. *The Elephant's Nest.* New York: Harper & Row, 1981.

Craig, Helen. *Mouse House Months.* New York: Random House, 1981.

de Paola, Tomie. *The Hunter and the Animals.* New York: Holiday House, 1981.

de Paola, Tomie. *Pancakes for Breakfast.* New York: Harcourt Brace, 1978.

Goodall, John S. *The Ballooning Adventures of Paddy Pork.* New York: Harcourt Brace, 1969.

Goodall, John S. *Creepy Castle.* New York: Atheneum, 1975.

Goodall, John S. *Lavinia's Cottage.* New York: Atheneum, 1983.

Hoban, Tana. *Is It Red? Is It Yellow? Is It Blue?* New York: Greenwillow, 1978.

Hutchins, Pat. *Changes, Changes.* New York: Macmillan, 1971.

Krahn, Fernando. *Catch That Cat!* New York: Dutton, 1978.

Mari, Iela, and Enzo Mari. *The Apple and the Moth.* New York: Pantheon, 1970.

Mayer, Mercer. *Frog Goes to Dinner.* New York: Dial, 1974.

Mayer, Mercer. *Frog, Where Are You?* New York: Dial, 1969.

Turkle, Brinton. *Deep in the Forest.* New York: Dutton, 1976.

Van Soelen, Philip. *A Cricket in the Grass.* New York: Scribner's, 1981.

[3] For a list of 162 wordless picture books published in the United States, see DiAnn Waskul Ellis and Fannie Wiley Preston, "Enhancing Beginning Reading Using Wordless Picture Books in a Cross-Age Tutoring Program," *The Reading Teacher* 37 (April 1984): 692–98.

Chapter 3

Word Recognition

Introduction

Good readers differ from poor readers both in size of sight vocabularies and in the ability to decode words. Good readers tend to have larger sight vocabularies than poor readers, resulting in a decreased need to stop and analyze words. However, when they do have to analyze words, they often have a more flexible approach than do poor readers, since they generally have been taught several strategies and have been encouraged to try a new one if one fails (Jenkins et al., 1980). Poor readers frequently know only a single strategy for decoding words, and there is not one strategy that is appropriate for all words. Thus these children are at a disadvantage when they encounter words for which their strategy is not useful. Even if they have been taught several strategies, poor readers may not have learned a procedure to follow that will allow them to decode unfamiliar words as efficiently as possible. "Research suggests that, no matter which strategies are used to introduce them to reading, the children who earn the best scores on reading comprehension tests in the second grade are the ones who made the most progress in fast and accurate word identification in the first grade" (Anderson et al., 1985, pp. 10–11).

This chapter presents a variety of methods of word recognition and stresses a flexible approach to unfamiliar words, encouraging application of those word recognition skills that are most helpful at the moment. It also explains how to use a number of word recognition skills in conjunction to help in decoding a word.

Setting Objectives

When you finish reading this chapter, you should be able to

1. Describe some ways to help a child develop a sight vocabulary.
2. Describe some activities for teaching use of context clues.
3. Discuss the place of phonics in the reading program.
4. Define each of the following terms: *consonant blend, consonant digraph, vowel digraph, diphthong.*
5. Describe how to teach a child to associate a particular sound with a particular letter or group of letters.
6. Discuss ways of teaching the various facets of structural analysis.
7. Name the skills that children need in order to use a dictionary as an aid in word recognition.

Key Vocabulary

Pay close attention to these terms when they appear in the chapter.

analytic approach to
    phonics instruction
derivatives
homographs
inflectional endings

irregularly spelled words
phonics
semantic clues
sight words
structural analysis

syntactic clues
synthetic approach to
    phonics instruction
variants
word configuration

In addition, pay close attention to the specific phonics terms that are discussed on pages 118–119.

WORD RECOGNITION SKILLS

Word recognition skills help a reader recognize words while reading. They include developing a store of words that can be recognized immediately on sight and being able to use context clues, phonics, structural analysis, and dictionaries for word identification. The last four skills are sometimes referred to as word attack skills.

Children need to be able to perform all of the different word recognition skills, since some will be more useful in certain situations than others. Teaching a single approach to word identification is not wise, because a child may be left without the proper tools for specific situations. Additionally, some word recognition skills are easier to learn than others, depending on the student's abilities. For example, a child who has a hearing loss may not become very skillful at using phonics but may learn sight words easily and profit greatly from the use of context clues.

Development of decoding skill to the point of automaticity (application without conscious thought) is necessary. This automatic decoding leaves the reader's attention free to focus upon comprehension of the message (Anderson et al., 1985).

Sight Words

Developing a store of sight words, or words that are recognized immediately without having to resort to analysis, is important to a young reader. The larger the store of sight words a person has, the more rapidly and fluently he or she can read a selection. Comprehension of a passage and reading speed suffer if a person has to pause too often to analyze unfamiliar words. The more mature and experienced a reader becomes, the larger his or her store of sight words becomes. For instance, most, if not all, of the words used in this textbook are a part of the sight vocabularies of college students. One goal of reading instruction is to turn all of the words that students continuously need to recognize in print into sight words.

A sight word approach (also referred to as a look-and-say or whole word approach) to teaching beginning reading makes sense for several reasons.

100

Teaching
Reading in
Today's
Elementary
Schools

1. The English language contains a multitude of irregularly spelled words, that is, words that are not spelled the way they sound. Many of these are among the most frequently used words in our language. The spellings of the following common words are highly irregular as far as sound-symbol associations are concerned: *of, through, two, know, give, come,* and *once.* Rather than trying in vain to sound out these words, children need to learn to recognize them on sight as whole configurations.

2. Learning several sight words at the very beginning of reading instruction gives the child a chance to engage in a successful reading experience very early and consequently promotes a positive attitude toward reading.

3. Words have meaning for youngsters by the time they arrive at school, but single letters have no meaning for them. Therefore, presenting children with whole words at the beginning allows them to associate reading with meaning rather than with meaningless memorization.

4. After children have built up a small store of sight words, the teacher can begin phonics instruction with an analytic approach. More about this approach can be found later in this chapter.

A teacher must carefully choose which words to teach as sight words. Extremely common irregularly spelled words (*the, of, to, two*) and frequently used regularly spelled words (*at, it, and, am, go*) should be taught as sight words so children can read connected sentences early in the program. The first sight words should be useful and meaningful; a child's name should be one of them. Days of the week, months of the year, and names of school subjects are other prime candidates. Words that stand for concepts that are unfamiliar to youngsters are poor choices. Before children learn *democracy* as a sight word, they need to have an understanding of what a democracy is. Therefore, this word is not a good one to teach in the primary grades.

Teaching some words with regular spelling patterns as sight words is consistent with the beliefs of linguists who have become involved with development of reading materials (see Chapter 6 for further details). Words with regular spelling patterns are also a good base for teaching "word families" in phonics—for example, the *an* family consists of *ban, can, Dan, fan, man, Nan, pan, ran, tan,* and *van.*

Sight Word Lists

Lists of basic sight words may give teachers an indication of what words are used most frequently in reading materials and therefore needed most frequently by students. Some of these lists are included or discussed in the following publications:

Dolch, Edward W. *A Manual for Remedial Reading.* 2nd ed. (Champaign, Ill.: Garrard, 1945).

Dreyer, Lois G., Karen R. Futtersak, and Ann E. Boehm. "Sight Words for the Computer Age: An Essential Word List." *The Reading Teacher* 39 (October 1985): 12–15.

Durr, William. "Computer Study of High Frequency Words in Popular Trade Juveniles." *The Reading Teacher* 27 (October 1973): 37–42.

Ekwall, Eldon E. *Diagnosis and Remediation of the Disabled Reader*. (Boston: Allyn and Bacon, 1976), p. 70.

Fry, Edward. *Elementary Reading Instruction*. (New York: McGraw-Hill, 1977), p. 73.

Harris, Albert J., and Milton Jacobson. *Basic Elementary Reading Vocabularies*. (New York: Macmillan, 1976).

Hillerich, Robert L. "Word Lists—Getting It All Together." *The Reading Teacher* 27 (January 1974): 353–60.

Mangieri, John N., and Michael S. Kahn. "Is the Dolch List of 220 Basic Sight Words Irrelevant?" *The Reading Teacher* 30 (March 1977): 649–51.

Moe, A. J. "Word Lists for Beginning Readers." *Reading Improvement* 10 (Fall 1973): 11–15.

Otto, Wayne, and R. Chester. "Sight Words for Beginning Readers." *Journal of Educational Research* 65 (July 1972): 435–43.

Palmer, Barbara. "Dolch List Still Useful." *The Reading Teacher* 38 (March 1985): 708–709.

Walker, Charles Monroe. "High Frequency Word List for Grades 3 Through 9." *The Reading Teacher* 32 (April 1979): 803–12.

Garrard Press (Champaign, Illinois) publishes basic vocabulary flash cards, including the words on the Dolch list of 220 most common words found in reading materials (excluding nouns). Garrard also publishes sets of 95 picture word cards, which have a common noun printed on the front of each card and the identifying picture printed on the back. Games for learning these basic sight words are also available through this publisher.

Another well-known list of basic sight words is Fry's list of "Instant Words" shown in Table 3.1. This list presents the words most frequently used in reading materials.

Dreyer, Futtersak, and Boehm (1985) have compiled a supplementary list of words found in computer-assisted instructional materials for elementary school children, because many of the special terms used in these materials are not found on traditional word lists. The list contains major procedural and feedback words found in thirty-five representative computer programs in the areas of reading comprehension, grammar, spelling, word processing, logic/problem solving, basic verbal concepts, and mathematics. This list will help teachers introduce children to the words they need to know in order to use computer-assisted instructional programs successfully.

Culyer (1982) recommends developing a locally relevant basic sight word list by charting the levels at which words are introduced in the basal series a school system uses. In other words, the words found in the different series used in a school system are combined into a single list, based on the point of introduction of each word in the pertinent series. Teachers can then use words of concern to the children in their area, rather than words determined on a nationwide basis, in their sight word instruction.

TABLE 3.1 Fry's List of "Instant Words"

First Hundred Words (approximately first grade)				Second Hundred Words (approximately second grade)				Third Hundred Words (approximately third grade)			
Group 1a	Group 1b	Group 1c	Group 1d	Group 2a	Group 2b	Group 2c	Group 2d	Group 3a	Group 3b	Group 3c	Group 3d
the	he	go	who	saw	big	may	fan	ask	hat	off	fire
a	I	see	an	home	where	let	five	small	car	sister	ten
is	they	then	their	soon	am	use	read	yellow	write	happy	order
you	one	us	she	stand	ball	these	over	show	try	once	part
to	good	no	new	box	morning	right	such	goes	myself	didn't	early
and	me	him	said	upon	live	present	way	clean	longer	set	fat
we	about	by	did	first	four	tell	too	buy	those	round	third
that	had	was	boy	came	last	next	shall	thank	hold	dress	same
in	if	come	three	girl	color	please	own	sleep	full	tell	love'
not	some	get	down	house	away	leave	most	letter	carry	wash	hear
for	up	or	work	find	red	hand	sure	jump	eight	start	yesterday
at	her	two	put	because	friend	more	thing	help	sing	always	eyes
with	do	man	were	made	pretty	why	only	fly	warm	anything	door
it	when	little	before	could	eat	better	near	don't	sit	around	clothes
on	so	has	just	book	want	under	than	fast	dog	close	through
can	my	them	long	look	year	while	open	cold	ride	walk	o'clock
will	very	how	here	mother	white	should	kind	today	hot	money	second
are	all	like	other	run	got	never	must	does	grow	turn	water
of	would	our	old	school	play	each	high	face	cut	might	town
this	any	what	take	people	found	best	far	green	seven	hard	took
your	been	know	cat	night	left	another	both	every	woman	along	pair
as	out	make	again	into	men	seem	end	brown	funny	bed	now
but	there	which	give	say	bring	tree	also	coat	yes	fine	keep
be	from	much	after	think	wish	name	until	six	ate	sat	head
have	day	his	many	back	black	dear	call	gave	stop	hope	food

102

The Second 300 Words
(approximately fourth grade)

Group 4a	Group 4b	Group 4c	Group 4d	Group 4e	Group 4f	Group 4g	Group 4h	Group 4i	Group 4j	Group 4k	Group 4l
told	time	word	wear	hour	grade	egg	spell	become	herself	demand	aunt
Miss	yet	almost	Mr.	glad	brother	ground	beautiful	body	idea	however	system
father	true	thought	side	follow	remain	afternoon	sick	chance	drop	figure	line
children	above	send	poor	company	milk	feed	became	act	river	case	cause
land	still	receive	lost	believe	several	boat	cry	die	smile	increase	marry
interest	meet	pay	outside	begin	war	plan	finish	real	son	enjoy	possible
government	since	nothing	wind	mind	able	question	catch	speak	bat	rather	supply
feet	number	need	Mrs.	pass	charge	fish	floor	already	fact	sound	thousand
garden	state	mean	learn	reach	either	return	stick	doctor	sort	eleven	pen
done	matter	late	held	month	less	sir	great	step	king	music	condition
country	line	half	front	point	train	fell	guess	itself	dark	human	perhaps
different	remem-ber	fight	built	rest	cost	hill	bridge	nine	them-selves	court	produce
bad	large	enough	family	sent	evening	wood	church	baby	whose	force	twelve
across	few	feet	began	talk	note	add	lady	minute	study	plant	rode
yard	hit	during	air	went	past	ice	tomor-row	ring	fear	suppose	uncle
winter	cover	gone	young	bank	room	chair	snow	wrote	move	law	labor
table	window	hundred	ago	ship	flew	watch	whom	happen	stood	husband	public
story	even	week	world	business	office	alone	women	appear	himself	moment	consider
sometimes	city	between	airplane	whole	cow	low	among	heart	strong	person	thus
I'm	together	change	without	short	visit	arm	road	swim	knew	result	least
tried	sun	being	kill	certain	wait	dinner	farm	felt	often	continue	power
horse	life	care	ready	fair	teacher	hair	cousin	fourth	toward	price	mark
something	street	answer	stay	reason	spring	service	bread	I'll	wonder	serve	president
brought	party	course	won't	summer	picture	class	wrong	kept	twenty	national	voice
shoes	suit	against	paper	fill	bird	quite	age	well	impor-tant	wife	whether

Source: From *Elementary Reading Instruction* (p. 73) by Edward Fry. Copyright © 1977. Used with permission of the author.

Teaching Sight Words

Before children begin to learn sight words, they must have developed visual discrimination skills. That is, they must be able to see likenesses and differences among printed words. It is also helpful, although not essential, for them to know the names of the letters of the alphabet, because this makes discussion of likenesses and differences in words easier. For example, a teacher could point out that, whereas *take* has a *k* before the *e*, *tale* has an *l* in the same position.

A potential sight word must initially be identified for the learners. A teacher should show the children the printed word as he or she pronounces it, or pair the word with an identifying picture. Regardless of the method of presentation, one factor is of paramount importance: the children must *look* at the printed word when it is identified in order to associate the letter configuration with the spoken word or picture. If children fail to look at the word when it is pronounced, they have no chance of remembering it when they next encounter it.

Teachers should also encourage children to pay attention to the details of the word by asking them to notice ascending letters (such as *b, d, h*), descending letters (such as *p, g, q*), word length, and particular letter combinations (such as double letters). Careful scrutiny of words can greatly aid retention.

Children learn early to recognize some sight words by visual configurations, or shapes. This technique is not one teachers should stress too much, since many words have similar shapes. But since many children seem to use the technique in the early stages of reading, regardless of the teacher's methods, a teacher can use configuration judiciously to develop early sight words. One way to do this is to call attention to shape by having the children frame the words to be learned.

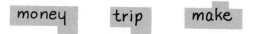

That word configuration soon loses its usefulness is demonstrated by the following words:

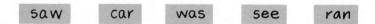

Teachers can call attention to word makeup through comparison and contrast, comparing a new word to a similar known word: *fan* may be compared to *can* if the children already have *can* in their sight vocabularies. The teacher can point out the fact that the initial letters of the words are different and the other letters are the same, or the students can discover this on their own. The latter method is preferable because the students are likely to remember their own discoveries longer than they will remember something they have been told by the teacher.

Few words will be learned by the students after a single presentation, although Ashton-Warner (1963) claims that children will instantly learn words that are extremely important to them. Generally, a number of repetitions will be necessary before a word actually becomes a sight word.

The teacher should carefully plan practice with potential sight words. It should be varied and interesting, because children will more readily learn those things in which they have an interest. Games are useful if they emphasize the words being learned rather than the rules of the game.

Practice with potential sight words should generally involve using the words in context. Out of context, children cannot pronounce many words with certainty, for example, *read, desert,* and *record.* The following sentences indicate the importance of context.

I *read* that book yesterday.

We drove for miles through the *desert.*

Will you *record* these figures for me?

I can't *read* without glasses.

How can you *desert* him when he needs you most?

I bought a new *record* today.

Another reason for using context when presenting sight words is that many commonly used words have little meaning when they stand alone. Prime examples are *the, a,* and *an.* Context for words may be a sentence (*The* girl ate *a* pear and *an* apple) or short phrases (*the* girl, *a* pear, *an* apple). Context is also useful in a situation where pronunciation is not as clear as it should be. Children may confuse the word *thing* with *think* unless the teacher has presented context for the word: "I haven't done a useful thing all day."

Hood (1972) suggests using phrase cards or, even better, story context for sight word practice. She correctly asserts that if readers can be encouraged to pay attention to context, they can learn to correct their own errors. She and her associates reward children verbally or with special privileges for paying attention to context and correcting their own mistakes.

The language experience approach, in which students' own language is written down and used as the basis for their reading material, is good for developing sight vocabulary. This approach (described in detail in Chapter 6) provides meaningful context for learning sight words, and it can be used productively with individuals or groups. The word-bank activities associated with it are particularly helpful.

Another context for presenting a word is a picture. Teachers may also present words in conjunction with the actual objects they name, such as chairs and tables, calling attention to the fact that the labels name the items. These names can be written on the board, so that youngsters can try to locate the items in the room by finding the matching labels.

106

Teaching
Reading in
Today's
Elementary
Schools

Constructing picture dictionaries, in which children illustrate words and file the labeled pictures alphabetically in a notebook, is a good activity for helping younger children develop sight vocabulary. This procedure has been effective in helping children whose primary language is not English learn to read and understand English words.

Teachers can use labels to help children learn to recognize their own names and the names of some of their classmates. On the first day of school, the teacher can give each child a name tag and label each child's desk with his or her name. The teacher may also label the area where the child is supposed to hang a coat or store supplies. The teacher should explain to the children that the letters written on the name tags, desks, and storage areas spell their own names and that no one else is supposed to use these areas. The children should be encouraged to look at the names carefully and try to remember them when locating belongings. Although the children may initially use the name tags to match the labels on the desks and storage areas, by the time the name tags are worn out or lost the children should be able to identify their printed names without assistance.

The teacher can generally accelerate this process by teaching children how to write their names. Children may first trace the name labels on their desks with their fingers. Next, they can try to copy the names on sheets of paper, using primary-sized pencils or crayons. At first the teacher should label all students' work and drawings with the students' names, but as soon as the children are capable of writing their names, they should label their own papers. From the beginning, the children's names should be written in capital and lower-case letters, rather than all capitals, since this is the way names most commonly appear in print.

The days of the week can also be taught as sight words. The teacher can write "Today is" on the chalkboard and fill in the name of the appropriate day each morning. At first the teacher may read the sentence to the children at the beginning of each day, but soon some children will be able to read the sentence successfully without help.

Function words—words that have only syntactic meaning rather than concrete content—are often particularly difficult for children to learn, because of their lack of concrete meaning and because many of them are similar in physical features. Jolly (1981) suggests the following ideas for teaching these troublesome words:

1. Teach only one word at a time of a pair that is likely to be confused (for example, *was* and *saw*).
2. First teach words that have large differences in features, then those that have finer differences. For example, teach *that* with words like *for* and *is* before presenting it with *this* and *the*.
3. Teach three or four dissimilar words in each session in a small group setting. Present them on individual cards to each student, in isolation and in context. Identify them and let the students analyze them, helping them learn to spell each word. The students read the words in context orally

after you read the phrases to them; then they are given some simple sentences in which they have multiple choices for target words and are asked to underline the correct words. Finally the students have a flash card drill.

4. Give parents suggestions for helping children practice these words in a game.

5. Use the cloze procedure (deleting target words and leaving blanks for the children to fill in) for a review method.

Much teaching of sight word recognition takes place as a part of basal reader lessons. The teacher frequently introduces the new words, possibly in one of the ways discussed above, before reading, discussing meanings at the same time. Then students have a guided silent reading period during which they silently read material containing the new words in order to answer questions asked by the teacher. Purposeful oral rereading activities offer another chance to use the new words. Afterward, teachers generally provide practice in workbooks or on the worksheets suggested in the teacher's manual of the basal reading series. Other follow-up activities include games, manipulative devices, and special audiovisual materials.

Bridge, Winograd, and Haley (1983) found that patterned (predictable) books were more effective than basal preprimers for teaching beginning sight words. The patterned books had repetitive lines and familiar themes, making it possible for the children to predict the next line or phrase. The patterned books and the preprimer chosen for this study contained many of the same words. The words found in the preprimer, but not in the patterned books, were taught through dictated language experience stories (see Chapter 6 for a detailed explanation of this technique), since they are also highly predictable. Teachers first presented the patterned books to the children by reading them aloud. Teachers then read the books a second time, inviting the children to join in when they were able to predict what was about to occur. Next, the children participated in choral reading from the book and from a chart that had no picture clues. Finally, they matched sentence strips with lines from the story and matched individual words with words from the story. Teachers followed the instructions in the teacher's manual to teach the preprimer stories. Children taught by the procedure using predictable books learned significantly more target sight words and nontarget sight words than the children who used the preprimers. (A list of predictable books is located in Chapter 2.)

Writing new words is helpful to some learners, especially to kinesthetic learners, who learn through muscle movement. Recent basal readers have made use of writing by providing incomplete sentences with choices of words that the children can use to complete the sentences. The children choose the words that fit the sentences and write each word in the blank provided. Example:

Janet forgot _____ she put the doll. (where, which)

108

Teaching
Reading in
Today's
Elementary
Schools

This approach forces the children to pay attention to small details in the words presented as choices and is likely to increase their word retention because the writing activity reinforces the letter sequence.

Games such as word bingo are useful for practice with sight words. The teacher or a leader calls out a word, and the children who recognize that word on their cards cover it. (Cards may look something like the ones shown.) When a child covers an entire card, he or she says "cover," and the teacher or leader checks the card to see if all the covered words were actually called.

saw	can	on
have	FREE	again
never	said	will

have	was	no
want	FREE	many
even	so	here

can	want	on
was	FREE	see
to	will	many

Card games in which children accumulate "books" of matching cards can be developed into word recognition games. Use a commercial pack of Old Maid cards with sight words carefully lettered on them, or form an original deck. Use the regular rules of the game, except in order to claim a book a child must name the word on the matching cards.

Another technique is to list sight words on a circular piece of cardboard and to have children paper-clip pictures to appropriate words. The teacher can make this activity self-scoring by printing the matching words on the backs of the pictures as shown below.

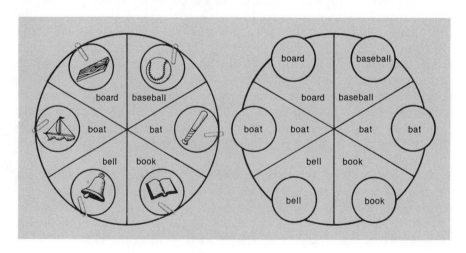

Dickerson (1982) compared the use of physically active games, passive games, and worksheets in an attempt to discover which would be most effective in increasing the sight vocabularies of remedial first graders. The

physically active games proved to be most effective, followed by the passive games. Worksheets were the least effective, although the children who used the worksheets did gain some sight vocabulary.

Some teachers use tachistoscopes to expose words rapidly for sight-word recognition practice. The advantage of this technique is that children become accustomed to the idea of recognizing the word immediately, not sounding it out. Special equipment is not necessary; the teacher can slide a file card with a slot cut out of it down a list of words, exposing each word for a brief period of time and thereby controlling the presentation.

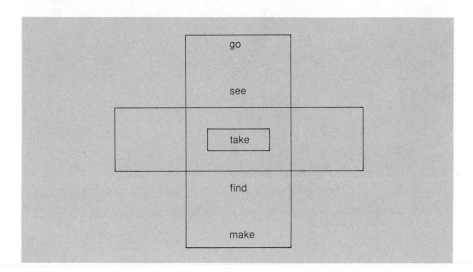

Ceprano (1981) reviewed research on methods of teaching sight words and found that no one method alone was best for every student. She found evidence that teaching the distinctive features of words helped children learn. She also found evidence that use of picture clues along with specific instruction to focus attention on the words facilitated learning. However, she reported that some research indicates that teaching words in isolation or with pictures does not assure the ability to read words in context. In fact, indications are "that most learners need directed experience with written context while learning words in order to perceive that reading is a language process and a meaning-getting process" (p. 321). Therefore, when teachers are working with sight word instruction, it seems wise to include presentation of words in context rather than in isolation.

✔ Self-Check: Objective 1
Should sight words be presented alone or in context? Justify your answer. Describe two activities that can be used for teaching sight words.
(See Self-Improvement Opportunities 1 and 2.)

110

Teaching
Reading in
Today's
Elementary
Schools

New sight words should be introduced to children in context and may be presented in a variety of ways, including word-bank activities and games involving word and phrase cards.   (© Carol Palmer)

Context Clues

Context clues—the words, phrases, and sentences surrounding the words to be decoded—help readers determine what the unfamiliar words are. Here we will focus on the function of context clues as *word recognition* aids; Chapter 5 offers a consideration of the function of context clues as *comprehension* aids.

Since research has found that readers' identification of a word is influenced by syntactic and semantic context, it is important that word recognition skills be introduced and practiced in context (Jones, 1982). Much of the written material that primary-level readers are introduced to is well within their comprehension as far as vocabulary and ideas are concerned, but these youngsters cannot always recognize in printed form the words that are familiar in oral form. Context clues can be of great help in this process. Research also shows that context clues are more helpful in word recognition for younger and poorer readers than they are for older and better readers (Gough, 1984).

Picture Clues

Picture clues are generally the earliest context clues used by children. In readiness materials, exposure to many pictures of a character, such as one named Sally, may develop the situation in which children recognize the character instantly. When shown a page containing a picture of Sally and a single word, they may naturally assume that the word names the picture and that the word is *Sally*. If they do not relate the picture to the word in this manner, the teacher can ask a question, such as "Who is in the picture?" to lead them toward understanding the relationship. If a child responds, "A girl," the teacher might ask, "What kind of letter is at the beginning of the word?" The response "A capital letter" would prompt the question, "What kinds of words have we talked about that begin with capital letters?" After eliciting the answer "Names," the teacher can then ask, "What is the name of the girl in the picture?" This question should produce the response "Sally." Finally, the teacher asks, "Now what do you think the word is?" At this point a correct response is extremely likely. The teacher should use a procedure that encourages the use of picture clues *along with*, rather than apart from, the clues available in the printed word.

Teachers should not overemphasize picture clues. They may be useful in the initial stages of instruction, but they become less useful as the child advances to more difficult material, which has a decreasing number of pictures and an increasing proportion of print. Encouraging too much reliance on pictures may result in too little time spent on developing word analysis skills.

Semantic and Syntactic Clues

As soon as possible, teachers should encourage first-grade children to use written context as a clue to unknown words. The idea of using context clues can be introduced by oral activities like this one.

● **MODEL ACTIVITY:** *Use of Oral Context*

Read sentences such as the ones below to the children, leaving out words as indicated by the blanks. After reading each sentence, ask the children what word they could use to finish the sentence in a way that would make sense. The children will find that the sentences that have missing words at the end are easier. In some cases, the children may suggest several possibilities, all of which are appropriate. Accept all of these contributions.

Sample sentences:
1. Jane went out to walk her _____.
2. John was at home reading a _____.
3. They were fighting like cats and _____.

112

Teaching
Reading in
Today's
Elementary
Schools

4. I want ham and _____ for breakfast.
5. Will you _____ football with me? ●

In the sample sentences above, children could use both semantic (meaning) and syntactic (grammar) clues in choosing words to fill in the blanks. Youngsters generally utilize these two types of clues in combination, but for the purpose of clarifying their differences, we will first consider them separately.

Semantic clues are clues derived from the meanings of the words, phrases, and sentences surrounding the unknown word. In the example just given, children can ask themselves the following questions to decide what words would make sense:

Sentence 1—What are things that can be walked?
Sentence 2—What are things that can be read?
Sentence 3—What expression do I know about fighting that has "like cats and" in it?
Sentence 4—What food might be eaten with ham for breakfast?
Sentence 5—What things can you do with a football?

There are various kinds of semantic clues, including the following:

1. Definition clues. A word may be directly defined in the context. If the child knows the word in oral form, he or she can recognize it in print through the definition.

    The *register* is the book in which the names of the people who come to the wedding are kept.

    The *dictionary* is a book in which the meanings of words can be found.

2. Appositive clues. An appositive may offer a synonym or description of the word, which will cue its recognition. Children need to be taught that an appositive is a word or phrase that restates or identifies the word or expression it follows, and that it is usually set off by commas, dashes, or parentheses.

    They are going to *harvest,* or gather in, the season's crops.

    That model is *obsolete* (outdated).

    The *rodents*—rats and mice—in the experiment learned to run a maze.

3. Comparison clues. A comparison of the unfamiliar word with one the child knows may offer a clue. In the examples the familiar words *sleepy* and *clothes* provide the clues for *drowsy* and *habit*.

Like her sleepy brother, Mary felt *drowsy.*

Like all of the clothes she wore, her riding *habit* was very fashionable.

4. Contrast clues. A contrast of the unknown word to a familiar one may offer a clue. In the examples the unfamiliar word *temporary* is contrasted with the familiar word *forever,* and the unfamiliar word *occasionally* is contrasted with the familiar word *regularly.*

It will not last forever; it is only *temporary.*

She doesn't visit regularly; she just comes by *occasionally.*

5. Common-expression clues. Familiarity with the word order in many commonly heard expressions, particularly figurative expressions, can lead children to the identity of an unknown word. In the context activity discussed earlier, children needed to know the expression "fighting like cats and dogs" to complete the sentence. Children with varied language backgrounds are more likely to be able to use figurative expressions to aid word recognition than are children with less developed backgrounds.

He was as quiet as a *mouse.*

Daryl charged around like a bull in a *china* shop.

6. Example clues. Sometimes examples are given for words that may be unfamiliar in print, and these examples can provide the needed clues for identification.

Mark was going to talk about *reptiles,* for example, snakes and lizards.

Andrea wants to play a *percussion* instrument, such as the snare drum or the bells.

Syntactic clues are contained in the grammar or syntax of our language. Certain types of words appear in certain positions in spoken English sentences. Thus, word order can give readers clues to the identity of an unfamiliar word. Because most children in schools in the United States have been speaking English since they were preschoolers, they have a feeling for the grammar or syntax of the language. Syntactic clues help them discover that the missing words in sentences 1 through 4 in the oral-context activity on pages 111–112 are nouns, or naming words, and that the missing word in sentence 5 is a verb, or action word.

Looking at each item, we see that in number 1 *her* is usually followed by a noun. *A* is usually followed by a singular noun, as in number 2. Items 3 and 4 both employ *and,* which usually connects words of the same type. In number 3 children are likely to insert a plural animal name because of the absence of an article (*a, an, the*). Similarly, in number 4 *and* will signal insertion of another food. Number 5 has the verb marker *will,* which is often found in the sequence "Will you (verb) . . . ?"

114

Teaching
Reading in
Today's
Elementary
Schools

As we pointed out earlier, semantic and syntactic clues should be used *together* to unlock unknown words.

Teaching Strategies

Early exercises with context clues may resemble the oral exercise explained above. Sometimes teachers supply multiple-choice answers and ask the children to circle or underline the correct choice in a written exercise. An example follows.

Sandy ate the ———. (cookie, store, shirt)

The child might need to apply some knowledge of phonics as well as context clues to complete the following sentence.

Pat wore a new ———. (hate, hat, heat)

It is good practice for a teacher to introduce a new word in context and let the children try to identify it, rather than simply to tell them what the word is. Then children can use any phonics and structural analysis knowledge that they have, along with context clues, to help identify the word. The teacher should use a context in which the only unfamiliar word is the new word; for example, use the sentence "My *umbrella* keeps me from getting wet when it rains" to present the word *umbrella*. The children will thus have graphic examples of the value of context clues in identifying unfamiliar words.

When a child encounters an unfamiliar word in oral reading to the teacher, instead of supplying the word, the teacher can encourage the child to read on to the end of the sentence (or even to the next sentence) to see what word would make sense. The teacher can encourage use of the sound of the initial letter or cluster of letters, sounds of other letters in the word, or known structural components, along with context. In a sentence where *hurled* appears as an unknown word, in the phrase *hurled the ball*, a child might guess *held* from the context. The teacher could encourage this child to notice the letters *ur* and try a word that contains that sound and makes sense in the context. Of course, this approach will be effective only if the child knows the meaning of the word *hurled*. Encouraging the child to read subsequent sentences could also be helpful, since these sentences might disclose situations in which *held* would be inappropriate but *hurled* would fit.

Use of context clues can help children make educated guesses about the identity of unfamiliar words. Context clues are best used with phonics and structural analysis skills since they help identify words more quickly than use of phonics or structural analysis clues alone would do. But without the confirmation of phonics and structural analysis, context clues provide only guesses. As we mentioned earlier, when a blank is substituted for a word in a sentence, students can often use several possibilities to complete the sentence and still make sense. When a child encounters an unknown word, he or she should make an educated guess based on the context and verify that guess by using other word analysis skills.

If a child encountered the sentence below, containing a blank instead of a word at the end, she might fill in the blank with either *bat* or *glove*.

> Frank said, "If I am going to play Little League baseball this year, I need a new ball and _____."

If the sentence gave the initial sound of the missing word, the child would know that *bat* was the appropriate word, instead of *glove*.

> Frank said, "If I am going to play Little League baseball this year, I need a new ball and *b*_____."

Structural analysis clues can be used in the same way. In the sentence below, a child might insert such words as *stop* or *keep* in the blank.

> I wouldn't want to _____ you from going on the trip.

The child would choose neither if he had the help of a familiar prefix to guide his choice. The word *prevent* would obviously be the proper choice.

> I wouldn't want to *pre*_____ you from going on the trip.

Suffixes and ending sounds are also very useful in conjunction with the context to help in word identification. Teachers can use exercises similar to the one below to encourage children to use phonics and structural analysis clues along with context clues.

● **WORKSHEET:** *Word Identification*

Directions: From the clues given, identify the incomplete words in the following sentences. Fill in the missing letters.

1. This package is too *h* __ __ __ *y* for me. Let someone else carry it.
2. I want to join the Navy and ride in a *s u b* __ __ __ __ __ __.
3. If you keep up that arguing, you will *s p* __ __ __ the party for everyone.
4. If you want to be strong, eat your *v* __ __ __ __ __ __ __ __ *s*.
5. John rides a *m* __ __ __ __ __ __ *c l e* to school.
6. You can't hurt it. It's *i n* __ __ *s t r* __ __ __ *i b l e*.
7. She lives in a *p e n t* __ __ __ __ __ apartment.
8. My grandmother has a home *r* __ __ __ *d y* for any disease. ●

116

Teaching
Reading in
Today's
Elementary
Schools

Some words are difficult to pronounce unless they are in context, for example, homographs—words that look alike but have different meanings and pronunciations, such as *row, wind, bow, read, content, rebel, minute, lead, record,* and *live.* Here are examples of how context can clarify pronunciations of these words.

1. I'll let you *row* the boat when I get tired.
   If I had known it would cause a *row,* I would never have angered you by mentioning the subject.
2. The *wind* is blowing through the trees.
   Did you *wind* the clock last night?
3. She put a *bow* on the gift.
   You should *bow* to the audience when you finish your act.
4. Can you *read* the directions to me?
   I *read* Tom Sawyer to my class last year.
5. I am *content* living in the mountains.
   The book has a nice cover, but I didn't enjoy the *content.*
6. Would you *rebel* against that law?
   I have always thought you were a *rebel.*
7. I'll be there in a *minute.*
   You must pay attention to *minute* details.
8. Nikki wants to *lead* the parade.
   Some gasoline has *lead* in it.
9. Did your father *record* his gas mileage?
   Suzanne broke Jill's *record* for the highest score in one game.
10. I *live* on Main Street.
    We saw a *live* octopus.

Although most of the examples in this section show only a single sentence as the context, children should be encouraged to look for clues in surrounding sentences as well as the sentence in which the word occurs. Sometimes an entire paragraph will be useful in defining a term.

A cloze passage, in which words have been systematically deleted and replaced with blanks of uniform length, can be a good way to work on context-clue use. For this purpose, the teacher can delete certain types of words (nouns, verbs, adjectives, etc.) if he or she wishes, rather than have random deletion. The class should discuss reasons for the words chosen to be inserted in the blanks, and the teacher should accept synonyms and sometimes nonsynonyms for which the students have a good rationale. The point of the exercise is to have the students think logically about what would make sense in the context.

Bridge, Winograd, and Haley (1983) found that children who read patterned (predictable) books rely more on context clues than children who read preprimers. In their study, the group who used the preprimers relied entirely on graphophonic (symbol-sound relationship) information, appearing to lack awareness of semantic and syntactic cues. This may have occurred

because of the sparse contexts available in preprimers and the fact that preprimers often lack natural language patterns and standard story structure, making prediction of the next word or phrase difficult for children accustomed to stories in natural language.

✔ Self-Check: Objective 2
**Describe a procedure to help children learn to use context clues.
(See Self-Improvement Opportunities 6 and 7.)**

Phonics

Before you read this section, go to "Test Yourself" at the end of the chapter and take the multiple-choice phonics test. It will give you an idea of your present knowledge of phonics. After you study the text, go back and take the test again to see just what you've learned.

Phonics is the association of speech sounds (phonemes) with printed symbols (graphemes). In some languages this sound-symbol association is fairly regular, but not in English. A single letter or combination of letters in our alphabet may stand for many different sounds. For example, the letter *a* in each of the following words has a different sound: *cape, cat, car, father, soda.* On the other hand, a single sound may be represented by more than one letter or combination of letters. The long *e* sound is spelled differently in each of the following words: *me, mien, meal, seed,* and *seize.* To complicate matters further, the English language abounds with letters that stand for no sound, as in island, *k*night, *w*rite, lam*b*, *g*nome, *p*salm, and r*h*yme.

The existence of spelling inconsistencies does not imply that phonics is not useful in helping children decode written language. We discuss inconsistencies to counteract the feeling of some teachers that phonics is an infallible guide to pronouncing words in written materials. Teaching phonics does not constitute a complete reading program; rather, phonics is a valuable aid to word recognition when used in conjunction with other skills, but it is only *one* useful skill among many. Mastering this skill, with the resulting ability to pronounce most unfamiliar words, should not be considered the product of the reading program. Children can pronounce words without understanding them, and getting *meaning* from the printed page should be the objective of all reading instruction.

Groff (1986) found in a 1983 study that, if beginning readers can attain an approximate pronunciation of a written word through applying phonics generalizations, they can then infer the true pronunciation of the word. For example, "100% of the second graders tested could infer and produce the *o* of *from* as /u/ after first hearing it as /o/. The pronunciation /from/ was close enough to /frum/ for these young pupils to infer its correct pronunciation" (p. 921). Groff concluded that children need practice in making such inferences. First they need to apply phonics generalizations to unfamiliar

118

Teaching
Reading in
Today's
Elementary
Schools

words, producing approximate pronunciations of the words. Then they can infer the real pronunciations of the words by thinking of words they know that are close in sound to the approximations achieved by the generalizations.

Skilled readers appear to identify unfamiliar words by finding similarities with known words (Anderson et al., 1985). For example, a reader might work out the pronunciation of the unknown word *lore* by comparing it with the known word *sore* and applying the knowledge of the sound of *l* in other known words, such as *lamp*. Cunningham (1978, 1979) suggests using a similar approach to identify polysyllabic words as well as single-syllable words.

Using twenty-four phonetically regular consonant-vowel-consonant words, Carnine (1977) studied the transfer effects of phonics and whole word approaches to reading instruction and found superior transfer to new words for the students who were taught phonics. The phonics group even had greater transfer to irregular words, although it was not extensive. Carnine pointed out that E. D. Gibson and H. Levin have interpreted research with adults as indicating that teachers should present *several* sound-symbol correspondences for each grapheme rather than one-to-one correspondences, thereby providing their students with a set for diversity. If such a procedure had been used in this study, it might have produced more transfer to irregular words; further examination of this possibility is needed.

✔ Self-Check: Objective 3

Can you justify teaching phonics as the only approach to word recognition? Why or why not?
(See Self-Improvement Opportunity 3.)

Terminology

To understand written material about phonics, teachers need to be familiar with the terms discussed below.

Vowels The letters *a, e, i, o,* and *u* represent vowel sounds, and the letters *w* and *y* take on the characteristics of vowels when they appear in the final position in a word or syllable. The letter *y* also has the characteristics of a vowel in the medial (middle) position in a word or syllable.

Consonants Letters other than *a, e, i, o,* and *u* generally represent consonant sounds. *W* and *y* have the characteristics of consonants when they appear in the initial position in a word or syllable.

Consonant Clusters (or Blends) Two or more adjacent consonant sounds blended together—with each individual sound retaining its identity—constitute a consonant cluster. For example, although the first three sounds in the word *strike* are blended smoothly, listeners can detect the separate sounds of *s, t,* and *r* being produced in rapid succession. Other examples are the *fr* in *frame,* the *cl* in *click,* and the *br* in *bread,* to mention only a few. Many teaching materials refer to these letter combinations as consonant blends rather than consonant clusters.

Consonant Digraphs Two adjacent consonant letters that represent a single speech sound constitute a consonant digraph. For example, *sh* is a consonant digraph in the word *shore,* since it represents one sound and not a blend of the sounds of *s* and *h.* Further examples of consonant digraphs can be found on page 125.

Vowel Digraphs Two adjacent vowel letters that represent a single speech sound constitute a vowel digraph. In the word *foot, oo* is a vowel digraph. Further examples of vowel digraphs can be found on page 126.

Diphthongs Vowel sounds that are so closely blended that they can be treated as single vowel units for the purposes of word identification are called diphthongs. These sounds are actually vowel blends, since the vocal mechanism produces two sounds instead of one, as is the case with vowel digraphs. An example of a diphthong is the *ou* in *out.* Further examples of diphthongs can be found on page 126.

Some authorities object to the use of the terms *long* and *short* vowel sounds, since some readers may think that these terms refer to the duration of the sound. For this reason the terms *glided* (for long) and *unglided* (for short) have been used in some publications. A majority of readers are more familiar with *long* and *short,* however, so we have used them in this text.

Of course, teachers may choose to use neither set of terms. Instead of saying, "The vowel sound is usually long," a teacher may say, "The vowel has the sound of its alphabet name." For short vowel sounds, the teacher can say that the sound is the same as the one heard in a key word like *pet, cat, mitt, cot,* or *cup.*

✔ **Self-Check: Objective 4**
Define and give an example of a consonant blend, a consonant digraph, a vowel digraph, and a diphthong.

Sequence for Presenting Phonics Skills

Teachers do not usually determine the sequence for presenting phonics materials, which is usually dictated by materials chosen for use in the school, but they might find it helpful to understand the reasoning behind a particular order. Teachers who understand a reasonable sequence for presenting phonics elements are better equipped to choose new materials when given the opportunity to do so.

120

Teaching
Reading in
Today's
Elementary
Schools

There seems to be agreement on the fact that good auditory and visual discrimination are prerequisites for learning sound-symbol relationships. We know that a child must be able to distinguish one letter from another and one sound from another before he or she can associate a particular letter with a particular sound. However, some controversy exists over the relative merits of teaching vowel sounds or consonant sounds first. Those who favor teaching vowel sounds first point out that every syllable of every word has a vowel sound and that vowels can be pronounced in isolation without undue distortion, whereas many consonants must be accompanied by vowels in order to be pronounced properly. These educators do not agree among themselves about *which* vowels should be presented first. Some prefer to teach the long vowels first because their sounds correspond to their letter names, while others believe that the short vowels should be presented first because they occur in more words in the beginning reading materials. Still others advocate teaching both types at the same time in order to take advantage of contrasts available in the children's vocabularies (*tap–tape, cot–coat*). They do seem to agree that the *r*- and *l*-controlled vowels, the schwa (ə) sound, and diphthongs should be presented after the long and short vowel sounds.

A majority of the authorities on reading instruction favor the presentation of consonant sounds before the introduction of vowel sounds, citing the following reasons:

1. Consonant letters are more consistent in the sounds they represent than vowel letters are. Many consonants represent a single sound (although they are not always sounded in a word), whereas all vowels represent numerous sounds. *B, f, h, k, l, m, p, r,* and *t* are among the most consistent consonant sounds.
2. Consonants usually make up the more identifiable features of a word. As an example, decide which of these representations of the word *tractor* is easiest to decipher: *t r __ c t __ r* or *__ __ a __ __ o __*.
3. More words start with consonants than with vowels, and words are generally attacked in a left-to-right sequence.

These reasons seem more practical than the reasons for presenting vowels first. We can overcome the problem that many consonants cannot be pronounced in isolation through an analytic approach to phonics, which is explained later in this chapter.

Words with consonants in the initial position are usually presented first, then words with consonants in the final position. Consonants that represent fairly consistent sounds are usually presented before those that represent several sounds (*c, g, s, x,* and so on). Consonant digraphs (voiced *th*, voiceless *th, sh, wh, ch, ck, ng, ph,* and so on) and consonant blends (*br, bl, st, str, gl,* and so on) are usually not presented until students have been taught the

Learning phonics skills involves learning about letter-sound associations such as those of consonants, consonant digraphs, and consonant clusters (or blends). (© Teri Leigh Stratford/Monkmeyer)

single consonant sounds in the initial positions. Consonant letters that appear in words but are not sounded ("silent" letters) must also receive attention, for they occur quite often (lamb, pneumonia, gnat).

Some authorities suggest teaching vowel and consonant sounds simultaneously, thus making possible the complete sounding of entire short words early in the program. For example, a teacher can present the short *a* sound along with several consonants (perhaps *m, t, f, c*) to make the building of several words possible (*mat, fat, cat*).

A sequence for presenting letter-sound correspondences is reproduced below. The first part of the sequence was suggested by Dale Johnson.

122

Teaching
Reading in
Today's
Elementary
Schools

Single Consonants
  Set 1: *d, n, l, m, b*
  Set 2: *p, f, v, r, h, k, y, s, c, t*
  Set 3: *j, w, z, x, q (u), g*
Consonant Clusters
  Digraphs: *sh, th, ch, ng, ph*
Double Consonants
  ss, ll, rr, tt, mm, nn, ff, pp, cc, dd, gg, bb, zz
Single Vowels
  i, a, o, u, e
Vowel Clusters
  Set 1: *io, ea, ou, ee, ai, au*
  Set 2: *oo, ow, oi, ay*
  Set 3: *ia, oa, ie, ue, iou, ua, ui*[1]
Consonant Blends
  consonant plus *l*, consonant plus *r*, *s* plus consonant
Patterned Irregularities
  knee, knife, knew, bomb, comb, lamb
Syllabication
  VCV [Vowel-Consonant-Vowel] *ba/by*
  VCCV [Vowel-Consonant-Consonant-Vowel] *nap/kin*
  VCle [Vowel-Consonant-le] *a/ble*

Phonics Generalizations

Many teachers believe that good phonics instruction is merely the presentation of a series of principles that children are expected to internalize and
utilize in the process of word identification. Difficulties may arise from this
conception.

First, pupils tend to internalize a phonics generalization more rapidly and effectively when they can arrive at it inductively. That is, by analyzing words to
which a generalization applies and by deriving the generalization themselves
from this analysis, children will understand it better and remember it longer.

Second, the irregularity of our spelling system results in numerous exceptions to phonics generalizations. Children must be helped to see that
generalizations help them to derive *probable* pronunciations rather than
infallible results. When applying a generalization does not produce a word
that makes sense in the context of the material, readers should try other
reasonable sound possibilities. For example, in cases where a long vowel
sound is likely according to a generalization but results in a nonsense word,
the child should be taught to try other sounds, such as the short vowel sound,
in the search for the correct pronunciation. Some words are so totally

[1] Dale D. Johnson, "Suggested Sequences for Presenting Four Categories of Letter-Sound
Correspondence," *Elementary English* 50 (September 1973): 888–96. Copyright © 1973 by the
National Council of Teachers of English. Reprinted with permission of the publisher.

irregular in spelling that even extreme flexibility in phonic analysis will not produce a close approximation of the correct pronunciation. In a situation such as this, the child should be taught to turn to the dictionary for help in word recognition. Further discussion of this approach to word recognition can be found later in this chapter.

Third, students can be so deluged with rules that they cannot memorize them all. This procedure may result in failure to learn any generalization well.

Teachers can enhance a phonics program by presenting judiciously chosen phonics generalizations to youngsters. Authorities vary on which ones to present (Bailey, 1967; Burmeister, 1968, Clymer, 1963; Emans, 1967), but they agree on some of them. Considering the findings of phonics studies and past teaching experience, we feel that the following generalizations are useful under most circumstances:

1. When the letters *c* and *g* are followed by *e, i,* or *y,* they generally have soft sounds: the *s* sound for the letter *c* and the *j* sound for the letter *g.* (Examples: *cent, city, cycle, gem, ginger, gypsy.*) When *c* and *g* are followed by *o, a,* or *u,* they generally have hard sounds: *g* has its own special sound, and *c* has the sound of *k.* (Examples: *cat, cake, cut, go, game, gum.*)

2. When two like consonants are next to each other, only one is sounded. (Examples: *hall, glass.*)

3. *Ch* usually has the sound heard in *church,* although it sometimes sounds like *sh* or *k.* (Examples of usual sound: *child, chill, china.* Examples of *sh* sound: *chef, chevron.* Examples of *k* sound: *chemistry, chord.*)

4. When the letters *ght* are side by side in a word, the *gh* is not sounded. (Examples: *taught, light.*)

5. When *kn* are the first two letters in a word, the *k* is not sounded. (Examples: *know, knight.*)

6. When *wr* are the first two letters in a word, the *w* is not sounded. (Examples: *write, wrong.*)

7. When *ck* are the last two letters in a word, the sound of *k* is given. (Examples: *check, brick.*)

8. The sound of a vowel preceding *r* is neither long nor short. (Examples: *car, fir, her.*)

9. In the vowel combinations *oa, ee,* and *ay,* the first vowel is generally long and the second one is not sounded. This may also apply to other double vowel combinations. (Examples: *boat, feet, play.*)

10. The double vowels *oi, oy,* and *ou* usually form diphthongs. While the *ow* combination frequently stands for the long *o* sound, it may also form a diphthong. (Examples: *boil, boy, out, now.*)

11. In a word that has only one vowel which is at the end of the word, the vowel usually represents its long sound. (Examples: *me, go.*)

12. In a word that has only one vowel which is *not* at the end of the word, the vowel usually represents its short sound. (Examples: *set, man, cut, hop, list.*)

124

Teaching
Reading in
Today's
Elementary
Schools

13. If there are two vowels in a word and one is a final *e,* the first vowel is usually long and the final *e* is not sounded. (Examples: *cape, cute, cove, kite.*)

14. The letter combination *qu* often stands for the sound of *kw,* although it sometimes stands for the sound of *k.* (Examples of *kw* sound: *quick, queen.* Example of *k* sound: *quay.*)

15. The letter *x* most often stands for the sound of *ks,* although at times it stands for the sound of *gz* or *z.* (Examples of *ks* sound: *box, next.* Example of *gz* sound: *exact.* Example of *z* sound: *xylophone.*)

Rosso and Emans (1981) tried to determine whether knowledge of phonic generalizations helps children decode unrecognized words and whether children have to be able to state the generalizations to use them. They found statistically significant relationships between knowledge of phonic generalizations and reading achievement, but pointed out that this does not necessarily indicate a cause-and-effect relationship. They also discovered that "inability to state a phonics rule did not seem to hinder these children's effort to analyze unfamiliar words . . . this study supports Piaget's theory that children in the concrete operations stage of development may encounter difficulty in describing verbally those actions they perform physically" (p. 657). Teachers may need to investigate techniques for teaching phonics generalizations that do not require children to verbalize a generalization.

It is wise to teach only one generalization at a time, presenting a second only after students have thoroughly learned the first. The existence of exceptions to generalizations should be freely acknowledged, and children should be encouraged to treat the generalizations as *possible* rather than *infallible* clues to pronunciation.

Consonants   Although consonant letters are more consistent in the sounds they represent than vowel letters are, they are not perfectly consistent. The list below shows some examples of variations with which a child must contend.

Consonant	Variations	Consonant	Variations
b	board, lamb	n	never, drink
c	cable, city, scene	p	punt, psalm
d	dog, jumped	q(u)	antique, quit
f	fox, of	s	see, sure, his,
g	go, gem, gnat		pleasure, island
h	hit, hour	t	town, listen
j	just, hallelujah	w	work, wrist
k	kitten, knee	x	fox, anxiety, exit
l	lamp, calf	z	zoo, azure, quartz

Consider the cases in which *y* and *w* take on vowel characteristics. Both of these letters represent consonant sounds when they are in the initial position in a word or syllable, but they represent vowel sounds when they are in a final or medial position. For example, *y* represents a consonant sound in the word *yard,* but a vowel sound in the words *dye, myth,* and *baby.* Notice that actually three different vowel sounds are represented by *y* in these words.

Consonant Digraphs Several consonant digraphs represent sounds not associated with either of the component parts. These are shown in the list below.

Consonant Digraph	*Example*
th	then, thick
ng	sing
sh	shout
ph	telephone
gh	rough
ch	chief, chef, chaos

Other consonant digraphs generally represent the usual sound of one of the component parts, as in *wr*ite, *pn*eumonia, and *gn*at. Some sources consider one of the letters in each of these combinations as a "silent" letter and do not refer to these combinations as digraphs.

Vowels The variability of the sounds represented by vowels has been emphasized before. Some examples of this variability are given in the list below.

Vowel Letter	*Variations*
a	ate, cat, want, ball father, sofa
e	me, red, pretty, kitten, her, sergeant
i	ice, hit, fir, opportunity
o	go, hot, today, women, button, son, work, born
u	use, cut, put, circus, turn

In the examples here, the first variation listed for each vowel is a word in which the long vowel sound, the same as its letter name, is heard. In the second variation the short sound of the vowel is heard. These are generally the first two sounds taught for each vowel.

Another extremely common sound that children need to learn is the schwa sound, a very soft "uh" or grunt usually found in unaccented syllables. It is heard in the following words: sof*a*, kitt*e*n, opportun*i*ty, butt*o*n, circ*u*s. The schwa sound is, as you can see, represented by each of the vowel letters.

Three types of markings represent the three types of vowel sounds we have discussed:

126

Teaching
Reading in
Today's
Elementary
Schools

Marking	Name of Mark	Designation
ā, ē, ī, ō, ū	macron	long vowel sound
ă, ĕ, ĭ, ŏ, ŭ	breve	short vowel sound
ə	schwa	soft "uh" sound

Some dictionaries place no mark at all over a vowel letter that represents the short sound of the vowel.

Vowel Digraphs   Some vowel digraphs represent sounds not associated with either of the letters involved. These digraphs are illustrated below:

Vowel Digraph	Example
au	taught
aw	saw
oo	food, look

Other vowel digraphs generally represent the usual sound of one of the component parts, as in break, bread, boat, seed, and aim. Some sources treat one of the letters in these combinations as "silent" and do not refer to them as digraphs.

Diphthongs   There are four common diphthongs, or vowel blends.

Diphthong	Example in Context
oi	foil
oy	toy
ou	bound
ow	cow

Notice that the first two diphthongs listed (*oi* and *oy*) stand for identical sounds, as do the last two (*ou* and *ow*). Remember that the letter combinations *ow* and *ou* are *not always diphthongs*. In the words *snow* and *blow*, *ow* is a vowel digraph representing the long *o* sound. In the word *routine*, *ou* represents an $\overline{oo}$ sound.

Teaching Strategies

There are two major approaches to phonics instruction, the synthetic approach and the analytic approach.

In a synthetic method the teacher first instructs children in the speech sounds that are associated with individual letters. Since letters and sounds have no inherent relationships, this task is generally accomplished by repeated drill on sound-symbol associations. The teacher may hold up a card on which the letter *b* appears and expect the children to respond with the sound ordinarily associated with that letter. The next step is blending the sounds together to form words. The teacher encourages the children to pronounce the sounds associated with the letters in rapid succession so that they produce a word or an approximate pronunciation of a word, which they can then recognize and pronounce accurately. This blending process generally begins with two- and three-letter words and proceeds to much longer ones.

Although blending ability is a key factor in the success of a synthetic phonics approach, many commercial materials for reading instruction do not give much attention to its development. Research findings indicate that children must master both segmentation of words into their component sounds and blending before they are able to apply phonics skills to the decoding of unknown words and that the ability to segment is a prerequisite for successful blending. Research also indicates that a teacher cannot assume that children will automatically transfer the skills they have been taught to unknown words. Direct instruction for transfer is needed, in order to ensure that it will occur (Johnson and Baumann, 1984).

When a synthetic phonics approach is used, the children will sometimes be asked to pronounce nonsense syllables because these syllables will appear later in written materials as word parts. Reading words in context does not generally occur until these steps have been repeatedly carried out and the children have developed a moderate stock of words.

The analytic approach involves teaching some sight words and then the sounds of the letters within those words. It is preferred by many educators and is used in many basal reader series, partly because it avoids the distortion that occurs when consonants are pronounced in isolation. For example, trying to pronounce a *t* in isolation is likely to result in the sounds *tə*. Pronouncing a schwa sound following the consonant can adversely affect the child's blending, since the word *tag* must be sounded as *tə-a-gə*. No matter how fast the child makes those sounds, he or she is unlikely to come very close to *tag*. The same process may be used to introduce other consonants, consonant blends, consonant digraphs, vowels, diphthongs, and vowel digraphs in initial, medial, and final positions. One possible problem when analytic phonics is used, however, is that children may not be able to extract an individual sound just from hearing it within a word.

The analytic method is illustrated in the three sample lesson plans presented below. The first two lesson plans are *inductive*. The children look at a number of specific examples related to a generalization and then derive the generalization. A *deductive* plan consists of the teacher's first stating a generalization and then having the children apply the generalization in decoding unfamiliar words. The third lesson plan illustrates this approach.

● **MODEL ACTIVITY:** *Analytic-Inductive Lesson Plan for Initial Consonant* D

Write on the chalkboard the following words, all of which the children have learned previously as sight words:

128
Teaching
Reading in
Today's
Elementary
Schools

dog	did
daddy	donkey
do	Dan

Ask the children to listen carefully as you pronounce the words. Then ask: "Did any parts of these words sound the same?" If you receive an affirmative reply, ask, "What part sounded the same?" This should elicit the answer that the first sound in each word is the same or that the words sound alike at the beginning.

Next ask the children to look carefully at the words written on the board. Ask: "Do you see anything that is the same in all these words?" This should elicit the answer that all of the words have the same first letter or all of the words start with *d.*

Then ask what the children can conclude about words that begin with the letter *d.* The expected answer is that words that begin with the letter *d* sound the same at the beginning as the word *dog* (or any other word on their list).

Next invite the children to name other words that have the same beginning sound as *dog.* Write each word on the board. Ask the children to observe the words and draw another conclusion. They may say, "Words that sound the same at the beginning as the word *dog* begin with the letter *d.*"

Ask the children to watch for words in their reading that begin with the letter *d* in order to check the accuracy of their conclusions. ●

● **MODEL ACTIVITY:** *Analytic-Inductive Lesson Plan for Short Vowel Sound Generalizations*

Write the following list of words on the board, all of which are part of the children's sight vocabularies:

sit	in
at	man
hot	Don
met	wet
cut	bun

Ask the children how many vowels they see in each of the words in the list. When you receive the answer "one," write on the board "One vowel letter."

Then ask: "Where is the vowel letter found in these words?" The children will probably say, "At the beginning in some and in the middle in others." Write on the board, "At the beginning or in the middle."

Then ask: "Which of its sounds does the vowel have in the word *sit*? In the word *at*? and so on until the students have discovered that the short sound is present in each word. Then write "Short sound" on the board.

Next ask the children to draw a conclusion about the vowel sounds in the words they have analyzed. The generalization may be stated, "In words that contain only one vowel letter, located at the beginning or in the middle of the word, the vowel usually has its short sound." The children will be likely to insert the word "usually" if they have been warned about the tentative nature of phonics generalizations.

Finally, ask the children if they should have included in their generalization words having only one vowel letter located at the end of the word. The children can check sight words such as *he, no,* and *be* in order to conclude that these words do not have a short vowel sound and therefore should not be included in the generalization. ●

● **MODEL ACTIVITY:** *Analytic-Deductive Lesson Plan for Soft Sound of* c

Tell the children: "When the letter *c* is followed by *e, i,*or *y,* it generally has its soft sound, which is the sound you have learned for the letter *s.*" Write the following examples on the chalkboard: *city, cycle,* and *cent.* Point out that in *cycle* only the *c* that is followed by *y* has the soft sound. Follow this presentation with an activity designed to check the children's understanding of the generalization. The activity might involve a worksheet with items like this:

Directions: Place a checkmark beside the words that contain a soft *c* sound.

_____ cite	_____ cider	_____ cape
_____ cord	_____ cede	_____ cymbal
_____ cut	_____ cod	_____ cell

The soft *c* sound is the sound we have learned for the letter _____. ●

Johnson and Bauman (1984) cite research indicating that "programs emphasizing a phonics or code approach to word identification produce superior word-calling ability when compared to programs applying an analytic phonics or meaning emphasis" (p. 590). But they continue by pointing out that "there seem to be distinct differences in the quality of error responses made by children instructed in the two general methodologies—readers' errors tend to be real words, meaningful, and syntactically appropriate when instruction emphasizes meaning, whereas code-emphasis word-identification instruction results in more nonword errors that are graphically and aurally like the mispronounced words" (p. 590). Because the goal of reading is comprehension, not word calling, the analytic approach, which uses meaning-emphasis techniques, should probably be chosen for instruction.

Teachers should keep in mind a caution concerning the teaching of phonics generalizations, involving the use of such terms as *sound* and *word.* Studies by Reid and Downing indicate that young children (five-year-olds) have trouble understanding terms used to talk about language, such as *word, letter,* and *sound* (Downing, 1973), and Meltzer and Herse (1969) found that first-grade children do not always know where printed words begin and end. In addition, Tovey (1980) found that the group of second through sixth

130

Teaching
Reading in
Today's
Elementary
Schools

graders that he studied had difficulty in dealing with abstract phonics terms such as *consonant, consonant blend, consonant digraph, vowel digraph, diphthong, possessive, inflectional ending,* and others. His study also showed that the children had learned sound-symbol associations without being able to define the phonics terms involved. Lessons such as those described are worthless if the students do not have these basic concepts. Before teaching a lesson using linguistic terms, the teacher should check to be sure that students grasp such concepts. Technical terminology should be deemphasized when working with students who have not mastered the terms.

Cordts (1965) suggests using key words to help children learn the sounds associated with vowels, consonants, vowel digraphs, consonant digraphs, diphthongs, and consonant blends. These words in all cases should already be part of the children's sight vocabularies. Cordts suggests that a key word for a vowel sound be one that contains that vowel sound and can be pictured, while a key word for a consonant sound should be one that can be pictured and has that consonant sound at the end. She feels that consonant sounds can be more clearly heard at the ends than at the beginnings of words.

From the suggestions given by Cordts, we have constructed the list of key words shown in Table 3.2.

TABLE 3.2 Sample Key Words

Sample Key Words for Vowel Sounds			
Short Vowels	*Long Vowels*	*Diphthongs*	*Special Vowel Digraphs*
cat	snake	coin	saw
bed	key	boy	auto
ship	dime .	house	moon
top	cone	cow	foot
bug	fuse		

Sample Key Words for Consonant Sounds			
Single Consonants	*Single Consonants (cont'd)*	*Special Consonant Digraphs*	*Only Heard at the Beginning of Words*
b—tub	p—hoop or pipe	ch—match	h—hat
d—head	s—glass	th—cloth	w—wing
f—chief	t—coat	sh—dish	j—jail
g—rug	v—sleeve or	ng—ring	wh—whale
k—chalk	dove		y—yard
l—rail	x—box		
m—arm	z—prize		
n—pen			
r—rope (The *r* sound is more consistent at the beginning than at the end of words.)			

Other authorities also encourage the use of key words, but most suggest using words with the consonant sounds at the beginning. The sounds may be harder to distinguish, but usable key words are much easier to find when initial sounds are used.

Key words are valuable in helping children remember sound-symbol associations which are not inherently meaningful. People remember new things through associations with things that they already know. The more associations that a person has for an abstract relationship, such as the letter *d* and the sound of *d,* the more quickly that person will learn to link the sound and symbol. The person's retention of this connection will also be more accurate. Schell (1978) refers to a third-grade boy who chose as key words for the consonant blends *dr, fr,* and *sp* the character names *Dracula, Frankenstein,* and *Spiderman.* These associations were both concrete and personal for him. The characters were drawn on key-word cards to aid his memory of the associations.

Consonant substitution activities are useful for helping students see how their knowledge of some words helps them to decode other words. To teach consonant substitution, the teacher writes a known word, such as *pat,* on the board and asks the students to pronounce the word. Then he or she writes on the board a letter for which the sound has been taught (for example, *m*). If the letter sound can be pronounced in isolation without distortion, the teacher asks the students to do so; if not, he or she asks for a word beginning with this sound. Then the students are asked to leave the *p* sound off when they pronounce the word on the board. They will respond with "at." Next they are asked to put the *m* sound in front of the "at," and they produce "mat." The same process is followed with other sounds, such as *s, r,* and *b.*

This procedure is also useful with sounds at the ends of words or in medial positions. Vowel substitution activities, in which the teacher may start with a known word and have the students omit the vowel sound and substitute a different one (for example: m*a*t, m*e*t, m*i*tt; p*a*t, p*e*t, p*i*t, p*o*t), can also be helpful.

Drill on letter-sound associations does not have to be dull. Teachers can use many game activities, and activities that are more businesslike in nature will not become boring if they are not overused. Always remember when planning games that, although competitive situations are motivational for some youngsters, others are adversely affected by being placed in win/lose situations, especially if they have little hope of being winners at least part of the time. Continuously being forced into losing situations can negatively affect a child's self-concept and can promote negative attitudes toward the activity involved in the game (in this instance, reading). This effect is less likely if children with similar abilities compete with each other; however, even then competitive games should be used with caution. Game situations in which children cooperate or in which they compete with their *own previous records* rather than with one another are often more acceptable. Here are some practical examples.

132 *ACTIVITIES*

Teaching
Reading in
Today's
Elementary
Schools

1. Construct cards resembling bingo cards, like the ones below. Pronounce a word beginning with the sound of one of the listed consonants or consonant digraphs. Instruct the children to check their cards for the letter or letter combination that represents the word's initial sound. Tell those who have the correct grapheme on the card to cover it with a token. Continue to pronounce words until one child has covered his or her entire card. The first child to do this can be declared the winner, or the game may continue until all cards are covered.

b	d	f	g
h	j	k	l
m	n	p	r
s	t	v	w

y	z	th	sh
h	ch	b	p
r	m	t	k
n	s	g	n

d	y	g	th
h	ch	k	p
m	r	s	v
sh	n	l	j

2. Give each child a sheet of paper that is blank except for a letter at the top. Have the children draw pictures of as many items as they can think of that have names beginning with the sound of the letter at the top of the page. Declare the child with the most correct responses the winner.

3. Make five decorated boxes, and label each with a short vowel. Have the children locate pictures of objects whose names contain the short vowel sounds and file them in the appropriate boxes. Each day take out the pictures, ask the children to pronounce the names, and check to see if the appropriate sounds are present. Do the same thing with long vowel sounds, consonant sounds, consonant blends, digraphs, diphthongs, and rhyming words.

4. Use worksheets such as those that follow. In each case, read the directions for the worksheet to the children before they begin.

● **WORKSHEET:** *Medial Vowels*

Directions: Listen to the word that the teacher says for each line. Circle the word that you hear.

1.	cat	cut	cot
2.	sit	set	sat
3.	hit	hat	hut
4.	fan	fun	fin
5.	cop	cap	cup
6.	pup	pip	pop
7.	mad	mod	mud ●

Directions: Draw a line connecting the words in Column 1 with the words in Column 2 that rhyme.

Column 1	Column 2
lake	coat
pig	big
size	cake
mat	mail
boat	prize
sail	sat ●

● **WORKSHEET:** *Long o Sound*

Directions: Underline the words that contain the long *o* sound.

1. cot
2. coat
3. snow
4. cow
5. cone
6. pole

7. soul
8. hog
9. won
10. moose
11. cold
12. tone ●

5. Place a familiar word ending on a cardboard disc like the one pictured here. Pull a strip of cardboard with initial consonants on it through an opening cut in the disc. Show the children how to pull the strip through the disc, pronouncing each word that is formed.

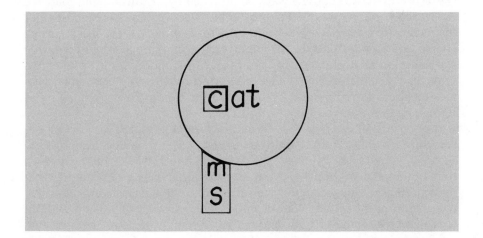

134

Teaching
Reading in
Today's
Elementary
Schools

6. Divide the children in the room into two groups. Give half of them initial consonant, consonant blend, or consonant digraph cards. Give the other half word-ending cards. Instruct the children to pair up with other children holding word parts that combine with their parts to form real words. Have the children hold up their cards and pronounce the word they have made when they have located a combination.

7. Use riddles. For example, "I have in mind a word that rhymes with *far*. We ride in it. It's called a _____."

8. Give students silly sentences to read orally. Construct these sentences so that they require the application of phonics skills taught previously. Examples: She said it was her fate to be fat. Her mate sat on the mat. He charged a high rate to kill the rat.

9. Let the children find a hidden picture by shading in all of the spaces that contain words with long vowel sounds.

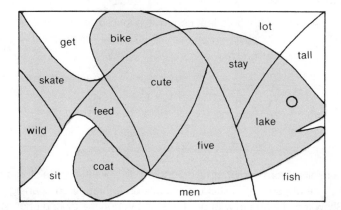

Practice exercises should always be preceded by instruction and followed by feedback on results if they are to be effective. The absence of prior instruction may cause practice of the wrong response. Feedback, which should come either directly from the teacher or through a self-correcting procedure (posted answers, for example), will inform students of errors immediately so that they do not learn incorrect responses. When students fail to see reasons for errors, the teacher will need to provide explanations and reteaching of the skill.

A phonics skill is a means to an end, not an end in itself. If a reader can recognize a word without resorting to letter-by-letter sounding, he or she will recognize it more quickly, and the process will interfere less with the reader's train of thought. When the words to be recognized are seen in context, as in most normal reading activities, the sound of the first letter alone may elicit recognition of the whole word. Context clues can provide a child with an idea about the word's identity, and the initial sound can be used to verify an educated guess. This procedure is efficient and is a good method of quickly identifying unfamiliar words. Of course, the ultimate goal of instruction in phonics and other word identification skills is to turn initially unfamiliar words into automatically recognized sight words.

Phonics skills receive extensive attention in the primary grades (1–3), and teachers of these grades are generally aware that they need to be well-informed in this area. Review and reteaching of phonics skills should, however, take place at successively higher grade levels. Not all children internalize phonics principles during the first three grades, and these children should have help until they have attained proficiency. Therefore, intermediate and upper-grade teachers should also be well versed in teaching these skills.

✔ Self-Check: Objective 5

Describe a procedure for teaching one of the phonics generalizations listed in this section.
(See Self-Improvement Opportunity 4.)

Structural Analysis

Structural analysis skills are closely related to phonics skills and have several significant facets:

1. inflectional endings
2. prefixes, suffixes
3. contractions
4. compound words
5. syllabication and accents

Structural analysis skills enable children to decode unfamiliar words by using units larger than single graphemes; this procedure generally expedites the decoding process. Structural analysis can also be helpful in understanding word meanings, a function discussed in Chapter 4.

Inflectional Endings

Inflectional endings are added to nouns to change number, case, or gender; added to verbs to change tense or person; and added to adjectives to change degree. They may also change the part of speech of a word. Since inflectional endings are letters or groups of letters added to the endings of root words, some people call them inflectional suffixes. The words that result are called variants, and some examples are found in the list below.

Root Word	Variant	Change
boy	boys	Singular noun changed to plural noun
host	hostess	Gender of noun changed from masculine to feminine

136

**Teaching
Reading in
Today's
Elementary
Schools**

Root Word	Variant	Change
Karen	Karen's	Proper noun altered to show possession (change of case)
look	looked	Verb changed from present tense to past tense
make	makes	Verb changed from first or second person singular to third person singular
mean	meaner	Simple form of adjective changed to the comparative form
happy	happily	Adjective changed to adverb

Generally, the first inflectional ending that children are exposed to is *s*. This ending often appears in preprimers and primers and should be learned early in the first grade. Other inflectional endings that children are likely to encounter in these early materials are *ing* and *ed*.

A child can be shown the effect of the addition of an *s* to a singular noun by illustrations of single and multiple objects. An activity such as that shown in Worksheet: Recognizing Inflectional Ending *s* can be used to practice this skill. Another sample worksheet for various inflectional endings and a commercial workbook activity (Example 3.1) demonstrate further practice with different inflectional endings.

● **WORKSHEET:** *Recognizing Inflectional Ending* s

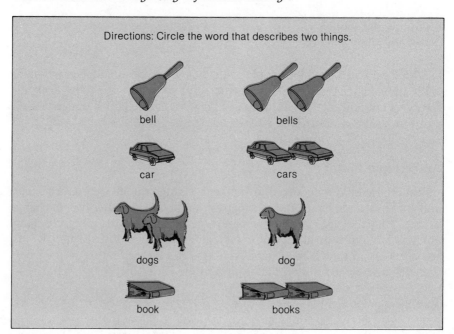

● **WORKSHEET:** *Recognizing Inflectional Endings*

Directions: In each sentence below, circle the endings you have studied.

1. He walk(ed) around the block with the boy(s.)
2. She found Jane('s) grape(s) in her lunchbox.
3. Bob is going with Jack('s) group.
4. Ray('s) motorcycle need(ed) to be fix(ed.)
5. Kristy has many toy truck(s.)
6. Toby pick(ed) up my glass(es.) ●

▶ **EXAMPLE 3.1:** Practice Sheet for Word Endings

● Read each pair of sentences.
Underline the word with the **est** ending.
Then circle the picture that answers
the question.

1. They are happy.
   Which one is happiest?

2. One is not big.
   Which is the biggest?

3. Which is tiniest?
   Not all are tiny.

4. One is not hungry.
   Who looks the hungriest?

★ Read the sentence. Find the base word
for the word in heavy black letters.
Mark the space for the answer.

Which day of the week was the **hottest**?
   ◯ hott   ◯ ho   ◯ hot

Source: ADVENTURES (Houghton Mifflin Reading Series), by William
K. Durr et al. Workbook, Teacher's Annotated Edition, p. 53. Copyright
© 1986 by Houghton Mifflin Company. Used by permission. ◀

138

Teaching
Reading in
Today's
Elementary
Schools

Children should not be given the impression that the inflectional ending *s* always sounds like the *s* in *see;* this pronunciation occurs only after an unvoiced *th, t, p, k,* and *f.* After other consonant sounds and after long vowel sounds, the ending *s* has the sound associated with the letter *z.*

The teacher should also emphasize variations in pronouncing the inflectional ending *ed.* When the *ed* follows *d* and *t,* the *e* is sounded, but after other letters the *e* is silent. When the *e* is sounded, a separate syllable is formed, but when it is not sounded, the inflectional ending does not form a separate syllable. (Examples: dusted—dust' ed; begged—begd.) In addition, the *d* in *ed* is given the sound ordinarily associated with *t* in many words, especially those ending with *s, ch, sh, f, k,* and *p.* (Examples: asked—askt; helped—helpt; wished—wisht.)

An activity that can help children recognize the varied sounds of the *d* in the ending *ed* follows.

● **MODEL ACTIVITY:** *Sounds of* d *in* ed *Ending*

Distribute worksheets containing the following words to the children:

1. dropped _____
2. canned _____
3. worked _____
4. passed _____
5. stopped _____

Then say: "Listen carefully as I pronounce each of the words on your paper. If the *d* in the ending *ed* sounds like *d,* write a *d* after the word. If the *d* sounds like *t,* write a *t* after the word." Give the children time to fill in their worksheets, and then say: "Now check your answers. Do you have a *t* for 1, 3, 4, and 5 and *d* for 2? If so, you have a perfect paper. If you missed some, please come to the skills corner, and I will help you." ●

Children in the primary grades are frequently exposed to the possessive case formed by *'s.* An activity designed for work with this inflectional ending follows.

● **MODEL ACTIVITY:** *The* 's *Ending*

Tell the children: "When I say, 'This is the book of my brother,' I mean that the book belongs to my brother. Another, shorter way of saying the same thing is 'This is my brother's book.' The apostrophe *s* on the end of the word *brother* shows that the noun following *brother* (book) belongs to brother. Reword these phrases without changing their meaning by using the apostrophe *s* ending." Pass out the following phrases on a handout or write them on the chalkboard or a transparency.

Example: the coat of my aunt   *my aunt's coat*
1. the cat that belongs to my friend _____
2. the hat of my father _____
3. the sister of my mother _____
4. the brother of Bill _____
5. the ball that belongs to Merryl _____
6. the house of my grandmother _____
7. the ranch of my uncle _____ ●

This activity could also become a matching exercise. For example:

the cat that belongs to my friend	my father's hat
the hat of my father	my friend's cat
the sister of my mother	my mother's sister

✔ Self-Check: Objective 6
Describe a procedure for teaching the inflectional ending *s*.

Prefixes and Suffixes

Prefixes and suffixes are affixes or sequences of letters that are added to root words to change their meanings and/or parts of speech. A prefix is placed before a root word, and a suffix is placed after a root word.

Children can learn the pronunciations and meanings of some common prefixes and suffixes. Good readers learn to recognize common prefixes and suffixes instantly; this helps them recognize words more rapidly than they could if they had to resort to sounding each word letter by letter. Knowledge of prefixes and suffixes can help readers decipher the meanings as well as the pronunciations of unfamiliar words. Common, useful prefixes and suffixes are shown in the list below.

Prefix	*Meaning*	*Example*
un-	not	unable
in-	in or not	inset, inactive
bi-	two, twice	bicycle, biweekly
dis-	apart from, reversal of	displace, dismount
multi-	many	multicolored
non-	not	nonliving
pre-	before	preview
re-	again	reread
pro-	in favor of	prolabor
post-	after	postscript
semi-	partly	semicircle
sub-	under	subway

140

Teaching
Reading in
Today's
Elementary
Schools

Prefix	Meaning	Example
super-	over	superhuman
trans-	across	transatlantic
tri-	three	tricycle

Suffix	Meaning	Example
-ful	full of	careful
-less	without	painless
-ment*	state of being	contentment
-ship*	state of being	friendship
-ous	full of	joyous
-ward	in the direction of	westward
-tion*	state of being	action
-sion*	state of being	tension
-able*	capable of being	likable
-ness*	state of being	happiness

NOTE: The starred (*) suffixes are best taught simply as visual units because their meanings are abstract.

Some very common prefixes, such as *ad-, com-,* and *con-,* are not included in the list above because they generally occur with word parts that do not stand alone and are not recognizable meaning units to children. Examples are *admit, advice, combine, commerce, commit, conceal,* and *condemn.*

The suffixes *-ment, -ous, -tion,* and *-sion* have especially consistent pronunciations. Thus, they are particularly useful to know. The suffixes *-ment* and *-ous* generally have the pronunciations heard in the words *treatment* and *joyous.* The suffixes *-tion* and *sion* have the sound of *shun,* as heard in the words *education* and *mission.*

When prefixes and suffixes are added to root words, the resulting words are called derivatives. Whereas prefixes simply modify the meanings of the root words, suffixes may change the parts of speech in addition to modifying the meanings. Some of the modifications that can result are listed below.

Root Word	Affix	Derivative	New Meaning or Change
happy	un-	unhappy	not happy
amuse	-ment	amusement	verb is changed to noun
worth	-less	worthless	meaning is opposite of original meaning

Use worksheets like the two shown below following instruction in prefixes and suffixes.

● **WORKSHEET:** *Recognition of Prefixes and Suffixes*

Directions: Circle the prefixes and suffixes you see in the words below.

1. disagree
2. reuse
3. inhuman
4. honorable
5. contentment
6. joyful
7. unusable

8. premeditate
9. transport
10. reload
11. likely
12. treatment
13. dangerous
14. westward ●

● **WORKSHEET:** *Adding Prefixes and Suffixes*

Directions: Make as many new words as you can by adding prefixes and suffixes to the following root words.

1. *agree*

2. *move*

3. *construct*

_____ _____ _____

_____ _____ _____

_____ _____ _____

_____ _____ _____ ●

Contractions

The apostrophe used in contractions indicates that one or more letters have been left out when two words were combined into one word. Children need to be able to recognize the original words from which the contractions were formed. The following are common contractions, with their meanings, that teachers should present to children:

can't/cannot
couldn't/could not
didn't/did not
don't/do not
hadn't/had not
hasn't/has not
he'll/he will
he's/he is
I'd/I had or I would
they'd/they had or they would
they'll/they will
they're/they are
they've/they have

I'll/I will
I'm/I am
I've/I have
isn't/is not
let's/let us
she'd/she would or she had
she'll/she will
she's/she is
shouldn't/should not
we've/we have
won't/will not
wouldn't/would not
you'll/you will

142

Teaching
Reading in
Today's
Elementary
Schools

wasn't/was not
we're/we are
weren't/were not

you're/you are
you've/you have

Use a worksheet such as the following for practice with contractions.

● **WORKSHEET:** *Contractions*

Directions: Match the contractions in Column 1 with their proper meanings in Column 2 by drawing a line from each contraction to its meaning.

Column 1	Column 2
don't	cannot
can't	do not
he's	we are
we're	I am
you'll	he is
I'm	will not
won't	you will ●

Compound Words

Compound words consist of two (or occasionally three) words that have been joined together to form a new word. The original pronunciations of the component words are usually maintained, and their meanings are connected to form the meaning of the new word. For example, *dishpan* is a pan in which dishes are washed. Children can be asked to underline or circle component parts of compound words or to put together familiar compound words. Examples of exercises illustrating these activities follow.

● **WORKSHEET:** *Recognizing Parts of Compound Words*

Directions: Circle the two words that make up each of the following compound words.

1. dishwasher
2. newspaper
3. beehive
4. earthquake

5. workbook
6. weekend
7. footprint
8. daylight ●

● **WORKSHEET:** *Building Compound Words*

Directions: Find a word in Column 2 that, when combined with a word in Column 1, will form a compound word. Write the words you form in Column 3. One example word has been filled in for you.

Column 1	Column 2	Column 3
pocket	burn	pocketbook
letter	hive	_____
sun	book	_____
grass	carrier	_____
bee	hopper	_____ ●

Syllabication/Accent

Since many phonics generalizations apply not only to one-syllable words but also to syllables within longer words, many people feel that breaking words into syllables can be helpful in determining pronunciation. Glass (1967), however, says that syllabication is usually done after the reader has recognized the sound of the word. Most of the participants in his study used the sounds to determine syllabication rather than syllabication to determine the sounds. If this procedure is the one normally used by children in attacking words, syllabication would seem to be of little use in a word analysis program. On the other hand, many authorities firmly believe that syllabication is helpful in decoding words. For this reason, a textbook on reading methods would be incomplete without discussions of syllabication and a related topic, stress or accent.

A syllable is a letter or group of letters that forms a pronunciation unit. Every syllable contains a vowel sound. In fact, a vowel sound may form a syllable by itself (a mong'). Only in a syllable that contains a diphthong is there more than one vowel sound. Diphthongs are treated as single units, although they are actually vowel blends. While each syllable has only one vowel sound or diphthong, there may be more than one vowel letter in a syllable. Letters and sounds should not be confused. For example, the word *peeve* has three vowel letters, but the only vowel sound is the long *e* sound. Therefore, *peeve* contains only one syllable.

There are two types of syllables: open syllables and closed syllables. Open syllables end in vowel sounds; closed syllables end in consonant sounds. Syllables may in turn be classified as accented (given greater stress) or unaccented (given little stress). Accent has much to do with the vowel sound that we hear in a syllable. Multisyllabic words may have primary (strongest), secondary (second strongest), and even tertiary (third strongest) accents. The vowel sound of an open accented syllable is usually long (*mī' nus, bā' sin*); the second syllable of each of these example words is unaccented, and the vowel sound represented is the schwa, often found in unaccented syllables. A single vowel in a closed accented syllable generally has its short sound, unless it is influenced by another sound in that syllable (*căp' sule, cär' go*).

Several useful rules concerning syllabication and accent are given below.

1. Words contain as many syllables as they have vowel sounds (counting diphthongs as a unit). Examples: *se/vere*—final *e* has no sound; *break—e*

144

Teaching
Reading in
Today's
Elementary
Schools

is not sounded; *so/lo*—both vowels are sounded; *oil*—diphthong is treated as a unit.

2. A word with more than one sounded vowel, when the first vowel is followed by two consonants, is generally divided between the two consonants. Examples: *mar/ry, tim/ber.* If the two consonants are identical, the second is not sounded.

3. Consonant blends and consonant digraphs are treated as units and are not divided. Examples: *ma/chine, a/bridge.*

4. A word with more than one sounded vowel, when the first vowel is followed by only one consonant or consonant digraph, is generally divided after the vowel. Examples: *ma/jor, ri/val* (generally long initial vowel sounds). There are, however, many exceptions to this rule, which make it less useful. Examples: *rob/in, hab/it* (generally short initial vowel sounds).

5. When a word ends in *le* preceded by a consonant, the preceding consonant plus *le* constitutes the final syllable of the word. This syllable is never accented, and the vowel sound heard in it is the schwa. Examples: *can/dle, ta/ble.*

6. Prefixes and suffixes generally form separate syllables. Examples: *dis/taste/ful, pre/dic/tion.*

7. Some syllable divisions come between two vowels. Examples: *cru/el, qui/et.*

8. A compound word is divided between the two words that form the compound, as well as between syllables within the component words. Examples: *snow/man, thun/der/storm.*

9. Prefixes and suffixes are usually not accented. (*dis/ grace' ful*)

10. Words that can be used as both verbs and nouns are accented on the second syllable when they are used as verbs and on the first syllable when they are used as nouns. (*pre/sent'*—verb; *pres' ent*—noun)

11. In two-syllable root words, the first syllable is usually accented, unless the second syllable has two vowel letters. (*rock' et, pa/rade'*)

12. Words containing three or more syllables are likely to have secondary (and perhaps tertiary) accents, as well as primary accents. (*reg' i/men/ta' tion*)

Readiness for learning syllabication includes the ability to hear syllables as pronunciation units. Teachers can have youngsters listen to words and clap for every syllable heard as early as first grade. An early written exercise on syllabication follows.

● *WORKSHEET: Syllabication*

Directions: On the line following each word, write the number of syllables that the word contains. If you need to do so, say the words aloud and listen for the syllables. Pay attention to the sounds in the words. Don't let the letters fool you!

1. ruin _____
2. break _____
3. table _____
4. meaningful _____
5. middle _____
6. excitement _____
7. disagreement _____
8. human _____
9. cheese _____
10. happen _____
11. right _____
12. person _____
13. fingertip _____
14. hotel _____
15. grandmother _____
16. elephant _____
17. name _____
18. schoolhouse _____
19. scream _____
20. prepare _____ ●

Generalizations about syllabication can be taught by the same process, described earlier in this chapter, as phonic generalizations can. Present many examples of a particular generalization, and lead the children to state the generalization.

Waugh and Howell (1975) point out that in dictionaries it is the syllable divisions in the phonetic respellings, rather than the ones indicated in the boldface entry words, that are of use to students in pronouncing unfamiliar words. The divisions of the boldface entry words are a guide for hyphenations in writing, not for word pronunciation.

Accentuation is generally not taught until children have a good background in word attack skills and is often presented in conjunction with the study of the dictionary as a tool for word attack. More will be said about that in the next section of this chapter.

Dictionary Study

Dictionaries are valuable tools to use in many different kinds of reading tasks. They can help students determine pronunciations, meanings, derivations, and parts of speech for words they encounter in reading activities. They can also help with spellings of words, if children have some idea of how the word is spelled and need only to confirm the order of letters within the word. Picture dictionaries are primarily used for sight word recognition and spelling assistance. This section deals mainly with the part the dictionary plays in helping children with word recognition; discussion of the dictionary as an aid to comprehension can be found in Chapter 4.

Although the dictionary is undeniably useful in determining the pronunciation of unfamiliar words, students should turn to it only as a last resort for this purpose. They should consult it only after they have applied phonics and structural analysis clues along with knowledge of context clues. There are two major reasons for this. First, applying the appropriate word recognition skills immediately, without having to take the time to look up the word in the dictionary, is less of an interruption of the reader's train of thought and therefore less of a hindrance to comprehension. Second, a person does not

146

Teaching
Reading in
Today's
Elementary
Schools

always have a dictionary readily available; however, if he or she practices other word recognition skills, they will always be there when they are needed.

When using other word attack skills has produced no useful or clear result, a child should turn to the dictionary for help. Obviously, before a child can use the dictionary for pronunciation, he or she must be able to locate a word in it. This skill is discussed in Chapter 7.

After the child has located the word, he or she needs the following two skills to pronounce the word correctly.

Interpreting Phonetic Respellings and Accent Marks

The pronunciation key and knowledge of sounds ordinarily associated with single consonants help in interpreting phonetic respellings in dictionaries. There will be a pronunciation key somewhere on every page spread of a good dictionary. Pupils do not need to memorize the diacritical (pronunciation) markings used in a particular dictionary. Different dictionaries use different markings, and learning the markings for one could cause confusion when students are using another. The sounds ordinarily associated with relatively unvarying consonants may or may not be included in the pronunciation key. Because they are not always included, it is important for children to master a knowledge of phonics.

Here are four activities for interpretation of phonetic spellings.

ACTIVITIES

1. Have the pupils locate a particular word in their dictionaries. (Example: *cheat* [*chēt*]) Call attention to the phonetic respelling beside the entry word. Point out the location of the pronunciation key and explain its function. Have the children locate each successive sound-symbol in the key—*ch, ē, t.* (If necessary, explain why the *t* is not included in the key.) Have the children check the key word for each symbol to be sure of its sound value. Then have them blend the three sounds together to form a word. Repeat with other words. (Start with short words and gradually work up to longer ones.)

2. Code an entire paragraph or joke using phonetic respellings. Provide a pronunciation key. Let the children compete to see who can write the selection in the traditional way first. Let each child who believes he or she has done so come to your desk. Check his or her work. If it is correct, keep it and give it a number indicating the order in which it was finished. If it is incorrect, send the student back to work on it some more. Set a time limit for the activity. The activity may be carried out on a competitive or a noncompetitive basis.

3. Give the children a pronunciation key and let them encode messages to friends. Check the accuracy of each one before it is passed on to the friends to be decoded.

4. Use a worksheet such as the following.

Directions: Pretend that the following list of words is part of the pronunciation key for a dictionary. Choose the key word or words that would help you pronounce each of the words listed below. Place the numbers of the chosen key words in the blank beside the appropriate word.

Pronunciation Key: (1) cat, (2) āge, (3) fär, (4) sōfə, (5) sit

1. cape (cāp) _____
2. car (cär) _____
3. ago (ə/gō') _____
4. aim (ām) _____
5. fad (fad) _____
6. race (rās) _____
7. rack (rak) _____
8. affix (ə/fiks') _____ ●

   Some words will have only one accent mark, whereas others will have marks to show different degrees of accent within a single word. Children need to be able to translate the accent marks into proper stress when they speak the words. Following are two ideas for use in teaching accent marks.

ACTIVITIES

1. Write several familiar multisyllabic words on the board. (*Bottle* and *apartment* are two good choices.) Explain that when words of more than one syllable are spoken, certain syllables are stressed or emphasized by the breath. Pronounce each of the example words, pointing out which part (or parts) of each word received stress. Next, tell the class that the dictionary uses accent marks to indicate which part of a word receives stress. Look up each word in the dictionary and write the dictionary divisions and accent marks for the word on the board. Pronounce each word again, showing how the accent marks indicate the parts of the words that you stressed when you pronounced them. Then have the children complete the following worksheet.

● **WORKSHEET:** *Accent Marks*

Directions: Pronounce the following words and decide where the accent is placed in each one. Indicate its placement by putting an accent mark (') after the syllable where you feel the accent belongs. Look up the words in the dictionary and check your placement. Make the correction on the line to the right of the word if you were wrong.

1. truth ful   _____
2. lo co mo tion   _____

148

Teaching
Reading in
Today's
Elementary
Schools

3. fric tion   _____

4. at ten tion   _____

5. ad ven ture   _____

6. peo ple   _____

7. gig gle   _____

8. emp ty   _____

9. en e my   _____

10. ge og ra phy   _____ ●

After the children have completed the worksheet, discuss the results. Have volunteers pronounce each word and indicate which syllable (or syllables) were stressed.

2. Introduce the concept of accent in the same way that is described in the first activity. Then distribute sheets of paper with a list of words such as the following.

(1) des' ti na' tion

(2) con' sti tu' tion

(3) hob' gob' lin

(4) mys' ti fy'

(5) pen' nant

(6) thun' der storm

Ask volunteers to read the words, applying the accents properly. When they have done so, give them a list of unfamiliar words with both accent marks and diacritical (pronunciation) marks inserted. (Lists will vary according to the ability of the children.) Once again, ask the children to read the words, applying their dictionary skills.

✔ Self-Check: Objective 7

Name two skills needed to enable a child to pronounce correctly words found in a dictionary.

(See Self-Improvement Opportunity 8.)

Introducing the Dictionary

Children can be introduced to picture dictionaries as early as the first grade. They can learn how dictionaries are put together and how they function by making their own picture dictionaries. Intermediate-grade pupils can develop dictionaries of special terms like *My Science Dictionary* or *My Health Dictionary*. From these they can advance to beginning and intermediate dictionaries. See Example 3.2 for a sample page of an intermediate dictionary.

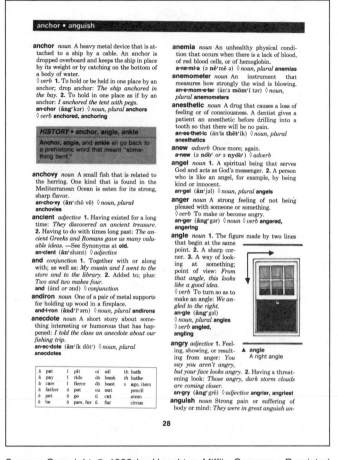

anchor • anguish

anchor *noun* A heavy metal device that is attached to a ship by a cable. An anchor is dropped overboard and keeps the ship in place by its weight or by catching on the bottom of a body of water. ◊ *verb* **1.** To hold or be held in one place by an anchor; drop anchor: *The ship anchored in the bay.* **2.** To hold in one place as if by an anchor: *I anchored the tent with pegs.*
an·chor (ăng′kər) ◊ *noun, plural* **anchors** ◊ *verb* **anchored, anchoring**

HISTORY • anchor, angle, ankle
Anchor, angle, and ankle all go back to a prehistoric word that meant "something bent."

anchovy *noun* A small fish that is related to the herring. One kind that is found in the Mediterranean Ocean is eaten for its strong, sharp flavor.
an·cho·vy (ăn′chō vē) ◊ *noun, plural* **anchovies**

ancient *adjective* **1.** Having existed for a long time: *They discovered an ancient treasure.* **2.** Having to do with times long past: *The ancient Greeks and Romans gave us many valuable ideas.* —See Synonyms at **old.**
an·cient (ān′shənt) ◊ *adjective*

and *conjunction* **1.** Together with or along with; as well as: *My cousin and I went to the store and to the library.* **2.** Added to; plus: *Two and two makes four.*
and (ănd *or* ənd) ◊ *conjunction*

andiron *noun* One of a pair of metal supports for holding up wood in a fireplace.
and·i·ron (ănd′ī ərn) ◊ *noun, plural* **andirons**

anecdote *noun* A short story about something interesting or humorous that has happened: *I told the class an anecdote about our fishing trip.*
an·ec·dote (ăn′ĭk dōt′) ◊ *noun, plural* **anecdotes**

ă	pat	ĭ	pit	oi	oil	th	bath
ā	pay	ī	ride	ōō	book	th	bathe
â	care	î	fierce	ōō	boot	ə	ago, item
ä	father	ŏ	pot	ou	out		pencil
ĕ	pet	ō	go	ŭ	cut		atom
ē	be	ô	paw, for	û	fur		circus

anemia *noun* An unhealthy physical condition that occurs when there is a lack of blood, of red blood cells, or of hemoglobin.
a·ne·mi·a (ə nē′mē ə) ◊ *noun, plural* **anemias**

anemometer *noun* An instrument that measures how strongly the wind is blowing.
an·e·mom·e·ter (ăn′ə mŏm′ĭ tər) ◊ *noun, plural* **anemometers**

anesthetic *noun* A drug that causes a loss of feeling or of consciousness. A dentist gives a patient an anesthetic before drilling into a tooth so that there will be no pain.
an·es·thet·ic (ăn′ĭs thĕt′ĭk) ◊ *noun, plural* **anesthetics**

anew *adverb* Once more; again.
a·new (ə nōō′ *or* ə nyōō′) ◊ *adverb*

angel *noun* **1.** A spiritual being that serves God and acts as God's messenger. **2.** A person who is like an angel, for example, by being kind or innocent.
an·gel (ān′jəl) ◊ *noun, plural* **angels**

anger *noun* A strong feeling of not being pleased with someone or something. ◊ *verb* To make or become angry.
an·ger (ăng′gər) ◊ *noun* ◊ *verb* **angered, angering**

angle *noun* **1.** The figure made by two lines that begin at the same point. **2.** A sharp corner. **3.** A way of looking at something; point of view: *From that angle, this looks like a good idea.* ◊ *verb* To turn so as to make an angle: *We angled to the right.*
an·gle (ăng′gəl) ◊ *noun, plural* **angles** ◊ *verb* **angled, angling**

▲ **angle**
A right angle

angry *adjective* **1.** Feeling, showing, or resulting from anger: *You say you aren't angry, but your face looks angry.* **2.** Having a threatening look: *Those angry, dark storm clouds are coming closer.*
an·gry (ăng′grē) ◊ *adjective* **angrier, angriest**

anguish *noun* Strong pain or suffering of body or mind: *They were in great anguish un-*

28

Source: Copyright © 1986 by Houghton Mifflin Company. Reprinted by permission from the HOUGHTON MIFFLIN INTERMEDIATE DICTIONARY. ◄

Some thesauruses are also available for children. Four of them are listed below.

In Other Words: A Beginning Thesaurus, rev. ed., by Andrew Schiller and William A. Jenkins. New York: Lothrop, Lee & Shepard, 1977.

Junior Thesaurus: In Other Words, by W. Cabell Greet et al. New York: Lothrop, Lee & Shepard, 1978.

Right Word: A Concise Thesaurus Based on the American Heritage Dictionary. Boston: Houghton Mifflin Company, 1978.

Webster's Students Thesaurus. Springfield, Mass.: G. & C. Merriam Company, 1978.

WORD RECOGNITION PROCEDURE

It is helpful if children know a procedure for decoding unfamiliar words. A child may discover the word at any point in the following procedure; he or she should then stop the procedure and continue reading. Sometimes it is necessary to try all of the steps.

Step 1.   Apply context clues.
Step 2.   Try sound of initial consonant, vowel, or blend along with context clues.
Step 3.   Check for structure clues (prefixes, suffixes, inflectional endings, compound words, or familiar syllables).
Step 4.   Begin sounding out the word using known phonics generalizations. (Go only as far as necessary to determine the word.)
Step 5.   Consult the dictionary.

A teacher may explain this five-step procedure in the following way:

1. First try to decide what word might reasonably fit in the context where you found the unfamiliar word. Ask yourself: "Will this word be a naming word? A word that describes? A word that shows action? A word that connects two ideas?" Also ask yourself: "What word will make sense in this place?" Do you have the answer? Are you sure of it? If so, continue to read. If not, go to Step 2.
2. Try the initial sound(s) along with the context clues. Does this help you decide? If you are sure that you have the word now, continue reading. If not, go to Step 3.
3. Check to see if there are familiar word parts that will help you. Does it have a prefix or suffix that you know? If this helps you decide upon the word, continue reading. If not, go to Step 4.
4. Begin sounding out the word, using all your phonics skills. If you discover the word, stop sounding and go back to your reading. If you have sounded out the whole word and it does not sound like a word you know, go to Step 5.
5. Look up the word in the dictionary. Use the pronunciation key to help you with the pronunciation of the word. If the word is one you have not heard before, check the meaning. Be sure to choose the meaning that fits the context.

For example, a reader who is confronted with the unfamiliar word *chamois* might apply the procedure in the following way.

1. "He used a chamois to dry off the car. I've never seen the word *c-h-a-m-o-i-s* before. Let's see . . . , is it a naming word? . . . Yes, it is, because *a* comes before it. . . . What thing would make sense here? . . . It

is something that can be used to dry a car. Could it be *towel*? . . . No, that doesn't have any of the right sounds. Maybe it is *cloth*?. . . . No, *cloth* starts with *cl*."

2. "*Ch* usually sounds like the beginning of *choice*. . . . I can't think of anything that starts that way that would fit here. . . . Sometimes it sounds like *k*. . . . I can't think of a word that fits that either. . . . *Ch* even sounds like *sh* sometimes. . . . The only word that I can think of that starts with the *sh* sound and fits in the sentence is *sheet*, and I can tell that none of the other sounds are right."

3. "I don't see a prefix, suffix, or root word that I recognize either."

4. "Maybe I can sound it out. Chămois. No, that's not a word. Kămois. That's not a word either. Shămois. I don't think so. . . . Maybe the *a* is long. Chāmois. No. Kāmois. No. Shāmois. No."

5. "I guess I'll have to use the dictionary. What? Shăm' ē? Oh, I know what that is. I've seen Dad use one! Why is it spelled so funny? Oh, I see! It came from French."

A crucial point for teachers to remember is that children should not consider use of word recognition skills important *only* during reading classes. They should apply these skills whenever they encounter an unfamiliar word, whether it happens during reading class, science class, during a free reading period, or in out-of-school situations. Teachers should emphasize to their students that the procedure explained above is applicable to *any* situation in which an unfamiliar word occurs.

Teachers should also encourage students to self-correct reading errors when the words they read do not combine to make sense. This can be accomplished with some well-planned instruction. Taylor and Nosbush (1983) had children individually read orally from material at their instructional levels. They praised each child for things that he or she did well when reading, especially any self-correcting behavior the student exhibited when miscues (unexpected responses) affected the meaning. They encouraged each student to try to make sure the material being read made sense. They also discussed some miscues that the student did not self-correct, particularly ones that did not make sense but for which good context clues were available. Students instructed in this way did better at self-correction than did students who read orally without being asked to pay attention to meaning.

Summary

Word recognition skills help a reader identify words while reading. Sight word recognition refers to the development of a store of words that can be recognized immediately on sight. Use of context clues to help in word identification involves using the surrounding words to decode an unfamiliar word. Both semantic and syntactic clues can be helpful. Phonics is the

152

Teaching
Reading in
Today's
Elementary
Schools

association of speech sounds (phonemes) with printed symbols (graphemes). Although the sound-symbol associations in English are not completely consistent, phonics is very helpful in the identification of unfamiliar words. Structural analysis skills enable readers to decode unfamiliar words using units larger than single graphemes. The process of structural analysis involves recognition of prefixes, suffixes, inflectional endings, contractions, and compound words, and is also concerned with syllabication and accent. Dictionaries can be used for word identification also. The dictionary respelling that is given in parentheses after the word supplies the word's pronunciation, but the reader has to know how to use the dictionary's pronunciation key in order to interpret the respellings appropriately.

Children need to learn to use all of the word recognition skills. Because different ones will be needed for different situations, they must also learn to use them appropriately.

Children need a procedure for approaching the decoding of words that are not in their sight vocabularies. The following five-step procedure is a good one to teach. The first step is to use context clues. The next step is to try the sound of the initial consonant, vowel, or blend in addition to context clues. Step 3 is to check for structure clues, and Step 4 is to use phonics generalizations to sound out as much of the word as necessary. The final step is to consult the dictionary.

Test Yourself

True or False

_____ 1. It is wise to teach a single approach to word attack.

_____ 2. All word recognition skills are learned with equal ease by all children.

_____ 3. Sight words are words that readers recognize immediately without needing to resort to analysis.

_____ 4. The English language is noted for the regularity of sound-symbol associations in its written words.

_____ 5. Teaching a small store of sight words can be the first step in inaugurating an analytic approach to phonics instruction.

_____ 6. Early choices for sight words to be taught should be words that are extremely useful and meaningful.

_____ 7. Games with complex rules are good ones to use for practice with sight words.

_____ 8. Most practice with sight words should involve the words in context.

_____ 9. If teachers teach phonics well, they do not need to bother with other word recognition skills.

_____ 10. Consonant letters are more consistent in the sounds they represent than vowel letters are.

_____ 11. Phonics generalizations often have numerous exceptions.

_____ 12. It is impossible to teach too many phonics rules, since these rules are extremely valuable in decoding unfamiliar words.

_____ 13. In a word that has only one vowel letter at the end of the word, the vowel letter usually represents its long sound.

_____ 14. It is wise to teach only one phonics generalization at a time.

_____ 15. Structural analysis skills include the ability to recognize prefixes and suffixes.

_____ 16. The addition of a prefix to a root word can change the meaning.

_____ 17. Inflectional endings can change the tense of a verb.

_____ 18. The apostrophe in a contraction indicates possession or ownership.

_____ 19. Every syllable contains a vowel sound.

_____ 20. There is only one vowel letter in each syllable.

_____ 21. Open syllables end in consonant sounds.

_____ 22. The vowel sound in an open accented syllable is usually long.

_____ 23. The schwa sound is often found in unaccented syllables.

_____ 24. When dividing words into syllables, we treat consonant blends and consonant digraphs as units and do not divide them.

_____ 25. Prefixes and suffixes generally form separate syllables.

_____ 26. Prefixes and suffixes are usually accented.

_____ 27. Picture clues are the most useful word recognition clues for sixth-grade pupils.

_____ 28. A comparison or contrast found in printed material may offer a clue to the identity of an unfamiliar word.

_____ 29. Context clues used in isolation provide only educated guesses about the identities of unfamiliar words.

_____ 30. Children should be expected to memorize the diacritical markings used in their dictionaries.

_____ 31. Accent marks indicate which syllables are stressed.

_____ 32. Some words have more than one accented syllable.

_____ 33. Another term meaning short vowel sound is "unglided" vowel sound.

_____ 34. Writing new words is helpful to some learners in building sight vocabulary.

_____ 35. The language experience approach is good for developing sight vocabulary.

_____ 36. One method of teaching sight words is best for all students.

Multiple Choice

_____ 1. In the word _myth_ the _y_

    a. has the characteristics of a vowel.

    b. is silent.

    c. has the characteristics of a consonant.

154

Teaching
Reading in
Today's
Elementary
Schools

_____ 2. When it occurs in the initial position in a syllable, the letter _w_
   a. stands for a vowel sound.
   b. is silent.
   c. stands for a consonant sound.

_____ 3. In the word _strong,_ the letters _str_
   a. represent a consonant blend.
   b. are silent.
   c. represent a single sound.

_____ 4. Consonant digraphs
   a. represent two blended speech sounds.
   b. represent a single speech sound.
   c. are always silent.

_____ 5. The word _sheep_ is made up of
   a. five sounds.
   b. four sounds.
   c. three sounds.

_____ 6. In the word _boat,_ the _oa_ is
   a. a vowel digraph.
   b. a diphthong.
   c. a blend.

_____ 7. In the word _boy,_ the _oy_ is
   a. a vowel digraph.
   b. a consonant digraph.
   c. a diphthong.

_____ 8. The word _diphthong_ contains
   a. three consonant blends.
   b. three consonant digraphs.
   c. a consonant digraph and two consonant blends.

_____ 9. In the word _know,_ the _ow_ is
   a. a diphthong.
   b. a vowel digraph.
   c. a consonant blend.

_____ 10. In the word _his,_ the letter _s_ has the sound usually associated with
   the letter
   a. _s._
   b. _z._
   c. _sh._

_____ 11. When the inflectional ending _ed_ follows the letter _d_ or the letter
   _t,_ the _e_ is
   a. sounded.
   b. silent.
   c. long.

_____ 12. In the word _helped,_ the _d_
   a. is silent.

b. has the sound of *d*.

c. has the sound of *t*.

_____ 13. In the word *canned*, the *d*

a. is silent.

b. has the sound of *d*.

c. has the sound of *t*.

_____ 14. Which type of accent mark indicates the heaviest emphasis?

a. primary

b. secondary

c. tertiary

Self-Improvement Opportunities

1. Compare the Dolch List of 220 Service Words and the Dolch List of 95 Picture Words with the words found in the preprimers and primers of a contemporary basal reading series. Are the words on the Dolch lists still high-usage words, even though the lists were compiled many years ago?

2. Plan exercises for presenting the words on a basic sight word list in context; many of these are function words and have meanings that are hard for the child to conceptualize. For example, *for* and *which* produce no easy images, but a child would understand the following sentences:

   I bought this *for* you.

   Which one is mine?

   Try your exercises in a classroom if you have the opportunity.

3. React to the following statement: "Going back to teaching basic phonics skills will cure all of our country's reading ills."

4. Make arrangements to observe a phonics lesson in which the teacher uses the synthetic approach and another lesson in which the teacher uses the analytic approach. Evaluate the two approaches. Be sure you evaluate the methods rather than the instructors.

5. Look up references related to the controversy concerning the value of teaching syllabication as part of a word recognition program. Prepare a paper on this topic.

6. React to the following statement: "I do not believe in teaching children to use context clues. It just produces a group of guessers."

7. Compile a list of words whose pronunciation depends upon the context. Plan a lesson for presenting some of these words to a group of youngsters in the grade level of your choice.

8. Compare the dictionary pronunciations of the following words in old and new dictionaries and in dictionaries published by different companies. Analyze the differences among diacritical markings. Use the words *gypsy*, *ready*, *lecture*, *away*, *ask*, *believe*, *baker*, and *care*.

156

Teaching
Reading in
Today's
Elementary
Schools

9. Gather the necessary material and construct a skill-development game for some aspect of word recognition.
10. Construct and try out the mind-reading game described in Virginia L. Poe's article in the April 1985 issue of *The Reading Teacher*, cited in the Bibliography.

Bibliography

Anderson, Richard C., Elfrieda H. Hiebert, Judith A. Scott, and Ian A. G. Wilkinson. *Becoming a Nation of Readers: The Report of the Commission on Reading.* Washington, D.C.: National Institute of Education, 1985.

Ashton-Warner, Sylvia. *Teacher.* New York: Simon and Schuster, 1963.

Bailey, Mildred Hart. "The Utility of Phonic Generalizations in Grades One Through Six." *The Reading Teacher* 20 (February 1967): 413–18.

Bridge, Connie A., Peter N. Winograd, and Darliene Haley. "Using Predictable Materials vs. Preprimers to Teach Beginning Sight Words." *The Reading Teacher* 36 (May 1983): 884–91.

Burmeister, Lou E. "Usefulness of Phonic Generalizations." *The Reading Teacher* 21 (January 1968): 349–56, 360.

Carnine, Douglas W. "Phonics Versus Look-Say: Transfer to New Words." *The Reading Teacher* 30 (March 1977): 636–40.

Ceprano, Maria A. "A Review of Selected Research on Methods of Teaching Sight Words." *The Reading Teacher* 35 (December 1981): 314–22.

Clymer, Theodore. "The Utility of Phonics Generalizations in the Primary Grades." *The Reading Teacher* 16 (January 1963): 252–58.

Cordts, Anna D. *Phonics for the Reading Teacher.* New York: Holt, Rinehart and Winston, 1965.

Culyer, Richard. "How to Develop a Locally-Relevant Basic Sight Word List." *The Reading Teacher* 35 (February 1982): 596–97.

Cunningham, Patricia M. "A Compare/Contrast Theory of Mediated Word Identification." *The Reading Teacher* 32 (April 1979): 774–78.

Cunningham, Patricia M. "Decoding Polysyllabic Words: An Alternative Strategy." *The Reading Teacher* 21 (April 1978): 608–14.

Dickerson, Dolores Pawley. "A Study of Use of Games to Reinforce Sight Vocabulary." *The Reading Teacher* 36 (October 1982): 46–49.

Downing, John. "How Children Think About Reading." In *Psychological Factors in the Teaching of Reading,* Eldon E. Ekwall, comp. Columbus, Ohio: Charles E. Merrill, 1973, pp. 43–58.

Dreyer, Lois G., Karen R. Futtersak, and Ann E. Boehm. "Sight Words for the Computer Age: An Essential Word List." *The Reading Teacher* 39 (October 1985): 12–15.

Emans, Robert. "The Usefulness of Phonic Generalizations Above the Primary Grades." *The Reading Teacher* 20 (February 1967): 419–25.

Fry, Edward. *Elementary Reading Instruction.* New York: McGraw-Hill, 1977.

Glass, Gerald G. "The Strange World of Syllabication." *The Elementary School Journal* 67 (May 1967): 403–405.

Gough, Philip B. "Word Recognition." In *Handbook of Reading Research,* P. David Pearson, ed. New York: Longman, 1984.

Groff, Patrick. "The Maturing of Phonics Instruction." *The Reading Teacher* 39 (May 1986): 919–23.

Hood, Joyce. "Why We Burned Our Basic Sight Vocabulary Cards." *The Reading Teacher* 27 (March 1972): 579–82.

Jenkins, Barbara L., et al. "Children's Use of Hypothesis Testing When Decoding Words." *The Reading Teacher* 33 (March 1980): 664–67.

Johnson, Dale D. "Suggested Sequences for Presenting Four Categories of Letter-Sound Correspondence." *Elementary English* 50 (September 1973): 888–96.

Johnson, Dale D., and James F. Baumann. "Word Identification." In *Handbook of Reading Research,* P. David Pearson, ed. New York: Longman, 1984.

Jolly, Hayden B., Jr. "Teaching Basic Function Words." *The Reading Teacher* 35 (November 1981): 136–40.

Jones, Linda L. "An Interactive View of Reading: Implications for the Classroom." *The Reading Teacher* 35 (April 1982): 772–77.

Meltzer, Nancy S., and Robert Herse. "The Boundaries of Written Words as Seen by First Graders." *Journal of Reading Behavior* I (Summer 1969): 3–14.

Palmer, Barbara. "Dolch List Still Useful." *The Reading Teacher* 38 (March 1985): 708–709.

Poe, Virginia L. "Mind Reading Made Easy: A Game for Practicing Word Recognition Skills." *The Reading Teacher* 38 (April 1985): 822–24.

Rosso, Barbara Rak, and Robert Emans. "Children's Use of Phonic Generalizations." *The Reading Teacher* 34 (March 1981): 653–57.

Schell, Leo M. "Teaching Decoding to Remedial Readers." *Journal of Reading* 31 (May 1978): 877–82.

Taylor, Barbara M., and Linda Nosbush. "Oral Reading for Meaning: A Technique for Word Identification." *The Reading Teacher* 37 (December 1983): 234–37.

Tovey, Duane R. "Children's Grasp of Phonics Terms vs. Sound-Symbol Relationships." *The Reading Teacher* 33 (January 1980): 431–37.

Waugh, R. P., and K. W. Howell. "Teaching Modern Syllabication." *The Reading Teacher* 29 (October 1975): 20–25.

Chapter 4

Meaning Vocabulary

Introduction

Meaning vocabulary (words for which meanings are understood) is essentially the set of labels for the clusters of concepts that people have learned through experience. These clusters of concepts or knowledge structures are called schemata. (Schemata are also discussed in detail in Chapter 5.) Because students must call upon their existing schemata to comprehend, meaning vocabulary development is an important component of comprehension skill (Jones, 1982). Therefore, direct instruction in word meanings is a valuable part of reading instruction.

In Chapter 3 we referred to the importance of decoding words and developing a sight vocabulary, but these abilities have little value if students do not understand the words. Children's sight vocabularies should be built from words they already comprehend, words that are a part of their meaning vocabularies. This chapter is concerned with the development of extensive meaning vocabularies and the difficulties that certain types of words may present to youngsters.

Setting Objectives

When you finish reading this chapter, you should be able to

1. Discuss some factors involved in vocabulary development.
2. Name and describe several techniques of vocabulary instruction.
3. Name some special types of words and explain how they can cause problems for children.

Key Vocabulary

Pay close attention to these terms when they appear in the chapter.

analogies	denotations	morphemes
antonyms	etymology	schema
appositive	figurative language	semantic feature analysis
categorization	homographs	semantic maps
connotations	homophones	synonyms
context clues	metaphoric language	word webs

VOCABULARY DEVELOPMENT

It is difficult to pinpoint the age at which children learn the precise meanings of words. Early in the language development process, they learn to differen-

160

Teaching
Reading in
Today's
Elementary
Schools

tiate between antonyms (opposites), making more discriminating responses as they grow older. Sometimes they overgeneralize about word meanings: for example, once a very young child learns the word *car*, he or she may apply it to any motor vehicle, making no discrimination between cars and trucks or other kinds of vehicles. Carol Chomsky's research has shown that some children as old as nine years have trouble distinguishing between the meanings of *ask* and *tell*, as well as between other words—a finding in congruence with Piaget's discovery that some children as old as ten years had not yet differentiated between the words *brother* and *boy* and the words *sister* and *girl* (McConaughy, 1978). As children mature they learn more about choosing specific words.

Eve Clark has indicated that words can be broken down into semantic features, or smaller components of meaning, which a child learns in order to develop understanding of words. When a child first uses a word, he or she may be aware of only one or two of its semantic features and therefore may use it incorrectly—for example, calling all birds *ducks*. As the child develops the meaning of the word more fully, he or she narrows down application of the word to the correct category—for example, adding the feature of webbed feet to eliminate robins from the *duck* category.

Clark has predicted that in order to recognize the overlapping meanings of synonyms, a child has to learn the semantic features of each word separately. Clark represents the features with positive (+) and negative (−) indicators. For example, children first find the word *before* to be related to time (+ time) and later to be related to sequence of time (− simultaneous). Finally, they add the feature that distinguishes *before* from *after* (+ prior). The semantic-features theory even explains figurative usage, such as metaphor. In this case, the child chooses only specific semantic features in the particular context; a "blanket of snow" would utilize the covering feature of a blanket and a snowfall.

Emotional reactions to words can also be expressed as semantic features. All readers do not develop the same emotional features for the same word, because of their varied backgrounds (McConaughy, 1978).

Children increase their vocabularies at a rapid rate during the elementary school years. It has been estimated that the typical child increases his or her vocabulary at a rate of about 1,000 words a year in the primary grades and 2,000 words a year in the intermediate grades, and some suggest that the rate is even higher. While estimates vary, they do reflect the general trend of a growing vocabulary with increasing age.

Vocabulary building is a complex process involving many kinds of words: words with *multiple meanings* (The candy is *sweet*. Mary has a *sweet* disposition.); words with *abstract definitions* (*Justice* must be served.); *homophones* (She will take the *plane* to Lexington. He has on *plain* trousers.); *homographs* (I will *read* the newspapers. I have *read* the magazine.); *synonyms* (Marty was *sad* about leaving. Marty was *unhappy* about leaving.); and *antonyms* (Bill is a *slow* runner. Mary is a *fast* runner.). Children must also acquire meanings for a number of relational terms, such as *same, more, less, different, taller/ shorter, older/younger, higher/lower,* and so on.

✔ Self-Check: Objective 1

What are some factors to be considered in vocabulary development? (See Self-Improvement Opportunity 4.)

VOCABULARY INSTRUCTION

Teachers can approach vocabulary instruction in a variety of ways, but some vocabulary instructional techniques appear to be more effective than others. The most desirable instructional techniques are those that

1. assist students in relating new words to their background knowledge,
2. assist students in developing elaborated (expanded) word knowledge,
3. actively involve students in learning new words, and
4. help students acquire strategies for independent vocabulary development (Carr and Wixson, 1986).

Four commonly used techniques for vocabulary instruction are the context method (in which students read new words in meaningful contexts), the association method (in which an unknown word is paired with a familiar synonym), the category method (in which students place words in categories), and the dictionary method (in which students look up the word, write a definition, and use the word in a sentence). Gipe (1980) expanded the context method to include having children apply the words based upon their own experiences and then studied the relative effectiveness of these four methods. She found that the expanded context method was the most effective method of teaching vocabulary. The application of new words may have been the most important aspect of the context method that Gipe used. After the students derived the meaning of the word from a variety of contexts, including a definition context, they *applied* the word to their own personal experiences in a written response, thus following the first guideline for desirable instructional techniques listed above.

Beck and McKeown (1983) described another program of vocabulary instruction that emphasized relating vocabulary to students' experiences. Students generated their own context for the terms being taught by answering questions about the words (for example, the teacher might say, "Tell about something you might want to *eavesdrop* on" [p. 624].) The program also helped the students to further their word knowledge by introducing new words in global semantic categories, such as *people* or *places,* and by requiring the students to work with the relationships among words. The children were asked to differentiate critical features of words and to generalize from one word to similar ones. They were also asked to complete analogies involving

162

**Teaching
Reading in
Today's
Elementary
Schools**

One effective means of vocabulary instruction involves students' deriving the meaning of a word from a variety of sources and then applying the word, in a written response, to their own experiences.   (© Sybil Shelton/Peter Arnold)

the words and to pantomime words. These activities were in keeping with Carr and Wixson's second and third suggestions about vocabulary instruction, because the students were actively involved in the activities described, rather than being passive observers. They discussed words, generated meanings, and applied meanings. In order to ensure thorough learning of the words, students were given a number of exposures to each word in a variety of contexts. The final aspect of Beck and McKeown's program was development of rapid responses to words by using timed activities, some of which were somewhat gamelike. These activities, which certainly kept the students actively involved, probably increased their interest as well.

The children involved in Beck and McKeown's program learned the words taught, developed speed and accuracy in making semantic decisions, showed superior comprehension on stories containing the target words to that of a control group, and evidently learned more than the specific words taught, as indicated by the size of their gains on a standardized measure of reading comprehension and vocabulary. The success of this program seems to emphasize the value of Carr and Wixson's evaluation guidelines.

Teachers can help students relate their personal experiences to new words by having them put personal connections on vocabulary word cards (Carr,

1985). For example, a student might connect the personal reaction "Mother's Thanksgiving dinner" with the adjective *elaborate* and write this personal reaction on the word card for *elaborate,* along with other notes about the word.

Instruction that gradually moves the responsibility for determining new word meanings from the teacher to the student helps students become independent learners. Teachers can guide students to use context clues to define words independently by using a four-part procedure. First, students are given categorization tasks. Next, students practice determining meanings from complete contexts. The third step is to practice determining meaning in incomplete contexts. Finally, students practice defining new vocabulary by means of context clues (Carr and Wixson, 1986).

Another procedure to help teachers focus on vocabulary instruction has been developed by Blachowicz (1986). Teachers first activate what the students know about the target words in the reading selection, using either exclusion brainstorming (in which students exclude unrelated words from a list of possible associated words) or knowledge rating (in which students indicate their degree of familiarity with the words). Then the teachers can elicit predictions about "connections between words or between words and the topic and structure of the selection" (p. 644), emphasizing the words' roles in semantic networks. (Word webs or semantic feature analysis, discussed later in this chapter, may be used.) Next the students are asked to construct tentative definitions of the words. They read the text to test these definitions, refining them as they discover additional information. Finally, the students use the words in other reading and writing tasks to make them their own. Blachowicz (1985, p. 877) pointed out that "the harder one works to process stimuli . . . the better one's retention." The approach that Blachowicz has devised causes the students to work harder by predicting and constructing definitions, rather than just memorizing material that is presented. Students seem to retain more information when they have learned it using active tasks than when they have learned it using passive tasks, such as memorization.

Another active way to clarify word meanings by associating situations with them is the dramatization of words. This technique provides a vicarious (indirect) experience that is more effective than mere verbal explanation of terms, and under some circumstances it has proved to be more effective than use of context clues, structural analysis, or dictionaries (Duffelmeyer, 1980; Duffelmeyer and Duffelmeyer, 1979).

Jiganti and Tindall (1986) compared the effects of a vocabulary program consisting of categorization activities and dramatic interpretations of new words with those of a dictionary method of instruction. In the dictionary activity, which was assigned as homework, students were given a list of words to look up in the dictionary, define, and use in a sentence. The classroom program was more successful and enjoyable than the homework approach. Good readers learned more than poor readers from the homework

164

Teaching
Reading in
Today's
Elementary
Schools

approach, but both good and poor readers benefited from the classroom approach.

Duffelmeyer (1985) has also urged teaching word meaning from an experience base. He believes that, without such teaching, students may have a store of words for which they have only a shell of meaning without substance. Duffelmeyer suggests four techniques to link word meaning and experience: use of synonyms and examples, use of positive and negative instances of the concepts, use of examples and definitions, and use of definitions together with sentence completion. His techniques are all teacher-directed and involve verbal interaction between the teacher and the students.

Duffelmeyer's four techniques may be used in the ways described below. In each case, the teacher first shows the students the target word, pronounces it for them, and then has them pronounce it.

1. When using synonyms and examples for a target word (*difficult*), the teacher tells the students that another word for *difficult* is *hard,* and that, if a task is *difficult,* it is hard to do. He or she may then ask the children to name *difficult* tasks and to tell why the tasks are difficult. Next, the teacher shows the students a sentence containing the word *difficult.* (It is *difficult* to do well on a test if you do not study for it.) The teacher asks why this is a true statement, and the children suggest answers.

2. When using positive and negative instances for a target word (*rude*), the teacher gives a simple definition for the word (*not polite*). Then he or she asks the students, "If a person holds the door open for someone who has both hands full of packages, is that person being rude?" The children should decide that this is not a rude act. Then the teacher may ask, "If a person interrupts someone who is speaking, is that person being rude?" The children should decide that this is a rude act. Finally, the teacher may ask the children if they have ever seen anyone do something that was rude. They may offer several examples.

3. When using examples and definitions for a target word (*generous*), the teacher might write on the chalkboard a paragraph containing the word in context and a contextual definition. For *generous,* a teacher in the upper grades might write:

    The president of the company was *generous* when he was asked to contribute to charities. His employees, following his example, gave freely also.

    Next, the teacher asks the students to read the paragraph and tell what they think *generous* means. The teacher then asks the students to give other examples of this concept.

4. When using definition together with sentence completion, the teacher gives the students a worksheet containing simple definitions of several words to be taught and sentence fragments containing each of these words. One entry might be:

1. crust: the hard outer covering of something—The crust of the earth is the part _____.

Before the students begin the worksheet, the class discusses the meaning of *crust* and ways to complete the sentence. Then they fill in the blank with an answer and discuss the word further. For example, the teacher might ask, "What other things besides the earth have crusts?" This should elicit much discussion. The other words on the worksheet are handled in the same way.

All four of Duffelmeyer's strategies are effective methods of vocabulary instruction that are congruent with Carr and Wixson's first three suggestions for good vocabulary instruction discussed on page 161. More detail about these approaches and other examples of use in teaching can be found in *The Reading Teacher* (Duffelmeyer, 1985).

Kaplan and Tuchman (1980) suggest an additional technique that can help children relate their past experiences to new vocabulary. In this approach the teacher selects a concept word related to something currently being studied, writes it on the board, and gives the children a specified time within which to write down related words. Then the children share their word lists. If the children do not respond well under time pressure, the teacher can write related words on the board as the children call them out.

In summarizing the findings of a vast amount of research concerning vocabulary instruction, Nelson-Herber (1986) says that "extensive reading can increase vocabulary knowledge, but direct instruction that engages students in construction of word meaning, using context and prior knowledge, is effective for learning specific vocabulary and for improving comprehension of related materials (p. 627). For this reason, she suggests intensive direct teaching of vocabulary in the content areas to help students read the content materials successfully. She endorses building from the known to the new, helping students understand the interrelationships among words in concept clusters (groups of related concepts), and encouraging students to use new words in reading, writing, and speaking. Construction of word meaning by the students from context, experience, and reasoning is basic to her approach. At times the students work in cooperative groups on vocabulary exercises, and they are involved with vocabulary learning before, during, and after reading of assigned material.

Stahl (1986) states that, according to research findings, vocabulary instruction improves comprehension only when both definitions and context are given, and has the largest effect when a number of different activities or examples using the word in context are used (p. 663). He further points out that techniques requiring students to think "deeply" about a term and its relationships to other terms are most effective. Class discussion seems to make students think more deeply about words as they make connections between their prior knowledge and new information. Multiple presentations

166

Teaching
Reading in
Today's
Elementary
Schools

of information about a word's meaning and multiple exposures to the word in varying contexts are both beneficial to comprehension. Additionally, the more time spent on vocabulary instruction, the better the results. Vocabulary programs that extend over a long period of time give students a chance to encounter the words in a number of contexts and to make use of them in their own language.

There are clearly a great number of programs for vocabulary development. Although they vary widely, many of them have produced good results, and teachers should be familiar with a variety of approaches. Many of the programs described above have combined several approaches, and good teachers will also use combinations of approaches in their classrooms. Graves and Prenn (1986) point out that "there is no one best method of teaching words . . . various methods have both their costs and their benefits and will be very appropriate and effective in some circumstances and less appropriate and effective in others" (p. 597).

Teaching strategies in which the teacher and the students work together are generally more effective than those in which the students are expected to learn new words without the teacher's help (Graves and Prenn, 1986). In addition, each instructional activity related to a word advances the students' mastery of that word to some degree. But many encounters may be necessary before complete mastery is achieved.

Vocabulary instructional techniques used in basal reading series tend to treat all words alike, even though some words are harder to learn than others and would be better learned through different methods. In addition, basal reading series often teach only a single meaning for a word, which limits the benefits of the instruction. Teachers must be aware of these weaknesses in basal reader vocabulary programs and provide supplementary instructional techniques that will counteract them (Sorenson, 1985).

Although almost all teachers feel that vocabulary instruction is important, many rely on workbook exercises alone to provide this instruction. Relatively few tend to relate new vocabulary words to students' experiences. This trend needs to be reversed, based upon evidence from current vocabulary research.

Several common methods of vocabulary development are discussed below. Each one has possibilities for enhancing the word knowledge of students.

Concept Development and Vocabulary Learning

Vocabulary terms are labels for people's schemata, or the clusters of concepts they have developed through experience. Sometimes children cannot understand the terms that they encounter in books because they do not know the concepts to which the terms refer. In this case, concept or schemata development involving the use of direct and vicarious experiences is necessary. Blachowicz (1985) affirms the fact that building a conceptual base for word learning is important.

A good technique for concept development is to offer as concrete an experience as possible with the concept. Then the class should discuss the attributes of the concept. The teacher should give examples and nonexamples of the concept, pointing out the attributes that distinguish examples from nonexamples. Next, the students should try to identify other examples and nonexamples that the teacher supplies, giving their reasons. Finally, the students should suggest additional examples and nonexamples. This sequence is closely related, although not identical, to that suggested by Graves and Prenn (1986).

For example, to develop the concept of *banjo,* the teacher could bring a banjo to class. The teacher would show it to the students, play it for them (or get someone to do so), and let them touch it and pluck or strum the strings. A discussion of its attributes would follow. The children might decide that a banjo has a circular body and a long neck, that it has a tightly stretched cover over the body, that it has strings, and that music can be played on it. The teacher might show the children pictures or real examples of a variety of banjos, some with five and some with four strings, and some with enclosed backs and some with open backs. Then the teacher might show the children a guitar, pointing out the differences in construction (different shape, different material covering the body, different number of strings, etc.). He or she may also show several other instruments, at first following the same procedure, and then letting the students identify the differences from and similarities to banjos. The students can provide their own examples of banjos by bringing in pictures or actual instruments. They will note that, although there may be some variation in size and appearance, the essential attributes will be present. They can also name and bring pictures or actual examples of instruments that are not banjos, explaining why these do not fit the concept. For example, a child might name a harp, a mandolin, or a violin.

Concrete experiences for abstract concepts are difficult to provide, but the teacher can use approximations. For example, to develop the concept of *freedom,* the teacher can say, "You may play with any of the play equipment in the room for the next ten minutes, or you may choose not to play at all." After ten minutes have passed, he or she can tell the class that they were given the freedom to choose their activity; that is, they were not kept from doing what they chose to do. The teacher may then offer several examples of freedom. One might be the freedom to choose friends. No one else tells the children who their friends have to be; they choose based on their own desires. The teacher should also offer several nonexamples of freedom. He or she might point out that during a game, players are restrained by a set of rules and do not have the freedom to do anything they want to do. Then the teacher should ask the students to give examples of freedom and explain why these examples are appropriate. A student may suggest that the freedom that we have in this country to say what we think about our leaders is a good example, because we are not punished for voicing our views. After several

168

Teaching
Reading in
Today's
Elementary
Schools

examples, the students will be asked for nonexamples. They may suggest that people in jail do not have freedom, because they cannot go where they wish or do what they wish. After a number of nonexamples have been offered, the teacher may ask the students to be alert for examples and nonexamples of freedom in their everyday activities and to report to the class on their findings. Some may discover that being "grounded" by their parents is a good nonexample of freedom.

Thelen (1986) indicates that meaningful learning is enhanced by a top-down approach to vocabulary development, which means that general concepts are taught before specific concepts. Then the children have the schemata they need to incorporate new facts that they encounter. With this approach, the teacher would present the concept "dog" before the concept "poodle." The children would have a prior pool of information to which the new information about "poodle" could be related. Isabel Beck has stated that ownership of a word, or being able to relate the word to an existing schema, is necessary for meaningful learning. In other words, students need to relate the word to information that they already know. Semantic mapping and semantic feature analysis (discussed later in this chapter) are two particularly good methods for accomplishing this goal.

Firsthand experiences, such as field trips and demonstrations, can help students associate words with real situations. These experiences can be preceded and followed up by discussion of the new concepts, and written accounts of the experiences can help students gain control of the new vocabulary. For example, a field trip to a data processing facility can be preceded by a discussion of the work that is done in the facility (generating bills, producing payroll checks, etc.). During the field trip, each activity that the students witness can be explained as they watch. This explanation should include the proper terms for the data processing equipment, processes, and personnel. After the trip, the students can discuss computers, keyboards, monitors, printers, printouts, word processing, operators, programmers, and other things and people to which they were exposed. They can make graphic displays of the new terms (see the sections on semantic maps and word webs), classify the new terms (see the section on categorization), make comparison charts for the words (see the section on semantic feature analysis), analyze the structure of the words (see the section on structural analysis), or manipulate the new terms in some other way. They may write individual summaries of the experience or participate in writing a class summary. They may wish to use reference books to expand their knowledge about some of the new things that they have seen. All of these activities will build both the children's concepts and their vocabulary and thereby enhance comprehension of material containing this vocabulary.

Vicarious experiences can also help to build concepts and vocabulary. Audiovisual aids, such as pictures, films, filmstrips, records, and videotapes, can be used to illustrate words that students have encountered in reading and to provide other words for discussion. Books such as thesauruses, children's dictionaries, and trade books about words (for example, *Words from the Myths*, by Isaac Asimov, Boston: Houghton Mifflin, 1961) are also useful sources of information about words.

Storytelling and story reading are good ways to provide vicarious experiences. Studies by Roe (1985, 1968) and Pigg (1986) have shown that a seven-week program of daily one-hour storytelling/story reading sessions with language follow-up activities can improve vocabulary skills in kindergarten, first-grade, and second-grade students. Students in the experimental groups in these studies produced more words in stories, more different words, and more multisyllabic words than did students in the control groups. The language follow-up activities that were used included creative dramatics, creative writing (or dictation), retelling stories with the flannel board, and illustrating scenes from the stories and describing them to the teacher.

Emphasizing Words Throughout the Day

Children learn much vocabulary by listening to the conversation of those around them. Therefore, a language-rich environment promotes vocabulary acquisition. Teachers can provide such environments in their classrooms. They can be very influential in children's vocabulary development, simply through being good models of vocabulary use. For example, when teachers read aloud or give explanations to the class, they should discuss any new words used and encourage the children to use them. Teachers should not "talk down" to children but should use appropriate terminology in describing things to them and participating in discussions with them.

Most teachers realize the importance of vocabulary instruction as a part of reading and language arts classes. The importance of teaching word meanings and of encouraging variety in word choice and exactness in expressing thoughts is generally accepted. Teachers therefore usually give attention to many aspects of vocabulary instruction, such as structural analysis, use of context clues, and use of reference books, such as dictionaries and thesauruses, during language classes.

Vocabulary instruction should take place throughout the day, not just during the language arts or reading period, however. Vocabulary knowledge is important in all subject areas covered in the curriculum. Children need to develop their vocabularies in every subject area so that the specialized or technical words they encounter are not barriers to learning. The techniques described in this chapter and the ideas presented in Chapter 8 will help teachers plan adequately for vocabulary instruction in the content areas.

Context Clues

We discussed use of context clues to help recognize words that are familiar in speech but not in print, in Chapter 3. Context clues can also key the meaning of an unfamiliar word by directly defining the word, providing an

170

Teaching
Reading in
Today's
Elementary
Schools

appositive, or comparing or contrasting the word with a known word. For example:

A *democracy* is a government run by the people being governed. (definition)

He made an effort to *alleviate*, or relieve, the child's pain until the doctor arrived. (appositive)

Rather than encountering hostile Indians, as they had expected, many settlers found the Indians to be *amicable*. (contrast)

Context can also offer clues in different sentences from that in which the new word is found, so children should be encouraged to read surrounding sentences for clues to meaning. Sometimes an entire paragraph embodies the explanation of a term, as in the following example:

I've told you before that measles are *contagious*! When Johnny had the measles, Beatrice played with him one afternoon, and soon Beatrice broke out with them. Joey caught them from her, and now you tell me you have been to Joey's house. I imagine you'll be sorry when you break out with the measles and have to miss the party on Saturday.

When introducing new words in context, teachers should use sentences that students can relate to their own experiences and that have only one unfamiliar word each. It is best not to use the new word at the very beginning of the sentence, since the children will not have had any of the facilitating context before they encounter it (Duffelmeyer, 1982).

Teachers can use a "think-aloud" strategy to help students see how to use context clues. Using the sentence about Indians above, which would be written on the board or on a transparency so that the students could see it, the teacher would say: "Rather than encountering hostile Indians, as they had expected, many settlers found the Indians to be amicable. I wonder what 'amicable' means? Let's see; the sentence says '*Rather than* encountering hostile Indians.' That means the Indians weren't hostile. 'Hostile' means unfriendly; so maybe 'amicable' means friendly."

Another example of the "think-aloud" strategy, geared to a primary-level task, might proceed as follows. The sentence to be discussed is "David wants to keep his new shirt, but Mark wants to *exchange* his for another color." The teacher could write the sentence on the board or show it to the children on a transparency. Then the teacher could read the sentence aloud and say: "I wonder what 'exchange' means? Let's see; the sentence says that David wants to keep his shirt, *but* Mark wants to exchange his. It also mentions another color of shirt. The *but* means that Mark wants to do something different from keeping his shirt. When I get something and don't like the color, I take it back and swap it for another color. Maybe that is what Mark wants to do. I guess 'exchange' means 'swap.'"

After several example "think-aloud" activities with context clues, the
teacher should ask student volunteers to "think aloud" the context clues to specific words. Students may work in pairs on a context clues worksheet and verbalize their context usage strategies to each other. Finally, the students should work alone to determine meanings from context clues.

ACTIVITIES

1. Using a selection the students are going to read, take an unfamiliar word, put it into a title, and construct several sentences that offer clues to its meaning. Show the title on the overhead projector; then show one sentence at a time, letting the students guess the meaning of the word at each step (Kaplan and Tuchman, 1980).
2. Use a technique called musical cloze. First select a song appropriate for the children and the unit of study. Make deletions in its text: certain parts of speech, words that fit into a particular category, words that show relationships, or something else. Using the original text, have the children practice until they learn the song; then sing it with the deletions and ask the children to suggest alternatives for the omitted words or phrases. Write these on the board and sing the song several times, using the children's suggestions in place of the original words. Afterward lead the students in a discussion of their replacement choices (Mateja, 1982).

Teachers can have students apply context clues fruitfully in conjunction with structure clues, which are discussed below.

Structural Analysis

Structural analysis, discussed in Chapter 3 as a word recognition skill, can also be used as an aid in discovering meanings of unknown words. Knowing meanings of common affixes and combining them with meanings of familiar root words can help pupils determine the meanings of many new words. For example, if a child knows the meaning of *joy* and knows that the suffix *-ous* means *full of,* he or she can conclude that the word *joyous* means *full of joy.* Students can often determine meanings of compound words by relating the meanings of the component parts to each other (*watchman* means a *man* who *watches*). After some practice, they can be led to see that the component parts of a compound word do not always have the same relationships to each other (*bookcase* means a *case* for a *book*).

Children begin to learn about word structure very early. First they deal with words in their simplest, most basic forms, as morphemes, the smallest units of *meaning* in a language. The word *cat* is one morpheme. If an *s* is added to form the plural, *cats,* the final *s* is also a morpheme, since it changes

172

Teaching
Reading in
Today's
Elementary
Schools

the word's meaning. There are two classes of morphemes, distinguished by function: *free* morphemes, which have independent meaning and can be used by themselves (*cat, man, son*), and *bound* morphemes, which must be combined with another morpheme in order to have meaning. Affixes and inflectional endings are bound morphemes; the *er* in *singer* is an example.

Worksheets and activities can help children see how prefixes and suffixes change meanings of words. An example of each is shown.

● **MODEL ACTIVITY:** *Prefix* un-

Say to students: "The word *unhappy* is made up of the prefix *un-* and the root word *happy*. The prefix *un-* means *not*, so the word *unhappy* means *not happy*." Then write the following words on the chalkboard and ask students to come forward to write the meanings for each of the following words.

1. unable
2. unbelievable
3. undeserving
4. undesirable
5. untrue
6. unused
7. unavailable
8. unappreciated

After the words have been defined, discuss the answers with the class. Ask students to give other examples of words with this prefix and encourage them to look for such words in their reading materials. ●

The teacher may also personalize the study of the prefix *un-* by having the students complete sentences such as the following.

● **WORKSHEET:** *Prefix* un-

Directions: Each of the sentences below contains a word with the prefix *un-* added and the same word without the prefix. The prefix *un-* means *not*. Fill in the blanks below with words or phrases that will make the sentences true. For example, "When I *laugh* I am happy, but when I *cry*, I am unhappy."

1. I am able to _____, but I am unable to _____.
2. The story about _____ is believable, but the one about _____ is unbelievable.
3. I have a _____ that is used and a _____ that is unused.
4. I am available for _____, but I am unavailable for _____. ●

Worksheets such as the one that follows can offer practice in determining meanings of compound words.

Directions: Using the meanings of the two words that make up each of the compound words below, write a definition for each word on the line beside it.

1. snowfall _____
2. coverall _____
3. doorstep _____
4. driveway _____
5. bookcase _____
6. bedroom _____ ●

During the follow-up discussion of this worksheet, the teacher should encourage the students to use the words in sentences and to generate other compound words using some of the same base words. For example, students might suggest *workroom* and *bookmark*. The teacher should also encourage the students to search for compound words in their reading material; jot them down, along with the sentence context; and mention them in class discussions.

Categorization

Categorization is grouping together things or ideas that have common features. Classifying words into categories can be a good way to learn more about word meanings. Young children can begin learning how to place things into categories by grouping concrete objects according to their traits. Once the children have developed some sight vocabulary, it is a relatively small step for them to begin categorizing the words they see in print according to their meanings. Very early in their instruction, children will be able to look at the list below and classify the words into such teacher-supplied categories as "people," "things to play with," "things to eat," and "things to do."

Word List

doll	bicycle	ball
candy	cookie	boy
toy	dig	sing
run	girl	mother
baby	sit	banana

The children may discover that they want to put a word in more than one category. This desire will bring up the opportunity for discussion that a word may fit in two or more different places for different reasons. The children should give reasons for all their placements.

174

Teaching
Reading in
Today's
Elementary
Schools

After the children become adept at classifying words into categories supplied by the teacher, they are ready for the more difficult task of generating the categories needed for classifying the words presented. The teacher may give them a list of words such as the following and ask them to place the words in groups of things that are alike and to name the trait that the items named have in common.

Word List

horse	cow	goose
gosling	mare	filly
colt	gander	bull
stallion	foal	hen
chick	calf	rooster

Children may come up with several different categories for the words above: various families of animals; four-legged and two-legged animals; feathered and furred animals; winged and wingless animals; or male animals, female animals, or animals that might be either sex. They might also use a classification that the teacher has not considered. As long as the classification system makes sense and the animals are correctly classified according to the stated system, the categorization is considered correct. No one way of categorization is more correct than any other, as long as it is based upon groups with common features. Teachers should encourage students to discover varied possibilities for classifications. Discussion of the various classification systems may help to extend the children's concepts about some of the animals on the list, and it may help some children develop concepts related to some of the animals for the first time. The classification system allows them to relate the new knowledge about some of the animals to the knowledge they already have about these animals or others.

The usefulness of categorization activities is supported by current research indicating that presenting words in semantically related clusters can lead to improvement in students' vocabulary knowledge and reading comprehension (Marzano, 1984). Marzano has identified a number of vocabulary clusters that teachers might find useful. Information on these clusters can be found in the November 1984 issue of *The Reading Teacher*.

Bufe (1983) suggested a categorization activity to promote comprehension of stories. It is designed to be used as a prereading strategy. When using it, the teacher writes four headings on the chalkboard: "Setting," "Actions," "Characters," and "Words about the characters." Then the teacher adds words from the story under each of these categories. The children may know some, but not all, of the words. The teacher then presents each list to the children, asking them if there are any words that they cannot pronounce, if there are any words that they do not know meanings for, and what the words tell them about the story that is going to be read. Pronunciations and meanings are cleared up through discussion, and predictions about the story are made. The predictions may be written in a few sentences. Students can also look for relationships among the words on the four lists.

A classification game such as the one below could provide an interesting way to work on categorization skills.

● **MODEL ACTIVITY:** *Classification Game*

Divide the children into groups of three or four and make category sheets like the one below for each group. When you give a signal, the children should start writing as many words as they can think of that fit in each of the categories; when you signal that time is up, a person from each group should read the group's words to the class. Have the children compare their lists and discuss why they placed certain words in certain categories.

Cities	States	Countries

Other appropriate categories are meats, fruits, and vegetables; mammals, reptiles, and insects; or liquids, solids, and gases. ●

Many of the other activities described in this chapter depend upon the use of categorization. For example, the activities for analogies, semantic maps, and semantic feature analysis all use categorization.

Analogies and Word Lines

Analogies compare two similar relationships and thereby bolster word knowledge. Educators may teach analogies by displaying examples of categories, relationships, and analogies; asking guiding questions about the examples; allowing students to discuss the questions; and applying the ideas that emerge (Bellows, 1980).

Students may need help in grouping items into categories and understanding relationships among items. For example, the teacher might write *nickel, dime,* and *quarter* on the board and ask, "How are these things related? What name could you give the entire group of items?" (Answer: *money.*) Teachers can use pictures instead of words in the primary grades; in either case, they might ask students to apply the skill by naming other things that would fit the category (*penny* and *dollar*). Or the teacher could write *painter* and *brush*

176

Teaching
Reading in
Today's
Elementary
Schools

and ask, "What is the relationship between the two items?" (Answer: A *painter works with a brush.*) Teachers should remember to simplify their language for discussions with young children, and to have students give other examples of the relationship (*butcher* and *knife*). After working through many examples such as these, the students should be ready for examples of simple analogies, such as "Light is to dark as day is to night," "Glove is to hand as sock is to foot," "Round is to ball as square is to block." Students can discuss how analogies work—"How are the first two things related? How are the second two things related? How are these relationships alike?" They can then complete incomplete analogies, such as "Teacher is to classroom as pilot is to _____." Younger children should do this orally; older ones can understand the standard shorthand form of *come : go : : live : die* if they are taught to read "*:*" as *is to* and "*: :*" as *as* (Bellows, 1980). Once children are familiar with analogies, they can use worksheets such as the following in class.

● **WORKSHEET:** *Analogies*

Directions: Fill in the blanks with words that complete the same relationship in the second word pair that was indicated in the first word pair.

1. hot is to cold as black is to _____.
2. milk is to drink as steak is to _____.
3. toe is to foot as finger is to _____.
4. blue is to blew as red is to _____.
5. coat is to coats as mouse is to _____.
6. up is to down as top is to _____. ●

Teachers may use word lines to show the relationships among words, just as they use number lines for numbers. They can arrange related words on a graduated line that emphasizes their relationships. For young children, they can use pictures and words to match or ask them to locate or produce appropriate pictures. Upper-grade students can be asked to arrange a specified list of words on a word line themselves. Word lines can concretely show antonym, synonym, and degree analogies, as in this example:

| enormous | large | medium | small | tiny |

Analogies that students could develop include "enormous is to large as small is to tiny" (synonym); "enormous is to tiny as large is to small" (antonym); and "large is to medium as medium is to small" (degree). The teacher can have the children make their own word lines and analogies (Macey, 1981).

Semantic maps can be used to teach related concepts (Johnson and Pearson, 1984; Johnson, Pittelman, and Heimlich, 1986). "Semantic maps are diagrams that help students see how words are related to one another. . . . Students learn the meanings and uses of new words, see old words in a new light, and see relationships among words" (Heimlich and Pittelman, 1986). In constructing a semantic map with a class, the teacher writes on the board or a chart a word that represents a concept that is central to the topic under consideration. He or she asks the students to name words related to this concept. The students' words are listed on the board or chart grouped in broad categories, and the students name the categories. They may also suggest additional categories. A discussion of the central concept, the listed words, the categories, and the interrelationships among the words follows. The discussion step appears to be the key to the effectiveness of this method, because it allows the students to be actively involved in the learning. After the class has discussed the semantic map, the teacher can give an incomplete semantic map to the children and ask them to fill in the words from the map on the board or chart and add any categories or words that they wish to add. The children can work on their maps as they do the assigned reading related to the central concept. After the reading, there can be further discussion, and more categories and words can be added to the maps. The final discussion and mapping allow the children to recall and graphically organize the information they gained from the reading (Johnson, Pittelman, and Heimlich, 1986; Stahl and Vancil, 1986). A semantic map constructed by one class is shown in Example 4.1.

Because a semantic map shows both familiar and new words under labeled categories, the procedure of constructing one helps students make connections between known and new concepts (Johnson, Pittelman, and Heimlich, 1986). The graphic display makes relationships among terms easier to see.

According to research findings, semantic mapping is effective in promoting vocabulary learning; furthermore, it is equally effective with homogeneous small groups and heterogeneous whole classes. The critical element may be the discussion, which allows the teacher to assess the children's background knowledge, clarify concepts, and correct misunderstandings (Stahl and Vancil, 1986).

Schwartz and Raphael (1985) used a modified approach to semantic mapping to help students develop a concept of definition. The students learned what types of information are needed for a definition, and they learned how to use context clues and background knowledge to help them understand words better. Word maps are really graphic representations of definitions. The word maps used by Schwartz and Raphael contained the information about the general class to which the concept belonged, answering the question, "What is it?"; the properties of the concept, answering the question, "What is it like?"; and examples of the concept (see Example 4.2).

178

Teaching
Reading in
Today's
Elementary
Schools

▶ **EXAMPLE 4.1:** Semantic Map of the Concept "Tennis"

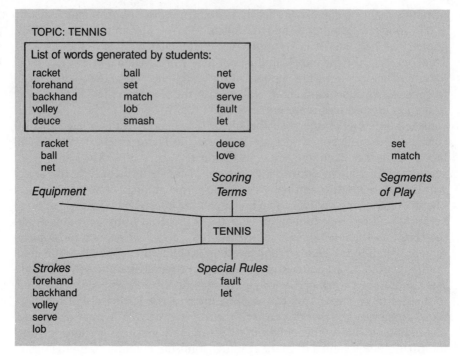

With the basic information contained in such a map, students have enough information to construct definitions. This procedure for understanding the concept of definition is effective from fourth-grade level through college. The approach used by Schwartz and Raphael started with strong teacher involvement, but control was gradually transferred to the children. Children were led to search the context of a sentence in which the word occurred for the elements of definition needed to map a word. Eventually the teachers provided only partial context for the word, leading the children to go to outside sources, such as dictionaries, for information to complete the maps. Finally teachers asked the students to write definitions including all the features previously mapped without actually mapping the word on paper.

Word webs are another way to represent the relationships among words graphically. Students construct them by connecting related words with lines. The words used for the web may be taken from material students have read in class. Example 4.3 shows such a web, based on the selection "Teaching Snoopy to Dance: Bill Melendez and the Art of Animation," by Valerie Tripp, from the Houghton Mifflin Reading Series. The words in parentheses would not be provided to the children; they would be asked to fill in these words, based upon the selection that they have read, and to check their answers by referring to the selection.

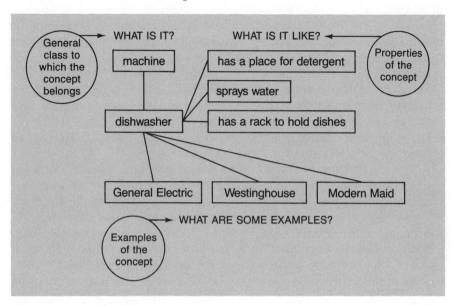

► **EXAMPLE 4.3:** Word Web for Basal Reader Selection

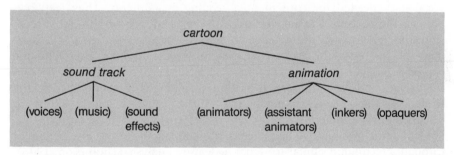

Source: EXPLORATIONS (Houghton Mifflin Reading Series), by William K. Durr et al. Teacher's Guide, p. 80. Copyright © 1986 by Houghton Mifflin Company. Used by permission. ◄

Semantic Feature Analysis

Semantic feature analysis is a technique that can help children understand the uniqueness of a word as well as its relationships to other words (Johnson and Pearson, 1984). To use such an analysis, the teacher lists in a column on the board or a chart some known words with common properties. Then the children generate a list of features possessed by the various items in the list. A feature need apply to only one item to be listed. The teacher writes these features in a row across the top of the board or chart, and the students fill in the cells of the resulting matrix with pluses to indicate the presence of

180

Teaching
Reading in
Today's
Elementary
Schools

the feature and minuses to indicate the absence of the feature. A partial matrix developed by children for various buildings is shown in Example 4.4. "Walls," "doors," and "windows" were other features suggested by the children for the matrix shown in Example 4.4; they were omitted from the example only for space considerations. These features all received a plus for each building, emphasizing the similarities of the terms *jail, garage, museum,* and *church.*

The children discussed the terms as they filled in the matrix. In the places where the question marks occur, the children said: "Sometimes it may have that, but not always. It doesn't have to have it." The group discussion brought out much information about each building listed, and served to expand the children's existing schemata.

A class can continue to expand such a matrix after it has initially been filled out by adding words that share some of the listed features. For example, the children added "grocery store" to the list of buildings in Example 4.4, since it shared the walls, doors, and windows, and they added other features showing the differentiation, such as "food," "clerks," and "shopping carts."

Johnson and Pearson (1984) suggest that, after experience with these matrices, children may begin to realize that some words have different degrees of the same feature. At this time, the teacher may want to try using a numerical system of coding, using 0 for *none,* 1 for *some,* 2 for *much,* and 3 for *all.* For example, under the feature "fear," "scared" might be coded with a 1, whereas "terrified" might be coded with a 3.

Anders and Bos (1986) suggest using semantic feature analysis with vocabulary needed for content area reading assignments. They feel that, because the analysis activates the students' prior knowledge through discussion and relates prior knowledge to new knowledge, students will have increased interest in the reading and therefore will learn more. This technique can be used before, during, and after the reading. A chart can be started in the background-building portion of the lesson, added to or modified by the students as they read the material, and refined further during the follow-up discussion of the material.

Metaphoric or figurative language (nonliteral language) can also be taught through a technique similar to semantic feature analysis (Thompson, 1986). A comparison chart can clarify differences and similarities between concepts

▶ **EXAMPLE 4.4:** Semantic Feature Analysis Chart

	barred windows	exhibits	steeple	cross	cars	lift-up doors	guards	oil stains
jail	+	–	–	–	–	–	+	–
garage	?	–	–	–	+	+	–	+
museum	?	+	–	–	?	–	+	–
church	–	–	+	+	–	–	–	–

that are not literally members of the same category. Finding similarities among essentially dissimilar things helps children understand the comparisons used in metaphoric language. For example, both *eyes* and *stars* might have the characteristic "shining" or "bright," leading to the source of the intended comparison in the expression of "her eyes were like stars." (Chapters 5 and 8 contain more information on figurative language.)

Dictionary Use

The dictionary can be an excellent source to use in discovering meanings of unfamiliar words, particularly for determining the appropriate meanings of words that have multiple definitions or specific, technical definitions. In some instances children may be familiar with several common meanings of a word, but not with a specialized meaning found in a content area textbook. For example, a child may understand a reference to a *base* in a baseball game but not a discussion of a military *base* (social studies material), a *base* that turns litmus paper blue (science material), or *base* motives of a character (literature). Words that have the greatest number of different meanings are frequently very common, such as *run* or *bank*.

Dictionaries are not always used properly in schools, however. Teachers should instruct children to consider the context surrounding a word, to read the different dictionary definitions, and to choose the definition that makes most sense in the context. Without such instruction, children have a strong tendency to read only the first dictionary definition and to try to force it into the context. The teacher should model the choice of the correct definition for the students, so that they can see what the task is. Students will then need to practice the task under teacher supervision.

The following worksheets are good to use for supervised practice immediately following instruction and for later independent practice.

● **WORKSHEET:** *Appropriate Dictionary Definitions*

Directions: Find the dictionary definition of *sharp* that fits each of the sentences below. Write the appropriate definition on the line following each sentence.

1. Katherine's knife was very sharp. _____
_____

2. There is a sharp curve in the road up ahead. _____
_____

3. Sam is a sharp businessman. That's why he has been so successful. _____
_____

4. I hope that when I am seventy my mind is as sharp as my grandmother's is. ___
_____

5. We are leaving at two o'clock sharp. _____
_____ ●

182
Teaching
Reading in
Today's
Elementary
Schools

In order to use the dictionary properly for vocabulary development, students must be instructed to consider a word's context, to read the different definitions, and then to choose a definition for the word in its specific context.   (© Ed Lettau/Photo Researchers)

● **WORKSHEET:** *Multiple Meanings of Words*

Directions: Some words mean different things in your textbooks from what they mean in everyday conversation. In each of the following sentences, find the special meanings for the words and write these meanings on the lines provided.

1. Frederick Smith has decided to *run* for mayor. _____
_____

2. The park was near the *mouth* of the Little Bear River. _____
_____

3. The management of the company was unable to avert a *strike.*_____
_____

4. That song is hard to sing because of the high *pitch* of several notes. _____
_____

5. That numeral is written in *base* two. _____
_____   ●

When using activities that involve workbooks or worksheets such as the ones shown above, teachers should go over the pages with the children after they have completed their work and discuss reasons for right and wrong responses.

Students can also use dictionaries to study etymology, the origin and history of words. Dictionaries often give the origin of a word in brackets after the phonetic respelling (although not all dictionaries do this in the same way), and archaic or obsolete definitions are frequently given and labeled so that pupils can see how words have changed. Older students may be introduced to the *Oxford English Dictionary,* whereas younger children may appreciate such sources as *The First Book of Words,* by S. Epstein and B. Epstein (New York: Franklin Watts, 1954), or *They Gave Their Names,* by Richard A. Boning (Baldwin, N.Y.: Barnell Loft, 1971).

Teaching word meanings through use of the dictionary has been widely criticized, but it is nevertheless a useful technique for vocabulary development if it is applied properly. There is research to support this view (Graves and Prenn, 1986).

Word Origins and Histories

The study of word origin and history is called etymology. Children in the intermediate grades will enjoy learning about the kinds of changes that have taken place in the English language by studying words and definitions that appear in very old dictionaries and by studying differences between American English and British English. Some sources that are useful follow:

Epstein, Sam, and Beryl Epstein. *The First Book of Words.* New York: Franklin Watts, 1954.
Funk, Wilfred. *Word Origins and Their Romantic Stories.* New York: Funk & Wagnalls, 1950.
Nurnburg, Maxwell. *Fun with Words.* Englewood Cliffs, N.J.: Prentice-Hall, 1970.

The teacher can place a "word tree," with limbs labeled Greek, Latin, Anglo-Saxon, French, Native American, Dutch, and so on, on the bulletin board. The class can then put appropriate words on each limb (Gold, 1981). A word tree such as this can be allowed to "grow" as a unit of study on words progresses.

Teachers need to help children understand the different ways in which words can be formed. Portmanteau words are formed by merging the sounds and meanings of two different words (for example, *smog,* from *smoke* and *fog*). Acronyms are words formed from the initial letters of a name or by combining initial letters or parts from a series of words (for example, *radar,* from *radio detecting and ranging*). Some words are just shortened forms of other words (for example, *phone,* from *telephone*), and some words are borrowed from other languages (for example, *lasso,* from the Spanish *lazo*). The class should discuss the origins of such terms when students encounter them while reading. In addition, students should try to think of other words

184

Teaching
Reading in
Today's
Elementary
Schools

that have been formed in a similar manner. The teacher may also wish to contribute other examples from familiar sources.

Denotations and Connotations

A word's denotation is its dictionary definition. Although many words (called multiple-meaning words) have more than one denotation, each one can be associated with particular contexts. For example, in the first sentence below, *light* means "not heavy," and in the second sentence, *light* means "illumination."

> The suitcase was light, so I had no trouble carrying it.
> The light was not good enough to read by, so I went to bed.

Connotations of words are the feelings and shades of meaning that a word tends to evoke (Cooper, 1986). They are not really a part of the word's denotation at all. For example, in the two sentences below, the word for the vehicle is all that is different, and the denotations of the two words are not extremely different. However, the second sentence evokes an image of important, wealthy people, whereas the first sentence gives no such picture.

> Their car was parked in front of the hotel.
> Their limousine was parked in front of the hotel.

Teachers should present words with different connotations to children and "think aloud" their reactions to the words, telling the connotations that the words have for them. Then the children should verbalize their reactions to some new words. Teachers should help them differentiate between the denotations of the words and the connotations that their feelings lend to the words.

Student-Centered Vocabulary Learning Techniques

Some vocabulary learning techniques focus upon the students and their particular needs and interests. Several examples follow.

Vocabulary Self-Collection Strategy

Haggard (1986) suggests the following approach for general vocabulary development.

1. Ask each child to bring to class a word that the entire class should learn. (The teacher brings one too.) Each child should determine the meaning of his or her word from its context, rather than looking it up in the dictionary.

2. Write the words on the board. Let each participant identify his or her word and tell where it was found, the context-derived meaning, and why the class should learn the word. The class should then discuss the meaning of the word in order to clarify and extend it and to construct a definition that the class agrees upon. This may be checked against a dictionary definition, if desired.

3. Narrow the list down to a manageable number, and have the students record the final list of words and definitions in vocabulary journals. Some students may want to put eliminated words on their personal lists.
4. Make study assignments for the words.
5. Test the children on the words at the end of the week.

This technique can also be adjusted to be used with basal reader assignments or content area assignments. Students using a basal reader can use the approach above, with the exception that they choose words from the basal reader story. With content area assignments, students can choose terms that are important for learning the content. Haggard feels that the act of choosing words increases students' sensitivity to new words and their enjoyment of learning words.

Study Based on Students' Names

Teachers can use students' names as springboards for vocabulary development, devoting a day to each child's name. For example, the class can discuss several meanings of the name ("Bill" is good for this one); find words that contain the name ("Tim" is in "Timbuktu"); study the etymology of one ("Patricia" means "high born" in Latin and is related to *patriotic* and *paternal*); or relate the name to colloquialisms or figurative language ("Jack of all trades"). The children may find examples of the name in literature in stories such as *Heidi* and *Kim;* in biographies of real people, such as Rachel Jackson and George Washington; in mythology (Diana, Jason, and Helen); or in authors' names (Carl Sandburg and Robert Frost). Children can relate a name to geography (Charleston, for example) or to the language of its origin ("Juan" is Spanish), or they can write limericks or poems with names that have easy rhymes. There are many other possibilities (Crist, 1980), and a class might even spend a week doing different activities with one name.

Study Based on Product Names

Familiar product names can be utilized to initiate vocabulary activities. Students can bring in empty product containers and place them in a box. Each student draws an item out of the box and uses its name in a sentence, giving it a common meaning. For example, the sentence for Joy dishwashing liquid could be "It is a joy to use this product" or "My new bicycle brought me much joy."

Word Banks or Vocabulary Notebooks

Students can form their own word banks by writing on index cards words they have learned, their definitions, and sentences showing the words in meaningful contexts. They may also want to illustrate the words or include personal associations or reactions to the words. Students can carry their word banks around and practice the words in spare moments, for example, while waiting for the bus or the dentist. In the classroom the word banks can be used in word games and in classification and other instructional activities.

Vocabulary notebooks are useful for recording new words found in general reading, or heard in conversations or on radio or television. New words may be alphabetized in the notebook and defined, illustrated, and processed in much the same way as word bank words.

Both word banks and vocabulary notebooks can help children maintain a record of their increasing vocabularies. Generally word banks are used in primary grades and notebooks are used in intermediate grades and above, but there are no set limits for either technique.

Word Play

Word play is an enjoyable way to learn more about words. It can provide multiple exposures to words in different contexts that are important to complete word learning. Gale (1982, p. 220) states, "Children who play with words show a stronger grasp of meaning than those who do not. To create or comprehend a pun, one needs to be aware of the multiple meanings of a word."

Some other ways that teachers can engage children in word play are described below.

ACTIVITIES

1. Have students write words in ways that express their meanings—for example, they may write *backward* as *drawkcab,* or *up* slanting upward and *down* slanting downward.
2. Ask them silly questions containing new words. Example: "Would you have a terrarium for dinner? Why or why not?"
3. Discuss what puns are and give some examples; then ask children to make up or find puns to bring to class. Let them explain the play on words to classmates who do not understand it. Example: "What is black and white and read all over?" Answer: A newspaper (word play on homophones *red* and *read*).
4. Use Hink Pinks, Hinky Pinkies, and Hinkety Pinketies, rhyming definitions for terms with one, two, and three syllables, respectively. Give a definition, tell whether it is a Hink Pink, Hinky Pinky, or Hinkety Pinkety, and let the children

guess the expression. Then let the children make up their own terms. Several examples follow.

Hink Pink: Unhappy father—Sad dad
Hinky Pinky: Late group of celebrators—Tardy party
Hinkety Pinkety: Yearly handbook—Annual manual

5. Give the students a list of clues ("means the same as . . ." "is the opposite of . . .", and so forth) to words in a reading selection, along with page numbers, and tell them to go on a scavenger hunt for the words, writing them beside the appropriate clues (Criscuolo, 1980).
6. Students might also enjoy crossword puzzles or hidden word puzzles that highlight new words in their textbooks or other instructional materials.

Riddles are a very effective form of word play. To use riddles, children must interact verbally with others, and to create riddles, they have to organize information and decide upon significant details. Riddles can help children move from the literal to the interpretive level of understanding (Gale, 1982). Tyson and Mountain (1982) point out that riddles provide both context clues and high-interest material. Both of these factors promote vocabulary learning.

Riddles can be classified into several categories: those based on homonyms, on rhyming words, on double meanings, and on figurative/literal meanings, for example. (See the section on "Special Words" later in this chapter.) An example of a homonym riddle is: "What does a grizzly *bear* take on a trip? Only the *bare* essentials" (Tyson and Mountain, 1982, p. 170).

Riddles work best with children who are at least six years old (Gale, 1982), and they continue to be especially effective with children through eleven years of age. After that, interest wanes in this form of word play.

Computer Techniques

Computers are present in many elementary school classrooms in this age of high technology, and the software available for them includes many programs for vocabulary development. Although some of these programs are simply drill-and-practice programs, which are meant to provide practice with word meanings that the teacher has already taught, some tutorial programs provide initial instruction in word meanings. (These programs may also include a drill-and-practice component.) Programs focusing on synonyms, antonyms, homonyms, and words with multiple meanings are available, as are programs providing work with classification and analogies. Since the available programs are increasing daily, teachers must select them carefully. Programs vary greatly in pedagogical soundness, technical accuracy, and ease of use; also, some are more appropriate to particular age and ability groups

188

Teaching
Reading in
Today's
Elementary
Schools

of students. Well-chosen software can provide a teacher with much useful material to supplement his or her vocabulary program.

✔ **Self-Check: Objective 2**

What are some techniques that can be used for vocabulary instruction? Which ones appear to be the best, according to Carr and Wixson's suggestions for evaluating techniques?
(See Self-Improvement Opportunities 1, 2, 5, 6, 7, and 8.)

Special Words

Special types of words, such as the ones mentioned below, need to be given careful attention.

Homophones

Homophones (also known as *homonyms*) can trouble young readers because they are spelled differently but pronounced the same way. Some common homophones are

I want to *be* a doctor.
That *bee* almost stung me.

She has *two* brothers.
Will you go *to* the show with me?
I have *too* much work to do.

I can *hear* the bird singing.
Maurice, you sit over *here*.

That is the only *course* they could take.
The jacket was made from *coarse* material.

Mark has a *red* scarf.
Have you *read* that book?

I *ate* all of my supper.
We have *eight* dollars to spend.

ACTIVITIES

1. Have children play a card game to work on meanings of homophones. Print homophones on cards and let the children take turns drawing from each other, as in the game of Old Maid. When a child has a pair of homophones, he or she can put them down if he or she can give a correct sentence using each word. The child who claims the most pairs wins.

2. Have the children play a game called Homophone Hunt, in which they are given a list of words for which they are to locate as many homophones as possible. Some words to use follow:

be	one
beat	pain
dear	pair
eight	peace
fair	red
hair	road
hall	sea
hour	sum
knew	sun
knight	tale
made	waste
mail	way

3. Have students web homophones in the following way:

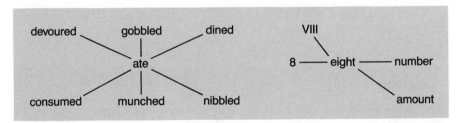

Homographs

Homographs are words that have identical spellings but not the same meanings. Their pronunciations may or may not be the same. Readers must use context clues to identify the correct pronunciations, parts of speech, and meanings of homographs. Examples include:

I will *read* my newspaper. (pronounced *rēd*)
I have *read* my newspaper. (pronounced *rĕd*)

I have a *contract* signed by the president. (noun: pronounced *cŏn' trăkt*; means a document)
I didn't know it would *contract* as it cooled. (verb: pronounced *cən/trăkt'*; means to reduce in size)

Synonyms

Synonyms are words that have the same or very similar meanings. Work with synonyms can help expand children's vocabularies.

190

Teaching
Reading in
Today's
Elementary
Schools

ACTIVITIES

1. Provide a stimulus word and have the pupils find as many synonyms as they can. Discuss the small differences in meaning of some words suggested as synonyms. For example, ask: "Would you rather be called 'pretty' or 'beautiful'? Why?"

2. Use a worksheet like the following one.

● **WORKSHEET:** *Synonyms*

Directions: Rewrite each sentence, substituting a synonym for the word in italics.

1. Gretchen had a *big* dog.
2. We *hurried* to the scene of the fire.
3. Will you *ask* him about the job?
4. I have *almost* enough money to buy the bicycle.
5. Curtis made an *error* on his paper.
6. Suzanne is a *fast* runner.
7. It was a *frightening* experience.
8. Marty was *sad* about leaving. ●

Antonyms

Antonyms are two words that have opposite meanings. Their meanings are not merely different; they are balanced against each other on a particular feature. For example, in the continuum of *cold, cool, tepid, warm,* and *hot, cold* is the opposite of *hot,* being equally close to the extreme in a negative direction as *hot* is in a positive direction. Thus *cold* and *hot* are antonyms. *Tepid* and *hot* are different, but not opposites. *Cool* and *warm* are also antonyms. Similarly, *buy* and *sell* are antonyms because one is the reverse of the other. But *buy* and *give* are not antonyms, because no exchange of money is involved in the giving. The words are different, but not opposite. Powell (1986) points out that the use of opposition (citing antonyms) in defining terms can help to set the extremities of a word's meaning and provide its shading and nuances. Research has shown that synonym production is helped by antonym production, but the reverse has not been shown to be true. Therefore, work with antonyms may enhance success in synonym exercises.

Exercises similar to the ones mentioned for use with synonyms can be used with antonyms, as can the one below. After this activity has been completed by the children, the teacher and children should discuss the antonym pairs, bringing out the points upon which the decisions about opposition were made.

Directions: Draw lines connecting the words in Column A with their antonyms in Column B.

Column A	Column B
slow	small
big	skinny
weak	young
fat	fast
ugly	pretty
old	strong ●

New Words

New words are constantly being coined to meet the new needs of society and are possible sources of difficulty. Have students search for such words in their reading and television viewing and then compile a dictionary of words so new that they are not yet in standard dictionaries. The class may have to discuss these words to derive an accurate definition for each one, considering all the contexts in which the students have heard or seen it (Koeller and Khan, 1981).

✔ Self-Check: Objective 3

What are some special types of words that may cause children comprehension problems? What types of problems may they cause? (See Self-Improvement Opportunity 3.)

Summary

Development of meaning vocabulary is the development of labels for the schemata, or organized knowledge structures, that a person possesses. Because vocabulary is an important component of reading comprehension, direct instruction in vocabulary can be helpful in enhancing reading achievement. Although pinpointing the age at which children learn the precise meanings of words is difficult, children generally make more discriminating responses about word meanings as they grow older, and vocabulary generally grows with increasing age.

There are many ways to approach vocabulary instruction. Techniques that link new terms to the children's background knowledge, that help them develop expanded word knowledge, that actively involve them in learning, and that help them become independent in acquiring vocabulary tend to be best. Techniques that cause children to work harder to learn words tend to

192

Teaching
Reading in
Today's
Elementary
Schools

aid retention. Teachers may need to spend time on concept development before working with specific vocabulary terms. Vocabulary development should be emphasized throughout the day, not just in reading and language classes; children can learn much vocabulary from the teacher's modeling vocabulary use. Context clues, structural analysis, categorization, analogies and word lines, semantic maps and word webs, semantic feature analysis, dictionary use, study of word origins and histories, study of denotations and connotations of words, a number of student-centered learning techniques, word play, and computer techniques can be helpful in vocabulary instruction.

Some special types of words can cause comprehension problems for children. They include homophones (homonyms), homographs, synonyms, antonyms, and newly coined words.

Test Yourself

True or False

_____ 1. Context clues are of little help in determining the meanings of unfamiliar words, although they are useful for recognizing familiar ones.

_____ 2. Structural analysis can be an aid to determining meanings of new words containing familiar prefixes, suffixes, and root words.

_____ 3. When looking up a word in the dictionary to determine its meaning, a child needs to read only the first definition listed.

_____ 4. Homophones are words that have identical, or almost identical, meanings.

_____ 5. Antonyms are words that have opposite meanings.

_____ 6. Word play is one good approach to building vocabulary.

_____ 7. Children sometimes make overgeneralizations in dealing with word meanings.

_____ 8. The development of vocabulary is essentially a child's development of labels for his or her schemata.

_____ 9. Work with analogies bolsters word knowledge.

_____ 10. Semantic mapping involves systematically deleting words from a printed passage.

_____ 11. Instruction in vocabulary that helps students relate new terms to their background knowledge is good.

_____ 12. Active involvement in vocabulary activities has little effect on vocabulary learning.

_____ 13. Pantomiming word meanings is one technique to produce active involvement in word learning.

_____ 14. Children should have multiple exposures to words they are expected to learn.

_____ 15. Working hard to learn words results in better retention.

_____ 16. There is no one best way of teaching words.

_____ 17. Basal reader vocabulary instructional techniques are universally excellent.

_____ 18. Both concrete and vicarious experiences can help to build concepts.

_____ 19. Vocabulary instruction should receive attention during content area classes.

_____ 20. "Think-aloud" strategies can help students see how to use context clues.

_____ 21. Use of worksheets should be followed by discussion of the students' responses.

_____ 22. Although use of categorization activities is motivational, according to current research findings it is not an effective approach.

_____ 23. Semantic mapping can be used to help students develop a concept of definition.

_____ 24. Semantic feature analysis is the same thing as structural analysis.

_____ 25. Semantic feature analysis can help students see the uniqueness of each word studied.

_____ 26. The study of word origins is called etymology.

_____ 27. Connotations of words are dictionary definitions.

_____ 28. Word banks can help students maintain a record of their increasing vocabularies.

_____ 29. There are at present no computer programs available for vocabulary development.

Self-Improvement Opportunities

1. Plan a dictionary exercise that requires children to locate the meaning of a word that fits the context surrounding that word.

2. In a chapter of a textbook for a content area such as science, social studies, math, language arts, or health, locate examples of difficult words whose meanings are made clear through context clues. Decide which kind of clue is involved in each example.

3. Construct a board game that requires the players to respond with synonyms and antonyms when they land on certain spaces or draw certain cards. Demonstrate the game with your classmates role-playing elementary students, or as an alternative, actually use the game with children in a regular classroom setting.

4. Ask four 6-year-old children, four 7-year-old children, four 8-year-old children, and four 9-year-old children the meanings of *ask* and *tell* and of *brother* and *boy*. Discuss your findings with your classmates. Were there differences in knowledge of precise meanings among the children? Was there a trend in these differences?

5. Plan a lesson designed to teach the concept of justice to a group of sixth graders.

194

Teaching
Reading in
Today's
Elementary
Schools

6. Identify important vocabulary terms in a textbook chapter. Decide which ones could be defined, or partially defined, through structural analysis. Share your findings with your classmates.

7. Develop a semantic map based upon a content area topic with a group of intermediate grade children. After they have done a reading assignment on the topic, revise the map with them.

8. Locate some commercial computer software designed for some aspect of vocabulary development. Try out the program, evaluating it on the basis of pedagogical soundness, ease of use for teachers and students, and appropriateness for the particular age or ability level of students you are teaching (or are preparing to teach). Write an analysis of the program and share your findings with your classmates.

Bibliography

Anders, Patricia L., and Candace S. Bos. "Semantic Feature Analysis: An Interactive Strategy for Vocabulary Development and Text Comprehension." *Journal of Reading* 29 (April 1986): 610–16.

Beck, Isabel L., and Margaret G. McKeown. "Learning Words Well—A Program to Enhance Vocabulary and Comprehension." *The Reading Teacher* 36 (March 1983): 622–25.

Bellows, Barbara Plotkin. "Running Shoes Are to Jogging as Analogies Are to Creative/Critical Thinking." *Journal of Reading* 23 (March 1980): 507–11.

Blachowicz, Camille L. Z. "Making Connections: Alternatives to the Vocabulary Notebook." *Journal of Reading* 29 (April 1986): 643–49.

Blachowicz, Camille L. Z. "Vocabulary Development and Reading: From Research to Instruction." *The Reading Teacher* 38 (May 1985): 876–81.

Bufe, Bruce N. "Word Sort to Improve Comprehension." *The Reading Teacher* 37 (November 1983): 209–10.

Carr, Eileen. "The Vocabulary Overview Guide: A Metacognitive Strategy to Improve Vocabulary Comprehension and Retention." *Journal of Reading* 21 (May 1985): 684–89.

Carr, Eileen, and Karen K. Wixson. "Guidelines for Evaluating Vocabulary Instruction." *Journal of Reading* 29 (April 1986): 588–95.

Cooper, J. David. *Improving Reading Comprehension.* Boston: Houghton Mifflin, 1986.

Criscuolo, Nicholas P. "Creative Vocabulary Building." *Journal of Reading* 24 (December 1980): 260–61.

Crist, Barbara. "Tim's Time: Vocabulary Activities from Names." *The Reading Teacher* 34 (December 1980): 309–12.

Duffelmeyer, Frederick A. "The Influence of Experience-Based Vocabulary Instruction on Learning Word Meanings." *Journal of Reading* 24 (October 1980): 35–40.

Duffelmeyer, Frederick A. "Introducing Words in Context." *The Reading Teacher* 35 (March 1982): 724–25.

Duffelmeyer, Frederick A. "Teaching Word Meaning from an Experience Base." *The Reading Teacher* 39 (October 1985): 6–9.

Duffelmeyer, Frederick A., and Barbara Blakely Duffelmeyer. "Developing Vocabulary Through Dramatization." *Journal of Reading* 23 (November 1979): 141–43.

Gale, David. "Why Word Play?" *The Reading Teacher* 36 (November 1982): 220–22.

Gipe, Joan P. "Use of a Relevant Context Helps Kids Learn New Word Meanings." *The Reading Teacher* 33 (January 1980): 398–402.

Gold, Yvonne. "Helping Students Discover the Origins of Words." *The Reading Teacher* 35 (December 1981): 350–51.

Goldstein, Bobbye S. "Looking at Cartoons and Comics in a New Way." *Journal of Reading* 29 (April 1986): 647–61.

Graves, Michael F., and Maureen C. Prenn. "Costs and Benefits of Various Methods of Teaching Vocabulary." *Journal of Reading* 29 (April 1986): 596–602.

Haggard, Martha Rapp. "The Vocabulary Self-Collection Strategy: Using Student Interest and World Knowledge to Enhance Vocabulary Growth." *Journal of Reading* 29 (April 1986): 634–42.

Heimlich, Joan E., and Susan D. Pittelman. *Semantic Mapping: Classroom Applications.* Newark, Del.: International Reading Association, 1986.

Jiganti, Mary Ann, and Mary Anne Tindall. "An Interactive Approach to Teaching Vocabulary." *The Reading Teacher* 39 (January 1986): 444–48.

Johnson, Dale D., and P. David Pearson. *Teaching Reading Vocabulary.* 2nd ed. New York: Holt, Rinehart and Winston, 1984.

Johnson, Dale D., Susan D. Pittelman, and Joan E. Heimlich. "Semantic Mapping." *The Reading Teacher* 39 (April 1986): 778–83.

Jones, Linda L. "An Interactive View of Reading Implications for the Classroom." *The Reading Teacher* 35 (April 1982): 772–77.

Kaplan, Elaine M., and Anita Tuchman. "Vocabulary Strategies Belong in the Hands of Learners." *Journal of Reading* 24 (October 1980): 32–34.

Koeller, Shirley, and Samina Khan. "Going Beyond the Dictionary with the English Vocabulary Explosion." *Journal of Reading* 24 (April 1981): 628–29.

Macey, Joan Mary. "Word Lines: An Approach to Vocabulary Development." *The Reading Teacher* 35 (November 1981): 216–17.

Marzano, Robert J. "A Cluster Approach to Vocabulary Instruction: A New Direction from the Research Literature." *The Reading Teacher* 38 (November 1984): 168–73.

Mateja, John. "Musical Cloze: Background, Purpose, and Sample." *The Reading Teacher* 35 (January 1982): 444–48.

McConaughy, Stephanie H. "Word Recognition and Word Meaning in the Total Reading Process." *Language Arts* 55 (November/December 1978): 946–56, 1003.

196

Teaching
Reading in
Today's
Elementary
Schools

Nelson-Herber, Joan. "Expanding and Defining Vocabulary in Content Areas." *Journal of Reading* 29 (April 1986): 626–33.

Pigg, John R. "The Effects of a Storytelling/Storyreading Program on the Language Skills of Rural Primary Students." Unpublished paper. Summer 1986.

Powell, William R. "Teaching Vocabulary Through Opposition." *Journal of Reading* 29 (April 1986): 617–21.

"The Right Vocabulary Instruction." *The Reading Teacher* 39 (March 1986): 743–44.

Roe, Betty D. *Use of Storytelling/Storyreading in Conjunction with Follow-up Language Activities to Improve Oral Communication of Rural First Grade Students: Phase I.* Cookeville, Tenn.: Rural Education Consortium, 1985.

Roe, Betty D. *Use of Storytelling/Storyreading in Conjunction with Follow-up Language Activities to Improve Oral Communication of Rural Primary Grade Students: Phase II.* Cookeville, Tenn.: Rural Education Consortium, 1986.

Schwartz, Robert M., and Taffy E. Raphael. "Concept of Definition: A Key to Improving Students' Vocabulary." *The Reading Teacher* 39 (November 1985): 198–205.

Sorenson, Nancy L. "Basal Reading Vocabulary Instruction: A Critique and Suggestions." *The Reading Teacher* 39 (October 1985): 80–85.

Stahl, Steven A. "Three Principles of Effective Vocabulary Instruction." *Journal of Reading* 29 (April 1986): 662–68.

Stahl, Steven A., and Sandra J. Vancil. "Discussion Is What Makes Semantic Maps Work in Vocabulary Instruction." *The Reading Teacher* 40 (October 1986): 62–67.

Thelen, Judith N. "Vocabulary Instruction and Meaningful Learning." *Journal of Reading* 29 (April 1986): 603–609.

Thompson, Stephen J. "Teaching Metaphoric Language: An Instructional Strategy." *Journal of Reading* 30 (November 1986): 105–109.

Tierney, Robert J., and James W. Cunningham. "Research on Teaching Reading Comprehension." In *Handbook of Reading Research,* P. David Pearson, ed. New York: Longman, 1984, pp. 609–55.

Tyson, Eleanore S., and Lee Mountain. "A Riddle or Pun Makes Learning Words Fun." *The Reading Teacher* 36 (November 1982): 170–73.

Chapter 5

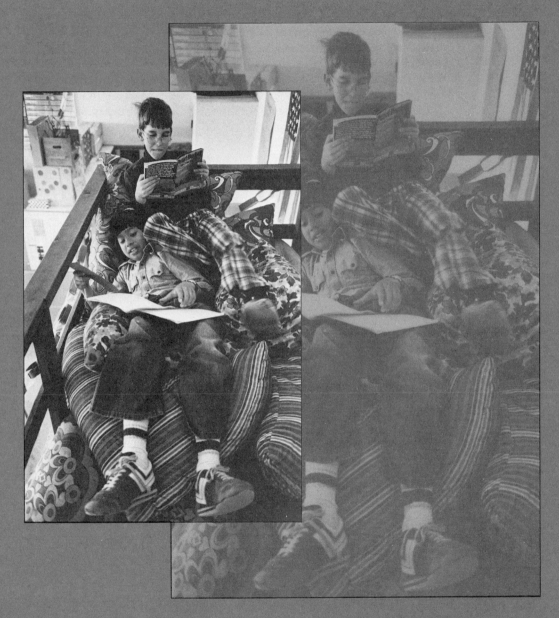

Comprehension

Introduction

The objective of all readers is, or should be, comprehension of what they read. This chapter discusses how to achieve that comprehension through background information and important comprehension skills, suggests methods of developing those skills, and points out techniques for ascertaining how well children have comprehended. It explores comprehension from two angles: the written units that a child must understand and the different types of comprehension that he or she should achieve. As Pearson and Johnson have pointed out, "reading comprehension is at once a unitary process and a set of discrete processes" (1978, p. 227). We discuss the individual processes separately, yet teachers must not lose sight of the fact that there are many overlaps and many interrelationships among the processes. There are even close relationships between comprehension and decoding. Research has shown that good comprehenders are able to decode quickly and accurately (Eads, 1981). Thus, developing decoding skills to the automatic stage seems to be important. However, teachers should always keep in mind that decoding skills are merely a means of accessing the meaning of the written material.

This chapter is a logical continuation of Chapter 4, "Meaning Vocabulary," for vocabulary knowledge is a vital component of comprehension. Therefore, these chapters cannot truly be considered separately. They are divided here only for convenience of presentation.

Example 5.1 shows the relationships among the ideas presented in this chapter. Readers approach a text with much background knowledge (many schemata) concerning their world, and they use this knowledge along with the information found in the text to construct the meanings represented by the printed material. In order to access the information supplied by the text, they must use word recognition skills (covered in Chapter 3) and comprehension skills (covered in Chapter 4 and in this chapter). They combine their existing knowledge with new information supplied by the text in order to achieve understanding of the material.

The written units of comprehension that readers must process are words, sentences, paragraphs, and whole selections. This chapter is concerned with the last three of these units, since words were covered extensively in Chapter 4. It presents ways of working with these units.

The types of comprehension discussed are literal, interpretive, critical, and creative. This chapter includes approaches for developing each type.

Questioning techniques that can be used to guide reading, enhance comprehension and retention, and assess comprehension are also covered. Preparing questions, helping students answer questions, and helping students question are three important topics that receive attention.

The content of this chapter is particularly important in view of research findings by Durkin (1978–79) and her associates. They observed fourth-grade classrooms chosen by principals as exemplary to determine how much time

▶ **EXAMPLE 5.1:** Chapter Organization

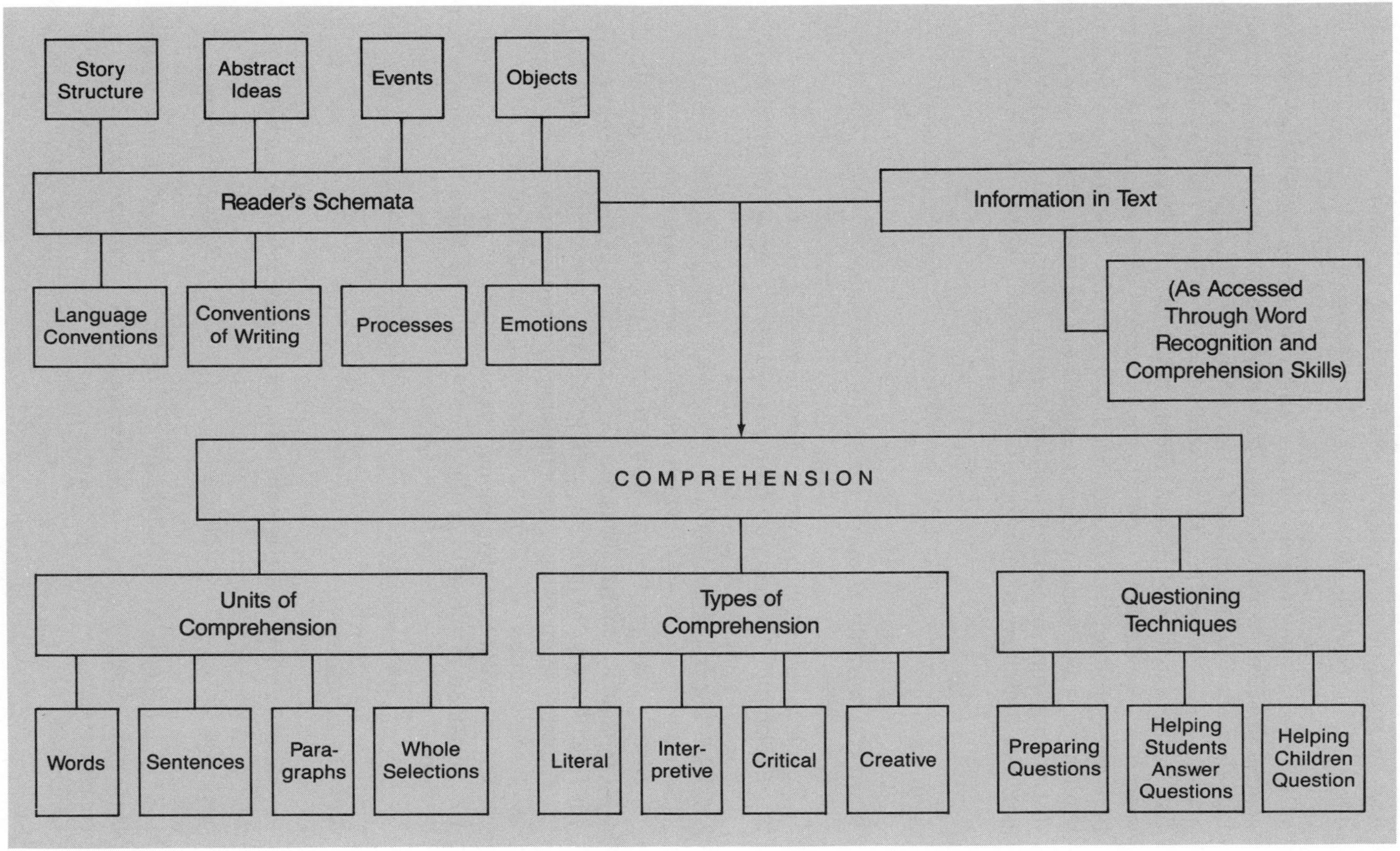

200

Teaching
Reading in
Today's
Elementary
Schools

teachers spend on instruction in reading comprehension. They found that less than 1 percent of instructional time was taken up by such instruction, while children spent a great deal of time on noninstructional activities such as answering questions in writing and completing workbook pages. In general, teachers spent more time on testing comprehension than on teaching. They often just mentioned a skill, saying just enough about it to justify making a related assignment. In another study Durkin (1981a) discovered that teacher's manuals for basal reading series did not always make adequate suggestions for teaching comprehension; instead, they emphasized practice and assessment activities and often only briefly described instructional procedures. This finding underscores the need for teachers to know a great deal about comprehension instruction, for they cannot depend completely on guidance from teacher's manuals.

Setting Objectives

When you finish this chapter, you should be able to

1. Explain how schema theory relates to reading comprehension.
2. Explain how to help pupils understand the meanings of sentences.
3. Suggest some ways to teach children to recognize main ideas of varied types of paragraphs.
4. Describe some ways in which selections are organized.
5. Discuss some prereading, during reading, and postreading activities that can enhance comprehension.
6. Describe ways to promote reading for literal meanings.
7. Explain the importance of being able to make inferences.
8. Discuss some of the things a critical reader must know.
9. Explain what "creative reading" means.
10. Explain how to construct questions that will check depth of comprehension.

Key Vocabulary

Pay close attention to these terms when they appear in the chapter.

analogies	ellipsis	knowledge-based
anaphora	idiom	processing
anticipation guides	InQuest	literal comprehension
cloze procedure	interpretive reading	metacognition
creative reading	juncture	nonrestrictive clauses
critical reading		propaganda techniques

In addition, when you read the section on propaganda techniques, pay close attention to the terms used there.

IMPORTANCE OF SCHEMATA

Educators have long believed that if a reader has not been exposed to the language patterns used by a writer or to the objects and concepts referred to by a writer, his or her comprehension will at best be incomplete. This belief is supported by recent theories holding that reading comprehension involves relating textual information to pre-existing knowledge structures, or schemata (Pearson et al., 1979). "These schemata represent . . . what is believed to be generally true, based on experience of a class of objects, actions, or situations" (Hacker, 1980, p. 867). In other words, each schema held by a person represents what the person knows about a particular concept and the interrelationships among the known pieces of information. For example, a schema for *car* may include a person's knowledge about its construction, its appearance, and its operation, as well as many other facts about it. Two people may have quite different schemata for the same basic concept; for example, a race-car driver's schema for *car* (or, to be more exact, his or her cluster of schemata about cars) will be different from that of a seven-year-old child.

People may have schemata for things, events, sequences of actions, emotions, roles, conventions of writing, and so forth. In fact, "schemata can represent knowledge at all levels—from ideologies and cultural truths . . . to knowledge about what patterns of excitations are associated with what letters of the alphabet" (Rumelhart, 1981, p. 13). Each schema a person has is incomplete, as though it contained empty slots that could be filled with information collected from new experiences. Reading of informational material is aided by the existing schemata and also fills in some of the empty slots in them (Durkin, 1981b).

Students need schemata of a variety of types to be successful readers. They must have concepts about the arrangement of print on a page, about the purpose of printed material (to convey ideas), and about the relationship of spoken language to written language. They need to be familiar with vocabulary and sentence patterns not generally found in oral language and with the different writing styles associated with different literary genres (Roney, 1984).

202

Teaching
Reading in
Today's
Elementary
Schools

A story schema is a set of expectations about the internal structure of stories (Mandler and Johnson, 1977; Rand, 1984). Studies have shown that well-structured stories are easier to recall and that unstructured passages are harder to summarize. Possession of a story schema appears to have a positive effect on recall, and good readers seem to have a better grasp of text structure than poor readers. Having children retell stories is a good way to discover their grasp of a story schema (Rand, 1984).

Rand (1984) hypothesized that having many experiences with well-formed stories helps children develop a story schema. Storytelling and story reading appear to be excellent ways to develop children's schemata related to stories or other materials that they will be expected to read. Hearing a variety of stories with standard structures helps children develop a story schema that allows them to anticipate or predict what will happen next. This ability enables children to become more involved in stories they read and more able to make and confirm or reject predictions—a process that fosters comprehension—more effectively. The sentence structure in the stories that are told and read to children expose them to patterns they will encounter when reading literature and will help make these patterns more understandable (Nessel, 1985; Pigg, 1986; Roe, 1985; Roe, 1986). Other ways of helping to develop children's story schemata include direct teaching of story structure and story grammars, which will be covered in a later section of this chapter.

Perhaps as much as anything else children need to know, they need to have the understanding that reading can be fun and can help them do things. Of course, in addition to the need for extensive background knowledge about the reading task, they need general background knowledge on the topics about which they are reading (Roney, 1984). Often children do not comprehend well because they know very little about their world (Cunningham, 1982b).

Schema theory has been supported by many research studies. For instance, Anderson, Reynolds, Schallert, and Goetz "found that recall and comprehension of passages which invited two schematic interpretations (wrestling versus a prison break or card-playing versus a music rehearsal) were highly related to the background knowledge of the readers and/or environment in which the testing occurred" (Pearson et al., 1979, p. 3). Bransford and Johnson discovered that college students' recall of obscure passages was increased if a statement of the passage's topic or a picture related to the passage was provided.

A study by Pearson et al. (1979) focused on younger students (second graders), who were tested on their background knowledge of spiders, given a selection about spiders to read, and then given a posttest including questions to elicit both implicit (implied) and explicit (directly stated) information. The researchers found that background knowledge had more effect on understanding of implied than of explicit information. Such studies suggest that the prior development of background information is likely to enhance reading comprehension, especially inferential comprehension. Stevens (1982) found

similar results among ninth graders reading about topics of which they had
high and low levels of prior knowledge. She then provided tenth graders with background information about a topic before reading and discovered that their reading on that topic was improved.

These studies indicate that teachers should plan experiences that will give children background information to help them understand written material they are expected to read or to help them choose appropriate schemata to apply to the reading. When children have trouble using their backgrounds of experience to help with reading comprehension, teachers need to find out whether the children lack the necessary schemata or whether they possess the needed schemata, but cannot use them effectively when reading (Jones, 1982). If the children lack the schemata, the teacher should plan direct and vicarious experiences to build them, such as examining and discussing pictures that reveal information about the subject, introducing new terminology related to the subject, and taking field trips or watching demonstrations. An obvious way to obtain background information about some topics is to read about them in other books (Crafton, 1982). Poor readers, in particular, frequently need more help with concept development than teachers provide. They need more discussion time before reading (Bristow, 1985). If children already know about the subject, letting them share their knowledge, preview the material to be read, and predict what might happen can be helpful (Jones, 1982).

Sheridan has pointed out that research on schemata provides evidence of the holistic nature of comprehension. Although she acknowledges that educators will still need to teach reading skills, Sheridan believes that schema theory has made the overlapping nature of those skills more apparent. Along with many others in the field of reading education, she hopes that the teaching of skills in isolation will cease through the application of schema research (Lange, 1981). Teachers should always approach comprehension skills by emphasizing their application in actual reading of connected discourse. One way to accomplish this is to relate the skills to whole selections in which students can apply the skills immediately after learning about and practicing them with less complex material. Another way is to stress the relationships of the various skills (for example, point out that details are the building blocks used to recognize main ideas and that following directions necessitates integrating the skills of recognizing details and detecting sequence).

Spiro (1979) and his colleagues have conducted studies that indicate that readers vary in the relative degrees to which they emphasize two processes of comprehension. Text-based processes are those in which the reader is primarily trying to extract information from the text. Knowledge-based processes are those in which the reader primarily brings prior knowledge and experiences to bear on the interpretation of the material. For example, consider this text: "The children were gathered around a table upon which sat a beautiful cake with *Happy Birthday* written on it. Mrs. Jones said, 'Now

204

Teaching
Reading in
Today's
Elementary
Schools

Maria, make a wish and blow out the candles.'" Readers must use a text-based process to answer the question "What did the cake have written on it?" because the information is directly stated in the material. They must use a knowledge-based process to answer the question "Whose birthday was it?" Prior experience will provide them with the answer, "Maria," because they have consistently seen candles blown out by the child who has the birthday at parties they have attended. Of course, before they use the knowledge-based process they have to use a text-based process to discover that Maria was told to blow out the candles.

Skilled readers may employ one type of process more than the other when the situation allows them to do this without affecting their comprehension. Less able readers may tend to rely too much on one type of processing, with the result of poorer comprehension. Unfortunately, some students have the idea that knowledge-based processing is not an appropriate reading activity, so they fail to use knowledge they have.

Rystrom presents a good argument that reading cannot be exclusively knowledge-based, or "top-down": if it were, two people reading the same material would rarely arrive at the same conclusions, and the probability that a person could learn anything from written material would be slight. He has an equally convincing argument that reading is not exclusively text-based, or "bottom-up": if it were, then all people who read a written selection would agree about its meaning. It is far more likely that reading is interactive, involving both information supplied by the text and information brought to the text by the reader, which combine to produce a person's understanding of the material (Strange, 1980). (See Chapter 1 for more elaboration of this idea.)

If reading performance results from interaction between information in the text and information possessed by the reader, then anything that increases a reader's background knowledge may also increase reading performance. Singer, McNeil, and Furse (1984) discovered that, in general, students at schools with broad curricular scopes scored higher on inferential reading comprehension than did students at schools with narrow curricular scopes. Increased exposure to social studies, science, art, music, mathematics, and other content areas should therefore enhance reading achievement.

Background knowledge that students possess needs to be activated through discussion or other means, just as related concepts that the students do not possess need to be developed before reading begins. Children need to realize that what they already know can help them understand the things discussed in their reading materials (Wilson, 1983). The prediction strategies in a Directed Reading-Thinking Activity (described in Chapter 6) may help with activation of schemata, as may the preview step of the SQ3R study method (described in Chapter 7) (Hacker, 1980) and the purpose questions of the directed reading activity (described in Chapter 6). A good way for teachers to help children learn to activate schemata is for them to "think aloud" for the students, modeling the activation of schemata for a passage while reading

(Bristow, 1985). Knowledge about a topic cannot be activated, however, if no knowledge is possessed (Cunningham, 1982).

Teachers should make sure that the material students are asked to read is not too difficult for them. When reading material that is too difficult, students cannot use the knowledge they have to assist them in comprehending material they do not understand (Wilson, 1983). Difficult materials tend to work against students' use of meaning-seeking activities because these materials cause students to focus too much on decoding and not enough on comprehension.

✔ Self-Check: Objective 1
What aspects of schema theory have direct application to the teaching of reading?
(See Self-Improvement Opportunity 1.)

UNITS OF COMPREHENSION

The basic comprehension units in reading are words, sentences, paragraphs, and whole selections. Since vocabulary is one of the most important factors affecting comprehension, Chapter 4 was devoted to the area of vocabulary instruction, addressing the word unit. This chapter includes consideration of comprehension of sentences, paragraphs, and whole selections. Even though units of comprehension are considered separately, it is important to re-member that comprehension is a unitary act, and eventually all of the procedures discussed here must work together. Ideas for improving word, sentence, and paragraph knowledge build up to the reading of whole selections, but sometimes difficulties are easier to address in smaller units.

Sentences

Children may find complicated sentences difficult to understand, so they need to know ways to attack them, or derive their meaning. Research has shown that systematic instruction in sentence comprehension increases reading comprehension. For example, Weaver had students arrange cut-up sentences in the correct order by finding the action word first and then asking who, what, where, and why questions (Durkin, 1978–79). Another approach is to have children discover the essential parts of sentences by writing them in telegram form, as illustrated in the Model Activity that follows.

● **MODEL ACTIVITY:** *Telegram Sentences*

Write a sentence such as this one on the chalkboard: "The angry dog chased me down the street." Tell the children that you want to tell what happened in the fewest words possible, because when you send a telegram, each word used

206

Teaching
Reading in
Today's
Elementary
Schools

costs money. Then think aloud about the sentence: "Who did something in this sentence? Oh, the dog did. My sentence needs to include the dog. . . . What action did he perform? He chased. I'll need that action word, too. Dog chased. . . . That doesn't make a complete thought though. I'll have to tell whom he chased. He chased me. Now I have a complete message that leaves out the extra details." My telegram is 'Dog chased me.'" ●

Teachers should help children learn that sentences can be stated in different ways without changing their meanings. For example, some sentence parts can be moved around without affecting the meaning of the sentence, as is true with these two sentences: (1) On a pole in front of the school, the flag was flying. (2) The flag was flying on a pole in front of the school.

Sentence Difficulty Factors

A number of types of sentences, including those with relative clauses, complex sentences, those in the passive voice, those containing pronouns, those with missing words, those with implicit (implied) relationships, and those expressing negation, have been found to cause comprehension difficulty for children. Children understand material better when the syntax is like their oral language patterns, but the text in some primary-grade basal readers is syntactically more complex than the students' oral language.

For example, relative clauses (including restrictive and nonrestrictive clauses) are among the syntactic patterns that do not appear regularly in young children's speech. Both restrictive clauses, which restrict the information in the main clause by adding information, and nonrestrictive or appositive clauses, which add information, are troublesome. In the example "The man *who called my name* was my father," the restrictive clause indicates which particular man to designate as "my father." "My father, who is a doctor, visited me today" is an example of a sentence with a nonrestrictive clause. Bormuth and associates found that 33 percent of the fourth graders they studied made errors in processing singly embedded restrictive clauses such as those in the examples given above when reading paragraphs (Kachuck, 1981).

Teachers should ask questions that test understanding of particular syntactic patterns in the reading material, and, when misunderstanding is evident, they should point out the clues that help children discover the correct meanings (Kachuck, 1981). Teachers may find it necessary to read aloud sentences from assigned passages to children and explain the functions of the relative clauses found in the sentences. Then teachers may give other examples of sentences with relative clauses and ask the children to explain the meanings of these clauses. Feedback on correctness or incorrectness and further explanation should be given at this point. Finally, teachers should provide children with independent practice activities to help them set the new skill in memory.

Students who need more work with relative clauses can be asked to turn
two-clause sentences into two sentences (Kachuck, 1981). Teachers can model this also, as in the example above: "The man called my name. The man was my father." Supervised student practice with feedback and independent practice could follow. For instruction in breaking down even more complex sentences into main ideas in order to discover the information included, the teacher may use a chalkboard activity with an example such as the following:

Although they don't realize it, people *who eat too much* may be shortening the amount of time *that they will live.*

1. People may shorten their lifespan.
2. They may do this by overeating.
3. They may not realize this possible bad effect of overeating.

The teacher can use the instructional sequence described above to teach the students how to break down this sentence. Students could move from this activity into sentence combining (explained below). Finally, they should apply their understanding in reading whole passages (Kachuck, 1981). Until they have used the skill in interpreting connected discourse, it is impossible to be sure that they have mastered it.

Sentence combining involves giving students two or more short sentences and asking them to combine the information into a single sentence. Such activities bring out the important fact that there are always multiple ways of expressing an idea in English (Pearson and Camperell, 1981). The teacher would write the sentences to be combined on the board and then model possible combinations. The following sentences might be used:

Joe is my brother.
He is little.

The teacher might combine the two sentences by saying "Joe is my little brother," "My little brother is Joe," or "Joe, my brother, is little." All of these ways of stating the sentence combine the information from both single sentences. The first construction is the most likely one for the children to produce, but they need to see the other possibilities so that they will not perceive the task as a closed one. Discussion of a number of sentence combinations may bring out much about the syntactic knowledge of the children.

Younger children also find it hard to understand sentences that delete linguistic units; for example, in "The man *calling my name* is my father," the words *who is* have been deleted and must be inferred (Kachuck, 1981). Yet Kachuck found that in second-grade readers, relative clauses occurred from six to twenty times per one hundred sentences. When reduced relative clauses—constructions such as "calling my name"—were considered, the

208

Teaching
Reading in
Today's
Elementary
Schools

incidence rose to twenty-eight to sixty-eight times per one hundred sentences. In higher-grade materials, an increase in such clauses was usual. When researchers examined standardized reading tests, they found that the proportions of relative clauses rose dramatically in fourth-grade materials, which could account for the apparent decline in reading progress of many children in the fourth grade: the children's inability to deal with these syntactic patterns may affect their scores. Procedures similar to the one described for working with relative clauses that are complete should be repeated with relative clauses that delete linguistic units.

Children should explore other ways in which sentences may be altered and still say the same thing, for example: (1) Jackie kicked the ball. (2) The ball was kicked by Jackie. Here the sentence has been transformed from the active to the passive voice. Children can work on understanding this without using the technical labels. The teacher can show the children a sentence such as "Jamie hit Ronnie," and show them that "Ronnie was hit by Jamie" says the same thing. The structure of both sentences can be discussed. Then the teacher can give the children another sentence, such as "Bob threw the ball," and tell them to write a sentence that says the same thing, but begins with "The ball." The students should discuss their sentences, and the teacher should provide feedback about accuracy. After several such examples, independent practice can take place.

Anaphora refers to "the use of a word as a substitute for a preceding word or group of words" (Harris and Hodges, 1981, p. 15). Both Barnitz (1979) and Irwin (1986) emphasize that anaphora may refer to a word or group of words that comes later in the material. (Harris and Hodges, 1981, label this construction "cataphora.") When the reference goes in this direction, the reading task is more difficult. Pearson and Johnson (1978) have compiled a table of anaphoric relationships that illustrates the breadth of the topic (see Table 5.1).

Teachers will probably need to address in class all forms of anaphora at some point, but the approaches used can be similar. Modeling of the thought processes used is important. Pearson and Johnson's comprehension probes shown in Table 5.1 can be used for discussion purposes and for the basis of practice exercises. Since children frequently have trouble identifying the noun to which a pronoun refers, they need practice in deciding to whom, or to what, pronouns refer. The Model Activity that follows offers ideas for instruction and practice on pronouns.

● *MODEL ACTIVITY: Pronoun Referents*

Write a sentence, such as the following one, containing a pronoun on the chalkboard and read it to the class: "Joan put the license plate on *her* bicycle." Model the process involved in determining the referent in the sentence by saying: "*Her* is a pronoun that stands for a noun [or with younger children, 'a person, place, or thing']. The noun usually comes before the pronoun that stands for it. The two nouns in this sentence that come before *her* are *Joan* and *plate. Her* indicates a woman or a girl.

A plate isn't a woman or a girl, so *her* probably stands for *Joan*." Then write a second
sentence, such as the following one, on the chalkboard: "Since the book was old,
it was hard to replace." Use this sentence to provide guided practice for the
children, and have them support their responses with reasons. Follow the guided
practice with independent practice using other sentences. ●

Problems also sometimes arise when sentences have words that are left out
but are supposed to be "understood." In sentences such as the following,
children need to practice determining what word or words are left out:

1. I have plenty of flower seeds. Do you need any more?
2. Tony knows he shouldn't drink so many soft drinks, but he claims he can't stop.

Once more, teacher explanation and modeling can be followed by guided
and independent practice by the students.

More information on working with anaphora may be found in this chapter
in the section "Interpretive Reading."

Still other sentence factors are sources of difficulty. When short sentences
such as those found in many primary readers are used to make reading
"easier" but in the process leave out the connectives that signal relationships,
students may find the material harder to read than longer sentences with
explicit causal, conditional, and time-sequence relationships. When these are
not explicitly stated, as below,

Because he was angry, he screamed at his brother.

they must be inferred by the reader, as in this example:

He was angry. He screamed at his brother.

Implicit relationships are harder for children to comprehend than explicit
ones. Teachers must be aware of this problem and attempt to help children
deal with it by focusing discussions and questions on implicit connective
relationships and talking about the need to discover them (Irwin, 1980).
More information related to implicit relationships is offered in the discussion
of interpretive reading in this chapter.

Negative constructions can cause students comprehension problems
(Mathewson, 1984). Teachers need to explain that negative sentences deny
something. A particular statement can be made negative in a number of
ways. For example, the following sentences are several ways to negate the
statement, "John plans to finish the work."

1. John does not plan to finish the work.
2. John doesn't plan to finish the work.
3. John never plans to finish the work.

TABLE 5.1 Anaphoric Relations

Relation	Example	Possible Comprehension Probe
1. Pronouns: I, me, we, us, you, he, him, they, them.	Mary has a friend named John. *She* picks *him* up on the way to school. *They* walk home together too.	Who gets picked up? Who picks him up? Name the person who gets picked up.
2. Locative (location) pronouns: here, there.	The team climbed to the top of Mt. Everest. Only a few people have been *there*.	Where have only a few people been? Name the place where only a few people have been.
3. Deleted nouns: usually an adjective serves as the anaphora.	The students scheduled a meeting but only a *few* attended. Apparently *several* went to the beach. *Others* attended a dance in the gym. *Only the most serious* actually came to the meeting. (Notice that each adjective phrase or adjective refers to students.)	Who went to the beach? Who attended the dance in the gym? What does the word *others* refer to?
4. Arithmetic anaphora.	Mary and John entered the building. The *former* is tall and lovely. The *latter* is short and squatty. The *two* make an interesting couple.	Who is tall and lovely? Who makes an interesting couple?
5. Class inclusive anaphora: a superordinate word substitutes for another word.	1. The dog barked a lot. The *animal* must have seen a prowler. 2. The lion entered the clearing. The *big cat* looked graceful as it surveyed its domain. 3. John was awakened by a siren. He thought the *noise* would never stop.	1. What animal must have seen a prowler? What does the word *animal* refer to? 2. What cat looked graceful? What does the word *cat* refer to? 3. What noise did John think would never stop?

210

Type	Examples	Questions
6. Inclusive anaphora: that, this, the idea, the problem, these reasons. Can refer back to an entire phrase, clause, or passage.	1. (After twenty pages discussing the causes of the Civil War.) For *these reasons*, the South seceded from the Union. 2. Someone was pounding on the door. *This* (or *it* surprised Mary. 3. Crime is getting serious in Culver. The police have to do a better job with *this problem*. 4. "Do unto others as you would have them do unto you." *Such an idea* has been the basis of Christian theology for 2000 years.	1. Why did the South secede from the Union? 2. What surprised Mary? 3. What do the police have to do a better job with? 4. What has been the basis of Christian theology for 2000 years?
7. Deleted predicate adjective: so is, is not, is too (also), *as* is.	1. John is dependable. *So* is Henry. 2. John is dependable. Susan *is not*. 3. The lion was large but graceful. The tiger *was too*. 4. The lion, *as is* the tiger, is large but graceful.	1. Is Henry dependable? 2. Is Susan dependable? 3. Describe the tiger. 4. Describe the tiger.
8. Proverbs: *so does, can, will, have, and so on* (or), *can, does, will too* (or), *can, does, will not, as did, can, will.*	1. John went to school. *So did* Susan. 2. John went to school. Susan *did too*. 3. Henry will get an A. *So will* Theresa. 4. Amy can do a cartwheel. Matthew *cannot*. 5. Mom likes bologna. Dad *does not*. 6. John likes, *as does* Henry, potato chips.	1. What did Susan do? 2. What did Susan do too? 3. What will Theresa do? 4. Can Matthew do a cartwheel? What can't Matthew do? 5. Does Dad like bologna? 6. What does Henry like? Does Henry like potato chips?

Source: TEACHING READING COMPREHENSION by P. David Pearson and Dale D. Johnson. Copyright © 1978 by Holt, Rinehart and Winston, Inc. Reprinted by permission of Holt, Rinehart and Winston, Inc.

212

Teaching
Reading in
Today's
Elementary
Schools

4. John plans to leave the work unfinished.
5. John does not intend to complete the work.
6. John hardly plans to finish the work.

Students may be less familiar with negation that is accomplished without use of the word *not*, and they may need help in recognizing this condition. They also need to recognize *not* in its contracted form.

Teachers should model both negative and affirmative sentences for the students, discuss the characteristics of each type of sentence, provide children with practice in negating affirmative statements, provide them with practice in recognizing negative and affirmative statements in print, and allow them to write negative sentences with different structures, as was shown above. Practice with negative constructions should continue with exposure to them in extended contexts of more than one sentence.

Punctuation

Punctuation can greatly affect the meaning conveyed by a sentence: it represents pauses and pitch changes that would occur if the passage were read aloud. While punctuation marks imperfectly represent the inflections in speech, they greatly aid in turning written language into oral language.

A period occurs at the end of a statement, a question mark at the end of an interrogative sentence, and an exclamation point at the end of an emphatic utterance. All of these punctuation marks signal a pause between sentences and also alter the meaning:

He's a crook. (Making a statement)
He's a crook? (Asking a question)
He's a crook! (Showing surprise or dismay at the discovery)

Commas and dashes indicate pauses within sentences and are often used to set off explanatory material from the main body of the sentence. Commas are also used to separate items in a series or to separate main clauses joined by coordinate conjunctions.

To help students see how punctuation can affect the meaning of the material, use sentences such as the following:

Mother said, "Joe could do it."
Mother said, "Joe could do it?"
"Mother," said Joe, "could do it."

We had ice cream and cake.
We had ice, cream, and cake.
We had ice cream and cake?

Discuss the differences in meaning among each set of sentences, highlighting the function of each punctuation mark.

Underlining and italics, which are frequently used to indicate that a word or group of words is to be stressed, are also clues to underlying meaning. For example, here are several stress patterns for a single sentence:

> *Pat* ate a snail.
> Pat *ate* a snail.
> Pat ate *a* snail.
> Pat ate a *snail.*

In the first example, the stress immediately indicates that Pat, and not anyone else, ate the snail. In variation two, stressing the word *ate* shows that the act of eating the snail was of great importance. In variation three, the writer indicates that only one snail was eaten, whereas the last variation implies that eating a snail was unusual and that the word *snail* is more important than the other words in the sentence.

Teachers need to be sure that children are aware of the aids to comprehension found in punctuation and that they practice interpreting these marks.

✔ Self-Check: Objective 2

Explain how children can discover essential parts of sentences by writing them in telegram form. Also, explain how children can break down complex sentences in order to discover the information included in them. Discuss the effect of punctuation marks on the meaning of sentences.

Paragraphs

Paragraphs are groups of sentences that serve a particular function within a whole selection or passage. They may be organized around a main idea or topic. Understanding their functions, their general organization, and the relationships between the sentences in a paragraph is important to reading comprehension.

Teaching students to make use of paragraphs that have specific functions can be beneficial. For example, students can be alerted to the fact that one or more *introductory paragraphs* inform the reader of the topics that will be covered in a selection. They usually occur at the beginnings of whole selections or major subdivisions of lengthy readings.

If children are searching for a discussion of a particular topic, they can check the introductory paragraph(s) of a selection to determine whether they need to read the entire selection. The "Introduction" sections that accompany each chapter in this book are intended to be used in this manner. Introductory paragraphs can also help readers establish a proper mental set for the material

214

Teaching
Reading in
Today's
Elementary
Schools

to follow; they may offer a framework for categorizing the facts that readers will encounter in the selection.

Summary paragraphs occur at the ends of whole selections or major subdivisions and summarize what has gone on before, stating the main points of the selection in a concise manner and omitting explanatory material and supporting details. They offer a tool for rapid review of the material. Students should be encouraged to use these paragraphs to check their memory for the important points in the selection.

Paragraph Patterns

The internal organization of paragraphs in informational material can have a variety of patterns (for example, listing, chronological order, comparison and contrast, and cause and effect). In addition, paragraphs of each of these types also generally have an underlying organization of main idea plus supporting details. Students' comprehension of informational material can be increased if they learn these paragraph patterns. Kaiden and Rice (1986) suggest having students look at different figures with geometric shapes and try to reproduce the figures. For example, two such figures might be:

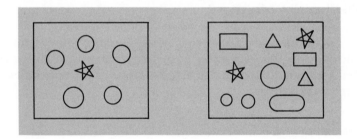

Patterned and unpatterned number sequences may also be used. In both cases, students will discover that patterned sequences are easier to remember than unpatterned ones. Then teachers can present related and unrelated lists of words to the children, and the children will discover that related words are easier to remember. These experiences prepare the students for the presentation of paragraph patterns. The Model Activities that follow show two examples of teaching procedures for paragraph patterns.

● **MODEL ACTIVITY:** *Chronological Order Paragraphs*

Write the following paragraph on the chalkboard:

    Jonah wanted to make a peanut butter sandwich. First, he gathered the necessary materials—peanut butter, bread, and knife. Then he took two slices of bread out of the package and opened the peanut butter jar. Next he dipped the knife into the peanut butter, scooping up some. Then he spread the peanut butter on one of the slices of bread. Finally, he placed the other slice of bread on the peanut butter he had spread, and he had a sandwich.

Discuss the features of this paragraph, pointing out the functions of the sequence words, such as *first, then, next,* and *finally.* Make a list on the board, showing the sequence of events, numbering them appropriately, or you may number them directly above their positions in the paragraph. Next, using another passage of the same type, have the students discover the sequence under your direction. Sequence words should receive attention during this discussion also. Then have the students practice detecting sequence in other paragraphs that you have duplicated for independent practice. Discuss these independent practice paragraphs in class after the students have completed the exercises. ●

● *MODEL ACTIVITY: Cause-and-Effect Paragraphs*

Write the following paragraph on the chalkboard:

Jean lifted the box and started for the door. Because she could not see where her feet were landing, she tripped on her brother's fire truck.

Discuss the cause-and-effect relationship presented in this paragraph by saying: "The effect is the thing that happened, and the cause is the reason for the effect. The thing that happened in this paragraph was that Jean tripped on the fire truck. The cause was that she could not see where her feet were landing. The word *because* helps me to see that cause."

Then use other cause-and-effect paragraphs with different key words (such as *since* or *as a result of*), or with no key words at all, for discussion, and provide the students with practice related to this paragraph pattern. ●

Teaching Main Ideas To understand written selections fully and to summarize long selections, children must be able to determine the main ideas of paragraphs. Teachers should provide them with opportunities to practice recognizing main ideas and help them to realize the following facts:

1. A topic sentence often states the main idea of the paragraph.
2. The topic sentence is often, though not always, the first sentence in the paragraph; sometimes it appears at the end or in the middle.
3. Not all paragraphs have topic sentences.
4. The main idea is supported by all of the details in a well-written paragraph.
5. When the main idea is not directly stated, readers can determine it by discovering the topic to which all of the stated details are related.

Donlan (1980) recommends a three-stage process for teaching the relationships in paragraphs and helping students locate main ideas. First he suggests exercises related to word relationships: equal relationships, such as *general*

216

Teaching
Reading in
Today's
Elementary
Schools

and *admiral;* opposite relationships, such as *war* and *peace;* superior/subordinate relationships, such as *corporal* and *private;* and no relationship, such as *tank* and *porch.* Next the teacher should use exercises on sentence relationships, which fall into the same four types. Finally students should try exercises dealing with complete paragraphs, analyzing them by examining the relationships among their sentences. The superior/subordinate relationships found in the paragraphs represent the main idea and supporting details. Consider the following paragraph:

> My brothers all joined the armed forces. Tom joined the Army. Robert joined the Navy. Bill became a Marine.

This paragraph could be diagrammed as follows:

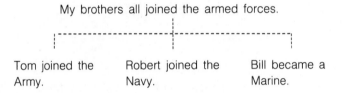

Exercises such as those below are helpful in giving pupils practice in locating main ideas in paragraphs.

● **WORKSHEET:** *Topic Sentences*

Directions: In the following paragraph, underline the sentence that states the main idea.

Edward Fong is a solid citizen of this city and this state. He is well educated, and he keeps his knowledge of governmental processes up-to-date. He has served our city well as a mayor for the past two years, exhibiting his outstanding skills as an administrator. Edward Fong has qualities that make him an excellent choice as our party's candidate for governor. ●

● **WORKSHEET:** *Unstated Main Ideas*

Directions: In the following paragraph, the main idea is implied rather than directly stated. On the line following the paragraph, write the main idea.

Scenic Lake is crowded each year with enthusiastic vacationers. The lake is extremely large and is an ideal place for water-skiing. It abounds with numerous varieties of fish and has an abundant supply of quiet inlets. The water is practically free of pollutants, making swimming a pleasant experience. Roped-off areas are available for swimmers, and lifeguards are provided by the state. The grounds near the swimming areas are supplied with picnic tables and grills.

Main idea: _____ ●

Directions: Read the following paragraph. Decide on a good title for it and place the title on the line provided.

_____ (Title)

   Johnny's teddy bear was five years old. It had dirty brown fur that was torn in two places. The cotton stuffing was visible at the torn spots. At one time there had been two button eyes, but only one was left. In spite of the bear's bad appearance, Johnny refused to throw him away. ●

✓ Self-Check: Objective 3
How can teachers help children understand paragraph patterns and recognize the main ideas of paragraphs?

Whole Selections

Entire selections consist of words, sentences, and paragraphs, and understanding of whole selections depends upon understanding the smaller units.

   Narrative (storylike) selections are generally composed of a series of narrative paragraphs, which present the unfolding of a plot. Though they are usually arranged in chronological order, paragraphs may be flashbacks, or narrations of events from an earlier time, to provide the reader with background information he or she needs to understand the current situation.

   Expository (explanatory) selections are composed of a variety of types of paragraphs, usually beginning with an introductory paragraph and primarily composed of a series of topical paragraphs, with transition paragraphs to indicate shifts from one line of thought to another and illustrative paragraphs to provide examples to clarify the ideas. These selections generally conclude with summary paragraphs, which present the main points of the selection in a concise manner. If a selection is extremely long, it may include summary paragraphs at the ends of the main subdivisions, as well as at the end of the entire work.

   The topical paragraphs within an expository selection are logically arranged in order to carry the reader through the author's presentation of an idea or process. Since the writer's purpose will dictate the order in which he or she arranges the material, a number of different types of organization are possible.

1. *Chronological order.* In some selections, events are presented in the order in which they occur.
2. *Cause-and-effect organization.* Some selections emphasize causes and effects. For example, a history textbook might present the causes of the Civil War and lead the reader to see that the war was the effect of these causes.
3. *Comparison-and-contrast organization.* Some written materials make points through comparison and contrast. For example, social studies materials

218

Teaching
Reading in
Today's
Elementary
Schools

may compare and contrast life in another country with life in the United States, or life in the past with present-day life.

4. *Enumeration.* Some selections are primarily lists of points that support the main idea. Material designed to explain how consumers can save energy might contain phrases such as "One way to help," "A second way," "Still another possibility," and so on.

5. *Topical order.* Some written material is organized around specific topics. For example, this textbook has a topical arrangement.

At times a writer may use more than one form of organization in a single selection, such as chronological order and cause-and-effect organization in history materials.

✔ Self-Check: Objective 4
**Name five ways in which entire selections are often organized.
(See Self-Improvement Opportunity 2.)**

To encourage comprehension of whole selections, teachers usually incorporate prereading, during reading, and postreading activities into the lessons. Some techniques include activities for more than one of these lesson parts.

Prereading Strategies and Activities

Prereading activities are often intended to activate students' problem-solving behavior and their motivation to examine the material (Tierney and Cunningham, 1984). The making of predictions in the Directed Reading-Thinking Activity described in Chapter 6 is a good example of this type of activity. These activities also can serve to activate schemata related to the subject of the text or the type of text to be read to enhance comprehension of the material, and they can actually be used to build background for topics covered by the reading material.

Previews Story previews, which contain information related to story content, can be beneficial to comprehension of the stories. Research has shown that having students read story previews designed partially to build background knowledge about the stories increased students' learning from the selections impressively (Tierney and Cunningham, 1984). Explanations using analogies have often been used to connect the familiar background experiences to the unfamiliar material to be read. Analogies vary in usefulness according to the degree to which they fit the situation. Students may also fail to use analogies unless they are prompted to do so, and they may need specific instruction in understanding analogies. (See Chapter 4 for more on analogies.)

Research has also indicated that story previews can help students make inferences when they read. The previews help children to activate their prior knowledge and to focus their attention before reading (Tierney and Cunningham, 1984).

Computer Use   Computer simulation programs, which provide models of actual activities, can provide students with background experiences as well as with motivation to do the reading required to complete the program activities (Balajthy, 1984). These programs are often available for content area topics, such as running a business or a country or performing a scientific experiment. They may be used before reading in these areas to build and/or activate schemata, just as written previews are used.

Anticipation Guides   Anticipation guides can be useful prereading devices. Designed to stimulate thinking, they consist of declarative statements, some of which may not be true, related to the material about to be read. Before the children read the story, they respond to the statements according to their own experiences (Wiesendanger, 1985). After reading, they discuss the statements again. An example of an anticipation guide for the story "The Little Red Hen" follows:

Anticipation Guide
1. You should have to work for your rewards.
2. You should be generous to others with your possessions.
3. It is important to cooperate to get work done in the fastest and easiest way.
4. Some people should work to support others who do not want to work.

VLP   Wood and Robinson (1983) suggest an approach to prereading activities that they call the VLP (vocabulary, oral language, and prediction) approach. They assert that the important vocabulary in a reading selection can be used to predict the content of the selection. Prediction of the content provides the students with a valid purpose for reading: verifying their predictions.

When using the VLP approach, the teacher determines the important and difficult words in a selection to be read, thinks of ways to associate the decoding skills the students know or are being taught with the chosen words, makes flash cards with the chosen words or writes them on the board, and plans oral language activities that emphasize the structural and conceptual elements of the words. For example, the students may be asked to find synonyms, antonyms, and homonyms for the words. They may place the words in categories and use the words in oral cloze activities (filling in omitted words in sentences). Students may analyze the structure of the words and look them up in the dictionary. When the children understand the meanings of all the selected words, the teacher asks them to predict what the story is about or what will happen next, based on the words that will appear in the selection. The children should then confirm, deny, or change their predictions as the reading takes place.

220

Teaching
Reading in
Today's
Elementary
Schools

Semantic Mapping   Semantic mapping is a good prereading strategy because it introduces important vocabulary that will be encountered in the passage and activates students' schemata related to the topic of the reading assignment. This makes possible the students' connecting of new information in the assignment to their prior knowledge. The procedure also may provide them with motivation to read the selection (Johnson, Pittelman, and Heimlich, 1986). (Semantic mapping receives attention in Chapter 4.)

During Reading Strategies and Activities

Metacognition   Recently there has been much attention given to students' use of metacognitive strategies during reading. Certainly, effective use of metacognitive techniques has a positive effect upon comprehension. Since the learning of metacognitive strategies is very much a study skill, this topic will be covered in detail in Chapter 7. Some information related to the use of metacognitive skills during reading as an aid to comprehension is included here to show the interrelationships of these two aspects of reading.

Metacognition refers to a person's knowledge of the intellectual functioning of his or her own mind and that person's conscious efforts to monitor or control this functioning. It involves analyzing the way that thinking takes place. In reading tasks, the reader who displays metacognition selects skills and reading techniques that fit the particular reading task (Babbs and Moe, 1983).

Part of the metacognitive process is deciding what type of task is needed to achieve understanding. The reader needs to ask: "Is the answer I need stated directly?"; "Does the text imply the answer by giving strong clues that help determine it?"; or "Does the answer have to come from my own knowledge and ideas as they relate to the story?" If the answer to the first question is "yes," the reader looks for the author's exact words for an answer. If the answer to the second question is "yes," the reader searches for clues related to the question and reasons about the information provided to determine an answer. If the answer to the third question is "yes," the reader relates what he or she knows and thinks about the topic to the information given and includes both sources of information in the reasoning process in order to come to a decision about an answer. (See Poindexter and Prescott, 1986, for specific application.)

Good readers monitor their comprehension constantly, and they take steps to correct situations when they fail to comprehend. They may reread passages or adjust their reading techniques or rates. Poor readers, on the other hand, often fail to monitor their understanding of the text read. They make fewer spontaneous corrections in oral reading than do good readers and also correct miscues that affect meaning less frequently than do good readers. They seem to regard reading as a decoding process, whereas good readers see it as a comprehension-seeking process (Bristow, 1985).

Palincsar and Brown (1986) suggest use of reciprocal teaching to promote comprehension and comprehension monitoring. In this technique the teacher

and the students take turns being the "teacher." The "teacher" leads the
discussion of material that the students are reading. The participants have four common goals: "predicting, question generating, summarizing, and clarifying" (p. 772). Predictions made by the students provide them with a purpose for reading—to test their predictions. Text features such as headings and subheadings help students form predictions. Question generation provides a basis for self-testing and interaction with others in the group. Summarizing, which can be a joint effort, helps students to integrate the information presented. Clarifying calls attention to reasons why the material may be hard to understand. Students are encouraged to reread or ask for help when their need for clarification becomes obvious.

If reciprocal teaching is used, the teacher must explain to the students each component strategy and the reason for it. Instruction in each strategy is important. At first, the teacher leads the discussion, modeling the strategies for the children. The children add their predictions, clarifications, and comments on the teacher's summaries and respond to the teacher's questions. Gradually the responsibility for the process is transferred from the teacher to the students. The teacher participates, but the students take on the "teacher" role too. The interactive aspect of this procedure is very important.

Palincsar and Brown (1986) found that reciprocal teaching resulted in improved comprehension and that students applied the skills learned through this teaching to content area reading, resulting in better performance in both social studies and science. This technique has proved successful in classes with as many as eighteen students, as well as in small groups. Reciprocal teaching has also proved successful in peer tutoring situations in which there is close teacher supervision.

Questions   During reading, guiding questions are often used to enhance comprehension. Research indicates that questions inserted by the teacher when students are reading seem to facilitate comprehension (Tierney and Cunningham, 1984). Some authorities have suggested that the extensive use of self-questioning while reading also will facilitate comprehension. Although this approach may hold promise, information from the research on the effectiveness of self-questioning is conflicting and incomplete (Tierney and Cunningham, 1984). (Questioning techniques are covered in detail later in this chapter.)

Shoop (1986) describes the Investigative Questioning Procedure (InQuest), a comprehension strategy that encourages reader interaction with text. The technique, which combines student questioning with creative drama, is used in the following way. The teacher stops the reading at a critical point in the story; one student takes the role of a major character; and other students take the role of investigative reporters "on the scene." The reporters question the character with interpretive and evaluative questions about story events. More than one character may be interviewed to delve into different viewpoints. Then the children resume reading, although the teacher may interrupt it

222

Teaching
Reading in
Today's
Elementary
Schools

several more times for other "news conferences." When first introducing the procedure, the teacher may occasionally participate as a story character or as a reporter in order to model the processes involved. The class should evaluate the process when the entire story has been covered.

InQuest lets students monitor comprehension. They actively keep up with "what is known." Before this procedure can be effective, however, students must have had some training in question generation. One means to accomplish such training is to give students opportunities to view and evaluate actual questioning sessions on news shows. They need to learn to ask questions that produce information, evaluations, and predictions; and they need to try to ask a variety of types of questions and to use *why* questions judiciously to elicit more in-depth responses.

Cloze Procedure   The cloze procedure is sometimes used as a strategy for teaching comprehension. When using the cloze procedure, the teacher deletes some information from a passage and asks students to fill it in as they read, utilizing their knowledge of syntax, semantics, and graphic clues. Cloze tasks can involve deletions of letters, word parts, whole words, phrases, clauses, or whole sentences. In macrocloze activities, even entire story parts are deleted. The deletions are generally made for specific purposes to focus upon particular skills. When a whole word is deleted and a standard-sized blank is left, the readers must use semantic and syntactic clues to decide on a replacement. If the blanks are varied in length, according to word length, word recognition skill also can be incorporated. If a short underline is provided for each letter, additional clues become available, and the task of exact replacement becomes easier. However, the discussion of alternatives when standard-sized blanks are used can be extremely beneficial in developing comprehension skills. Although random or regularly spaced deletions can be helpful in encouraging students to make predictions and confirm predictions based on their language knowledge, such systems of deletion will not focus on a particular skill. Discussion of alternative answers is very important in cloze instruction with any deletion pattern that is used, but some cloze tasks provide more varied possibilities than do others (Schoenfeld, 1980; Valmont, 1983). Teachers should always elicit reasons for use of particular choices and should give positive reinforcement for good reasoning.

When preparing a cloze passage designed for teaching, rather than testing, teachers should leave the initial and final sentences of the selection intact and delete no more than 10 percent of the words. They can choose passages of any length. Cloze lessons can focus on any specific comprehension skill, such as relating pronouns to their referents, but they should only be used after the teacher gives instruction about the skill (Schoenfeld, 1980).

When multiple-choice answers are provided for completing passages, the task is not a true cloze procedure, but is referred to as a maze procedure. Maze techniques are probably less effective in encouraging learners to use their linguistic resources (Valmont, 1983).

In postreading activities children should be given an opportunity to decide what else they would like to know about the topic and where they can find out more (Crafton, 1982). They may read about the topic and share their findings with the class.

Whereas prereading questions may focus children's learning more than postreading questions, there are indications that postreading questions may facilitate learning for all information in the text. There appears to be an advantage to using higher-level, application-type, and structurally important questions. Children obtain greater gains from postreading questions if feedback on answers is provided, especially feedback on incorrect answers (Tierney and Cunningham, 1984).

A good postreading activity for use with content area selections that explain how to do something (for example, how to work a particular type of mathematics problem or how to perform a science experiment) is to have the students perform the task, applying the information that was read. Postreading activities that are often appropriate for reading in the area of social studies are construction of time lines of events included in the reading selection and construction of maps of areas discussed. Many of the activities included under "Creative Reading" in this chapter are good postreading activities that ask the student to go beyond the material just read and create something new based upon the reading.

General Strategies and Activities

Semantic Webbing and Story Mapping "Semantic webbing is a process for constructing visual displays of categories and their relationships" (Freedman and Reynolds, 1980, p. 877) that can help students organize and integrate concepts. Each web consists of a core question, strands, strand supports, and strand ties. The teacher chooses a core question, which becomes the center of the web, to which the entire web is related. The students' answers are web strands; facts and inferences taken from the story and students' experiences are the strand supports; and the relationships of the strands to each other are strand ties. Example 5.2 shows a semantic web based on "How D. Y. B. Worked for April," an excerpt from *Bright April,* by Marguerite de Angeli, included in the basal reader *Panorama* (Houghton Mifflin, 1974). In preparing to construct this web, children were given the task of reading a portion of the story to predict what would happen next. The core question focuses on this. Students answered the question, and their answers became web strands (for example, "cry") if the other children judged them reasonable. Support for strands was drawn from the story and from their experiences. The support was also accepted or excluded according to the class's evaluation. If strands were found to be unsupportable, they were rejected at this point, just before the strands were related through strand ties (shown in the example with

224 ▶ **EXAMPLE 5.2:** Semantic Web

Teaching
Reading in
Today's
Elementary
Schools

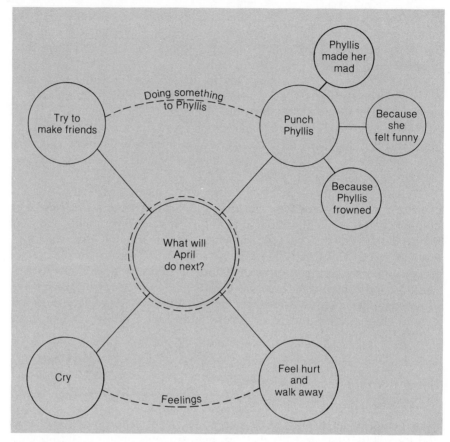

Source: Reprinted with permission of Glenn Freedman and Elizabeth Reynolds and the International Reading Association. ◀

broken lines). The web was then used as a basis for further activity, such as reading the end of the story to see what really happened (Freedman and Reynolds, 1980).

Story maps, which are visual representations of stories that resemble semantic maps or webs, help readers perceive the way their reading material is organized. They can be used as advance organizers for a story that is about to be read or as a means to focus postreading discussion. When the story map is used as an advance organizer, the students may try to predict the contents of the story from it and then read to confirm or reject their predictions. Students may also refer to the map as reading progresses to help them keep their thoughts organized. After reading, the students could try to reconstruct the map from memory or could just discuss it and its relationship to story events (Reutzel, 1985).

In story maps, specific relationships of story elements are made clear. Main ideas and sequences, comparisons of characters, and cause-effect relationships are some of the features of stories that can be shown in maps (Reutzel, 1985).

Reutzel (1985) compared the effectiveness of using story maps as part of a basal reader lesson to use of a regular directed reading activity. He found the lessons using story maps to be effective in improving comprehension of narrative and expository text.

Cloze story maps can be useful in comprehension instruction (Reutzel, 1986). To make a cloze story map, the teacher first puts the main idea in the center of the map; then connects key words for major concepts or events symmetrically around the main idea in a clockwise direction; and finally places subevents and subconcepts around the major concepts or events to which they relate, also in a clockwise order. Then the teacher deletes every fifth item in the map, again moving in a clockwise direction around events and their subevents. Such a deletion pattern is illustrated in Example 5.3.

▶ **EXAMPLE 5.3:** Sample Deletion Pattern for a Cloze Story Map

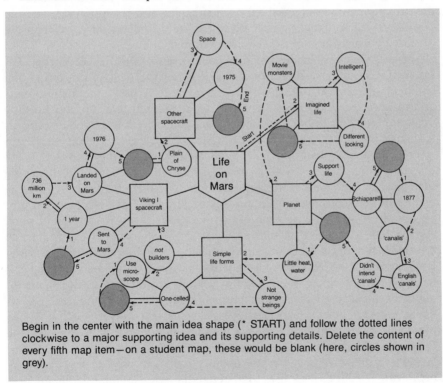

Begin in the center with the main idea shape (* START) and follow the dotted lines clockwise to a major supporting idea and its supporting details. Delete the content of every fifth map item—on a student map, these would be blank (here, circles shown in grey).

Source: Reprinted with permission of D. Ray Reutzel and the International Reading Association. ◀

226

Teaching
Reading in
Today's
Elementary
Schools

The teacher can introduce the cloze map in the prereading stage and discuss it with the students, having them speculate about the material that has been deleted. Then the teacher can give the students reproductions of the cloze map to fill in as they read the passage. After the reading, correct information for deleted items can be discussed. The teacher may then wish to see if the students can reproduce the map from memory, allowing them to self-check their responses (Reutzel, 1986).

Story Grammar and Story Frame Activities A story schema is a person's mental representation of story structures and the way they are related. Knowledge of such structures appears to facilitate both comprehension and recall of stories. The reading-writing connection is evident from the fact that children's written stories can serve as a source for understanding their concepts of story. Children's retellings of stories also reveal story knowledge (Golden, 1984).

A story grammar provides rules that define these story structures. Jean Mandler and Nancy Johnson developed a story grammar that includes six major structures: setting, beginning, reaction, attempt, outcome, and ending (Whaley, 1981). In a simplified version of Perry Thorndyke's story grammar, the structures are setting, characters, theme, plot, and resolution (McGee and Tompkins, 1981). Teachers may be able to help students develop a concept of story by using these or other story grammars.

There are many activities teachers could use to develop the concept. For instance, they may read stories and talk about the structure in terms that children understand (folktales and fairy tales have easily identifiable parts and make good choices), or they may have children retell stories. Reading or listening to stories and predicting what comes next is a good activity, as is discussion of the predicted parts. Teachers may give students stories in which whole sections are left out, indicated by blank lines in place of the material (macrocloze activity), and ask students to supply the missing material and then discuss the appropriateness of their answers. By dividing a story into different categories and scrambling the parts, teachers can provide students with the opportunity to rearrange the parts to form a good story. Or they can give all the sentences in the story on strips of paper to the children and ask them to put together the ones that fit (Whaley, 1981). Each student may start by writing a setting for a story; then the paper is passed to a classmate who adds a beginning and passes the paper to another classmate. Reactions, attempts, outcomes, and endings, respectively, are added as the papers are passed to each successive student. When the stories are complete, they are read aloud to the class (Spiegel and Fitzgerald, 1986).

Fowler (1982) suggests the use of story frames to provide a structure for organizing a reader's responses to material that is read. Frames are sequences of blanks linked by transition words that reflect a line of thought. Frames like the ones in Example 5.4 can be used with a variety of selections.

▶ **EXAMPLE 5.4:** Story Frames

Figure 1
Story summary with one character included

Our story is about _____. _____ is an important
character in our story. _____ tried to _____. The
story ends when _____.

Figure 2
Important idea or plot

In this story the problem starts when _____. After that,
_____. Next, _____
_____. Then, _____. The
problem is finally solved when _____. The story ends
_____.

Figure 3
Setting

This story takes place _____. I know this because the
author uses the words "_____." Other clues
that show when the story takes place are _____
_____.

Figure 4
Character analysis

_____ is an important character in our story. _____ is
important because _____. Once, he/she
_____. Another time, _____. I think
that _____ is _____ because _____
   (character's name)   (character trait)
_____.

Figure 5
Character comparison

_____ and _____ are two characters in our story.
_____ is _____ while
   (character's name)   (trait)
_____ is _____. For
   (other character)   (trait)
instance, _____ tries to _____ and _____
tries to _____. _____ learns a lesson when _____
_____.

Source: Reprinted with permission of Gerald L. Fowler and the International Reading Association. ◀

228

Teaching
Reading in
Today's
Elementary
Schools

The frames can be the basis of class discussion of a story that has been read. Because the frames are open-ended, the discussion will include much varied input. The teacher should stress that the information used in subsequent blanks should relate reasonably to the material that came before it. Students may use frames independently after the process has been modeled and practiced in class, and the results may also be discussed by the class. This technique is especially useful with primary-grade students and remedial reading students (Fowler, 1982).

A technique called "probable passages" also makes use of story frames (Wood, 1984). In this procedure the teacher takes words the children are about to read and has the children categorize them under "setting," "characters," "problem," "problem solution," and "ending." Then the teacher sets up a story frame based on these categories and asks the children to predict a story line by placing selected terms in the frame. The class can change this "probable passage" to reflect the story more accurately after reading takes place.

Teaching story parts to less able fourth graders and clarifying temporal and causal relationships among the parts aided both the students' literal and their inferential comprehension of stories (Spiegel and Fitzgerald, 1986). Similarly, instruction in story parts and causal relationships among them resulted in improved story comprehension for learning-handicapped students (Varnhagen and Goldman, 1986). In both cases instruction involved production of story elements, another example of positive use of the reading-writing connection.

To provide independent practice for beginning readers and prereaders, teachers can videotape stories, giving an introduction to the story and the story structure to be studied. The children should receive directions for listening that focus attention on that structure, as well as directions for follow-up activities such as drawing pictures of characters, setting, or resolution; choosing pictures related to theme from several provided by the teacher; and arranging pictures that relate the plot in sequence. To make sure the procedures are clear, the entire group should do the activity under the teacher's direction the first time such tapes are used (McGee and Tompkins, 1981).

Even though there is much interest among educators in the use of story grammars, questions remain about this technique. Results of studies on the effectiveness of story grammar instruction in increasing reading comprehension have been contradictory (Dreher and Singer, 1980; Greenewald and Rossing, 1986; Sebesta, Calder, and Cleland, 1982; and Spiegel and Fitzgerald, 1986). Some have shown positive effects and others have shown no benefits.

Other Story Structure Techniques To help children with comprehension of stories that start and end at the same place, with a series of events in between, the circle story can be effective (Jett-Simpson, 1981; Smith and Bean, 1983). The teacher draws a circle on a large sheet of paper and divides it into the same number of pie-shaped sections as there are events in the story. The teacher reads the story to the children, who then decide upon the events that need to be pictured in each section of the circle. Circle story completion can be done in small groups, with each child responsible for illustrating a different event. If the paper is large, all the children can work at the same time.

Creative dramatics proved to be superior to discussion and drawing for developing story comprehension for kindergartners and first graders (Galda, 1982; Pellegrini and Galda, 1982). Other studies have shown that dramatics can improve readiness, vocabulary development, and oral reading skills of students in kindergarten through junior high school. The active reconstruction of a story through drama focuses children's minds on the characters, setting, and plot of a story. Interpretation conflicts can be resolved through discussion (Miller and Mason, 1983).

Reading-Writing Connection Composition and comprehension both involve planning, composing, and revising. Although it may seem clear what these steps are in composition, their equivalents in reading may be less obvious. Teachers may need to think of the prereading activities related to background building, schema activation, and prediction as the planning phase in comprehension; developing tentative meanings while reading as the composing phase; and revising the meanings when new information is acquired as the revision phase. Many writing acts that accompany comprehension instruction are composition activities (Pearson, 1985). Writing story predictions based upon questioning or prereading word webs is an example of writing in the prereading phase. Note-taking during reading may be in the form of outlines or series of summary statements (another obvious link between reading and writing activities). Macrocloze activities related to story grammars and the use of story frames are other ways that writing can be used to enhance reading. Interpretive reading activities, such as rewriting sentences containing figurative expressions into literal forms and rewriting sentences containing pronouns by using their referents instead, are composition activities. Many writing activities are a part of creative reading instruction. Several of these are mentioned in the section on creative reading in this chapter under the heading "Producing New Creations." More on the reading-writing connection can be found in Chapters 1, 6, 8, and 9.

Listening-Reading Transfer Lesson A listening-reading transfer lesson can also be useful in improving comprehension skills. In such a lesson, the teacher asks students to listen to a selection and respond to a purpose (such as determining sequence of events) that he or she has set. As the class discusses the detected sequence, the teacher provides guidance, helps children explain how they made their decisions, and rereads the material if it is necessary to resolve controversies. Then the children read a different selection for the same purpose, and a similar follow-up discussion is conducted. Teachers can use this type of lesson with any comprehension skill (Cunningham, 1982).

230

Teaching
Reading in
Today's
Elementary
Schools

✔ **Self-Check: Objective 5**

Describe some good prereading, during reading, and postreading activities for promoting comprehension.
(See Self-Improvement Opportunities 3 and 4.)

TYPES OF COMPREHENSION

Readers employ a number of types of comprehension in order to understand fully what they read. To take in ideas that are directly stated is literal comprehension; to read between the lines is interpretive comprehension; to read for evaluation is critical reading; and to read beyond the lines is creative reading. Perhaps because literal comprehension is easiest to attain, teachers have given it a disproportionate amount of attention in the classroom; but children need to achieve higher levels of reading comprehension to become informed and effective citizens.

Literal Reading

Reading for literal comprehension, which involves acquiring information that is directly stated in a selection, is important in and of itself and is also a prerequisite for higher-level understanding. Examples of the skills involved are the ability to follow directions and the ability to restate the author's material in other words. For instance, if the author wrote, "The man's tattered coat was not effective against the cold," a child could show evidence of literal comprehension by saying, "The man's ragged coat didn't keep him warm."

Recognizing *stated* main ideas, details, causes and effects, and sequences is the basis of literal comprehension. Exercises for developing literal comprehension include those described earlier under "Units of Comprehension," as well as those below.

Details

The specific, explicitly stated parts of a paragraph or passage that contain the basic information are the details upon which main ideas, cause-and-effect relationships, inferences, and so on are built. For example, in the sentence "The man wore a red hat," the fact that a red hat was being worn is one detail that readers can note.

In order to locate details effectively, students may need some direction about the types of details signaled by specific questions. For example, a *who* question asks for the name or identification of a person, or sometimes an animal; a *what* question asks for a thing or event; a *where* question asks for a place; a *when* question asks for a time; a *how* question asks for the way something is or was accomplished; and a *why* question asks for the reason for something. After discussing these question words and their meanings, the teacher can model for the students the location of answers to each type of question in a passage displayed on the chalkboard or a transparency. Then the students can use a worksheet such as the one below to practice the skill. The teacher should provide feedback on the correctness of responses as expediently as possible after the students complete the worksheet.

● **WORKSHEET:** *Locating Details in a Newspaper Story*

Directions: Read this newspaper article and answer the questions.

Jane and John Stone, who own the local grocery, had one hundred dollars stolen from them as they left the store last night at eleven o'clock. The robber stepped from behind a shrub outside the door of the grocery store and pulled a gun from his pocket, saying, "Hand over that cash sack!" Stone handed the robber the sack of money he had just removed from the cash register, and the man turned and fled, leaving both Mr. and Mrs. Stone unharmed.

1. Who was involved in this event?
2. What took place?
3. Where did it take place?
4. When did it take place?
5. How or why did it take place? ●

Some activities for developing the skill of locating details are presented below. (Recognizing details is also important in completing exercises under the topics "Sequence" and "Following Directions.")

ACTIVITIES

1. After students have read a paragraph, ask them questions for which the answers are directly stated in the paragraph. Have them show where the answers were found in the paragraph.

   Tom's favorite toy was his dump truck. Although Tom was usually a generous boy, he never offered to let anyone else play with the truck. He had had the truck for three years, and it was still as good as new. Tom was afraid that other children would be careless with his toy.

   a. What was Tom's favorite toy?
   b. Describe the condition of Tom's toy.
   c. How long had Tom had his favorite toy?

2. Give the children a set of directions, and have them number the important details (or steps), as in the following example. Go through one or more examples before you ask them to work alone.

232

Teaching
Reading in
Today's
Elementary
Schools

To make a good bowl of chili, first (1) sauté the onions for about ten minutes. Then (2) add the ground beef and brown it. (3) Stir the mixture frequently so that it will not burn. Finally, (4) add the tomatoes, tomato sauce, Mexican-style beans, salt, pepper, and chili powder. (5) Cook over low heat for forty-five minutes to one hour.

3. Make some copies of a menu. After showing pupils how to locate items and prices, ask them to read it and answer specific questions such as these:

   a. What is the price of a soft drink?
   b. Can you order a baked potato separately? If so, under what heading is it found?
   c. What else do you get when you order a rib steak?
   d. How many desserts are available?

4. Using a description like the one below and reading each step aloud, draw an object on the board. Then give the children a written description of another object and ask them to draw it.

   The flower has five oval petals. The petals are red. The center, at which the petals meet, is brown. The flower has a long green stem. At the bottom of the stem are overlapping blade-shaped leaves, which are half as tall as the stem.

5. Have the children read paragraphs from newspaper articles and answer literal questions. Newspaper articles are good for practice of this sort, since lead paragraphs tend to include information about *who, what, where, when, why,* and *how.*

Main Ideas

As was discussed earlier, the main idea of a paragraph is the central thought around which a whole paragraph is organized. It is often, but not always, expressed in a topic sentence in expository writing; in narrative writing even fewer explicitly stated topic sentences will be found.

Finding the main idea in whole selections of nonfiction generally is a categorizing process in which the topic is located and the information given about the topic is then examined (Moldofsky, 1983). In fiction, however, there is not a "topic" but a central problem, which is rarely stated explicitly. Therefore, in this section the activities for locating directly stated main ideas will focus on expository writing.

Different people mean different things when they request main ideas from students, and, when asked to give the main idea of a passage, some students produce topics, some topic sentences, and some brief summaries. However, a description of the task that is expected may be all they need to cause them to produce the desired response (Moore and Cunningham, 1984).

A topic merely identifies the subject matter; a main idea also includes the type of information given about the topic. For example, a topic of a paragraph or selection could be "football," whereas the main idea could be "There are several different ways to score in football."

Some activities for working with directly stated main ideas are given below. Activities for working with implied main ideas are found under the heading "Interpretive Reading."

ACTIVITIES

1. Demonstrate the idea that the topic sentence is the main idea and that the other sentences in the paragraph relate to it by taking a paragraph, locating the topic sentence, and showing the relationship of each of the other sentences to the topic sentence. Then give the students paragraphs and ask them to underline the topic sentence and tell how each of the other sentences relates to it.

2. Have the students read a story that has a clearly stated main idea and point it out, explaining why you chose that idea. Then ask them to read another story, select the main idea from a list of options, and explain why they chose as they did.

3. Gather old newspapers and cardboard for mounting. Tell the children that a rim rat is a newspaper worker who writes headlines and that they will pretend to be "rim rats" in this activity. Cut from the newspaper a number of articles that you feel will be of interest to the children and separate the text of each article from its headline. The child's task is to read each article and locate the most suitable headline for it. Mount article and title on cardboard. To make the task easier, have them match captions to pictures, use very short articles, or use articles that are completely different in subject matter. Discuss the reasons for their choices.

For evaluation purposes, make the activity self-checking by coding articles and headlines. To follow up you might use these ideas: have children make pictures and captions to share in the skills center; write articles and prepare headlines separately and let children match them; have them try to match advertisements to pictures or captions to cartoons.

4. Again working with newspaper articles without titles, have students construct titles using the information in the lead paragraph. Show them how to do this before you ask them to work on the task alone.

234

Teaching
Reading in
Today's
Elementary
Schools

5. Discuss how main headings and subheadings in textbooks give information about the main ideas in sections.

Cause and Effect

Recognizing and understanding a cause-and-effect relationship in a written passage is an important reading skill. It is considered a literal skill when the relationship is explicitly stated ("Bill stayed out *because* he was ill"). Teachers can use the following activities when the cause and the effect are directly stated in the passage; when they are implied, teachers can use procedures similar to the ones listed in the section on interpretive reading.

ACTIVITIES

1. Display (by writing on the board or by showing a transparency) a paragraph that contains a cause-and-effect relationship. Model the process of locating the cause and the effect. Point out clue words, such as *because,* if they are present, but make sure that the students know that they cannot always expect such clues to be present. Then show the children another paragraph. State the cause of the action and have them identify the effect. Discuss the children's responses. A paragraph such as the one below could be used for instruction.

   Bobby, Jill, Leon, and Peggy were playing softball in Bobby's yard. Peggy was up at bat and hit the ball squarely in the direction of Bobby's bedroom window. As the group watched in horror, the softball crashed right through the window, shattering the glass.

   Question: What happened when the softball hit the window?

2. Use the procedure described in the first activity, but describe the effect and have the children identify the cause. Using the same paragraph as an example, the question would be "What made the window break?"

Sequence

Sequence—the order in which events in a paragraph or passage occur—is signaled by time-order words such as *now, before, when, while, yet, after,* and so on. Children must learn to recognize straightforward chronological sequence, as well as flashbacks and other devices that describe events "out of order."

Teachers must model the process of finding the correct sequence of events in a passage for the students before expecting them to locate such sequences independently. Helpful time-order words should be discussed and pointed out in selections. Then students need to engage in practice activities related to this skill.

ACTIVITIES

1. Have the children read a short selection. Then list the events in the selection out of sequence and show students how to reorder them. Using another selection—like that in the Worksheet below—ask the children to list the events in sequence. (Use shorter selections for younger children.)

● **WORKSHEET:** *Placing Story Events in Order*

Directions: Read this story and then place the list of events in order.

We were all excited on Friday morning because we were going to go to the circus. We had trouble concentrating on eating breakfast, but Mother wouldn't allow us to leave the table before we were finished.

Immediately after breakfast we piled into the station wagon. Everyone was talking at once and bouncing around on the seats as Dad started the car and backed out of the driveway. We were making so much noise and moving around so much that Dad didn't hear or see the truck turn the corner. The truck driver honked his horn, but it was too late. Dad backed right into the side of the truck.

The angry driver jumped out of his truck, but when he saw the crowd of us in the station wagon, he calmed down. He and Dad talked to each other for a while, staring at the damaged side of the truck occasionally. Then they went into the house to report the accident to the police.

Mother immediately recovered from the shock and told us to get out of the car. "We'll have a long wait before we will be able to leave," she said.

Story Events
The family got into the station wagon.
The truck driver honked his horn.
The family ate breakfast.
Dad backed out of the driveway.
Dad and the truck driver talked.
Mother told the children to get out of the car.
Dad backed into the side of the truck.
Dad and the truck driver went into the house.
The driver jumped out of his truck.   ●

2. After they have read a selection, ask the children to answer questions about the order of events. For example, using an article entitled "Wars in Which United States Citizens Have Fought," ask the children questions such as "Which came first, the Civil War or the War of 1812?" "Was the Korean Conflict before or after World War II?"

3. Cut the separate frames of comic strips apart, back them with cardboard to make them durable, scramble them, and place them in envelopes; then ask the children to read the separate frames and arrange them in the correct order. If you wish to have students check this activity themselves, indicate the correct

236

Teaching
Reading in
Today's
Elementary
Schools

order by assigning a number to each frame on the back. To vary the difficulty of this task, use some strips that have little or no dialogue, some with a moderate amount, and some with a great deal of dialogue, or strips with different numbers of frames.

4. A similar activity is to cut a story apart so that each paragraph forms a separate section, back the sections with cardboard, scramble them, and give them to pupils to place in the proper sequence. You may put numbers on the backs of the sections to indicate the order if you want students to do a self-check.

5. Help students construct time lines of their lives (Baker, 1982). Parents may be called upon to provide information about the years in which significant events occurred. A time line of a typical day or of the current school year could also be used. Then have the children construct a time line of a story that they have read or listened to in class, using the skill learned by making personal time lines.

6. Give students a passage of text that contains a number of time-order terms and ask them to circle the terms.

Following Directions

The ability to read and follow directions is a prerequisite for virtually all successful schoolwork. This skill is considered a part of literal reading comprehension. It involves understanding details and sequence; therefore, some of the exercises under those headings are appropriate to use in teaching children to follow written directions.

The teacher should take a set of directions for performing a task and should model following these directions carefully, reading the directions aloud as each step is completed and commenting on the meaning of each instruction. Then he or she should follow the directions again, leaving out a vital step. There should be class discussion about the results of not following directions carefully. In addition, the activities below may prove useful.

ACTIVITIES

1. Discuss with the children the functions of such key words as *first, next, last,* and *finally*. Then give them a paragraph containing these words and ask them to underline the words that help to show the order of events.

2. Prepare handouts with uncolored pictures. Have the children color the pictures according to directions such as "Color the girl's sweater red. Color her skirt gray. Color her hair brown."

3. Use a practice sheet similar to the one that follows.

● **WORKSHEET:** *Following Directions*

Directions: Read all of the items before you begin to carry out each instruction. Work as quickly as you can; you have five minutes to finish this activity.

1. Write your name at the top of the paper.
2. Turn the paper over and add 15 and 25. Write the answer you get on this line: _____.
3. Stand up and clap your hands three times.
4. Count the number of times the word *the* is written on this page. Put the answer on this line: _____.
5. Subtract 9 from 99. Put your answer on this line: _____.
6. Go to the board and write your name.
7. Count the people in this room. Put the answer under your name at the top of the page.
8. Now that you have read all of the directions, take your paper to the teacher. It should have no marks on it. ●

4. Make it a practice to refer children to written directions instead of telling them how to do everything orally. Ask them to read the directions silently and then tell you in their own words what they should do.

5. Teach the children the meanings of words commonly encountered in written directions, such as *underline, circle, divide, color, example, left, right, below, over,* and *match.* Other words that might need attention are listed in an article by Newcastle (1974).

6. Write directions for a project and have the students complete the steps (Baker, 1982). Construction and cooking projects, as well as science experiments and magic tricks, can be used. Discussion can center on the results that occur if the correct sequence is not followed. Directions can be cut apart, scrambled, and reconstructed to show comprehension of the necessary sequence.

7. Write directions on slips of paper, place them in a box, and let each child in turn draw a slip of paper and follow the instructions. In the initial stages of learning to follow written directions, each slip should list one step; later, two or more steps may be included per slip. Individualize this activity by giving one-step directions to those who are just beginning to learn to follow directions and multistep directions to those who have acquired some facility.

> Close the door. (one step)
> Walk to the pencil sharpener. Turn around in a circle. (two steps)
> Hop three times on your left foot. Hop two times on your right foot. Bow to the class. (three steps)

✔ Self-Check: Objective 6
Describe a procedure for developing literal comprehension of
1. the main idea.
2. details.
3. cause and effect.
4. sequence.
5. following directions.
(See Self-Improvement Opportunities 5 and 6.)

Interpretive Reading

Interpretive reading involves reading between the lines or making inferences. It is the process of deriving ideas that are implied rather than directly stated. Skills for interpretive reading include

1. inferring main ideas of passages in which the main ideas are not directly stated,
2. inferring cause-and-effect relationships when they are not directly stated,
3. inferring referents of pronouns,
4. inferring referents of adverbs,
5. inferring omitted words,
6. detecting mood,
7. detecting the author's purpose in writing,
8. drawing conclusions, and
9. interpreting figurative language.

A text is never fully explicit. Some relationships among events, motivations of characters, and other factors are left out of texts with the expectation that readers will figure them out on their own. Readers, therefore, have to play an active role in constructing the meanings represented by the text. They must infer the implied information by combining the information in the text with their background knowledge of the world. Stories requiring more inferences are more difficult to read (Carr, 1983; Pearson, 1985).

Lange has pointed out that "readers make inferences consistent with their schemata" (1981, p. 443), but it is important to realize that children have less prior knowledge than adults and do not always make inferences spontaneously, even when they possess the necessary background knowledge.

Even very young children can, during their daily activities, make inferences by connecting new information to information they already possess, but they do not necessarily apply this skill to reading without teacher direction. Active involvement with the printed message enhances the students' abilities to make inferences related to it. Comparing things in students' own lives with things that might occur in stories they are about to read is one way to help them see the thinking processes they should use when they read. Even poor readers show the ability to draw inferences about their reading when such a procedure is used (Hansen and Hubbard, 1984).

Using a group setting in which children heard about each other's experiences, listened to each other's predictions about a story, and then wrote down their own experiences and guesses, Hansen (1981b) found that primary-grade children were able to increase their ability to make inferences about the story. Hansen (1981a) also tested two methods designed to convince children that they can and should make inferences about what they read, drawing from their prior knowledge. The Strategy method employed prereading activities to relate children's knowledge to the text; the Question method provided

practice in answering inferential questions. Using a control group that was
asked to answer primarily literal questions, Hansen found that the Strategy method increased the likelihood that the children would draw inferences spontaneously in the instructional setting, and the Question method also enhanced the children's ability to draw inferences spontaneously.

McIntosh (1985) suggests that teachers should ask first graders to make inferences based only on information located close together in the text. When the information is not adjacent in the text, the teacher can use guiding questions to lead the students to the information. This type of instruction helps students to become aware of the need to search actively for the meaning of written passages. Older children increase in their ability to draw inferences, possibly because of their increased knowledge of the world.

Students are expected to make inferences about a number of things: locations, people who act in certain ways, time, actions, devices or instruments, categories, objects, causes and/or effects, solutions to problems, and feelings. They can relate important vocabulary in the reading material to their backgrounds of experience, in order to make these inferences. First, the teacher should explain how important words in a passage can help in drawing a particular inference about the passage. Then the teacher should provide students with the opportunity to practice and apply this procedure. During the application phase, students are asked to make an inference based on the first sentence and then retain, modify, or reject it as each subsequent sentence is read (Johnson and Johnson, 1986). Such instruction is needed because some students will make hypotheses about the reading material but will fail to modify them when additional information shows them to be incorrect. Instead, they may distort later information in an attempt to make it conform to their original hypotheses. These children may have problems with passages that present one idea and follow it with a contrasting idea or that present an idea and subsequently refute it. They may also have difficulty with passages that give examples of a topic, followed by a topic statement, or with passages that never give a topic statement (Kimmel and MacGinitie, 1985).

Using a passage that contains a word with multiple meanings, asking for possible meanings for the word based on initial sentences, and then reading to confirm or disprove these predictions about meanings can be a good way to help students learn to revise hypotheses when reading. Reading stories written from unusual points of view can also help (for example, "Little Red Riding Hood" rewritten from the wolf's point of view). Introducing students to various organizational patterns for texts, such as the ones mentioned in this chapter under the heading "Whole Selections," can also help (Kimmel and MacGinitie, 1985).

Pearson (1985) succinctly describes a method related to teaching inference skills that was developed by Gordon and Pearson (1983). It is "(1) ask the inference question, (2) answer it, (3) find clues in the text to support the inference, and (4) tell how to get from the clues to the answer (i.e., give a

240

Teaching
Reading in
Today's
Elementary
Schools

'line of reasoning')" (Pearson, 1985, p. 731). First, the teacher models all four steps; then the teacher performs steps 1 and 2, while requiring the students to complete steps 3 and 4; then the teacher performs steps 1 and 3, requiring the students to complete steps 2 and 4; and finally the teacher asks the question (step 1) and the students perform all the other steps. Therefore, the responsibility for the task is gradually transferred from teacher to students. This is an excellent procedure and can be used for other skills as well.

Holmes (1983) developed a confirmation strategy for improving the ability of poor readers to respond to inferential questions. First, the children read a passage and an inferential question to be answered about the passage. Then they try to answer the question, checking their responses against key words in the passage to see if they are reasonable. For example, if the question is "When did this happen?", the answer "at night" will be discarded if the passage contains the key word *sun* in the phrase *the sun beamed*. The children may need practice in recognizing phrases that answer questions starting with *who*, *what*, *where*, *when*, *why*, and *how*. They may need to be helped to identify key words also, starting with the first sentence and continuing through the passage. The teacher can show the children how to ask themselves "yes-no" questions to help them decide if their answers are confirmed by the key words. For example, they might be encouraged to ask, "If the sun beamed, could it be night?" Students need to learn to ask these questions of themselves, but they may practice by asking the questions of classmates in relation to the responses given by the classmates. If a "no" response is obtained, the answer (hypothesis) is discarded, and another one is developed and tested. If all "yes" responses are obtained, the answer has a good chance of being correct. This strategy has been shown to be more effective in improving the comprehension of poor readers in the fourth and fifth grades than was a strategy in which the students just practiced answering inferential questions.

Main Ideas

For some selections readers must infer the main idea from related details. A good way to develop readiness to make such inferences is to ask children to locate the main ideas of pictures first. Then ask them to listen for main ideas as you read to them, and finally have them look for main ideas of passages they read.

The teacher should model the thought process students need to follow in deciding upon the main idea of a selection before asking them to try this independently. In the sample worksheet on inferring unstated main ideas the teacher could compare each of the possible choices to the details in the selection, rejecting those that fail to encompass the details. As students practice and become more proficient at identifying implied main ideas, the teacher should delete the choices and ask them to state the main idea in their own words (Moore and Readence, 1980). In addition, teachers can increase passage length as the children gain proficiency, beginning with paragraphs that do not have directly stated topic sentences and moving gradually to entire selections. Because of the obvious morals, Aesop's fables are good for teaching implied main ideas; the teacher can give students a fable and ask them to state the moral, then compare the actual morals to the ones the children stated, discuss any variations, and examine reasoning processes.

● **WORKSHEET:** *Inferring Unstated Main Ideas*

Directions: In the selection below, the main idea is implied but not directly stated. Choose the correct main idea from the list of possible ones.

The mayor of this town has always conducted his political campaigns as name-calling battles. Never once has he approached the basic issues of a campaign. Nevertheless, he builds himself up as a great statesman, ignoring the irregularities that have been discovered during his terms of office. Do you want a man like this to be re-elected?

The main idea of this selection is
1. The current mayor is not a good person to re-elect to office.
2. The mayor doesn't say nice things about his opponents.
3. The mayor is a crook.
4. The mayor should be re-elected. ●

Another activity on inferring unstated main ideas appears in the discussion on comprehending paragraphs.

In fiction, the main idea may be a central problem, rather than a topic and the information presented about the topic. To help students learn to locate a central problem in a fictional work, the teacher should first activate their schemata for problems and solutions, perhaps by talking about background experiences or stories previously read. Then the class may identify and categorize types of problems. Finally, the teacher should model the process of identifying a central story problem with a familiar, brief story. Pauses when reading to hypothesize about the central problem and to confirm or modify hypotheses can show the students how to search for the thing the central character wants, needs, or feels that provides a problem. The teacher should let the children see how the story's events affect the hypotheses made. Events of a story may be listed on the board to be analyzed for the needs or desires of the main character (Moldofsky, 1983).

Cause and Effect

Sometimes a reader needs to be able to infer a cause or effect that has been implied in the material, as in the following activity. Brainstorming out loud about causes and effects may help children develop more skill in this area.

242

Teaching
Reading in
Today's
Elementary
Schools

The teacher can ask: "What could be the effect when a person falls into the lake? What could be the cause of a crying baby?" Then he or she should elicit the reasoning behind children's answers.

● **WORKSHEET:** *Inferring Cause-and-Effect Relationships*

Directions: Read the following paragraphs and answer the question.

Jody refused to go to bed when the babysitter told her it was time. "This is a special occasion," she said. "Mom and Dad said I could stay up two hours later tonight."

Reluctantly, the babysitter allowed Jody to sit through two more hour-long TV shows. Although her eyelids drooped, she stubbornly stayed up until the end of the second show.

This morning Jody found it hard to get out of bed. All day there was evidence that she was not very alert. "What is wrong with me?" she wondered.

Question: What caused Jody to feel the way she did today?   ●

Pronoun Referents

Writing seldom, if ever, explicitly states the connection between a pronoun and its referent, so the task of determining the referent is an inferential one. Working with third graders, Margaret Richek found that, given a sentence paraphrase choice such as the one shown below, children understood the repeated subject most easily, the pronominalized form next, and the deleted form least easily (Barnitz, 1979).

Bill saw Jane, and Bill spoke to Jane.
Bill saw Jane, and he spoke to her.
Bill saw Jane and spoke to her.

Barnitz (1979) found that students recalled structures in which the referent was a noun or noun phrase more easily after reading than ones in which the referent was a clause or sentence.

Mark wanted an ice-cream cone but did not have enough money for it. (noun phrase referent)
Mike plays the guitar for fun, but he does not do it often. (sentence referent)

Similarly, children found it easier to remember structures in which the pronoun followed its referent than ones in which the pronoun came first (Barnitz, 1979).

Because it was pretty, Marcia wanted the blouse.
Marcia wanted the blouse because it was pretty.

Teachers should present these structures in the order of difficulty indicated by the studies just cited. They should explain the connections between the pronouns and referents in a number of examples before giving students exercises in which to make the relationship themselves.

After presenting all of the structures separately, teachers could use a worksheet such as the following to provide practice in integrating learning.

● **WORKSHEET:** *Pronoun Referents*

Directions: Circle the word or group of words to which each italicized word refers.

1. Don hit Jasper and then ran away from *him*.
2. Janice wanted a five-string banjo, but Janice's mother would not buy *it*.
3. Daniel works at the car wash, but he does not do *it* on school days.
4. Because *it* was the last one left, Terry did not take the piece of cake.
5. Sandra mopped the floor because she had gotten *it* dirty. ●

Adverb Referents

At times adverbs refer to other words or groups of words without an explicitly stated relationship. Teachers can explain these relationships, using examples such as the ones below, and then let children practice making the connections independently.

I'll stay at home, and you come here after you finish. (In this sentence, the adverb *here* refers to *home*.)

I enjoy the swimming pool, even if you do not like to go there. (In this sentence, the adverb *there* refers to *swimming pool*.)

Omitted Words

Sometimes in writing, words are omitted and said to be "understood," a structure known as ellipsis. Ellipsis can cause problems for some students, so again teachers should provide examples and explain the structure and then give children practice in interpreting sentences.

Are you going to the library? Yes, I am. (In the second sentence, the words *going to the library* are understood.)

Who is going with you? Bobby. (The words *is going with me* are understood.)

I have my books. Where are yours? (Here the second sentence is a shortened form of *Where are your books?*)

After this structure has been thoroughly discussed, students may practice by restating the sentences, filling in the deleted words.

Detecting Mood

Certain words and ways of using words tend to set a mood for a story, poem, or other literary work. Teachers should have children discuss how certain words trigger certain moods—for example, *ghostly, deserted, haunted,* and *howling* convey a scary mood; *lilting, sparkling, shining,* and *laughing* project a happy mood; *downcast, sobbing,* and *dejected* indicate a sad mood. They should model for the children the process of locating mood words in a paragraph and using these words to determine the mood of the paragraph. Then they can give the children copies of selections in which they have underlined words setting the mood and let them decide what the mood is, based on the underlined words. Finally, teachers can give the students a passage such as the one below and tell them to underline the words that set the mood. After they complete the worksheet, they should discuss the mood that was set by the words.

● *WORKSHEET:* *Detecting Mood*

Directions: Underline the words that set the mood of the paragraph.

Jay turned dejectedly away from the busy scene made by the movers as they carried his family's furniture from the house. "We're going away forever," he thought sadly. "I'll never see my friends again." And a tear rolled slowly down Jay's cheek, further smudging his unhappy face. ●

Detecting the Author's Purpose

Writers always have a purpose for writing: to inform, to entertain, to persuade, or to accomplish something else. Teachers should encourage their students to ask, "Why was this written?" by presenting them with a series of stories and explaining the purpose of each one, then giving them other stories and asking them to identify the purposes. The class should discuss reasons for the answers.

● *WORKSHEET:* *Detecting Author's Purpose*

Directions: Read the following materials and decide for each one whether the author was trying to inform, entertain, or persuade.

Television Works Like This, by Jeanne and Robert Bendick. New York: McGraw-Hill, 1965.

The Story of Doctor Doolittle, by Hugh Lofting. Philadelphia: Lippincott, 1920.

"Put Safety First," a pamphlet. ●

Drawing Conclusions

In order to draw conclusions, a reader must put together information gathered from several different sources or places within the same source. Students may develop readiness for this skill by studying pictures and drawing conclusions from them. Answering such questions as the following may also help. The teacher should model the process before having the students attempt it.

1. What is taking place here?
2. What happened just before this picture was taken?
3. What are the people in the picture preparing to do?

Cartoons may be used to good advantage in developing this comprehension skill. The teacher can show the students a cartoon such as the one below and ask a question that leads them to draw a conclusion, such as "What kind of news does Dennis have for his father?" Putting together the ideas that an event happened today and that Dennis's father needs to be relaxed to hear about it enables students to conclude that Dennis was involved in some mischief or accident that is likely to upset his father. The teacher can model the necessary thinking process by pointing out each clue and describing how

DENNIS the MENACE

"LET ME KNOW WHEN YOU'RE RELAXED ENOUGH TO HEAR ABOUT SOMETHIN' THAT HAPPENED TODAY."

DENNIS THE MENACE® used by permission of Hank Ketcham and © by Field Enterprises, Inc.

246

Teaching
Reading in
Today's
Elementary
Schools

he or she related it to a personal knowledge about how parents react. Then students can practice on other cartoons.

In the early grades, riddles such as "I have a face and two hands. I go tick-tock. What am I?" are good practice in drawing conclusions. Commercial riddle books, which allow readers to answer riddles and explain the reasoning behind their answers, may also be used for developing this skill.

● **WORKSHEET:** *Drawing Conclusions*

Directions: Read each paragraph and answer the question that follows it.

1. Ray went through the line, piling his plate high with food. He then carried his plate over to a table, where a waitress was waiting to find out what he wanted to drink. Where was Ray? _____

2. Cindy awoke with pleasure, remembering where she was. She hurried to dress so that she could help feed the chickens and watch her uncle milk the cows. Then she would go down to the field, catch Ginger, and take a ride through the woods. Where was Cindy? _____ ●

Another way to help children draw conclusions is to ask questions about sentences that imply certain information. For example, the teacher may write on the chalkboard, "The uniformed man got out of his truck and climbed the telephone pole with his tools." Then he or she may ask, "What do you think is this man's job? What are your reasons for your answers?" Even though the sentence does not directly state that the man is a telephone repair person, the details all imply this occupation. With help, children can become adept at detecting such clues to implied meanings.

In order to draw conclusions about characters' motives in stories, children must have some knowledge about how people react in social situations. This knowledge comes from their backgrounds of experience. Teachers' questions can encourage inferences by requiring students to consider events from the viewpoints of different characters; to think about the characters' likely thoughts, feelings, and motives; and to anticipate consequences of the actions of various characters (Moss and Oden, 1983).

Interpreting Figurative Language

Interpreting figurative language is an inferential task. Idioms abound in the English language. An idiom is a phrase that has a meaning different from its literal meaning. A person who "pays through the nose," for example, does not make use of that body part but does pay a great deal. Idioms make written language more difficult to comprehend, but they also add color and interest (Bromley, 1984).

Eustolia Perez found that third-grade Mexican-American children benefited from oral language activities that included practice with idioms (Bromley,

1984). Non-native students often lack the backgrounds of experience with the culture to help them interpret idioms. They may be confused over the idea that a word or phrase has different meanings in different contexts.

It may be helpful to teach idioms by defining them and explaining them when they occur in reading materials or in oral activities. Studying the origin of the expressions may also be helpful. After an idiom's meaning has been clarified, students need to use it in class activities. They may rewrite sentences to include newly learned idioms, or replace these idioms with more literal language. Illustrating idioms is another helpful activity. Students can also listen for idioms in class discussion or try using them. Creative writing about possible origins of idioms could elicit interest in discovering their real origins (Bromley, 1984).

More extensive coverage of figurative expressions is located in Chapter 8 in the section entitled "Literature." Different types of figures of speech are identified, and teaching suggestions are offered.

✔ Self-Check: Objective 7
Explain why children need to know how to make inferences.

Critical Reading

Critical reading is evaluating written material—comparing the ideas discovered in the material with known standards and drawing conclusions about their accuracy, appropriateness, and timeliness. The critical reader must be an active reader, questioning, searching for facts, and suspending judgment until he or she has considered all of the material. Critical reading depends upon literal comprehension and interpretive comprehension, and grasping implied ideas is especially important.

If people are to make intelligent decisions based upon the material that they read, such as which political candidate to support, which products to buy, which movies to attend, which television programs to watch, and so on, they must read critically. Since children are faced with many of these decisions early in life, they should receive instruction in critical reading early.

Teachers can begin promoting critical reading in the first grade, or even kindergarten, by encouraging critical thinking. When reading a story to the class, they can ask, "Do you think this story is real or make-believe? Why do you think so?" If the children have difficulty in answering, questions such as "Could the things in this story really have happened? Do you know of any children who can fly? Have you ever heard of any *real* children who can fly? Have you ever heard of anyone who stayed the same age all of the time? Do all people grow up after enough years have passed?" can be helpful. By asking "Can animals really talk? Have you ever heard an animal talk?" teachers can help children understand how to judge the reality or fantasy in a story.

Critical thinking can also be promoted at an early stage through critical reading of pictures. If children are shown pictures that contain inaccuracies

248

Teaching
Reading in
Today's
Elementary
Schools

(for example, a car with a square wheel), they can identify the mistakes. Children's magazines often contain activities of this type, and illustrators of books often inadvertently include incorrect content. After the children have read (or have been read) a story containing such a picture, ask them to identify what is wrong in the picture, according to the story.

Research has shown that critical listening and critical reading instruction can be effective with students in grades one through six, regardless of whether basic decoding skills have already been mastered or not. Therefore, such instruction is appropriate for remedial, as well as developmental, readers. In a study by Boodt (1984), critical listening instruction resulted in an increase in critical reading and general reading comprehension for remedial readers in grades four through six.

To foster critical reading skills in the classroom, teachers can encourage pupils to read with a questioning attitude. Lead them to ask questions such as the following when reading nonfiction.

1. Why did the author write this material?
2. Does the author know what he or she is writing about? Is he or she likely to be biased? Why?
3. Is the material up-to-date?
4. Is the author approaching the material logically or emotionally? What emotional words does he or she use?
5. Is the author employing any undesirable propaganda techniques? Which ones? How does he or she use them?

Fiction can be read critically also, but the questions that apply are a little different.

1. Could this story really have happened?
2. Are the characters believable within the setting furnished by the story? Are they consistent in their actions?
3. Is the dialogue realistic?
4. Did the plot hold your interest? What was it that kept your interest?
5. Was the ending reasonable or believable? Why, or why not?
6. Was the title well chosen? Why, or why not?

Careful questioning by the teacher to extend limited and stereotyped depictions of people in reading materials can help children develop critical reading expertise. Children must be encouraged to relate their personal experiences to the materials (Zimet, 1983). Children can examine stereotyped language in relation to stories in which it occurs, and teachers can point out the problems caused by looking at people and ideas in a stereotyped way (Zimet, 1983). For example, some books give the impression that certain nationalities have particular personality characteristics, but it should be easy to demonstrate that not all people of that nationality are alike, just as not all Americans are alike.

Children need to learn to judge what information is significant and what is insignificant. They do not need to struggle with insignificant information (Crafton, 1982).

Critical thinking is often important to the interpretation of humor (Whitmer, 1986). Therefore, humorous literature can be an enjoyable vehicle for teaching critical reading skills. It is especially good for determining the author's purpose (often to entertain, but sometimes also to convince through humor) and for evaluating content (especially distinguishing fact from fantasy and recognizing assumptions).

Author

The mature critical reader must consider and evaluate the person who wrote the material, considering the four categories that follow.

Author's Purpose The critical reader will try to determine whether the author wrote the material to inform, to entertain, to persuade, or for some other purpose. This is an interpretive reading skill.

Author's Point of View The critical reader will want to know if the writer belonged to a group, lived in an area, or held a strong view that would tend to bias any opinions about a subject in one way or another. Two accounts of the Civil War might be very different if one author was from the North and the other from the South.

Author's Style and Tone The author's style is the manner in which he or she uses vocabulary (vividness, precision, use of emotional words, use of figurative language) and sentence structure (the order within the language). Special attention should be given to use of *figurative language,* expressions that are not meant to be taken literally, and use of emotional words, which do much to sway the reader toward or away from a point of view or attitude. Note the effects of the two sentences below.

Author 1: Next we heard the *heartrending* cry of the wounded tiger.
Author 2: When the tiger was shot, it let out a *vicious* roar.

Teachers should be aware of undesirable aspects of the style or tone of some writers of material for youngsters. A condescending tone, for example, will be quickly sensed and resented.

Author's Competence The reliability of written material is affected by the competence of the author to write about the subject in question. If background information shows that a star football player has written an

250

Teaching
Reading in
Today's
Elementary
Schools

article on the nation's foreign policy, intermediate grade youngsters will have little trouble determining that the reliability of the statements in this article is likely to be lower than the reliability of a similar article written by an experienced diplomat.

To determine an author's competence, students should consider his or her education and experience, referring to books such as *Current Biography* (H. W. Wilson, 1987) and *Fifth Book of Junior Authors and Illustrators* (H. W. Wilson, 1983) or to book jacket flaps to find such information. Teachers can give students a topic and ask them to name people who might write about it. Students can discuss which people might be most qualified, or they can compare two authors of books on the same subject and decide which one is better qualified. Class members who are knowledgeable about a topic and others who are not can write reports on that topic, while remaining pupils predict which people are likely to have the most accurate reports. The students can follow up with a comparison for accuracy (Ross, 1981).

Material

In addition to comprehending the material literally, the critical reader needs to be able to determine and evaluate the following things about it.

Timeliness   The critical reader will wish to check the date that the material was published, because the timeliness of an article or book can make a crucial difference in a rapidly changing world. For example, an outdated social studies book may show incorrect boundaries for countries or fail to show some countries that now exist; similarly, an outdated science book may refer to a disease as incurable when a cure has recently been found. A science or history book with a 1950 copyright date would contain no information about astronauts or moon shots.

Accuracy and Adequacy   Nonfiction material should be approached with this question in mind: "Are the facts presented here true?" The importance of a good background of experience becomes evident here. A reader who has had previous experience with the material will have a basis of comparison not available to one lacking such experience. A person with only a little knowledge of a particular field can often spot such indications of inadequacy as exaggerated statements, one-sided presentations, and opinion offered as fact. Obviously, readers can check reference books to see if the statements in the material are supported elsewhere.

Appropriateness   Critical readers must be able to determine whether the material is suitable for their purposes. A book or article can be completely accurate and not be applicable to the problem or topic under consideration. For example, a child looking for information for a paper entitled "Cherokee Indian Ceremonies" needs to realize that an article on the invention of the Cherokee alphabet is irrelevant to the task at hand.

Differentiation of Fact from Opinion This skill is vital for good critical readers. People often unquestioningly accept as fact anything they see in print, though printed material is often composed of statements of opinion. Some authors intermix facts and opinions, giving little indication that they are presenting anything but pure fact. Also, many readers are not alert to clues that signal opinions. By pointing out these clues and providing practice in the task of discrimination, teachers can promote the ability to discriminate between facts and opinions.

Some readers have trouble reading critically because they do not have a clear idea of what constitutes a fact. Facts are statements that can be verified through direct observation, consultation of official records of past events, or scientific experimentation. The statement "General Lee surrendered to General Grant at Appomattox" is a fact that can be verified by checking historical records. For various reasons, opinions cannot be directly verified. For example, the statement "She is the most beautiful girl in the world" is unverifiable and is therefore an opinion. Even if every girl in the world could be assembled for comparison, different people's standards of beauty are different, and a scale of relative beauty would be impossible to construct.

Knowledge of key words that signal opinions, such as *believe, think, seems, may, appears, probably, likely,* and *possibly,* can be extremely helpful to readers. Teachers often find that pointing out such indicators to children and giving the children practice in locating them is highly beneficial.

Children must also understand that not all opinions are of equal value, since some have been based upon solid facts, whereas others are unsupported. Critical readers try to determine the relative merits of opinions as well as to separate the opinions from facts.

Newspaper editorials offer one good way, especially in the intermediate grades, for children to practice distinguishing fact from opinion. Students can underline each sentence in the editorial with colored pencils, one color for facts and another for opinions. They can then be encouraged to discuss which opinions are best supported by facts. Worksheets similar to the following one might also be used to help children differentiate fact from opinion.

● **WORKSHEET:** *Fact or Opinion?*

Directions: Read each sentence carefully. Decide whether it states a fact or an opinion. Write an *F* on the line after the sentence if the statement is a fact; write an *O* if it is an opinion.

1. Harrison Ford is a great actor. _____
2. Austin is the capital of Texas. _____
3. There are twelve inches in a foot. _____
4. I believe that people were never intended to visit other planets. _____
5. Mark thinks that there is other intelligent life in our solar system. _____
6. The discovery of polio vaccine was probably the most important discovery of the century. _____

252

Teaching
Reading in
Today's
Elementary
Schools

7. Emily has brown eyes. _____
8. Everyone who is worth knowing will be at the party. _____
9. It appears that Martin is the most eager worker in the plant. _____
10. There are two pints in a quart. _____ ●

Recognition of Propaganda Techniques Elementary school children, like adults, are constantly deluged with writing that attempts to influence their thinking and actions. Some of these materials may be used for good purposes and some for bad ones. For example, most people would consider propaganda designed to influence people to protect their health "good," whereas they would label propaganda designed to influence people to do things that are harmful to their health "bad." Since propaganda techniques are often utilized to sway people toward or away from a cause or point of view, children should be made aware of them so that they can avoid being unduly influenced by them.

The Institute for Propaganda Awareness has identified seven undesirable propaganda techniques that good critical readers should know about:

1. name calling—using derogatory labels (*yellow, reactionary, troublemaker*) to create negative reactions toward a person without providing evidence to support such impressions
2. glittering generalities—using vague phrases to influence a point of view without providing necessary specifics
3. transfer technique—associating a respected organization or symbol with a particular person, project, product, or idea, thus transferring that respect to the person or thing being promoted
4. plain-folks talk—relating a person (for example, a politician) or a proposed program to the common people in order to gain their support
5. testimonial technique—using a highly popular or respected person to endorse a product or proposal
6. bandwagon technique—playing on the urge to do what others are doing by giving the impression that everyone else is participating in a particular activity
7. card stacking—telling only one side of a story by ignoring information favorable to the opposing point of view.

Teachers should describe the propaganda techniques to the class and model the process of locating these techniques in printed materials, such as advertisements. Then the children should practice the skill.

Children can learn to detect propaganda techniques by analyzing newspaper and magazine advertisements, printed political campaign material, and requests for donations to various organizations. Activities like the first two in the list below are also helpful. The other twelve activities can be used to provide children with practice in other critical reading skills.

1. Number several newspaper advertisements and attach them to the bulletin board. Have children number their papers and write beside the number of each advertisement a description of the propaganda technique or techniques it uses.

2. Have a propaganda hunt. Label boxes with the names of the seven propaganda techniques discussed above, and ask children to find examples of these techniques in a variety of sources and drop their examples into the boxes. As a class activity, evaluate each example for appropriateness to the category in which it was placed.

3. Use computer simulation programs to provide practice in making critical judgments. These programs provide simulated models of real-life experiences with which students can experiment in a risk-free manner. Students enjoy seeing the results of their decision making (Balajthy, 1984).

4. Ask students to compare two biographies of a well-known person by answering questions such as "How do they differ in their treatment of the subject? Is either of the authors likely to be biased for or against the subject? Are there contradictory statements in the two works? If so, which one seems most likely to be correct? Could the truth be different from both accounts?"

5. Have students compare editorials from two newspapers with different philosophies or from different areas. Have them decide why differences exist and which stand, if any, is more reasonable, based on facts.

6. Ask students to examine newspaper stories for typographical errors and to determine whether or not each typographical error changed the message of the article.

7. Have the class interpret political cartoons from various newspapers.

8. Ask students to examine the headlines of news stories and decide whether or not the headlines fit the stories.

9. Using a list of optional topics—school policies, parental restrictions, and so forth—ask students to write editorials, first presenting facts, then their opinions, and finally their reasons for the opinions (Rabin, 1981).

10. Locate old science or geography books containing statements that are no longer true and use them to show the importance of utilizing current sources. Let students compare old books with new ones to find the differences (new material included, "facts" that have changed, etc.), and discuss what types of material are most and least likely to be dependent on recent copyright dates for accuracy (Ross, 1981).

11. Have students become acquainted with the typical point of view of a particular writer or newspaper and then predict the position that writer or newspaper will take on an issue, later checking to discover the accuracy of their predictions (Ross, 1981).

12. Let children compare the results when they write about the same topic from different viewpoints (Ross, 1981).

13. Direct students to write material that will persuade their classmates to do something. Then examine the results for the techniques they used.

254

Teaching
Reading in
Today's
Elementary
Schools

14. Discuss the nutritional aspects of sugar and chemical food additives and the foods that contain them. Then have students examine the ingredient lists from popular snacks. What food value do various snacks have, based upon their labels (Neville, 1982)?

✔ Self-Check: Objective 8

What does a critical reader need to know about the authors of the selections he or she is reading?

React to this statement: "I know it is correct because it is here in this book in black and white."

Name seven commonly used propaganda techniques. Give an example of each.

(See Self-Improvement Opportunity 7.)

Creative Reading

Creative reading involves going beyond the material presented by the author. It requires readers to think as they read, just as critical reading does, and it also requires them to use their imaginations. According to Huus (1967), it "is concerned with the production of new ideas, the development of new insights, fresh approaches, and original constructs." Teachers must carefully nurture creative reading, trying not to ask only questions that have absolute answers, since these will tend not to encourage the diverse processes characteristic of creative reading. In order to go beyond the material in the text, the readers must make use of their background schemata, combining this prior knowledge with ideas from the text to produce a new response based on, but not completely dictated by, the text. Creative readers must be skilled in the areas discussed below.

Cause and Effect

Creative readers must understand cause-and-effect relationships in a story so well that they know why a character acts as he or she does at a particular time. For example, by analyzing the reasons for the actions in the story "Stone Soup," the creative reader will know why the townspeople finally produced their food supplies to be used in the soup after being so careful to hide them and deny their existence. Such readers will also be able to imagine what might have happened in a story if a particular event had not occurred or if something quite different had happened.

To help students acquire the skill of reading creatively, teachers should model the thought process involved. After the students practice on various texts, ask them to explain their reasons for thinking as they did. Some questions they might answer for *Heidi*, for example, are presented below:

What would have happened in the book if Peter had not pushed Klara's wheelchair down the side of the mountain?

What would have happened if Herr Sessman had refused to send Heidi back to the Alm, even though the doctor advised it?

Some questions for *Wind in the Willows* include:

Why was Mole so dissatisfied with life at the beginning of the story?

Why did Ratty search for Mole in the Wild Woods? Why was Toad boastful?

Visualization

Visualization is seeing pictures in the mind, and readers draw upon their existing schemata in order to accomplish this. It is possible for a person to visualize things previously experienced, things heard, or things read. By vividly visualizing the events depicted by the author's words, creative readers allow themselves to become a part of the story—they see the colors, hear the sounds, feel the textures, taste the flavors, and smell the odors described by the writer. They will find that they are living the story as they read. By doing this, they will enjoy the story more and understand it more deeply.

Creating mental pictures during silent reading can help children with recall of events read, and creating such images before reading has been shown to produce better literal comprehension than was produced by creating the images after reading (Fredericks, 1986).

Training in visualization has been found effective for third through sixth-grade students. There is, however, some indication from research that imagery attempts may not help very young children. These students may not be able to form images on command (Tierney and Cunningham, 1984).

Dee Mundell suggested four steps for helping children develop techniques for visualization. First, teachers should lead students to visualize concrete objects after they have seen and closely examined them in the classroom. Then teachers can ask children to visualize objects or experiences outside the classroom. They can draw concrete objects they visualize and compare their drawings to the actual objects later. Next, teachers can read high-imagery stories to the children, letting individuals share their mental images with the group and having small groups illustrate the stories after the reading. Finally, teachers should encourage students to visualize as they read independently (Fredericks, 1986).

Open-ended questions can aid development of imagery (Fredericks, 1986). For example, if a child says she sees a house, the teacher can ask, "What does it look like?" If she then replies that it is white with green trim, the teacher may ask, "What is the yard like?"

Exercises that encourage visualization are listed below.

256 *ACTIVITIES*

Teaching
Reading in
Today's
Elementary
Schools

1. Give students copies of a paragraph that vividly describes a scene or situation and have them illustrate the scene or situation in a painting or a three-dimensional art project.

2. Using a paragraph or statement that contains almost no description, ask students questions about details they would need in order to picture the scene in their minds.

   Example: The dog ran toward Jane and Susan. Jane held out her hands toward him and smiled.

   Questions: What kind of dog was it? How big was it? Why was it running toward the girls? Were the girls afraid of the dog? What happened when the dog reached the girls? Where did this action take place? Was the dog on a leash, behind a fence, or running free?

3. Have the children dramatize a story they have read, such as the folktale "Caps for Sale."

THE FAMILY CIRCUS   **By Bil Keane**

3-4
Copyright 1983
The Register and Tribune
Syndicate, Inc.

"I like reading. It turns on pictures in your head."

Reprinted with special permission of King Features Syndicate, Inc.

Making Value Judgments

Creative readers need to be able to determine whether actions of characters are reasonable or unreasonable. In order to help them develop this ability, teachers may ask questions such as the following:

Was the little red hen justified in eating all of the bread she had made, refusing to share with the other animals? Why, or why not?

Was it a good thing for Heidi to save bread from the Sessmans' table to take back to the grandmother? Why, or why not?

Readers draw upon their schemata related to right and wrong actions in order to complete this type of activity. Not all children will answer in the same way, because of their varying schemata.

Solving Problems

Creative readers relate the things they read to their own personal problems, sometimes applying the solution of a problem encountered in a story to a different situation. For instance, after reading the chapter in *Tom Sawyer* in which Tom tricks his friends into painting a fence for him, a child may use a similar ruse to persuade a sibling to take over her chores or even her homework.

To work on developing this problem-solving skill, teachers need to use books in which different types of problems are solved, choosing an appropriate one to read or to let the children read and then asking the children questions, such as the following:

1. What problem did the character(s) in the story face?
2. How was the problem handled?
3. Was the solution a good one?
4. What other possible solutions can you think of?
5. Would you prefer the solution in the book or one of the others?

Predicting Outcomes

In order to predict outcomes, readers must put together available information and note trends, then project the trends into the future, making decisions about what events might logically occur next. A creative reader is constantly predicting what will happen next in a story, reacting to the events he or she is reading about and drawing conclusions about their results. Stauffer and Cramer (1968) describe in detail ways of promoting this approach to reading, and a condensed version of their approach is presented in Chapter 6 under the heading "Alternatives to Use of the DRA."

An enjoyable way to work on this skill is to have students read one of the action comic strips in the newspaper for several weeks and then predict what will happen next, based upon their knowledge of what has occurred until that time. The teacher can record these predictions on paper and file them; later, students can compare the actual ending of the adventure with their predictions. The teacher should be sure that students can present reasons to

258

Teaching
Reading in
Today's
Elementary
Schools

justify what they predict. When judging their theories, the teacher should point out that some predictions may seem as good a way to end the story as the one the comic-strip artist used. On the other hand, some may not make sense, based on the evidence, and reasons for this should be made clear.

Improving Story Presentation

Creative readers may be able to see how a story could be improved in order to make it more interesting—for example, excessive description may cause a story to move too slowly, and certain parts could be deleted or changed to be more concise. For another story, students may suggest that the story did not have enough description to allow them to picture the setting and characters well enough to really become involved. In this case, the teacher should ask them to add descriptive passages that make visualization easier. Perhaps one child will feel that a story would be better with more dialogue and will write scenes for the characters, to replace third-person narration. Another child may feel that a story needs a more gripping opening paragraph. The possibilities for skill development are extensive, but the teacher must remember that this skill is extremely advanced and may only be attained by the best readers in the elementary grades, although many others will attain it before their school years are finished.

Producing New Creations

Art, drama, and dance can be useful in elaborating on what students read. By creating a new ending for a story, adding a new character, changing some aspect of a character, or adding an additional adventure within the framework of the existing story, students approach reading creatively. Possible activities are listed below. Many of them involve responding to literature through writing. (More on the reading-writing connection is found in Chapter 9.)

ACTIVITIES

1. Have students write plays or poems based on books of fiction they have read and enjoyed.
2. Ask students to illustrate a story they have read, using a series of pictures or of three-dimensional scenes.
3. Have the students write a prose narrative based upon a poem they have read.
4. After the children have read several stories of a certain type (such as *Just So Stories*), ask them to write an original story of the same type.
5. Transfer the story of *Heidi* to the Rocky Mountains or to Appalachia.

✔ **Self-Check: Objective 9**   **259**
Define creative reading and discuss some of the things that creative   Comprehension
readers must be able to do.

QUESTIONING TECHNIQUES

All reading done by children should be purposeful, because (1) children who are reading with a purpose tend to *comprehend* what they read better than those who have no purpose, and (2) children who read with a purpose tend to *retain* what they read better than those who have no purpose. For these reasons teachers should set purposes for youngsters by giving them questions rather than merely telling them, "Read chapter seven for tomorrow." This approach avoids presenting children with the insurmountable task of remembering everything they read and allows them to know that they are reading to determine main ideas, locate details, understand vocabulary terms, or meet some other well-defined goal. As a result, they can apply themselves to a specific, manageable task. However, if teachers always use the same type of purpose question, children may not develop the ability to read for a variety of purposes.

Basal reader manuals tend to offer a variety of types of purpose questions. Teachers may not make use of these ready-made questions, however. Shake and Allington (1985) found that the second-grade teachers who participated in a research study on questioning procedures used more of their own questions than they did questions from the basal reader manual. Seventy-nine percent of the questions asked were original. Even when using the questions from the manual, the teachers tended to paraphrase them. The teachers' questions tended to be literal ones, focusing on trivial facts, and they were frequently poorly formed.

Prereading questions should focus on predicting and relating text to prior knowledge. Purpose questions should cover as much of the story as possible. They should be asked about the details that relate to problems, goals, attempts to solve problems, characters' reactions, resolutions, and themes (Pearson, 1982, 1985). (More about this type of questioning can be found under the heading "Other Bases for Questioning.")

Shanahan (1986) found that, for the fifth graders in his study, prereading questions did not have a significant effect on the children's total amount of recall, but they did cause the children to have better recall of information cued by the questions. Making predictions based upon prereading questions improved recall of cued information even more than did the prereading questions alone. Students need to generate the predictions themselves, not just listen to predictions made by others, for this approach to be effective.

Even when teachers do not provide purpose questions, children are often guided in the way they approach their reading assignments by the types of

260

Teaching
Reading in
Today's
Elementary
Schools

Teachers should prepare their questions carefully, for the types of questions they ask can affect the type of information about a reading selection that children will remember.   (© Elizabeth Crews)

questions that teachers have used in the past, on tests. If a teacher tends to ask in test questions for factual recall of small details, children will concentrate on such details, perhaps overlooking the main ideas entirely. In class discussion, the teacher may be bewildered by the fact that the children know many things that happened in a story without knowing what the basic theme was. In general, research has shown that simply asking more inference questions during and after reading stories improves inferential comprehension (Hansen, 1981a; Hansen and Pearson, 1983; Pearson, 1985). Thus the types of questions that teachers ask about selections affect the types of information that students recall about selections, and students remember best information about which they have been directly questioned (Wixson, 1983).

Whether teachers prepare only test questions or both purpose and test questions, they all use both written and oral questions as a part of class activities. And it is significant that the bulk of research indicates that regardless of when they are used, questions foster increased comprehension, apparently because readers give more time to the material related to answering them (Durkin, 1981b). Since this situation exists, teachers need to understand thoroughly the process of preparing questions.

Farrar (1983) believes that oral questioning for comprehension should be carried out differently from written questioning. Whereas written questions need to be clear, concise, and complete, oral questions are part of complex social interactions and may need to be stated differently in order to be less threatening. Questions stated in less threatening ways encourage responses. Hints and chains of questions that bring out needed background information and lead to successful answers to complex questions reduce the threat of questioning.

Farrar (1984a) asserts that the phrasing of questions should depend on the amount of challenge individual children need. Questions can be phrased differently and still address the same content. The phrasing can make questions easier or harder to answer and can require simple or complex answers. It may take several questions requiring simple responses to obtain all of the information that can be obtained from one question requiring a complex response.

Another problem that may arise, related to the form of questioning used, is unfamiliarity of some children with the question-answer-feedback sequence that is often used for instructional purposes. Some children have not been exposed to this language pattern at home and feel that it is strange and confusing that the teacher is asking for information he or she already knows. Teachers may need to actively teach the question-answer-feedback strategy in oral and written situations so that students will respond appropriately (Farrar, 1984b).

Preparing Questions

Teachers often ask questions they devise on the spur of the moment. This practice is no doubt due to the pressure of the many different tasks that a teacher must perform during the day, but it is a poor one for at least two reasons. First, questions developed hastily, without close attention to the material involved, tend to be detail questions ("What color was the car? Where were they going?"), since detail questions are much easier to construct than most other types. But detail questions fail to measure more than simple recall. Second, many hastily constructed questions tend to be poorly worded, vague in their intent, and misleading to students.

Questions Based on Comprehension Skills

One of the bases for planning questioning strategies is to try to construct questions of particular types to tap different types of comprehension and different comprehension skills. Seven major types of questions are generally useful in guiding reading.

1. Main idea—ask the children to identify the central theme of the selection.
2. Detail—ask for bits of information conveyed by the material.

262

Teaching
Reading in
Today's
Elementary
Schools

3. Vocabulary—ask for the meanings of words used in the selection.
4. Sequence—require knowledge of events in their order of occurrence.
5. Inference—ask for information that is implied but not directly stated in the material.
6. Evaluation—ask for judgments about the material.
7. Creative response—ask the children to go beyond the material and create new ideas based on the ideas they have read.

Main Idea Questions   These may give children some direction toward the nature of the answer. The question "What caused Susie to act so excited?" could direct readers toward the main idea of a passage in which Susie was very excited because she had a secret. An example of a question that offers no clues to the main idea is "What would be a title for this selection that would explain what it is about?" Main idea questions help children to be aware of details and the relationships among them.

Detail Questions   These ask for information such as "Who was coming to play with Maria? What was Betty bringing with her? What happened to Betty on the way to Maria's house? When did Betty finally arrive? Where had Betty left her bicycle?" Whereas it is important for students to assimilate the information conveyed by these questions, very little depth of comprehension is necessary to answer them all correctly. Therefore, even though these questions are easy to construct, they should not constitute the bulk of the questions the teacher asks.

Vocabulary Questions   Such questions check children's understanding of word meaning. For discussion purposes, a teacher might ask children to produce as many meanings of a particular word as they can, but purpose questions and test questions should ask for the meaning of a word as it is used in the selection under consideration.

Sequence Questions   These check the child's knowledge of the order in which events occurred in the story. The question "What did Alex and Robbie do when their parents left the house?" is not a sequence question, since children are free to list the events in any order they choose. The question "What three things did Alex and Robbie do, in order, when their parents left the house?" requires children to display their grasp of the sequence of events.

Inference Questions   These require some reading between the lines. The answer to an inference question is implied by statements in the selection, but it is not directly stated, as in the example below.

Passage:
Margie and Jan were sitting on the couch listening to Bruce Springsteen records. Their father walked in and announced, "I hear that Bruce Springsteen is giving a

concert at the Municipal Auditorium next week." Both girls jumped up and ran toward their father. "Can we go? Can we go?" they begged.

Question:
Do you think Margie and Jan liked to hear Bruce Springsteen sing? Why, or why not?

Evaluation Questions   Such questions require children to make judgments. Although these judgments are inferences, they depend upon more than the information implied or stated by the story; the children must have enough experience related to the situations involved to establish standards for comparison. An example of an evaluation question is "Was the method Kim used to rescue Dana wise? Why, or why not?" These questions are excellent for open-ended class discussion but hard to grade as test questions.

Creative Response Questions   Questions requiring creative response are also good for class discussions. As a means of testing comprehension of a passage, however, they are not desirable, since almost any response could be considered correct. Examples of creative response questions include "If the story stopped after Jimmy lost his money, what ending would you write for it?" and "If Meg had not gone to school that day, what do you think might have happened?"

Other Question Types   Crowell and Au (1981), who recommend use of different question types, have developed a scale of comprehension questions arranged in order from easiest to most difficult:

1. Association—designed to discover any detail from a story that a child can recall. Example: "What was this story about?"
2. Categorization—requires a simple categorization. Example: "Did you like Anna Marie? Why, or why not?"
3. Seriation—asks for interrelationships among details, such as sequence of events or cause and effect. Example: "What happened first? What happened next? And then what?"
4. Integration—requires combining elements in the story into a coherent structure. Example: "What was the problem in this story?" followed by a question specific to the story, such as "What problem did Nino have?"
5. Extension—asks for application beyond the bounds of the immediate story structure. Example: "Tell me another way this story could have ended."

Pearson and Johnson (1978) suggest three question types. They label questions as textually explicit when they have answers that are directly stated in the text, textually implicit when they have implied answers, and scriptually implicit when they must be answered by the reader from his or her background knowledge.

264

Teaching
Reading in
Today's
Elementary
Schools

Characteristics of the reader interact with the text and the question to determine the actual demands of the question-answering task. A reader's interest, background knowledge, and reading skill affect the difficulty and type of question for each reader. The structure of a question may lead a teacher to expect a textually explicit response, whereas the background of the student may cause a scriptually implicit response to a question (Wixson, 1983). For example, the text may have told the readers how to construct a kite. If the child had actually made a kite before reading the material, he or she might answer the question on the basis of direct experience, rather than from information presented in the text.

Inability to take the perspective of another person can affect comprehension. Students who can take the perspective of another person do better on scriptually implicit questions (Gardner and Smith, 1987).

Other Bases for Questioning

Two other bases for questioning deserve attention: use of story grammar and use of a story map.

A story is a series of events related to each other in particular ways. As people hear and read many stories, they develop expectations, sometimes called story schemata, about the types of things they will encounter; these help them organize information. Related story schemata are described by a *story grammar*. As Sadow (1982) suggests, questions based on story grammar may help children develop story schemata. The questions should be chosen to reflect the logical sequence of events.

David Rumelhart proposed a simple story grammar that "describes a story as consisting of a setting and one or more episodes" (Sadow, 1982, p. 519). The setting includes the main characters and the time and location of the events, and each episode contains an initiating event, the main character's reaction to it, an action of the main character caused by this reaction, and a consequence of the action, which may act as an initiating event for a subsequent episode. (Sometimes some of the elements of an episode are not directly stated.) Sadow suggests the following five generic questions as appropriate types to ask about a story:

1. Where and when did the events in the story take place and who was involved in them? (Setting)
2. What started the chain of events in the story? (Initiating Event)
3. What was the main character's reaction to this event? (Reaction)
4. What did the main character do about it? (Action)
5. What happened as a result of what the main character did? (Consequence) (Sadow, 1982, p. 520)

Such questions can help students see the underlying order of ideas in a story, but of course teachers should reword them to fit the story and the particular children. For example, Question 1 can be broken into three questions (where, when, who), and the teacher can provide appropriate focus by using words or phrases from the story. After pupils address these story grammar questions, which establish the essential facts, they should answer questions that help them relate the story to their experiences and knowledge (Sadow, 1982).

Each of Sadow's generic questions could include detail or inference questions, as described in the suggested list of seven question types on pages 261–262. For example, her setting question would fit under the detail category if the answer was directly stated in the material and under the inference category if the answer was implied. Similarly, Sadow's initiating-event question is a type of sequence question, whereas her reaction question could be a detail or an inference question, according to the listed types, as could her action and consequence questions.

Marshall (1983) has also suggested using story grammar as a basis for developing comprehension questions and for evaluating student retellings, which are sometimes used instead of questions. A checklist for story retellings can be used to indicate if story parts were included and whether they were included with or without prompts. In her questioning scheme, *theme* questions are similar to main idea questions and ask about the major point or moral of the story. As is true in Sadow's questioning scheme, *setting* questions are "where" and "when" questions. *Character* questions ask about the main character and/or other characters. *Initiating events* questions often ask about a problem faced by a particular character. *Attempts* questions ask what a character did about a situation or what he or she will do. *Resolution* questions ask how a character solved the problem or what the reader would do to solve the problem. *Reactions* questions focus on what a character felt, the reasons for a character's actions or feelings, or the feelings of the reader.

Beck and McKeown (1981) suggest use of a story map as a basis for questioning. In order to develop a story map, the teacher first determines the premise or starting point of the story and then lists the major events and ideas that make up the plot, including implied ideas and relationships. Then he or she designs questions (both detail and inference types) that elicit the information in the map and follow the sequence of the story. Extension questions (evaluation or creative-response type) can be used to extend discussion to broader perspectives; such questions that elicit tangential information should not be placed in the story-map question sequence. (Story maps are discussed more thoroughly on pages 224–225.)

Guidelines for Preparation

Some guidelines for preparing questions may be of use to teachers who wish to improve their questioning techniques. The following suggestions may help teachers avoid the pitfalls that have been detected by other educators.

1. When trying to determine overall comprehension skills, ask a variety of questions designed to reflect different types of comprehension. *Avoid overloading the skill evaluation with a single type of question.*

266

Teaching
Reading in
Today's
Elementary
Schools

2. Don't ask questions about obscure or insignificant portions of the selection. Such questions may make a test harder, but they don't convey realistic data about comprehension. *"Hard" tests and "good" tests are not necessarily synonymous.*

3. Avoid ambiguous or tricky questions. *If a question has two or more possible interpretations, more than one answer for it has to be acceptable.*

4. Questions that a person who has not read the material can answer correctly offer you no valuable information about comprehension. *Avoid useless questions.*

5. Don't ask questions in language that is more difficult than the language of the selection the question is about. *Sometimes you can word questions so as to prevent a child who knows the answer from responding appropriately.*

6. Make sure the answers to sequence questions require knowledge of the *order* of events. *Don't confuse questions that simply ask for lists with sequence questions.*

7. Don't ask for unsupported opinions when testing for comprehension. Have children give support for their opinions, by asking, "Why do you think that?" or "What in the story made you think that?" *If you ask for an unsupported opinion, any answer would be correct.*

8. Don't ask for opinions, if you want facts. *Ask for the type of information you want to receive.*

9. Avoid questions that give away information. Instead of saying, "What makes you believe the boy was angry?" say, "How do you think the boy felt? Why?" *Questions may lead students to the answers by supplying too much information.*

10. If a question can be answered with a *yes* or a *no,* or if a choice of answers is offered, the child has a chance to answer the question correctly without having to read the selection at all. *Avoid questions that offer choices.*

Helping Students Answer Questions

Raphael and Pearson (1982) taught students three types of Question-Answer Relationships (QARs). QAR instruction encourages students to consider both information in the text and their own background knowledge when answering questions (Raphael, 1986). The relationship for questions that had answers directly stated in the text in one sentence was referred to as "Right There." The students looked for the words in the question and read the sentence containing those words to locate the answer. The relationship for questions with an answer in the story that required information from multiple sentences or paragraphs was referred to as "Think and Search," and the relationship for questions for which answers had to come from the reader's own knowledge was referred to as "On My Own" (Raphael and Pearson, 1982). Modeling the decision about question-answer relationships and correct answers based upon them was an important part of the teaching. Supervised practice following the modeling, with immediate feedback on student responses, was also important. The practice involved gradually increased passage lengths, progressing from simpler to more difficult tasks (Raphael, 1982). Students who had been taught the three types of QARs answered questions more successfully than did a control group. Average and low-ability students showed the greatest improvement after training (Raphael, 1984). More repetition was needed for primary-grade children to learn QARs than for intermediate-grade children to learn them (Raphael, 1986).

Raphael (1986) has recently modified QAR instruction to include four categories, clustered under two headings. The following diagram illustrates this modification.

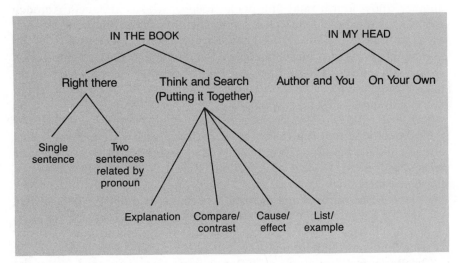

Source: Reprinted with permission of Taffy E. Raphael and the International Reading Association.

In the modified scheme, the "In My Head" category is divided into questions that involve both the text information and the reader's background of experiences (Author and You) and those that can be answered from the reader's experience without information from the story (On My Own) (Raphael, 1986).

Discussing the use of the QAR categorization to plan questioning strategies, Raphael (1986, p. 521) states: "Questions asked prior to reading are usually On My Own QARs. They are designed to help students think about what they already know and how it relates to the upcoming story or content text. In creating guided reading questions, it is important to balance text-based and inference questions. For these, Think and Search QARs should dominate, since they require integration of information and should build to the asking of Author and You QARs. Finally, for extension activities, teachers will want to create primarily On My Own or Author and You QARs, focusing again on students' background information as it pertains to the text."

Helping Students Question

Many authorities currently believe that having the reader generate questions throughout the reading process is important to comprehension. The reader is in control of the reading process when reading in this manner (Nolte and Singer, 1985). In one study, third-grade students were trained to ask literal questions about material being read. They learned to discriminate questions from nonquestions and good literal questions from poor ones, and they practiced producing good literal questions for paragraphs and then for stories, which they read to answer the questions. Their comprehension was enhanced by the question-generation and answering procedure (Cohen, 1983). In another study, fourth- and fifth-grade students who were taught (through modeling, with gradual phasing out of teacher involvement) to generate their own questions based on a story grammar outperformed a control group on a comprehension measure administered at the end of the training period (Nolte and Singer, 1985). Bristow (1985) believes that provision of interspersed questions in the text to provide a transition from teacher questioning to self-questioning may be helpful.

Kitagawa (1982, p. 43) encouraged children to become questioners by asking questions that had to be answered by a question, such as "What question did the author mainly answer in the passage we just read?" She also encouraged them to develop questions they wished to have answered through educational activities, such as field trips, and to construct preview questions, based on titles and pictures, for reading selections. Students were asked what questions they would ask the author of a selection or a character, if they could, and they were asked to predict the questions that would be answered next in the selection.

The Reciprocal Questioning (ReQuest) procedure, developed by Manzo (1969), seems a promising way of improving reading comprehension as well as of helping children develop questioning techniques. ReQuest is a one-to-one teaching technique that encourages children to think critically and formulate questions. A condensed outline of the procedure is given below.

1. Both child and teacher have copies of the selection to read.
2. Both silently read the first sentence. The child may ask the teacher as many questions as he or she wishes about that sentence. The child is told to try to ask the kind of questions that the teacher might ask, in the way the teacher might ask them.
3. The teacher answers the questions but requires the child to rephrase those questions that he or she cannot answer because of their poor syntax or incorrect logic.
4. After the teacher has answered all the child's questions, both read the second sentence, and the teacher asks as many questions as he or she feels will profitably add to the child's understanding of the content.
5. The teacher periodically requires the child to verify his or her responses.

All through this interaction, the teacher constantly encourages the child to imitate the teacher's questioning behavior, reinforcing such behavior by saying, "That's a good question" or by giving the fullest possible reply.

This procedure continues until the child can read all the words in the first paragraph, can demonstrate literal understanding of what he or she has read, and can formulate a reasonable purpose, stated as a question, for completing the remainder of the selection.[1]

✔ Self-Check: Objective 10

Name seven types of questions that are useful in guiding reading and checking comprehension.
Name five of the ten guidelines for question preparation mentioned in this section.
(See Self-Improvement Opportunity 8.)

Summary

The central factor in reading is comprehension of the material read. Since reading is an interactive process that involves both the information brought to the text by readers and the information supplied by the text, good comprehension depends upon readers' backgrounds of experience as well as their facility with various comprehension skills that help them unlock the meanings within the text. The schemata built through these experiences aid the comprehension of printed material and are themselves modified by input from the printed material.

Readers must learn to comprehend sentences, paragraphs, and whole selections. Sentences that are complex, contain relative clauses, are in the passive voice, contain pronouns, have missing words, have implied relationships, or express negation may need special attention because students may have difficulty in comprehending them. The meaning conveyed by punctuation in sentences should also receive attention. Students also need help in understanding the functions and organizational patterns of paragraphs. They then have to understand the ways that whole selections are organized and how prereading, during reading, and postreading activities can foster comprehension of these selections. Prereading activities such as previews, computer use, anticipation guides, the VLP approach, and semantic mapping can be

---

[1] For a specific illustration of helping children to ask questions by using a technique called DRTA, see Elaine Schwartz and Alice Sherf, "Student Involvement in Questioning for Comprehension," *The Reading Teacher* 29 (November 1975): 150–54. See also Barbara Olmo, "Teaching Students to Ask Questions," *Language Arts* 52 (November/December 1975): 1116–19 for more ideas on questioning.

270

Teaching
Reading in
Today's
Elementary
Schools

helpful. Metacognitive strategies, questioning, and the cloze procedure are among the techniques that can be used during reading. Postreading activities usually involve extending knowledge on the topic and questioning. Some activities, such as semantic webbing and story mapping, story grammar and story frame activities, other story structure techniques, and writing activities related to reading may be involved in prereading, during reading, and postreading activities at various times.

Four types of comprehension are discussed in this chapter. Literal reading is reading for directly stated ideas; interpretive reading is reading for implied ideas; critical reading is reading for evaluation; and creative reading is reading beyond the lines. Teachers can generally teach skills in all of these areas most effectively through explanation and modeling, guided student practice, and independent student practice.

Questioning techniques are important to instruction because teachers use questions to provide purposes for reading, to elicit and focus discussion, and to check comprehension of material read. Questions may be based on comprehension skills or story structure. Students may need to be taught how to approach answering questions. Self-questioning by the reader is also a valuable comprehension and comprehension-monitoring technique. Teachers can help students develop the skill of self-questioning.

Test Yourself

True or False

_____ 1. Each schema that a person has represents what the person knows about a particular concept and the interrelationships among the known pieces of information.

_____ 2. Anything that increases a reader's background knowledge may also increase comprehension.

_____ 3. Anaphoric relationships are easy ones for children to comprehend.

_____ 4. Students may have trouble understanding sentences involving negation.

_____ 5. Previews for stories that build background related to the stories have a positive effect on comprehension.

_____ 6. Punctuation marks are clues to pauses and pitch changes.

_____ 7. The main idea of a paragraph is always stated in the form of a topic sentence.

_____ 8. Literal comprehension involves acquiring information that is directly stated in a selection.

_____ 9. Students must attend to details when they follow directions.

_____ 10. Comic strips can be used to develop an activity for recognizing sequence.

_____ 11. Critical reading is reading for evaluation.

_____ 12. Critical reading skills are easier to teach than literal reading skills.

_____ 13. Readers at the critical and interpretive levels are interested in determining the author's purpose.

_____ 14. Critical readers are not interested in copyright dates of material they read.

_____ 15. An inference is an idea that is implied in the material rather than directly stated.

_____ 16. Elementary school children are too young to be able to recognize propaganda techniques.

_____ 17. A bandwagon approach takes advantage of the desires of people to conform to the crowd.

_____ 18. Critical thinking skills should first be given attention in the intermediate grades.

_____ 19. Critical readers read with a questioning attitude.

_____ 20. Creative reading involves going beyond the material presented by the author.

_____ 21. Teachers should give little class time to creative reading because it is not practical.

_____ 22. All reading that children do should be purposeful.

_____ 23. When making out comprehension questions for testing purposes, teachers should use several different types of questions.

_____ 24. A good test is a hard test and vice versa.

_____ 25. Listing questions and sequence questions are the same thing.

_____ 26. Comprehension-monitoring techniques are metacognitive strategies.

_____ 27. Punctuation marks do not function as clues to sentence meaning.

_____ 28. Children sometimes make overgeneralizations in dealing with word meanings.

_____ 29. Research has shown that teachers spend the majority of their time on instruction in reading comprehension.

_____ 30. Reading comprehension involves relating textual information to pre-existing knowledge structures.

_____ 31. Comprehension skills should be taught in a way that emphasizes their application when students are actually reading connected discourse.

_____ 32. Less able readers may rely too much on either text-based or knowledge-based processing.

_____ 33. Richard Rystrom has presented an argument that reading is exclusively a top-down process.

_____ 34. InQuest combines student questioning with creative drama.

_____ 35. Story grammar activities can increase understanding of story structure and serve as a basis for questioning.

_____ 36. Restrictive clauses cause few comprehension problems for children.

_____ 37. Semantic webbing involves systematically deleting words from a printed passage.

272

Teaching
Reading in
Today's
Elementary
Schools

_____ 38. Children make inferences that are consistent with their schemata.

_____ 39. Some children have difficulty determining referents of pronouns and adverbs.

_____ 40. Young children are unable to make inferences.

Self-Improvement Opportunities

1. Choose a short selection about an uncommon subject. Question your classmates to find out how complete their schemata on this topic are. Give them copies of the selection to read. Discuss the reading difficulties some of them had because of inadequate prior knowledge.
2. Construct a time line for a chapter in a social studies text that has a chronological order organizational pattern. Describe to your classmates how you could use the time line with children to teach this organizational pattern.
3. Write an anticipation guide for a well-known folktale. Discuss the guide in class.
4. Construct a story map for a story. Display the map in class and let your classmates try to predict the contents of the story from it.
5. Use old newspapers to devise teaching materials for
   a. finding main ideas.
   b. locating propaganda techniques.
   c. distinguishing fact from opinion.
   d. recognizing sequence.
6. Make a "Following Directions" board game.
7. Make a file of examples of each of the propaganda techniques listed in the chapter. File ideas for teaching activities, games, bulletin boards, and so on, and show your files to your classmates, sharing with them the possible instructional uses of your file.
8. Make up questions of the seven types listed on the content found in this chapter or on the content of another chapter in this book. Bring the questions to class and ask classmates to respond.

Bibliography

Babbs, Patricia J., and Alden J. Moe. "Metacognition: A Key for Independent Learning from Text." _The Reading Teacher_ 36 (January 1983): 422–26.

Baker, Deborah Tresidder. "What Happened When? Activities for Teaching Sequence Skills." _The Reading Teacher_ 36 (November 1982): 216–18.

Balajthy, Ernest. "Computer Simulations and Reading." _The Reading Teacher_ 37 (March 1984): 590–93.

Barnitz, John G. "Developing Sentence Comprehension in Reading." *Language Arts* 56 (November/December 1979): 902–908, 958.

Beck, Isabel L., and Margaret G. McKeown. "Developing Questions That Promote Comprehension: The Story Map." *Language Arts* 58 (November/December 1981): 913–18.

Boodt, Gloria M. "Critical Listeners Become Critical Readers in Remedial Reading Class." *The Reading Teacher* 37 (January 1984): 390–94.

Bristow, Page Simpson. "Are Poor Readers Passive Readers? Some Evidence, Possible Explanations, and Potential Solutions." *The Reading Teacher* 39 (December 1985): 318–25.

Bromley, Karen D'Angelo. "Teaching Idioms." *The Reading Teacher* 38 (December 1984): 272–76.

Carr, Kathryn S. "The Importance of Inference Skills in the Primary Grades." *The Reading Teacher* 36 (February 1983): 518–22.

Cohen, Ruth. "Self-Generated Questions as an Aid to Reading Comprehension." *The Reading Teacher* 36 (April 1983): 770–75.

Crafton, Linda K. "Comprehension Before, During, and After Reading." *The Reading Teacher* 36 (December 1982): 293–97.

Crowell, Doris C., and Kathryn Hu-pei Au. "A Scale of Questions to Guide Comprehension Instruction." *The Reading Teacher* 34 (January 1981): 389–93.

Cunningham, Pat. "Improving Listening and Reading Comprehension." *The Reading Teacher* 35 (January 1982a): 486–88.

Cunningham, Pat. "Knowledge for More Comprehension." *The Reading Teacher* 36 (October 1982b): 98–101.

Donlan, Dan. "Locating Main Ideas in History Textbooks." *Journal of Reading* 24 (November 1980): 135–40.

Dreher, Mariam Jean, and Harry Singer. "Story Grammar Instruction Unnecessary for Intermediate Grade Students." *The Reading Teacher* 34 (December 1980): 261–68.

Durkin, Dolores. "Reading Comprehension Instruction in Five Basal Reader Series." *Reading Research Quarterly* 16 (1981a): 515–44.

Durkin, Dolores. "What Classroom Observations Reveal About Reading Comprehension Instruction." *Reading Research Quarterly* 14 (1978–79): 481–533.

Durkin, Dolores. "What Is the Value of the New Interest in Reading Comprehension?" *Language Arts* 58 (January 1981b): 23–43.

Eads, Maryann. "What to Do When They Don't Understand What They Read—Research-Based Strategies for Teaching Reading Comprehension." *The Reading Teacher* 34 (February 1981): 565–71.

Farrar, Mary Thomas. "Another Look at Oral Questions for Comprehension." *The Reading Teacher* 36 (January 1983): 370–74.

Farrar, Mary Thomas. "Asking Better Questions." *The Reading Teacher* 38 (October 1984a): 10–15.

Farrar, Mary Thomas. "Why Do We Ask Comprehension Questions? A

274

Teaching
Reading in
Today's
Elementary
Schools

New Conception of Comprehension Instruction." *The Reading Teacher* 37 (February 1984b): 452–56.

Fowler, Gerald. "Developing Comprehension Skills in Primary Students Through the Use of Story Frames." *The Reading Teacher* 36 (November 1982): 176–79.

Fredericks, Anthony D. "Mental Imagery Activities to Improve Comprehension." *The Reading Teacher* 40 (October 1986): 78–81.

Freedman, Glenn, and Elizabeth G. Reynolds. "Enriching Basal Reader Lessons with Semantic Webbing." *The Reading Teacher* 33 (March 1980): 667–84.

Galda, Lee. "Playing About a Story: Its Impact on Comprehension." *The Reading Teacher* 36 (October 1982): 52–55.

Gardner, Michael K., and Martha M. Smith. "Does Perspective Taking Ability Contribute to Reading Comprehension?" *Journal of Reading* 30 (January 1987): 333–36.

Golden, Joanne M. "Children's Concept of Story in Reading and Writing." *The Reading Teacher* 37 (March 1984): 578–84.

Gordon, Christine, and P. David Pearson. *Effects of Instruction in Metacomprehension and Inferencing on Students' Comprehension Abilities.* Technical Report No. 269. Urbana: University of Illinois, 1983.

Greenewald, M. Jane, and Rosalind L. Rossing. "Short-Term and Long-Term Effects of Story Grammar and Self-Monitoring Training on Children's Story Comprehension." In *Solving Problems in Literacy: Learners, Teachers, and Researchers,* Jerome A. Niles and Rosary V. Lalik, eds. Rochester, N.Y.: National Reading Conference, 1986, pp. 87–91.

Hacker, Charles J. "From Schema Theory to Classroom Practice." *Language Arts* 57 (November/December 1980): 866–71.

Hansen, Jane. "The Effects of Inference Training and Practice on Young Children's Reading Comprehension." *Reading Research Quarterly* 16, no. 3 (1981a): 391–417.

Hansen, Jane. "An Inferential Comprehension Strategy for Use with Primary Grade Children." *The Reading Teacher* 34 (March 1981b): 665–69.

Hansen, Jane, and Ruth Hubbard. "Poor Readers Can Draw Inferences." *The Reading Teacher* 37 (March 1984): 586–89.

Hansen, Jane, and P. David Pearson. "An Instructional Study: Improving the Inferential Comprehension of Fourth Grade Good and Poor Readers." *Journal of Educational Psychology* 75, no. 6 (1983): 821–29.

Harris, Theodore L., and Richard E. Hodges, eds. *A Dictionary of Reading and Related Terms.* Newark, Del.: International Reading Association, 1981.

Holmes, Betty C. "A Confirmation Strategy for Improving Poor Readers' Ability to Answer Inferential Questions." *The Reading Teacher* 37 (November 1983): 144–47.

Huus, Helen. "Critical and Creative Reading." In *Critical Reading,"* Martha L. King, Bernice Ellinger, and Willavene Wolf, eds. New York: J. B. Lippincott, 1967, pp. 84–89.

Irwin, Judith Westphal. "Implicit Connectives and Comprehension." *The Reading Teacher* 33 (February 1980): 527–29.

Irwin, Judith Westphal. *Teaching Reading Comprehension Processes.* Englewood Cliffs, N.J.: Prentice-Hall, 1986.

Jett-Simpson, Mary. "Writing Stories Using Model Structures: The Circle Story." *Language Arts* 58 (March 1981): 293–300.

Johnson, Dale D., and Bonnie von Hoff Johnson. "Highlighting Vocabulary in Inferential Comprehension Instruction." *Journal of Reading* 29 (April 1986): 622–25.

Johnson, Dale D., Susan D. Pittelman, and Joan E. Heimlich. "Semantic Mapping." *The Reading Teacher* 39 (April 1986): 778–83.

Jones, Linda L. "An Interactive View of Reading: Implications for the Classroom." *The Reading Teacher* 35 (April 1982): 772–77.

Kachuck, Beatrice. "Relative Clauses May Cause Confusion for Young Readers." *The Reading Teacher* 34 (January 1981): 372–77.

Kaiden, Ellen, and Linda Rice. "Paragraph Patterns and Comprehension: A Tactical Approach." *Journal of Reading* 30 (November 1986): 164–66.

Kimmel, Susan, and Walter H. MacGinitie. "Helping Students Revise Hypotheses While Reading." *The Reading Teacher* 38 (April 1985): 768–71.

Kitagawa, Mary M. "Improving Discussions or How to Get the Students to Ask the Questions." *The Reading Teacher* 36 (October 1982): 42–45.

Lange, Bob. "Making Sense with Schemata." *Journal of Reading* 24 (February 1981): 442–45.

Mandler, Jean M., and Nancy S. Johnson. "Remembrance of Things Parsed: Story Structure and Recall." *Cognitive Psychology* 9 (January 1977): 111–51.

Manzo, Anthony V. "The ReQuest Procedure." *Journal of Reading* 13 (November 1969): 123–26.

Marshall, Nancy. "Using Story Grammar to Assess Reading Comprehension." *The Reading Teacher* 36 (March 1983): 616–20.

Mathewson, Grover C. "Teaching Forms of Negation in Reading and Reasoning." *The Reading Teacher* 37 (January 1984): 354–58.

McGee, Lea M., and Gail E. Tompkins. "The Videotape Answer to Independent Reading Comprehension Activities." *The Reading Teacher* 34 (January 1981): 427–33.

McIntosh, Margaret E. "What Do Practitioners Need to Know About Current Inference Research?" *The Reading Teacher* 38 (April 1985): 755–61.

Miller, G. Michael, and George E. Mason. "Dramatic Improvisation: Risk-Free Role Playing for Improving Reading Performance." *The Reading Teacher* 37 (November 1983): 128–31.

Moldofsky, Penny Baum. "Teaching Students to Determine the Central Story Problem: A Practical Application of Schema Theory." *The Reading Teacher* 36 (April 1983): 740–45.

Moore, David W., and James W. Cunningham. "Task Clarity and

276

Teaching
Reading in
Today's
Elementary
Schools

Sixth-Grade Students' Main Idea Statements." In *Changing Perspectives on Research in Reading/Language Processing and Instruction,* Jerome A. Niles and Larry A. Harris, eds. Rochester, N.Y.: National Reading Conference, 1984, pp. 90–94.

Moore, David W., and John E. Readence. "Processing Main Ideas Through Parallel Lesson Transfer." *Journal of Reading* 23 (April 1980): 589–93.

Moss, Joy F., and Sherri Oden. "Children's Story Comprehension and Story Learning." *The Reading Teacher* 36 (April 1983): 784–89.

Nessel, Denise. "Storytelling in the Reading Program." *The Reading Teacher* 38 (January 1985): 378–81.

Neville, Rita. "Critical Thinkers Become Critical Readers." *The Reading Teacher* 35 (May 1982): 947–48.

Newcastle, Helen. "Children's Problems with Written Directions." *The Reading Teacher* 28 (December 1974): 292–94.

Nolte, Ruth Yopp, and Harry Singer. "Active Comprehension: Teaching a Process of Reading Comprehension and Its Effects on Reading Achievement." *The Reading Teacher* 39 (October 1985): 24–31.

Olmo, Barbara. "Teaching Students to Ask Questions." *Language Arts* 52 (November/December 1975): 1116–19.

Palincsar, Annemarie Sullivan, and Ann L. Brown. "Interactive Teaching to Promote Independent Learning from Text." *The Reading Teacher* 39 (April 1986): 771–77.

Pearson, P. David. *Asking Questions About Stories.* Occasional Paper No. 15. Columbus, Ohio: Ginn and Company, 1982.

Pearson, P. David. "Changing the Face of Comprehension Instruction." *The Reading Teacher* 38 (April 1985): 724–38.

Pearson, P. David, and Kaybeth Camperell. "Comprehension of Text Structures." In *Comprehension and Teaching: Research Reviews,* John T. Guthrie, ed. Newark, Del.: International Reading Association, 1981, pp. 27–55.

Pearson, P. David, and Dale D. Johnson. *Teaching Reading Comprehension.* New York: Holt, Rinehart and Winston, 1978.

Pearson, P. David, et al. *The Effect of Background Knowledge on Young Children's Comprehension of Explicit and Implicit Information.* Urbana: University of Illinois, Center for the Study of Reading, 1979.

Pellegrini, A. D., and Lee Galda. "The Effects of Thematic-Fantasy Play Training on the Development of Children's Story Comprehension." *American Educational Research Journal* 19 (Fall 1982): 443–52.

Pigg, John R. "The Effects of a Storytelling/Storyreading Program on the Language Skills of Rural Primary Students." Unpublished paper. Cookeville: Tennessee Technological University, 1986.

Poindexter, Candace A., and Susan Prescott. "A Technique for Teaching Students to Draw Inferences from Text." *The Reading Teacher* 39 (May 1986): 908–11.

Rabin, Annette T. "Critical Reading." *Journal of Reading* 24 (January 1981): 348.

Rand, Muriel K. "Story Schema: Theory, Research and Practice." *The Reading Teacher* 37 (January 1984): 377–82.

Raphael, Taffy E. "Question-Answering Strategies for Children." *The Reading Teacher* 36 (November 1982): 186–90.

Raphael, Taffy E. "Teaching Learners About Sources of Information for Answering Comprehension Questions." *Journal of Reading* 27 (January 1984): 303–11.

Raphael, Taffy E. "Teaching Question Answer Relationships, Revisited." *The Reading Teacher* 39 (February 1986): 516–22.

Raphael, Taffy E., and P. David Pearson. *The Effect of Metacognitive Awareness Training on Children's Question Answering Behavior.* Technical Report No. 238. Urbana: University of Illinois, Center for the Study of Reading, 1982.

Reutzel, D. Ray. "Clozing in on Comprehension: The Cloze Story Map." *The Reading Teacher* 39 (February 1986): 524–28.

Reutzel, D. Ray. "Story Maps Improve Comprehension." *The Reading Teacher* 38 (January 1985): 400–404.

Roe, Betty D. *Use of Storytelling/Storyreading in Conjunction with Follow-up Language Activities to Improve Oral Communication of Rural First Grade Students: Phase I.* Cookeville, Tenn.: Rural Education Consortium, 1985.

Roe, Betty D. *Use of Storytelling/Storyreading in Conjunction with Follow-up Language Activities to Improve Oral Communication of Rural Primary Grade Students: Phase II.* Cookeville, Tenn.: Rural Education Consortium, 1986.

Roney, R. Craig. "Background Experience Is the Foundation of Success in Learning to Read." *The Reading Teacher* 38 (November 1984): 196–99.

Ross, Elinor Parry. "Checking the Source: An Essential Component of Critical Reading." *Journal of Reading* 24 (January 1981): 311–15.

Rumelhart, David E. "Schemata: The Building Blocks of Cognition." In *Comprehension and Teaching: Research Reviews*, John T. Guthrie, ed. Newark, Del.: International Reading Association, 1981, pp. 3–26.

Sadow, Marilyn W. "The Use of Story Grammar in the Design of Questions." *The Reading Teacher* 35 (February 1982): 518–22.

Schoenfeld, Florence G. "Instructional Uses of the Cloze Procedure." *The Reading Teacher* 34 (November 1980): 147–51.

Schwartz, Elaine, and Alice Sheff. "Student Involvement in Questioning for Comprehension." *The Reading Teacher* 29 (November 1975): 150–54.

Sebesta, Sam Leaton, James William Calder, and Lynne Nelson Cleland. "A Story Grammar for the Classroom." *The Reading Teacher* 36 (November 1982): 180–84.

Shake, Mary C., and Richard L. Allington. "Where Do Teacher's Questions Come From?" *The Reading Teacher* 38 (January 1985): 432–38.

Shanahan, Timothy. "Predictions and the Limiting Effects of Prequestions." In *Solving Problems in Literacy: Learners, Teachers, and Researchers*, Jerome A. Niles and Rosary V. Lalik, eds. Rochester, N.Y.: National Reading Conference, 1986, pp. 92–98.

278

Teaching
Reading in
Today's
Elementary
Schools

Shoop, Mary. "InQuest: A Listening and Reading Comprehension Strategy." *The Reading Teacher* 39 (March 1986): 670–74.

Singer, Harry, John D. McNeil, and Lory L. Furse. "Relationship Between Curriculum Scope and Reading Achievement in Elementary Schools." *The Reading Teacher* 37 (March 1984): 608–12.

Smith, Marilyn, and Thomas W. Bean. "Four Strategies That Develop Children's Story Comprehension and Writing." *The Reading Teacher* 37 (December 1983): 295–301.

Spiegel, Dixie Lee, and Jill Fitzgerald. "Improving Reading Comprehension Through Instruction About Story Parts." *The Reading Teacher* 39 (March 1986): 676–82.

Spiro, Rand J. *Etiology of Comprehension Style.* Urbana: University of Illinois, Center for the Study of Reading, 1979.

Stauffer, Russell G., and Ronald Cramer. *Teaching Reading at the Primary Level.* Newark, Del.: International Reading Association, 1968.

Stevens, Kathleen C. "Can We Improve Reading by Teaching Background Information?" *Journal of Reading* 25 (January 1982): 326–29.

Strange, Michael. "Instructional Implications of a Conceptual Theory of Reading Comprehension." *The Reading Teacher* 33 (January 1980): 391–97.

Tierney, Robert J., and James W. Cunningham. "Research on Teaching Reading Comprehension." In *Handbook of Reading Research,* P. David Pearson, ed. New York: Longman, 1984, pp. 609–55.

Valmont, William J. "Cloze Deletion Patterns: How Deletions Are Made Makes A Big Difference." *The Reading Teacher* 37 (November 1983): 172–75.

Varnhagen, Connie K., and Susan R. Goldman. "Improving Comprehension: Causal Relations Instruction for Learning Handicapped Learners." *The Reading Teacher* 39 (May 1986): 896–904.

Whaley, Jill Fitzgerald. "Story Grammars and Reading Instruction." *The Reading Teacher* 34 (April 1981): 762–71.

Whitmer, Jean E. "Pickles Will Kill You: Use Humorous Literature to Teach Critical Reading." *The Reading Teacher* 39 (February 1986): 530–34.

Wiesendanger, Katherine D. "Comprehension: Using Anticipation Guides." *The Reading Teacher* 39 (November 1985): 241–42.

Wilson, Cathy Roller. "Teaching Reading Comprehension by Connecting the Known to the New." *The Reading Teacher* 36 (January 1983): 382–90.

Wixson, Karen K. "Questions About a Text: What You Ask About Is What Children Learn." *The Reading Teacher* 37 (December 1983): 287–93.

Wood, Karen D. "Probable Passages: A Writing Strategy." *The Reading Teacher* 37 (February 1984): 496–99.

Wood, Karen D., and Nora Robinson. "Vocabulary, Language and Prediction: A Prereading Strategy." *The Reading Teacher* 36 (January 1983): 392–95.

Zimet, Sara Goodman. "Teaching Children to Detect Social Bias in Books." *The Reading Teacher* 36 (January 1983): 418–21.

Chapter 6

Major Approaches to
Reading Instruction

Introduction

Over the years educators have developed many approaches to teaching reading. Some of the more widely accepted ones are discussed in this chapter. These approaches are not mutually exclusive; in many instances teachers use more than one method simultaneously. In fact, educators who advocate an eclectic approach urge teachers to use the best techniques and materials from each approach in order to meet the varied needs of the individuals in any classroom. The authors of this text take this position, believing that no one approach is best for all students or for all teachers.

Setting Objectives

When you finish reading this chapter, you should be able to

1. Name the types of materials that are a part of most basal reader series.
2. Compare and contrast a directed reading activity with a directed reading-thinking activity.
3. Explain the rationale behind the language experience approach.
4. Discuss the characteristics of the individualized reading approach.
5. Name some other ways of individualizing reading instruction.
6. Discuss the features of linguistic approaches.

Key Vocabulary

Pay close attention to these terms when they appear in the chapter.

computer-assisted instruction
computer-managed instruction
directed reading activity
directed reading-thinking activity
eclectic approaches
expectation outline

experience charts
individualized reading approach
interest inventory
language experience approach
linguistics
minimally contrasting spelling patterns

objective-based approach
prereading guided reading procedure
programmed instruction
Reconciled Reading Lesson
word bank
Word Wonder

BASAL READER APPROACH

Basal reader series are the most widely used materials for teaching reading in the elementary schools of America. They help children become ready for reading and they provide for development and practice of reading skills in each grade. Series generally have one or more readiness books (paperback), several preprimers (paperback), a primer (hardback), a first reader (hardback), and one or two readers for each succeeding grade level through grade six or eight (hardback). For example, the Houghton Mifflin Reading Program has two readiness books, three preprimers, a primer, a first reader, a 2^1 (first half of second grade) reader, a 2^2 (second half of second grade) reader, a 3^1 reader, a 3^2 reader, and one reader for each of the grades four through eight. Basal reader series are generally referred to by their publishers' names (for example, the Houghton Mifflin series, the Scott Foresman series, the Ginn series, and so on).

In addition to the student readers, basal reader series include teacher's manuals, which have detailed lesson plans that help teachers use the readers to best advantage. Teachers who follow these plans use what is called a directed reading activity (DRA), described later in this chapter. Basal reader series also include workbooks that children can use to reinforce skills they have previously learned in class. Workbooks are not designed to teach the skills and should not be used for this purpose. Many publishing companies offer other supplementary materials to be used in conjunction with basal series, such as "big books" (chart-sized replicas of readiness book pages and preprimer stories), read-aloud libraries for the teacher, duplicating masters, unit tests, and various other items.

The major strengths of basal reader programs are listed below.

1. The books are carefully graded in difficulty. The vocabularies of most series are carefully controlled so that children do not meet too many unfamiliar words in a single lesson, and repetition of words is planned so that the children have a chance to fix them in their memories.
2. The teacher's manuals have many valuable suggestions about teaching reading lessons, and thus can save much lesson preparation time.
3. Most basal reader series deal with all phases of the reading program, including word recognition, comprehension, oral reading, silent reading, reading for information, and reading for enjoyment. This comprehensive coverage helps a teacher avoid overemphasis or underemphasis of any aspect.
4. The series provide for systematic teaching of skills and systematic review.

Nevertheless, basal readers have frequently been the object of criticism in the past. The weaknesses that have been mentioned most often are:

1. Controlled vocabularies result in dull, repetitive stories with little literary merit.
2. The sentence structure found in most basal readers is not like that used by children who read them. It is too stiff and formal, devoid of the contractions and sentence fragments used in normal conversation.

282

**Teaching
Reading in
Today's
Elementary
Schools**

3. Settings and characters tend to be familiar to middle-class suburban white children from intact families, but not to other racial and socioeconomic groups or to groups from rural or urban backgrounds.

4. The characters tend to be presented in stereotyped male/female roles and situations.

5. Basal series are often advertised as *total* reading programs. If teachers accept this assertion, they may fail to provide the variety of experiences that children need for a balanced program.

6. Teachers are often led to believe that if they do not carry out *all* the suggestions in the teacher's manuals, they will fail to provide adequate instruction. By trying to do everything suggested, they use up valuable time with inappropriate activities for some groups of children, leaving no time for appropriate ones. Basal readers should not be used from front to back in their entirety without considering the special needs of particular children in the class.

Authors of basal readers have been trying, with a good deal of success, to overcome the causes of these criticisms. In order to provide stories with high quality, limited vocabulary, and extensive repetition, they have included folktales in some of the early readers. Other good literature is also included. Authors have tried to make the language more like normal conversation, and they have diversified the characters, introducing people of various races, roles, and backgrounds. Female children now sometimes wear jeans and play ball rather than being permanently relegated to the kitchen to bake cookies. Dad has ceased to dress perpetually in a business suit, and Mom appears without an apron. All of these modifications show sensitivity to the needs of textbook users and the changes in society.

Recently other complaints have surfaced. One is based on research by Durkin (1981), which uncovered the fact that teacher's manuals of basal reader series give much more attention to comprehension assessment and practice than to direct, explicit instruction. The teaching suggestions that are included tend to be very brief, and often ideas for instruction in comprehension are offered *after* a selection, when such instruction would have been helpful in understanding the selection itself. In addition, manuals only infrequently bring together related materials (such as different ways of showing possession) in review so that teachers can emphasize the relationships.

Sorenson (1985) found that basal reader teacher's manuals often use the same instructions to teach all vocabulary words, regardless of the particular words involved or the grade level of the reader. Since individual words have characteristics that require different teaching approaches for most effective learning (concrete versus abstract words, for example), teachers must adjust instruction when manuals fail to do so. In addition, basal reader manuals often give more attention to the pronunciations of new words than to their meanings, and they often ignore the fact that words have more meanings than the one found in a particular story. They often assume that words that have been previously presented have been learned, giving no attention to the possible need for reteaching. They also assume that words not previously taught in the basal reader are new, an assumption that is also not necessarily true. Furthermore, some basal readers offer little vocabulary instruction for students in upper grade levels; those that do offer vocabulary instruction often fail to adjust the strategies to the increased concept difficulty of words presented in higher-level readers.

Another complaint relates to the style of writing that is common in basal readers, especially those at the lower levels. Bridge, Winograd, and Haley (1983) point out that the plotless strings of disconnected sentences found in preprimer and primer selections may adversely affect the comprehension of beginning readers because the structures of these selections are not predictable in the way that those of normal stories are. In many cases the selections' sentences are disconnected because of efforts to make the readability of the selections lower and therefore more appropriate to younger children. Chopping up longer sentences and leaving out connectives, however, may make the sentences harder for children to read because of the inferences about sentence relationships that must be made. In addition, typical story parts, such as settings or reactions, may be omitted from stories in basal readers because of the vocabulary limitations of the particular grade level. Such omissions may violate the knowledge that young children possess about story structure, however, and the children may be unable to make sense out of the narratives. Egan (1983) has pointed out that many traditional folktales appearing in reading texts have been so transformed by rewriting that they have lost much of their original impact. Vocabulary limitations may also adversely affect the integrity of the story. In one adaptation of "The Shoemaker and the Elves," the words *shoes, elves,* and *shoemaker* are not used (Holbrook, 1985). In such a case, a claim of using traditional literature seems unfounded. The story has lost its traditional character.

Picture-dependent stories are frequent in first-grade basal readers. These stories require children to understand both words and pictures in order to obtain the meaning. This requirement causes divided attention and may be particularly hard for less able readers (Elster and Simons, 1985). In addition, this approach may discourage readers from looking for meaning in the words presented. They may become too picture-dependent, which is undesirable because pictures generally are gradually phased out as major content transmitters in later grades.

The readability levels of the workbooks accompanying basal readers, as opposed to the readability levels of the readers themselves, have also generated complaints. Fitzgerald (1979) and Stensen (1982) found that, in general, workbooks were too difficult for the grade levels for which they were intended and that workbooks for grades four through six were especially difficult, being at seventh-grade level or above.

Basal reader workbook pages often fail to relate directly to the story in the reader and also fail to give sufficient attention to higher-level comprehension

284

Teaching
Reading in
Today's
Elementary
Schools

skills. Therefore, Scheu, Tanner, and Au (1986) suggest that it may be beneficial for teachers to construct skill worksheets for seatwork that reinforce comprehension instruction given in basal reader lessons and that relate to the story just read.

Basal reader readiness materials have also been brought under scrutiny. Templeton (1986) points out that they tend to work on sounds first and print second, even though the use of print can facilitate the development of metalinguistic awareness, because print is not as hard to study as speech. Speech is too transitory to be studied readily. Additionally, because basal reader readiness materials often present letter-sound associations before children have a concept of *word*, children are unable to apply these associations usefully. Finally, the value of writing activities in developing metalinguistic awareness has not generally been recognized by developers of basal readiness activities.

Recently, interest in the characteristics and content of basal readers has increased, as reflected by several studies that have discovered pertinent information. Hare (1982) studied the teacher's manuals of four series, two of which had an early meaning-getting emphasis and the other two of which had an early decoding emphasis, to determine whether comprehension questions reflected the philosophical stance of the series. She hypothesized that the meaning-emphasis series would have more questions requiring inferential thinking and use of prior knowledge, whereas the decoding-emphasis series would use more literal and text-based questions. This hypothesis was affirmed to some extent, but Hare found many similarities between the two types of readers. Both had larger numbers of literal questions in the first-grade text than at the higher levels, although the decoding-emphasis texts had slightly larger percentages of these questions than the meaning-emphasis texts did. When Hare also considered grades three and five, however, she found no significant differences in the number of strictly literal questions in the two types of series. In the fifth-grade texts, both types of series had more questions requiring children to integrate passage information with prior knowledge, although the meaning-emphasis series had a higher percentage of these than the decoding-emphasis series did. This study appears to indicate that a series' philosophy is only somewhat evident in the relative concentration of question types asked.

Some teachers feel assured that their students will learn the most common English words as long as they follow the adopted basal program. According to a study by Fry and Sakiey (1986), however, only about 50 percent to 59 percent of the 3,000 most common English words are introduced in basal readers for kindergarten to grade six. Teachers who wish to present more of the common words will need to supplement the vocabulary presented in basal readers. The results of this study may be somewhat misleading, however, since students can easily decode some of the words not presented after they have learned standard word recognition techniques. For example, students who have learned the phonics generalization about words that have

Basal reading series, the most widely used materials for teaching reading in elementary schools, include graded reading texts and accompanying teacher's manuals. (© Susan Lapides)

only one vowel that is not at the end of the word (generalization 12 in Chapter 3) should be able to decode the word *cub,* and those who have learned the phonics generalization concerning words that have two vowels, one of which is a final *e,* should be able to decode the word *cube,* even though these words are not presented in a series. Therefore, students could learn to read words with these patterns even if the particular words were not formally presented.

Even though basal reader publishers have made strides in including more content-type material in readers in recent years, there is evidently still an imbalance in the types of material presented. An examination of preprimer through second-grade basal readers by Flood, Lapp, and Flood (1984) revealed that narrative selections still dominate, followed by poetry. Only a small percentage of the total selections was expository, and biographies and autobiographies were nearly nonexistent.

In an analysis of the content of basal reader selections by the Institute for Research on Teaching's Language Arts Project, language skills content was found "in 20.3% of the selections, social science content in 19.9%, and science content in 11.9%. Only 4.6% of the selections had content in any of

286

Teaching
Reading in
Today's
Elementary
Schools

the other major subject areas, such as art, mathematics, or music" ("Basal Reading Texts," 1984). There was functional (skills) content in 29.1 percent of the selections and ethos (right action) content in 12.3 percent of them. These figures suggest that there may not be a great deal to comprehend in some basal reader texts. The content available varied widely from publisher to publisher, however; thus educators who select texts must choose wisely.

Aaron and Anderson (1981) analyzed three basal reader series to discover the values expressed in them, and learned that the series were alike in stressing work/success/failure, cooperation/helpfulness/togetherness, solicitude for others/kindness, good and bad moral rules, strength/activity/power, novelty/excitement, cleanliness/orderliness, responsibility, independence/toughness, trying hard/don't give up, courage, smartness/cleverness/thinking, generosity/doing more than required/noncommercialism, sense of emergency, fairness, and honesty. Each of these values appeared in at least three of the sixty-three stories analyzed. Many of them were found in basals of earlier periods. Unlike earlier readers, however, today's basals were found to have strong female models in nontraditional roles.

One concern about the content of basal readers is their inadequate representation of women and members of ethnic groups. Although evidence of better representation of women and ethnic groups has been found in current basal reading series, room for improvement exists. Basal readers appear to ignore a large percentage of working women. In six 1980–1982 basal reading series that were studied, women were shown more frequently in the role of a full-time mother than in any other career, and, whereas 64 percent of careers depicted in basal readers were assigned to white males and 17 percent to minority males, only 14 percent of careers depicted were assigned to white females and 5 percent to ethnic females. It is obvious that females are not being given as many career models as are males, nor are ethnic groups being given as many models as white readers. Nevertheless, female roles in basal series have increased in 1980–1982 series from their frequency in 1977–1979 series, while male roles have decreased in frequency. During the same time period, both ethnic female and ethnic male roles have increased. The changes are slow but seem to be in the right direction. Another concern, however, is that ethnic minorities and women tend to be depicted primarily in historic career roles (Britton, Lumpkin, and Britton, 1984). More change is needed to depict both ethnic minorities and women more realistically.

Elderly people were underrepresented in 1980–1982 series also, according to the study by Britton, Lumpkin, and Britton (1984). Serra and Lamb (1984) came to the same conclusion about the elderly. Of the stories in four basal reading series, they found that only 6.8 percent dealt with elderly characters. They did find, encouragingly, that the elderly were generally depicted in a positive manner. Close relationships between them and relatives were typically shown, and many stories showed them to be wise and inspirational. The stories of the elderly dealing with hurt, problems, and challenges were sensitive. Some stories showed the elderly in relationships with special friends or helpers, and some showed them as socially active, breaking stereotyped roles.

Both Hopkins (1982) and Britton, Lumpkin, and Britton (1984) found that the handicapped were also underrepresented in basal readers. Selections about people with handicaps do not generally appear in primary materials, and many basal readers at all levels fail to include such material. In the stories that do include people with handicaps, blindness is the condition that is most often depicted.

In another research effort, Snyder (1979) studied basal stories to see if they offered role models of people reading. The results were somewhat disappointing. Although the readers depicted people reading a wide variety of printed forms, the different forms (for example, blueprints, labels, addresses on letters) did not appear often. Characters were shown reading storybooks and signs most frequently, generally in the home, and males were shown reading more than females. Even animals were shown reading more than females. Green-Wilder and Kingston (1986) also found that examples of reading behavior on the part of characters in basal reader selections were sparse. They occurred in only 7 percent to 15 percent of the selections in five basal reader series for kindergarten through grade eight, and many of the references were fleeting. Generally these activities were not central to the plots of the stories.

Finally, Pieronek (1980) studied the degree to which basal readers reflect the interests of intermediate students and found that, with minor exceptions, the books reflect the students' interests reasonably well. Only mystery and humor seem to be somewhat slighted.

Teachers should voice their feelings about the shortcomings of basal series that have been indicated by research studies. Publishers have been responsive to user reactions in the past and are likely to continue to be responsive.

Despite the fact that many negative findings have been obtained in studies of basal materials, it is still true that they are very useful to elementary school teachers. Even though improvements are possible, these materials provide positive guidance for many teachers, helping them to include all aspects of the reading program systematically. The manner in which basal materials are used, however, should receive some attention.

Use of Basal Materials

Any material, good or bad, can be used well or can be misused. Some information about the use of basal materials is therefore needed.

Many teachers form basal reading groups based upon achievement. They place the best readers in the top group, the average readers in a middle group or groups, and the poorest readers in the lowest group. In this way, these teachers feel that they can provide all of the children with basal materials that are appropriate for their reading levels. In actuality, however, the match of materials with children is not always good. Forell (1985) has pointed out that good readers are often placed in comfortable reading materials where

288

Teaching
Reading in
Today's
Elementary
Schools

word recognition problems are not frequent and attention can be given to meaning, using context clues to advantage. Poor readers, however, are often placed in "challenging" material that promotes frustration and is not conducive to comprehension, since so much attention is needed for word recognition. This arrangement thus denies them a chance for fluent reading. All readers should be given material that is comfortable enough to allow reasonable application of comprehension skills. Teachers may be reluctant to place students at as low a level as they need to be placed in order to allow this to happen, but doing so will be beneficial in the long run.

It is also true that lower reading groups will sometimes need to have more instruction at a particular level than is available in a single series. Teachers should not just move students up to higher levels when they are not ready, but should use additional books at the appropriate level from other series (Wilson, 1983).

In a study of teachers' use of basal manuals, Durkin (1984) found that teachers tended not to use recommended prereading activities but did use postreading activities. They spent little time on developing new vocabulary, building background, and providing prereading questions but spent more time on comprehension assessment questions and written practice assignments. The teachers tended to use questions from the manual, rather than original ones. The teachers also used the phonics instructional goals from the manuals, but did not follow the suggested instructional procedures. They did use the suggested written practice exercises.

It is unfortunate if Durkin's findings about usage of prereading activities is accurate, since these activities are important to comprehension. It is probably also unfortunate if the manuals' procedures for phonics instruction are being ignored by teachers, since most of these procedures are well developed and helpful. Research findings by Shake and Allington (1985) conflict with those of Durkin concerning the use of questions from the manuals. They found that second-grade teachers used more of their own questions than they did basal reader questions and that they paraphrased the basal questions when they did use them.

Blanton, Moorman, and Wood (1986) suggest that teachers use direct instruction in basal reader skill lessons. First, the students' background knowledge related to the skill should be assessed by the teacher; then the teacher should explain the skill in detail, including when it is needed and why it is important. Next, the students should try to explain the skill in their own words. Following this, the teacher should model the use of the skill for the students and then provide them with guided practice with the skill. Students should apply the skill in regular reading materials, with the teacher monitoring and providing instruction as needed. Finally, the teacher should lead the students in discussion of real-world encounters with the skill. Some of these steps may be included in basal manual instructions already. Teachers can add the other steps for more complete skills lessons.

Some educators have expressed concern that teachers do not allow students to do a sufficient amount of contextual reading (as opposed to reading isolated words and sentences). Gambrell (1984) studied the average amounts of time spent on silent and oral contextual reading experiences during teacher-directed reading instruction in grades one through three. In the first grade, during a thirty-minute lesson, a child read silently for about two minutes and orally for about one minute. In the second grade, during a twenty-nine-minute lesson, a child read silently for about four minutes and orally for about one-fourth minute. In the third grade, during a twenty-three-minute lesson, a child read silently for about five-and-a-half minutes and orally for about one-fourth minute. Obviously, contextual reading was not given heavy priority by the teachers in this study.

There is no reason for basal readers to be used *only* as indicated in the manual. Reutzel (1986) believes that basal readers can also provide effective material for use with sentence-combining activities (see Chapter 5). These writing activities can enhance reading comprehension skills. Basal reader selections are good to use because many of them contain short and choppy sentences that students can combine into longer, more interesting sentences. In addition, when very complex sentences are encountered in upper-grade basal readers, sentence reduction techniques, in which long sentences are broken down into shorter ones, may be used. Such techniques help link reading and writing instruction.

Educators have expressed considerable concern about the misuse of workbooks that accompany basal readers—some teachers use them to keep children busy while they meet with other children or do paperwork. It is important to note that the fault here is with the teachers' procedures and not with the workbooks. Workbook activities should always be purposeful, and a teacher should never assign a workbook page simply to keep students occupied. He or she should grade and return completed workbook assignments promptly, since children need to have correct responses reinforced immediately and to be informed about incorrect responses so that they will not continue to practice them.

Schachter (1981) has suggested ways in which teachers can increase the effectiveness of their use of workbooks. First, teachers should decide to use the pages to provide children with appropriate practice needed to master a skill previously taught and to provide successful experiences. To achieve these goals in a group setting, a teacher can use the every-pupil response technique, having all students respond to instructions ("underline," "circle," and so forth) at the same time. When a spoken response is required, the teacher asks the question and then calls on a specific child to answer. By giving the question before calling on a specific pupil, the teacher encourages all pupils to listen to and consider the question since they do not know who will be asked to respond. Incorporation of trimodal responses, in which children respond to each task in visual, auditory, and kinesthetic or tactile modes, is also helpful. For example, they see the word, hear its pronunciation, and write it. At times the teacher may wish to do an exercise with the children to be sure they complete it successfully. And some children may need more practice than others, which they can get without extra pages if

290

Teaching
Reading in
Today's
Elementary
Schools

the teacher offers multiple practice for each item on one page. For example, first the teacher might read himself or herself, then have the students underline, and then ask the students to read.

This discussion has contained generalizations about basal readers; the intention is not to imply that all basal reader series are alike. On the contrary, series differ in their basic philosophies, their order of presentation of skills, their degree and type of vocabulary control, their types of selections, and the practice activities in their workbooks. Most are eclectic in approach, but some emphasize one particular method, such as a linguistic or an intensive phonics approach. Some contain no pictures; some have line drawings or photographs; and some provide a mixture of drawings and photographs. Before a school system adopts a basal series, teachers should examine many series. The one that best fits the student population should be selected.

✔ Self-Check: Objective 1

List some types of materials that are a part of most basal reading series and explain the purpose of each.
(See Self-Improvement Opportunities 1, 7, 8, and 9.)

Directed Reading Activity (DRA)

The DRA is a teaching strategy used to extend and strengthen a child's reading abilities. It can be used with a basal story or with any other reading selection, including content area materials. The five steps that usually compose the DRA are summarized below.

1. *Motivation and development of background.* During this part the teacher attempts to interest pupils in reading about the topic by helping them associate the subject matter with their own experiences or by using audiovisual aids to arouse interest in unfamiliar areas. It may not be necessary to work on motivation for all stories.

   At this point the teacher can determine whether the children have the backgrounds of experience and language necessary for understanding the story, and if necessary, he or she can develop new concepts and vocabulary before the story is read.

2. *Directed story reading (silent and oral).* Before children read the story silently the teacher provides them with purpose questions (or a study guide) to direct their reading (on a section-by-section basis at lower grade levels). Following the silent reading, the teacher may ask the children to read aloud their answers to the purpose or study-guide questions or to read orally for a new purpose. This section of the lesson is designed to aid children's comprehension and retention of the material.

3. *Skill-building activities.* Either before the silent reading or after it, the teacher provides direct instruction in one or more word recognition or comprehension skills.

4. *Follow-up practice.* During this portion of the lesson, children practice skills they have already been taught, frequently by doing workbook exercises.
5. *Enrichment activities.* These activities may connect the story with art, music, or creative writing, or may lead the children to read further material on the same topic or by the same author.

Although the steps may vary from series to series, most basal reading lessons have parts that correspond to the preceding list of components. Directed reading of a story generally involves the teacher asking questions and the children reading to find the answers.

To illustrate the directed reading activity used in a basal reading series, a sample lesson for a sixth-grade-level story is presented in Example 6.1. This lesson is taken from the teacher's manual for the reader *Celebrations* (Houghton Mifflin, 1986). The "Skill Preparation for Unit 14" is presented before the lesson related to the specific story begins, making the skill taught available for use in reading the selection for which it is designed. This part corresponds to the third step listed for the DRA, while the practice activities offered here correspond to the fourth step. The skill lesson covers the comprehension skill of noting sequence. If the lesson is not successful for all of the students, there is a reteaching lesson available (not shown here). The section entitled "Reading the Selection" contains a "Preparation" section to guide the teacher through vocabulary and concept development, corresponding to the first step listed for the DRA, and a "Reading" section that provides directed reading, corresponding to the second step of the DRA. The "Thinking It Over" section has comprehension questions to guide discussion of the material that has been read silently, and the "Optional Resources" section offers additional follow-up practice. Finally, the "Review and Enrichment" section offers still more practice and extension activities that correspond to the fifth step listed for the DRA.

Reconciled Reading Lesson

Reutzel (1985) developed the Reconciled Reading Lesson because he felt that the organization of basal reader lessons did not fit into the framework of schema theory. The prereading phase does need to be fully developed to be in line with schema theory, and Reutzel devised a plan that allows teachers to use the parts of the DRA in a different order to accomplish this objective more fully. In a way, Reutzel has reversed the DRA with some modifications, because the material under "Enrichment Activities" is used to build background and activate schemata, along with the introduction of new vocabulary. Next the skill instruction activities can be used to develop needed skills *before* the reading takes place. Although some basal readers use this placement already, many do not. The reading skills being developed should be directly related to the story to be read. Some of the discussion questions designated by the basal teacher's manual for use after the reading can be

292

Teaching
Reading in
Today's
Elementary
Schools

asked before the reading to elicit predictions about the story from the students. Both lower- and higher-order questions should be included. Silent reading guided by the predictions is next, followed by brief postreading activities. Postreading activities should include questioning and discussion for the purpose of comprehension and vocabulary assessment and assessment of skills learning. Inservice teachers have reported excellent results with Reutzel's plan.

Incorporating Metacognition into Basal Lessons

Comprehension monitoring can be made a natural part of a DRA. A plan for incorporating it into a lesson has been developed by Schmitt and Baumann (1986). During the prereading period, students can be encouraged to activate their background knowledge about the topic to enhance comprehension. They can use the title and pictures to decide what they already know about the topic. Then they can be asked to make predictions about the story elements, using the title, pictures, and their background knowledge. They should set purposes related to these predictions, reading to find out if the predictions are true. They should also be urged to generate questions to be answered as the reading progresses, to keep them actively involved with the material.

As the children read, they should stop at logical story breaks and summarize the main points to check for continuing comprehension. They should check their prereading predictions as they read and should change or modify them, if necessary, as new information is gained. For each new piece of information, they should also try to activate prior knowledge that they have about the topic. Generating new questions to answer as they read is also profitable.

After reading, the children should summarize the entire selection and evaluate their predictions. They should make sure they can answer the prereading purpose question and should generate other questions about key story features, which they may ask of their classmates.

An example of incorporating metacognition into the basal reading story in Example 6.1 follows.

During the prereading period the children could be asked to read the title of the story and look at the pictures and think about what they already know about the topic. One student, Mike, might ask himself, "What is a mural?" Then he might think, "We have pictures on the walls in the hall that are called murals, I think." Then, as he looked at the pictures, the thought might become, "Yes, it seems to be about a picture like the ones in the hall. They are painting on a wall." Mike might read the dark print directly under the title, and, considering the people's names in conjunction with the appearance of the people in the picture, think, "The people in the story are probably Mexican or Spanish." He might predict that the story would be about two Mexican girls painting a picture on a wall of their school.

▶ **EXAMPLE 6.1:** DRA as Presented in a Basal Reading Series

293
Major
Approaches
to Reading
Instruction

3 Skill Preparation for Unit 14

The Mural

Comprehension

Noting Sequence:
  Events (C2 · C1)
  Clue Words (C2 · C2) Lesson 13

To understand stories and articles that you read, you need to know the order in which the events in the story or article happened. Today you will learn more about using clues to determine the sequence of events.

Instruction
Listen to these sentences:

> Ann and June spoke in whispers. The baby fell asleep.

If you read those sentences in a story, you might not be able to tell which event happened first. Ann and June might have spoken in whispers before the baby fell asleep, after the baby fell asleep, or at the same time the baby was falling asleep.

For clarity, authors often use clue words to help you understand the order in which events happened. For example, an author might say, "Before the baby fell asleep, Ann and June spoke in whispers" or "Ann and June spoke in whispers until the baby fell asleep." In either case, you would know that the girls' whispering happened first, and the baby's falling asleep happened next.

If the author had said, "Ann and June spoke in whispers after the baby fell asleep," you would know that the baby fell asleep first. Now listen to this sentence:

> Ann and June spoke in whispers as the baby fell asleep.

The clue word as tells you that the two events occurred at the same time.

Sometimes events are not mentioned in the same order in which they happened. Authors often use clue words such as before, earlier, previously, until, after, then, next, soon, later, finally, and eventually to help the reader understand the order in which events occurred.

Sometimes dates are mentioned in stories and articles. They are also clues to the sequence in which events happened.

Even when clue words or dates are not included in the text, you can often tell the order in which events occurred by thinking about the logical sequence.
Listen to this sentence:

> Barry took out the snow shovel and cleared the walk.

You know that Barry took out the shovel before clearing the walk because that is the logical sequence of events.

Read this paragraph, and identify the words that are clues to sequence. Then decide in which order things happened.

Display *Guide dogs are selected on the basis of physical fitness, sense of responsibility, and intelligence. At fourteen months of age, a guide dog begins a training program that lasts from three to five months. First, the dog becomes adjusted to the leather harness and handle worn when guiding. Then, after learning to watch traffic and cross streets safely, the dog learns to obey commands. Finally, after mastering these skills, the dog and its new owner train together for a four-week period.*

In this paragraph, the author has used the words first, then, after, and finally as clues to the sequence of the guide dog's training. **What happens first?** . . . *(The dog becomes adjusted to the harness and handle.)* **What happens**

294
**Teaching
Reading in
Today's
Elementary
Schools**

next? . . . *(The dog learns to watch traffic and cross streets safely.)* **Then what happens?** . . . *(The dog learns to obey commands.)* **What is the final step in the dog's training?** . . . *(The dog and its new owner train together for four weeks.)*

Guided Practice

Workbook page 63, or **Teacher's Notebook
Guided Practice** page 11

Read the first paragraph silently. Notice that the order in which events are mentioned in this paragraph is not exactly the same as the order in which things happened. Find and underline each word in the paragraph that is a clue to the sequence in which the events happened.
Now read the list of events below the paragraph. Which of these events happened first, and how do you know? . . . *(Wasps made nests of wood and plant fibers — logical sequence)* **Write the number 1 beside that sentence to show that it was the first thing that happened.**

. . . What happened next? . . . *(Ancient Chinese learned to make paper.)* **Write the number 2 beside that sentence.**

Continue to work through the remaining four sentences with the students in the same way, calling on a volunteer to read each successive event in turn and having students mark the number beside the sentence that tells the next event.

Now read the second paragraph. Think about the sequence in which the events in the paragraph happened. Use the numbered lines below the paragraph to write each event in the order that it happened.

Summary

Encourage students to express in their own words the following understandings:

* Noticing the sequence of events in a story or article is an aid to understanding and remembering what is read.

* In a story or article, events are not always in the same order in which they happened.

* Noticing clue words and dates and thinking about the logical order of events helps in determining the correct sequence.

Independent Practice

Have students open to **Workbook** page 64 and complete the exercise independently.

**Workbook page 63
or Teacher's Notebook Guided Practice page 11**

Sequence • Events and Clue Words
Guided Practice

A. Paper, as we know it, is a mixture of wood, plant fibers, and rags. It is said that the ancient Chinese discovered the art of paper making after watching wasps make paperlike nests of a combination of old wood and tough plant fibers. Several ancient Chinese paper makers were captured in a battle in what is now part of the Soviet Union. Encouraged to continue their profession in prison, these paper makers taught others who later made the art known in Spain and, eventually, in all of Europe. From 1750 to 1882, various inventions improved the art of paper making until the process became similar to that used today.

___ The Chinese taught the art of paper making to others.
___ Several ancient Chinese paper makers were captured.
___ Paper making was made known in Spain.

___ Wasps made nests of wood and plant fibers.
___ Ancient Chinese learned to make paper.
___ Inventions improved the art of paper making.

B. Before Milly left for the library, she grabbed her umbrella. She had gone to the store earlier in the day and had gotten soaked in a sudden downpour. She didn't want that to happen again. As Milly was walking to the library, it started to rain once more. She tried to open the umbrella, but it broke right in her hand. Milly got soaked again!

1. _____
2. _____
3. _____
4. _____
5. _____
6. _____

Name _____ Date _____

Comprehension: Noting Correct Sequence — Events and Clue Words   Unit 13 • CELEBRATIONS   63

Reteaching Lesson:
Noting Sequence: Order of Events, Clue
Words
See page 683 in this Guide.

Optional Resources

Instruction Charts or **Instruction Transparencies:**
Unit 13

Teacher's Notebook:
Assessment Forms A and B pages 31, 32

3

Workbook page 64
Independent Practice

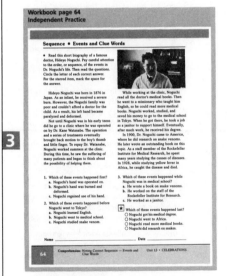

Sequence • Events and Clue Words

• Read this short biography of a famous
doctor, Hideyo Noguchi. Pay careful attention
to the order, or sequence, of the events in
Dr. Noguchi's life. Then read the questions.
Circle the letter of each correct answer.
For the starred item, mark the space for
the answer.

Hideyo Noguchi was born in 1876 in
Japan. As an infant, he received a severe
burn. However, the Noguchi family was
poor and couldn't afford a doctor for the
child. As a result, his left hand became
paralyzed and deformed.
Not until Noguchi was in his early teens
did he go to a clinic where he was operated
on by Dr. Kane Watanabe. The operation
and a series of treatments eventually
brought back motion to the boy's thumb
and little finger. To repay Dr. Watanabe,
Noguchi worked summers at the clinic.
During this time, he saw the suffering of
many patients and began to think about
the possibility of helping them.

While working at the clinic, Noguchi
read all the doctor's medical books. Then
he went to a missionary who taught him
English, so he could read more medical
books. Noguchi worked, studied, and
saved his money to go to the medical school
in Tokyo. When he got there, he took a job
as a janitor to support himself. Eventually,
after much work, he received his degree.
In 1900, Dr. Noguchi came to America,
where he did research on snake venoms.
He later wrote an outstanding book on this
topic. As a staff member of the Rockefeller
Institute for Medical Research, he spent
many years studying the causes of diseases.
In 1928, while studying yellow fever in
Africa, he caught the disease and died.

1. Which of these events happened first?
a. Noguchi's hand was operated on.
b. Noguchi's hand was burned and
deformed.
c. Noguchi regained use of his hand.

2. Which of these events happened before
Noguchi went to Tokyo?
a. Noguchi learned English.
b. Noguchi went to medical school.
c. Noguchi studied snake venom.

3. Which of these events happened while
Noguchi was in medical school?
a. He wrote a book on snake venoms.
b. He worked on the staff of the
Rockefeller Institute for Research.
c. He worked as a janitor.

★ Which of these events happened last?
○ Noguchi got his medical degree.
○ Noguchi went to Africa.
○ Noguchi read more medical books.
○ Noguchi did research on snakes.

Name _____ Date _____

64 Comprehension: Noting Correct Sequence — Events and   Unit 13 • CELEBRATIONS
Clue Words

296

Teaching
Reading in
Today's
Elementary
Schools

1 Reading the Selection

The Mural

1

by Emilia Durán
pages 178–189

Summary

Mercedes had hoped to win the art contest and be the person chosen to paint a mural depicting Chicano culture. To her dismay, the contest ended in a tie between Mercedes and her cousin Inez, who, Mercedes felt, always got the bigger half of everything.

To make matters worse, the girls had different ideas of what the mural should be like. Mercedes preferred a scene depicting the history of Mexico; Inez had a futuristic vision of cities and rockets. Mercedes's anger and frustration came to a head when Inez later began painting a sun on her half of the wall. A sunrise had been a major feature of Mercedes's painting, and she did not see how the painting could have two suns.

After a conversation with her grandmother, who pointed out that traditionally Hispanic muralists include many scenes in the same mural, Mercedes returned to Inez with the suggestion that they paint the family in the center of their mural.

Preparation

Vocabulary/Concept Development

Tell students that they will read a story about the painting of a mural. Explain that before they read, you will introduce some vocabulary words from the story.

Display the sentences below containing underlined words; do not show the meanings. Use these suggestions to introduce the vocabulary words to students:

● Remind students to use their knowlege of phonics, base words, word parts, and syllables, as well as the context, to help them pronounce each word and figure out its meaning.

● Have students read the sentences silently.

● Call on volunteers to read each sentence aloud and to explain the meaning of each underlined word. Then have them tell how they arrived at the meaning.

● Guide students in using the Glossary or a dictionary for meaning and pronunciation when necessary. When the underlined word also appears in the Glossary, the context sentence is preceded by an asterisk.

`Display` **1. As the artist traveled from agency to agency looking for a job, he carried a leather portfolio containing his best drawings.** ("a portable briefcase")

2. Each star in the American flag symbolizes one state in the Union. ("stands for, represents")

3. Before the carpenter began to build the new room, he laid a board between two upright X-shaped forms. He would cut wooden planks on this sawhorse. ("a rack on which lengths of wood can be sawed")

4.* When the artist discovered that he no longer had his portfolio, he was filled with dismay. ("discouragement about a problem one does not know how to solve")

5.* Shirley had made several commitments, offering her time and skill in helping Ned fix his car. ("pledges or promises")

6. Jan is incorporating everyone's birthday into the painting by using flowers to symbolize the months. ("blending, uniting, joining")

Discuss with students what they know about the history and culture of Mexico. Tell students that they will read a story about two American girls whose ancestors came from Mexico. Explain that the girls and their families refer to themselves as *Chicanos* (chĭ **kä'**nōz), a shortened form of *Mexicano* (mä'hē **kä'**nō), the Spanish word for *Mexican*. If necessary, give students the following information about these Native American groups:

• Mayan and Aztec peoples built great civilizations before Spanish explorers arrived in Mexico in the 1500's.

• Both were known for their stone pyramids. The Aztecs were also known for a large, disc-shaped stone, a type of calendar with images of the sun surrounded by the days of the week and a history of the Aztec people.

Point out that three different cultures — Mayan, Aztec, and Spanish — are all part of Chicano heritage.

Reading
Purpose Setting/Silent Reading

Have students turn to page 178 in their books. Ask them to read the story title, the author's name, and the opening sentences. If students have seen one, ask them to explain what a mural is. *(a large picture painted on a wall)* Otherwise, give the meaning of the word. Remind students to use the footnotes in the story to find out the pronunciations of the Spanish words. Have students read to see how, in the process of growing up, two people learn to accept their differences and work together.

Skill Reminder

Comprehension: Sequence — Events and Clue Words (C2 · C1,2)
Students will apply this skill as they read the selection and in the Additional Questions in Thinking It Over. Remind students that clues indicating sequence can be single words or phrases.

THE MURAL
by Emilia Durán

Mercedes knew how she wanted the mural to look, but Inez had other ideas. How could they paint it together?

178

The class party was almost over when Mercedes saw Mr. Alva standing in the door. He was holding a large portfolio. Here it was, the moment she had been waiting for all those weeks, ever since she had entered the art contest. The winner would paint a mural on the side of Mr. Alva's store, overlooking the little park. The mural would symbolize the neighborhood's Chicano heritage, and all the students in the school had been invited to submit ideas for its design. Mr. Alva had brought the winning picture to show the class.

Mercedes held her breath. "Please," she thought, "please let it be mine — I've never wanted anything so much!" She could hardly sit quietly through Mr. Alva's long introduction, but finally she heard him say, ". . . in fact, it was impossible for us to choose between two such excellent entries. The contest is a tie between two members of this class — Mercedes and Inez Gálvez. We want them to paint the mural together."

Mr. Alva took two pictures from his portfolio and held them side by side. Mercedes's painting represented the history of Mexico. It showed a pyramid, a large calendar stone, Spanish *conquistadores*[1] on their horses, and a Mexican figure in the center to represent the blending of the Aztec, Mayan, and Spanish cultures. The sky flamed with the colors of a brilliant sunrise.

"Oh, no," Mercedes thought. "Not a tie. That's almost worse than not winning at all!" She looked at Inez's picture and wondered, "What did they see in *that*?" Inez had painted the city of the future, with many buildings and machines. In the sky there were rockets and moving sidewalks. A large banner was decorated with symbols of Chicano achievements. It was exciting, with a lot of action, but Mercedes couldn't see that it had much to do with the purpose of the contest. "I *hate* it!" she thought.

[1] conquistadores (kŏn kēs'tä **dôr'**ās) Conquerors.

179

1

Then the other thoughts crowded in, the ones Mercedes had been trying not to have. "Why do I have to share everything with Inez, just because we are cousins and were born on the same day? They try to treat us the same, but it never comes out the same. The same clothes look better on Inez; when I make 95 on a test, she makes 98. Why does she always seem to get the bigger half of everything?"

Mercedes hated being jealous of Inez. What would her family think of her if they knew, she wondered. Her parents; her big brother, Daniel; Abuelita¹; Tío³ Ernesto; and Tía⁴ Diana — all seemed to think she and Inez were twins, or something. What if they knew she didn't want to be a twin? They would be ashamed of her for being so selfish, especially Abuelita, who had brought them all up always to respect one another.

Mercedes managed to smile through the rest of the party, the congratulations of her teachers and friends, and their farewells for the summer, but she was thinking, "What a way to start a vacation — having to act all enthusiastic about painting my half of a mural with rockets zooming all over the other half. What kind of mural is that? It will look stupid!"

She hoped to slip away without having to talk to Mr. Alva or Inez, but they stopped her at the door. "Mr. Alva wants us to go with him to the paint store and pick out the colors and the brushes we want to use," Inez told her. "We must call Abuelita and tell her we will be late. She is expecting us to help with the plans for Daniel's homecoming party."

When they had delivered their supplies to Mr. Alva's store, he suggested, "Let's have a look at the wall you're going to paint. I've put a barricade of sawhorses around it so the children won't get underfoot while you paint. When you come tomorrow, we will stretch a plank between two ladders, and

---
¹ **Abuelita** (ä'bwĕ lē'tə)   ³ **Tío** (tē'ō)   ⁴ **Tía** (tē'ə)

180

you can stand on the plank to reach the top of the wall. You must tell me if there's anything else you need."

As they walked around to the side of the building, Mercedes remembered how excited she had been the year before, when Mr. Alva had bought the store and the vacant lot beside it, and had donated the lot to the community for a playground. Until then, the lot had been an eyesore, full of weeds and rusty tin cans.

What a difference now! It had been a lot of work, but everybody on the block had pitched in last summer to clean up and plant things — grass and flowers and a hedge to keep children from chasing balls into the street. By the end of the summer, the neighbors had begun bringing picnic suppers and spending long evenings eating, playing games with the children, singing songs, and telling stories. It was wonderful.

There was still work to be done. Several of the neighbors had volunteered to build benches and equipment for the little children to play on. Best of all, the mural would give the neighbors something nicer than a blank concrete wall to look at. Or at least half the wall would be nice to look at. Mercedes wasn't so sure about the other half.

All the way home, Mercedes wondered how she would get through the family dinner that night, with everybody congratulating her on winning the contest. As things turned out, it wasn't so bad after all because everyone was full of plans for Daniel's return from college the next evening. Mercedes was grateful for the opportunity to slip away quietly and go to bed early.

After tossing and turning for most of the night, Mercedes overslept the next morning. When she finally arrived at Mr. Alva's store, Inez was already up on the plank — looking great in an old pair of coveralls and whistling a little tune. How could she be so cheerful, so early?

181

Mercedes climbed onto her end of the plank and began quickly to fill in the blue part of her sky. She could hardly wait to get the background filled in so she could start on the sunrise. Now that they had started painting, Mercedes realized that some parts of the mural were going to be tricky. With a picture of the past on one side and the future on the other, what were they going to paint in the middle? Something about the present, obviously, but what?

When she stepped down to change brushes, she sneaked a quick glance to see what Inez was doing over on her side of the picture. She could hardly believe what she saw — Inez busily

182

painting a big yellow sun peeking out from behind a skyscraper. "Why are you putting that sun there?" Mercedes asked.

"Oh, I just thought of it," Inez replied airily. "The picture seemed to need something else up in this corner."

"What this picture *needs* is my sunrise," thought Mercedes. "Inez knew that was an important part of my painting, and now she has put the sun on her side instead. We can't have two suns, one on each side of the picture. It just wouldn't make sense. Now that she has taken the sun away from my half, what am I going to paint over here? How thoughtless can she be?"

183

Furious, Mercedes climbed back onto the plank and began slapping blue paint on the wall.

"Hey, look out!" shouted Inez. "You're splashing paint all over. It's all running down in streaks." She stepped down to get a better look at what Mercedes was doing. "Besides," she continued, "that shade of blue you are using is too dark. Your sky should match my sky."

For a moment Mercedes stood absolutely still. Then, very slowly and without speaking she stepped down, picked up the broadest paintbrush, dipped it into the black paint, climbed back up, painstakingly painted a broad black stripe down the middle of the wall, and stepped back down on the ground.

"What are you doing?" Inez demanded. "What's the matter with you today, anyway? What is this all about?"

Controlling her anger, Mercedes looked directly at Inez for the first time and spoke slowly and quietly. "This is not one picture any longer. It is two. That is your side. This is my side. What happens over here is none of your business. Now, if you will excuse me, I think I won't paint any more today."

All the way home, Mercedes was torn between anger at Inez and dismay at her own behavior. Never in all her life had she behaved so rudely toward her cousin — or anyone else, for that matter. What would Abuelita think of her, if she knew?

Mercedes had hoped to sneak into her room unnoticed, but as soon as she opened the door, she heard her grandmother moving about in the kitchen. Abuelita must be starting to prepare the *empanadas*,[1] Daniel's favorites, for tonight's celebration dinner. Later, the whole family would pitch in to help, since it took many hands to prepare the large number of *empanadas* needed for all the aunts and uncles and cousins who would be coming to dinner.

---
[1] empanadas (ĕm′pä nä′däs)

184

Abuelita must have heard the door open because she called to Mercedes to come and help her. As Mercedes sidled into the kitchen, Abuelita gave her a sharp look and handed her a mixing bowl and a spoon.

Working silently alongside Abuelita, Mercedes realized how much she wanted her grandmother's help in straightening out her feelings, but how could she ask for it when she felt so ashamed? Why didn't Abuelita say something — anything? Were they going to go on like this all afternoon?

Finally, Abuelita put down her mixing bowl and asked, "Why are you looking so angry? What has happened?"

"It's Inez," Mercedes burst out. "She is ruining the mural. Furthermore, she is trying to tell me how to paint my half." Little by little, the whole story of the argument came out, and the more Mercedes talked, the angrier she felt. Then she concluded, ". . . and I'm going to let her paint it all by herself. Let her ruin things without any help from me. I quit."

Abuelita spoke sternly. "Mercedes, you surprise me. In this house, we do not speak ill of our family. We also honor our commitments. There will be no more criticism of Inez, and no more talk of quitting. Now, what is behind this? What is this ruining you say Inez is doing?"

"The mural is supposed to show something about Chicano life. When I made my picture, I was remembering the time when I was just a little girl and you took Daniel and me to Mexico City to that museum. I saw where part of our culture came from. Later when we climbed the old Aztec pyramids, I felt a sense of drama.

"I wanted to put the drama and importance of our history into my picture, but Inez wants to show a lot of tall buildings and rockets. She calls it the city of the future. I hate it, and it doesn't have anything to do with us!"

Abuelita was silent for a long time. Finally, she spoke, "Mercedes, it is true that the past is important, but so are the

185

present and the future. You and Daniel have done things I never dreamed of. Now Daniel is in college, and one day you will be. Daniel plans to be an architect, and the buildings he designs will probably look more like Inez's city than your pyramid. Those tall buildings do have something to do with us. Do you see?"

Mercedes nodded silently, and Abuelita continued. "Do you remember the murals that we saw in Mexico City? Most of them were not one scene, or two scenes, but many small scenes incorporating many different things. If great artists have room for such variety in their paintings, surely you and Inez can find room for all your ideas in one mural. You will have to work it out together.

"However, I find it hard to believe that all this anger comes about because of what is to be painted on a wall. It seems to me that there is something more involved here — something that you perhaps have not wanted to tell me. Is it not true?"

Hardly daring to look at Abuelita, Mercedes managed to mumble, "Having to share everything with Inez gets to be a real pain sometimes."

Abuelita spoke thoughtfully. "The family has always kept you together, as if you were sisters. Both of you have only brothers, and it is a fine thing to have a sister. When you were small, the two of you wanted to do everything together.

"Now you are growing older, and I remember how it was with my sisters. We had always done things together, but as I grew older, I did not always want to be with them. Sometimes, I wanted to do things alone. I still loved them just as much as ever, but I also needed some time to learn to be by myself. Perhaps it is the same with you two. It may be that Inez, also, feels that there can be too much of a good thing.

"I will speak to the family tonight after dinner. They will understand. In the meantime, you and Inez must settle your differences concerning the mural. Have you sat down and

187

186

300

Teaching
Reading in
Today's
Elementary
Schools

1

talked together about what you should paint, or has each of you tried to go her own way? In this family, we talk to one another."

"In this family. . . ." thought Mercedes. "I've been so busy being angry with Inez that I haven't even thought about how wonderful it is going to be when we are all together tonight. Of course they will understand. They always do."

Mercedes hugged her grandmother and said, "Abuelita, I have to go now. It is high time I did talk with Inez about the mural. Besides, I think I am getting an idea about how to do it, and I want to share it with her. I can't tell you because it's a surprise."

On the way to Mr. Alva's store, Mercedes thought about the middle of the mural — the part that would have to show something important about the present. The most important thing that she could think of was the family. Inez would think so too — the family as the link between the past and the future. They could paint pictures of their family and their neighbors and their families in the center. Of course — that was what the park and the mural were all about.

Mercedes began to hum a little tune, the same tune Inez had been whistling that morning. Maybe working together on this mural wasn't such a bad idea, after all.

Author

Emilia Durán has enjoyed an extensive career working with young people of various ages. Her experiences as a teacher and mother have contributed to her writing for children.

188

Thinking It Over

Comprehension Questions

1. How were Mercedes's ideas about the mural different from Inez's?
2. Why didn't Mercedes talk with Inez about their differences of opinion?
3. How did her conversation with Abuelita change Mercedes's ideas about the mural?
4. How do you think Abuelita would feel about Mercedes's new idea for the mural, and why?

Vocabulary

In this story, Abuelita was preparing Daniel's favorite food, *empanadas*. Interview your classmates and ask them to name their favorite foods. Make a chart with the following headings, and list each food under the heading where it belongs on the chart. Some foods may go under more than one heading.

  Meat, Fish, Eggs, and Legumes
  Milk and Milk Products
  Vegetables and Fruits
  Grains and Cereals

Writing a Description

Imagine that an artist is going to paint a picture as a gift to you and has asked what you would like to have the picture portray. Write a description of the picture that you would like to have painted.

189

Thinking It Over

Comprehension
Page 189

Comprehension Questions: Text

1. Purpose **How were Mercedes's ideas about the mural different from Inez's?** (Mercedes's ideas concerned the traditions of the past; Inez's ideas were about her vision of the community's future.) **Pages 179, 185–186**

Literal: making comparisons

2. **Why didn't Mercedes talk with Inez about their differences of opinion?** (Answers may vary. Examples: *Mercedes was ashamed of her jealousy of Inez. Mercedes valued the tradition of respect for members of the family and would be uncomfortable about insisting on her own interpretation of their task.*) **Pages 180, 184, 185, and 186**

Interpretive: character's actions

3. **How did her conversation with Abuelita change Mercedes's ideas about the mural?** (It made her aware that there was room within the traditional mural to incorporate a variety of scenes and messages. It also helped her to solve the problem of which aspect of the present would be most appropriate to portray in the center of the mural.) **Pages 185 and 187**

Interpretive: making inferences

4. **How do you think Abuelita would feel about Mercedes's new idea for the mural, and why?** (Answers will vary. Students can assume that Abuelita values the family and would be pleased to see this concept featured prominently in the mural. She would also be pleased to have the girls work together on the mural.)

Evaluative: thinking creatively

Additional Questions

1. Skill Application **Turn to page 181 and read from paragraph 1 through paragraph 3. What sequence of events is described here?** *(A short history of the park — as it was before last year, as it was by the end of last year, and as it will be when it is finished.)* **What clue words and phrases show the sequence?** *("until then," "last summer," "by the end of the summer," "There was still work to be done.")* **Page 181**

Literal: sequence of events

2. **How would you describe the difference between Mercedes's and Inez's personalities?** *(Answers will vary. Examples: Mercedes was more traditional and old-fashioned in her outlook, and perhaps somewhat more timid. Inez was more modern and perhaps more confident and assertive.)*

Evaluative: making comparisons

3. **Imagine that it had been Inez rather than Mercedes who had gone to talk with Abuelita. How might she have described what had happened while she and Mercedes were painting that morning?** *(Answers will vary, but should include the following: Inez probably does not know that Mercedes is jealous, nor does she understand Mercedes's ideas about the mural.)*

Evaluative: thinking critically

4. **What do you think Mercedes may have learned from this experience that could make it easier for her to handle difficult situations in the future?** *(She probably learned to deal with difficult situations somewhat more directly. Even sensitive and difficult issues may be more easily resolved when one is able to discuss them with others. Mercedes realized that she should have trusted her family to understand her feelings and help her resolve her problem.)*

Evaluative: character's feelings

5. **How did the author let you know that Daniel is still a very important part of the family, even though he no longer lives at home for most of the year?** *(The whole family is planning a homecoming party for him; preparations have already been started on the day before he is to arrive. Story says family was eager to see Daniel. In her discussion with Mercedes, Abuelita refers with pride to Daniel's plans to become an architect.)*

Interpretive: making inferences

1

Vocabulary
Page 189

Ask students to read and follow the Vocabulary directions on page 189 in *Celebrations*. You may want to write the headings on the chalkboard and fill in the food items after students complete their charts.

Writing a Description
Page 189

Ask students to read and follow the Writing directions on page 189 in *Celebrations*. Have students refer to Writing Aids on page 573 in their readers. Remind students that because the artist will have only words, not pictures, to go by, their descriptions must be very clear. Suggest they include specific details and color suggestions.

302

**Teaching
Reading in
Today's
Elementary
Schools**

page 65 Vocabulary Reinforcement
page 66 Story Comprehension

Optional Resources

1

Instruction Charts or **Instruction Transparencies:**
Unit 14

Enrichment Book:
Vocabulary Reinforcement and Story
Comprehension Unit 14

Spelling Bonus:
Unit 14

**Workbook page 65
Vocabulary Reinforcement**

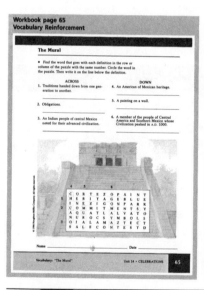

**Workbook page 66
Story Comprehension**

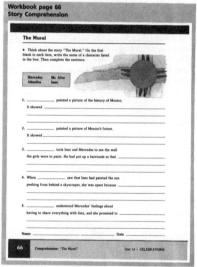

2 Review and Enrichment

Recommended Review
Vocabulary

Recognition Vocabulary:
Choosing Correct Forms

Display the following list of words and sentences with blanks. Explain to students that the words in the list are forms of words that were introduced in the story. Have students read the list of words and complete each sentence, using the correct form of the word from the list.

Display   *symbol   symbolize   symbolic
commit   committed   commitment*

1. *A ___ is something that is used to stand for something else.*

2. *A blindfolded figure holding a balance scale is often used to ___ justice.*

3. *It is said to have a ___ meaning.*

4. *George was ready to ___ himself to a weekend of study.*

5. *He was invited to a party on Saturday, but decided to honor his ___ to spend the weekend studying.*

6. *By Saturday night, he had ___ a whole chapter to memory.*

Answers: 1. *symbol* 2. *symbolize* 3. *symbolic* 4. *commit* 5. *commitment* 6. *committed*

Meaning Vocabulary:
Compound Words

Display the following list of scrambled compounds. Explain to students that these words were made up from compound words in the story. However, the parts have been mixed up; the first part of one compound word has been joined to the last part of a different compound word. Have students take each word apart and put the correct first and last parts together to make a real compound word.

Display   *coversore   eyescraper   farefoot
sawalls   underwell   skyhorses*

Answers: *coveralls, eyesore, farewell, sawhorses, underfoot, skyscraper*

Some students may enjoy inventing meanings and sentences for the mixed-up compounds as they were originally displayed.

Skills

Comprehension:
Using Context (C1 · A1)

Remind students that they should use the context, the surrounding words and ideas in a sentence or passage, to help them get the meanings of unfamiliar words. Briefly discuss synonyms, appositions, and cause-effect relationships as context clues to meaning.

Have students read the following paragraphs from "The Mural" and answer the questions:

Read page 179, paragraph 3.
   What does the word *portfolio* mean in that paragraph? What context clues tell you that? . . . *("a case in which papers can be carried" — Mr. Alva took the pictures out of it.)*

304

**Teaching
Reading in
Today's
Elementary
Schools**

Read page 180, paragraph 3.
> **What does the word** *congratulations* **mean in that paragraph? What context clues tell you that?** . . . *("speak with praise"; cause-effect — Mercedes had just won the contest)*

`Workbook` page 67

Comprehension:
Understanding Punctuation — Commas (C1 · B1b)

Remind students that commas are used to help prevent misreading of a sentence by separating words and ideas. Review with students the following uses of commas:

- Commas separate the names of three or more persons or things in a series.

- Commas set apart the name of a person or persons being addressed.

- Commas set apart words that explain or tell about something or someone mentioned in the sentence. The word *or* appears in an explanation that tells the meaning of a preceding word or phrase.

Tell students that they will read sentences from "The Mural" and answer questions about the author's use of commas.

Read page 179, paragraph 3, sentence 3.
> **How many objects in Mercedes's painting are mentioned in the sentence?** . . . *(four: a pyramid, a calendar stone,* conquistadores, *and a Mexican figure)*
> **How many cultures were represented by these objects?** . . . *(three: Aztec, Mayan, and Spanish)*

Read page 185, paragraph 8, sentence 2.
> **Why is there a comma after Mercedes in this sentence?** . . . *(the name of a person being addressed)*

2

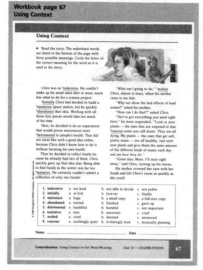

Read page 184, paragraph 6, sentence 2.
　　　What word in the sentence does the
phrase "Daniel's favorites" explain? . . .
(empanadas)

Workbook page 68

Optional Review
Vocabulary

**Meaning Vocabulary:
　　Borrowed Words**

　　Display the following list of words. Explain
to students that these are words the English language has borrowed from Spanish. Have students
use dictionaries to investigate the meanings of any
words on the list with which they are unfamiliar.

Display　*fiesta　renegade　rodeo　　chili
bonito　avocado　sombrero　lariat*

　　Have students write sentences using the
borrowed words. They should include in their sentences context clues from which other students can
derive the meanings.

Skills

**Comprehension:
　　Using Context** (C1 · A1)

　　Display the following sentences and have
students use the context to get the meanings of the
underlined words. Call on volunteers to explain
meanings of the underlined words and identify the
context clues that gave them the meanings.

Display　　1.　*Mother* <u>*lauded*</u> *me for the good
grade I had received on my paper.*

　　　2.　*Harvey is not usually stubborn, but
yesterday he was* <u>*obstinate*</u>*.*

　　　3.　*Jed is so* <u>*taciturn*</u> *that it is very hard
to know what he thinks.*

　　　4.　*Anita worked* <u>*meticulously*</u>*, or carefully, on her science project.*

　　5.　*The old dog's* <u>*debility*</u> *prevented him
from chasing the squirrel.*

　　6.　*Although few dogs seem to dislike
swimming, most dogs display a strong*
<u>*antipathy*</u> *toward being bathed.*

　　Answers: 1. "praised"; cause-effect
2. "stubborn"; synonym 3. "silent"; cause-
effect 4. "carefully"; apposition
5. "weakness"; cause-effect 6. "dislike";
synonym

**Comprehension:
　　Understanding Punctuation —
　　Commas** (C1 · B1b)

　　If necessary, remind students that authors
use commas to help prevent misreading of a sentence. Examples of the use of commas include separating three or more items in a series, setting apart
the name of a person or persons addressed, and
explaining another word mentioned in the sentence.
　　Display the following sentences with commas and ask the following questions:

Display　　1.　*I chose Mary Beth and Joyce for my
team.*

　　　2.　*I chose Mary, Beth, and Joyce for
my team.*

　　　3.　*This is a photograph of Fritz Kreisler, a well-known concert violinist and
composer.*

　　　4.　*While I was running with Bill, my
brother passed us on his bicycle.*

　　　5.　*I made a template, or stencil, to
help in painting the border.*

　　　6.　*My lunch included salad, tomato
soup, and cheese.*

Say　　How many players were chosen for the
team in sentence 1? *(two)*
　　　　How many were chosen in sentence 2? *(three)*
　　　　How many people are mentioned as being in the photograph in
sentence 3? *(one)*

2

306

Teaching
Reading in
Today's
Elementary
Schools

Who was Fritz Kreisler? *(a well-known violinist and composer)*

How many people are mentioned in sentence 4? *(three)*

Which word in sentence 5 tells the meaning of the word template? *(stencil)*

Was a tomato included in the list mentioned in sentence 6? *(no)*

To what does the word tomato **in that sentence refer?** *(a kind of soup)*

Teacher's Notebook

Extra Practice Master page 15

2

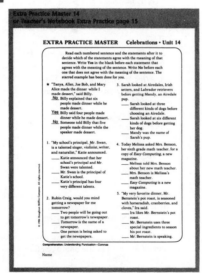

Extra Practice Master 14
or Teacher's Notebook Extra Practice page 15

EXTRA PRACTICE MASTER Celebrations • Unit 14

Read each numbered sentence and the statements after it to decide which of the statements agree with the meaning of that sentence. Write **Yes** in the blank before each statement that agrees with the meaning of the sentence. Write **No** before each one that does not agree with the meaning of the sentence. The starred example has been done for you.

★ "Tanya, Allen, Joe Bob, and Mary Alice made the dinner while I made dessert," said Billy.
 No Billy explained that six people made dessert while she made dessert.
 Yes Billy said four people made dinner while he made dessert.
 No Someone told Billy that five people made dinner while the speaker made dessert.

1. "My school's principal, Mr. Swan, is a talented singer, violinist, writer, and naturalist," Katie announced.
 ___ Katie announced that her school's principal and Mr. Swan were talented.
 ___ Mr. Swan is the principal of Katie's school.
 ___ Katie's principal has four very different talents.

2. Robin Craig, would you mind getting a newspaper for me tomorrow?
 ___ Two people will be going out to get tomorrow's newspaper.
 ___ Tomorrow is the name of a newspaper.
 ___ One person is being asked to get the newspapers.

3. Sarah looked at Airedales, Irish setters, and Labrador retrievers before getting Mandy, an Airedale pup.
 ___ Sarah looked at three different kinds of dogs before choosing an Airedale.
 ___ Sarah looked at six different kinds of dogs before getting her dog.
 ___ Mandy was the name of Sarah's pup.

4. Today Melissa asked Mrs. Benson, her sixth grade math teacher, for a copy of *Easy Computing*, a new magazine.
 ___ Melissa told Mrs. Benson about her new math teacher.
 ___ Mrs. Benson is Melissa's math teacher.
 ___ *Easy Computing* is a new magazine.

5. "My very favorite dinner, Mr. Bernstein's pot roast, is seasoned with horseradish, cranberries, and cloves," Ira said.
 ___ Ira likes Mr. Bernstein's pot roast.
 ___ Mr. Bernstein uses three special ingredients to season his pot roast.
 ___ Mr. Bernstein is speaking.

Comprehension: Understanding Punctuation—Commas

Name

Enrichment
Vocabulary-Related Activities

Challenge: Gazetteer of Spanish Names
Many cities, towns, rivers, and mountain ranges in the United States have names that came from the Spanish language. Have students use reference sources to compile a list of such names and to investigate the meanings of the names in Spanish. Their findings can be compiled into a gazetteer of places in the United States that have Spanish names.

Embedded Words
Students may enjoy making pictures that contain the embedded letters of a word from the story. First they should choose a story word. Next, they should write the letters of the word at various places on a sheet of paper. Then they should draw a picture that incorporates the letter forms as part of the drawing, and in such a way as to camouflage the letters. When they have finished, their pictures can be assembled into a bulletin board display. Students can try to find the hidden words in one another's pictures.

Skills-Related Activities

Creating a Cloze Paragraph
Have students imagine a day in which they could do anything they wished for twelve hours. Have them write a paragraph about what they would do that day, using such sequence clue words as *first, then, next,* and *finally.* Then have them copy the paragraph, this time leaving blanks for the sequence clue words. Have students exchange papers and fill in the blanks.

Selection-Related Activities

Planning a Mural

Have a small group of students design and make a mural for the school bulletin board. Tell students that the mural should represent something important about their local community. Have a volunteer serve as a group scribe to record the decisions made by the group in their cooperative effort.

Class Celebration

A favorite food in Mercedes's family was *empanadas*. Students may enjoy planning a class celebration in which they share their favorite foods. A committee of students can plan an occasion on which those who wish to do so may bring a favorite dish for others to sample. Students may also wish to exchange recipes for family favorites.

Suggestions for Wider Reading

The Art of the Spanish in the United States and Puerto Rico (nonfiction)
by Shirley Glubock (Macmillan)

Felita
by Nicholasa Mohr (Westminster)

Ferris Wheel
by Mary Stoltz (Harper)

Optional Resources

Instruction Charts or **Instruction Transparencies:**
Unit 14

Teacher's Notebook:
Extra Practice Master page 15

Enrichment Book:
Unit 14

2

Source: CELEBRATIONS (Houghton Mifflin Reading Series), by William K. Durr et. al. Teacher's Guide, pp. 226–243. Copyright © 1986 by Houghton Mifflin Company. Used by permission. ◄

308

Teaching
Reading in
Today's
Elementary
Schools

After prereading predictions have been made, the teacher could instruct the children to read the story for the purpose specified on page 233 of the manual or for another purpose chosen by the teacher. Mike could then begin to read to find out if his prediction was true. Before completing the first paragraph, Mike should realize that the mural is not being painted on the school, although the people involved are of Mexican background. He might also generate the question, "Why does it talk about the winner when two girls are shown in the picture?" Reading further, he would find out that two girls were involved because a contest had ended in a tie. Mike might then think about how unhappy one girl in the first picture looked and ask himself the question, "Is one of the girls unhappy about the way the contest turned out?" After reading two more paragraphs, he would know that Mercedes was unhappy and that she had a bad attitude toward the project of painting the mural.

Mike might also search his memory for information about Mexico as he reads the story and try to link his background knowledge of Mexico with pyramids, calendar stones, and conquistadores. If *conquistadores* were a new word, he might think: "I don't know the word *conquistadores*. I wonder how I can figure out what it means. Oh! Here it says they were 'on their horses.' That might be a picture of them on the wall. Maybe they are soldiers." At this point Mike might summarize what he knew in this way: "Two girls tied for winner of an art contest. They were to work together on a mural on a store. One of them was unhappy about sharing the honor." He might then think, "I wonder how the other girl will feel," and continue to read to discover Inez's reaction. Mike would proceed to read the story in this way until he reached the end. Then he would summarize the entire story and think about the accuracy of his initial and subsequent predictions. Mike might think: "I was right about the activity the girls were doing, but I was wrong about the location of the activity when I first started reading. I was right about most of my other predictions. I think I understood the story pretty well." He then might generate a question about the story to ask his classmates: "How did Mercedes's attitude toward painting the mural change at the end of the story, and what caused the change?"

✔ Self-Check: Objective 2
What are the parts of a directed reading activity?
(See Self-Improvement Opportunity 2.)

Alternatives to Use of the DRA

The directed reading activity has for many years been the format for basal reader lessons, and it is a valuable procedure. However, because teachers desire variety in lessons to add spice to reading instruction, Spiegel (1981) has suggested alternatives to the DRA, including the directed reading-thinking activity (DRTA), the expectation outline, the prereading guided reading procedure, and Word Wonder (all described in this chapter), as well as ReQuest and semantic webbing (described in Chapter 5). Horizontal reading (Cunningham, 1980), the "probable passages" suggested by Wood (1984), and the story frames suggested by Fowler (1982) are other good options. Horizontal reading is described in this chapter, and the last two techniques are described in Chapter 5.

The DRTA is a general plan for directing children's reading of either basal reader stories or content area selections and for encouraging children to think as they read and to make predictions and check their accuracy. Stauffer offers some background for understanding the DRTA.

Inquiry is native to the mind. Children are by nature curious and inquiring, and they will be so in school if they are permitted to inquire. It is possible to direct the reading-thinking process in such a way that children will be encouraged to think when reading—to speculate, to search, to evaluate, and to use. (1968, p. 348)

Stauffer (1969) further points out that teachers can motivate effort and concentration by a student by involving the student intellectually and encouraging him or her to formulate questions and hypotheses, to process information, and to evaluate tentative solutions. The DRTA is directed toward accomplishing these goals. It has two components—a process and a product.

The process consists of

1. identifying purposes,
2. guiding the reader's adjustment of rate to fit his or her purposes and the material,
3. observing the reading in order to diagnose difficulties and offer help, and
4. developing comprehension.

The product component consists of skill-building activities.

Perhaps because the student is interacting with the material during reading, the DRTA is extremely useful for improving children's comprehension of selections.

The lesson plan in Example 6.2 illustrates the steps of a directed reading-thinking activity. It is designed for use with the basal reading selection "The Mural," found in Example 6.1. The skill-building activities in the basal teacher's manual can be used with this guided reading procedure.

▶ **EXAMPLE 6.2:** DRTA Plan for a Basal Reading Selection

Step 1: Making predictions from title clues.
Write the title of the story or chapter to be studied on the chalkboard and have a child read it. For this selection, write "The Mural." Ask the children, "What do you

310

Teaching
Reading in
Today's
Elementary
Schools

think this story will say about a mural?" Give them time to consider the question thoroughly and let each child have an opportunity to make predictions. All student predictions should be accepted, regardless of how reasonable or unreasonable they may seem, but the teacher should not make any predictions during this discussion period.

Step 2: Making predictions from picture clues.
Have the students open their books to the beginning of the selection. Ask them to examine carefully the picture on the first page of the story. Then, after they have examined it, ask them to revise the predictions they made earlier, based on the additional information in the picture.

Step 3: Reading the material.
Have the students read page 179 of the story to check the accuracy of their predictions.

Step 4: Assessing the accuracy of predictions, adjusting predictions.
When all the children have read page 179, lead a discussion by asking such questions as "Who was right about what the story was going to say about a mural?" Ask the children who believe they were right to read orally to the class the parts of the selection that support their predictions. Children who were wrong can tell why they believe they were wrong. Let them revise their predictions, if necessary, and then ask them, "What will happen now that Mercedes and Inez are expected to paint the mural together?"

Step 5: Repeating the procedure until all parts of the lesson have been covered.
Have the children read pages 180–183 to check the accuracy of their predictions. Have them read selected parts orally to justify predictions they think were correct and tell why they believe incorrect predictions were incorrect. Have them revise or adjust their predictions, based upon their reading. Then pose the question, "What do you think Mercedes will do now?" Ask them to read page 184 to check their predictions. After a discussion of the accuracy of the predictions and revisions of predictions, ask them, "What will Mercedes do now? Will she change her mind or let Inez finish the mural alone? What will cause her to act the way she does?" Have them read pages 185–188 to check their predictions for the final time. ◀

Making predictions about what will occur in a text encourages children to think about the text's message. In order to make predictions, students use their background knowledge about the topic and their knowledge of text organizational patterns. In preparing a DRTA, the teacher should select places to pause so that the children can make predictions. During pauses, the teacher may use one or more open-ended questions to elicit student predictions about the next part of the story (Blachowicz, 1983). (See Chapter 8 for an example of the DRTA applied to a content area lesson.)

✔ **Self-Check: Objective 2**

311

Major
Approaches
to Reading
Instruction

What are the steps in a DRTA?
(See Self-Improvement Opportunity 6.)

An expectation outline is most appropriate for a factual story and can be used with content area materials as well as basal readers. The teacher asks children to tell what they think they will learn about the topic, writing questions that the children expect to have answered on the chalkboard, in related groups. Vocabulary words are emphasized during this procedure, and the teacher clarifies them as necessary, also filling in some needed background information. The children make up titles for each related group of questions, then read the story to find the answers. They read the proof of their answers orally.

The prereading guided reading procedure is also particularly useful with factual material. The teacher asks the children to tell everything they know about the topic while she or he writes their contributions on the board. Then the children analyze the contributions for inconsistencies, connecting the numbers of inconsistent statements with lines and noting information of questionable accuracy with a question mark. After categorizing the information, the children read to discover whether or not it is correct.

With Word Wonder, children name the words they expect to encounter in a story they are about to read, and then they read to check their predictions. The teacher may also list words and let the children decide whether each one is likely to appear in the story, offering their reasons for choosing particular words. After reading, discussions of why certain words were not included may help clear up misconceptions. Students may read orally the parts in which they found specific vocabulary words.

A final instructional technique is horizontal reading (Cunningham, 1980), which can be used as an adjunct to the basal reader approach. Horizontal reading gives children additional experiences and practice at the level they have just completed instead of moving them on to the next level immediately. It allows students to review skills in their current level and practice them while reading different stories, thus developing automaticity at each level. *Encore Readers*, published by Scott, Foresman, are horizontal readers correlated with grades one to three of that publisher's *Basics in Reading* program; *Text Extenders*, published by Scholastic, include collections of books correlated with each level (grades one through six) of basal readers published by Houghton Mifflin, Ginn, Holt, Macmillan, Economy, Harcourt Brace Jovanovich, and Scott, Foresman.

LANGUAGE EXPERIENCE APPROACH (LEA)

The language experience approach interrelates the different language arts and uses the experiences of the children as the basis for reading materials.

312

Teaching
Reading in
Today's
Elementary
Schools

The rationale for this approach has been stated very concisely by one of its leading proponents, R. V. Allen.

What I can think about, I can talk about.
What I can say, I can write—or someone can write for me.
What I write, I can read.
I can read what I write, and what other people can write for me to read. (1973, p. 158)

This approach to reading is not totally new; in fact, one of its major components, the experience chart, has been used since the 1920s. Originally, experience charts were group-composed stories that were transcribed by the teacher on the chalkboard or chart paper and then read by the children. Today, they may be either group or individual compositions: stories about field trips, school activities, or personal experiences outside of school; or charts that contain directions, special words, observations, job assignments, questions to be answered, imaginative stories or poems, or class rules.

Because the charts used in the language experience approach are developed by the children, they are motivational, and because they use the language of the children, the reading material on them is meaningful to the children. Frequently, basal reader stories are not meaningful to many children, because the language is unfamiliar. The language experience approach has been used effectively with students who speak English as a second language, providing material for reading instruction that they can understand (Moustafa and Penrose, 1985).

A child's background may be limited, but every child has experiences that can be converted into stories. In addition, the teacher can plan interesting first-hand experiences that can result in reading material that is meaningful for all pupils.

The language experience approach is consistent with schema theory. Because it uses the child's experiences as the basis for written language, the child necessarily has adequate schemata to comprehend the material and can thus develop a schema for reading that includes the idea that written words have meaning (Hacker, 1980). The language patterns found in stories composed by children are usually much more mature than those found in basal readers, since children use compound and complex sentences and a wide vocabulary. Nevertheless, children seem to find their own language patterns much easier to read than those in a basal reader, probably because clues in a familiar context are easier to use. In fact, pupils often pick up the long, unusual words in experience stories faster than many of the short service words, probably because the distinctive configurations of these words contribute to recognition.

With the language experience approach, reading grows out of natural, ongoing activities. Children can see the relationships between reading and their oral language. This approach helps them to visualize reading as "talk written down" and offers good opportunities for developing the concepts of *writing, word,* and *sentence.* During the language experience process children see the transformation from oral language to print take place, including directionality, the spacing between words, and punctuation and capitalization. Framing the individual language units with the hands is also helpful in illustrating their meanings (Blass, Jurenka, and Zirzow, 1981).

Implementation in Kindergarten

In order to use the language experience approach in the kindergarten, the teacher should fill the classroom with stimulating things, such as building blocks, a kitchen corner, a science corner, and so on. He or she must also provide children with opportunities to engage in many concrete and vicarious experiences designed to enrich their backgrounds, including field trips, demonstrations, experiments, and movies.

At the kindergarten level, experience charts are usually individual ones, although group charts may be composed following a special activity. The child (or group of children) dictates the experience story to the teacher, who either writes the story in manuscript or types it. The teacher then reads the story back to the child. Although an especially adept pupil may begin to recognize some of the words on the chart, at this point the teacher should emphasize that writing is just talk written down rather than have the child read the chart. Watching the teacher write the chart also helps the child become accustomed to the left-to-right progression of print, which the teacher can emphasize by sweeping the hand across the page under each line when he or she reads the chart.

In addition to using experience charts, the teacher can label desks with the owners' names to show students that everything has not only an oral name but a written name. As time passes children will recognize many of these names by sight. Lists of class helpers, the date of each day, and other regularly used announcements (for example, "today's weather," "library day") also provide opportunities for learning words by sight, as does labeling children's drawings with a word or phrase.

Those children who are ready to read may move into a program similar to the one described below, which is appropriate for use in the primary grades.

Implementation in the Primary Grades

After the children have participated in a common experience and have talked it over thoroughly, the group is ready to compose an experience story. First the teacher may ask for suggestions for a title, allowing the students to select their favorite by voting. The teacher then records the title on the chalkboard or a transparency. Each child offers details to add to the story, which the teacher also records. She may write "Joan said" by Joan's contribution, or she may simply write the sentence, calling attention to capitalization and punctuation as she does so. After she writes each idea, the teacher reads it

314

Teaching
Reading in
Today's
Elementary
Schools

aloud. After all contributions have been recorded, she reads the entire story to the class, sweeping her hand under each line to emphasize the left-to-right progression. Then she asks the class to read the story with her as she moves her hand under the words. Under cover of the group, no child will stand out if he or she doesn't know a word.

If this is the group's first actual reading experience, the teacher will probably stop at this point. On the second day, the class can be divided into three or four groups, with which the teacher can work separately. To begin each group session, the teacher rereads the story to the children, using a master chart she made the day before. Then the group rereads it with her. Next she asks for a volunteer who reads the story with her, filling in the words he or she knows while the teacher supplies the rest. After each child in the group has had a chance to read, the teacher asks students to find certain words on the chart. She may also show the children sentence strips (also prepared the day before) and have the children match these with the lines on the chart, either letting volunteers reconstruct the entire chart from the sentence strips or using this as a learning-center activity to be completed individually while other groups are meeting. Group charts can be useful in developing many skills and are commonly utilized for lessons in word endings, compound words, long and short vowels, rhyming words, initial consonants, capitalization, punctuation, and other areas.

If the teacher makes a copy of the story for each student, she may underline on that copy the words that the student recognizes as he or she reads the story. The teacher may then make word cards of these words, which serve as the beginnings of the children's "word banks." (Word cards containing the words a child has used in stories can eventually be used to drill on sight vocabulary, to work on word recognition skills, and to develop comprehension skills.) As a group of students finishes meeting with the teacher, the students may be given the opportunity to illustrate their stories individually.

After this first attempt, students will write most experience stories in small groups, sometimes working on a story together and sometimes producing and sharing individual stories. At times, slower learners may dictate their stories to the faster learners or to helpers from higher grades. Some teachers use tape recorders for dictation.

When students are dictating individual stories, the teacher should accept stories of any length (Mallon and Berglund, 1984). Some children will be ready to produce longer stories sooner than the others. When children dictate very brief stories, however, the teacher can ask questions to prompt them to expand the narratives (Reimer, 1983). If a student suggests an irrelevant sentence, the teacher may wish to question the student about its appropriateness for the story before recording it. If a child rambles through a lengthy description, the teacher may ask, "How do you want that written down for your story?" This question may result in a more focused response (Mallon and Berglund, 1984).

Class stories do not always have to be in the same format. They may take the form of reports, newspaper articles, descriptive essays, or letters, or they can be creative in content while using a particular writing style to which the children have been exposed. For example, after reading predictable books to the children, the teacher can encourage the children to produce the same kind of story. The repetition and predictability in these stories make sharing these child-developed books with classmates a profitable way to provide much practice in reading familiar words and language structures (Reimer, 1983).

Computers can be useful in a language experience lesson. The teacher can type in student-dictated material and modify it as the students direct. When using the computer in this way, the children should be facing the large monitor directly, with the teacher sitting at an angle to the monitor. This arrangement gives the students who are composing the story an unobstructed view (Smith, 1985). The students may use one beginning and develop different endings, printing out the different versions for comparison. The teacher can give students individual printed copies to illustrate and/or expand (Grabe and Grabe, 1985).

Another way to use the computer that takes advantage of its graphics capabilities is to provide a sequence of pictures that tell a story and let the students dictate a title and a story to fit the pictures. The teacher can enter the dictated material into the computer, and the children can read their stories from the computer screen. Then the teacher can print the story and pictures for them (Grabe and Grabe, 1985).

At some point the students may be able to enter their stories into the computer themselves. Several word-processing programs are easy enough for even primary students to learn to use. *Snoopy Writer* (Random House Software, New York, N.Y.) is an illustrated word processor suitable for children as young as six to eight years old ("What's in Store Software Guide," 1986). *Magic Slate* (Sunburst Communications, Pleasantville, N.Y.), has twenty-, forty-, and eighty-column versions and can accommodate users as young as first graders as well as adult users. *PlayWriter: Tales of Me* (Woodbury Software, Old Bridge, N.J.) goes beyond being a simple word processor. It presents children with questions that can guide them in writing, editing, and illustrating a book about themselves or someone else ("What's in Store," 1985). IBM's *Listen to Learn* also goes beyond simple word processing—it "talks" through a speech synthesizer. Text can be displayed on the computer monitor and spoken simultaneously or the children can type in text and listen as it is spoken. This program can help children to build sight vocabulary, among other skills, and, as is true of the other programs listed here, it can be used very effectively with the language experience approach.

Children can write stories on the computer most effectively when several students work together. One child can decide what to write and can enter the text, while one or more "advisers" offer help with mechanics, spelling, grammar, or computer operation (Starshine and Fortson, 1984); or the group

316

Teaching
Reading in
Today's
Elementary
Schools

of children can collectively decide what to say, taking turns entering sentences as they are agreed upon.

A noncomputer variation of individual language experience productions suggested by Reimer (1983) is writing notes in order to have a conversation. The teacher writes a note; the student responds in writing; and the exchange continues, with the student reading and writing for the purpose of communication.

Sharing stories, whether orally or in written form, is very important, since group members will soon see that certain words occur over and over again and that they can read the stories written by their classmates. The experience stories written by the group as a whole may be gathered into a booklet under a general title chosen by the group, and individuals may also bind their stories into booklets. Recopying a story to be included in a booklet is excellent motivation for handwriting practice. Pupils will enjoy reading each other's booklets, and a collection of their own stories provides both a record of their activities and evidence of their growth in reading and writing.

In one school a multicultural group of first graders wrote language experience stories, illustrated them, made them into books, and set up a classroom library. The books were given library pockets and check-out cards and were catalogued and shelved as they might be in a regular library, and children assumed jobs as reference librarians, check-out librarians, check-in librarians, and so forth. Both older and younger children in the school were scheduled for visits to use the library, which was operated for six days, and the student librarians accomplished an extensive amount of learning during the progress of the project (Powers, 1981).

As time passes and the children learn to write and spell, they may wish to write experience stories by themselves, asking the teacher or turning to their word banks or dictionaries for help in spelling. Teachers should allow them to spell phonetically when they are writing, since they can go back and correct spelling and rewrite the story in a neater form later if the story is to be read by others.

Rereading and editing require children to make judgments about syntax, semantics, and the topic and whether the written account can be understood by others. They provide ways to emphasize comprehension when using language experience stories. At first this should be done with extensive teacher guidance; later children can work more independently (Sulzby, 1980).

Word banks offer many opportunities for instructional activities. When children have accumulated a sufficient number of word cards in their word banks, they can use them to compose new stories or to play word-matching or visual and auditory discrimination games. To develop comprehension skills a teacher can use classification games, asking such questions as "How many of you have a color word? A word that shows action? A word that names a place?" When each student has as many as ten word cards, the children can begin to alphabetize them by the first letter, which gives them a practical reason to learn alphabetical order. They can also develop a picture dictionary representing the words on their cards. Or they can search for their words in newspapers and magazines. After they recognize that their words appear in books, they will realize that they can read the books. The uses for word banks seem to be limited only by the teachers' and pupils' imaginations.

Implementation in Higher Grades

The language experience approach can still have many applications above the primary grades. These applications are often in content area instruction—writing the results of scientific experiments; comparing and contrasting people, things, or events; writing directions for performing a task; and so forth.

Many computer applications lend themselves to upper-grade activities, for the children often can enter their stories easily and are encouraged to do so by the ease of revision without the drudgery of recopying. A good computer application is the production of a newspaper based upon experiences around the school. Programs are available that make the production of a nice-looking newspaper relatively easy for children. There can be reporters, who initially enter the stories into the computer; editors, who edit the work of the reporters; and "typesetters," who format the edited material (Mason, 1984b).

Grabe and Grabe (1985) suggest that student-generated interactive fiction stories (like *Microzine*'s Twist-a-Plots from Scholastic Inc., New York) can be enjoyable for students to write and for their classmates to read. Some knowledge of computer programming on the part of the teacher is necessary to promote this type of activity, although the stories can also be produced off of the computer (like Bantam Books' Choose Your Own Adventure Series).

Text structures that are found in content area textbooks, such as comparison-and-contrast patterns, can initially be taught through language experience activities. Then the students will be more likely to understand them when they encounter them in content materials. First, the teacher can present children with two items and ask them how these items are alike. Then the teacher can ask how the items are different. The class can construct a chart of these likenesses and differences during the discussion. After the discussion, the children can dictate a language experience story based on the information listed on their chart. The teacher can encourage them to write first about likenesses and then about differences. Practice activities with the completed story can include matching the two parts of a contrast, for example, matching "a marble is round" with "a jack has points." Parts of the story can be scrambled, and then the story can be rearranged with the comparisons and contrasts lined up appropriately (Kinney, 1985).

LEA: Pros and Cons

The language experience approach offers something for children regardless of the modes through which they learn best, as it incorporates all modes. For instance, the learners use the auditory mode when stories are dictated or read

318

Teaching
Reading in
Today's
Elementary
Schools

aloud, the kinesthetic (motor) mode when they write stories, and the visual mode when they read stories.

Use of the language experience approach promotes a good self-concept. It shows children that what they have to say is important enough to write down and that others are interested. It also promotes close contact between teachers and pupils. Finally, this approach has been highly successful as a remedial technique in the upper grades, allowing remedial readers to read material that interests them rather than lower-level materials that they quickly recognize as being designed for younger children.

Of course, there are some potential disadvantages to the LEA. They are as follows:

1. The lack of sequential development of reading skills because of the unstructured nature of the approach is seen as a disadvantage by some. It must be remembered, however, that there is no one correct sequence for presenting reading skills. Children learn from a variety of programs that provide different skill sequences, and with careful planning a good teacher can provide some sequence when using this approach.
2. Some educators regard the lack of systematic repetition of new words and the lack of vocabulary control in general as drawbacks.
3. The charts may be lacking in literary quality.
4. Charts can be memorized, resulting in recitation rather than actual reading.
5. Repetition of the same reading material may become boring, causing students to "tune it out." An alert teacher, however, can avoid allowing repetition to continue to this point.
6. Making charts is very time-consuming.
7. If this approach is used to the exclusion of other methods of reading instruction, at some point the limitations of the children's backgrounds of experience may keep them from developing in reading as they should; but this approach is rarely used in isolation.

Some teachers fail to use the children's own language in the language experience stories because it does not fit the teachers' ideas of basic words. These teachers are not likely to reap the full benefits of this approach.

✔ Self-Check: Objective 3
What is the rationale behind the language experience approach? What are some advantages of the LEA? Some disadvantages? (See Self-Improvement Opportunity 3.)

INDIVIDUALIZED APPROACHES

There are many ways to individualize reading instruction. This section contains a description of the traditional individualized reading approach, which has a number of well-defined characteristics, and other ways to individualize reading instruction, including objective-based approaches, programmed instruction, and use of computers.

Individualized Reading Approach

The individualized reading approach encourages children to move at their own pace through reading material that they have chosen, rather than requiring them to move through teacher-prescribed material at the same pace as other children placed in the same group for reading instruction. With the individualized reading approach, which is designed to encourage independent reading, each child receives assistance in improving performance when need for such assistance becomes apparent.

A number of characteristics are nearly always attributed to the individualized reading approach, including the following:

1. *Self-selection*. Children are allowed to choose material that they are interested in reading. Each child in the class may choose a different book. The teacher may offer suggestions or give help if it is requested, but the decision ultimately rests with the child. Thus, the individualized reading approach has built-in motivation—children want to read the material because they have chosen it.
2. *Self-pacing*. Each child reads the material at his or her own pace. Slower students are not rushed through material in order to keep up with the faster ones, and faster children are not held back until others have caught up with them.
3. *Skills instruction*. The teacher helps students, either on an individual basis or in groups, develop their word recognition and comprehension skills as these skills are needed.
4. *Record-keeping*. The teacher keeps records of the progress of each child. He or she must know the levels of a child's reading performance in order to know which books the child can read independently, which are too difficult or frustrating, and which the child can read with the teacher's assistance. The teacher must also be aware of a student's reading strengths and weaknesses, and should keep a record of the skills help that has been planned and given to the child. Each child must keep records of books read, new words encountered, and new ways of attacking words experienced.
5. *Student-teacher conferences*. One or two times a week, the teacher schedules a conference with each child, varying from three to fifteen minutes depending on the purpose.
6. *Sharing activities*. The teacher plans some time each week for the children to share books that they have read individually. The children may share with the entire class or with a small group. Sharing can sometimes be in the form of book auctions in which the children bid with play money on the opportunity to read a book next. The "auctioneer" tries to make the students interested in bidding by telling about the book (Bagford, 1985).

320

Teaching
Reading in
Today's
Elementary
Schools

7. *Independent work.* The children do a great deal of independent work at their seats, rather than spending the majority of the assigned reading period in a group with the teacher. Better readers and older children can benefit more from time with individualized reading than can poorer readers and younger students, who need more teacher direction (Bagford, 1985).

Since exposure to different types of literature can help children build schemata for these types and should thus increase their efficiency in processing the text, this approach is congruent with schema theory (Hacker, 1980). In addition, the variety of material pupils read provides vicarious experiences that help build other schemata and thus enhance future comprehension. Children encounter words in a variety of meaningful contexts, thus extending their vocabulary knowledge (Bagford, 1985).

Individualized reading also helps students realize that reading is enjoyable. At the same time, reading of books at comfortable reading levels develops fluency and can contribute to improved reading rate (Bagford, 1985).

To set up an individualized reading program, a teacher must have available a large supply of books, magazines, newspapers, and other reading materials—at least three to five books per child, covering a variety of reading levels and many different interest areas. This collection will need to be supplemented continuously after the program begins, for many children will quickly read all of the books that are appropriate for them. Sources of books are school, city, and county libraries; book clubs; parent-teacher associations; and class members' personal collections.

The teacher should have read a large number of the books available to the children, since doing so makes it much easier to check the comprehension of pupils. Starting a file of comprehension questions and answers for the books being used in the program is a good idea; these questions will be available year after year and will help refresh the teacher's memory of the books.

The teacher will also find it convenient to have a file of skill-developing activities, covering the entire spectrum of word recognition and comprehension skills and a wide range of difficulty levels.

When starting an individualized program, the teacher should determine the reading levels and interests of the children through either standardized or informal tests in order to choose books for the program. Informal reading inventories that provide information about a child's levels of performance (discussed at length in Chapter 10) yield a great deal of useful information, as does an interest inventory, such as the one shown in Example 6.3. The teacher must administer the inventory to primary-level children orally.

▶ **EXAMPLE 6.3:** Interest Inventory

1. The things I like to do after school are:

    a. _____

    b. _____

    c. _____

2. The television programs I enjoy most are:

   a. _____

   b. _____

   c. _____

3. My hobbies are:

   a. _____

   b. _____

   c. _____

4. If I could take a trip, I would like to go to:

   a. _____

   b. _____

   c. _____

5. The sports I like best are:

   a. _____

   b. _____

   c. _____

6. The school subjects I like best are:

   a. _____

   b. _____

   c. _____

7. I like to hear these types of stories read to me:

   a. _____

   b. _____

   c. _____

8. I like to read these types of stories on my own:

   a. _____

   b. _____

   c. _____ ◀

Before initiating an individualized program, the teacher can plan routines to follow in the classroom, considering questions such as (1) How are books to be checked out? (2) How will conferences be set up? (3) What should a child who is working independently at his or her desk do when in need of assistance? The room arrangement can also be planned in advance to allow for good traffic flow. If books are located in a number of places instead of bunched together in a single location, pupils will have less trouble finding them and the potential noise level in the room will be lower.

The teacher may find that having a file folder for each child will help in organizing and record-keeping. Each file folder could contain both a reading skills checklist on which to record skill strengths and weaknesses and a form noting conference dates and skill help given. Students can keep their own records in file folders that are accessible to both teacher and children. These records will take different forms, depending upon the maturity of the children. A primary-level record might look like the one shown on the following page.

322

Teaching
Reading in
Today's
Elementary
Schools

Name of Book	Author	Evaluation (Circle One)		
		Good	O.K.	Bad
		Good	O.K.	Bad
		Good	O.K.	Bad
		Good	O.K.	Bad

An intermediate-level record might look like this one.

Name of Book	Author	Comments

A form that could be used by children at all levels might look like this one.

New Words from Reading		
Word	Pronunciation	Definition

Student-teacher conferences serve a variety of purposes, including:

1. To help with book choices. To overcome the fear that children will not be able to select books wisely, teachers should spend some time showing children how to choose appropriate books. The teachers can encourage them to read one or two pages of the books that they think might appeal to them and to consider the number of unfamiliar words they encounter. If there are more than five unfamiliar words per page, the book might be too difficult, whereas if there are no unfamiliar words, the child should consider the possibility that he or she could read more difficult material. If the teacher has given an interest inventory, he or she can suggest potentially interesting books to pupils who find it hard to make a choice.
2. To check comprehension. Conferences help determine how well the children are comprehending the books and other materials they are reading. The teacher should ask a variety of types of comprehension

questions—main idea, detail, inference, cause and effect, sequence, and vocabulary.

3. To check word attack and oral reading skills. The teacher can ask a child to read orally, observing his or her methods of attacking unfamiliar words and of using oral reading skills, such as appropriate phrasing and good oral expression.
4. To give skill assistance. If a child is the only one in the room who needs help with a particular reading skill, the teacher can help him or her on a one-to-one basis during a conference.
5. To plan for sharing. Some conferences help children prepare for sharing their reading experiences with others. If a child wishes to read a portion of a book to the other class members, the teacher might use a conference to listen to the child practice audience reading and to give help with the presentation.

There is nothing contradictory about using group instruction in an individualized reading program. A teacher can group together children with similar skill difficulties to give help. The important thing is to be sure that all children get the instruction they need when they need it and are not forced to sit through instruction they do not need.

When an individualized reading program is in effect, each child is expected to be involved in independent silent reading a great deal of the time. This time should be uninterrupted by noisy surroundings, classmates' projects, or non-task-oriented activities such as daydreaming, wandering around the room, or talking to other students. The teacher should make the rules for the quiet reading time very clear, and acceptable activities should be well defined: taking part in student-teacher conferences, selecting a book, reading silently, giving or receiving specific reading assistance, taking part in a skills group, completing a skill-development practice activity, or keeping records concerned with reading activity. Strict adherence to the rules will make the program run more smoothly.

Individualizing a reading program is a huge undertaking, but such a program can be introduced gradually in two ways.

1. Use part of the time. Introduce the individualized program one day a week while using the basal program the other four days. Then increase time spent in the individualized program one day at a time over a period of weeks until all five days of the week are devoted to it.
2. Use part of the class. Introduce the program to one reading group at a time while the remaining groups continue the basal program. If the children are grouped by ability, the top group will be a good first choice because they are likely to have more independent work habits and will probably learn the routines more quickly than the other children would. After one group has become familiar with the approach, other groups can

324

Teaching
Reading in
Today's
Elementary
Schools

be introduced to it, until the entire class is participating in the individualized reading program.

The program may be entirely supplemental also. A class or school reading club could participate in individualized reading on particular themes, from particular authors, or in a particular genre and share their reading experiences with one another (Bagford, 1985).

The main advantages of an individualized reading approach follow.

1. There is built-in motivation in reading books that the child chooses himself or herself.
2. A child is not compared negatively with other children, since every child has a different book and the books are primarily trade books, which have no visible grade designation.
3. Each child has an opportunity to learn to read at his or her own rate.
4. A great deal of personal contact with students is made possible by the pupil-teacher conferences.

Characteristics of this approach that are considered disadvantages by some are listed below.

1. The teacher must amass and continually replenish a large quantity of reading material.
2. There are time difficulties inherent in trying to schedule so many individual conferences and skill-group meetings.
3. An enormous amount of bookkeeping is necessary.
4. It lacks a sequential approach to skill development.

Some recent research concerning the effectiveness of a modification of the individualized reading approach has shown positive results from its use (Eldredge and Butterfield, 1986). Although the individualized reading approach has not been in the forefront of usage in schools in recent years, it may attract more attention in the future because of its emphasis on reading connected passages of literature and the positive research results.

✔ Self-Check: Objective 4

Name seven characteristics that are usually associated with an individualized reading approach.

What are some advantages and disadvantages of this approach?

(See Self-Improvement Opportunity 4.)

Other Means of Individualizing Reading Instruction

The individualized reading approach described above is only one of many ways that have been developed to individualize reading instruction. Descriptions of several other approaches that have been used for this purpose follow.

Objective-Based Approach

An objective-based approach offers each child instruction based upon his or her needs, as indicated by criterion-referenced tests that check on the student's mastery of a list of skill objectives (see Chapter 10 for a description of these tests). Instruction is prescribed to help the child master skills in which he or she shows weakness. Materials of various types and from various sources are used, including basal readers, filmstrips, mechanical devices (such as controlled readers), programmed materials, games, and so on. These materials may be placed in learning centers for individual use, or they may be used with teacher direction.

The Wisconsin Design (Interpretive Scoring Systems/National Computer Systems), which uses commercial materials from a variety of publishers along with some specially developed techniques as a basis for prescriptions, serves as an example of an objective-based program (also called "management systems" and "diagnostic/prescriptive"). It has the following characteristics:

1. It has a set of behavioral objectives for the various reading skills.
2. Special tests determine whether children have mastered the skills.
3. Materials are specially designed or listed to correspond to these skills, to be used with those who fail to attain a particular level of achievement on the tests.
4. It has a method for recording and reporting results.

The major operations called for in the Wisconsin Design's framework for organizing instruction are identification of essential content, statement of objectives, assessment, identification of appropriate teaching/learning activities, and evaluation. A management component, included in the framework because systematic student accounting is necessary, is composed of mechanisms for keeping records of students' skill development—a card-sorting system in which the basic skill data for each pupil are kept on a profile card. An "Outline of Reading Skills" is essentially a scope and sequence statement of reading skills for kindergarten through grade six.

The remaining components of the Design—the assessment exercises, profile cards, and aids to instruction—are keyed to the specific skills listed in the outline. A "Statement of Skills and Objectives" states the objectives of the first three skill areas—word attack, comprehension, and study skills—as closed, behavioral objectives. The objectives of the last three areas—self-directed reading, interpretive reading, and creative reading—are stated as open, describing behaviors and activities. *The Wisconsin Tests of Reading Skill Development* test for most of the skills in word attack, comprehension, and study skills, either as written tests or in the form of directions for teacher observation. Skills in each of the six areas are clustered at levels that correspond generally to traditional grade levels.

The Teacher's Resource Files key the skills in the outline to selected published materials and techniques in the teacher's resource file and include

326

Teaching
Reading in
Today's
Elementary
Schools

a variety of materials and procedures that can be used to develop a specific skill. "Guides to Individual Skill Assessment" are filed in the appropriate folders of the Teacher's Resource File for Word Attack and are intended to assist teachers in observing specific skill-related behaviors and to serve as models for the development of additional individual guides or exercises. The file also includes a list of ten concept development activities, along with materials and procedures for each activity.

Some basal reading series that have a self-contained objective-based approach have their own identified skill objectives, criterion-referenced tests, and materials designed for development of each objective. Ginn's *Reading 720* series is an example of such a series.

Some of the advantages of management systems in general are the following:

1. They work well with many approaches to reading, although they do not fit into some of the less rigid methods, such as the language experience approach.
2. The teacher has an overall picture of the child's strengths and weaknesses.
3. Children work on the skills they need the most.
4. Success is likely because children work at their own levels; self-concepts are thus enhanced.
5. Learners may have as much time as they need for skill mastery.
6. Grouping can be flexible to include children's short-term common skills needs.
7. Teachers can report progress in specific skills to parents.

Some of the disadvantages are:

1. It takes planning and time to organize a room to facilitate needed skill practice.
2. The wide variety of materials needed may be discouraging to some teachers.
3. Record-keeping is a vital element but is time-consuming.
4. Some important aspects of reading may be neglected; more attention is given to skills than reading interests.[1]

Diagnostic/prescriptive programs include the following:

Fountain Valley Support System. Richard L. Zweig Associates, 20800 Beach Blvd., Huntington Beach, CA 92648

---

[1] For other evaluations of such systems, see Robert T. Rude, "Objective-Based Reading Systems: An Evaluation," *The Reading Teacher* 28 (November 1974): 169–75. Also see Dale D. Johnson and P. David Pearson, "Skills Management Systems: A Critique," *The Reading Teacher* 28 (May 1975): 757–64.

Prescriptive Reading Inventory. CTB/McGraw-Hill, Del Monte Research Park, Monterey, CA 93940

Teachers who use these systems have generally expressed positive attitudes toward the approach, but they indicate feeling pressured to cover too many of the objectives in a given time. There is also some concern about excessive testing, overemphasis on skills, availability of sufficient teaching material, and the large amount of record-keeping that is needed (Otto, Wolf, and Eldridge, 1984).

If management systems are used by teachers, they may wish to supplement their programs with sustained silent reading (see Chapter 9), the individualized reading approach, or at least some regularly scheduled recreational reading for the children. Doing this can help develop the concept that reading is more than just skill building and that the skills can be used in a functional setting.

Programmed Instruction

Some attempts to individualize instruction include programmed materials, which instruct in small, sequential steps, each of which is referred to as a frame. The pupil is required to respond in some way to each frame and is instantly informed of the correctness of his or her response (giving immediate reinforcement). Because the instruction is presented to an individual child, rather than to a group, each child moves through the material at his or her own pace, thereby benefiting from some individualization. An even greater degree of individualization is provided by branching programs, which offer review material to children who respond incorrectly to frames, thereby indicating that they have not mastered the skills being presented.

Programmed instruction can also provide follow-up reinforcement for instruction presented by the teacher, thereby freeing the teacher from many drill activities and allowing him or her more time to spend on complex teaching tasks. The programmed materials are designed to be self-instructional and do not require direct teacher supervision.

On the other hand, programmed instruction does not lend itself to teaching many complex comprehension skills, such as those involving analysis and interpretation, nor does it promote flexibility of reading rate. Word analysis and vocabulary-building skills are most prominently treated in programmed materials, so teachers may wish to use other materials (for example, basal texts) or techniques (for example, semantic webbing) to present and provide practice for the complex comprehension skills.

Perhaps the best-known programmed material for reading instruction is Sullivan Associates' *Programmed Reading,* published by McGraw-Hill. The program consists of two readiness kits and three programmed reading series, including teacher's guides and other available support materials such as duplicating masters, cassette tapes, alphabet strips, pupil alphabet cards,

328

Teaching
Reading in
Today's
Elementary
Schools

teacher alphabet cards, sound-symbol cards, activity books, achievement tests, filmstrips, teacher's guides to film strips, two Read and Think Series, duplicating masters for Read and Think Series, response books and vinyl overlays which make readers reusable, and placement tests. Criterion-referenced tests follow each unit in the programmed readers, and the teacher's guide contains suggestions for appropriate corrective exercises that do not repeat previously presented materials. Both word attack and comprehension receive attention in this program: Series I focuses on word attack but introduces comprehension skills in the sixth of seven books, and comprehension receives increasing emphasis in Series II and Series III.

Computer Approaches

There are two broad categories of computer use for individualizing instruction: computer-assisted instruction (CAI), in which a computer administers a programmed instructional sequence to a student, and computer-managed instruction (CMI), in which the computer takes care of such tasks as record-keeping, diagnosis, and prescription of individualized assignments. These two approaches are sometimes available in a single coordinated package.

Computer-Assisted Instruction   Of the two basic types of CAI that are currently used for reading instruction—drill-and-practice and tutorial (Blanchard, 1980)—the simplest and most common is the drill-and-practice program, which consists of practice lessons on skills that students have previously been taught. Students receive material in a programmed sequence (as described above, under Programmed Instruction) and immediate feedback on correctness of answers; sometimes they are given more than one opportunity to answer before they are told the correct answer.

Practice is important for developing accuracy in and automaticity of reading skills (see Chapter 1). Computer drill-and-practice programs can provide repetition without the impatience sometimes manifested by teachers. When the goal is development of accuracy, the computer can be used to present a few exercises accompanied by clear, immediate feedback, particularly for incorrect answers. After the children have attained accuracy, the teacher can have them practice using computer programs with larger numbers of exercises, sometimes emphasizing speed, which are accompanied by less extensive feedback. Some drill-and-practice programs recirculate missed items for further practice, without the teacher having to plan or execute such repetition (Balajthy, 1984).

Game characteristics can add interest to computer drills. With or without the game format, computers have the capability to provide graphics that increase the appeal of the programs (Balajthy, 1984).

Tutorial programs are really advanced forms of drill-and-practice programs in which the computer actually presents instruction, then follows it with

Software available for microcomputers enables students to either practice skills they have already learned or to interact with the computer to solve problems. (© Janice Fullman/The Picture Cube)

practice activities. Depending upon the correct and incorrect responses a student gives as the program progresses, he or she may be branched to a remedial sequence of instruction, taken back through the initial instruction, directed through the typical sequence for the instruction, or skipped ahead in the program to avoid unnecessary practice. In some programs the student has no direct control over the sequence; in others, he or she may request review, remedial help, or additional practice as part of the program design.

Programs may be self-paced or computer-paced. Self-paced programs allow the student to move at his or her own rate through the material, thereby providing more attention to individual differences than computer-paced programs, which progress through the material at a predetermined rate (Balajthy, 1984). Sometimes the programs are self-paced on a page-by-page basis—the student presses "Return" when he or she wants to continue. Other programs are designed to allow the student to choose a pace for the entire program when the study session starts.

Programs can also be linear or branching. Linear programs take all students through the same sequence of material, although they generally allow the

330

Teaching
Reading in
Today's
Elementary
Schools

students to progress at their own rates. Branching programs, on the other hand, adjust the instructional sequence according to the student's performance. Branching programs are obviously more helpful for individualizing instruction.

Recently, teachers have been using word-processing programs in the schools more than they did a few years ago. Word processing on the computer allows children to experiment with language and to control their own learning processes (Heffron, 1986). As was indicated under the section on the language experience approach in this chapter, word processing can ease the task of writing and revising for both the teacher and the student.

Teachers who are unfamiliar with computer technology in general may find it difficult to determine how to implement CAI in the school; therefore, some knowledge of computer equipment (hardware) can be helpful to teachers. In schools today, microcomputers are used, rather than the massive mainframe computers that were sometimes used in the past. Most of these systems were "plagued by high cost, low reliability, inadequate programming, and, as the number of users grew, extremely slow response time" (Gersten et al., 1981, p. 45). Because of these problems, some educators felt that they were not reasonable tools for instruction.

Microcomputers, on the other hand, are considerably less expensive than mainframe computers, are portable, and have rapid response capabilities. These characteristics have helped to move microcomputers into education's mainstream. Most microcomputers used in reading education vary from the size of an electric typewriter to a little over twice that. They have a typewriter keyboard for student input, a video display for presenting instruction to students, and a built-in microprocessor and memory, allowing them to operate as discrete units. A printer may be attached to provide printed output. A microcomputer system can be so inexpensive that an individual classroom might have one or more of its own.

Minicomputers are smaller than mainframe computers but larger than microcomputers and range in price between the two. Minicomputers generally serve an entire school rather than a single classroom.

The heart of a CAI system is the software, the programs that actually provide the instruction. These programs are developed by people and therefore vary in quality; the computer can only carry out the instructions the programmer has given it. Programs may be written on printed pages so that someone has to enter them into the computer's memory by using a typewriterlike keyboard, or they may be on prerecorded cassettes or disks. Teachers are wise to try out software before purchasing it (Spindle, 1981), because, as Botterell (1982) points out, "the lack of good software is the biggest barrier to the growth of educational computing. . . . There is a great deal of bad educational software on the market" (p. 149). Botterell goes on to state that commercial publishers and materials developers have been slow to enter the field of educational computing. Fortunately, they now are moving in this direction.

In the meantime teachers will need to be careful about programs they purchase, asking themselves such questions as the following:

1. Is the material instructionally sound?
2. Is the program easy for the learner to use?
3. Does use of the program accomplish something that is needed in this classroom?

To be instructionally sound, the program should present accurate information in a reasonable sequence with an appropriate amount of pupil interaction. It should not give responses to incorrect answers that reward the learner with clever messages or graphics, while not doing this for correct answers. Ease of use encompasses clear instructions on what to do to advance material on the screen, to respond to questions (Do students use a letter or an entire typed-out answer to respond to a multiple-choice question? Do they touch the screen on or beside the correct answer?), and to receive help when needed. Erroneous keystrokes should not "dump" a student out of the program but allow him or her to recover in a clear and easy way.

Even good programs are not useful if they do not accomplish something that needs to be done. Only the teacher can decide that. Herriott (1982, p. 82) has noted that the computer can:

1. Impart information on a one-to-one basis with a high success rate when well-written and thoroughly validated programs are used.
2. Provide imbedded remedial instruction of which the student may not necessarily be aware.
3. Provide enrichment material within the program.
4. Keep accurate track of progress throughout the program, and indeed, throughout a series of programs on varied material.
5. (Perhaps most important.) Allow the student to progress at his own rate.
6. Provide video and audio support via peripheral devices linked directly to the computer.
7. Provide a massive information retrieval base—either by direct display of the material itself or by directing the student to the appropriate medium.[2]

Esbensen (1981) points out that drill-and-practice routines can conserve a teacher's time while providing individualized instruction for students who need help learning facts and skills. The interactive nature of CAI can make this drill more interesting, and it helps keep the learner involved with the task.

Computer-assisted instruction has been successfully used to teach initial reading skills. One early system was developed at Stanford University primarily to teach decoding skills. It utilized a "Model 33" teletypewriter and

[2] REPRINTED FROM CREATIVE COMPUTING MAGAZINE, Copyright © 1982 AHL COMPUTING, INC.

332

Teaching
Reading in
Today's
Elementary
Schools

an audio headset.[3] Children using this CAI program along with regular instruction scored better on tests given at the end of first grade than a control group, and the same group also scored better on tests given at the end of second grade, although no CAI was administered to either group during the second grade.

Programs that are currently available come in all levels of complexity and involve the use of many different skills. Some examples follow:

1. In *Dragon's Keep* (Sierra On-Line, Coursegold, Calif.), children use the computer to locate animals in a building and free them. To accomplish this, the children have to read simple words and phrases (Dudley-Marling, 1985).
2. DLM Teaching Resources (Allen, Tex.) offers programs for drill and practice that use arcade-game formats. One of these programs, *Word Master*, deals with antonyms, synonyms, and homonyms (Mason, 1984a).
3. *Snooper Troops* (Spinnaker Software Corporation, Cambridge, Mass.) presents students with mysteries to be solved by collecting and following clues and testing hypotheses (Dudley-Marling, 1985). This material is obviously good for developing higher-order comprehension skills.
4. *Deadline* (Infocom, Cambridge, Mass.) is an interactive story in which the student makes decisions that affect the story (Dudley-Marling, 1985). Such a program demands involvement with the story on the part of the reader and application of critical reading skills.
5. *The Cave of Time* (Bantam Software, New York, N.Y.) is one of a number of interactive fiction stories based on Bantam Books' "Choose Your Own Adventure Series" ("What's in Store Software Guide," 1986). It causes students to use higher-order comprehension skills as they create an adventure.

Some computer-based programs for teaching reading employ a multisensory approach. For example, the IBM *Writing to Read* program attempts to teach reading through an approach that involves tactile, visual, and auditory senses (Heffron, 1986).

When Lois Avaunne Hed examined "the effects math, reading and language arts CAI had on regular classroom, special education, and disadvantaged elementary school students in fifteen different studies, she concluded that students advanced because the CAI approach compressed learning time, individualized instruction, and provided more hours of concentrated instruction for each learner" (Gersten, Schuyler, and Czechowicz, 1981, p. 45).

Of the many public schools that use CAI, the Chicago public school system has a particularly large program incorporating commercial drill-and-practice

---

[3] For more information, see Richard C. Atkinson and John D. Fletcher, "Teaching Children to Read with a Computer," *The Reading Teacher* 25 (January, 1972): 319–27.

programs in reading instruction for grades two through six. Decoding, literal and figurative comprehension, and some study skills are covered (Blanchard, 1980).

Although comprehension materials are not yet as numerous as word recognition materials, attempts are being made to develop good programs in this area. The Center for the Study of Reading (University of Illinois at Urbana-Champaign) designed two microcomputer-based reading activities based on how comprehension occurs and what makes up effective instructional software: "Story Maker" and "Textman."

In "Story Maker," which works on problem-solving, reasoning, inference, and evaluation skills, a child can work toward a goal the computer has generated, which describes something that will happen in a story. An inverted tree design allows the child to make choices that add to the story line at each branch; when he or she has made decisions from the top to the bottom of the tree, the child has a complete story. Early decisions affect the ending, and, as the child moves through the story, he or she has to assess new information, make predictions about consequences, and decide which choice will lead to the desired outcome. If the outcome does not match the child's goal, the computer responds that the result is not the one expected. A printer provides a copy of the completed story to the child, which has motivated some children to do creative things, such as making books.

In "Textman" students guess which sentences go together to form a paragraph in a specific selection. The child is informed about what kind of text is involved. He or she may be told about the purpose of the material and the author and given some paragraphs that come before and after the missing one. He or she tries to choose the sentence that comes next in the paragraph from a list of choices; incorrect answers result in parts being added to a hanging figure, as in the familiar game of Hangman. The computer also gives feedback on whether incorrectly chosen sentences are elsewhere in the text or do not occur in the text at all. Such programs obviously are educationally desirable (Zacchei, 1982). These programs are available from Bolt, Beranak and Newman (Cambridge, Massachusetts).

Some traditional educational publishers who are currently producing CAI programs for reading and some educational software houses are listed below, along with sample selections from these companies. Other publishers and programs are referred to earlier in this section. These lists and programs are merely representative of the array of publishers and available programs. *Swift's Educational Software Directory* (Austin, Tex.: Sterling Swift) is one good reference source for these materials and for noncommercial software. Reviews in periodicals such as *Electronic Learning* and *The Computing Teacher*, as well as those in *The Reading Teacher*, can also be helpful. The Minnesota Educational Computing Consortium (MECC) is a large distributor of educational software that has an extensive catalogue of offerings that may also be a useful resource.

334

Teaching
Reading in
Today's
Elementary
Schools

1. Milliken Publishing Company
   1100 Research Blvd.
   St. Louis, MO 63132
   (*Comprehension Power; Cloze Plus*)
2. Random House School Division
   2970 Brandywine Road
   Atlanta, GA 30341
   (*Fundamental Word Focus; Tutorial Comprehension; Homonyms in Context*)
3. Borg-Warner Educational Systems
   600 W. University Drive
   Arlington Heights, IL 60004
   (*Critical Reading; Word Structure*)
4. Educational Activities
   P.O. Box 392
   Freeport, NY 11520
   (*Read and Solve Math Problems; How to Read in the Content Areas; Literal Comprehension Program; Reading with Understanding; Critical Reading Program: Reading with Critical Understanding*)
5. Houghton Mifflin Company
   One Beacon Street
   Boston, MA 02108
   (*Base Words and Affixes: Noting Details/Visualization; Comprehension—Sequence and Cause/Effect; Comprehension—Interpretive Thinking Skills; Vowel Sounds; Following Directions*)
6. Orange Cherry Media
   7 Delano Drive
   Bedford Hills, NY 10507
   (*The Cloze Technique for Developing Comprehension; Word Factory; Vocabulary Builders; Active Reading—World of Nature Series; Adventures Around the World; Strange Encounters: You Decide*)
7. Weekly Reader Family Software
   Xerox Educational Publications
   245 Long Hill Road
   Middletown, CT 06457
   (*Stickybear Reading; Stickybear ABC; Stickybear Opposites*)
8. Learning Well
   200 South Service Road
   Roslyn Heights, NY 11577
   (*Fact or Opinion; Fantasy Land; Galaxy Search; Hinky Pinky*)
9. Sunburst Communications, Inc.
   39 Washington Avenue
   Pleasantville, NY 10570
   (*M-ss-ng L-nks; Puzzler*)
10. IBM Software
    P.O. Box 1328

1000 Northwest 51st Street
Boca Raton, FL 33432
(*Reading Comprehension Skills; Reading for Information; Reading for Meaning*)

11. Hartley Courseware
123 Bridge
Dimondale, MI 48821
(*Antonyms/Synonyms; Word Families; Roots/Affixes*)

Computer-Managed Instruction Computer-managed instruction can help teachers keep track of student performance and guide learning activities. For example, some systems provide tests on specific objectives that are computer-scored. The computer then matches the student's deficiencies to available instructional materials, suggests instructional sequences for the teacher to use, or assigns material directly to the student. The computer may also perform tasks such as averaging grades on a series of tests, thereby removing quite a bit of burdensome record-keeping from the teacher's shoulders (Hedges, 1981; Coburn et al., 1982).

Houghton Mifflin Company supplies a CMI program for reading that gives an on-the-computer survey test, made up of items from the Individual Pupil Monitoring System's criterion-referenced test, after the teacher has provided instruction. Evidence of mastery of a skill allows a student to move to the next skill, but if the student needs to practice, the computer can assign appropriate materials. A posttest then determines whether reteaching is needed; if a student fails, the computer can prescribe work in outside materials. The system provides the teacher with thirteen types of reports on pupils' learning, including a Work Report, which provides a skill-by-skill analysis of each student's progress; a Survey Statistics Report, which shows at a glance how the class has performed overall on the survey; a Survey Alert Report, which tells which students failed to show mastery of a particular skill; and an Assignment Status Report, which indicates skills assigned, mastered, and bypassed. This CMI system was originally available only on a minicomputer. Now it is available for Apple II and IBM microcomputers. Some other companies, such as Milliken and Educational Development Corporation, have systems that run on microcomputers.

Management systems are built into some individual CAI programs. They allow the teacher to see how well the children perform, and sometimes they even indicate which items were answered incorrectly. The management systems in some programs tell the students when to move on to more difficult levels of the program or to drop back to easier ones. Some of these management systems, however, do not save results from session to session but erase data when the computer's power is turned off (Balajthy, 1984).

The computer generation is here. Children are unintimidated by computers, and teachers need to keep in step. The use of computers holds much promise for education, but the technology is changing rapidly, so teachers need to stay up-to-date.

336

Teaching
Reading in
Today's
Elementary
Schools

What are some advantages of programmed instruction?
What kinds of questions should teachers ask about the computer
software that they purchase for reading instruction?
(See Self-Improvement Opportunities 5 and 10.)

LINGUISTIC APPROACHES

Linguistics is the scientific study of human speech. Linguistic scientists (also referred to as linguists) have attempted to provide an accurate description of the structure of the English language by identifying the sound units, the meaning units, and the patterns that occur in the language, concentrating upon the oral aspects rather than the written aspects of the language.

There is no *one* linguistic approach to teaching reading; however, a number of approaches have been built around linguistic principles. The earliest such program for teaching reading was developed for parents by Leonard Bloomfield, who was not an educator but who had strong feelings about the impact of linguistic principles on reading instruction. (See Leonard Bloomfield and Clarence Barnhart, *Let's Read, A Linguistic Approach,* Detroit, Mich.: Wayne State University Press, 1961, for Bloomfield's approach.) Some other materials built upon linguistic principles are Mildred K. Rudolph et al., *Merrill Linguistic Readers* (Columbus, Ohio: Charles E. Merrill, 1986), and Ralph F. Robinett et al., *Miami Linguistic Readers* (Boston: D.C. Heath, 1971).

Some ways in which linguistic studies have affected instructional materials are explained below.

1. Beginning readers are presented with material in which each letter has only a single phonetic value (sound); therefore, if the short *a* sound is being used in early material, the long *a* sound or other sounds associated with the letter *a* are not used. Naturally, after students have thoroughly learned one phonetic value of a letter, other values are presented.
2. Irregularly spelled words are avoided in beginning reading material, although some (for example, *a* and *the*) are used to construct sentences that have somewhat normal patterns.
3. Word-attack skills are taught by presenting minimally contrasting spelling patterns, words that vary by a single letter. For example, one lesson may contain the words *can, tan, man, ban, fan, ran,* and *pan.* This exposure to minimally contrasting patterns is believed to help the child understand the difference that a certain letter makes in the pronunciation of a word. However, sounds are not isolated from words, because when the sounds are pronounced outside the environment of a word they are distorted. This is particularly true of isolated consonant sounds; *buh, duh,* and *puh* are sounds incorrectly associated with the letters *b, d,* and *p.*
4. Reading orally in a normal speaking fashion is emphasized. Reading is looked upon as turning writing back into speech.

Among linguists' many disagreements about the proper ways of presenting reading material to children, two of the most prominent concern the context of words. First, some linguistic reading materials present children with lists of words (with minimally contrasting spelling patterns) to pronounce. Structural linguists object to this because it isolates words from context. They point out that sentences are basic meaning-bearing units and that many words that do not appear in context cannot be pronounced, defined, or categorized as to part of speech. Second, some linguistic reading materials (for example, *Merrill Linguistic Readers*) have no illustrations because the authors feel that a child, using extraneous picture clues, may fail to perceive and use the clues to word identification inherent in the language. Other linguistic readers use pictures to provide a context that the limited vocabulary cannot provide.

Example 6.4 conveys a feeling for the type of material contained in linguistic readers.

▶ **EXAMPLE 6.4:** Sample of Linguistic Reading Material

SKILLS DEVELOPMENT

Before Reading Page 6

Comprehension: Phrase Development

Write the phrase *a cat* on the chalkboard. Have pupils read the phrase. (Have them pronounce the word *a* as it is pronounced in natural speech, not as its letter name is pronounced.)

Ask the pupils, "What word follows the word *a*?" After they have answered *cat*, ask them, "What other words could follow the word *a*?" Have them say the word *a* along with their words, and have them listen to the way their words sound with the word *a*. To help them get started, give them some examples, such as "a horse" or "a book."

You could also have the pupils make up several descriptive phrases beginning with the word *a*. Write the phrase *a fat cat* on the chalkboard and have the pupils read this phrase. Give them several oral examples, such as "a brown horse" or "a big book." Then have the pupils offer several descriptive phrases of their own.

After pupils have given their phrases, return their attention to the phrase *a cat* on the chalkboard. Write *A Cat* beneath it. Tell pupils that each word remains the same when a capital is used for the first letter. Read the phrases *a cat* and *A Cat* to the pupils, and then have the pupils read the phrases. Point to the phrase *A Cat* and tell pupils that this will be the title of their first story. Have pupils open their Readers to page 6. *Continue with the Guided Reading of the story on page 6.*

GUIDED READING

Direct pupils' attention to the title of the story. Have them place their markers below it. Have the title read aloud. Then say, "Let's read the story to see what we can find out about a cat."

Guide the silent reading of each sentence by asking the suggested question above it. At this early stage, have oral reading follow the silent reading of each sentence. Demonstrate moving the marker down the page as each sentence is read.

A Cat

What is Nat?

Nat is a cat.

What can you tell about how he looks?

Nat is fat.

What does the last sentence
say about Nat?

Nat is a fat cat.

Discuss the story. Use these questions: "Who is the cat? What does Nat look like?"

Proceed to the oral reading of the entire story. Encourage pupils to use normal stress and intonation in their oral reading. Allow each pupil the opportunity to read the entire story orally. If a particular pattern word proves difficult, offer help in the following sequence. First, have the pupil spell the word. If this procedure does not activate recall, write other words of the pattern on the chalkboard. If neither plan is successful, supply the word and provide practice at a later time. If a circle word is not recognized, pronounce it for the pupil who is having difficulty.

Continue with the Skills Development on the next page at this time or the next day.

Source: Mildred K. Rudolph et al., *I Can, Teacher's Edition, Merrill Linguistic Reading Program* (Columbus, Ohio: Charles E. Merrill, 1986), p. T-12. ◄

✔ **Self-Check: Objective 6**
Describe some features of linguistic reading approaches.

ECLECTIC APPROACHES

Eclectic approaches combine the desirable aspects of a number of different methods rather than strictly adhering to a single one. Teachers often choose an eclectic approach to fit their unique situations. Following are some examples; they are only possibilities, and teachers should remember that the only limitations are school resources and their own imaginations.

1. Language experience stories can be based on characters, events, or ideas in basal stories. The teacher can plan an experience related to the story, lead a discussion of the experience, and record the students' dictated account. If an experience such as this is used prior to reading the basal story, it can help to activate the children's schemata related to the story. It will also probably involve use of some of the same vocabulary in the

story, providing an introduction to this vocabulary in context. The story may also be used as a basis for skills instruction suggested in the basal reader (Jones and Nessel, 1985). Grabe (1981) also suggests having the teacher supplement the basal reader approach by having children write "books about the book." They dictate stories about the basal selection using the new vocabulary. This approach has been found to enhance comprehension and vocabulary skills. In a classroom in which there are two reading periods each day, the teacher may use the basal reader during the first period and the language experience approach during the second, relating the experience story to the basal story and thereby helping the children gain additional practice with much of the same vocabulary.

2. To encourage sequential skill development, use a basal reader approach two or three days a week; then use an individualized reading approach for the remaining days to gain the motivational value of self-selected activities.

3. For children who are reading at grade level and below, a basal reader approach might be better because these children have a greater need for direct teacher interaction and structured materials. The children reading above grade level could be involved in an individualized reading approach, doing much more work independently at their seats and being given skill instruction only when specific needs become evident.

4. Programmed instruction can be utilized with any approach, as can computer-assisted instruction. The use of the word-processing function of the computer, as described by Kleiman and Humphrey (1982) and as discussed earlier in this chapter, makes the computer a natural tool for implementation of the language experience approach. Children who tend to always produce short stories, due to difficulties in writing, are freed to write more extensively with the ease of editing offered by the computer.

5. Teacher Support Software provides games for the Apple, TRS 80, and Atari computers that use the words from particular lessons in Ginn, Harper and Row, Holt, Houghton Mifflin, and Macmillan basal reader series. Teachers simply specify the series being used when ordering. The disks contain word lists for each story in the series (Mason, 1984a).

Classroom Example

The discussion below shows how a teacher who embraces an eclectic approach to reading instruction might operate during one reading period. The following activities might be taking place:

1. The teacher is working with a grade-level basal reading group in a corner of the room.

2. Children from another reading group are illustrating a language experience story that they wrote on the previous day. As they finish their illustrations, pairs of children from this group are forming sentences with their word-bank words.

340

Teaching
Reading in
Today's
Elementary
Schools

3. Several children who are reading far above grade level are busy reading self-selected library books at their seats.
4. Three other children, also reading above grade level, have returned to the room from the library and seated themselves together to discuss some research reading they have been doing on space travel.
5. A boy who is reading two years below grade level is working independently in a programmed reading textbook.
6. A girl is in another corner of the room, working on a microcomputer program on prefixes and suffixes.

All of the students are busy at reading tasks, but the tasks involve many different approaches to reading instruction.

Summary

Basal reader series are the most widely used materials for teaching reading in elementary schools in this country. Although they have been criticized by some groups, basal readers are advantageous for teachers to use because of the balanced programs offered, the systematic presentation of skills, the systematic review offered, the careful grading of materials, and the valuable teaching suggestions in the manuals. The directed reading activity (DRA) is the teaching strategy presented in basal manuals. This strategy can be used with other reading materials as well. Reutzel's Reconciled Reading Lesson allows teachers to use the parts of the DRA in a different order to make it fit into the framework of schema theory better. Comprehension monitoring can also be made a natural part of a DRA. Alternatives to using the DRA include the directed reading-thinking activity (DRTA), the expectation outline, the prereading guided reading procedure, Word Wonder, ReQuest, semantic webbing, probable passages, story frames, and horizontal reading.

The language experience approach interrelates the different language arts and uses the experiences of the children as the basis for reading materials. This approach has many advantages: it incorporates the visual, auditory, and kinesthetic modes of learning; it promotes a positive self-concept and fosters close contact between teachers and pupils; and it serves as an effective remedial technique in the upper grades. On the other hand, some feel that the approach has several disadvantages: sequential skill development is lacking; systematic repetition of new words is not present; material may not have high literary quality; repetition of the material may become boring; and the making of charts is time-consuming. This approach can be introduced in kindergarten, but it continues to have applications for all students in higher grades, especially in conjunction with content area activities.

The traditional individualized reading approach allows children to move at their own paces through reading material that they have chosen. Skills instruction is offered on the skills that the children need at a particular time, and only children who need the skills instruction receive it. Student-teacher conferences help the teacher monitor progress and build rapport with the students. Sharing activities allow group interaction. This approach requires much record-keeping by the teacher and the children. The built-in motivation in an individualized program is a positive feature, as are the self-pacing and lack of negative comparisons with other children. However, the large quantity of materials needed, the scheduling problems with conferences, the record-keeping demands, and the lack of sequential skill development are considered disadvantages by some.

Other means of individualizing instruction include objective-based approaches, programmed instruction, and computer approaches. An objective-based approach offers each child instruction based upon his or her needs, as indicated by criterion-referenced tests that check on mastery of a list of skill objectives. Instructional materials are prescribed, corresponding to skills needs, for children who fail to attain a specified level of achievement on the tests. Much record-keeping by the teacher is required to keep up with the children's individual programs.

Programmed instruction is administered through materials which present information in small, sequential steps. The student responds at each step and receives immediate feedback about the correctness of the response. The student is allowed to learn at his or her own pace.

Computer approaches include computer-assisted instruction (CAI), in which a computer administers a programmed instructional sequence to a student, and computer-managed instruction (CMI), in which the computer takes care of such tasks as record-keeping, diagnosis, and prescription of individualized assignments. Drill-and-practice programs, tutorial programs, interactive fiction programs, game-type simulation programs, and word-processing programs are some of the computer-assisted instructional materials available. Computer-managed instruction can help teachers keep track of student performance and guide learning activities.

Linguistic approaches have been built around linguistic principles. Although there is no one linguistic approach to teaching reading, some of the more commonly used linguistic materials present regular spelling patterns for sounds first, use minimally contrasting spelling patterns to teach word-attack skills, and emphasize reading orally in a normal speaking fashion.

Eclectic approaches combine desirable aspects of a number of different methods. The only limitation to these combinations is the teacher's imagination.

Test Yourself

True or False

_____ 1. Teacher's manuals in basal reading series generally provide detailed lesson plans for teaching each story in a basal reader.

_____ 2. Basal reader workbooks are designed to teach reading skills and do not require teacher intervention.

342

Teaching
Reading in
Today's
Elementary
Schools

_____ 3. Workbook activities are only good to keep children busy while the teacher is engaged in other activities.

_____ 4. Authors of today's basal readers are trying to reflect today's world realistically.

_____ 5. The language experience approach (LEA) makes use of child-created material for reading instruction.

_____ 6. A word bank is a collection of words that the teacher believes the children should learn.

_____ 7. The language experience approach promotes a better self-concept in many children.

_____ 8. The individualized reading approach utilizes self-selection and self-pacing.

_____ 9. The individualized reading approach involves no direct skills instruction.

_____ 10. Student-teacher conferences are an integral part of the individualized reading approach.

_____ 11. A disadvantage of the individualized reading approach is the absence of sequential skill development.

_____ 12. Beginning linguistic reading materials make use of words that conform to regular spelling patterns.

_____ 13. Programmed instruction involves the presentation of instructional material in small, sequential steps.

_____ 14. Eclectic approaches combine the best features of a number of different approaches.

_____ 15. Sometimes computers are useful in diagnosing students' reading difficulties and prescribing corrective programs.

_____ 16. Basal readers should always be used from front to back in their entirety.

_____ 17. Behavioral objectives are provided for each of the elements in the Wisconsin Design.

_____ 18. The language experience approach is not consistent with schema theory.

_____ 19. Drill-and-practice programs are among the rarest and most complex CAI programs.

_____ 20. Microcomputers are much less expensive than mainframe computers, and therefore it is easier for schools to purchase them for CAI purposes.

_____ 21. No commercial educational publishers have as yet ventured into the field of CAI.

_____ 22. The directed reading-thinking activity is a good alternative to the directed reading approach to provide a more student-centered experience.

_____ 23. A Reconciled Reading Lesson has the same organization as a DRA.

_____ 24. Word processing on the microcomputer is useful for writing language experience stories.

_____ 25. The language experience approach is not useful above first grade.

Self-Improvement Opportunities

343

Major
Approaches
to Reading
Instruction

1. Visit an elementary school classroom and discuss the instructional materials used in the reading program with the teacher(s).
2. Visit a school and watch an experienced teacher using a DRA plan.
3. Develop a language experience chart with a group of youngsters. Use it to teach one or more word-attack skills.
4. Plan an individualized reading approach for a specific group of youngsters. Explain what materials will be used (include reading levels and interest areas of the materials) and where they will be obtained. Outline the record-keeping procedures; explain how conferences will be scheduled and the uses to which they will be put; and describe the routines the children will follow for selecting books, checking out books, and receiving help while reading.
5. Look into the possibility of utilizing CAI in the reading program of a school near you. Find out what computer programs that fit into the current reading program are available. See if there are programs that are designed to supplement the basal reading program being used. Decide what equipment would be needed to make use of these programs. Investigate the cost of the equipment and programs.
6. Develop a directed reading-thinking activity (DRTA) for a story in a basal reader. Then try it out in an elementary school classroom or present it to a group of your peers in a reading or content methods course.
7. Choose a basal reader for a grade level you might teach. Examine it for variety of types of writing (narrative, expository, poetry). Make a chart showing the frequency of the various types. Note also the frequency of different types of content (language skills, social studies, science, art, mathematics, music, and so on). Report your results to the class.
8. Choose a basal reader for a grade level you might teach. Examine it for career roles of the women and men and for white characters and minority characters. Make charts showing career frequencies for these factions of society.
9. Choose a basal reader for a grade level you might teach. Examine it for representation of elderly characters and handicapped characters. Notice also how these characters are portrayed. Report your findings to the class.
10. Choose a computer program that is designed to work on some aspect of reading for a grade level of your choice. Answer the three questions listed on page 331 in reference to the program, considering "this classroom" in Question 3 to refer to the grade level you chose. Write a narrative that tells why you would or would not recommend use of the program, considering all the factors presented in the section of this chapter related to computers.

Bibliography

Aaron, Robert L., and Martha K. Anderson. "A Comparison of Values Expressed in Juvenile Magazines and Basal Reader Series." *The Reading Teacher* 35 (December 1981): 305–13.

Allen, R. V. "The Language-Experience Approach." In *Perspectives on Elementary Reading: Principles and Strategies of Teaching*, Robert Karlin, ed. New York: Harcourt Brace Jovanovich, 1973.

Atkinson, Richard C., and John D. Fletcher. "Teaching Children to Read with a Computer." *The Reading Teacher* 25 (January 1972): 319–27.

Bagford, Jack. "What Ever Happened to Individualized Reading?" *The Reading Teacher* 39 (November 1985): 190–93.

Balajthy, Ernest. "Reinforcement and Drill by Microcomputer." *The Reading Teacher* 37 (February 1984): 490–94.

Barbe, Walter B., and Jerry Abbot. *Personalized Reading Instruction.* Englewood Cliffs, N.J.: Prentice-Hall, 1975.

"Basal Reading Texts: What's in Them to Comprehend?" *The Reading Teacher* 38 (November 1984): 194–95.

Baumann, James F. "How to Expand a Basal Reader Program." *The Reading Teacher* 37 (March 1984): 604–607.

Blachowicz, Camille L. Z. "Showing Teachers How to Develop Students' Predictive Reading." *The Reading Teacher* 36 (March 1983): 680–83.

Blanchard, Jay S. "Computer-assisted Instruction in Today's Reading Classrooms." *Journal of Reading* 23 (February 1980): 430–34.

Blanton, William E., Gary B. Moorman, and Karen D. Wood. "A Model of Direct Instruction Applied to the Basal Skills Lesson." *The Reading Teacher* 40 (December 1986): 299–304.

Blass, Rosanne J., Nancy Allan Jurenka, and Eleanor G. Zirzow. "Showing Children the Communicative Nature of Reading." *The Reading Teacher* 34 (May 1981): 926–31.

Botterell, Art. "Why Johnny Can't Compute." *Microcomputing* 6 (April 1982): 146–50.

Bridge, Connie, Peter N. Winograd, and Darlene Haley. "Using Predictable Materials vs. Preprimers to Teach Beginning Sight Words." *The Reading Teacher* 36 (May 1983): 884–91.

Britton, Gwyneth, Margaret Lumpkin, and Esther Britton. "The Battle to Imprint Citizens for the 21st Century." *The Reading Teacher* 37 (April 1984): 724–33.

Coburn, Peter, et al. *Practical Guide to Computers in Education.* Reading, Mass.: Addison-Wesley, 1982, pp. 46–49.

Cunningham, Pat. "Horizontal Reading." *The Reading Teacher* 34 (November 1980): 222–24.

Dudley-Marling, Curtis. "Microcomputers, Reading, and Writing: Alternatives to Drill and Practice." *The Reading Teacher* 38 (January 1985): 388–91.

Durkin, Dolores. "Is There a Match Between What Elementary Teachers

Do and What Basal Reader Manuals Recommend?" *The Reading Teacher* 37 (April 1984): 734–44.

Durkin, Dolores. "Reading Comprehension Instruction in Five Basal Reader Series." *Reading Research Quarterly* 16, No. 4 (1981): 515–44.

Egan, Owen. "In Defense of Traditional Language: Folktales and Reading Texts." *The Reading Teacher* 37 (December 1983): 228–33.

Eldredge, J. Lloyd, and Dennie Butterfield. "Alternatives to Traditional Reading Instruction." *The Reading Teacher* 40 (October 1986): 32–37.

Elster, Charles, and Herbert D. Simons. "How Important Are Illustrations in Children's Readers?" *The Reading Teacher* 39 (November 1985): 148–52.

Esbensen, Thorwald. "Personal Computers: The Golden Mean in Education." *Personal Computing* 5 (November 1981): 115–16, 120.

Fitzgerald, Gisela G. "Why Kids Can Read the Book But Not the Workbook." *The Reading Teacher* 32 (May 1979): 930–32.

Flood, James, Diane Lapp, and Sharon Flood. "Types of Writing Included in Basal Reading Programs: Preprimers Through Second-Grade Readers." In *Changing Perspectives on Research in Reading/Language Processing and Instruction,* Jerome A. Niles and Larry A. Harris, eds. Rochester, N.Y.: National Reading Conference, 1984, pp. 5–10.

Forell, Elizabeth. "The Case for Conservative Reader Placement." *The Reading Teacher* 38 (May 1985): 857–62.

Fowler, Gerald. "Developing Comprehension Skills in Primary Students Through Use of Story Frames." *The Reading Teacher* 36 (November 1982): 176–79.

Fry, Edward, and Elizabeth Sakiey. "Common Words Not Taught in Basal Reading Series." *The Reading Teacher* 39 (January 1986): 395–98.

Gambrell, Linda B. "How Much Time Do Children Spend Reading During Teacher-Directed Reading Instruction?" In *Changing Perspectives on Research in Reading/Language Processing and Instruction,* Jerome A. Niles and Larry A. Harris, eds. Rochester, N.Y.: National Reading Conference, 1984, pp. 193–98.

Gersten, Irene Fandel, James A. Schuyler, and Lesley I. Czechowicz. "The Personal Computer Phenomenon in Education." *Sourceworld* 2 (November/December 1981): 44–47.

Grabe, Mark, and Cindy Grabe. "The Microcomputer and the Language Experience Approach." *The Reading Teacher* 38 (February 1985): 508–11.

Grabe, Nancy White. "Language Experience and Basals." *The Reading Teacher* 34 (March 1981): 710–11.

Green-Wilder, Jackie L., and Albert J. Kingston. "The Depiction of Reading in Five Popular Basal Series." *The Reading Teacher* 39 (January 1986): 399–402.

Hacker, Charles J. "From Schema Theory to Classroom Practice." *Language Arts* 57 (November/December 1980): 866–71.

Hare, Victoria Chou. "Beginning Reading Theory and Comprehension Questions in Teacher's Manuals." *The Reading Teacher* 35 (May 1982): 918–23.

346

Teaching
Reading in
Today's
Elementary
Schools

Hedges, William D. "Lightening the Load with Computer-Managed Instruction." *Classroom Computer News* 1 (July/August 1981): 34.

Heffron, Kathleen. "Literacy with the Computer." *The Reading Teacher* 40 (November 1986): 152–55.

Herriott, John. "CAI: A Philosophy of Education and a System to Match." *Creative Computing* 8 (April 1982): 80–86.

Holbrook, Hilary Taylor. "The Quality of Textbooks." *The Reading Teacher* 38 (March 1985): 680–83.

Hopkins, Carol J. "Representation of the Handicapped in Basal Readers." *The Reading Teacher* 36 (October 1982): 30–32.

Jones, Margaret B., and Denise D. Nessel. "Enhancing the Curriculum with Experience Stories." *The Reading Teacher* 39 (October 1985): 18–22.

Karlin, Robert, ed. *Perspectives on Elementary Reading: Principles and Strategies of Teaching.* New York: Harcourt Brace Jovanovich, 1973.

Kinney, Martha. "A Language Experience Approach to Teaching Expository Text Structure." *The Reading Teacher* 38 (May 1985): 854–56.

Kleiman, Glenn, and Mary Humphrey. "Learning with Computers: Word Processing in the Classroom." *Compute* 4 (March 1982): 96, 98–99.

Mallon, Barbara, and Roberta Berglund. "The Language Experience Approach: Recurring Questions and Their Answers." *The Reading Teacher* 37 (May 1984): 867–71.

Mason, George. "Programs for Supplementing Your Basal." *The Reading Teacher* 37 (March 1984a): 680–81.

Mason, George. "The Word Processor and Teaching Reading." *The Reading Teacher* 37 (February 1984b): 552–53.

Moustafa, Margaret, and Joyce Penrose. "Comprehensible Input PLUS the Language Experience Approach: Reading Instruction for Limited English Speaking Students." *The Reading Teacher* 38 (March 1985): 640–47.

Otto, Wayne, Anne Wolf, and Roger G. Eldridge. "Managing Instruction." In *Handbook of Reading Research,* P. David Pearson, ed. New York: Longman, 1984, pp. 799–828.

Pieronek, Florence T. "Do Basal Readers Reflect the Interests of Intermediate Students?" *The Reading Teacher* 33 (January 1980): 408–12.

Powers, Anne. "Sharing a Language Experience Library with the Whole School." *The Reading Teacher* 34 (May 1981): 892–95.

Reimer, Beck L. "Recipes for Language Experience Stories." *The Reading Teacher* 36 (January 1983): 396–401.

Reutzel, D. Ray. "Reconciling Schema Theory and the Basal Reading Lesson." *The Reading Teacher* 39 (November 1985): 194–97.

Reutzel, D. Ray. "The Reading Basal: A Sentence Combining Composing Book." *The Reading Teacher* 40 (November 1986): 194–99.

Russavage, Patricia M., Larry L. Lorton, and Rhodessa L. Millham. "Making Responsible Instructional Decisions About Reading: What Teachers Think and Do About Basals." *The Reading Teacher* 39 (December 1985): 314–17.

Schachter, Sumner W. "Using Workbook Pages More Effectively." *The Reading Teacher* 35 (October 1981): 34–37.

Scheu, Judith, Diane Tanner, and Katheryn Hu-pei Au. "Designing Seatwork to Improve Students' Reading Comprehension Ability." *The Reading Teacher* 40 (October 1986): 18–25.

Schmitt, Maribeth Cassidy, and James F. Baumann. "How to Incorporate Comprehension Monitoring Strategies into Basal Reader Instruction." *The Reading Teacher* 40 (October 1986): 28–31.

Serra, Judith K., and Pose Lamb. "The Elderly in Basal Readers." *The Reading Teacher* 38 (December 1984): 277–81.

Shake, Mary C., and Richard L. Allington. "Where Do Teacher's Questions Come From?" *The Reading Teacher* 38 (January 1985): 432–38.

Smith, Nancy. "The Word Processing Approach to Language Experience." *The Reading Teacher* 38 (February 1985): 556–59.

Snyder, Geraldine V. "Do Basal Characters Read in Their Daily Lives?" *The Reading Teacher* 33 (December 1979): 303–306.

Sorenson, Nancy. "Basal Reading Vocabulary Instruction: A Critique and Suggestions." *The Reading Teacher* 39 (October 1985): 80–85.

Spiegel, Dixie Lee. "Six Alternatives to the Directed Reading Activity." *The Reading Teacher* 34 (May 1981): 914–20.

Spindle, Les. "Computer Corner: What Software Is, and What It Does." *Radio-Electronics* 52 (December 1981): 88, 90, 106.

Starshine, Dorothy, and Laura R. Fortson. "First Graders Use the Computer: Great Word Processing." *The Reading Teacher* 38 (November 1984): 241–43.

Stauffer, Russell G. "Reading as a Cognitive Process." *Elementary English* 44 (April 1968): 348.

Stauffer, Russell G. *Teaching Reading as a Thinking Process.* New York: Harper & Row, 1969.

Stenson, Carol M. "Yes, Workbooks Are Too Hard to Read." *The Reading Teacher* 35 (March 1982): 725–26.

Sulzby, Elizabeth. "Using Children's Dictated Stories to Aid Comprehension." *The Reading Teacher* 33 (April 1980): 772–78.

Templeton, Shane. "Literacy, Readiness, and Basals." *The Reading Teacher* 39 (January 1986): 403–409.

"What's in Store." *Family Computing* 3 (October 1985): 81–90.

"What's in Store Software Guide." *Family Computing* 4 (March 1986): 82–91.

Wilson, Carol Roller. "Teaching Reading Comprehension by Connecting the New to the Known." *The Reading Teacher* 36 (January 1983): 382–90.

Wood, Karen D. "Probable Passages: A Writing Strategy." *The Reading Teacher* 37 (February 1984): 496–99.

Zacchei, David. "The Adventures and Exploits of the Dynamic Storymaker and Textman." *Classroom Computer News* (May/June 1982): 28–30.

Chapter 7

Reading/Study Skills

Introduction

Reading/study skills are techniques that enhance comprehension and retention of information contained in printed material and thus help children cope successfully with reading assignments in content area classes. Students need to develop the ability to use good study methods that can help them in retaining material they read, the ability to take tests effectively, flexibility of reading habits, the ability to locate and organize information effectively, and the ability to use metacognitive strategies when studying. Knowledge of how to gain the greatest amount of information possible from graphic aids (maps, graphs, tables, and illustrations) in content area reading materials is also useful.

Teaching study skills is not exclusively the job of the intermediate-grade teacher, although the need for it is more obvious at this level than at the primary level. Primary-grade teachers must lay the foundation by developing readiness for this instruction and making children aware of the need for study skills. They can do this with activities such as making free-form outlines related to stories the children have heard or read, occasionally writing group experience charts in outline form, letting the children see them using indexes and tables of contents of books to find needed information, encouraging the children to watch them use the card catalog to help locate books, and reading aloud information related to content area study from a variety of reference books. Primary teachers can begin actual study skill instruction in use of some parts of books (tables of contents, glossaries), dictionary use (alphabetical order, use of picture dictionaries), library use (location of the easy-to-read books, check-in and check-out procedures), map-reading (titles, directional indicators, legends), graph-reading (picture graphs, circle graphs, simple bar graphs), and picture-reading.

Since some children are ready for more advanced skills, such as note-taking, much more quickly than others, intermediate-grade teachers should determine the readiness of particular children for study skills instruction and offer instruction to fit the students' capabilities. Those children who are ready for more advanced skills should be helped to develop these skills as early as possible, because study skills help children succeed in all subjects.

Teachers may present study skills during a content class when the need arises or during a reading class, but they should be sure the skills are applied to content soon after the reading class. Children will retain skills longer if they apply them, and they will see them as useful tools, not as busywork exercises. The likelihood of their applying their new knowledge is increased if they practice skills in the context in which they are to be used, so a teacher may find it very effective to set aside time during a content class to teach a study skill that students will need immediately in that class.

Setting Objectives

When you finish reading this chapter, you should be able to

350

Teaching
Reading in
Today's
Elementary
Schools

1. Discuss the features of the SQ3R study method.
2. Explain the importance of developing flexible reading habits.
3. Name some skills that a child needs in order to locate information in a book or in a library.
4. Describe how to help a child learn to take good notes, make a good outline, and write a good summary.
5. Discuss the metacognitive skills needed by children.
6. Explain how to teach a child to use graphic aids in textbooks.

Key Vocabulary

Pay close attention to these terms when they appear in the chapter.

arrays	line graphs	ReFlex Action
bar graphs	metacognition	scale
circle or pie graphs	picture graphs	SQRQCQ
guide words	reading rate	SQ3R
legend	reading/study skills	

STUDY METHODS

Study methods are techniques that students learn to help them study written material in a way that enhances comprehension and retention. They are student-directed, rather than teacher-directed, as are the directed reading activities (DRAs) found in teacher's manuals in basal reading series. (See Chapter 6 for a description of a DRA.)

SQ3R

Probably the best-known study method is Robinson's SQ3R Method— Survey, Question, Read, Recite, Review (Robinson, 1961).

Survey. As you approach reading assignments you should notice chapter titles and main headings, read introductory and summary paragraphs, and inspect any visual aids such as maps, graphs, or illustrations. This initial survey provides a framework for organizing the facts you later derive from the reading.

Question. Formulate a list of questions that you expect to be answered in the reading. The headings may give you some clues.

Read. Read the selection in order to answer the questions you have formulated. Since this is purposeful reading, making brief notes may be helpful.

Recite. Having read the selection, try to answer each of the questions that you formulated earlier without looking back at the material.

Review. Reread to verify or correct your recited answers and to make sure that you have the main points of the selection in mind and that you understand the relationships between the various points.

Using a study method such as this one will help a student remember content material better than simply reading the material would. Consequently, it is worthwhile to take time in class to show pupils how to go through the various steps. The teacher should have group practice sessions on SQ3R, or any study method, before he or she expects the children to perform the steps independently.

Material chosen for SQ3R instruction should be content material on which the students should normally use the method. The teacher should ask all the students to survey the selection together, reading aloud the title and main headings and introductory and summary paragraphs, and discussing the visual aids, in the first practice session.

The step that needs most explanation from the teacher is the Question step. The teacher should show children how to take a heading, such as "Brazil's Exports," and turn it into a question: "What are Brazil's exports?" This question should be answered in the section, and trying to find the answer provides a good purpose for reading. A chapter heading, such as "The Westward Movement," may elicit a variety of possible questions: "What is the Westward Movement?" "When did it take place?" "Where did it take place?" "Why did it take place?" "Who was involved?" The teacher can encourage children to generate questions like these in a class discussion in initial practice sessions.

After they have formulated questions, the class reads to find the answers. The teacher might make brief notes on the chalkboard to model behavior the children can follow. Then he or she can have students practice the recite step by asking each child to respond orally to one of the purpose questions, with the book closed. During the review step the children reread to check all the answers they have just heard.

In further practice sessions, the teacher can merely alert the children to perform each step and have them all perform the step silently at the same time. It will probably take several practice sessions before the steps are thoroughly set in the students' memories.

Although SQ3R is probably the most well-known study method, it is not the only one. Spache and Spache (1977) recommend use of a similar method that does not include prereading questions but has the following steps: Preview, Read, Summarize, Test. Both methods are most often applied in the areas of social studies and science.

SQRQCQ

Another method that seems simple enough to utilize with good results at the elementary level is one developed especially for use with mathematics

352
Teaching
Reading in
Today's
Elementary
Schools

materials—SQRQCQ (Fay, 1965). SQRQCQ stands for Survey, Question, Read, Question, Compute, Question. This approach may be beneficial because youngsters frequently have great difficulty reading statement problems in mathematics textbooks.

Survey. You read through the problem quickly to gain an idea of its general nature.

Question. You ask, "What is being asked in the problem?"

Read. You read the problem carefully, paying attention to specific details and relationships.

Question. You make a decision about the mathematical operations to be carried out and in some cases the order in which they are to be performed.

Compute. You do the computations you decided upon in the preceding step.

Question. You decide whether or not the answer seems to be correct, asking, "Is this a reasonable answer? Have I accurately performed the computations?"

As is true with SQ3R, the teacher should have the whole class practice the SQRQCQ method before he or she expects students to use it independently. The teaching of the method takes little extra time, since it is a good way to manage mathematics instruction. (You may wish to refer to this section again as you read the section in Chapter 8 on mathematics materials.)

Other Techniques to Improve Retention

In addition to providing pupils with a good study method, a teacher can increase their ability to retain content material by following the suggestions provided below.

1. Conduct discussions about all assigned reading material. Talking about ideas that they have read helps to fix these ideas in students' memories.
2. Teach your pupils to read assignments critically. Have them constantly evaluate the material that they read, and avoid giving them the idea that something is true "because the book says so" by encouraging them to challenge any statement in the book if they can find evidence to the contrary. The active involvement with the material that is necessary in critical reading aids retention. (See Chapter 5 for a thorough discussion of critical reading.)
3. Encourage your pupils to apply the ideas they have read about. For example, after reading about parliamentary procedure, students could conduct a club meeting; after reading about a simple science experiment, they could actually conduct the experiment. Children learn those things that they have applied better than those about which they have only read.

4. Always be certain that the children have in mind a purpose for reading before beginning each reading assignment, since this increases their ability to retain material. You may supply them with purpose questions or encourage them to state their own purposes. Some examples of purpose questions are:

   a. What was the route Josey and her parents took on their bicycle trip? (sequence question)
   b. What caused Ian to forget about the promise he had made? (cause-and-effect question)

   (More information about purpose questions is found in Chapter 5.)
5. Use audiovisual aids to reinforce concepts presented in the reading material.
6. Read background material to the class to give students a frame of reference to which they can relate the ideas that they read.
7. Prepare study guides for content area assignments. Study guides, duplicated sheets prepared by the teacher, help children retain their content area concepts by setting purposes for reading and providing appropriate frameworks for organizing material. (Study guides receive extensive attention in Chapter 8.)
8. Teach the students to look for the author's organization. Have them outline the material.
9. Encourage the children to picture the ideas the author is describing. Visualizing information will help them remember it longer.
10. Teach note-taking procedures and encourage note-taking. Writing down information often helps children retain it.
11. After the children have read the material, have them summarize it in their own words in either written or oral form.
12. Have children use spaced practice (a number of short practice sessions extended over a period of time) rather than massed practice (one long practice session) for material you wish them to retain over a long period of time.
13. Encourage *overlearning* (continuing to practice a skill for a while after it has been initially mastered) of material that you wish pupils to retain for long periods of time.
14. When appropriate, teach some simple mnemonic devices—for example, "there is 'a rat' in the middle of 'separate.' "
15. Offer positive reinforcement for correct responses to questions during discussion and review sessions.
16. Encourage students to look for words and ideas that are mentioned repeatedly, because they are likely to be important ones.

Test-taking Skills

Students need to have retained what they have read in order to do well on tests, but sometimes students who know the material fail to do as well as

354

Teaching
Reading in
Today's
Elementary
Schools

they could because they lack good test-taking skills. Students may study in the same way for essay tests and objective tests, for example. Helping them understand how to study for and take different types of tests can improve their performances.

Teachers can help students prepare for taking essay tests by helping them understand the meanings of certain words, such as *compare, contrast, describe,* and *explain,* that frequently appear in essay questions. The teacher can state a potential question using one of these terms and then model the answer to the question, explaining what is important to include in the answer. If a contrast is requested, the differences in the two things or ideas should be explained. If a comparison is requested, likenesses are also important to include.

Preparation for objective tests can include learning important terms and their definitions, studying for types of questions that have been asked in the past, and learning to use mnemonic devices (short phrases or verses used as memory aids) to help in memorizing lists. Teachers should encourage such techniques.

Teachers can also encourage students to consider the words *always, never,* and *not* carefully when answering true-false questions, since these words have a powerful effect on the meaning. They can make sure students realize that if any part of a true-false statement is false, the answer must be false. They can also caution students to read and consider all answers to a multiple-choice question before choosing an answer.

Children can also be helped to perform better on standardized tests through focused instruction. The classroom environment and procedures are greatly modified when standardized tests are being administered, and children will be better able to demonstrate their knowledge if they are not bewildered by the procedural changes (Stewart and Green, 1983).

Teachers should discuss with the children the purpose of the tests and the special rules that apply during testing well before the standardized tests are to be given. They should provide practice in completing test items within specified time limits. A practice test with directions, time limits, and item formats as similar to those of the test to be taken as possible should be given to familiarize the children with the overall testing environment. The teacher can help the children look upon the test as a game in which they are trying to get as many correct answers as possible. After the practice test, the children can ask the teacher about any problems they experienced (Stewart and Green, 1983).

Children need to learn to follow the directions for testing exactly, including those related to recording answers. They should learn to answer items they can answer quickly first and to check answers if they have time left. They need to realize the importance of reading all answers before choosing the best one and to understand that they should guess rather than leave an answer blank if there is not a severe penalty for guessing.

Flexible readers adjust their approaches and rates to fit the materials they are reading. Good readers continually adjust their reading approaches and rates without being consciously aware of it.

Adjustment of Approach

A flexible reader approaches printed material according to his or her purposes for reading and the type of material. For example, she may read poetry aloud so she can savor the beauty of the words, or she may read a novel for relaxation in a leisurely fashion, giving attention to descriptive passages that evoke visual imagery and taking time to think about the characters and their traits. If she is reading a novel simply to be able to converse with friends about its story line, she may read less carefully, only wishing to discover the novel's main ideas and basic plot.

Informational reading is approached with the idea of separating the important facts from the unimportant ones and paying careful attention in order to retain what is needed from the material. Rereading is often needed if materials contain a high density of facts or very difficult concepts and interrelationships. For such material, reading every word may be highly important, whereas it is not as important for materials that have few facts or less difficult concepts. Flexible readers approach materials for which they have little background with greater concentration than material for which they have extensive background.

Some purposes for reading do not demand the reading of every word in a passage. Sometimes skimming (reading selectively to pick up main ideas and general impressions about the material) or scanning (moving the eyes rapidly over the selection in order to locate a specific bit of information, such as a name or a date) is sufficient. Skimming is the process used in the survey step of SQ3R when students are trying to orient themselves to the organization and general focus of the material. Scanning is useful when searching for names in telephone books or entries in dictionaries or indexes.

Adjustment of Rate

Students will use study time more efficiently if they are taught to vary their rates to fit the reading purposes and materials. A student should read light fiction for enjoyment much faster than a mathematics problem that he hopes to solve. When reading to find isolated facts, such as names and dates, he will do better to scan a page rapidly for key words than to read every word of the material. When reading to determine main ideas or organization of a selection, he will find skimming more reasonable than reading each word of the selection.

356

Teaching
Reading in
Today's
Elementary
Schools

Children often make the mistake of trying to read everything at the same rate. Some of them read short stories as slowly and carefully as they read science experiments, and they will probably never enjoy recreational reading because they have to work so hard and it takes them so long to read a story. Other children read everything at a rapid rate, often failing to grasp essential details in content area reading assignments, although they complete the reading. Reading rate should not be considered separate from comprehension. The optimum rate for reading a particular piece is the fastest rate at which the child maintains an acceptable level of comprehension.

One way to help pupils fit their reading rates to reading materials is illustrated in the following activity.

● **MODEL ACTIVITY:** *Adjusting Reading Rates*

Ask pupils questions such as these:

1. What rate would be best for reading a science experiment?
   a. fast
   b. moderate
   c. slow
2. Which material could you read fastest and still meet your purpose?
   a. television schedule
   b. newspaper article
   c. science textbook

Follow up answers with the question "Why?" If students do not choose "slow" as the answer for the first question, analyze the reason they give and point out any problems, making clear to them that every step in a science experiment must be done accurately and in the proper sequence or the experiment will not work. In order to assure that he or she understands all details and follows the proper sequence, a person must read slowly enough not to overlook any detail, and may even have to reread to be absolutely accurate.

If children do not answer "a television schedule" for the second question, ask what purpose they would have in reading such a schedule. When they reply, "to find what is on at a particular time" or "to find out when a certain program is on," point out that it is possible to scan for this information and that scanning is the fastest type of reading. They might aim to locate specific facts in a newspaper or a science textbook, but the format of a television schedule facilitates scanning, and it would probably be faster to read one even if the purposes for reading each type of material were similar. ●

Another way to assist children in fitting appropriate rates to materials is to give them various types of materials and purposes, allow them to try different rates, and then encourage them to discuss the effectiveness of different rates for different purposes and materials. This will be particularly helpful if regular classroom materials are used for the practice. Emphasis on increasing reading speed is best left until children have a firm grasp of the basic word recognition and comprehension skills. By the time they reach the intermediate grades, some will be ready for help in increasing their reading rates. It is important to remember that speed without comprehension is useless, so the teacher must be sure they maintain comprehension levels as work on increasing reading rate progresses.

Students whose basic skills are good enough to qualify them for rate improvement exercises need to realize that they can save time when doing some functional reading and that they can read more recreationally in the same amount of time they currently use if they increase their reading rates (Bergquist, 1984). Some techniques teachers can use with students to help them increase their reading rates include the following.

ACTIVITIES

1. To encourage students to try consciously to increase their reading rates, time their reading for three minutes. At the end of that time period, have the students count the total words read, divide by three, and record the resulting number as their rate in average words per minute. To ensure focus on understanding, follow the timed reading with a comprehension check. The students can graph the results of these timed readings over a period of time, along with the comprehension results. Ideally, students will see their rates increase without a decrease in comprehension. If the children's comprehension does decrease, encourage them to slow down enough to regain an appropriate comprehension level.

2. To show students that they can read faster than they have been reading, use speed reading devices such as the tachistoscope, which presents printed material for brief periods of time; controlled reading machines, which project material at varying speeds; and reading pacers, which have arms that move down a page of printed material from top to bottom at regulated speeds.

3. To help children cut down on unnecessary regressions (going back to reread), have the children use markers to move down the page, covering the lines just read.

4. To help children cut down on vocalization and subvocalization while reading, have them hold tongue depressors or pencils in their mouths to decrease movements of the lips and tongue.

5. To help decrease children's anxiety about comprehension that could impede their progress, give them easy material for practice in building their reading rates.

ReFlex Action

One method for developing flexible readers is known as ReFlex Action. It is designed to supplement the readiness portion of a guided reading activity. Its objective is to have children select the processing strategies that best fit a

358

Teaching
Reading in
Today's
Elementary
Schools

given reading context. The first step is analysis of context through questioning, whether teacher-directed, student-initiated, or reciprocal. Readers should question the purpose for reading; the difficulty, structure, and organization of the material; their background and interest in a particular area; the aids (such as teacher assistance, study guides, etc.) available for working with the selection; the social setting in which the reading will take place; and the time constraints, if any. The second step of the approach is strategy selection—determining whether skimming, scanning, reading to comprehend all of the ideas presented by the author, or a combination of strategies is needed. If the reader decides he or she should use a combination of strategies, he or she should determine the order in which to apply them in this step also. Obviously, teachers must provide varied contexts for reading—not a single unvarying approach with the same purpose, the same difficulty level, and so forth—in order to make this approach work (Hoffman, 1979).

✔ Self-Check: Objectives 1 and 2

Describe the SQ3R study method.
Explain the reasons that children should learn to read different materials at different rates.
(See Self-Improvement Opportunity 1.)

LOCATING INFORMATION

In order to engage in many study activities, pupils need to be able to locate the necessary reading material. A teacher can help by showing them the location aids in textbooks, reference books, and libraries.

Books

Most books offer pupils several special features that are helpful for locating needed information, including prefaces, tables of contents, indexes, appendices, glossaries, footnotes, and bibliographies. Teachers should not assume that children can adjust from the basal reader format to the format of content subject books without assistance. Basal readers have a great deal of narrative (storylike) material that is not packed with facts to be learned, as is the content material that students will encounter. Although most basals have a table of contents and a glossary, they contain fewer of the special features mentioned above than do content area textbooks. Therefore, teachers should present content textbooks to the children carefully.

Preface/Introduction

When a teacher presents a new textbook to pupils in the intermediate or upper grades, he or she can ask them to read the preface or introduction to get an idea of why the book was written and of the manner in which the author or authors plan to present the material. Children should be aware that the prefaces and introductions of books they plan to use for reference can give them valuable information.

Table of Contents

The table of contents of a new textbook can also be examined on the day the textbook is distributed. Even primary-level pupils can learn that the table of contents tells what topics the book discusses on which pages and makes it unnecessary for a person to look through the entire book to find the section that is of interest at the moment. The teacher can hold a brief drill with the new textbook that will emphasize these points, asking questions such as the following ones:

What topics are covered in this book?
What is the first topic that is discussed?
On what page does the discussion about _____ begin? (This question can be repeated several times with different topics inserted in the blank.)

Indexes

Pupils in the intermediate and upper grades should become familiar with indexes. They should understand that an index is an alphabetical list of items and names mentioned in a book and the pages upon which these items or names appear, and that some books contain one general index and some contain subject and author indexes as well as other specialized ones (for example, a first-line index in a music or poetry book). Most indexes contain both main headings and subheadings, and students should be given opportunities to practice using these headings to locate information within their books. The following lesson should follow a preliminary lesson about what an index is. Since the children's own textbooks should be used to teach index use, this lesson can be used as a model for a lesson that the teacher designs for an actual index in a content area book being used in the classroom.

● **MODEL ACTIVITY:** *Lesson Plan for Index Practice*

Sample Index
Addition
   checking, 50–54
   meaning of, 4
   on number line, 10–16, 25–26
   number sentences, 18–19
   regrouping in, 75–91, 103–104
Checking
   addition, 50–54
   subtraction, 120–25

360

Teaching
Reading in
Today's
Elementary
Schools

Circle, 204–206
Counting, 2–4
Difference, 111–12
Dollar, 35
Dozen, 42
Graph, 300–306
    bar, 303–306
    picture, 300–303

Model the use of this index by "thinking aloud" how you would use it to find different pieces of information. Then ask the children to use the sample index to answer the following questions:

1. On what pages would you look to find out how to check addition problems? Under what main topics and subheadings do you have to look to discover these page numbers?
2. On what page will you find "dollar" mentioned?
3. What pages contain information about circles?
4. On what pages would you look to find out how to add using a number line? What main heading did you look under to discover this? What subheading did you look under?
5. Where would you look to find information about picture graphs? Would you expect to find any information about picture graphs on page 305? Why or why not?
6. Is there information on regrouping in addition on pages 103 and 104? Is this information on any other pages?

Ask the following questions if you are using an actual index.
    Find the meaning of addition and read it to me. Did you look in the index to find the page number? Could you have found it more quickly by looking in the index? ●

Thinking skills become important in using an index when the word being sought is not listed. Readers must then think of synonyms for the word or another form of the word that might be listed. Brainstorming possibilities for listings for a variety of terms could be a helpful class activity to prepare the students to be flexible when such situations occur.

Appendices

Students can also be shown that the appendices of books contain supplementary information that may be helpful to them—for example, bibliographies or tabular material. There are times when children need to use this material, but they will not be likely to use it if they do not know where to find it.

Glossaries

Primary-grade children can be shown that glossaries, which are often included in their textbooks, are similar to dictionaries but include only the words presented in the book in which they are found. Textbooks often contain glossaries of technical terms which can greatly aid students in understanding the book's content. The skills necessary for proper use of a glossary are the same as those needed for using a dictionary. (See Chapters 3 and 4 for discussions of dictionary use.)

Footnotes and Bibliographies

These aids refer students to other sources with information about the subject being discussed in a book, and teachers should encourage students to turn to these sources for clarification, for additional information on a topic for a report, or simply for their own satisfaction.

The bibliography, which appears at the end of a chapter or at the end of the entire textbook, is generally a list of references that the author consulted when researching the subject or that contain additional information. In some cases, bibliographies list books by a particular author or appropriate selections for particular groups.

Reference Books

Elementary school children are often called upon to find information in such reference books as encyclopedias, dictionaries, almanacs, and atlases. Unfortunately, many students reach high school still unable to use such aids effectively. Though some skills related to the use of reference books can be taught in the primary grades (for example, use of picture dictionaries), the bulk of the responsibility for teaching use of reference books rests with the intermediate-grade teacher.

Important skills for effective use of reference books include:

1. knowledge of alphabetical order and understanding that encyclopedias, dictionaries, and some atlases are arranged in alphabetical order.
2. ability to use guide words, knowledge of their location on a page, and understanding that they represent the first and last entry words on a dictionary or encyclopedia page.
3. ability to use cross-references (related primarily to use of encyclopedias).
4. ability to use pronunciation keys (related primarily to use of dictionaries).
5. ability to choose from several possible word meanings the one that most closely fits the context in which a word is found (related to use of dictionaries).
6. ability to interpret the legend of a map (related to use of atlases).
7. ability to interpret the scale of a map (related to use of atlases).

362
Teaching
Reading in
Today's
Elementary
Schools

Although reference books such as almanacs can be helpful tools, teachers should use caution in assigning work from these books because their readability is often high. (© Mimi Forsyth/Monkmeyer)

8. ability to locate directions on maps (related to use of atlases).
9. ability to determine which volume of a set of encyclopedias will contain the information needed.
10. ability to determine key words under which related information can be found.

Because of the fact that encyclopedias, almanacs, and atlases are often written on much higher readability levels than the basal materials used in the classroom, teachers must use caution in assigning work in these reference books. Children are not likely to profit from looking up material in books that are too hard for them to read; when children are asked to do so, they tend to copy the material word for word without trying to understand it.

MacCormick and Pursel (1982) found that the overall readability levels of three encyclopedias often used in schools—the *Academic American Encyclopedia*, the *Encyclopaedia Britannica*, and the *World Book*—were all too high for elementary students, being sixteenth, sixteenth, and eleventh grade in difficulty respectively. None of the selections checked in the *Academic American* and the *Britannica* were below ninth-grade level; these books are clearly not good choices for the majority of elementary students, though some *parts* of their articles, in particular opening paragraphs, are written on lower levels and thus are not totally unusable. About 16 percent of the *World*

Book's articles are written on fifth- through eighth-grade level, with the rest
on higher levels. The common use of this encyclopedia in elementary schools makes knowledge of this fact very important to teachers, who should make assignments requiring use of encyclopedias carefully, with specific students in mind.

Many skills related to the use of an atlas are included in the section of this chapter that is concerned with reading maps. Some aspects of dictionary use and use of encyclopedias are discussed below. (Other aspects of dictionary use are discussed in Chapters 3 and 4.)

Dictionaries

Before a child can use a dictionary for any of its major functions, he or she must be able to locate a designated word with some ease. Three important skills are necessary for this.

Alphabetical Order Since the words in a dictionary are arranged in alphabetical order, children must learn alphabetical order to gain access to the words they seek. Beginning with the first letter of the word, they gradually learn alphabetization by the first two or three letters, and learn that sometimes it is necessary to work through every letter in a word in the process.

Three ideas for developing and strengthening students' knowledge of alphabetical order are given below.

● *MODEL ACTIVITY: Alphabetical Game*

Divide the class into two teams and line players up in alphabetical order by names. For the first round of the game have students take turns answering when you call a letter of the alphabet by responding with the next letter of the alphabet. Give the player's team a point if he or she answers correctly and deduct a point if the player answers incorrectly. After an incorrect answer, give the other team an opportunity to answer correctly on the same letter. In the second round the team member must answer with the preceding letter of the alphabet, and in the third round he or she must give the two letters that immediately precede and follow the letter you call. The same activity can be carried out in class without using teams. ●

● *MODEL ACTIVITY: Alphabetical Order*

On the front side of each of 14 file cards write the words shown below. On the reverse side write the letters. Set the cards up at a learning center and have the children follow the directions shown below. (As you can see, this particular message is a seasonal one, but the activity can be redesigned for any number of cards with whatever message you choose.)

364

Teaching
Reading in
Today's
Elementary
Schools

1. apple—M
2. bear—E
3. great—R
4. happy—R
5. heart—Y
6. height—C
7. learn—H

8. monster—R
9. noticeable—I
10. noticed—S
11. powerful—T
12. puppy—M
13. steak—A
14. streak—S

Directions: Place the words printed on the file cards in alphabetical order. When you have done so, take the cards and arrange them on your desk in left-to-right order with Card 1 containing the word that comes first in the alphabet. Place them as shown below.

Order for Cards

1   2   3   4   5
6   7   8   9   10   11   12   13   14

Now turn the cards over. If you have alphabetized the cards correctly, they will spell out a message for you. If you do not find a message on the back of the cards, turn the cards over and study them carefully to see which ones are not in alphabetical order. Rearrange the cards correctly and look for the message again. The correct arrangement is in the answer key, if you find yourself unable to work this puzzle correctly. ●

● **MODEL ACTIVITY:** *Alphabetizing*

Write the following pairs of words on the board:

(1) baby
   donkey
(2) window
   tractor
(3) happen
   curve
(4) acorn
   antler
(5) teach
   bitter
(6) scold
   sample
(7) advise
   add
(8) straight
   stick
(9) church
   chief
(10) penthouse
   pentagon
(11) reaction
   reactor
(12) planter
   plantation

Ask the children which word in each pair would appear first in the dictionary and why. The pairs are arranged so that each set of three is harder than the previous set. You can ask the less able readers to respond to the easier pairs and the better readers to respond to the harder ones, if not all of the students are ready for the more difficult items. The last set of three pairs is quite difficult. ●

Guide Words Children need to learn that the guide words at the top of a dictionary page tell them the first and last words on that page. If they are proficient in use of alphabetical order, they should be able to decide whether or not a word will be found on a particular page by checking to see if the word alphabetically falls between the two guide words.

The following suggestions are for students' work with guide words in the dictionary.

ACTIVITIES

1. If the children each have copies of identical dictionaries, use dictionaries for this activity; otherwise, the glossary in the back of a textbook can be used. Tell the children to turn to a certain page and read the guide words. Then ask them to locate the first guide word on the page and tell where it is found. Follow the same procedure with the second guide word. Direct the students to repeat this activity with a number of different pages. Then ask them to explain what guide words tell dictionary users.
2. Write two guide words on the board. Have each child write as many words as possible that would be found on a dictionary page with those guide words. Set a time limit. The child with the largest number of correct words can be declared the winner, but this doesn't have to be a competitive activity.
3. Use worksheets such as those that follow.

● **WORKSHEET:** *Guide Words*

Directions: Pretend that the two words listed in all capital letters below are the guide words for a page of the dictionary. On the line beside each of the numbered words, write "yes" if the word would be found on that page and "no" if it would not. Be ready to explain your choices when the teacher checks this worksheet.

BRACE—BUBBLE

1. beaker_____
2. boil_____
3. break_____
4. braid_____
5. bud_____
6. buy_____
7. broke_____
8. bracelet_____
9. bunny_____
10. bribe_____
11. brave_____
12. border_____
13. bypass_____
14. brag_____
15. bring_____
16. brother_____
17. branch_____
18. bridge_____
19. brake_____
20. barber_____ ●

● **WORKSHEET:** *Guide Words*

Directions: Below are four guide words and the two dictionary pages on which they occur. Write the number of the page on which each of the numbered words would be found, unless it would be found on neither page; in that case, write "no" beside the word.

366

Teaching
Reading in
Today's
Elementary
Schools

Page 300 *RAINBOW—RAPID*
Page 301 *RAPPORT—RAVEN*

1. rare_____
2. ramble_____
3. ranch_____
4. rabbit_____
5. rash_____
6. razor_____
7. rave_____

8. ratio_____
9. range_____
10. raw_____
11. rank_____
12. raincoat_____
13. race_____
14. raise_____ ●

Locating Variants and Derivatives Variants and derivatives are sometimes entered alphabetically in a dictionary, but more often they are either not listed or are listed in conjunction with their root words. If they are not listed, the reader must find the pronunciation of the root word and combine the sounds of the added parts with that pronunciation. This procedure requires advanced skills in word analysis and blending.

Here are two ideas for exercises in locating variants and derivatives in the dictionary.

● **WORKSHEET:** *Determining the Correct Entry Word*

Directions: If you wanted to look up the following words in the dictionary, you might not be able to find them listed separately. These words have prefixes, suffixes, and inflectional endings added to root words, so you may need to locate their root words to find them. For each word, write the root word on the line.

1. happily_____
2. commonly_____
3. earliness_____
4. opposed_____
5. undeniable_____
6. gnarled_____
7. cultivating_____

8. customs_____
9. cuter_____
10. joyfully_____
11. computable_____
12. comradeship_____
13. concentrating_____
14. directness_____ ●

● **MODEL ACTIVITY:** *Locating Variants and Derivatives*

Write on the board a series of test words, all of which are variants or derivatives. See that each pupil has a dictionary. Then give a signal to the class members to begin to look up the words. The first one to locate each test word goes to the board and writes beside the word the entry under which he or she found the word.

Test Word   *Student's Entry*
donating   donate

Continue the process until all words have been located. It is a good idea to circulate and give assistance to children who are having difficulty. ●

Encyclopedia Use

Since different encyclopedias vary in content and arrangement, pupils should be exposed to several different sets. In addition to asking them to compare encyclopedias on an overall basis, noting such things as type of index used, number of volumes, and publication date, teachers should have them compare the entries on a specified list of topics. The following activities can be used to provide children with instruction and practice in use of the encyclopedia.

● *MODEL ACTIVITY: Encyclopedia Skills*

Have students find the correct volume for each of the following topics, without opening the volume:

George Washington
Declaration of Independence
Civil War
Turtles
Siamese Cats

Have them check their choices by actually looking up the terms. If they fail to find a term in the volume where they expected to find it, ask them to think of other places to look. Let them check these possibilities also. Continue the process until each term has been located. A possible interchange between teacher and pupil might be:

Teacher: In which volume of the encyclopedia would a discussion of George Washington be found?
Pupil: In Volume 23.
Teacher: Why did you choose Volume 23?
Pupil: Because *W* is in Volume 23.
Teacher: Why didn't you choose Volume 7 for the *G*'s?
Pupil: Because people are listed under their last names.
Teacher: Look up the term and check to see if your decision was correct.
Pupil: It was. I found "George Washington" on page 58.
Teacher: Very good. Now tell me where you would find a description of Siamese cats.
Pupil: In Volume 19 under *Siamese*.
Teacher: Check your decision by looking it up.
Pupil: It is not here. It must be under *C*. I'll check Volume 3.
Teacher: Good idea.
Pupil: Here it is. It is under *Cats*. ●

368

Teaching
Reading in
Today's
Elementary
Schools

● **WORKSHEET:** *Choosing the Right Volume*

Directions: Pretend you have an encyclopedia in which there is one volume for each letter of the alphabet. Look at the following names, decide which volume you should use to find each one, and write the letter of the volume in the space provided beside the name. When you finish, take the answer key and check your work. If you don't understand why you made your mistakes, ask the teacher or aide for help.

Abraham Lincoln _____
Clara Barton _____
Martin Luther King _____
Eleanor Roosevelt _____
Henry Wadsworth Longfellow _____
John Paul Jones _____
Martin Van Buren _____
Answer Key: L, B, K, R, L, J, V ●

● **WORKSHEET:** *Using the Encyclopedia*

Directions: Look up each of the following topics in the encyclopedia. Then write the letter of the volume in which you found the topic and the page numbers on which it is discussed on the line beside each topic.

1. Badminton _____
2. Constellations_____
3. U.S. Constitution_____
4. Lobster_____
5. Oleander_____
6. Sampan_____ ●

Note: Teachers should construct their own encyclopedia worksheets based on words and topics of importance to content material that is being taught.

Encyclopedia articles are very difficult to comprehend for intermediate-grade readers. This difficulty makes putting the information they find into their own words harder. Yonan (1982) suggests using a topic with a low difficulty level and high interest for first attempts at encyclopedia reports. Then the teacher can have the students take a viewpoint that makes copying word-for-word hard. For example, they can take the viewpoint of an animal being researched and write in the first person. The students and teacher can construct a list of things the students should look for about their topics and the students can list what they already know about each category of information. Next the children can read the captions for the graphic aids in the encyclopedia article to gather information. Then they can skim the written material to gather main ideas, before reading the material carefully and putting it into their own words. They should be encouraged to choose interesting facts for their reports and to consult other sources to check their facts and obtain additional ideas.

Other Reference Materials

Children are often asked to use materials other than books, such as newspapers, magazines, catalogues, transportation schedules, and pamphlets and brochures, as reference sources.

To help youngsters learn to locate information in newspapers, teachers can alert them to the function of headlines and teach them how to use the newspaper's index. Teachers also should devote some class time to explaining journalistic terms, which can help children better understand the material in the newspaper, and to explaining the functions of news stories, editorials, columns, and feature stories.

In helping children to use magazines, teachers can call attention to the table of contents and give the children practice in using it, just as they did with textbooks. Distinguishing between informational and fictional materials is important in magazines, as is analysis of advertisements to detect propaganda. Activities related to these critical reading skills are found in Chapter 5.

In order to use catalogues, children again need to be able to use indexes. Activities suggested in this chapter for using indexes in newspapers and textbooks can be profitably used here also. Ability to read charts giving information about sizes and information about postage and handling charges may also be important in the use of catalogues.

A variety of transportation schedules, pamphlets, and brochures may be used as reference sources in social studies activities. Since their formats may vary greatly, teachers will need to plan practice in reading the specific materials that they intend to use in their classes.

The following activities can be aids in helping students to use newspapers and catalogues as reference materials.

ACTIVITIES

1. Use activities related to developing the concept of main idea (see Chapter 5) to sensitize youngsters to the function of headlines.
2. During class discussion explain the meanings of any of the following terms and abbreviations with which the children are not familiar: AP, byline, dateline, editorial, UPI.
3. Use activities found in Chapters 5 and 8 concerning types of stories, columns, features, and advertisements in the newspaper.

370

Teaching
Reading in
Today's
Elementary
Schools

4. Develop worksheets similar to the following ones for use of the newspaper's index and for practice with charts in catalogues. Always model the skill to be practiced before expecting the students to perform it independently. Whenever possible, use real newspapers and catalogues as a basis for worksheets similar to the ones shown.

● **WORKSHEET:** *Use of a Newspaper's Index*

Directions: Below is an index from a newspaper. Study it and answer the questions that follow.

Index

Comics	B-11-12	Finance	A-4-7
Classified Ads	B-5-10	Horoscope	A-8
Crossword	B-11	Humor columns	A-8-9
Editorials	A-23	Obituaries	A-11
Entertainment	B-3-4		

1. Where in the newspaper would you find information concerning financial matters? _____
2. In what section would you look to find a movie that you would like to see or to find the television schedule? _____
3. On what page is the crossword puzzle found? _____
4. How many pages have comics on them? _____
5. Where would you look to find out which people had died recently? _____ ●

● **WORKSHEET:** *Reading Charts in Catalogues*

Directions: Study the chart below, which describes postage and handling charges assessed by one company. Answer the questions that follow it.

Postage and Handling Charges
If your order is:

up to $6.99	—	add 90¢
$7.00 to $10.99	—	add $1.30
$11.00 to $14.99	—	add $1.70
$15.00 to $18.99	—	add $2.10

1. Your order comes to $8.70. What are the postage and handling charges? _____ For what amount should you write your check? _____
2. Your order comes to $14.99. What are the postage and handling charges? _____
3. Your order is only 90¢. What are the postage and handling charges? _____ ●

Libraries

The teacher and the librarian should work together as a team to develop the skills that pupils need to use the library effectively. The librarian can help by showing students the location of books and journals, card catalogs, and reference materials (such as dictionaries, encyclopedias, atlases, and the *Reader's Guide to Periodical Literature*) in the library; by explaining the procedures for checking books in and out; and by describing the rules and regulations relating to behavior in the library. Demonstrations of the use of the card catalog and the *Reader's Guide* and explanations of the arrangement of books under the Dewey Decimal System, which is the system used most often in elementary school libraries, are also worthwhile. Prominently displayed posters can help remind children of check-out procedures and library rules.

By familiarizing children with reasons for using the library and by explaining to them why they may need to use such aids as the card catalog, the Dewey Decimal System, and the *Reader's Guide,* teachers can prepare students for a visit to the library. While they are still in the classroom, the children can learn that cards in the card catalog are arranged alphabetically and that the card catalog contains subject, author, and title cards. Sample cards of each type, similar to those shown in Example 7.1, can be drawn on posters and placed on the bulletin board. In addition, fifth and sixth graders will benefit from a lesson that explains the use of cross-reference cards (also shown in Example 7.1).

The teacher may want to construct a model of a card-catalog drawer and have the children practice using it. Children may enjoy constructing the three main types of cards for several books that they have read and then alphabetizing these cards to make a miniature card catalog.

Two other suggestions for practice with library skills follow.

1. The teacher can send the children on a scavenger hunt that requires use of the library by dividing the class into teams and giving the teams statements to complete or questions to answer (Example: The author of *The Secret Garden* is _____).
2. The teacher can give students questions and ask them to show on a map of the library where they would go to find the answers. (Muller and Savage, 1982).

✔ Self-Check: Objective 3

What are the special features of books that can help pupils locate desired information? Describe each feature briefly.

Name several types of reference books and enumerate special skills needed to use each one.

Describe three types of cards used in a card catalog.

(See Self-Improvement Opportunities 2, 3, and 4.)

372

Teaching
Reading in
Today's
Elementary
Schools

▶ **EXAMPLE 7.1:** Subject, Author, Title, and Cross-Reference Cards

Subject card

        HORSES

F

Hen   Henry. Marguerite

       Black gold; illus. by Wesley Dennis

       Rand McNally, © 1957

Author card

F

Hen   Henry Marguerite

       Black gold; illus. by Wesley Dennis

       Rand McNally, © 1957

Title card

        Black gold

F

Hen   Henry. Marguerite

       Black gold; illus. by Wesley Dennis

       Rand McNally, © 1957

Cross-reference card

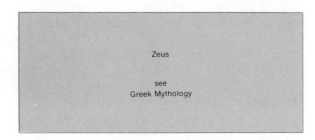

When engaging in such activities as writing reports, elementary school students need to organize the ideas they encounter in their reading. Too often teachers at the elementary level give little attention to organizational skills, such as note-taking, outlining, and summarizing, and too many youngsters enter secondary school without having mastered them.

Note-taking

Teachers may present note-taking skills in a functional setting when children are preparing written reports on materials they have read. Children should be taught

1. to include key words and phrases in their notes.
2. to include enough of the context to make the notes understandable after a period of time has elapsed.
3. to include bibliographical references (sources) with each note.
4. to copy direct quotations exactly.
5. to indicate carefully which notes are direct quotations and which are reworded.

Key words—the words that carry the important information in a sentence—are generally nouns and verbs, but they may include important modifiers. Example 7.2 shows a sample paragraph and a possible set of notes based upon this paragraph.

After reading the paragraph shown in Example 7.2, the note-taker first thinks, "What kind of information is given here?" The answer, "a problem for restaurant owners or managers—good help," is the first note. Then the note-taker searches for key words to describe the kind of help needed. For example, cooks who "are able to prepare the food offered by the restaurant" can be described as *good* cooks—ten words condensed into two that carry the idea. In the case of the nouns *dishwasher* and *waitresses* and *waiters*, descriptive words related to them are added; condensation of phrases is not necessary, although the *ands* between the adjectives may be left out, because the key words needed are found directly in the selection. The last part of the paragraph can be summed up in the warning "Hire with care." It is easy to see that key-word notes carry the message of the passage in a very condensed or abbreviated form.

A teacher can go through an example such as this one with the children, telling them what key words to choose and why, and then provide another example, letting the children decide as a group which key words to write down and having them give reasons for their choices. Finally, each child can do a selection individually. After completing the individual note-taking, the children can compare their notes and discuss reasons for choices.

374
Teaching
Reading in
Today's
Elementary
Schools

Among the organizational skills important for students to learn at the elementary-school level are note-taking, outlining, and summarizing.   (© Joel Gordon)

▶ **EXAMPLE 7.2:** Sample Paragraph and Notes

A restaurant is not as easy a business to run as it may appear to be to some people, since the problem of obtaining good help is ever-present. Cooks, dishwashers, and waitresses or waiters are necessary personnel. Cooks must be able to prepare the food offered by the restaurant. Dishwashers need to be dependable and thorough. Waitresses and waiters need to be able to carry out their duties politely and efficiently. Poorly prepared food, inadequately cleaned dishes, and rude help can be the downfall of a restaurant, so restaurant owners and managers must hire with care.

Sample note card

> Problem for restaurant owner or
> manager—good help; good cooks;
> dependable, thorough dishwash-
> ers; polite, efficient waitresses and
> waiters. Hire with care.

Students can take notes in outline form, in sentences, or in paragraphs.
Beginners may even benefit from taking notes in the form of semantic webs or maps. (See Chapters 4 and 5 for elaboration of these techniques.)

Example 7.3 shows several sample note cards.

▶ **EXAMPLE 7.3:** Sample Note Cards

1st reference from source

> Berger, Melvin. "Folk Music." *The World Book Encyclopedia*, 1983, VII, p. 283.
>
> Folk songs are passed along from person to person and gradually change in form through the years.

Source previously used

> Berger, p. 283.
>
> "Most American and European folk songs have a stanza form, which consists of a verse alternating with a chorus. The verses tell the story, and so each verse is different. The words of the chorus remain the same in most folk songs."

Incomplete sentences

> Berger, pp. 283–284.
>
> Kinds of folk music: ballads, work songs, union songs, prison songs, spirituals, dance songs, game songs, nonsense songs, American Indian "power" songs, call-response songs.

Outlining

Teachers can lead children to understand that outlining is writing down information from reading material in a way that shows the relationships

376

Teaching
Reading in
Today's
Elementary
Schools

between the main ideas and the supporting details, although, of course, children must already know how to recognize main ideas and details. Two types of outlines that are important for children to understand are the sentence outline, in which each point is a complete sentence, and the topic outline, which is composed of key words and phrases. Since choosing key words and phrases is in itself a difficult task for many youngsters, it is wise to present sentence outlines first.

The first step in forming an outline is to extract the main ideas from the material and to list these ideas beside Roman numerals in the order they occur. Supporting details are listed beside capital letters below the main idea they support and are slightly indented to indicate their subordination. Details that are subordinate to the main details designated by capital letters are indented still further and preceded by Arabic numerals. The next level of subordination is indicated by lower-case letters, though elementary pupils will rarely need to make an outline that goes beyond the level of Arabic numerals.

A blank outline form like the one shown in Example 7.4 may help students to understand how to write an outline in proper form.

▶ **EXAMPLE 7.4:** Sample Outline

Title
I. Main idea
   A. Detail supporting I
   B. Detail supporting I
      1. Detail supporting B
      2. Detail supporting B
         a. Detail supporting 2
         b. Detail supporting 2
      3. Detail supporting B
   C. Detail supporting I
II. Main idea
   A. Detail supporting II
   B. Detail supporting II
   C. Detail supporting II ◀

The teacher can supply pupils with partially completed outlines of chapters in their subject matter textbooks and ask them to fill in the missing parts, gradually leaving out more and more details until the pupils are doing the complete outline alone. In order to develop readiness for outlining as described above, use Model Activity: Readiness for Outlining.

1. Provide the children with a set of items to be categorized.
2. Ask them to place the items in categories. More than one arrangement may be possible; let them try several.
3. Provide the children with a blank outline form of this type:

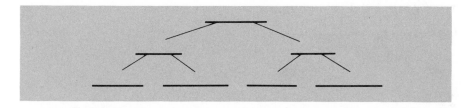

4. Have the children fill in the outline.
   Example:
   a. Provide plastic animals: horse, cow, chicken, pig, elephant, lion, sea gull, rooster, tiger.
   b. Give them time to categorize.
   c. Provide this outline.

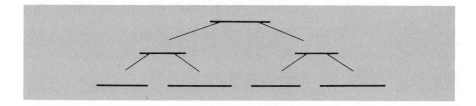

   d. Possible solution:

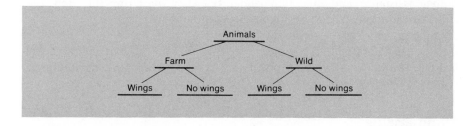

This activity can be used as a first step in teaching the concept of outlining to first and second graders. ●

The next step might be to have the students make free-form outlines, called arrays, for stories (Hansell, 1978). To make arrays, children use words, lines,

378

Teaching
Reading in
Today's
Elementary
Schools

and arrows to arrange key words and phrases from the story in a way that shows their relationships. Simple, very familiar stories allow children to concentrate on arranging the terms logically rather than on locating the details. Example 7.5 shows an array based upon the familiar story "The Three Little Pigs."

▶ **EXAMPLE 7.5:** Story Array

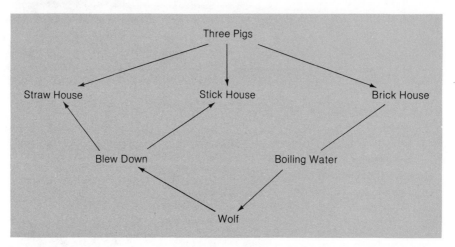

At first teachers will need to provide the key words and phrases. The children can then cooperatively develop arrays in small groups with help from teachers' probing questions about connecting lines, directions of arrows, and positions of phrases. The children may also ask the teacher questions about their decisions. As they develop proficiency with the task, the teacher can allow them to choose key words and phrases themselves, at first with his or her assistance and then independently. After mastering this step, the children can move on to forming arrays without assistance.

Children can obtain outlining practice by outlining material that the teacher has entered into a computer file. The children can move phrases and headings around with a word-processing program and make an outline in relatively painless fashion.

Summarizing

In a summary, a pupil is expected to restate what the author has said in a more concise form. Main ideas of a selection should be preserved, but illustrative material and statements that merely elaborate upon the main idea should not be included.

One possible way in which the teacher can build children's experience with summarizing is to give the children a long passage to read and three or four summaries of the passage. Then the teacher explains, step-by-step, why each of the poor summaries is not sufficient and why the best summary is acceptable. Finally, the teacher gives the children another passage, along with several possible summaries, and has them choose the best summary and tell why they did not choose each of the others.

Children should be led to see that, when making summaries, trivial and redundant material should be deleted. Superordinate terms can be used to replace lists of similar items or actions (for example, "people" for "men, women, and children"). Steps in an action may be replaced by a superordinate action ("baked a cake" for "took flour, butter, . . . and then placed it in an oven"). Each paragraph can be represented with its topic sentence or implied main idea sentence (Brown and Day, 1983; Brown, Day, and Jones, 1983; Recht, 1984).

The deletion of unnecessary material when constructing summaries should be modeled by the teacher and then it should be practiced by the students under supervision. The choice of superordinate terms and actions and the choice or construction of topic sentences should also be modeled and practiced. Easy material should be used for beginning instruction, and paragraphs should be used before proceeding to longer passages (Recht, 1984).

In addition, the following exercises may be helpful in providing practice with summarizing.

● **MODEL ACTIVITY:** *Writing Headlines*

Give the children copies of news stories without headlines, like the one below, and let them provide headlines that contain the main ideas of the stories.

Coopersville's pollution index has increased to a highly undesirable level this year. Chemists reveal that on a scale of 100, Coopersville's pollution is 95, compared to 75 for the average U.S. urban area. This report merely verifies what most residents of Coopersville have known for a long time—Coopersville exists under a cloud of smog. ●

● **MODEL ACTIVITY:** *Single-Sentence Summaries*

Have the children read a short passage, like the one below, and try to summarize its content in a single sentence.

Sometimes your hair makes a noise when you comb it. The noise is really made by static electricity. Static electricity collects in one place. Then it jumps to another place. Rub your feet on a rug. Now touch something. What happens? Static electricity collects on your body, but it can jump from your finger to other places. Sometimes you can see a spark and hear a noise. ●

✔ **Self-Check: Objective 4**
Three types of organizational skills have been discussed in this section. Name and explain the function of each.

METACOGNITION

Metacognitive skills (skills involving the ability to examine one's intellectual functioning) are important in reading for meaning and in reading for retention. Comprehension monitoring and taking steps to ensure comprehension when deficiencies are discovered are the skills associated with reading for meaning. Recognizing important ideas, checking mastery of the information read, and developing effective strategies for study are the skills involved in reading for retention (Baker and Brown, 1984). Metacognition involves knowing what is known already, knowing when understanding of new material has been accomplished, knowing how the understanding was reached, and knowing why something is or is not known. Children have shown some awareness of these aspects of learning. Catherine Canley and Frank Murray found that children realized that age, ability, and effort affected their success at pronouncing and defining easy and hard words. They showed understanding that effort, as well as ability, is important for success (Guthrie, 1983).

Research indicates that comprehension monitoring is a developmental skill that is not fully developed until adolescence. Ann Brown and Sandra Smiley discovered that low-ability students did not always benefit from monitoring strategies. These strategies may be beneficial only if students possess the background and understanding to make effective use of them. However, with attention to the level of maturity of the students, aspects of comprehension monitoring can be taught. It is important for teachers to guide students toward use of these skills, rather than just teaching *about* the skills (Meir, 1984).

To develop metacognitive skills in children, the teacher must convince the children of the need to become active learners. The children need to learn to set goals for their reading tasks, to plan how they will meet their goals, to monitor their success in meeting their goals, and to remedy the situation when their goals are not met. In order to plan ways to meet their goals, children need to know some techniques, such as relating new information to their background knowledge, previewing material to be read, paraphrasing ideas presented, and identifying the organizational pattern or patterns of the text. Students should learn the value of periodically questioning themselves about the ideas in the material to see if their goals are being met (Babbs and Moe, 1983). They need to learn to ask if the information they have read makes sense. If it does not make sense, they should learn to ask why it does not make sense. They should decide if there is a problem with decoding a word, understanding what a word means, understanding what a sentence is saying, understanding how a sentence relates to the rest of the passage, or grasping the focus or purpose of the passage (Wilson, 1983). If the goal has not been met because a word has not been recognized, then context clues, structural analysis, phonics, and possibly the dictionary must be used. If word meaning is the problem, any of these techniques except phonics may again be used. If sentence structure or sentence relationships are the problem, identification of key words, breaking down of sentences into separate meaning units, locating antecedents for pronouns, and other such techniques may help.

Teachers should teach specific strategies for students to use when comprehension is not attained. Moderately difficult material should be used for this instruction, so that there will be some comprehension problems to confront, although it should not be too difficult to be useful. Background information should be presented before the children read, so that they have the information needed to apply comprehension strategies. Teachers need to encourage children to make guesses in their efforts to comprehend the text (Fitzgerald, 1983).

The teacher can model strategies used to monitor comprehension by reading a passage aloud and "thinking aloud" his or her own monitoring behaviors and hypotheses. Noting things that are currently known and unknown and modifying these notes as more information is added can help. Students should be drawn into the process in subsequent lessons by using the "think-aloud" strategy. Eventually they need to apply the monitoring strategy independently (Fitzgerald, 1983).

Teachers can ask students to read difficult passages and then ask questions about the passages. The children write their answers and indicate their degree of confidence in the answers. Incorrect answers should have low confidence ratings and correct answers should have high ratings in order to indicate good comprehension monitoring (Fitzgerald, 1983).

Babbs (1984) found that fourth graders could obtain better literal recall when using comprehension-monitoring cards as they read. After each sentence, the cards prompted them to decide if they understood. If understanding had not been achieved, cards prompted them to use strategies such as reading on, rereading, looking in a glossary, or checking with others in order to resolve the confusion. After each paragraph, a card prompted them to decide what the paragraph said. After each page, another card prompted them to recite what was on the page. The children did not appear to internalize the monitoring strategy to the extent of using it when the cards were not present, even though they could state the steps in the monitoring procedure.

It appears that metacognitive strategies can be taught, but more study is needed concerning students who benefit most from such strategies and the best ways to teach the strategies. They do not seem to work equally well for all students.

✔ Self-Check: Objective 5
What can be done to develop metacognitive skills in children?

GRAPHIC AIDS

Textbooks contain numerous aids to readers that children often disregard because they have had no training in how to use these aids. We have already

382

Teaching
Reading in
Today's
Elementary
Schools

discussed glossaries, footnotes, bibliographies, and appendices in this chapter, but we also need to consider graphic aids such as maps, graphs, tables, and illustrations.

Fry (1981) believes that teachers should give more attention to the development of graphical literacy—the ability to read maps, graphs, pictures, and diagrams. As Singer and Donlan (1980) suggest, teachers can use reading comprehension questions (such as those discussed in Chapter 5) or a directed reading activity to teach how to understand these aids. Actually making graphic aids is also a good technique to help the students develop their communication abilities.

Maps

Many maps appear in social studies textbooks, and they are also sometimes found in science, mathematics, and literature books. As early as the first grade, children can begin developing skills in map reading, which they will use increasingly as they progress through school and maps appear with greater frequency in reading materials. Without comprehending the maps, children will find it more difficult to understand the concepts presented in narrative material.

A first step in map reading is to examine the title (for example, "Annual Rainfall in the United States") to determine what area is being represented and what type of information is being given about the area. The teacher should emphasize the importance of determining the information conveyed in the title before moving on to a more detailed study of the map. The next step is to teach the children how to determine directions. By helping students to locate directional indicators on maps and to use these indicators to identify the four cardinal directions, the teacher makes children aware that north is not always at the top nor south at the bottom of a map, although many maps are constructed in this manner.

Interpretation of the legend of the map is the next reading task. The legend contains an explanation of each of the symbols used on a map, and unless a reader can interpret it, he or she will be unable to understand the information conveyed by the map.

Learning to apply a map's scale is fairly difficult. Because it would be highly impractical to draw a map to the actual size of the area represented (for instance, the United States), maps show areas greatly reduced in size. The scale shows the relationship of a given distance on the map to the same distance on the earth.

Upper-elementary school pupils can be helped to understand about latitude and longitude, the Tropic of Cancer and the Tropic of Capricorn, the north and south poles, and the equator. Students should also become acquainted with map terms, such as *hemisphere, peninsula, continent, isthmus, gulf, bay,* and many others.

Each time children look at a map of an area, the teacher should encourage them to relate it to a map of a larger area—for example, to relate a map of

Tennessee to a map of the United States. This points out the position of
Tennessee within the entire United States.

Some suggestions for teaching map-reading skills are given below.

ACTIVITIES

1. In teaching children about directions on maps, give them pictures of directional indicators that are tilted in various ways, with north indicated on each one. Model the location of other directions, based upon the knowledge of where north is, for one of the indicators. Then let the students fill in *S, E,* and *W* (for south, east, and west) on each of the other indicators.
2. To teach children to apply a map's scale, help them to construct a map of their classroom to a specified scale. Provide step-by-step guidance.
3. Model the use of a map's legend. Then have the children practice using the map's legend by asking them questions such as the following:
   Where is there a railroad on this map?
   Where is the state capital located?
   Where do you see a symbol for a college?
   Are there any national monuments in this area? If so, where are they?
4. Let the children show that they understand terms such as *gulf* and *peninsula* by locating these features on a map.
5. Give the children maps such as the one presented in Example 7.6 and have them answer questions about them.

▶ **EXAMPLE 7.6:** Sample Map and Questions

Questions
1. What is this map about?
   a. American Indian Tribes of the U.S.
   b. Number of American Indians in U.S. counties in 1970
   c. Number of American Indians in U.S. counties today
2. The example shows a main map and two inset maps. What is true about these three maps?
   a. They all are drawn to the same scale.
   b. Two of them are drawn to the same scale.
   c. They are all drawn to different scales.
3. What indicates the densest population?
   a. Solid white
   b. Gray and white stripes
   c. Solid dark gray
4. What is the Indian population in most of Tennessee?
   a. Under 100
   b. 100–2,499
   c. 2,500–9,999

384

Teaching
Reading in
Today's
Elementary
Schools

5. The Indian population in Nevada varies from what to what?
   a. 100–2,499
   b. 2,500–10,000
   c. Under 100–10,000 and over

6. In what portion of the U.S. is there the largest concentration of Indians?
   a. Southwest
   b. Southeast
   c. Northeast

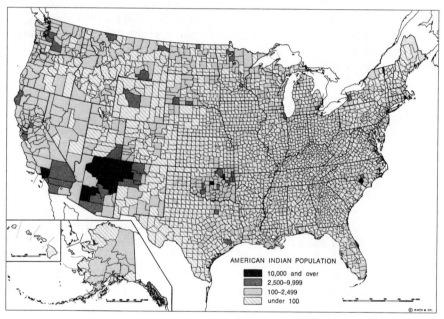

AMERICAN INDIAN POPULATION

10,000 and over
2,500–9,999
100–2,499
under 100

Source: Rand McNally and Company. Reprinted with permission. ◄

Graphs

Graphs are diagrams that often appear in social studies, science, and mathematics books to clarify written explanations. There are four basic types of graphs. These are described below and illustrated in Example 7.7.

1. *Picture graphs* express quantities through pictures.
2. *Circle* or *pie graphs* show relationships of individual parts to the whole.
3. *Bar graphs* use vertical or horizontal bars to compare quantities. (Vertical bar graphs are easier to read than horizontal ones.)
4. *Line graphs* show changes in amounts.

Students can learn to discover from the graph's title what comparison is being made or information is being given (for example, time spent in various

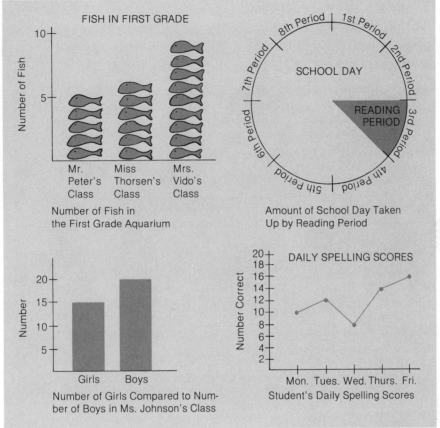

FISH IN FIRST GRADE

Number of Fish

Mr. Peter's Class / Miss Thorsen's Class / Mrs. Vido's Class

Number of Fish in
the First Grade Aquarium

SCHOOL DAY

READING PERIOD

1st Period, 2nd Period, 3rd Period, 4th Period, 5th Period, 6th Period, 7th Period, 8th Period

Amount of School Day Taken
Up by Reading Period

Number

Girls / Boys

Number of Girls Compared to Number of Boys in Ms. Johnson's Class

DAILY SPELLING SCORES

Number Correct

Mon. Tues. Wed. Thurs. Fri.

Student's Daily Spelling Scores

activities during the day or populations of various counties in a state), to interpret the legend of a picture graph, and to derive needed information accurately from a graph.

One of the best ways to help children learn to read graphs is to have them construct meaningful graphs such as the ones below.

1. A picture graph showing the number of festival tickets sold by each class. One picture of a ticket could equal five tickets.
2. A circle graph showing the percentage of each day that a child spends in sleeping, eating, studying, and playing.
3. A bar graph showing the number of books read by the class members each week for six weeks.
4. A line graph showing the weekly arithmetic or spelling test scores of one child over a six-week period.

386

Teaching
Reading in
Today's
Elementary
Schools

A teacher should also construct graphs like the one shown in Example 7.8 and model the location of information in the graphs. Then he or she can ask the children to answer questions about the graphs.

▶ **EXAMPLE 7.8:** Sample Graph and Questions

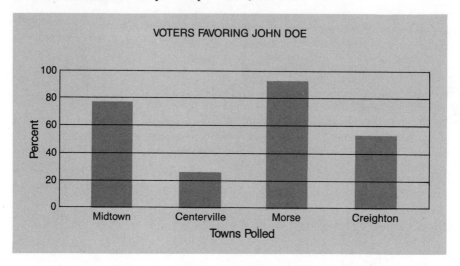

Questions
1. What percent of the voters from Midtown were for John Doe?
   a. 30
   b. 50
   c. 60
   d. 80
2. In which of the four towns shown was John Doe the least popular?
   a. Midtown
   b. Centerville
   c. Morse
   d. Creighton
3. In which of the four towns shown did John Doe have the most support?
   a. Midtown
   b. Centerville
   c. Morse
   d. Creighton
4. In which town were 95 percent of the voters for John Doe?
   a. Midtown
   b. Centerville
   c. Morse
   d. Creighton ◀

Tables

Tables may appear in reading materials of all subject areas, and may present a problem because children have trouble extracting the particular facts needed from a large mass of available information. The great amount of information provided in the small amount of space on tables can confuse children unless the teacher provides a procedure for reading tables.

Just as the titles of maps and graphs contain information about their content, so do the titles of tables. In addition, since tables are arranged in columns and rows, the headings can provide information. To discover specific information, students must locate the intersection of an appropriate column with an appropriate row. The teacher can model reading tables, verbalizing the mental processes involved in locating the information. Then the children can be asked to read a table, such as the multiplication table shown in Example 7.9, and answer related questions. Some sample questions are provided.

▶ **EXAMPLE 7.9:** Sample Table and Questions

Multiplication Table

	1	2	3	4	5	6	7	8	9
1	1	2	3	4	5	6	7	8	9
2	2	4	6	8	10	12	14	16	18
3	3	6	9	12	15	18	21	24	27
4	4	8	12	16	20	24	28	32	36
5	5	10	15	20	25	30	35	40	45
6	6	12	18	24	30	36	42	48	54
7	7	14	21	28	35	42	49	56	63
8	8	16	24	32	40	48	56	64	72
9	9	18	27	36	45	54	63	72	81

Questions
1. What is the product of $5 \cdot 6$?
2. What is the product of $9 \cdot 3$?
3. Is the product of $5 \cdot 4$ the same as the product of $4 \cdot 5$?
4. Which number is greater: the product of $3 \cdot 8$ or the product of $4 \cdot 7$?
5. When a number is multiplied by 1, what will the product always be?
6. Why is 24 where the 4 row and the 6 column meet?
7. How do the numbers in the 2 row compare with the numbers in the 4 row? ◀

Illustrations

Various types of illustrations are found in textbooks, ranging from photographs to schematic diagrams. All too often, children see illustrations merely as space fillers, reducing the amount of reading they will have to do on a page. As a result, they tend to pay little attention to illustrations even though

388

Teaching
Reading in
Today's
Elementary
Schools

illustrations are a very good source of information. For example, a picture of a jungle may add considerably to a child's understanding of that term, or a picture of an Arabian nomad may illuminate the term *Bedouin* in a history class. Diagrams of bones within the body can show a child things that he or she cannot readily observe first-hand.

✔ Self-Check: Objective 6

Name the four reading aids discussed in this section and briefly discuss the type of information each one offers.
(See Self-Improvement Opportunities 5, 6, and 7.)

Summary

Reading/study skills enhance comprehension and retention of printed material. Study methods, such as SQ3R and SQRQCQ, can help students to retain material that they read. A number of other techniques can also help children with retention.

Developing test-taking skills can allow students to show teachers more accurately what they have learned. Students need skills for taking objective and essay tests, and they need special skills for standardized testing situations.

Development of flexible reading habits can help children study more effectively. Children need to be able to adjust their approach to the reading and adjust their reading rates. ReFlex Action is one method for developing flexible readers.

Children need to learn skills for locating information in library books and textbooks, using the important parts of the books; in reference books, such as dictionaries and encyclopedias; and in the library. They also need to learn how to organize the information when it is found, and they need to learn how to monitor their comprehension and retention of material (metacognition).

Students need to know how to obtain information from the graphic aids found in textbooks. Maps, graphs, tables, and illustrations must all be read and understood.

Test Yourself

True or False

_____ 1. SQ3R stands for Stimulate, Question, Read, Reason, React.
_____ 2. SQ3R is a study method useful in reading social studies and science materials.
_____ 3. SQRQCQ is a study method designed for use with mathematical textbooks.

_____ 4. Students remember material better if they are given opportunities to discuss it.

_____ 5. Study guides are of little help to retention.

_____ 6. Writing information often helps children to fix it in their memories.

_____ 7. Massed practice is preferred over spaced practice for encouraging long-term retention.

_____ 8. Students should read all reading materials at the same speed.

_____ 9. Rereading is often needed for materials that contain a high density of facts.

_____ 10. Glossaries of technical terms are offered as reading aids in many content area textbooks.

_____ 11. Index practice is most effective when the children use their own textbooks rather than a worksheet index that has no obvious function.

_____ 12. Children need to be able to use subject, author, and title cards found in the card catalog.

_____ 13. Elementary-school pupils have no need to learn how to take notes, since they are not asked to use this skill until secondary school.

_____ 14. Subordination in outlines is indicated by lettering, numbering, and indentation.

_____ 15. The legend of a map tells the history of the area represented.

_____ 16. North is always located at the top of a map.

_____ 17. A good way to help children develop an understanding of graphs is to help them construct their own meaningful graphs.

_____ 18. Children may use newspapers, magazines, catalogues, and brochures as reference sources.

_____ 19. Teachers do not need to teach journalistic terms to elementary-level youngsters; this is a higher-level activity.

_____ 20. The ability to read charts is needed when using catalogues.

_____ 21. Key words are the words that carry the important information in a sentence.

_____ 22. Being able to recognize main ideas is a prerequisite skill for outlining.

_____ 23. Guide words indicate the first two words on a dictionary page.

_____ 24. ReFlex Action is an approach for developing flexible readers.

_____ 25. When making summaries, redundant material should be retained.

_____ 26. Some children fail to do well on essay tests because they do not understand terms like _compare_ and _contrast._

_____ 27. Standardized testing conditions need to be practiced, so that the children will be familiar with the situation when they take such a test.

_____ 28. Comprehension monitoring is a skill that can be fully developed in first grade.

_____ 29. Rereading can be a useful metacognitive strategy.

Self-Improvement Opportunities

1. Using materials of widely varying types, develop a procedure to help elementary students learn to be flexible in their rates of reading.
2. Take a content area textbook at the elementary level and plan procedures to familiarize children with the parts of the book and the reading aids the book offers.
3. Collect materials that youngsters can use as supplementary reference sources (newspapers, magazines, catalogues, brochures, etc.), and develop several short lessons to help the children read these materials more effectively.
4. Visit an elementary school library and listen to the librarian explaining the reference materials and library procedures to students. Evaluate the presentation and decide how you might change it if you were responsible for it.
5. After collecting a variety of types of maps, decide which features of each type will need most explanation for youngsters.
6. Make a variety of types of graphs into a display that you could use in a unit on reading graphs.
7. Collect pictures and diagrams that present information. Ask several children to study these pictures and extract as much information from them as possible. Then analyze the results.
8. Choose a textbook from a subject area and grade level of your choice. Examine closely the material on twenty consecutive pages and list the study skills needed to obtain information from these pages effectively.

Bibliography

Anderson, Thomas H., and Bonnie B. Armbruster. "Studying." In *Handbook of Reading Research,* P. David Pearson, ed. New York: Longman, 1984, pp. 657–97.

Babbs, Patricia J. "Monitoring Cards Help Improve Comprehension." *The Reading Teacher* 38 (November 1984): 200–204.

Babbs, Patricia J., and Alden J. Moe. "Metacognition: A Key for Independent Learning from Text." *The Reading Teacher* 36 (January 1983): 422–26.

Baker, Linda, and Ann L. Brown. "Metacognitive Skills and Reading." In *Handbook of Reading Research,* P. David Pearson, ed., New York: Longman, 1984, pp. 353–94.

Bergquist, Leonard. "Rapid Silent Reading: Techniques for Improving Rate in Intermediate Grades." *The Reading Teacher* 38 (October 1984): 50–53.

Brown, A. L., and J. D. Day. "Macrorules for Summarizing Texts: The Development of Expertise." *Journal of Verbal Learning and Verbal Behavior* 22, no. 1 (1983): 1–14.

Brown, A. L., J. D. Day, and R. Jones. "The Development of Plans for Summarizing Texts." *Child Development* 54 (1983): 968–79.

Fay, Leo. "Reading Study Skills: Math and Science." In *Reading and Inquiry*, J. Allen Figurel, ed. Newark, Del.: International Reading Association, 1965, pp. 93–94.

Fitzgerald, Jill. "Helping Readers Gain Self-Control over Reading Comprehension." *The Reading Teacher* 37 (December 1983): 249–53.

Fry, Edward. "Graphical Literacy." *Journal of Reading* 24 (February 1981): 383–90.

Guthrie, John T. "Children's Reasons for Success and Failure." *The Reading Teacher* 36 (January 1983): 478–80.

Hansell, Stevenson F. "Stepping Up to Outlining." *Journal of Reading* 22 (December 1978): 248–52.

Hoffman, James V. "Developing Flexibility Through ReFlex Action." *The Reading Teacher* 33 (December 1979): 323–29.

MacCormick, Kristina, and Janet E. Pursel. "A Comparison of the Readability of the *Academic American Encyclopedia, The Encyclopaedia Britannica,* and *World Book.*" *Journal of Reading* 25 (January 1982): 322–25.

Meir, Margaret. "Comprehension Monitoring in the Elementary Classroom." *The Reading Teacher* 37 (April 1984): 770–74.

Muller, Dorothy H., and Liz Savage. "Mapping the Library." *The Reading Teacher* 35 (April 1982): 840–41.

Recht, Donna. "Teaching Summarizing Skills." *The Reading Teacher* 37 (March 1984): 675–77.

Robinson, Francis P. *Effective Study.* Rev. ed. New York: Harper & Row, 1961, Chapter 2.

Singer, Harry, and Dan Donlan. *Reading and Learning from Text.* Boston: Little, Brown, 1980, Chapter 12.

Spache, George D., and Evelyn B. Spache. *Reading in the Elementary School.* 4th ed. Boston: Allyn & Bacon, 1977, Chapters 11 and 12.

Stewart, Oran, and Dan S. Green. "Test-Taking Skills for Standardized Tests of Reading." *The Reading Teacher* 36 (March 1983): 634–38.

Taylor, Barbara M. "A Summarizing Strategy to Improve Middle Grade Students' Reading and Writing Skills." *The Reading Teacher* 36 (November 1982): 202–205.

Wilson, Cathy Roller. "Teaching Reading Comprehension by Connecting the Known to the New." *The Reading Teacher* 36 (January 1983): 382–90.

Yonan, Barbara. "Encyclopedia Reports Don't Have to Be Dull." *The Reading Teacher* 36 (November 1982): 212–14.

Chapter 8

Reading in the
Content Areas

Introduction

In order to read well in content area textbooks, children need good general reading skills, including word recognition, comprehension, and reading/study skills. If they cannot recognize the words they encounter, they will be unable to take in the information that the material is intended to convey. Without good literal, interpretive, critical, and creative reading comprehension skills, they will not understand the textbook's message. And if they lack good reading/study skills, they will be less likely to comprehend and retain the material. These skills may be initially acquired in reading class. However, because of the special reading problems presented by content area books, teachers should be aware that simply offering their students instruction in basal readers during reading class is not sufficient if the children are to read well in content area texts. Special help with content area reading, at the time when they are asked to do such reading, is important to children. They learn reading skills appropriate to specific subject areas and general techniques useful for expository or content reading best if the skills and techniques are taught when they are needed. In this chapter each content area (language arts, social studies, mathematics, and science and health), along with its reading difficulties and activities to promote readiness and good comprehension, is discussed. In addition, general content area reading strategies are presented. These strategies are intended to be used in conjunction with the many strategies already described in Chapter 5 to aid readers in comprehending content area material fully.

Setting Objectives

When you finish reading this chapter, you should be able to

1. Use a cloze test to determine the difficulty of written materials.
2. Name some readability formulas that you can use to determine the difficulty of written materials.
3. Describe several general techniques for helping students read content area materials.
4. Describe some procedures and materials helpful in presenting material in language arts, social studies, mathematics, and science and health books.

Key Vocabulary

Pay close attention to these terms when they appear in the chapter.

394

Teaching
Reading in
Today's
Elementary
Schools

cloze procedure
concept-text-
  application approach
content area textbook
directed inquiry
  activity
directed reading-
  thinking activity
euphemism
expository text

figurative language
frustration level
guided reading
  procedure
hyperbole
independent level
instructional level
K-W-L Teaching Model
language arts

language experience
  approach
metaphor
oral reading strategy
question-only strategy
readability
SAVOR procedure
simile
study guides

CONTENT TEXTS COMPARED TO BASAL READERS

Content textbooks, with the exception of many literature books, contrast dramatically with basal readers in their demands upon students. English, mathematics, social studies, science, and health books are in most cases more difficult to read and often are not as carefully graded for reading difficulty as are basal readers. In addition, teachers and students use many supplementary materials, some of which have been prepared not as textbooks but as trade books, in content areas. Whereas basal readers generally have carefully controlled vocabularies and planned repetition of key words to encourage their acquisition, content area texts present many new concepts and vocabulary terms rapidly and give little attention to planned repetition. All of the content areas have specialized vocabularies that students must acquire; generally, little technical vocabulary is presented in basal readers.

Large portions of basal readers are written in a narrative style that describes the actions of people in particular situations. They do not present the density of ideas typical of content textbooks, which are generally written in an expository (explanatory) style, with facts presented in concentrated form. Students must give attention to every sentence in the content books, for nearly every one will carry important information that they must acquire before they can understand later passages. This is rarely true of basal readers, for each selection is generally a discrete entity.

Narrative material is easier for children to read than is expository material. One study showed that fourth-grade children can perceive differences in these types of writing and understand their different functions (Alvermann and Boothby, 1982). Therefore, at least by the time children are in the intermediate grades, teachers should probably stress reasons for the reading of expository materials.

Basal reader selections usually have entertaining plots that children can read for enjoyment. Content selections rarely offer this enticement; therefore, few content books tend to be chosen by students for recreational reading.

Content textbooks contain large numbers of graphic aids to be interpreted by the students, whereas basal readers contain a much smaller percentage of these aids. The illustrations found in basal readers above first-grade level are primarily for interest value, but those in content books are designed to help clarify concepts and should be studied carefully.

Recent research studies have found some content textbooks to lack unity and obvious purpose, thereby making comprehension more difficult (Holbrook, 1985). Even though in recent years social studies books have been found to have shorter sentences and easier vocabulary and to present fewer concepts, which would seem likely to make them easier to read, the absence of directly stated main ideas in many passages and even in paragraphs can cause comprehension problems. Texts that have been overly simplified may be a response to market forces seeking material for "the lowest common denominator" (Doyle, 1984). Basal readers, with their predominantly narrative style and the general lack of need to present a number of new concepts, do not exhibit these same difficulties, although there have been complaints that even the narratives in basal readers have been stripped of their effectiveness with the move toward easier texts. (See Chapter 6 for more on this topic.)

Whereas typographical headings that signal the organization of the selection are abundant in content area textbooks, few such headings are used in basal readers, and the ones that are used are not as informative as those in the content books. Children using content books can be helped to see that in many cases the typographical headings outline the material for them, indicating main ideas and supporting details.

READABILITY

The first step in helping children read content material is for teachers to be aware of the difficulty of the textbooks that they assign for reading. Teachers must adjust their expectations for each pupil's use of the book according to his or her reading ability, so that no child is assigned work in a book on his or her frustration level, that is, the level at which the material is so difficult it will immediately be frustrating and the student will be unable to comprehend it. Trying to read from such a book can prevent students from learning the content. If children are forced to try to read a book of this difficulty, they may develop negative attitudes toward the subject, the teacher, and even school in general. Students will probably learn best from printed material that is written on their independent levels, the levels at which they read with ease and comprehension. They can also learn from textbooks written on their instructional levels, the levels at which they read with understanding when given sufficient help by the teacher. (See Chapter 10 for further discussion of independent, instructional, and frustration levels.)

Cloze Tests

One way to estimate the suitability of a textbook for pupils is to use a cloze test, which is constructed and administered in the following manner.

1. Select a passage of approximately 250 consecutive words from the textbook. This should be a passage that the pupils have not read, or tried to read, before.
2. Type the passage, leaving the first sentence intact and deleting every fifth word thereafter. In the place of deleted words, substitute blanks of uniform length.
3. Give the pupils the passage and tell them to fill in the blanks, allowing them all the time they need.
4. Score the test by counting as correct only the exact words that were in the original text. Determine each pupil's percentage of correct answers. If a pupil had less than 44 percent correct, the material is probably at that individual's frustration level and is too difficult. Thus, you should offer alternative ways of learning the material. If he or she had from 44 percent to 57 percent correct, the material is probably at the instructional level for that student, and he or she will be able to learn from the text if you provide careful guidance in the reading by developing readiness, helping with new concepts and unfamiliar vocabulary, and providing reading purposes to aid comprehension. If the child had more than 57 percent correct, the material is probably at his or her independent level, and he or she should be able to benefit from the material when reading it independently (Bormuth, 1968).

If a teacher is using the percentages given above, he or she can count *only* exact words as correct, since the percentages were derived using only exact words. Synonyms must be counted as incorrect, along with obviously wrong answers and unfilled blanks.

Because all the material in a given textbook is unlikely to be written on the same level, teachers should choose several samples for a cloze test from several places in the book in order to make a decision about the suitability of the book for a particular child.

A cloze passage such as the one shown in this section, which contains 263 words, may be used to determine the difficulty of a science textbook. No words have been deleted from the first sentence in order to give the pupil an opportunity to develop an appropriate mental set for the material that follows. A score of less than 22 correct responses indicates that the material is too difficult; a score of 22 to 28 indicates that the child can manage the material if given assistance by the teacher; and a score of more than 28 indicates that the child can read the material independently.

Cloze tests are preferred to informal reading inventories, or IRIs (see Chapter 10 for a discussion of IRIs), for matching textbooks to pupils by some authorities because they put the child in direct contact with the author's language without having the teacher in between (through the written questions). Frequently a child can understand the text but not the teacher's questions related to it, which can result in underestimation of the child's comprehension of the material. On the other hand, some children react with frustration to the cloze materials, and these children would fare better if tested with an IRI.

Children should have experience with cloze-type situations before teachers use this procedure to help match pupils with the appropriate levels of textbooks. If they have not had such experiences, they may not perform as well as they otherwise would.

● **WORKSHEET:** *Cloze Passage*

Directions: Read the following passage and fill in each blank with a word that makes sense in the sentence.

The electricity of an electron is called a *negative charge.* The amount of electrical _____ of one electron is _____. But when millions of _____ move together, their
   (1)   (2)   (3)

energy _____ great. Sometimes they jump _____ the air from one _____ to
      (4)   (5)   (6)

another. This heats _____ air. You see the _____ air as a spark. _____ may also
         (7)   (8)   (9)

hear a _____. Did you ever get _____ electric shock? If you _____, you felt
    (10)   (11)   (12)

electrons moving. _____ of your body was _____ path on which negative _____
        (13)   (14)   (15)

of electricity traveled.

Static Electricity

Electrons _____ easy to take away _____ some atoms. Electrons can _____
      (16)   (17)   (18)

rubbed away from wool _____ a balloon. They collect _____ the balloon. This gives
         (19)   (20)

_____ balloon a negative charge _____ electricity. Atoms of the _____ are
 (21)   (22)   (23)

missing some electrons. _____ have less negative electricity _____ they had. A
          (24)   (25)

material _____ is missing electrons has _____ positive charge. A material _____
    (26)   (27)   (28)

has a positive charge _____ electricity can hold more _____.
          (29)   (30)

   The kind of electricity _____ by rubbing electrons from _____ material to
          (31)   (32)

another is _____ *static* (STAT ik) *electricity. Static* means "_____ stay in one
      (33)   (34)

place." _____ materials may keep charges _____ static electricity for a
    (35)   (36)

_____ time.
 (37)

398

Teaching
Reading in
Today's
Elementary
Schools

When charges of _____ electricity jump through the _____, you see lightning.

(38) (39)

Sometimes _____ happens when electrons jump _____ one cloud to another.

(40) (41)

_____ the electrons may jump _____ the earth. Electrons always _____ to a

(42) (43) (44)

place that _____ fewer electrons. The earth _____ things that touch it _____

(45) (46) (47)

always hold more electrons. _____ the electrons jump, they _____ no longer

(48) (49)

static electricity. _____ are *current* (KUHR-unt) *electricity.*

(50)

Answers: (1) energy (2) small (3) electrons (4) is (5) through (6) place
(7) the (8) hot (9) You (10) sound (11) an (12) did (13) Part
(14) a (15) charges (16) are (17) from (18) be (19) with (20) on
(21) the (22) of (23) wool (24) They (25) than (26) that (27) a
(28) that (29) of (30) electrons (31) made (32) one (33) called
(34) to (35) Some (36) of (37) long (38) static (39) air (40) it
(41) from (42) Or (43) to (44) jump (45) has (46) and (47) can
(48) Once (49) are (50) They

Source: George Mallinson et al. *SCIENCE: UNDERSTANDING YOUR ENVIRONMENT* (Level 4).
Copyright © 1972 General Learning Corporation. Reprinted by permission of Silver Burdett
Company. ●

After determining each student's ability to benefit from the class textbook, the teacher can form instructional groups. Group 1 (an independent-level group) will be able to read textbook assignments and prepare for class discussion independently, and its students will sometimes be able to set their own purpose questions to direct their reading. Group 2 (an instructional-level group) will need to have the teacher introduce material carefully, build concepts and vocabulary gradually, and assign purpose questions. Group 3 (a frustration-level group) will need to be introduced to the subject and, in order to understand the concepts and information involved, be given some simpler materials such as library books with a lower readability level than that of the text or selections written by the teacher on an appropriately low level.

All groups can participate together in discussing the material, and the teacher can record significant contributions on the board in the same way that he or she might do when recording a language experience story. (See Chapter 6 for a detailed discussion of the language experience approach.) When the teacher asks class members to read the contributions from the board at the end of the discussion period, even poor readers may be able to read fairly difficult contributions because they have heard the sentences being dictated and have seen them being written down. Before the next class, the teacher can duplicate the class summary for each student to use in reviewing for tests and he or she can help the youngsters in Group 3 to reread the notes, emphasizing the new words and concepts, during study periods.

Readability Formulas

Standardized tests are a good way to obtain information on the reading achievement levels of pupils. Teachers should remember, however, that a standardized test score is not necessarily a reliable measure of a child's reading ability in a content textbook, since these tests are not generally built on passages that are comparable in style and writing patterns. Informal tests based on actual content materials may be better indications of the material's difficulty. Having determined the pupils' reading levels, the teachers can determine whether a textbook is appropriate by testing it with a standard measure of readability. Among widely used readability formulas, the Spache Readability Formula is designed for primary-grade books (Spache, 1966); the Dale-Chall Readability Formula is designed for materials from fourth-grade through college level (Dale and Chall, 1948); and the Gunning Fog Index (Gunning, 1968) and the Fry Readability Graph (Fry, 1977) can be used on material at all levels.

Because readability formulas are strictly text-based, they do not give information related to the interactive nature of reading. For example, they cannot gauge a reader's background knowledge about the topic, motivation to read the material, or interest in the topic. In addition, they cannot separate reasonable prose from a series of unconnected words (Rush, 1985). They cannot measure the effects of an author's writing style or the complexity of concepts presented. For these reasons, no formula offers more than an approximation of level of difficulty for material. Formulas do, however, generally give reliable information about the relative difficulty levels of textbook passages and other printed materials, and this information can be extremely helpful to teachers. A quick way to estimate readability is shown in Example 8.1.

Microcomputer programs designed to test readability can ease the burden of making calculations by hand. Such programs are available for several formulas (Judd, 1981), including Dale-Chall, Fry, and Gunning. Application of readability formulas is "the type of repetitive, high precision task for which computers were originally designed" (Keller, 1982).

It is worth noting that research has shown that many content area textbooks are written at much higher readability levels than are basal readers for the corresponding grades. Researchers have also discovered that subject-matter textbooks often vary in difficulty from chapter to chapter. If a teacher is aware of various levels of difficulty within a text, he or she can adjust teaching methods to help the students gain the most from each portion of the book, perhaps by teaching easier chapters earlier in the year and more difficult chapters later on. Of course, this technique is not advisable for teaching material in which the concepts in an early, difficult chapter are necessary for understanding a later, easier chapter.

400

Teaching
Reading in
Today's
Elementary
Schools

▶ **EXAMPLE 8.1:** Graph for Estimating Readability

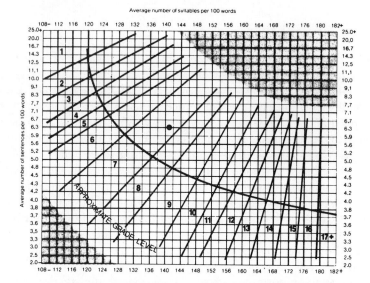

Average number of syllables per 100 words

Expanded Directions for Working Readability Graph

1. Randomly select three (3) sample passages and count out exactly 100 words each, beginning with the beginning of a sentence. Do count proper nouns, initializations, and numerals.
2. Count the number of sentences in the hundred words, estimating length of the fraction of the last sentence to the nearest one-tenth.
3. Count the total number of syllables in the 100-word passage. If you don't have a hand counter available, an easy way is to simply put a mark above every syllable over one in each word, then when you get to the end of the passage, count the number of marks and add 100. Small calculators can also be used as counters by pushing numeral 1, then push the + sign for each word or syllable when counting.
4. Enter graph with *average* sentence length and *average* number of syllables; plot dot where the two lines intersect. Area where dot is plotted will give you the approximate grade level.
5. If a great deal of variability is found in syllable count or sentence count, putting more samples into the average is desirable.
6. A word is defined as a group of symbols with a space on either side; thus, *Joe, IRA, 1945,* and *&* are each one word.
7. A syllable is defined as a phonetic syllable. Generally, there are as many syllables as vowel sounds. For example, *stopped* is one syllable and *wanted* is two syllables. When counting syllables for numerals and initializations, count one syllable for each symbol. For example, *1945* is four syllables, *IRA* is three syllables, and *&* is one syllable.

Note: This "extended graph" does not outmode or render the earlier (1968) version inoperative or inaccurate; it is an extension. (REPRODUCTION PERMITTED—NO COPYRIGHT)

Source: "Fry's Readability Graph: Clarifications, Validity, and Extension to Level 17," *Journal of Reading* 21 (December 1977): 249. Directions: Randomly select three 100-word passages from a book. Plot the average number of sylllables and sentences per 100 words on the graph. Grade level scores that fall in the shaded area are invalid. Example: An average of 141 syllables and 6.3 sentences per 100 words indicates 7th grade readability. ◀

Describe how to use a cloze test to estimate the suitability of a
textbook for a child or group of children.
Name two widely used readability formulas.
(See Self-Improvement Opportunity 1.)

GENERAL TECHNIQUES FOR CONTENT AREA READING

When working with students who are reading in the content areas, teachers
should do many of the things suggested in earlier chapters concerning
directing the reading of any material, such as developing vocabulary knowledge, activating background knowledge about the topic, and providing
purposes for reading. They should also suggest use of a study method, such
as SQ3R or another appropriate method, encourage note-taking, and provide
suggestions to promote retention of the material. (Information about these
activities can be found in Chapters 4, 5, and 7.) Teachers may also use a
number of other techniques to help their students read in content areas more
effectively. Several are discussed in this section.

Directed Reading-Thinking Activity (DRTA)

The DRTA can be used to direct children's reading of either basal reader
stories or content area selections. (A complete discussion of the DRTA is
found in Chapter 6.)

The lesson plan in Example 8.2 illustrates the steps of a directed reading-
thinking activity. It is designed for use with a chapter entitled "Exploring and
Settling the New Lands" from *The Country* by Gertrude Stephens Brown with
Ernest W. Tiegs and Fay Adams (Lexington, Mass.: Ginn and Company,
1983, pp. 122–39). It could also include activities for vocabulary or concept
development. The words *nomadic, moccasins, stockade, wagon train, jerky,
timber line,* and *compromise* may need attention. In addition, information
about the Native American tribes mentioned—the Shoshoni, the Mandans,
and the Nez Percés—could be useful background-building material. Questions for reflecting on the reading and related activities for extending the
learning experience appear at the end of the selection.

▶ **EXAMPLE 8.2:** Social Studies Lesson Plan Using the DRTA

Step 1: Making predictions from title clues.
Write the title of the chapter to be studied on the chalkboard and have a child read
it. Ask the children, "What do you think this chapter will cover?" or "What do you
think this section will tell about exploring and settling new lands?" Give them time
to consider the questions thoroughly and let each child have an opportunity to make
predictions. Then write the subheading of the first subsection, "A Shoshoni Girl

402

Teaching
Reading in
Today's
Elementary
Schools

Grows Up," on the chalkboard and allow the children to adjust predictions or make further predictions. Accept all predictions, regardless of how reasonable or unreasonable they may seem, and refrain from making predictions during this discussion period.

Step 2: Making predictions from picture clues.
Have the students open their books to the beginning of the selection. Ask them to examine carefully the pictures and the map shown in this selection. Then, after they have examined the illustrations, ask them to revise the predictions they made earlier.

Step 3: Reading the material.
Ask the children to read the selection to check their predictions. They may read this material in nine segments, corresponding to the nine subdivisions with main headings or paragraph headings, or they may read it in two segments corresponding to the main headings alone. After reading each segment, they move to Step 4.

Step 4: Assessing the accuracy of predictions, adjusting predictions.
When the children have read the first assigned segment, lead a discussion by asking such questions as, "Who correctly predicted what this section would tell?" Ask the children who believe they were right to read orally to the class the parts of the selection that support their predictions. Children who were wrong can tell why they believe they were wrong. Then have the children adjust their predictions on the basis of what they have just read and the heading of the second segment, "Lewis and Clark Explore the Northwest."

Step 5: Repeating the procedure until all parts of the lesson have been covered. ◀

Directed Inquiry Activity (DIA)

Keith Thomas has developed this procedure based on the directed reading-thinking activity for study reading in content areas. Here the children preview a part of the reading assignment and predict responses to the questions *who, what, when, where, how,* and *why,* which are recorded on the chalkboard. After class discussion of the ideas takes place, students read to confirm or alter their predictions. The predictions provide purposes for reading and, along with discussion, provide the mental set needed for approaching reading (Manzo, 1980).

Guided Reading Procedure

Anthony Manzo's guided reading procedure (GRP), designed to help readers improve organizational skills, comprehension, and recall, is appropriate for content area reading at any level. The steps in the procedure are as follows.

1. Set a purpose for reading a selection of about 500 words and tell the children to remember all they can. Tell them to close their books when they finish reading.

Content area textbooks are very demanding upon students; they are generally written in an expository style, with a high density of facts and with frequent use of specialized and technical terms.   (© James L. Shaffer/Lightwave)

2. Have the students tell everything they remember from the material, and record this information on the board.
3. Ask students to look at the selection again to correct or add to the information that they have already offered.
4. Direct the children to organize the information in an outline (see Chapter 7), semantic web (see Chapter 5), or some other arrangement.
5. Ask synthesizing questions to help students integrate the new material with previously acquired information.
6. Give a test immediately to check on the children's short-term recall.
7. Give another form of the test later to check medium or long-term recall.

A study of the GRP by Ankney and McClurg (1981) showed that it was superior to more conventional methods (vocabulary presentation, purpose questions, and postreading discussion) for social studies but not for science, and that it seemed to have no differential effect on better and poorer readers, males and females, or higher achievers and lower achievers. The researchers concluded that the GRP offered an effective approach to reading in content areas and added variety to classes. Although it was time-consuming, it caused children to be eager to return to their books to verify information and search for additional facts.

The SAVOR Procedure

This procedure, developed by Stieglitz and Stieglitz (1981), is based upon the semantic feature analysis technique, but its focus is reinforcement of essential content area vocabulary rather than merely increased awareness of likenesses and differences in words. It works well as a culminating activity for a lesson, since pupils must have some knowledge of the topic to use it.

To begin the procedure, the teacher introduces the topic and divides the class into groups of no more than five people each. The members of each group generate words related to the category involved, which one student lists in a column. Then the children identify features common to one or more of the examples. The student recorder writes these features across the top of the page. Group members then put pluses or minuses in the spaces where the category words and features intersect. If they disagree, the teacher should ask them to defend their choices, using any needed reference materials. A matrix developed for discussion of geometric shapes might be as shown in Example 8.3. After the matrix is filled in with pluses and minuses, the children can discuss which features different shapes have in common and which are unique to one shape.

▶ **EXAMPLE 8.3:** SAVOR Matrix for Geometric Shapes

	Straight lines	Curved lines	Four sides	Three sides	All sides must be equal in length
Triangle Rectangle Circle Square					

It is wise to introduce students to the SAVOR technique with a familiar topic, such as "vehicles," not related to the area of study, so that the focus is on the technique. The teacher should write the list on the board as the children name category members, then list the features as the children name them, giving examples if they have trouble starting. One such completed matrix is illustrated in Example 8.4.

When first using the procedure in content areas, the teacher might provide an incomplete matrix for the children to complete with pluses and minuses, under direct teacher supervision. The teacher should always discuss reasons

	Two-wheeled	Four-wheeled	motor-powered	pedal-powered
cars	−	+	+	−
bicycles	+	−	−	+
tricycles	−	−	−	+
motorcycles	+	−	+	−

for marks when there is disagreement. Then the pupils can work in small groups as the teacher circulates to assist and/or observe.

Oral Reading Strategy

Manzo (1980) has recommended using an oral reading strategy about once a week in a content class. The teacher reads aloud about two pages of the text while the children follow in their books. He or she stops at logical points and asks the children to summarize the information in their own words. This technique will reveal confusions, raise questions, and allow the teacher a chance to work on vocabulary and other points of concern.

Question-Only Strategy

With this strategy, the teacher first tells the students the topic for study and explains that they must learn all they can by asking questions about it. Then they will be given a test covering all the ideas the teacher believes are important, whether the questions have covered those ideas or not. The students then ask their questions, and the teacher answers them. Following the questions, a test is given. Later, the students discuss what questions they should have asked, but did not ask, during the questioning step. Finally they read their texts or use some other means of learning what they did not learn through their questions. A teacher may choose to give a follow-up test after the study (Manzo, 1980).

Learning Text Structure

Many students do not use text structure to help them comprehend and retain information from content area textbooks, but research has shown that text structure can be taught (McGee and Richgels, 1985). Five of the more common expository text structures that may be taught are cause/effect, comparison/contrast, problem/solution, description, and collection. Use of description and use of collection (a series of descriptions about a topic

406

Teaching
Reading in
Today's
Elementary
Schools

presented together) are more common in elementary-level texts than are the other three types.

Teachers can show with graphic organizers (such as structured overviews) how passages with the same text structure can have different content. Then they can prepare graphic organizers for each of the structures to be taught. Focusing on one structure at a time, they can present students with the graphic organizer for a passage and have them construct a passage based on this organizer, which will include appropriate clue words, such as *because*, *different from*, and so forth. Teachers should emphasize how the clue words help both readers and writers. After revising and refining their passages, students can compare them with the passage upon which the graphic organizer was based (McGee and Richgels, 1985).

Flood (1986) contends that teachers can help children understand expository text by having them read and write such material. Before teachers ask children to read the material, they should give them prereading help in relating the new material to their background knowledge, in extending their background knowledge, in clearing up their misconceptions about the topic, and in setting purposes for learning. New facts presented should be logically grouped for best learning.

Maps of the content may be developed and used before, during, and/or after students read it. (See Chapter 5 for a discussion of semantic mapping with examples. Also see the section "Webs Plus Writing" in this chapter.) Sometimes teachers may construct the maps, and other times students may do so (Flood, 1986). The teacher should also ask intelligent questions before, during, and after reading. (See Chapter 5 for a discussion of questioning techniques.)

Language Experience Approach (LEA) and Other Writing Techniques

The language experience approach is a good basic method to use in content area teaching (Jones and Nessel, 1985). Expository text structure can be taught through the LEA (Kinney, 1985). For example, if the teacher wishes to have the students learn the comparison-and-contrast pattern of writing, he or she can have them discuss how two objects are alike and different, make a chart showing the likenesses and differences, and dictate a story based on the chart. The teacher can ask first for likenesses and then for differences as the dictation takes place. Then the children can use their own story to locate the two related parts of a contrast and do other activities related to the structure. (This chapter contains several examples of use of the language experience approach in particular content areas to promote learning of the content.)

The Global Method is a content-oriented version of the language experience approach (Sullivan, 1986). The study of social studies and science, particularly, can be enhanced by this method. Students are encouraged to observe things around them, record their observations (in pictures or writing), and associate what they observe with their past experiences and prior knowledge. Children keep an observation notebook in which they record things observed in school, at home, on trips, or anywhere they happen to go. Then they organize their observations. Children are led by the teacher to draw conclusions about word parts in words that they can already identify, since they are chosen from the students' discussions of topics in their notebooks. This adds to decoding skill in the midst of content learning.

Another way to teach expository text structure also involves the reading-writing connection (Flood, Lapp, and Farnan, 1986). First, children are given directed practice in writing a paragraph with a directly stated main idea and supporting details. Each child selects a topic with the guidance of the teacher, activates prior knowledge about the topic, and searches for additional information on the topic. Next, the information that was gathered is categorized and a main idea about one of the categories is generated. Supporting details for the main idea are listed, and then the main idea and details are combined into a short paragraph. Peers then evaluate each other's paragraphs for clarity of presentation. Some rewriting and editing may occur after feedback is received from peers. After students write expository paragraphs, they may search for the main ideas and details in printed materials, including their textbooks.

Feature Analysis Plus Writing

A feature matrix can be helpful for gathering, comparing, and contrasting information about several items in the same category (Cunningham and Cunningham, 1987). The teacher first reads through the material and selects the members of the category and some features that some, all, or none of the category members have, forming them into a matrix like the ones shown in the section on the SAVOR procedure. Only the members of the category and the features are put in the matrix by the teacher, who then displays the matrix to the class. The students copy the matrix onto their papers, and then place pluses in cells for which they feel the category members display the respective features and minuses in cells for which they feel the members do not display the respective features. If a student is unsure about whether or not a category member has a particular feature, he or she leaves the cell blank. Then the students read the chosen assignment to confirm or revise the pluses and minuses they have indicated and to fill in any empty spaces. Erasing and changing marks is encouraged if information read refutes initial ideas. During class discussion following the reading, the students and teacher complete the class matrix cooperatively. If there is disagreement, students return to the text to find support for their positions. Library research may be needed on some points.

408

Teaching
Reading in
Today's
Elementary
Schools

The information on the feature matrix can then be used to write about the material that has been read. For example, if the second matrix under the SAVOR procedure is used, one type of vehicle can be chosen and the teacher can model the writing of a paragraph about it. Another paragraph can be cooperatively written about another type. Then each student or each small group of students may choose other types of vehicles to write about. (Note that the matrix can be expanded to include many more examples.) Using the information from a feature matrix for paragraph writing promotes retention of information covered in the matrix.

Webs Plus Writing

Webs are useful organizers in the content areas (Cunningham and Cunningham, 1987). Before the reading of the content material, the teacher records the information the students think they know about the topic of the chapter in the form of a web like the one shown in Example 8.5.

▶ **EXAMPLE 8.5:** Web for Content Material

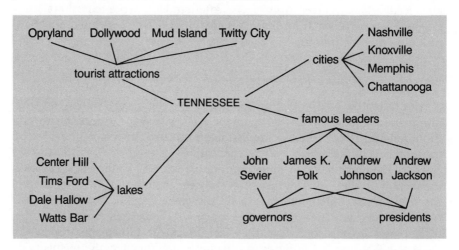

The students may make individual webs, containing only the points they think are correct. Then they read the material, checking the information on the web and adding new information that they find. In class discussion following the reading, the class web is revised and disagreements are settled by consulting the text. The class can write paragraphs about different strands of the web, for example, about famous leaders from Tennessee.

Concept-Text-Application (CTA) Approach

The concept-text-application approach is a way to organize lessons to help elementary school students understand expository text (Wong and Au, 1985). The phases in the approach are as follows:

1. *C—Concept assessment/development phase.* This phase consists of a prereading discussion in which the children's background knowledge about the topic is assessed and new concepts and terms needed for comprehension of the text may be developed.
2. *T—Text phase.* In this phase the teacher introduces the reading selection and sets purposes for reading. The class reads the text silently in segments, with guided discussion following the reading of each segment. During discussion, information brought out in the first two phases is organized graphically on the chalkboard.
3. *A—Application phase.* In this phase the teacher plans postreading activities to encourage the children to use the knowledge they have gained. This phase generally involves discussion that may include summarizing and synthesizing information, and students may be asked to evaluate and respond creatively to the material. Additional research and reports could be included.

K-W-L Teaching Model

Ogle (1986) has devised what she calls the K-W-L teaching model for expository text. The *K* stands for "What I *Know,* the *W* stands for "What I *Want* to Learn," and the *L* for "What I *Learned.*" In the first step the teacher and the students discuss what the group already knows about the topic of the reading material. The teacher may ask the students where they learned what they know or how they could prove the information. Students may also be asked to think of categories of information that they think may be found in the material they are about to read. The second step involves class discussion of what the students want to learn. The teacher may point out disagreements in the things that the students think they already know and may call attention to gaps in their knowledge. Then each student writes down personal questions to be answered by the reading. Students then read the material. After they have finished reading, they record what they have learned from the reading. If the reading did not answer all of their personal questions, students can be directed to other sources for the answers.

Study Guides

Study guides—duplicated sheets prepared by the teacher and distributed to the children—help guide reading in content fields and alleviate those

410

Teaching
Reading in
Today's
Elementary
Schools

difficulties that interfere with understanding. They can set purposes for reading as well as provide aids for interpretation of material through suggestions about how to apply reading skills, as shown in Example 8.7, which is in the social studies section of this chapter. There are many kinds of study guides, and the nature of the material and the reason for reading it can help teachers determine which kind to use.

Pattern guides are study guides that stress the relationship among the organizational structure, the reading/thinking skills needed for comprehension, and the important concepts in the material. The first step in constructing such a guide is identifying the important concepts in the material. Then information about each concept must be located within the selection, and the author's organizational pattern must be identified. The teacher then integrates the identified concepts, the writing pattern, and the skills necessary for reading the material with understanding in a guide that offers as much direction as the particular students need—whether it be the section of text in which the information is located; the specific page number; or the page, paragraph, and line numbers.

A pattern guide for a selection with a cause-and-effect writing pattern might be constructed in this manner.

1. Identify the reading/thinking process on the upper left portion of the guide and in the directions. Example:

   Cause/Effect
   As you read this material, look for the effects related to the causes listed below.

2. Offer page or page and paragraph numbers for each listed cause.
3. Consider offering some completed items to get the students started and model the correct responses (Olson and Longnion, 1982).

Teachers might want to turn the social studies activity on identifying contrasts and the science classification game found later in this chapter into pattern guides.

Anticipation guides, which are used before reading a selection, require students to react to a series of statements related to the selection to be read. The children can react to the anticipation guide again after the reading has taken place and can see the differences, if any, between their initial opinions and the correct responses. Use of these guides, therefore, is conceptually similar to pre- and postreading semantic webbing. The statements in an anticipation guide should relate to major concepts and significant details in the reading material. They may reflect common misconceptions about the topic. The guide may be used in a group setting, with students discussing and justifying their responses (Wood and Mateja, 1983). An anticipation guide for a selection on computers is shown in Example 8.6.

Directions: Read each sentence below. If you think the sentence says something that is right, write "yes" on the line that is beside the sentence and below the word *Before.* If you do not think what the sentence says is right, write "no" on the line that is beside the sentence and below the word *Before.* After you read, you will write your "yes" or "no" for each sentence under the word *After.*

Before   *After*

_____   _____   1. A computer can think by itself.
_____   _____   2. A computer has many uses.
_____   _____   3. A computer is useless without a program.
_____   _____   4. People control what a computer can do.
_____   _____   5. All computers are alike.
_____   _____   6. A computer can help people do work. ◀

Study guides should be prepared carefully and used with discrimination. Not all members of the class should be given the same study guide, since students should have questions geared to their levels of development in reading skills. Remember that a study guide will not increase the likelihood that a student will understand a selection if the selection is too difficult for that student to read.

Several students may cooperate to find the answers to questions on a study guide, or they may work individually. In any case, the teacher should be sure the class discusses the questions or items after reading the material.

Manipulative Materials

Teachers can use manipulative learning materials to teach both content objectives and the reading skills necessary to attain these objectives. Examples of manipulative materials are puzzles that require matching content vocabulary terms with pictures representing the terms and shapes to arrange as a good art composition with written directions on creating a good composition. After introducing and demonstrating these materials in whole class sessions, the teacher should place them in learning centers to be used independently by the students. The materials should have directions for easy reference, and there should be a way for the students to determine the accuracy of their answers or to receive reinforcement. If activities call for divergent thought, reinforcement is usually provided through a report or project. Among activities provided by the materials are matching technical vocabulary terms with illustrations of their meanings in a puzzle format, matching causes with effects, and following directions to produce an art product (Morrow, 1982).

Integrating Approaches

Because no single technique will make it possible for all students to deal with the many demands of content material, a teacher must know many approaches, must teach them directly, and must let the students know why they help. Children need to be able to pick out an appropriate approach for a particular assignment.

"The eight areas to be considered in planning a content lesson are objectives, vocabulary, background and motivation, survey and prediction, purposes for reading, guided reading, synthesis and reorganization, and application" (Gaskins, 1981, p. 324). The ultimate goal is to make students capable of studying effectively on their own.

To begin, the teacher should present to the class some content and process (reading/study skill) objectives for each lesson, then move on to vocabulary by presenting and teaching words through context clues or by relating the words to ones the children already know. Next comes a discussion designed to supply background information, motivate the students, and relate the material to things they already know. Then the teacher asks the students to survey the material and predict what it is going to tell. Purposes for reading are set, either through the predictions, or by other techniques. The teacher should guide the reading through use of a study guide; reading to verify hypotheses; reading to answer *who, what, when, where, how,* and *why* questions; or selective reading to discover important information. Then he or she should plan activities that guide students to synthesize and reorganize information—for example, use the guided reading procedure, construct main-idea statements, take notes, write a content-based language experience story on the material (first group, then individual), or make graphic representations of the content (graphs, charts, diagrams). Students need to be given an opportunity to apply in some way the concepts they have read about (Gaskins, 1981).

✓ Self-Check: Objective 3

Name several general techniques for helping students read content area materials.
Describe two in detail.
(See Self-Improvement Opportunities 2 and 5.)

SPECIFIC CONTENT AREAS

Special reading difficulties are associated with each of the content areas. It is best to teach skills for handling these difficulties when students need them in order to read their assignments.

Language Arts

The language arts block of the elementary school curriculum involves listening, speaking, reading, and writing instruction. It includes the subjects of reading, literature, and English. Since basal readers used during reading class have been discussed in other chapters in this textbook, they will not be considered here.

Literature

In literature classes children are asked to read and understand many literary forms, including short stories, novels, plays, poetry, biographies, and auto-biographies. (These forms are discussed in Chapter 9.) One characteristic of all these forms is the frequent occurrence of figurative or nonliteral language, which is sometimes a barrier to understanding. Children tend to interpret literally expressions that often have meanings different from the sums of the meanings of the individual words. For example, the expression "the teeth of the wind" does not mean that the wind actually has teeth, nor does "a blanket of fog" mean a conventional blanket. Context clues indicate the meanings of such phrases in the same ways that they cue word meanings.

Adults often assume that children have had exposure to an expression that is quite unfamiliar to them. Children need substantial help if they are to comprehend figurative language. Research has shown that even basal readers present many of these expressions. For instance, Groesbeck (1961) found many figurative expressions in third-grade basal readers, and she discovered that the frequency of such expressions increased as grade level increased. Some common kinds of figures of speech that cause trouble are

1. simile—a comparison using *like* or *as*
2. metaphor—a direct comparison without the words *like* or *as*
3. personification—giving the attributes of a person to an inanimate object or abstract idea
4. hyperbole—an extreme exaggeration
5. euphemism—substitution of a less offensive term for an unpleasant term or expression.

Teaching children to recognize and understand similes is usually not too difficult, because the cue words *like* and *as* help to show the presence of a comparison. Metaphors, however, may cause more serious problems. A metaphor is a comparison between two unlike things that share an attribute (Readence, Baldwin, and Head, 1986). Sometimes children do not realize that the language in metaphors is figurative; sometimes they do not have sufficient background knowledge about one or both of the things being

414

Teaching
Reading in
Today's
Elementary
Schools

compared; and sometimes they just have not learned a process for interpreting metaphors.

The two things compared in a metaphor may seem to be incompatible, but readers must think of past experiences with each, searching for a match in attributes that could be the basis of comparison. Visual aids can be helpful in this process. Thompson (1986) suggests a comparison chart, such as the one below.

COMPARISON CHART

Man	Mouse
–	small
–	squeaks
√	alive
–	four legs
√+	timid

A – indicates dissimilarity.
A √ indicates similarity.
A √+ indicates important similarity.

The teacher can "think aloud" about the operation of metaphors and their purposes. He or she can ask students questions related to the process being demonstrated. Group discussion of the comparison chart helps to activate students' prior knowledge about the items being compared, and the chart helps make similarities more obvious.

Readence, Baldwin, Rickelman, and Miller (1986) found specific word knowledge to be an important factor in interpreting metaphors. The traditional practice offered in many commercial materials may not be helpful to students in interpreting other metaphors. Readence, Baldwin, and Head (1986, 1987) suggest the following instructional sequence for teaching metaphorical interpretation:

1. The teacher can display a metaphor, such as "Her eyes were stars," together with the more explicit simile, "Her eyes were as bright as stars," and explain that metaphors have a missing word that links the things being compared (such as "bright" does). Other sentence pairs can also be shown and explained.
2. Then the students can be asked to find the missing word in a new metaphor, such as "He is a mouse around his boss." They can offer guesses, explaining their reasons aloud. At this point, the teacher can

explain that people have lists of words related to different topics stored in their minds. Examples can be modeled by the teacher and then produced by the students. At this point, the students can try to select the attribute related to the new metaphor. After two incorrect guesses, the attribute "timid" can be supplied and the reason for this choice given. This process can then be repeated with another new metaphor.

3. As more metaphors are presented, the teacher can do less modeling, turning over more and more control for the process to the students.

After teachers explain each type of figurative language, model its interpretation, and have students interpret it under supervision, they may provide independent practice activities such as the following ones. Ideally, the teachers should take examples of figurative expressions from literature the children are actually reading and use them in constructing practice activities.

ACTIVITIES

1. Show students pictures of possible meanings for figurative expressions and ask them to accept or reject the accuracy of each picture. (For example, if you illustrate the sentence "She worked like a horse" with a woman pulling a plow, children should reject the picture's accuracy.)

2. Ask children to choose the best explanation of a figurative expression from a number of possible choices. Example:

    "The sun smiled down at the flowers" means:
    a. The sun was pleased with the flowers.
    b. The sun shone on the flowers.
    c. The sun smiled with its mouth.

3. Give each child a copy of a poem that is filled with figures of speech and have the class compete to see who can "dig up" all the figures of speech first. You may require students to label all figures of speech properly as to type and to explain them.

4. Have the children participate in an "idioms search," in which they look in all kinds of reading material and try to find as many examples of idioms as they can. Students must define each one in a way that corresponds with its usage.

5. Use a worksheet such as the one shown in Worksheet: Figures of Speech.

Reading plays is quite different from reading the narrative and expository material discussed previously. Reading plays can help students see the relationship between print and spoken language (Manna, 1984). "A play's script, consisting mostly of dialogue, the sequence of events, and a limited description of the setting, stimulates children to pay close attention to textual details and helps them develop language skills basic to interpretive reading"

416 ● **WORKSHEET:** *Figures of Speech*

Teaching
Reading in
Today's
Elementary
Schools

Directions: Look at this cartoon and caption and answer the questions that follow.

DENNIS THE MENACE® used by permission of
Hank Ketcham and © by Field Enterprises, Inc.

a. What does "been through the mill" really mean, as Dennis's mother used it?
b. What does Dennis *think* it means?
c. How is the woman likely to react to Dennis's question?
d. How does Dennis's mother probably feel about the question?
e. Can misunderstanding figurative language cause trouble at times? Why do you
   say so? ●

(p. 712). Bringing the play to life involves many interpretive and creative
decisions about the setting, action, and characters. Discussion about the way
that dialogue should be delivered makes the students sensitive to language
styles and usage that fit the context and the characters.

Comparisons of narrative and script versions of the same stories can help
students see the differences in the writing styles and can help them learn to
look for information in the right places (Manna, 1984). Many plays based
upon children's stories are easily found. Basal readers often include such
plays, as do some trade books.

Both creative dramatizations of plays and dramatized reading, such as reader's theater, can be used in elementary classrooms. Tape-recording rehearsals for later evaluation is a good idea, and having children produce their own scripts for plays from narratives they have read is also a valuable procedure (Manna, 1984).

English

English textbooks cover the areas of listening, speaking, and writing and generally are composed of a series of sections of instructional material followed by practice exercises. The technical vocabulary involved includes such terms as *determiner, noun, pronoun, manuscript, cursive,* and *parliamentary procedure.* The concepts presented in the informational sections are densely packed; each sentence is usually important for understanding, and examples are frequently given. Children need to be encouraged to study the examples because they help to clarify the information presented in the narrative portion of the textbook.

Teachers are wise to plan oral activities in class to accompany the listening and speaking portions of the English textbook, since such practice allows immediate application of the concepts and facilitates retention of the material. Similarly, it is wise to ask pupils to apply the concepts encountered in the writing section as soon as possible in relevant situations to aid retention.

Composition instruction can form the basis for reading activities. The children can read their own material in order to revise it to enhance clarity or ensure correct use of language conventions. They may read it aloud to peers for constructive criticism, or their peers may read it themselves (Dionisio, 1983).

Children read to obtain information to include in their compositions, and they read to learn different styles of writing. For example, they read poems to absorb the style of writing before attempting to write poetry (Dionisio, 1983).

Social Studies

In social studies reading, youngsters encounter such technical terms as *democracy, communism, capitalism, tropics, hemisphere, decade,* and *century* as well as many words that have meanings different from their meanings in general conversation. When children first hear that a candidate is going to *run* for office, they may picture a foot race, an illusion that is furthered if they read that a candidate has decided to enter the *race* for governor. If the term *race* is applied to people in their texts, the children may become even more confused. Children who know that you *strike* a match or make a *strike* when bowling may not understand a labor union *strike.* Discussions about the *mouth* of a river could bring unusual pictures to the minds of youngsters. The

418

Teaching
Reading in
Today's
Elementary
Schools

teacher is responsible for seeing that the students understand the concepts represented by these terms.

Social studies materials also present children with maps, charts, and graphs to read. Ways of teaching the use of such reading aids have been suggested in Chapter 7. Social studies materials must be read critically. Students should be taught to check copyright dates to determine timeliness and to be alert for such problems as outdated geography materials that show incorrect boundaries or place names.

Fictionalized biographies and diaries used for social studies instruction are excellent for teaching children to evaluate the accuracy and authenticity of material, since authors have invented dialogue and thoughts for the characters to make the material seem more realistic. Teachers should lead children to see that these stories try to add life to facts but are not completely factual, perhaps by having them check in reference books for accuracy of dates, places, and names. Sometimes reading an author's foreword or postscript will offer clues to the fictional aspects of a story; for example, at times only the historical events mentioned are true. Students should also be aware that authors use first-person narrative accounts to make the action seem more personal, but that in reality the supposed speaker is not the one who did the writing. Also, any first-person account offers a limited perspective because the person speaking cannot know everything that all the characters in the story do or everything that is happening at one time. Alert students to look for the author's bias, and ask them to check to see how much the author depended on actual documents if a bibliography of sources is given (Storey, 1982).

Many other comprehension skills, such as the ability to recognize cause-and-effect relationships and to grasp chronological sequence, are necessary to understand social studies materials. (For more information on these comprehension skills, see Chapter 5.) These materials are generally written in a very precise and highly compact expository style in which many ideas are expressed in a few lines of print. Authors may discuss a hundred-year span in a single paragraph or on a single page or cover complex issues in a few paragraphs, even though whole books could be devoted to these issues. The sample content selection, "Problems Old and New," used for illustrating a study guide, is an example of expository writing (see Example 8.7). Because children's reading should be purposeful, the use of student study guides for social studies material is recommended.

▶ **EXAMPLE 8.7:** Sample Selection and Study Guide

Problems Old and New (Page 192)

The West promised many wonderful things. But getting there to enjoy them was not an easy task. Wagon trains starting out on the Oregon or Santa Fe Trail faced long, difficult journeys. Sometimes supplies ran out, or no water and firewood could be found, or the wagons got stuck in prairie mud. All these were new problems for the people moving west.

But there were some familiar problems, too. They had to keep order on the wagon train, and see that rules were followed. They also had to make sure that important jobs were done, like fixing broken wagons, taking care of animals, cooking, caring for the sick, and hunting antelope and buffalo for meat. In other words, each group had to organize a small government for itself.

You have learned that different countries had different kinds of government. It was the same with the wagon trains. Some of them elected committees to make rules for the whole group. Some asked one man to be the leader. And other groups allowed anyone over sixteen to have a say in making rules.

(Page 193)

When the wagon trains finally reached the places where they were going, the problem of making a government came up again. The rules made for wagon trains would not work in the new settlements. The westerners usually kept some of the rules they had followed in the towns and villages in the East. But all the older rules could not be used in the wilderness. Some new rules were needed. But who would make the new rules? How would they be made? What kind of rules would they be? The national government did not make rules for the West until most of it had become states. There was a government for each of the new territories in the West. But the territories were so big that the territorial governments had trouble keeping in touch with every town, city, and settlement. So the new westerners had to make these important decisions about government all by themselves.

Source: William R. Fielder, ed. *Inquiring About American History: Studies in History and Political Science* (New York: Holt, Rinehart and Winston, 1972), pp. 192–93. Reprinted with permission of the publisher.

Study Guide

Overview question: How did people govern themselves during and after journeys to the West?

1. Read the first paragraph on page 192 to discover what new problems were faced by people moving west on wagon trains.
   What is a synonym for each of the following words: *task, journeys*?
2. Read the second paragraph to discover what familiar problems people moving west on wagon trains faced.
   What kinds of animals did they use for meat? Do these animals resemble animals commonly used for meat by today's Americans?
3. Read paragraph three to discover three different forms of wagon train governments.
   What is a committee? What are some advantages and some disadvantages of having decisions made by a committee?
   How is allowing sixteen-year-olds to vote similar to or different from the United States government today?

420

Teaching
Reading in
Today's
Elementary
Schools

4. Study the picture at the top of the page [not reproduced here]. Describe the wagon in which the people traveled west.
5. Read the paragraph on page 193 to find out who made the important decisions about government after the people finally reached the places where they were going.

   What is a wilderness?
6. *Territory* is the root word from which *territories* and *territorial* are formed.

   What are the meanings of *territory*, *territories*, and *territorial*?
7. Why did territorial governments have trouble keeping in touch with the towns, cities, and settlements in the territories? ◄

The study guide in Example 8.7 directs students' reading in the following way. First, the overview question offers an overall purpose for the reading, helping students read the material with the appropriate mental set. In Number 1 students are given a purpose for reading the first paragraph (in order to enhance comprehension and retention of important content). Following the purpose is a question focusing upon important vocabulary. Number 2 provides a purpose for reading the second paragraph and asks two questions, the first of which guides the children to information directly stated in the passage and the second of which encourages them to relate what they discover from reading the passage to their own lives. In addition to providing a purpose for reading the third paragraph, Number 3 asks three questions: the first focuses on important vocabulary; the second calls for critical thinking about a concept in the passage; and the third tries to relate the past time students are reading about to the present. In Number 4 the children are encouraged to study a picture to gain information to add to that gained from the printed word. In Number 5 they are given a purpose for reading the next paragraph and are asked about important vocabulary. Number 6 encourages students to apply their structural-analysis skills to determine the meanings of vocabulary terms, and Number 7 requires them to make an inference from the facts presented.

Social studies materials are organized in a variety of ways, including cause-and-effect relationships, chronological order, comparisons and/or contrasts, and topical order (for example, by regions, such as Asia and North America, or by concepts, such as transportation and communication). The content selection "Problems Old and New" is an example of the comparison/contrast arrangement. To help children deal with cause-and-effect and chronological order arrangements, teachers can use the ideas found in Chapter 5 for helping students determine such relationships and sequences. Drawing time lines is one good way to work with chronological order, and an idea for working with the comparison/contrast style is shown in Model Activity: Identifying Contrasts.

Ask the children to make a chart showing the contrasts (or comparisons) in a selection, using the following format. (The ideas are based on the selection "Problems Old and New.")

Familiar Problems	New Problems
Need for order	Supplies ran out
Fixing broken wagons	No water
Caring for animals	No firewood
Cooking	Wagons stuck in prairie mud
Caring for the sick	
Hunting animals for meat ●	

If the teacher points out the organizational pattern of the selection, children approach the reading with an appropriate mental set, which aids greatly in comprehension of the material.

Social studies materials frequently are written in a very impersonal style and may be concerned with unfamiliar people or events that are often remote in time or place. Also, students may lack interest in the subject. For these reasons, teachers should use many interesting trade books to personalize the content and to expand on topics that are covered very briefly in the textbook. Hennings (1982) suggests a number of children's storybooks that can be used to teach social studies concepts. Some of them are as follows:

Aardema, Verna. *Why Mosquitoes Buzz in People's Ears: A West African Tale.* New York: Dial Press, 1975. (justice)

Burton, Virginia Lee. *The Little House.* Boston: Houghton Mifflin, 1942. (change)

Waber, Bernard. *"You Look Ridiculous," Said the Rhinoceros to the Hippopotamus.* Boston: Houghton Mifflin, 1966. (individual differences)

Hennings (1982) also suggests comparing and contrasting similar stories to gain a more complete understanding of the concepts being developed. Use of stories also can promote inferential thinking and reading, since the messages in stories are often implied, rather than being directly stated. Among supplementary reading materials that are not too difficult are the following. (Approximate difficulty levels are given.)

The Childhood of Famous Americans Series. Indianapolis: Bobbs-Merrill. (grade 4)

Follett Beginning Social Studies Series. Chicago: Follett. (grades 1–6)

Frontiers of America Books: American History for Reluctant Readers, by Edith McCall et al. Chicago: Children's Press. (grade 3)

422

Teaching
Reading in
Today's
Elementary
Schools

Indians of America Books. Chicago: Children's Press. (grades 2–4)
The Piper Books. Boston: Houghton Mifflin. (intermediate grades)
See and Read Beginning to Read Biographies. New York: G. P. Putnam. (grade 2)

Using the Newspaper

The newspaper is a living textbook for social studies through which youngsters learn about tomorrow's history when it is happening. Different parts of the newspaper require different reading skills, as noted below.

1. news stories—identifying main ideas and supporting details (who, what, where, when, why, how), determining sequence, recognizing cause-and-effect relationships, making inferences, drawing conclusions
2. editorials—discriminating between fact and opinion, discovering the author's point of view, detecting author bias and propaganda techniques, making inferences, drawing conclusions
3. comics—interpreting figurative language and idiomatic expressions, recognizing sequence of events, making inferences, detecting cause-and-effect relationships, drawing conclusions, making predictions
4. advertisements—detecting propaganda, making inferences, drawing conclusions, distinguishing between fact and opinion
5. entertainment section—reading charts (TV schedule and the like), evaluating material presented
6. weather—reading maps

All of these skills have been discussed fully in either Chapter 5 or Chapter 7.

Student newspapers such as *Weekly Reader* (Columbus, Ohio: Field Publications) and *Know Your World* (Columbus, Ohio: Xerox Education Publications) are often used in the elementary classroom. *Know Your World* is aimed at youngsters who are ten to sixteen years old but are reading on a second- to third-grade level, whereas *Weekly Reader* has a separate publication for each grade level.

Most regular newspapers vary in difficulty from section to section. A check with a readability formula of available newspapers, especially local ones, will help teachers decide if the students in their classes can use the newspapers profitably.

Teachers can begin newspaper study by determining what the students already know with an inventory such as that shown in Example 8.8.

▶ **EXAMPLE 8.8:** Newspaper Inventory

Directions: Answer the following questions about your use of the newspaper.

1. What newspaper(s) come to your home?
2. Do you read a newspaper regularly? How often?

3. What parts of the newspaper do you read? _____News _____Editorials _____Comics _____Entertainment section _____Features _____Advertisements _____Columns _____Other (Give names.) _____

4. How do you locate the part of the newspaper that you want? _____turn each page   _____use the index
5. Where is the index in a newspaper?
6. What do the following terms mean?
   a. AP   e. lead
   b. byline   f. masthead
   c. dateline   g. UPI ◀
   d. editorial

After administering such an inventory, the teacher can decide where the students need to begin in newspaper study. Some will need initial orientation to the parts of the newspaper and the information found in each part; some will need help with location skills; and others will need help with newspaper terminology.

Following are several activities to help children read the newspapers more effectively.

ACTIVITIES

1. Have pupils locate the *who, what, where, when, why,* and *how* in news stories.
2. Using news stories with the headlines cut off, have pupils write their own headlines and compare these with the actual headlines.
3. Have children scan a page for a news story on a particular topic.
4. Give children copies of news stories about the same event from two different newspapers. Then ask them to point out likenesses and differences and discuss.
5. Using copies of conflicting editorials, have students underline facts in one color and opinions in another color and discuss the results. Also have them locate emotional language and propaganda techniques in each editorial.
6. Discuss the symbolism and the message conveyed by each of several editorial cartoons. Then ask students to draw their own editorial cartoons.
7. Have pupils compare an editorial and a news story on the same topic. Discuss differences in approach.
8. Tell youngsters to locate comics that are funny. Then ask them to tell why.
9. Cut out the words in a comic strip, have the children fill in words they think would fit, and compare with the original. Or show children comic strips with the last frame missing, ask them what they think will happen, and let them compare their ideas with the real ending.

424

Teaching
Reading in
Today's
Elementary
Schools

10. By studying the entertainment section, pupils can decide what movie or play would be most interesting to them or locate time slots for certain television programs.
11. Encourage the children to try to solve crossword puzzles.
12. To discover which type of writing is more objective, which has more descriptive terms, and so on, pupils should compare human interest features with straight news stories. Have them dramatize appropriate ones.
13. Ask pupils to search grocery advertisements from several stores for the best buy on a specified item or to study the classified advertisements to decide what job they would most like to have and why. Then ask them to write their own classified ads.
14. Have the youngsters study the display advertisements for examples of propaganda techniques.
15. Ask pupils to locate examples of the following types of columns: medical advice, love advice, household hints, humor, and how-to-do-it.
16. Ask students to use the index of the paper to tell what page to look on for the television schedule, weather report, and so on.
17. Ask the children to search through the newspaper for typographical errors, and then discuss the effect of these errors on the material in which they have appeared.
18. Have pupils search the sports page for synonyms for the terms *won* and *lost.* Ask them why these synonyms are used.

Mathematics

Reading in mathematics has its own difficulties. For one thing, there is again the problem of specialized vocabulary. Young children have to learn terms like *plus, minus, sum,* and *subtraction,* whereas older children encounter such terms as *perimeter* and *diameter.* Words with multiple meanings also appear frequently. Discussions about *planes, figures,* numbers in *base* two, or raising a number to the third *power* can confuse children who know other, more common meanings for these words. Nevertheless, many mathematics terms have root words, prefixes, or suffixes that children can use in determining their meanings. (For example, *triangle* means three angles.)

To help build math vocabulary, teachers can assign a math word for each day, which students must identify and use in a sentence. One child may "own" the word, wearing a card on which the word is written and giving a presentation on it to the rest of the group, or students may have to identify or illustrate math terms written on cards before they can line up to leave the room. The teacher can ask questions about which terms being studied apply to a particular problem or ask the children to dramatize the problems or meanings of math terms (Kutzman and Krutchinsky, 1981).

Mathematical crossword puzzles provide good practice with specialized vocabulary. An example is shown in Worksheet: Mathematical Crossword Puzzle.

Across

1. Two _____ two equals four.
4. Abbreviation for inch
5. Ten _____ one equals nine.
8. In the decimal system base
 _____ is used.

Down

1. A decimal _____ shows place
 value.
2. Total
3. The same amount in all containers,
 or _____ amounts
6. 1/12 of a foot
7. One × _____ = one. ●

    Difficulties with words are not the only problems children have with math textbooks. They are also required to understand a different symbol system and to read numerals as well as words, which involves understanding place value. Children must be able to interpret such symbols as plus and minus signs, multiplication and division signs, symbols for union and intersection, equal signs and signs indicating inequalities, and many others, as well as abbreviations such as *ft., lb., in., qt., mm, cm,* and so on.

    Symbols often are particularly troublesome to children, perhaps partly because some symbols mean other things in other contexts; for example, "−" means "minus" in math but is a hyphen in regular print.

    Matching exercises such as the one shown in Worksheet: Matching Exercise for Symbols encourage youngsters to learn the meanings of symbols.

    To read numbers, pupils must understand place value. They must note, for example, that in the number 312.8 there are three places to the left of the decimal point (which they must discriminate from a period), which means that the leftmost numeral indicates a particular number of hundreds, the next numeral tells how many tens, and the next numeral tells how many ones (in

426

Teaching
Reading in
Today's
Elementary
Schools

● *WORSHEET:* *Matching Exercise for Symbols*

Directions: Draw a line from each symbol in Column 1 to its meaning in Column 2.

Column 1	Column 2
=	is greater than
>	is less than
≠	equals
<	plus
−	is not equal to
+	minus
÷	divided by ●

this case, three hundreds, one ten, and two ones, or three hundred twelve). To determine the value to the right of the decimal, they must realize that the first place is tenths, the second place hundredths, and so forth. In this example, there are eight tenths; therefore, the entire number is three hundred twelve and eight tenths. This is obviously a complex procedure, involving not merely reading from left to right but reading back and forth.

Mathematical sentences also present reading problems. Children must recognize numbers and symbols and translate them into verbal sentences, reading $9 \div 3 = 3$, for example, as "nine divided by three equals three."

Students will need help in reading and analyzing word problems as well. Teachers should arrange such problems according to difficulty and avoid assigning too many at one time (Schell, 1982).

Story problems can present special comprehension difficulties. They require the basic comprehension skills (determining main ideas and details, seeing relationships between details, making inferences, drawing conclusions, analyzing critically, and following directions). Dechant (1970) suggests that students follow a definite procedure in solving statement problems:

1. learn all word meanings
2. discover what is asked for in the problem
3. decide what facts are needed to solve the problem
4. decide what mathematical operations must be performed
5. decide upon the order in which the operations should be performed.

An additional step, "estimate the correctness of the answer," should be added to these five steps. Students need to decide if their answers are reasonable.

Collier and Redmond (1974) point out that mathematics material is very concise and abstract in nature and involves complex relationships. A high density of ideas per page appears in this kind of material, and understanding each word is very important, for one word may be the key to understanding an entire section. Yet elementary teachers too often approach a math lesson in terms of developing only computational skill, apparently not realizing that reading skills can be advanced during arithmetic lessons, or that arithmetic statement problems would be more comprehensible if attention were given to reading skills.

To understand mathematics materials, Collier and Redmond (1974) suggest students should

1. read the material rapidly or at a normal rate in order to get an overview and to see the main points.
2. read the material again, this time "more slowly, critically, and analytically" to determine details and relationships involved.
3. read some parts of the material a number of times, if necessary, varying the purpose each time.
4. look for relevant information.
5. decide what operations must be performed.
6. determine whether all needed information is given.
7. read the numbers and operation symbols needed to solve the problem.
8. adjust reading rate to the difficulty of the material.

Presenting story problems in abbreviated form, an approach used by some teachers and in some elementary mathematics textbooks, has not proved to be helpful for either good or poor readers (Threadgill-Sowder, 1984). In addition, high-ability problem solvers in one study found the abbreviated form to be harder than a regular verbal presentation, apparently because it does not provide sufficient context to make the problem understandable.

Sometimes children find it useful to draw a picture of the situation involved in a problem or to manipulate actual objects, and teachers should encourage such approaches to problem solving when they are appropriate. Teachers should watch their students solve word problems and decide where they need the most help: with computation, with problem interpretation (understanding of problems that they are not required to read for themselves), with reading, or with integration of the three skills in order to reach a solution. Small groups of students needing help in different areas of problem-solving can be formed (Cunningham and Ballew, 1983).

A recent research study showed that students who made up their own math story problems to solve performed better on tests of applications skills than did those who practiced textbook word problems. Children are likely to do better at interpreting a story problem if they have constructed a similar problem (Ferguson and Fairburn, 1985).

Cox and Weibe (1984) have developed a test that, when used with measures of computation, can help teachers determine three categories of children: (1) those who understand mathematical vocabulary but are deficient in computation, (2) those who are good at computation but are deficient in their ability to read mathematical terms with understanding, and (3) those who are deficient in both areas. The Wiebe/Cox Mathematical

428

Teaching
Reading in
Today's
Elementary
Schools

Vocabulary Reading Inventory can be found in the January 1984 issue of *The Reading Teacher*.

Since story problems are not written in a narrative style, children often lack the familiarity with the text structure needed for ease of comprehension. The pattern of writing for story problems is procedural, having important details at the beginning and the topic sentence near the end. This pattern fails to offer children an early purpose for their reading (Reutzel, 1983).

Reutzel (1983) suggests that children will benefit from creating story problems related to their own experiences. This activity can greatly help their comprehension of such problems.

Graphs, maps, charts, and tables, which often occur in mathematics materials, were discussed in Chapter 7.

Science and Health

Extremely heavy use of technical vocabulary is typical in science and health textbooks, where students will encounter terms like *lever, extinct, rodent, pollen, stamen, bacteria, inoculation,* and *electron*. Again, some of the words that have technical meanings also have more common meanings—for example, *shot, matter, solution,* and *pitch*. In these classes, as in all content area classes, the teacher has the responsibility of seeing that the pupils understand the concepts represented by the technical terms in their subjects. As an example, a science teacher might bring in a flower when explaining what the *stamen* are and where they are located. While diagrams are also useful, the more concrete an experience with a concept is, the more likely it is that the student will develop a complete understanding of the concept; a diagram is a step removed from the actual object.

Comprehension skills, such as recognizing main ideas and details, making inferences, drawing conclusions, recognizing cause-and-effect relationships, recognizing sequence, and following directions, are important in reading science and health materials, as are critical reading skills. Because material can rapidly become outdated, awareness of copyright dates of these materials is important. The inquiring attitude of the scientist is the same as that of the critical reader. Ability to use such reading aids as maps, tables, charts, and graphs is also necessary.

Science and health materials, like social studies materials, are written in a highly compact, expository style that often involves classification, explanations, and cause-and-effect relationships. The suggestions in Chapter 7 for teaching outlining skills can be especially useful in working with classification, which involves arranging information under main headings and subheadings. A classification game, such as that shown in Worksheet: Classification Game, may also be helpful.

Explanations in science and health materials often describe processes, such as pasteurization of milk, which may be illustrated by pictures, charts, or diagrams designed to clarify the textual material. Material of this type needs

Directions: Place the terms at the bottom of the page under the correct headings.

Animal	Vegetable	Mineral

Terms: fox, fish, grass, rock, tree, iron, dog, flower, silver, gold.   ●

to be read slowly and carefully and frequently requires rereading. Teachers might apply the material in Chapter 7 related to reading diagrams and illustrations, or the material in Chapter 5 on detecting sequence, since a process is generally explained in sequence. The oral reading strategy and the directed inquiry activity described earlier in this chapter would also be extremely useful in presenting material of this type. Similarly, the suggestions given in Chapter 5 for recognizing cause-and-effect relationships will help children handle this type of arrangement when it occurs in science textbooks.

Instructions for performing experiments are often found in science textbooks, and the reader must be able to comprehend the purpose of the experiment, read the list of materials to determine what he or she must assemble in order to perform the experiment and determine the order of steps to be followed. The suggestions in Chapter 5 on locating main ideas, details, and sequential order and learning to follow directions should be useful when reading material of this nature. Before they perform an experiment, children should attempt to predict the outcome, based upon their prior knowledge. Afterward, they should compare their predicted results with the actual results, investigating the reasons for differences. Did they perform each step correctly? Can they check special references to find out what actually should have happened?

Because science textbooks are often written at higher difficulty levels than are the basal readers for the same grade level, some children will need alternate materials to use for science instruction. Among these are:

Follett Beginning Science Books. Chicago: Follett.
Young Scott Science Books. New York: William Scott.
Science Picture Books. Herbert S. Zim. New York: William Morrow.

In addition, in some cases teachers can relate basal reader stories to science study by making science job cards to be used as follow-up activities to stories. An example of directions on one job card follows.

430

Teaching
Reading in
Today's
Elementary
Schools

These students use many diverse reading and study skills in their science class as they follow directions, interpret diagrams, and relate text exposition and description to scientific materials and models.   (© David S. Strickler/The Picture Cube)

"What kind of weather do you believe was occurring in the story? Tell why you think this is true. Share your ideas with your reading group" (Whitfield and Hovey, 1981).

Smardo (1982) suggests the use of children's literature, along with hands-on exploration, to clarify science concepts in early childhood programs. Teachers can use children's trade books that deal with scientific concepts to help the children distinguish between real and make-believe situations. Since the National Survey of Science, Mathematics, and Social Studies Education has indicated that teachers in early childhood programs spend only seventeen minutes a day on science, this use of literature in addition to traditional science instruction could bolster children's development of scientific schemata, which they can call on later when reading scientific textbooks. Discussion of the books offers children a chance to ask questions, share their opinions and background knowledge, make predictions, and engage in inferential and critical thinking. Smardo suggests books that can be useful for particular scientific concepts, including the following:

Carle, Eric. *Mixed up Chameleon.* Philadelphia: Thomas Y. Crowell, 1975. (animal changes)

Carle, Eric. *The Very Hungry Caterpillar.* New York: Philomel, 1969. (animal changes)

DeRegniers, Beatrice. *Shadow Book.* New York: Harcourt Brace Jovanovich, 1960. (shadow)

Krause, Ruth. *Carrot Seed.* New York: Harper & Row, 1945. (growing)

Provensen, Alice, and Martin Provensen. *A Year at Maple Hill Farm.* New York: Atheneum, 1978. (seasons)

Zion, Gene. *Summer Snowman.* New York: Harper & Row, 1955. (melting)

Science activities that involve direct experiences, such as using manipulative materials, doing experiments, or making observations of phenomena, can be used as the basis of language experience stories or charts that will provide reading material in science (Barrow, Kristo, and Andrew, 1984). The experience is accompanied and/or followed by class discussion, after which the children produce a chart or story about the experience. They may illustrate the story after it is written, or they may draw their observations first and then write about them. Reading related concept books, such as the ones mentioned above, may serve to provide children with material to use in expanding their stories.

✔ Self-Check: Objective 4

Name some social studies and science and health reading problems that could occur.

Describe a procedure that you can follow in solving verbal mathematical problems.

(See Self-Improvement Opportunities 3, 5, 6, and 8.)

Summary

Teachers must be aware that basal reading instruction alone is not likely to prepare children thoroughly to read in the content areas. They need to learn reading skills that are appropriate to specific subject areas, as well as general techniques that are helpful in reading expository text. Content texts offer more reading difficulties than do basal reader materials. They do not have

432

Teaching
Reading in
Today's
Elementary
Schools

carefully controlled vocabularies and planned repetition of key words. They have a greater density of ideas presented, and they do not have the narrative style that is most familiar to the children. They may contain many graphic aids which have to be interpreted.

Teachers need to be aware of the readability of the materials that they give to children to read, and they must adjust their expectations and reading assignments based upon the reading levels of the students in relationship to the readability of available instructional materials. Cloze tests and informal reading inventories can be used to tell how well children can read particular texts. Teachers can also use readability formulas in conjunction with the children's reading test scores to estimate the appropriate materials for particular children. Although readability formulas have the drawback of being completely text-based, they can offer assistance in deciding on the relative difficulty of material with fairly good results. Microcomputer programs can be used to help teachers apply readability formulas.

Many techniques can be used to help children read content area materials more effectively. Among these are the directed reading-thinking activity, the directed inquiry activity, the guided reading procedure, the SAVOR procedure, the oral reading strategy, the question-only strategy, the language experience approach, the global method, feature analysis plus writing, webbing, the concept-text-application approach, the K-W-L teaching model, use of study guides, use of manipulative materials, and integrated approaches.

Each content area presents special reading difficulties. For example, each one has specialized vocabulary that must be understood. Reading in literature involves comprehending many literary forms, such as short stories, novels, plays, poetry, biographies, and autobiographies. The figurative language that frequently occurs in these forms is sometimes a barrier to understanding. English textbooks cover the areas of listening, speaking, reading, and writing. The techniques presented in these areas need to be practiced through oral and written exercises. Social studies materials abound with graphic aids to be interpreted, and they require much application of critical reading skills. The newspaper is a good teaching aid for the social studies area. Mathematics has a special symbol system to be learned, but perhaps the greatest difficulty in this content area is the reading of story problems. Children need to learn a procedure for approaching the reading of such problems. Science and health materials contain many graphic aids. They also often include instructions for performing experiments, which must be read carefully in order to ensure accurate results.

Test Yourself

True or False

_____ 1. Content area textbooks are carefully graded as to difficulty and are generally appropriate to the grade levels for which they are designed.

_____ 2. One difficulty encountered in all content areas is specialized vocabulary, especially regarding common words that have additional technical meanings.

_____ 3. The cloze technique can be used to help determine whether or not a textbook is suitable for use with a specific child.

_____ 4. All children in the fifth grade can benefit from the use of a single textbook designated for the fifth grade.

_____ 5. Readability formulas are too complicated for classroom teachers to use.

_____ 6. Students often must acquire early concepts and vocabulary in content textbooks before they can understand later content passages.

_____ 7. Offering youngsters instruction in basal readers is sufficient to teach reading skills needed in content area textbooks.

_____ 8. Children instinctively understand figures of speech; therefore, figurative language presents them with no special problems.

_____ 9. Story problems in mathematics are generally extremely easy to read.

_____ 10. Mathematics materials require a child to learn a new symbol system.

_____ 11. Concrete examples are helpful in building an understanding of new concepts.

_____ 12. Science materials need not be read critically since they are written by experts in the field.

_____ 13. An expository style of writing is very precise and highly compact.

_____ 14. The cause-and-effect pattern of organization is found in social studies and science and health materials.

_____ 15. Social studies materials frequently have a chronological organization.

_____ 16. All parts of the newspaper require identical reading skills.

_____ 17. The SAVOR procedure is designed to reinforce essential content area vocabulary.

_____ 18. In Manzo's oral reading strategy, children read aloud to each other.

_____ 19. The directed inquiry activity involves predictions made by the children.

_____ 20. Study guides may set purposes for reading.

_____ 21. The directed reading-thinking activity is a general plan for teaching either basal reader stories or content area selections.

_____ 22. Readability formulas take into account the interactive nature of reading.

_____ 23. Expository text structure can be taught through the language experience approach.

_____ 24. Anticipation guides are used before reading a selection and sometimes responded to again after reading has taken place.

_____ 25. Comparison charts can help children to understand metaphors.

434

Teaching
Reading in
Today's
Elementary
Schools

_____ 26. Children's literature can be used to teach social studies and science concepts.

Self-Improvement Opportunities

1. As a test of your ability to use the Fry Readability Graph, turn to the sample selection "Problems Old and New" in the section on social studies and determine its readability. Start counting your sample with "The West. . . ." If you get an incorrect answer, study the procedure again and determine where you made your error.

    Answer
    137 syllables
    7.8 sentences
    6th grade
    (Did you count your sample right? Your last word should have been *taking.*)

2. Develop a directed reading-thinking activity (DRTA) for a content area lesson. Then try it out in an elementary school classroom or present it to a group of your peers in a reading or content methods course.

3. Develop a lesson for teaching students the multiple meanings of words encountered in science and health, social studies, mathematics, or literature. Try the lesson out in an elementary school classroom or present it to a group of your peers.

4. Collect examples of figurative language from a variety of sources and use them to develop a lesson on interpreting figurative language.

5. Select a passage from a social studies or science textbook. Prepare a study guide for children to use in reading/studying the passage.

6. Develop a bibliography of trade books that youngsters who are unable to read a particular content area textbook could use.

7. Demonstrate to your classmates the usefulness of newspaper reading in your particular content area.

8. Prepare a comparison/contrast chart as illustrated in the social studies section of this chapter for some topic in your content area.

Bibliography

Alvermann, Donna E., and Paula R. Boothby. "Text Differences: Children's Perceptions at the Transition Stage in Reading." *The Reading Teacher* 36 (December 1982): 298–302.

Ankney, Paul, and Pat McClurg. "Testing Manzo's Guided Reading Procedure." *The Reading Teacher* 34 (March 1981): 681–85.

Barrow, Lloyd H., Janice V. Kristo, and Barbara Andrew. "Building Bridges Between Science and Reading." *The Reading Teacher* 38 (November 1984): 188–92.

Bormuth, J. R. "The Cloze Readability Procedure." In *Readability in 1968,* J. R. Bormuth, ed. Champaign, Ill.: National Council of Teachers of English, 1968, pp. 40–47.

Collier, Calhoun C., and Lois A. Redmond. "Are You Teaching Kids to Read Mathematics?" *The Reading Teacher* 27 (May 1974): 804–808.

Cox, Juanita, and James H. Wiebe. "Measuring Reading Vocabulary and Concepts in Mathematics in the Primary Grades." *The Reading Teacher* 37 (January 1984): 402–10.

Cunningham, James W., and Hunter Ballew. "Solving Word Problem Solving." *The Reading Teacher* 36 (April 1983): 836–39.

Cunningham, Patricia M., and James W. Cunningham. "Content Area Reading-Writing Lessons." *The Reading Teacher* 40 (February 1987): 506–12.

Dale, Edgar, and Jeanne S. Chall. "A Formula for Predicting Readability." *Educational Research Bulletin* 27 (January 21, 1948): 11–20 and 28; (February 18, 1948): 37–54.

Dechant, Emerald. *Improving the Teaching of Reading.* 2nd ed. Englewood Cliffs, N.J.: Prentice-Hall, 1970, Chapters 12 and 13.

Dionisio, Marie. "'Write? Isn't This Reading Class?'" *The Reading Teacher* 36 (April 1983): 746–50.

Doyle, Denis P. "The 'Unsacred' Texts: Market Forces That Work Too Well." *American Educator* 8 (Summer 1984): 8–13.

Ferguson, Anne M., and Jo Fairburn. "Language Experience for Problem Solving in Mathematics." *The Reading Teacher* 38 (February 1985): 504–507.

Flood, James. "The Text, the Student, and the Teacher: Learning from Exposition in the Middle Schools." *The Reading Teacher* 39 (April 1986): 784–91.

Flood, James, Diane Lapp, and Nancy Farnan. "A Reading-Writing Procedure That Teaches Expository Paragraph Structure." *The Reading Teacher* 39 (February 1986): 556–62.

Fry, Edward. "Fry's Readability Graph: Clarifications, Validity, and Extension to Level 17." *Journal of Reading* 21 (December 1977): 249.

Gaskins, Irene West. "Reading for Learning: Going Beyond the Basals in the Elementary Grades." *The Reading Teacher* 35 (December 1981): 323–28.

Groesbeck, Hulda Gwendolyn. "The Comprehension of Figurative Language by Elementary Children: A Study in Transfer." Ph.D. dissertation, University of Oklahoma, 1961.

Gunning, R. *The Technique of Clear Writing.* New York: McGraw-Hill, 1968.

Hennings, Dorothy Grant. "Reading Picture Storybooks in the Social Studies." *The Reading Teacher* 36 (December 1982): 284–89.

Holbrook, Hilary Taylor. "The Quality of Textbooks." *The Reading Teacher* 38 (March 1985): 680–83.

Jones, Margaret B., and Denise D. Nessel. "Enhancing the Curriculum with Experience Stories." *The Reading Teacher* 39 (October 1985): 18–22.

436

Teaching
Reading in
Today's
Elementary
Schools

Judd, Dorothy H. "Avoid Readability Formula Drudgery: Use Your School's Microcomputer." *The Reading Teacher* 35 (October 1981): 7–8.

Keller, Paul F. G. "Maryland Micro: A Prototype Readability Formula for Small Computers." *The Reading Teacher* 35 (April 1982): 778–82.

Kinney, Martha A. "A Language Experience Approach to Teaching Expository Text Structure." *The Reading Teacher* 38 (May 1985): 854–56.

Klare, George R. "Readability." In *Handbook of Reading Research,* P. David Pearson, ed. New York: Longman, 1984, pp. 681–744.

Kutzman, Sandra, and Rick Krutchinsky. "Improving Children's Math Vocabulary." *The Reading Teacher* 35 (December 1981): 347–48.

Manna, Anthony. "Making Language Come Alive Through Reading Plays." *The Reading Teacher* 37 (April 1984): 712–17.

Manzo, Anthony V. "Three 'Universal' Strategies in Content Area Reading and Language." *Journal of Reading* 24 (November 1980): 147.

McGee, Lea M., and Donald J. Richgels. "Teaching Expository Text Structure to Elementary Students." *The Reading Teacher* 38 (April 1985): 739–48.

Morrow, Lesley Mandel. "Manipulative Learning Materials: Merging Reading Skills with Content Area Objectives." *Journal of Reading* 25 (February 1982): 448–53.

Ogle, Donna M. "K-W-L: A Teaching Model That Develops Active Reading of Expository Text." *The Reading Teacher* 39 (February 1986): 564–70.

Olson, Mary W., and Bonnie Longnion. "Pattern Guides: A Workable Alternative for Content Teachers." *Journal of Reading* 25 (May 1982): 736–41.

Readence, John E., R. Scott Baldwin, and Martha H. Head. "Direct Instruction in Processing Metaphors." *Journal of Reading Behavior* 18, no. 4 (1986): 325–39.

Readence, John E., R. Scott Baldwin, and Martha H. Head. "Teaching Young Readers to Interpret Metaphors." *The Reading Teacher* 40 (January 1987): 439–43.

Readence, John E., R. Scott Baldwin, Robert J. Rickelman, and G. Michael Miller. "The Effect of Vocabulary Instruction on Interpreting Metaphor." In *Solving Problems in Literacy: Learners, Teachers, and Researchers,* Jerome A. Niles and Rosary V. Lalik, eds. Rochester, N.Y.: National Reading Conference, 1986, pp. 87–91.

Reutzel, D. Ray. "C⁶: A Reading Model for Teaching Arithmetic Story Problem Solving." *The Reading Teacher* 37 (October 1983): 28–34.

Rush, R. Timothy. "Assessing Readability: Formulas and Alternatives." *The Reading Teacher* 39 (December 1985): 274–83.

Schell, Vicki J. "Learning Partners: Reading and Mathematics." *The Reading Teacher* 35 (February 1982): 544–48.

Smardo, Frances A. "Using Children's Literature to Clarify Science Concepts in Early Childhood Programs." *The Reading Teacher* 36 (December 1982): 267–73.

Spache, George D. *Good Reading for Poor Readers.* 6th ed. Champaign, Ill.: Garrard Press, 1966.

Stauffer, Russell G. "Reading as a Cognitive Process." *Elementary English* 44 (April 1968): 348.

Stauffer, Russell G. *Teaching Reading as a Thinking Process.* New York: Harper & Row, 1969.

Stieglitz, Ezra L., and Varda S. Stieglitz. "SAVOR the Word to Reinforce Vocabulary in the Content Areas." *Journal of Reading* 25 (October 1981): 46–51.

Storey, Dee C. "Reading in the Content Areas: Fictionalized Biographies and Diaries for Social Studies." *The Reading Teacher* 35 (April 1982): 796–98.

Sullivan, Joanne. "The Global Method: Language Experience in the Content Areas." *The Reading Teacher* 39 (March 1986): 664–68.

Thompson, Stephen J. "Teaching Metaphoric Language: An Instructional Strategy." *Journal of Reading* 30 (November 1986): 105–109.

Threadgill-Sowder, Judith, et al. "A Case Against Telegraphing Math Story Problems for Poor Readers." *The Reading Teacher* 37 (April 1984): 746–48.

Tinker, Miles A., and Constance M. McCullough. *Teaching Elementary Reading.* 4th ed. Englewood Cliffs, N.J.: Prentice-Hall, 1975, Chapter 13.

Whitfield, Edie L., and Larry Hovey. "Integrating Reading and Science with Job Cards." *The Reading Teacher* 34 (May 1981): 944–45.

Wong, Jo Ann, and Kathryn Hu-pei Au. "The Concept-Text-Application Approach: Helping Elementary Students Comprehend Expository Text." *The Reading Teacher* 38 (March 1985): 612–18.

Wood, Karen D., and John A. Mateja. "Adapting Secondary Level Strategies for Use in Elementary Classrooms." *The Reading Teacher* 36 (February 1983): 492–96.

Chapter 9

Literary Appreciation and Recreational Reading

Introduction

Elementary school teachers should make sure that there is a balance among developmental, functional, and recreational reading within the reading program. They should recognize that the recreational phase calls for planning just as the other phases do. In this chapter we consider the place of literature in the reading program, suggest ways for teaching literature skills, and give ideas for encouraging children to read for pleasure.

Without doubt, one of the most important long-range objectives for the elementary school reading program is the development of reading habits that will serve the individual throughout an entire lifetime. Evidence that a large percentage of adults are *able* to read but seldom *do* read for either information or enjoyment suggests that they were perhaps discouraged by too much reading instruction and not enough opportunities for informational and recreational reading. Therefore, it is crucial that children be exposed to experiences with literature that are designed to promote reading enjoyment.

Setting Objectives

When you finish reading this chapter, you should be able to

1. Identify ways to use children's literature in different areas of the curriculum.
2. Know some literary elements and forms that children should learn.
3. Locate sources for selecting and evaluating children's literature.
4. Recognize the different types of reading materials available for children.
5. Design a classroom environment conducive to recreational reading.
6. Discuss ways to motivate children to read for pleasure.
7. Identify ways to use literature for stimulating the reading-writing process.
8. Understand when and how children should read orally.
9. Identify several ways in which children can respond to literature through drama.
10. Discuss a variety of ways to interpret literature creatively.

Key Vocabulary

Pay close attention to these terms when they appear in the chapter.

antiphonal choral reading	choral reading/speaking	genre
author's chair	cinquain	haiku
book-recording device	creative dramatics	improvisation
Caldecott Award	diorama	Newbery Award
characterization	echoic verse	pantomime

plot

readers' theater

recreational reading

selection aids

setting

style

Sustained Silent Reading

theme

trade books

USING LITERATURE IN THE READING PROGRAM

The major purpose of using literature in the reading program is to promote a lifetime appreciation and enjoyment of fine reading materials. Ideally, a literature program should encourage students to learn about their literary heritage, expand their imaginations, develop reading preferences, evaluate literature, increase awareness of language, and grow socially, emotionally, and intellectually. These goals can be reached through a well-planned program in which the teacher reads aloud to students daily and provides them with opportunities to read and respond to literature.

Developmental, functional, and recreational reading can easily be incorporated into the school day. During the instructional period, when students are probably reading from their basal readers, developmental reading occurs. Functional reading takes place when students need to find information for a specific purpose or when they are studying in the content areas. Recreational reading and literary appreciation can occur throughout the day as the teacher reads a story or a chapter from a book to the class, as the students read trade books, or library books, when they finish their work, or during a special period set aside for interpreting literature through such activities as choral reading, book sharing, or creative dramatics. Teachers might teach literary skills directly through a unit on poetry or a novel, or they might integrate them with basal reader and language arts lessons, as shown in Table 9.1.

For students who find textbooks difficult or dull, supplementary trade books offer a viable option for learning content area material. Many children experience their first serious difficulties with reading as they begin reading textbooks, but the continued use of high-interest trade books along with textbooks may ease the transition. In selecting and using appropriate trade books, teachers should follow certain steps: identify concepts for further development; locate suitable trade books to help teach these concepts; present books to students by reading them aloud or making copies available for independent reading prior to textbook assignments; use trade books during and after reading the text to extend concept acquisition; and provide follow-up activities in the forms of creative writing, drama, and interviewing (Brozo and Tomlinson, 1986).

In social studies, award-winning trade books can be found for nearly every period of history. Elizabeth Speare's *The Bronze Bow* is a novel about a boy who encounters Jesus in Rome; Marguerite De Angeli's *The Door in the Wall* treats the situation of a crippled boy in fourteenth-century England; *The Courage of Sarah Noble* by Alice Dalgliesh describes a young girl who must face the difficulties of living in Connecticut in early pioneer days; Carol Brink's *Caddie Woodlawn* brings the reader into the excitement of living on

TABLE 9.1 Literary Skills and Recreational Reading During a Typical School Day

441

Literary
Appreciation
and
Recreational
Reading

Time	Activity	Purpose
8:30–8:45	Teacher reads aloud to children.	Children develop an interest in reading for pleasure.
9:00–10:30	Children read from basal readers.	Children learn some literary skills as they read a selection from good literature.
11:00–11:20	Several children demonstrate and explain a science experiment to the rest of the class.	Children use informational books for a purpose.
12:45–1:30	Children read biographies and historical fiction.	Children investigate materials related to the social studies unit.
2:00–2:30	Teacher introduces a poem during language arts class.	Children listen to the poem and respond to its rhythm, visual images, and mood.

Whenever children have free time, they may read a library book.

the Wisconsin frontier during the last half of the nineteenth century; and Paula Fox's *The Slave Dancer* tells the story of a boy who becomes involved in the slave trade with Africa during pre–Civil War days. Biographies of famous people who lived during different historical periods also add spice to textbook accounts.

Teachers can use trade books to develop mathematical and scientific concepts as well (Sharp, 1984; Sutherland and Arbuthnot, 1986). Starting with simple counting books, such as the vividly illustrated *Brian Wildsmith's 1, 2, 3's*, teachers can use books to expand concepts dealing with shapes, with comparative size, and with ordinal numbers. An activity and craft book, *Right Angles: Paper-Folding Geometry*, by Jo Phillips, helps young children work out mathematical concepts, and Robert Froman's *Bigger and Smaller* shows relative sizes of objects. The realistic photographs in Tana Hoban's *Count and See* help youngsters learn to count, whereas books on the metric system, including June Behrens's *The True Book of Metric Measurement* at the primary level and Franklyn Branley's *Think Metric!* at the intermediate level, explain the system and give reasons for converting to it. Science informational books help children understand the laws of nature, as in Laurence Pringle's *Into the Woods: Exploring the Forest Ecosystem*, or experience the delight of discovery, as in Vicki Cobb and Kathy Darling's *Bet You Can't, Science Impossibilities to Fool You*. The color photographs and realistic illustrations found in many science books increase a child's enjoyment and understanding (Norton, 1987).

Vocabulary lessons are lively and fun when the class uses trade books for word play and for learning interesting features of words (Blatt, 1978; Burke, 1978). In the Amelia Bedelia books, by Peggy Parish, Amelia takes everything literally, with disastrous results: her sponge cake is made of sponges! Fred Gwynne's *A Chocolate Moose for Dinner* illustrates figurative expressions and words with multiple meanings as a child might visualize them; William Steig's *CDB* uses letters of the alphabet to represent words for silly sayings; and Emily Hanlon uses homonyms to form nonsense verses in *How a Horse Grew Hoarse on the Site Where He Sighted a Bare Bear*.

Literature can also promote facility in the area of language arts, as demonstrated in the activities given later in this chapter for a folklore unit. Skills developed in a unit such as this are reading, reporting (orally and in written form), telling stories, literary appreciation, vocabulary, writing creatively, listening, and doing research.

✔ Self-Check: Objective 1

Suggest some ways in which you can use trade books to enrich teaching in the content areas.
(See Self-Improvement Opportunity 1.)

TEACHING LITERATURE SKILLS

When developing literature programs, teachers should plan diversity in children's exposure to literature rather than allow pupils to have random encounters with books (Stewig, 1980). They can organize instruction by genres (forms or categories), literary elements, or topics in order to vary students' experiences, and they should introduce students to the specialized vocabulary and skills they need to develop an appreciation of literature.

Literary Elements

In order to understand literary passages, children should be able to recognize and analyze plots, themes, characterization, settings, and authors' styles. The *plot* is the overall plan for the story; the *theme* is the main idea that the writer wishes to convey; and *characterization* refers to the way in which the writer makes the reader aware of the characteristics and motives of each person in the story. The *setting* consists of time and place and the *style* is the writer's mode of expressing thoughts. Teacher-directed questioning can make students aware of these literary elements and help children understand the interrelationships among them.

Literary Forms

Children's literature consists of a variety of genres or literary forms, including historical and realistic fiction, biographies, poetry, plays, informational books, and fantasy and folklore. Historical fiction, biographies, and informational books are all useful for integrating with content areas, whereas good realistic fiction serves as a model for helping children understand others and solve problems in their own lives. Poetry encourages children to explore their emotions, and plays offer the pleasure of acting out favorite stories. Both modern fantasy and folklore allow children to escape into worlds of imaginary characters and events. Teachers should use all of these forms in their literature programs, and they can enhance children's understanding of them by reading literature of all forms aloud and pointing out the characteristics of each genre.

↙ Self-Check: Objective 2

Name and describe several literary elements and forms that teachers should present to children in a well-balanced literature program.

(See Self-Improvement Opportunity 2.)

Story Reading and Storytelling

Reading aloud to children of all ages serves many purposes. Good oral reading by the teacher serves as a model and allows students to experience literature that they might not be able or inclined to read for themselves. It can also whet their appetites to read more on their own, since an exciting chapter or section of a book often stimulates children to read the entire book themselves. Based on a survey of 520 children, Mendoza (1985) reports that children throughout the elementary grades overwhelmingly enjoy hearing stories read to them, like to talk about books after they have been read aloud, and want a chance to look at them further or read them for themselves. Besides providing exposure to specific books, reading to children can also introduce them to creative and colorful use of language in prose and poetry, present new vocabulary and concepts, and acquaint them with the variety of language patterns found in written communication.

Teachers should read in natural tones and with expression, providing time for sharing the illustrations, exploring key words and phrases, and evaluating reactions. The best stories to read aloud are those that children cannot easily read for themselves, that the teacher personally likes and is thoroughly familiar with, and that possess the qualities characteristic of the best literature. Jim Trelease's *Read-Aloud Handbook* (1985) is an excellent source of information about how and what to read aloud to children.

Similarly, teacher storytelling acquaints children with literature and provides for good listening experiences. With no book between the storyteller and the audience, listeners focus their attention on each word and gesture, and they visualize the story to suit themselves because there are no illustrations (Nessel, 1985). Folktales are especially good for telling, for they were told and told again long before they were ever captured in print.

444

Teaching
Reading in
Today's
Elementary
Schools

Simply listening to stories is a valuable experience for children, but occasional follow-up discussions can bring out points that they might otherwise miss. The teacher should be prepared to lead discussions related to characters, theme, plot, or some other aspect of a story whenever the occasion warrants. A card file with questions to initiate a discussion about each book is useful. An example of a card for such a file is shown in Example 9.1.

To introduce children to books, teachers and librarians often use book talks about individual books or about several books that are related in some way. The teacher begins by telling a humorous or exciting part of the story and stops just short of the conclusion in order to make children want to read the ending for themselves.

Teachers can tape-record storybooks to build a library of recorded stories that children can listen to year after year. When the teacher has recorded several stories, he or she should place the tapes at a listening center along with the accompanying books. These teacher-recorded materials are better than commercially prepared tapes because they offer lower cost, wider choice of books, and pacing designed for the needs of special learners (Carbo, 1981).

ENCOURAGING RECREATIONAL READING

The test of a good recreational reading program is the quantity and quality of books that students read voluntarily. Teachers can encourage children to read for pleasure in a variety of ways.

Selecting Recreational Reading Materials

The kinds of literature that teachers make available to their students affect the success of their recreational reading programs. In order to satisfy their interests and accommodate their reading levels, students need a wide selection of materials. Achievement test scores may be used to establish a rough indication of reading levels. Teachers should make easier books available to encourage the slow reader and more difficult ones to challenge the gifted reader. In a study of fourth- and fifth-grade high, average, and low achievers, reading achievement levels seemed unrelated to areas of interest in reading, however (Anderson, Higgins, and Wurster, 1985).

According to Huck, Hepler, and Hickman (1987), children are interested in reading realistic fiction, biographies, stories about animals, tales of exploration and adventure, and stories of the past. They like suspense, action, humor, and make-believe. From a survey of research, Norton (1987) found that children like fast-paced books, detailed descriptions of settings, characters with warmth, and specific information about topics; they do not like sad books. At the intermediate level boys prefer sports, excitement, information, science, tall tales, and nonfiction, whereas girls like to read animal stories, fantasy, fairy tales, and stories about other children. Girls read more than

► **EXAMPLE 9.1:** Literature Discussion Card

445

Literary
Appreciation
and
Recreational
Reading

Class Discussion

The Giving Tree, Shel Silverstein, Harper & Row, 1964.
A tree responds to the needs of a boy by giving of itself in many ways.
Discuss the following topics.

1. Do you think it was right for the boy to take so much from the tree?
2. Did the boy give anything back to the tree? What might he have done for the tree?
3. Suppose the tree had not given so much of itself. What would be the advantages for others?
4. Do you know a person who is like the Giving Tree?

boys, but boys like nonfiction more than girls do. Increasingly, students become interested in seeking out information from nonfiction books on a wide range of subjects. Teachers can assess children's personal reading interests by simply asking them to list three things that interest them or by administering an interest inventory such as the one found in Chapter 6.

Students also have preferences regarding the use of illustrations in trade books (Sutherland and Arbuthnot, 1986). They insist that the illustrations accurately represent the description in the text, and they want to see the picture along with the description, not on a page before or after. They like illustrations with action and prefer bright colors, but can also accept some books with black and white or softly colored pictures.

Many selection aids, or references that identify and evaluate publications, are available to help teachers and librarians select literature for specific purposes. Among the most comprehensive are the *Children's Catalog* (Richard Isaacson et al., eds., 15th ed., New York: H. W. Wilson Co., 1986) and *The Elementary School Library Collection: A Guide to Books and Other Media, Phases 1, 2, 3* (Lois Winkel, ed., 15th ed., Williamsport, Pa.: Bro-Dart Foundation, 1986). Both of these contain author, title, and subject indexes and provide annotations of the books listed.

Each year since the 1974–1975 school year, the International Reading Association–Children's Book Council Joint Committee has published an annotated list of "Children's Choices," which appears in the October issue of *The Reading Teacher*. Each list is compiled by approximately 10,000 children, working in teams, who read new books and vote for their favorites. Since children are the ultimate critics of their literature, teachers and librarians should consider their choices seriously when purchasing and recommending books.

446

Teaching
Reading in
Today's
Elementary
Schools

Another useful source in selecting children's books is a listing of Newbery and Caldecott Award winners. The John Newbery Award is presented annually to the author whose book is selected by a special committee as the year's most distinguished contribution to American literature for children; excellence in illustration is the criterion used in granting the annual Randolph Caldecott Award.

When teachers choose books to read aloud or to shelve in class libraries, they should select books that are not stereotyped or sexist. Smith, Greenlaw, and Scott (1987) found that teachers' favorite read-aloud books contained more male than female protagonists, depicted females narrowly and often negatively, and portrayed traditional male stereotypes. Very few books included minorities, the elderly, or characters with physical or mental differences. Since youngsters are impressionable and often are first exposed to role expectations and other people through books, teachers should select literature that provides a balanced view of society. Kinman and Henderson (1985) found that Newbery Award books from 1977 to 1984 contained less-stereotyped characters and more situations that reflected society realistically than they did in the past, while Dougherty and Engel (1987) found that Caldecott Award winners showed a trend toward sex equality.

Selecting appropriate poetry for children is especially difficult. Poorly chosen poems can prejudice children against poetry, whereas a suitable poem will amuse, inspire, emotionally move, or intellectually interest listeners. According to Ingham (1984), children favor humorous narrative poetry with rhythm and rhyme about topics related to their lives. Among poetry collections that are popular with intermediate-level children, Shel Silverstein's *Where the Sidewalk Ends* and *The Light in the Attic* are favorites. They contain hilarious poems about children who think and behave much the same the world over, and the clever line drawings surrounded by open spaces help the reader visualize the scenes. The humor comes from alliteration, from plays on words, or from highly exaggerated situations, such as in "Sarah Cynthia Sylvia Stout Who Would Not Take the Garbage Out" (*Where the Sidewalk Ends*).

Most of the books that children use in school have sturdy library bindings and have been carefully selected for content, but students sometimes prefer other forms of reading material. Most children enjoy reading paperback books because they are easy to carry around and inexpensive to own. Many teachers prefer paperbacks because multiple copies of one book cost the same as a single library edition, so teachers can order enough for small groups of children to read and use in follow-up activities and discussions.

Paperback books are often available at special reduced rates through book clubs, such as the Scholastic Book Club (Englewood Cliffs, N.J. 07632). For over two decades "Reading is FUNdamental," or "RIF" (600 Maryland Avenue S.W., Smithsonian Institution, Washington, D.C. 20560), has offered an inexpensive book distribution program in which each child receives three free books a year. Since paperbacks are so easily available, they are one way to make recreational reading appealing to children.

447

Literary
Appreciation
and
Recreational
Reading

Promoting reading enjoyment and fostering good lifetime reading habits are among the most important objectives of a school reading program. (© Hugh Rogers/ Monkmeyer)

Easy-to-read books generally do not meet the criteria for good children's literature, but they are valuable in a beginning reading program. Written with a controlled vocabulary that a first grader can decode and understand, these books are intended to be read *by* young children instead of *to* them. Youngsters who have just learned to read experience great delight in being able to read an entire book independently.

448

Teaching
Reading in
Today's
Elementary
Schools

Many good children's magazines are available for different reading levels and different areas of interest. These periodicals are excellent classroom resources and offer several benefits for the reading program: (1) the material is current and relevant; (2) the reading range varies in levels of difficulty and content presented; (3) several genres usually appear in a single issue; (4) language activities, such as crossword puzzles, contests, and children's writings, are often included; (5) the illustrations and photographs are excellent and can improve comprehension; and (6) low cost makes them easily accessible (Seminoff, 1986). Classroom subscriptions to two or three favorites will enrich the reading program. Some popular choices are listed in Appendix B to this chapter.

During multimedia presentations children experience folk songs, story-telling with sound effects, and filmed versions of classics, through recordings, filmstrips, and films. Multimedia approaches can be springboards for getting children interested in reading good literature, since quite often a child who hears a story at a listening station later asks to read the book. Appendix B to Chapter 2 lists sources of multimedia materials.

The primary purpose of using comic books in the classroom is to motivate poor readers (Koenke, 1979; Wright, 1979). Though comics are not great literature and do not guarantee improvement in reading, they do offer a colorful, fast-paced alternative for the reluctant reader, and good teachers can find creative ways to use them. Those comics exhibiting the seal "Approved by the Comics Code Authority" on their front covers contain reasonably wholesome material for children aged nine to thirteen, their primary readers. In readability, comics range from first grade (*Archie* and *Casper the Friendly Ghost*) to seventh grade (*Prince Valiant*), according to the Fry Readability Graph.

TV tie-ins are a relatively new form of reading material for young people, but they are remarkably popular, especially with slow and reluctant readers. TV tie-ins are paperback books based on the story lines and characters from popular television series. They are fast moving, action filled, and easy to read. Students are enthusiastic about reading them because they are already familiar with the characters and can anticipate the action. Busch (1978) found that 89 percent of 595 students in grades two through twelve had read a book as a result of watching a commercial television program.

✔ Self-Check: Objectives 3 and 4

Identify alternative sources for selecting children's literature. What are some types of literature that have special appeal for students? (See Self-Improvement Opportunities 5, 6, 7, and 8.)

Creating an Environment for Recreational Reading

Lively and interesting responses to literature are likely to occur in classrooms with "nurturing environments" (Hickman, 1984, p. 381). Such environments provide many of the following features: an abundance of fine-quality books in both the classroom and school libraries; adequate time for selecting and reading books; introductions of new books; daily reading aloud; book discussions in whole classes, with small groups, and with individuals; use of correct literary terminology; and creative and long-term experiences with literature. Teachers who want to encourage children to read for pleasure provide special areas for recreational reading and design bulletin boards and displays that attract attention to books. Imagination helps to create an interesting place for children to relax and read. Discarded refrigerator cartons with the backs removed can be transformed into grass shacks, log cabins, moon rockets, or witches' dens for children to visit in their free time; a raised platform covered with carpet scraps in a secluded corner is a special place to escape with a favorite book; old telephone cable spools make round library tables for young children; and old-fashioned bathtubs piled with cushions are appealing hideaways. Children also appreciate having their own private places for reading where they will not be disturbed, so teachers should provide carpet scraps, large pillows, pieces of plywood, and chains of beads for creative private nooks and crannies. Bookshelves filled with books within reach of all reading areas are a necessity, and the selection should be changed periodically.

Bulletin boards and dioramas can create interest in specific books or special topics. Small, portable bulletin boards are suitable for featuring books and authors, perhaps with displays of book jackets, which are colorful and easy to use. (See Example 9.2 for a sample bulletin board.) Three-dimensional dioramas take time to make, but the tiny figures intrigue children. To make a diorama, cut the top and one side off a small carton and set up a scene from a story inside the box. For example, to illustrate *Charlotte's Web,* weave the word TERRIFIC into a piece of fishnet, place a tiny pipe-cleaner spider in it, tack the net up over a corner of the box, and put a model of a pig with some straw on the bottom of the carton. Beside the scene place a copy of the book.

Working together, a teacher and a librarian can arrange attractive displays of new books, perhaps along with projects at interest centers in any curricular area. For instance, James Daugherty's *Daniel Boone* and Roberta Strauss Feuerlecht's *The Legends of Paul Bunyan* could be displayed in connection with a unit on the westward movement. Other ideas for book displays are suggested below.

Madeline, by Ludwig Bemelmans. Use a French flag, a model of the Eiffel Tower, and a poster of Paris from a travel agency.

White Snow, Bright Snow, by Alvin Tresselt. Include a display of student-made white paper snowflakes on a dark background and marshmallow snowmen standing in detergent snowflakes.

The Story of Johnny Appleseed, by Aliki. Display a map of Johnny Appleseed's travels, along with an apple, seeds from an apple, and apple blossoms (if in season).

450

Teaching
Reading in
Today's
Elementary
Schools

▶ **EXAMPLE 9.2:** Bulletin-Board Display

For this bulletin board use a carpet scrap, a puff of cotton for a cloud, and some book jackets to accompany the artwork. ◀

A Gathering of Days: A New England Girl's Journal, 1830–32, by Joan Blos. Use a map of New England and a looseleaf notebook for students to record imaginary events that could have happened to them if they had been Catherine's friends.

Motivating Students to Read

With an abundant supply of books and a supportive reading environment, most children will be enthusiastic about recreational reading. Some will still need to be motivated, however, and even good readers occasionally appreciate added incentives for reading.

Book-recording devices, which are ways of keeping track of the number and type of books that students read, provide good incentives (Whitehead, 1968). Bulletin-board charts, card files, and reading wheels and ladders are examples. The most familiar recording device is simply a large piece of poster board with each child's name listed at the left side. Beside each name is space for students to place tiny replicas of books that they have read, with the title and the author printed on them. Different colors of construction paper can represent different categories of books, such as yellow for science fiction, orange for biography, and red for realistic fiction.

Another familiar recording device is the bookworm, which consists of a series of connected circles. Whenever a child finishes a book, he or she adds a circle with the title and author. The bookworm is a joint endeavor that can run up and down the walls of the classroom. Again, different colors can represent different types of reading material.

Reading wheels and ladders are used individually to encourage children to diversify their reading. Each spoke of the wheel or each rung of the ladder represents a different type of book, and students color in or cover up a space for each book read. A sample bookworm and a reading ladder are shown in Example 9.3.

▶ **EXAMPLE 9.3:** Bookworm and Reading Ladder

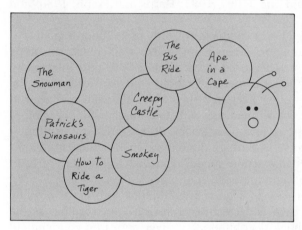

Students may keep personal card files or notebooks listing books they have read, or they may contribute to a class file. For their files, students should note brief comments on one side of the card and draw illustrations on the other. Some schools use special programs to promote interest in reading. One elementary school sponsors a contest called "Bring on the Books" to promote recreational reading and to involve parents (Gitelman and Rasberry, 1986), and some schools participate in nationwide reading incentive programs, such as those sponsored by the March of Dimes and Pizza Hut. Media specialists organize book clubs to attract readers with similar interests who wish to share their knowledge. A Reading Olympics program awards gold, silver, and bronze certificates to each child who completes a specified number of books. On RIF distribution days some teachers hold special motivational programs, which are often seasonal: witches tell spooky stories at Halloween, the Easter bunny makes the spring distribution, or the Abominable Snowman pulls books from a sack during the winter season.

452

Teaching
Reading in
Today's
Elementary
Schools

Sustained Silent Reading (SSR) is widely used as a means for stimulating interest in reading. The teacher sets aside a period of time, usually from fifteen to thirty minutes, each day for silent reading. SSR can be used by a single classroom or by the entire school—students and staff. Reading materials are freely chosen by the students, who now have the opportunity to use the skills that they have acquired for an uninterrupted period of reading for pleasure. As their teacher joins them, they realize that recreational reading has value even for adults. Of course, a wide selection of books, effective motivational strategies, and follow-up discussions of reading materials are important components of Sustained Silent Reading. Research on the effectiveness of SSR is somewhat inconclusive and subjective, but most studies indicate that SSR tends to improve students' attitudes and achievement in reading (Berglund and Johns, 1983; Harris and Smith, 1986; and Schaudt, 1983).

Manning and Manning (1984) conducted a study of 415 fourth graders to see what recreational reading programs would make a difference in reading attitudes and achievement. They used three models: SSR, peer interaction, and individual teacher-student conferences about students' reading. In the peer-interaction model, students selected their own materials and read at their own pace, but they also interacted with one another by engaging in such activities as small group and paired book discussions, oral reading to one another, and sharing books through dramatization and puppetry. Pupils participating in the peer-interaction model achieved significantly greater gains in both achievement and attitudes than other students.

Book fairs are another way of acquainting children with new books by offering them books to own and creating enthusiasm for reading. Media specialists arrange with book distributors to deliver books on consignment for about a week, and then advertise the fair in advance so that children can look forward to buying new books. Special book-related events, such as puppet shows, visiting storytellers, dramatic presentations, and special displays, are often held in conjunction with the book fair.

Some other ideas for stimulating reader interest are given below:

ACTIVITIES

1. Use free promotional materials (bookmarks, posters, etc.) available from the Children's Book Council, 67 Irving Place, New York, N.Y. 10003.
2. Using schedules from local television studios, announce in advance when book-related television shows will be shown. *The Wizard of Oz* has been shown every year for many years.
3. Set the mood for storytime with music, dim lights, a special room arrangement, or a feature related to a specific story.
4. Supply nonfiction and biographical books related to a current topic of great interest (a royal wedding, for example).

5. Promote Book Week and Library Week and use related materials (also available from the Children's Book Council).
6. Ask your school librarian to show the children special features of the library (where new books are placed, what story filmstrips are available and how to use them, how to use the card catalog, where award-winning books are located, and so on).
7. Make a "Who's Who" of famous story characters, to which each student contributes one or more pages.
8. Invite a local author to speak to your class and discuss what it is like to write a book.
9. Use crossword puzzles, charades, and games based on stories.

Some things actually discourage young people from reading. For example, most children intensely dislike required reading lists and formal book reports. Students also find prolonged analysis of books tedious, and they lose interest in reading if the teacher shows no interest in reading for pleasure.

✔ Self-Check: Objectives 5 and 6

Cite several ways to create a stimulating environment for recreational reading and motivate children to read for pleasure.
(See Self-Improvement Opportunity 9.)

Connecting Reading and Writing Through Literature

A natural bond exists between reading and writing. Although one is in a sense the reverse of the other, both call for an awareness of the elements and forms of literature, as well as the rhythm and flow of language. In understanding (reading) and creating (writing) stories, children use knowledge of story structure and other literary techniques. Literature serves as both a model and a spark for creative writing.

Instructional Procedures

In order to promote the connection between reading and writing through literature, teachers should immerse their students in an environment where they have purposes and opportunities for reading and writing throughout the day and across all areas of the curriculum. Teachers can read aloud daily to students from various forms of children's literature and provide a variety of good books for classroom library shelves. They might set up learning centers with activities for encouraging children to make written responses to books, being sure to allow time for such reading and writing to take place. They should integrate trade books with all curricular areas and make assignments that require thoughtful reactions to literature. Writing materials, including lined and unlined paper, pencils with erasers, colored pens for revising and editing, and folders for completed work, should be readily available. The classroom environment should be supportive and free from the risks that

454

Teaching
Reading in
Today's
Elementary
Schools

inhibit honest expression, such as being graded for initial attempts and being forced to share written work. According to Freeman (1983), teachers should recognize and accept all efforts at writing, but should praise only exceptional work. In classrooms with positive reading-writing environments, teachers write along with their students and share with them the frustrations and satisfactions of writing. Where trust is established between the teacher and class members and where reading and writing occur naturally, written responses to literature are likely to flourish.

Even in a positive environment, good creative writing doesn't just happen. Rather, teachers need to use a variety of strategies for helping students acquire writing skills. Just before reading aloud to the class, the teacher might ask students to listen to how the author uses a lead sentence to create interest in the story or uses dialogue for developing characterization. During the story the teacher could stop occasionally to point out a literary technique or to ask students to close their eyes and visualize a descriptive passage. After completing the story or chapter, the teacher might ask students what they specifically liked or disliked about the way the author wrote. When the teacher points out such features to the class, students learn to evaluate material, thus making them more critical readers and improving their writing abilities as well. One fourth-grade class of avid readers and writers reached the point where they expected certain things from books and made a chart entitled "What Makes a Book Good?", thus establishing their own criteria for evaluating books (Strickland and Cullinan, 1986).

Another useful strategy to help children overcome writing problems is to hold individual conferences and group or class minilessons. Teachers can determine children's difficulties by reading their written work and observing such problems as inconsistency in style, lack of clarity, stilted dialogue, and disconnected story lines. Then, by questioning students about possible alternatives and showing them examples of ways in which published authors have handled similar situations, they can help them recognize and resolve their problems. For instance, if a character in a child's story seems artificial, the teacher might suggest reading a chapter from one of the books about Ramona to see how Beverly Cleary developed her character. Occasionally, teachers can circulate among the students during writing sessions, making brief, individual comments that will cause students to re-examine or expand their writing (Dionisio, 1983).

When students and teachers share their written work, a great deal of learning takes place. One way of sharing is collaborative writing in which class members dictate ideas and words for a selection that the teacher writes on the chalkboard. Students continue to modify and improve upon the original version until they are satisfied with the final product. Another way is for the teacher to model creative writing on the chalkboard or an overhead projector by writing and editing a short paragraph while the students watch. Pupils can also work in pairs or small groups on writing projects and help each other by reading and critiquing rough drafts, suggesting literary sources as models, brainstorming words and ideas, and checking mechanics. Emphasis should be on the expression of ideas in response to literature rather than on mechanics, which should be stressed only in the final draft.

Working with the Elements of Literature

In order to write well-developed stories, students need to be familiar with the elements of literature discussed earlier in this chapter. They learn about these elements by analyzing stories they read or hear. Some suggestions for working with major story elements follow.

1. *Setting.* Teachers should point out how time and place affect the plot, characterization, and mood of stories. Stories must be true to their settings; characters behave differently today from the way they behaved a hundred years ago, and city life involves situations different from those that occur in country life. Teachers should advise children to place their stories in familiar settings so that they can draw on personal experiences.
2. *Characterization.* Children who examine literature with strong characterization find that writers develop their characters through dialogue, actions, interactions with others, and insights into their thoughts and feelings, as well as by description. Children might begin developing realistic characters by imagining the kinds of characters they want to use in their stories, writing character sketches about each one, and then writing stories in which these characters interact (Tway, 1985).
3. *Plot.* Before beginning to write, students need plans for their stories. They may analyze short, simple stories to see how writers introduce their stories, develop them through a series of incidents, create interest and suspense, and reach satisfying conclusions. Students should be encouraged to include action, dialogue, and description as they develop their plots.
4. *Style.* Perhaps a writer's first consideration is whether to write in the first or third person. Since much writing is personal narrative, children often write in the first person, although they may be tempted to write in the third person because it is more commonly found in published books. If children have problems with switching from the first to the third person, the teacher may talk to them about *who* is telling the story and remind them to be consistent (Tway, 1985).

Working with Literary Forms

Beginning writers are likely to use prose, but teachers can encourage them to try different forms of prose, as well as plays and poetry. By reading aloud from different literary genres and calling attention to the characteristics of each, teachers help students understand different forms of writing.

Folklore presents many possibilities for modeling different literary forms. Reading about legendary heroes, such as Paul Bunyan and Pecos Bill, stimulates children to create their own legendary heroes. With teacher

456

Teaching
Reading in
Today's
Elementary
Schools

guidance, they identify characteristics of legendary heroes, such as remarkable deeds and unusual appearance. A collaborative effort in writing a detailed character sketch of an imaginary legendary hero might lead to a series of adventures about this character written by individual students.

One of the easiest forms to use as a model is the fable, which is usually characterized by brevity, a moral, and use of animal characters. Writers can either start with a short story and find an appropriate moral, or begin with a moral and develop a short story to fit it.

Myths, *pourquoi* (why) tales, some Native American folklore, and Rudyard Kipling's *Just So Stories* provide explanations for universal origins. These stories are excellent ways for children to understand different cultures and become familiar with literary classics, and careful analysis of style and structure enables students to base creative writing on this story form. Students may wish to begin by creating stories for the origins of animal characteristics, such as how the horse got its mane or why the donkey has long ears (Tway, 1985).

In order to get students to express their reactions to books, the teacher might introduce them to diaries, journals, or letters, in which the authors write in the first person and express honest feelings in an informal style. Good sources of literature to use as models are *Anne Frank: Diary of a Young Girl* (diary), Joan Blos's *A Gathering of Days* (journal), and Beverly Cleary's *Dear Mr. Henshaw* (collection of letters). Children who use diaries or journals to write reactions to books they read can share their feelings with classmates and keep records of these books. Over a period of time they can observe how their tastes in reading change and notice differences in their abilities to analyze and evaluate literature (Sutherland and Arbuthnot, 1986).

Play writing requires students to pay close attention to form and style as they read examples of plays in books. Using these examples as models, students can write their own scripts, complete with dialogue, narration, provisions for stage directions, and logical divisions into scenes and acts. After they write a play and perform it, they may find that their dialogue is not realistic and may substitute more natural speech (Strickland and Cullinan, 1986).

Teachers can guide children in writing poetry by first immersing them in an environment rich in poetry and then asking them to respond freely and with feeling. As a third-grade teacher, Valentine (1986) placed poetry books on the shelves of her classroom library and began reading her favorite poems to the children. She told them to ask themselves, "What does this poem mean to me?" Looking at the works of published poets for inspiration, they began writing their own poetry by creating free narrative and adding line breaks later. Based on her experiences with sixth graders, Rogers (1985) advocated participation in poetry through listening, reading, writing, singing, and reciting, followed by expression of "poetic thought," in which students use language imaginatively for conveying their ideas. She suggested a three-step process: (1) mind stretching, in which children become more actively aware of things; (2) developing metaphoric minds for perceiving new and unusual relationships; and (3) sensitizing children to the sound systems of language, in particular repetitions, arrangements, and word choices.

Although Valentine and Rogers felt no need to use sequential activities and poetry forms, other teachers prefer to follow a series of structured activities in teaching poetry. Describing a poetry-writing program for fourth and fifth graders in her school, Freeman (1983) identifies a series of activities, beginning with visits by a consultant who reads poetry aloud and directs children's attention to the ideas expressed in the poems. The program continues with attention to basic language patterns and alliterative word games before moving to various poetry forms (such as cinquains and haiku, discussed below). Attention to rhyming forms (couplets and quatrains) and free verse concludes the series of activities. The school's poetry-writing program uses modeling as the instructional method and the children's own experiences as the content for poetry writing.

Two structured forms of poetry that teachers often use to help children start writing their own poetry are cinquain and haiku. A *cinquain* is a simple five-lined poem that has the following structure (Burns and Broman, 1983):

Line 1: one word, giving title
Line 2: two words, describing title
Line 3: three words, expressing action
Line 4: four words, expressing a feeling in a phrase
Line 5: one word, repeating title or giving synonym for title

The cinquains below were written by fourth graders:

Snakes	Butterfly
Long, slimy	Quiet, delicate
Sliding, hissing, creeping	Fluttering, flying, gliding
Small and scaly creatures	Silently through the sky
Reptiles	Butterfly

Haiku is a short three-lined Japanese poem with seventeen syllables—five in the first line, seven in the second line, and five in the third line. It should capture a moment or an image in relation to nature or the seasons of the year. Using Ann Atwood's *Haiku: The Mood of the Earth* as a model, teachers can help students acquire a sensitivity for expressing feelings about the wonders of nature. The following examples of haiku were also written by fourth graders:

The highway looks at	Scary shadows move
the mountain in the daybreak	heavily across the room
as the sun rises	darkening my bed

Publishing

Occasionally poetry, stories, and illustrations created by children are published in magazines, but most children will see their work "published" only if their teacher arranges to publish it in the classroom. Sutherland and Arbuthnot (1986) stress the importance of providing an audience for a story that has been carefully written, revised, and edited. They state, "The sense of audience should be impressed on children so that they begin to recognize the responsibility a writer has toward potential readers and to think about the kinds of responses they hope to get from readers" (p. 591). Children should experience writing for different audiences, including teachers and parents, younger children, and their peers.

Classroom publishing can take many forms. Children might begin by writing stories to go along with pictures they have drawn or with wordless picture books in their library. They might use features that they have seen in published books, including tables of contents, title pages, and biographical sketches of themselves as authors. Pages could be fastened with brads, taped together, sewn, or professionally bound. Finished books might be shelved or placed on tables in the classroom, or they might be taken to the school library, fitted with pockets, and checked out. Some types of books that teachers might help children make are listed below.

Individual books. Students write individual stories or series of short articles on such topics as "All About Me" or "My Dog Freckles."

Class books. A class book is a collection of students' writings centered on a particular theme. For example, a class book could be an ABC book, for which each child contributes a page about a different letter of the alphabet; a recipe book for which each child submits a recipe; or a poetry book, for which each child writes a poem.

Patterned books. From a story they read or hear read to them, children create a similar story using the same language pattern or theme. For instance, Judith Viorst's *Alexander and the Terrible, Horrible, No Good, Very Bad Day* might trigger a class book on each child's worst day or individual books on a disastrous series of events in each child's life. (See Appendix B at the end of Chapter 2 for a list of patterned or predictable/repetitive books to use for this purpose.)

Yearbooks. Children select their best creative writing of the year and compile it into a yearbook (Tway, 1985).

The "author's chair" is a popular feature in classrooms in which first graders are learning about the relationship between reading and writing as they become authors themselves (Graves and Hansen, 1983). The children read books by professional authors and write their own stories, which the teacher sometimes publishes in hard cover and shelves along with books by professional authors. Each day children take turns sitting in the author's chair while they read trade books or their own stories to peers. After a first grader reads an original story, classmates comment on what they think the story is about and then direct questions about the story to the child-author. When a trade book is read, both the teacher and the class think about what the author might say in response to their questions. Although the author's chair is the focus of activity in this classroom, much reading and writing take place throughout the day. Children read their own books to each other, often from "satellite" chairs, and then teach interested classmates how to read them also.

According to Graves and Hanson, reading and writing are both acts of composing (1983, p. 177). In the author's chair program, the children move through three stages—replication, transition, and sense of option—as they grow in their understanding of what it means to be an author. During the replication stage, they make drawings, invent spellings, and at first place words erratically on pages as they imitate versions of writing, and during oral reading they mimic the intonation of other readers. They are learning to put their ideas on paper and to discuss them with others. The transition stage partially consists of realizing the importance of choosing the right topic (usually related to personal experiences) and identifying with professional authors. The children's interest gradually shifts from artwork to print as their decoding and encoding skills develop and they perceive the connection between pictures and writing. Striving for meaning, they do considerable rereading as they write so that their stories will make sense to their audiences. During the third stage, the children learn that they have options: stories can be imaginary or real, or the same story can appear in different versions. They rewrite their stories to organize and clarify them as they consider what they might be asked when they read from the author's chair. By this time the children understand the processes of reading and writing and can make and defend their decisions as authors.

There is currently a great deal of interest in writing as a process and in ways of combining reading and writing to promote natural growth in literacy. Other references to the reading-writing connection appear throughout the text, particularly in Chapter 2, in which it is related to emerging literacy, and in Chapter 6, in which it is discussed as part of the reading lesson.

Reading-Writing Activities

In addition to the ideas already presented in this section for linking reading and writing, teachers may want to use ideas from the learning center (see Example 9.6) and unit later in this chapter, as well as the activities below.

ACTIVITIES

1. Let the students write a class newspaper on one of these themes: (a) news stories that are modern adaptations of fairy tales and Mother Goose rhymes,

460

Teaching
Reading in
Today's
Elementary
Schools

(b) a newspaper written at the same time and place as the setting of the book that the teacher is reading, or (c) a literary digest of news about books. Children may compose advertisements for favorite books to place in the newspaper.

2. Ask the children to prepare an annotated list of their favorite books and then get together with other students, alphabetize the complete list, and compile a class bibliography for other students to use.

3. Ask students to collect as many Newbery Award books and Honor books (runners-up to Award books) as they can find, read several of them, and ask their friends to read others. After making up and filling out an evaluation checklist for each book, with criteria such as characterization, author's style, authenticity of setting, and plot development, they may add to the checklist comments about the merit of each book.

4. Encourage students to write a radio or television script based on a story. First they should read some plays to become familiar with directions for staging and appropriate writing style for dialogue.

5. Let the students write a different ending for a story or complete an unfinished story.

6. Let students make original book jackets for favorite books by illustrating the cover, writing a brief biographical sketch of the author on one flap, and writing a "blurb" to make the book sound appealing on the other flap.

7. Encourage students who read books about different geographical regions or countries to keep imaginary travel diaries.

8. Have each student choose a favorite character from literature, such as Pippi Longstocking or Curious George, and write a story about an imaginary visit to the school or a day spent in her or his company.

9. Let each student read a biography of a famous person from history and write a story about what would happen if that person lived today—for example, how he or she would bring peace to the world, solve medical problems, or protect the environment.

10. Ask students to choose unusual settings from books—perhaps something from science fiction or historical fiction—and write stories about themselves in these different settings.

Cowin (1986) based a writing/literature unit on Chris Van Allsburg's Caldecott winner *Jumanji,* a story of two children who play a board game that brings a jungle, complete with wild animals and natural disasters, into their home with every roll of the dice. The unit began with prewriting exercises in which children were to write directions for a board game and evaluate the adequacy of their directions. The teacher then read the story and asked the students to write follow-up stories for it. She typed their follow-ups and made them into transparencies to use as a basis for a lesson on writing to create specific visual images. The students rewrote their stories, including more specific details on these second drafts, and shared them with partners who constructively criticized the stories. After a final editing for mechanics, the compositions were mounted and displayed for parents at an open house.

461
Literary
Appreciation
and
Recreational
Reading

✔ Self-Check: Objective 7
What are several strategies for using literature to support the reading-writing connection?
(See Self-Improvement Opportunities 10 and 12.)

Providing Other Opportunities for Responding to Literature

Writing activities in which children respond to books help them develop an appreciation for literature or an interest in recreational reading. On the next few pages are some suggestions for other types of creative activities based on literature.

Creative Book Sharing

Even though children dislike formal book reports, they should be encouraged to respond to and share books on certain occasions. Teachers can devise dozens of ways for children to react to books, including the ones below.

ACTIVITIES

1. Set up mock interviews between the student and a character in the book, between two book characters, between the student and the author, or between a character and the author.
2. Arrange a panel discussion in which several students who have read different books by the same author talk about similarities and differences in the books, the writer's strengths and weaknesses, the writer's general philosophy, and how the author's style has changed over a period of time.
3. Once a month let students share in groups of four or five what they liked or did not like about a book they read, showing the book while they are telling about it.
4. When more than one student reads the same book, try the following suggestions: dramatize a scene from the story; set up a puppet show and tape-record the voices of the characters; compare views about character development, conflicts in the story, and the ending of the book.
5. For biographies, have students discuss the childhoods of famous people, what influences caused them to become famous, and what struggles they faced to accomplish their goals.
6. When students have read biographies of creative people, ask them to include examples of the subjects' famous works in their reviews: playing a recording by a well-known composer, showing an art print by a painter, or displaying a product of an inventor.

462

Teaching
Reading in
Today's
Elementary
Schools

7. For books about travel, students might read several books about the same country and compare points of view or give an illustrated lecture on the country by locating it on the map and showing postcards and other travel materials.
8. For realistic fiction, encourage students to identify the problems of the characters and how they are solved, relate the situation in the book to the students' own environments, or propose alternate solutions for the characters' problems.
9. Encourage students to compare books with movie or television versions of the same story.

Interpreting Literature Orally

Fluent oral reading with intonation and phrasing that accurately reflects the mood and tone of the story or poem is another way of responding to literature. Oral reading is more difficult than silent reading because, in order to convey the author's message to an audience, the reader must pronounce words correctly, phrase appropriately, enunciate distinctly, use proper intonation, and pace the reading appropriately. To accomplish these goals, the oral reader should have an opportunity to read silently first in order to become acquainted with the author's style of writing, determine the author's message, and check the correct pronunciation of unfamiliar words. If the passage is particularly difficult, the reader may need to practice it aloud in order to ensure proper phrasing and intonation.

Oral reading skills require special attention. The teacher may demonstrate good and poor oral reading, let the children analyze these performances, and then help students draw up a list of standards or guidelines such as the one that follows.

1. Be sure you can pronounce each word correctly before you read your selection to an audience. If you are not sure of a pronunciation, check the dictionary or ask for help.
2. Say each word clearly and distinctly. Don't run words together, and take care not to leave out word parts or to add parts to words.
3. Pause in the right places. Pay attention to punctuation clues.
4. Emphasize important words. Help the audience understand the meaning of the selection by the way you read it. Read slowly enough to allow for adequate expression and speak loudly enough to be easily heard.
5. Prepare carefully before you read to an audience.

Possible activities for developing good reading before an audience include the following.

1. Give the children opportunities to listen to good readers. Be a good model by preparing diligently before reading literature selections to the class. Good models are also available on tape recordings.

463

Literary
Appreciation
and
Recreational
Reading

2. Let the children listen to tapes of their own oral reading efforts and analyze their own performances, using the class-developed guidelines.

3. Discuss the reading clues offered by punctuation marks and give the children practice in interpreting these marks in short selections or single sentences.

4. Discuss how voice inflection helps to convey meaning. Have the children say "She is going" in a way that indicates a fact, that denotes dislike of the idea, that emphasizes that the action will be taken, and that shows happiness about the information.

5. Give special attention to reading poetry in a way that avoids a singsong effect. Emphasize the value of punctuation marks for this purpose.

6. Have children do repeated readings of the same passage so that they try to improve their fluency with each rereading. This method was effective for increasing fluency with third graders (Koskinen and Blum, 1984).

Teachers should guide children's choices of materials for oral reading by helping them find selections that flow smoothly, contain realistic dialogue, and have natural rhythm. The materials should be interesting and easy to read so that pupils are unlikely to have difficulties with sentence structure and vocabulary (Ross, 1986). Several sources of material for helping children with specific oral reading skills are available; a sample page from one source is presented in Example 9.4.

▶ **EXAMPLE 9.4:** Sample Oral Reading Exercise

Using Your Voice in Oral Reading

Here are some sentences that have contrasts. Read one pair of sentences. See how the second sentence differs from the first. Make sure your voice changes to show the contrast.

1. The roaring wind banged the door shut.
   A gentle breeze drifted softly by.

2. The giant pounded his fist on the table.
   A wee fairy flitted to the rosebud.

3. The bass drum boomed like thunder.
   The silver bells tinkled softly.

4. The Indian slipped silently through the trees.
   The speeding car crashed into the bridge.

5. The great clock boomed out the hours.
   The tiny watch ticked gently and steadily.

6. The girls tiptoed past the sickroom door.
   The shouting boys dived with a great splash.

464

Teaching
Reading in
Today's
Elementary
Schools

7. The sneaky cat crept up on the birds.

The elephant crashed through the brush.

Source: Mildred Dawson and Georgiana Newman, *Oral Reading and Linguistics*, Book 3, "Loud and Clear," p. 41. Westchester, Ill.: Benefic Press, 1969. ◀

When well-rehearsed oral reading occurs, there should be one or more people with whom the reader is attempting to communicate through reading. Audience members should not have access to the book from which the performer is reading and should not be allowed to follow the reading with their eyes. Instead, they should listen to the reader in order to grasp the author's meaning, or, if the reader is reading to prove a point, to agree or disagree. The reader must attempt to hold the audience's attention through oral interpretation of the author's words. A stumbling performance will lead to a restless, impatient audience and a poor listening situation.

Some examples of purposes for audience reading are:

1. Confirming an answer to a question by reading the portion of the selection in which the answer is found.
2. Reading aloud the part of an assigned story that is funniest or saddest or that tells about a particular person, thing, or event.
3. Reading a news story in which the class should be interested or background information for a topic of discussion from a reference or trade book.
4. Making announcements or issuing invitations.
5. Reading the part of a character in a play or the narration for a play or other dramatic presentation.
6. Reading news for a school radio broadcast.
7. Sharing a part of a published story, a poem (poems are written to be read aloud), or an experience story that the reader has enjoyed.
8. Participating in choral reading or readers' theater.
9. Reading aloud directions for a group activity, such as performing an experiment, making a model, or playing a game.
10. Participating in a class read-aloud program. Spend about forty-five minutes each week on an oral reading session in which different students each read aloud for a few minutes from favorite trade books.
11. Sharing riddles, jokes, and tongue twisters to entertain classmates.
12. Reading stories aloud to children in lower grades.
13. Impersonating characters in stories by reading the lines and using appropriate expressions and gestures.
14. Reading descriptive passages or poems aloud and letting classmates draw pictures of the visual images they see.

✔ Self-Check: Objective 8

465

Literary
Appreciation
and
Recreational
Reading

List the purposes for having children read aloud that seem most important to you.
(See Self-Improvement Opportunity 10.)

Responding Through Drama

The dramatic process includes such activities as

1. pantomiming story situations.
2. characterizing objects or persons.
3. improvising situations and dramatizing stories.
4. reading and creating plays (and using aids, such as puppets).
5. readers' theater.
6. reading/speaking choral verse.

Through the ages, communication has taken place through body actions. Movement stories or poems delight children, and *pantomiming* is one way of dramatizing through movement. Beginning with simple activities such as being a toad under a mushroom, it can then progress to pantomimes involving the cooperation of several children. Since young children usually know some nursery rhymes when they enter school, these rhymes can be used for pantomime. It's fun to be Jack or Jill and run up the hill, to be Little Bo Peep looking for her sheep, or to be the scary spider chasing Miss Muffet away from her tuffet. Fables (such as Aesop's) are also good for a group to act out, as are folktales like *Little Red Riding Hood*.

Teachers can focus on *characterization* (being an animal or another person) by asking children to interpret the giant in *Jack and the Beanstalk*. How does he walk? What kind of person is he? How old is he? What should his facial expressions be like? What is his relationship with the other characters in the story?

Acting without a script is called *improvisation* or *creative dramatics,* and children who participate in this form of drama must have the main points of a story firmly in mind and understand the roles of the characters. Usually the teacher reads a favorite story to the students and tells them in advance that they may act it out. Children volunteer to play different parts and interpret the story as they understand it. At the primary level children may dramatize such stories as *The Three Billy Goats Gruff* or *The Three Bears,* while intermediate students may act out scenes from *Rip Van Winkle* or Katherine Paterson's *The Great Gilly Hopkins*.

Puppets—either simple hand puppets that the children have made, in which the head is moved by the index finger and the arms by the third finger and thumb, or rod puppets, controlled by one or more rigid rods to which the puppet is attached—are very useful for presenting plays. Puppets may be

466

Teaching
Reading in
Today's
Elementary
Schools

constructed from paper sacks, Styrofoam, rubber balls, papier-mâché, old socks, fruits or vegetables, sticks, and so on. Tape-recording the script as the children read it (or act it out) and then playing it during the puppet performance may help some children concentrate on hand movements until they can coordinate both speaking and manipulating the puppets.

Readers' theater is a form of drama in which a narrator and several characters present a dramatic reading from a story that has been selected for its strong characterization and smoothly flowing style (Sutherland and Arbuthnot, 1986). The narrator should be a fluent oral reader, and the other readers must understand their characters fully in order to interpret their roles in the story. The performers should rehearse their parts, perhaps adding sound effects or background music when appropriate, and then perform their story for an audience. No scenery or costumes are necessary.

Another form of drama is *choral reading/speaking,* in which students listen and respond to the sounds and rhythms of speech. As children become aware of language patterns, they often improve their oral reading skills. Among the various types of choral reading/speaking are the following:

Echoic verse. The reader says a line and the audience repeats it, word for word, intonation for intonation, and sometimes even action for action. Poems that lend themselves well to echoic treatment include Vachel Lindsay's "The Mysterious Cat" and Eleanor Farjeon's "The Night Will Never Stay."

Unison. The entire class speaks the lines together with attention to consistency in timing, intonation, and voice quality. Appropriate selections are those with strong rhythm and strong contrasting moods, such as nursery rhymes, limericks, and nonsense verse (Miccinati, 1985).

Line-a-child. Each child reads one or two lines individually. When the climax is reached, a few lines may be read in unison. Barbara Cooney's *Cock Robin* is a good choice.

Refrain. One individual reads or speaks the narrative part and the whole group joins in on the refrain. Example:

> "Never, No Never"
>
> Leader: Did you ever see an elephant
> Sitting in a tree?
> Group: Never, no never, no never.
> Leader: Did you ever see a rooster
> Swimming in the sea?
> Group: Never, no never, no never.
> Leader: Did you ever see a dog
> Carry doughnuts on his tail?
> Group: Never, no never, no never.
> Leader: Did you ever see a cat
> With green spots on his back?

467

Literary
Appreciation
and
Recreational
Reading

Group: Never, no never, no never.
Leader: Did you ever see a monkey
            Striped all pink and black?
Group: Never, no never, no never.
Leader: Did you ever see the mailman
            Bring milk instead of mail?
Group: Never, no never, no never.
Author Unknown

Two-part or antiphonal. Two groups of children are involved, such as boys and girls, light voices and deep voices, or questions and answers. Example:

"Cats"
Group 1: "Pussycat, pussycat, where have you been?"
Group 2: "I've been to London to look at the Queen."
Group 1: "Pussycat, pussycat, what did you there?"
Group 2: "I frightened a little mouse under a chair."
Author Unknown

✔ Self-Check: Objective 9

What are several ways that children can respond to literature through drama? Consider ways that you might want to use drama in your classroom.
(See Self-Improvement Opportunities 13 and 14.)

Responding Through Art

Students can interpret stories through many art media, including clay, paint, papier-mâché, scraps of felt and ribbon, and collage. Four specific ways of responding to literature through art are suggested here.

ACTIVITIES

1. *Murals* are designed around a central theme: a scene from a story, a parade of characters, a series of episodes, or a synthesis of popular characters in an "animal fantasy" (Huck, Hepler, and Hickman, 1987, pp. 679–80). For example, *A Tree Is Nice,* by Janice Udry, would be a good basis for a mural that shows many kinds of trees. With the aid of the teacher, children plan how their mural will look; then each child sketches one part and attaches it to the appropriate place to get a general idea of the total effect. When they are satisfied with the plan, the children begin drawing with crayon, chalk, or tempera paint.
2. As with murals, *mobiles* begin with a theme and a plan for developing that theme. Tiny objects or two-dimensional cutouts of characters are attached to nylon

468

Teaching
Reading in
Today's
Elementary
Schools

thread, fishing line, or fine wire and are suspended from rods or some sort of frame. The balancing rods may be cut from metal coat hangers, or students can use a tree branch or umbrella frame for support. The mobile must be carefully balanced so that objects can move freely. Children might draw monsters from Maurice Sendak's *Where the Wild Things Are,* color them on both sides, cut them out, and fasten them to a mobile.

3. Students can make a *box movie,* or a series of drawings that represent scenes from a story, by drawing the scenes on a roll of shelf paper or on individual sheets of manila paper that are fastened together in sequence. The paper is attached at both ends to rods and rolled around one rod like a scroll. Then the roll is placed inside a box that has an opening the size of one frame. A student turns the rollers as the narrator tells the story. For instance, children could depict *Julie of the Wolves,* by Jean George, by showing Julie's developing relationship with the wolves, one scene at a time.

4. *Time lines* are drawn on long, narrow strips of paper to show time relationships within stories or of events. Each interval on the time line represents a specified span of time. Students can also make a *map* from the description of the setting of almost any story, such as one tracing the route of the slave ship in Paula Fox's *The Slave Dancer.*

✔ Self-Check: Objectives 9 and 10

Recall some books that were your favorites when you were a child. What types of response to literature would be appropriate to use with these books?

(See Self-Improvement Opportunities 10 and 11.)

Responding at Learning Centers

Basically, a learning center is a collection of activities related to a central theme. Its physical arrangement should be attractive and practical but can vary according to the amount of space, the kinds of materials, and the locations available. Procedures for organizing and managing learning centers are given in Chapter 11.

A teacher may wish to use one center for literature throughout the year, with collections of cards for students to use independently. A sample card is shown in Example 9.5. The teacher can introduce special themes periodically to encourage students to react critically to certain types of literature. Such themes might include

a study of mythology.

a comparison of biographical books about a famous person.

an investigation of the history of children's books.

an analysis of authors' styles of writing.

a study of a particular author and his or her works.

▶ **EXAMPLE 9.5:** Learning Center Card

469

Literary
Appreciation
and
Recreational
Reading

CREATIVE WRITING   Independent Work

Many Moons, James Thurber, Harcourt Brace Jovanovich, 1943.

A young princess desires the moon, and the king sends for his wise men for help. It is the court jester, however, who solves the problem with the princess's help.

Choose one idea and write a story about it.

1. Imagine you are the Royal Magician. How would you keep Princess Lenore from seeing the moon?
2. Make a list of the things you would tell the king you had done for him if you were the Royal Magician.
3. Who was the cleverest of the king's assistants? Why do you think so?

Activities built around the theme of "Judy Blume and Her Books" are provided in Example 9.6 as a model for a literature center. This theme is used because of Judy Blume's great popularity with intermediate-level readers. Her books contain humor, insight into the feelings of young adolescents, characters with whom readers can identify, and a straightforward treatment of contemporary issues. To use the center, students need multiple copies of several of Blume's books.

▶ **EXAMPLE 9.6:** A Literature Learning Center: Judy Blume and Her Books

Directions: Read several Judy Blume books and think about them. Then read the activities at the literature center and choose two or more from each category. Keep your work in a file folder at the center. You may wish to work with other readers.

A. *About the Author*
   1. Write a letter to Judy Blume in care of the publisher and ask her
      a. Why did you become a writer?
      b. Are the characters real people?
      c. How do you know so much about how we feel?
      d. Whatever you would like to know.
   2. Name a theme that you would like Judy Blume to write about next.
      a. Write a paragraph suggesting a story line.
      b. Describe what you think the main character would be like.
   3. Find out all you can about Judy Blume. Consult magazine articles, books about authors, and information on book jackets. Then

470

Teaching
Reading in
Today's
Elementary
Schools

a. design a bulletin-board display using book jackets, a picture of Judy Blume, and interesting facts about her life.

b. make an illustrated booklet containing reviews of her books and information about her background as a writer.

c. prepare a presentation about her and her books to give to another class.

4. Prepare a mock interview with Judy Blume for radio or television. After you have rehearsed it, present it to the class.

5. Plan a panel discussion or debate with other Blume readers about whether or not authors should write on the kinds of themes that Judy Blume chooses.

B. *About the Books*

1. Make a collage of magazine pictures related to the themes in Judy Blume's books.

2. Choose favorite scenes from Blume's books. Find others who have read the same books and act out the scenes for your class.

3. Write diary entries for five consecutive days in the life of one of the characters.

4. Identify the theme for each book you read. Then relate these themes to yourself and people you know.

5. Predict what the characters in the books you have read will be doing in five or ten years.

6. Think about the characters and choose one to be your friend. Give reasons for your choice. Is there someone you would not like for a friend? If so, why?

7. Should Judy Blume's books be translated into other languages for boys and girls in other countries to read? Why or why not?

8. Create a television commercial to advertise one or more of Blume's books. You may want to include a musical jingle.

9. Could one of Blume's books be made into a television series? Consider possible story lines and audience reactions.

10. Make riddles of character descriptions for others to guess.

11. Make and play a game of Concentration using book titles and character names from Judy Blume's books.

12. Choose one book that several of you have read and talk about all the emotions or feelings that are discussed in the book. Make a list.

C. *About Specific Books*

1. *Freckle Juice* (New York: Four Winds Press, 1971).

a. Make up your own recipe for freckle juice.

b. How would you like to change your appearance? What difference would it make? How important is appearance?

2. *Then Again, Maybe I Won't* (Scarsdale, N.Y.: Bradbury Press, 1971).

a. How would you feel if you suddenly became rich? poor?

3. *Blubber* (Scarsdale, N.Y.: Bradbury Press, 1974).

a. Write a page in Blubber's diary expressing her feelings about being fat.

b. Suggest ways that Blubber could have defended herself.

4. *Are You There God? It's Me, Margaret* (Scarsdale, N.Y.: Bradbury Press, 1970).

471

Literary
Appreciation
and
Recreational
Reading

a. What kind of relationship does Margaret have with God? How does her relationship compare with yours?

b. What were some of the problems that Margaret had in moving to a new place? Make a list of the problems you might face if you moved. ◄

Participating in a Literature Unit

To help children appreciate a certain aspect of literature, a teacher can plan a unit around a story. The unit might actually replace basal reader instruction for a time, or it might be taught in addition to the basal reader, perhaps near the end of the school day. Such a unit might involve children in a number of related language arts skills, as in the following example. In it children read, report (orally and in written form), tell stories, write creatively, listen, learn new vocabulary words, and do research. At the same time they are learning to appreciate fables, folklore, fairy tales, legends, and myths.

ACTIVITIES FOR A UNIT ON FOLKLORE

1. Let children read and compare folktale variants, beginning with the Brothers Grimm tales and moving toward contemporary versions. (Reference source: *Household Stories,* New York: McGraw-Hill, 1966).
2. Encourage children to tell stories, repeating familiar favorites or creating new tales.
3. Read and/or tell classic folktales to the students.
4. Provide opportunities for discovering word origins and literary allusions, especially in myths (examples: echo, Pandora's box, Mercury, Atlas).
5. Let children dramatize folktales using puppets, pantomime, readers' theater, and creative dramatics.
6. Encourage children to write creatively. Have them
   a. study the characteristics of a fable (brevity, animal characters, a moral) and create new fables.
   b. write modern versions of fairy tales.
   c. make up a ballad based on folklore and set it to music.
   d. make up original *pourquoi* tales, such as "Why the Rabbit Has Long Ears."
   e. write new endings for fairy tales after changing a major event in the story, such as having the First Little Pig build his house out of stone and the Third Little Pig build his house out of spaghetti.
   f. select a newspaper story, find a moral for it (example: Theft doesn't pay), and write a fable about this moral.
7. Help students find out how folktales were originally communicated and how they came to be written.
8. Invite storytellers for children to listen to. Ask students to interview the storytellers about techniques and about the origins of the tales they tell.

472

Teaching
Reading in
Today's
Elementary
Schools

Media specialists, librarians, and other support personnel can work with teachers to encourage children's reading and to develop a complete recreational reading program. (© Robert A. Issacs/Photo Researchers)

9. Encourage students to compare similarities in characters and motifs of folktales from around the world (examples: the Jackal in India, the Weasel in Africa, and Brer Rabbit in the United States).

Working with Support Personnel

Teachers and librarians should work together to use the library's resources both to reinforce subject matter and to encourage students to read for pleasure. By suggesting books and materials that will complement units of study and relate to the interests of their students, teachers work with librarians. By introducing new books, presenting stories to the class, and showing students how to use the library, librarians cooperate with teachers. In one program the teachers and the librarian work together to find books to use for individualized reading and classroom learning centers (Noyce, 1979).

In an all-school oral literature program coordinated by a media specialist, teachers select a theme around which four units are planned for the year (Boothroy and Donham, 1981). The media specialist helps teachers select books for reading aloud in keeping with the theme, and students make first, second, and third choices of unit topics. Each unit meets for two 25-minute periods per week for nine weeks. At oral literature time groups of children visit the rooms of teachers to whom they have been assigned for the nine-week period. The teacher reads aloud from a book and leads a discussion about it during the session, asking children to respond creatively through art, drama, or writing projects.

473

Literary
Appreciation
and
Recreational
Reading

Parents and the community should also be part of a school's literature program. If they realize the value of literature in their child's reading program, parents can encourage him or her to read for pleasure. Parent-teacher organizations can sponsor programs to review children's books and magazines that might be unfamiliar to parents and to suggest ways in which parents can provide a home atmosphere that promotes interest in reading. Parents or members of the community might also like to join children during an SSR or storytelling session; some nonschool personnel may be excellent storytellers or have books that they are willing to contribute. The school, the home, and the community can work together to encourage recreational reading.

Summary

A well-balanced reading program should include developmental, functional, and recreational reading. Some major purposes for recreational reading are creating a lifelong interest in reading for pleasure, developing the abilities to appreciate and evaluate literature, and acquiring knowledge of one's literary heritage. Teachers can achieve these purposes by reading aloud to students and providing them with opportunities to respond to literature throughout the school day. Trade books can supplement textbooks and help students develop understanding of each curricular area. Students can learn about literature by examining different literary elements and forms, and teachers can present literature through story reading and storytelling at all levels.

In selecting appropriate reading materials, teachers need to be aware of children's reading levels, interests, and preferences for different types of literature. Interest inventories and selection aids are useful in choosing books, as are lists of Caldecott and Newbery Award winners and Children's Choices. Many students prefer reading paperback books and periodicals.

Literary environments with an abundance of interesting books and attractive displays help create interest in reading. Book-recording devices and special incentive programs motivate children to read, and Sustained Silent Reading provides time for free reading.

Literature can serve as a basis for connecting reading with writing when children model their writing on different literary forms. Teachers who pose questions about style and form, character development and use of dialogue, and literary techniques are making their students aware of various literary elements. Children can create and publish their own books.

Students can also respond to books through creative book sharing, fluent oral reading, various types of dramatization, and art. Teachers may wish to

474

Teaching
Reading in
Today's
Elementary
Schools

develop units and learning centers for literature in order to support these types of activities. Teachers, parents, librarians, and members of the community can work together in developing a complete recreational reading program.

Test Yourself

True or False

_____ 1. Children's literature can be a part of the entire curriculum.

_____ 2. The major purpose of teaching literature is to enable children to know the titles and authors of children's books.

_____ 3. A book's theme is the overall plan for the story.

_____ 4. Style is the author's mode of expressing thoughts in words.

_____ 5. When reading aloud, teachers should speak in natural tones and with expression.

_____ 6. Selection aids are people who advise librarians about which books to order.

_____ 7. The Newbery Award is for excellence in illustration.

_____ 8. Easy-to-read books are high-quality literature for children.

_____ 9. The RIF program is an inexpensive book-distribution program.

_____ 10. Many good children's magazines are being published.

_____ 11. TV tie-ins are copies of television scripts.

_____ 12. The classroom environment has little or no effect on recreational reading.

_____ 13. SSR is a Russian reading program.

_____ 14. Book fairs offer children opportunities to buy books and enjoy book-related activities.

_____ 15. Among good ways of motivating children to read books are required reading lists and formal book reports.

_____ 16. Since audience reading is an exercise in communication, it therefore demands a real audience.

_____ 17. In readers' theater the performers read aloud from their scripts in a dramatic style.

_____ 18. Choral reading is a useful activity for developing oral reading skills.

_____ 19. A cinquain is a three-lined verse with seventeen syllables.

_____ 20. When writing responses to literature, the children's first priority should be the mechanics of writing.

_____ 21. Boys generally read more books than girls.

_____ 22. There is no need for teachers to read aloud to children after they learn to read for themselves.

_____ 23. Children in the elementary school should not be expected to write any type of poetry.

_____ 24. Parents, librarians, and the community should all support the reading program.

Self-Improvement Opportunities

475

Literary
Appreciation
and
Recreational
Reading

1. Think of some ways to use children's literature to enrich each area of the curriculum. Then choose one subject and find three books that you could use to supplement the textbook.
2. Read a selection from children's literature. Identify its genre and literary elements. Outline a plan for using this selection to teach a lesson on the elements of literature.
3. Select a read-aloud story for an age level of your choice. Then share it with a small group of children or your peers. Tape your reading and evaluate it.
4. After thinking about the best time of day for reading orally to a class, choose a grade level that you would like to teach and make a list of books that you would like to read aloud to your class.
5. Ask children to name their favorite books and see if some books are named by several children. If you have a chance, administer an interest inventory to these children to find out their reading interests.
6. Ask a child to evaluate a book by answering questions that you have prepared. Then see if your own evaluation agrees with the child's analysis.
7. Find a selection aid and analyze its usefulness in helping you choose appropriate books for an elementary classroom.
8. Find copies of children's magazines and choose two or three that you would like for your classroom. Write a brief review of each.
9. List five techniques that you would like to use for motivating children to read for pleasure.
10. With some other students, make up a list of creative ways for children to report on books.
11. Find a group of children to work with you and make one of the four special art projects described in this chapter.
12. Choose a favorite book from children's literature and write a lesson plan that involves children in a writing activity based on the book you have chosen.
13. Look through a children's poetry book and find poems that you might use for any three types of choral reading/speaking. Decide how you would present each poem.
14. Select a story with strong characterization to adapt for a readers' theater production. Get together with other students and write a script based on the story that elementary children could use.

Bibliography

Anderson, Gary, Diana Higgins, and Stanley R. Wurster. "Differences in the Free-Reading Books Selected by High, Average, and Low Achievers." *The Reading Teacher* 39 (December 1985): 326–30.

476

Teaching
Reading in
Today's
Elementary
Schools

Berglund, Roberta L., and Jerry L. Johns. "A Primer on Uninterrupted Sustained Silent Reading." *The Reading Teacher* 36 (February 1983): 534–39.

Blatt, Gloria T. "Playing with Language." *The Reading Teacher* 31 (February 1978): 487–93.

Boothroy, Bonnie, and Jean Donham. "Listening to Literature: An All-School Program." *The Reading Teacher* 34 (April 1981): 772–74.

Brozo, William G., and Carl M. Tomlinson. "Literature: The Key to Lively Content Courses." *The Reading Teacher* 40 (December 1986): 288–93.

Burke, Eileen M. "Using Trade Books to Intrigue Children with Words." *The Reading Teacher* 32 (November 1978): 144–48.

Burns, Paul C., and Betty L. Broman. *The Language Arts in Childhood Education.* 5th ed. Boston: Houghton-Mifflin, 1983, p. 210.

Busch, Jackie S. "Television's Effects on Reading: A Case Study." *Phi Delta Kappan* 59 (June 1978): 668–71.

Carbo, Marie. "Making Books Talk to Children." *The Reading Teacher* 35 (November 1981): 186–91.

Children's Magazine List. Glassboro, N.J.: Educational Press Association of America, 1985.

Cowin, Gina. "Implementing the Writing Process with Sixth Graders: *Jumanji,* Literature Unit." *The Reading Teacher* 40 (November 1986): 156–61.

Dionisio, Marie. "Write? Isn't This Reading Class?" *The Reading Teacher* 36 (April 1983): 746–50.

Dougherty, Wilma Holden, and Rosalind E. Engel. "An 80s Look for Sex Equality in Caldecott Winners and Honor Books." *The Reading Teacher* 40 (January 1987): 394–98.

Freeman, Ruth H. "Poetry Writing in the Upper Elementary Grades." *The Reading Teacher* 37 (December 1983): 238–43.

Gitelman, Honore F., and Gayle Burgess Rasberry. "Bring on the Books: A Schoolwide Contest." *The Reading Teacher* 39 (May 1986): 905–907.

Golden, Joanne M. "Children's Concept of Story in Reading and Writing." *The Reading Teacher* 37 (March 1984): 578–84.

Graves, Donald, and Jane Hansen. "The Author's Chair." *Language Arts* 60 (February 1983): 176–83.

Harris, Larry A., and Carl B. Smith. *Reading Instruction.* New York: Macmillan, 1986.

Hickman, Janet. "Children's Response to Literature: What Happens in the Classroom." In *Readings on Reading Instruction,* Albert J. Harris and Edward R. Sipay, eds. 3rd ed. New York: Longman, 1984, pp. 377–82.

Huck, Charlotte S., Susan Hepler, and Janet Hickman. *Children's Literature in the Elementary School.* 4th ed. New York: Holt, Rinehart and Winston, 1987.

Ingham, Rosemary Oliphant. "Poetry Preferences with Great References." *Kentucky Reading Journal* 5 (Spring 1984): 11–15.

Kinman, Judith R., and Darwin L. Henderson. "An Analysis of Sexism in Newbery Medal Award Books from 1977 to 1984." *The Reading Teacher* 38 (May 1985): 885–89.

Koenke, Karl. "ERIC/RCS: The Careful Use of Comic Books." *The Reading Teacher* 34 (February 1981): 592–95.

Koskinen, Patricia S., and Irene H. Blum. "Repeated Oral Reading and the Acquisition of Fluency." In *Changing Perspectives on Research in Reading/Language Processing and Instruction,* Thirty-Third Yearbook of the National Reading Conference, Jerome A. Niles, ed., and Larry A. Harris, assoc. ed. Rochester, N.Y.: National Reading Conference, 1984, pp. 183–87.

Manning, Gary L., and Maryann Manning. "What Models of Recreational Reading Make a Difference?" *Reading World* 23 (May 1984): 375–80.

Mendoza, Alicia. "Reading to Children: Their Preferences." *The Reading Teacher* 38 (February 1985): 522–27.

Miccinati, Jeannette L. "Using Prosodic Cues to Teach Oral Reading Fluency." *The Reading Teacher* 39 (November 1985): 206–12.

Nessel, Denise D. "Storytelling in the Reading Program." *The Reading Teacher* 38 (January 1985): 378–81.

Norton, Donna. *Through the Eyes of a Child.* 2nd ed. Columbus, Ohio: Charles E. Merrill, 1987.

Noyce, Ruth M. "Team Up and Teach with Trade Books." *The Reading Teacher* 32 (January 1979): 442–48.

Radebaugh, Muriel Rogie. "Using Children's Literature to Teach Mathematics." *The Reading Teacher* 34 (May 1981): 902–906.

Rogers, Wanda C. "Teaching for Poetic Thought." *The Reading Teacher* 39 (December 1985): 296–300.

Ross, Elinor P. "Classroom Experiments with Oral Reading." *The Reading Teacher* 40 (December 1986): 270–75.

Schaudt, Barbara A. "Another Look at Sustained Silent Reading." *The Reading Teacher* 36 (May 1983): 934–36.

Seminoff, Nancy Wiseman. "Children's Periodicals Throughout the World: An Overlooked Educational Resource." *The Reading Teacher* 39 (May 1986): 889–95.

Serebrin, Wayne. "A Writer and an Author Collaborate." *Language Arts* 63 (March 1986): 281–83.

Sharp, Peggy Agostino. "Teaching with Picture Books Throughout the Curriculum." *The Reading Teacher* 38 (November 1984): 132–37.

Silvers, Penny. "Process Writing and the Reading Connection." *The Reading Teacher* 39 (March 1986): 684–88.

Smith, Nancy J., M. Jean Greenlaw, and Carolyn J. Scott. "Making the Literate Environment Equitable." *The Reading Teacher* 40 (January 1987): 400–407.

Stewig, John Warren. *Children and Literature.* Chicago: Rand McNally, 1980.

478

Teaching
Reading in
Today's
Elementary
Schools

Strickland, Dorothy S., and Bernice E. Cullinan. "Literature and Language." *Language Arts* 63 (March 1986): 221–25.

Sutherland, Zena, and May Hill Arbuthnot. *Children and Books.* 7th ed. Glenview, Ill.: Scott, Foresman, 1986.

Trelease, Jim. *The Read-Aloud Handbook.* New York: Viking Penguin, 1985.

Tway, Eileen. *Writing Is Reading: 26 Ways to Connect.* Urbana, Ill.: National Council of Teachers of English, 1985.

Valentine, Sonia L. "Beginning Poets Dig for Poems." *Language Arts* 63 (March 1986): 246–52.

Whitehead, Robert. *Children's Literature: Strategies of Teaching.* Englewood Cliffs, N.J.: Prentice-Hall, 1968, pp. 37–44.

Wright, Gary. "The Comic Book—A Forgotten Medium in the Classroom." *The Reading Teacher* 33 (November 1979): 158–61.

CHAPTER APPENDIX A: CHILDREN'S BOOKS CITED IN CHAPTER 9

Alcott, Louisa May. *Little Women.* Boston: Little, Brown, 1868.

Alexander, Martha. *Nobody Asked Me If I Wanted a Baby Sister.* New York: Dial, 1971.

Aliki. *The Story of Johnny Appleseed.* Englewood Cliffs, N.J.: Prentice-Hall, 1963.

Ashbjornsen, Peter Christian, and Jorgen E. Moe. *The Three Billy Goats Gruff.* New York: Harcourt, Brace and World, 1957.

Atwood, Ann. *Haiku: The Mood of the Earth.* New York: Scribner's, 1971.

Behrens, June. *The True Book of Metric Measurement.* Chicago: Children's Press, 1975.

Bemelmans, Ludwig. *Madeline.* New York: Viking, 1962.

Blos, Joan W. *A Gathering of Days: A New England Girl's Journal, 1830–32.* New York: Scribner's, 1979.

Blume, Judy. *It's Not the End of the World.* Scarsdale, N.Y.: Bradbury, 1972.

Branley, Franklyn M. *Think Metric!* New York: Crowell, 1973.

Brink, Carol. *Caddie Woodlawn.* New York: Macmillan, 1936.

Byars, Betsy. *Summer of the Swans.* New York: Viking, 1970.

Cleary, Beverly. *Dear Mr. Henshaw.* New York: Morrow, 1983.

Cleary, Beverly. *Ramona Quimby, Age 8.* New York: Morrow, 1981.

Cobb, Vicki, and Kathy Darling. *Bet You Can't, Science Impossibilities to Fool You.* New York: Lothrop, Lee and Shepard, 1980.

Collodi, Carlo. *Pinocchio.* New York: Franklin Watts, 1967.

Cooney, Barbara. *Cock Robin.* New York: Charles Scribner's Sons, 1965.

Dalgliesh, Alice. *The Courage of Sarah Noble.* New York: Charles Scribner's Sons, 1954.

Daugherty, James. *Daniel Boone.* New York: Viking, 1932.

De Angeli, Marguerite. *The Door in the Wall.* New York: Doubleday, 1949.

Feuerlecht, Robert Strauss. *The Legends of Paul Bunyan.* New York: Macmillan, 1966.

Fox, Paula. *The Slave Dancer.* Scarsdale, N.Y.: Bradbury, 1974.

Frank, Anne. *Anne Frank: The Diary of a Young Girl,* B. M. Mooyaart, trans. New York: Doubleday, 1952.

Froman, Robert. *Bigger and Smaller.* New York: Crowell, 1971.

Galdone, Paul. *The Gingerbread Boy.* New York: Seabury, 1973.

George, Jean. *Julie of the Wolves.* New York: Harper & Row, 1973.

Gwynne, Fred. *A Chocolate Moose for Dinner.* New York: Dutton, 1973.

Hanlon, Emily. *How a Horse Grew Hoarse on the Site Where He Sighted a Bare Bear.* New York: Delacorte, 1976.

Hoban, Tana. *Count and See.* New York: Macmillan, 1972.

Irving, Washington. *Rip Van Winkle and the Legend of Sleepy Hollow.* New York: Macmillan, 1965 (from *The Sketch Book,* 1819).

Kipling, Rudyard. *Just So Stories.* New York: Doubleday, 1972.

Lindgren, Astrid. *Pippi Longstocking.* New York: Viking, 1950.

Parish, Peggy. *Amelia Bedelia.* New York: Harper & Row, 1963.

Parish, Peggy. *Teach Us, Amelia Bedelia.* New York: Greenwillow, 1977.

Paterson, Katherine. *The Great Gilly Hopkins.* New York: Crowell, 1979.

Phillips, Jo. *Right Angles: Paper-Folding Geometry.* New York: Crowell, 1972.

Pringle, Laurence. *Into the Woods: Exploring the Forest Ecosystem.* New York: Macmillan, 1973.

Sendak, Maurice. *In the Night Kitchen.* New York: Harper & Row, 1970.

Sendak, Maurice. *Where the Wild Things Are.* New York: Harper & Row, 1964.

Silverstein, Shel. *The Light in the Attic.* New York: Harper & Row, 1981.

Silverstein, Shel. *Where the Sidewalk Ends.* New York: Harper & Row, 1974.

Speare, Elizabeth. *The Bronze Bow.* Boston: Houghton Mifflin, 1961.

Steig, William. *CDB.* New York: Simon and Schuster, 1968.

Steptoe, John. *Stevie.* New York: Harper & Row, 1969.

Tolkien, J. R. R. *The Hobbit.* Boston: Houghton Mifflin, 1938.

Tresselt, Alvin. *White Snow, Bright Snow.* New York: Lothrop, 1947.

Twain, Mark. *The Adventures of Huckleberry Finn.* New York: Harper & Row, 1884.

Udry, Janice. *A Tree Is Nice.* New York: Harper & Row, 1957.

Viorst, Judith. *Alexander and the Terrible, Horrible, No Good, Very Bad Day.* New York: Atheneum, 1972.

Van Allsburg, Chris. *Jumanji.* Boston: Houghton Mifflin, 1981.

White, E. B. *Charlotte's Web.* New York: Harper & Row, 1952.

Wildsmith, Brian. *Brian Wildsmith's 1, 2, 3's.* New York: Franklin Watts, 1965.

480

Teaching
Reading in
Today's
Elementary
Schools

CHAPTER APPENDIX B: CHILDREN'S PERIODICALS[1]

Boy's Life   (1325 Walnut Lane, Irving, TX 75038-3096). Age range 8–18. Boys in Scouting.

Chickadee   (The Young Naturalist Foundation, 59 Front Street E, Toronto, Ontario, Canada M5E 1B3). Age range 4–9. Children's environment.

Child Life   (P.O. Box 10681, Des Moines, IA 50381). Age range 7–9. Safety, health, and nutrition.

Children's Digest   (P.O. Box 10681, Des Moines, IA 50381). Age range 8–10. Safety, health, and nutrition.

Children's Playmate   (P.O. Box 10681, Des Moines, IA 50381). Age range 5–7. Safety, health, and nutrition.

Classical Calliope   (Cobblestone Publishing Inc., 20 Grove Street, Peterborough, NH 03458). Age range 10–17. Literature.

Cobblestone   (Cobblestone Publishing Co., 20 Grove Street, Peterborough, NH 03458). Age range 8–14. History.

The Electric Company   (200 Watt Street, P.O. Box 2923, Boulder, CO 80322). Age range 6–10. General interest.

Faces   (20 Grove Street, Peterborough, NH 03458). Age range 8–14. People in history.

Highlights for Children   (P.O. Box 269, Columbus, OH 43272-0002). Age range 2–12. General interest.

Jack and Jill   (P.O. Box 10681, Des Moines, IA 50381). Age range 6–8. Safety, health, and nutrition.

National Geographic World   (Dept. 01085, 17th and M Streets, NW, Box 2330, Washington, DC 20036). Age range 8–13. General interest.

Odyssey   (P.O. Box 92788, Milwaukee, WI 53202). Age range 8–14. Astronomy and space science.

Owl   (The Young Naturalist Foundation, 59 Front Street E, Toronto, Ontario, Canada M5E 1B3). Age range 8–14. Children's environment.

Penny Power   (P.O. Box 2878, Boulder, CO 80322). Age range 8–14. Consumer education.

Ranger Rick's Nature Magazine   (The National Wildlife Federation, 1412 16th Street, NW, Washington, DC 20036-2266). Age range 6–12. Nature study.

Stone Soup   (P.O. Box 83, Santa Cruz, CA 95063). Age range 6–13. Literature.

3-2-1 Contact   (Box 2933, Boulder, CO 80322). Age range 8–14. Science and technology.

---

[1] Selected from *Children's Magazine List*, Educational Press Association of America, Glassboro State College, Glassboro, N.J. 08028, updated November 1985.

Chapter 10

Assessment of Pupil Progress

Introduction

Assessing children's mastery of what is being or has been taught is indispensable to good teaching and is frequently an integral part of instructional procedures. Such a statement as "Doing these exercises will give you an opportunity to see how well you can read and interpret tables" illustrates the close relationship between instruction and evaluation. Some evaluative procedures, however, such as standardized (and other) tests designed to measure pupil achievement at any particular time, are less easily identified with instruction.

This chapter is divided into four major parts. The first is concerned with informal (nonstandardized) assessment procedures and devices; the second is concerned with norm-referenced (standardized) assessment instruments; the third with criterion-referenced tests; and the fourth with process-oriented, or holistic, assessment. Samples of different kinds of tests are provided throughout the chapter, and the purposes and uses of various assessment devices and instruments are discussed. By knowing what the child needs, the teacher will know what to teach. Therefore, as is further explained in Chapter 12, adjusting instruction in the light of appropriate information makes all the difference. Teachers must assess pupils frequently to detect the ongoing changes in their achievement. They must not consider assessment a once- or twice-a-year practice.

Among kinds of assessment procedures that a teacher will find useful are diagnosing specific reading skills on a day-by-day basis as reading instruction proceeds, determining the appropriate level of reading instruction for each individual in a class, estimating each student's potential reading level, and assessing general reading achievement and areas of strengths and weaknesses in a class.

Setting Objectives

When you finish reading this chapter, you should be able to

1. Know how to assess the following types of reading skills informally: sight vocabulary, word attack, comprehension, study, and oral reading.
2. Evaluate the development of literary interests.
3. Explain how to use a graded word list to determine reading level.
4. Construct and interpret an Informal Reading Inventory (IRI) to find a child's reading level.
5. Recognize and analyze the significance of a reading miscue.
6. Name several ways to assess a child's ability to read content materials.
7. Describe tests for different aspects of reading readiness.
8. Use norm-referenced reading survey tests effectively.
9. Describe the types and content of some norm-referenced reading tests.

10. Identify some limitations of norm-referenced tests.
11. Differentiate between a norm-referenced and a criterion-referenced test.
12. Describe ways that process-oriented assessment differs from traditional assessment.

Key Vocabulary

Pay close attention to these terms when they appear in the chapter.

achievement test
aptitude test
cloze procedure
criterion-referenced test
diagnostic test
dialectal miscue
frustration level
grade-equivalent scores
graded word list
graphic cues
holistic assessment

independent level
informal assessment
informal reading
  inventory
insertions
instructional level
miscue
norm-referenced test
percentile rank
performance sample
potential reading level

process-oriented
  assessment
reading readiness test
reliability
reversals
stanine
survey test
syntactic cues
underachiever
validity

INFORMAL (NONSTANDARDIZED) ASSESSMENT

In the day-to-day program, the classroom teacher will necessarily depend more upon informal assessment devices than upon formal assessment instruments. (Formal instruments are commercially available tests that have been standardized against a specific norm or objective). In simple terms, this means that the effective teacher is observing and recording individual strengths and weaknesses during the educational process in order to adjust instruction to meet individual needs.

Assessment of Specific Skill Areas

Reading Readiness Skills

The importance of assessing a child's readiness for reading is discussed in Chapter 2, and some types of assessment are presented in this chapter. The use of performance samples, or systematic observations of a child's work (i.e., tapes of oral reading and samples of written work), provides information needed for comprehensive assessment of a child's literacy development (Teale, Hiebert, and Chittenden, 1987). This form of assessment is based on the following principles: (1) assessment is an integral part of instruction; (2) methods of assessment vary and include readiness tests, analyses of

484

Teaching
Reading in
Today's
Elementary
Schools

students' reading and writing, and teacher observations; (3) assessment includes a variety of skills and knowledge related to different forms of literacy; (4) systematic assessment occurs regularly; (5) assessment takes place in many different contexts; (6) informal assessments resemble regular classroom activities; and (7) assessments are appropriate for children's cultural backgrounds and developmental levels.

Teachers may use a variety of techniques for implementing these principles while assessing children's levels of literacy (Teale, Hiebert, and Chittenden, 1987). Teachers can evaluate children's awareness of the function or purpose of writing by observing youngsters' responses to printed labels and messages, and they can learn about comprehension skills by noting children's answers to questions about stories that are read to them. Children also reveal a great deal about their emergent literacy when they pretend to read books, especially by the way they use pictures or print as a guide, by the formality of their language, and by their ability to construct stories. Their use of invented spellings when they write and their perceptions of the connections between reading and writing as they "read" their writings are also indicative of their literacy development. Other indications include the ability to dictate coherent stories and to recognize environmental print (words on signs, for example).

Other types of informal assessment are suggested below.

1. The teacher can create his or her own informal checklist of readiness skills and behaviors. He or she can make several copies of this checklist for each pupil, keeping them in individual file folders. By filling out the forms periodically and dating each one, the teacher has a written record of each child's progress.
2. It is possible to evaluate a child's readiness for any type of prereading skill through use of informal activities designed for that purpose. For example, naming the pictures on charts of people, animals, or things gives an indication of the extent of the student's vocabulary. Teachers can use sets of word pairs (such as *wall, fall,* and *cat, can*) to ask the child which rhyme and which do not, or alphabet cards (of capital letters and lower-case letters) to assess progress toward alphabet reading.
3. Story retelling is useful for evaluating the language of students. After the teacher tells a short story to an individual student in a quiet setting, the child retells it into a tape recorder. This method also tests a child's ability to organize, comprehend, and express connected speech under controlled conditions (Pickert and Chase, 1978).
4. To assess children's prereading phonics abilities, use a prereading phonics inventory, such as the one designed by Durrell and Murphy (1978), which tests pupils' ability to recognize and write letters and their awareness of letter names. Children are asked to match spoken words with words in print.
5. Anecdotal records, or detailed running accounts of a child's activities, are useful in analyzing a child's social-emotional readiness, language develop-

ment, interests, and attitudes. A teacher may focus attention on one child for a period of time and jot down exactly what the child is doing at each moment—sitting, walking, playing, talking, watching, listening, or looking at a book. These records may be kept in a file along with checklists and samples of the child's work.

Sight Vocabulary

In addition to observing children and interacting with them to determine their levels of literacy, teachers may wish to check their knowledge of specific skills. Teachers who wish to assess a child's recognition of sight words may find index cards (3" × 5") useful. The cards should be numbered and arranged in the same order as the words on a test sheet, and the examiner should keep a copy of the test sheet with a record of words the child misses. If a teacher uses a test sheet in place of cards, the child should place a cardboard marker under each word as he or she proceeds down the page. Both the child and the examiner should have copies of the test sheet. The examiner proceeds as follows:

1. Tell the child to say the words he or she knows. For each correct response, check the corresponding word on the examiner's copy. Write in any miscalled word or types of errors a child makes while trying to pronounce each word.
2. The child should pronounce each word immediately, with no hesitation. If he or she miscalls the word but corrects it before going on, write "C" in front of the word that was corrected.
3. If the child makes no effort on the word, point to or present the next word.
4. If a child makes any of the following efforts, do not give credit for knowing the word:
   a. miscalls or omits the word and then a word or more later comes back and gives it correctly,
   b. miscalls the word and gives more than one mistaken word before getting the correct one,
   c. hesitates longer than five seconds before giving the word.
5. The child's score is the number of words checked.

Word Recognition

Several formal measures of this aspect of reading are available. Informal assessment of the various skills and techniques that relate to word recognition are discussed below.

Context The teacher can observe the child figuring out the meanings of words from sentences such as the following, which illustrate different types of contextual clues.

486

Teaching
Reading in
Today's
Elementary
Schools

A *dulcimer* is a musical instrument with wires stretched over a soundboard. (definition)

Fran likes to participate in sports, but I prefer being a *spectator*. (contrast)

We saw a *space shuttle* at the museum. (familiar—the child is already acquainted with the word, in this case through a field trip to a museum)

Please *cooperate* with your partner and help finish the work. (experience—the child is already acquainted with the idea through experience)

Noting the reactions of a child trying to identify the italicized words in these sentences, the teacher can ask the following questions:

1. Does the pupil rely primarily on phonics, context, or something else?
2. Does she use the entire sentence to help her figure out a word, or does she just stop to get help before having used all the clues?
3. Does her attitude toward an unknown word reflect confidence or frustration?

Other informal assessment procedures include

1. a cloze procedure, used on a basal reader or content passage to see if the child can use context clues to supply missing words or synonyms. (See Chapter 8.)
2. word recognition exercises at appropriate levels.

Phonics   Whereas several norm-referenced word-analysis tests are available, teachers may informally measure phonic analysis abilities by asking children to identify initial, medial, and final sounds in words.

What is the first sound you hear in *book, toy, forest, part, kitchen*? What are the first two letters in these words: *fright, snake, skate, praise, dwelling*?

What is the middle sound you hear in *cabbage, balloon, reading*?

What is the vowel with which each word begins: *Indian, olives, elephant, umbrella, apple*?

Moreover, teachers can prepare exercises for each of the phonic elements introduced to a group of children.

Element: consonant digraphs
Assessment: Ask the child to tell you what two consonants go together to make a new sound in the words

*sh*e   tee*th*   bea*ch*   tou*gh*

A more comprehensive informal inventory of phonics skills is presented in Example 10.1. It could be given to an entire class at one time as a pretest or posttest to help determine what skills students have or have not learned. Students should be given an answer form with categories and numbers on it to use in recording their responses. Teachers should realize that results may be affected by students' inability to spell the words, however. This type of inventory could also be given individually by having a child read each word orally so that the teacher can check knowledge of letter-sound correspondences. A child's inability to recognize the words on a list, however, might prevent him or her from pronouncing some known sounds.

▶ **EXAMPLE 10.1:** Informal Phonics Inventory

I. CONSONANT SOUNDS (initial)
Directions: Write the beginning letter of each word I say.

1. hit
2. just
3. go
4. pet
5. zoo
6. work
7. town
8. lamp
9. never
10. fox

II. CONSONANT SOUNDS (final)
Directions: Write the last letter of each word I say.

1. tub
2. head
3. chief
4. glass
5. hoop
6. walk
7. rug
8. pen
9. dog
10. arm

III. CONSONANT BLENDS (initial)
Directions: Write the first two letters of each word I say.

1. step
2. brown
3. spin
4. claw
5. draw
6. skate
7. glad
8. black
9. frown
10. slap

IV. CONSONANT BLENDS (final)
Directions: Write the last two letters of each word I say.

1. dark
2. last
3. lamp
4. ant
5. wasp
6. part
7. ask
8. stand
9. sharp
10. find

V. CONSONANT DIGRAPHS (initial)
Directions: Write the first two letters of each word I say.

488

**Teaching
Reading in
Today's
Elementary
Schools**

1. then   3. chief
2. shout   4. photo

VI. CONSONANT DIGRAPHS (final)
Directions: Write the last two letters of each word I say.
1. sing   3. dish
2. such   4. cloth

VII. LONG AND SHORT VOWELS
Directions: If the vowel is short as I say a word, write *short* and the vowel. If it is long, write *long* and the vowel.
1. hit   6. red
2. ate   7. hat
3. me   8. cut
4. go   9. hot
5. mule   10. ice

VIII. VOWEL DIGRAPHS AND DIPHTHONGS
Directions: Write the two vowels that go together to form a unit—such as *oo, oi, oy,* and *ou*—in each word I say.
1. taught   5. toy
2. saw   6. cow
3. food   7. book
4. oil   8. out ◄

The results from this type of inventory indicate what kinds of skills individual students need to learn. Using these results, the teacher can help children master those skills by working with them individually or in small groups. He or she may need to clear up misconceptions or review skills that children have studied previously; then students should practice applying the studied skills in new situations.

Generally, a student is considered to have adequate knowledge of a skill if he or she gets 75 percent to 80 percent of the answers correct in a particular category. A teacher might administer the informal phonics inventory in Example 10.1 and find the following information: all of the children got 75 to 80 percent of the answers correct in I, Consonant Sounds (initial) and II, Consonant Sounds (final). One child made only 60 percent in III, Consonant Blends (initial), and another child made just 50 percent in IV, Consonant Blends (final). Four children scored below 75 percent on both V, Consonant Digraphs (initial) and VI, Consonant Digraphs (final); eight children made below 75 percent on VII, Long and Short Vowels; and only three children made 75 percent or more on VIII, Vowel Digraphs and Diphthongs. Using these results, the teacher knows that the two children who scored below 75 percent in skill categories III and IV should receive individualized instruction and be required to complete skill sheets for practice. The students who did not make 75 percent in categories V, VI, and VII should meet with the teacher in special skills groups until they understand the skills. In category VIII, where nearly all of the students missed too many items, the teacher needs to teach most of the class. The three students who have already mastered this last skill should be allowed to work independently during this instructional time.

Teachers should apply this same diagnostic-prescriptive principle to other types of reading instruction as well. They should first make an assessment, next analyze the results to see which students are weak in certain areas, and then plan specific activities to help students reach certain levels of competence in these areas.

Structural Analysis Again, an informal performance checkup through observation is a reliable means of collecting data. The teacher can provide a series of sentences, such as those shown below, and have the child complete them by adding a correct beginning or ending to the word in parentheses.

An umbrella is _____ on a rainy day. (need)

A baby is _____ to drive a car. (able)

Teachers can prepare and administer an informal structural analysis inventory in the same way as a phonics inventory. Consisting of exercises related to prefixes and suffixes, inflectional endings, contractions, compound words, and syllabication and accent, the inventory might resemble the one in Example 10.2.

▶ **EXAMPLE 10.2:** Structural Analysis Inventory

Directions: Write the following parts of the words listed below.

prefix: unable _____
suffix: painful _____
root word: funny _____
contraction for: do not _____
words used in the contraction: we've _____ _____
words forming the compound: pancake _____ _____
words forming the compound: bookcase _____ _____
each syllable: window _____ _____
each syllable: arithmetic _____ _____ _____ _____
each syllable: handle _____ _____ ◀

Dictionary Usage To assess a specific objective or element of instruction related to working with dictionaries, a teacher can give the children a list of unfamiliar words and ask them to look the words up in the dictionary and

490

Teaching
Reading in
Today's
Elementary
Schools

then pronounce them by using information derived from the dictionary. Possible words are

anathematize
bludgeon
chimerical
dishabille
eustachian

The location skills and the pronunciation skills needed to use a dictionary (discussed in Chapters 3 and 7) are important elements to test in ongoing checkups. For example, can the child alphabetize words as to the first, first two, first three letters? Can he or she use guide words as clues to alphabetical position? Can the child use the symbols in the pronunciation key?

A more comprehensive informal inventory of dictionary skills is presented in Example 10.3.

▶ **EXAMPLE 10.3:** Informal Dictionary Inventory

1. Look up the word _____. What are the two guide words found on the page on which you found the word?
2. What does the word _____ mean?
3. In the dictionary, on what page are the pronunciation and meaning of the word _____ found?
4. What synonyms are provided for the term _____?
5. What is the derivation of the word _____?
6. What part of speech is the term _____?
7. What diacritical marks are used in the phonetic spelling of _____?
8. What is the dictionary entry for the word _____?
9. How many syllables does this word have: _____?
10. Which syllable of _____ receives a secondary emphasis?
11. What vowel sounds are given for each accented syllable for the word _____?
12. Which syllable of the word _____ contains a schwa sound? ◀

Comprehension

To measure meaning or comprehension abilities, teachers can ask questions about a passage that the child has read silently.

1. Literal—Ask identification questions, such as *who, what, when, where, how many.*
2. Interpretive—Ask explanatory questions, such as *how, why.*
3. Critical—Ask judgment or evaluation questions.

For more specific assessment of comprehension skills (such as discovering main ideas and specific facts, following sequences of events, drawing conclusions, reacting to mood, and the like), prepare an informal comprehension inventory by providing the child with passages to read and questions to answer. Teachers might use appropriately leveled or sequenced sets of materials, such as Richard Boning's series (1985), which covers the following nine skills, providing passages and questions of varying difficulty:

1. locating the answer
2. drawing conclusions
3. following directions
4. getting the main idea
5. detecting the sequence
6. getting the facts
7. using the context
8. working with sounds
9. making inferences.

In a day-to-day situation, accomplish informal assessment of comprehension through questions like the following:

1. What is the main idea of the third paragraph on page 150?
2. Read pages 88 through 91. What are the events that lead to finding the lost dog?

Study Skills

Study skills, such as the ability to use tables of contents and indexes; to locate and use basic reference materials; and to read maps, globes, tables, charts, and graphs, may be assessed directly when students are using such materials. Examination of oral and written reports will reveal strengths and weaknesses in students' abilities to organize, summarize, outline, and take notes.

Informal exercises that require children to use actual reference sources are also informative (for examples, see Chapter 7). Teachers might use the following means to prepare sample test items.

1. Parts of textbooks—Prepare questions that require children to make use of different aids in their textbooks, such as tables of contents, glossaries, and appendices.
2. Interpretation of graphic aids—Prepare questions related to examples from the students' textbooks.
3. Reference materials—Develop questions designed to determine if children know various reference sources and how to use them.

492

Teaching
Reading in
Today's
Elementary
Schools

4. Outlining and note-taking—Using a passage from a content area textbook, ask children to read and then outline it, giving a certain number of main ideas and subtopics.
5. Flexibility of rate—Use selections with different directions, such as "Skim to remember the main ideas of the author," "Scan to find the answers to these three questions in the selection," and the like.

In assessing the ability to adjust reading rate during silent reading, teachers should observe and provide exercises to answer the following questions: What are the pupil's rates of speed in reading various materials for various purposes? Is the reading speed appropriate to the purpose for reading? Does the pupil vary the rate according to the difficulty of the material? Does the pupil insist on comprehending what he or she reads?

✔ Self-Check: Objective 1
Prepare one "checkup" exercise for each of these word recognition skills: context clues, phonic analysis, structural analysis, and dictionary usage. Do the same for a comprehension and a study skill. (See Self-Improvement Opportunity 1.)

Oral Skills

Teachers often ask children to read orally in order to determine the extent of their sight vocabularies and their methods of deciphering unfamiliar words. When they use oral reading for this purpose, they should conduct the session on a one-to-one basis with the pupil, rather than publicly. This is the only situation for oral reading in which students should not do any prior silent reading, for the teacher needs to see the child's initial approach to words in order to gain useful information. A method for marking children's errors is offered later in this chapter in the section on informal reading inventories.

Teachers working with beginning readers will want to use oral reading much more frequently than teachers of more mature readers will, since the processes by which beginning readers attack unfamiliar words should be monitored daily so that teachers can offer appropriate skills instruction. They will also need to hear beginners read aloud in order to help them develop the ability to read in thought units. In addition, oral reading is an ego-satisfying experience for beginning readers, who are eager to read aloud to prove their ability to perform adequately.

Oral reading also provides the teacher with the opportunity to evaluate a child's oral reading fluency and expertise. For this purpose, silent reading should precede oral reading. Example 10.4 is a sample checklist of oral reading behaviors that teachers can consult when evaluating children's oral reading skills. Teachers may wish to make a check to indicate an acceptable level of proficiency, or they may want to rank the level of skill proficiency by using numbers (5 for high and 1 for low).

► **EXAMPLE 10.4:** Oral Reading Checklist

1. _____ Reads with appropriate expression and intonation.
2. _____ Reads by phrases and thought units, not word by word.
3. _____ Pauses for commas.
4. _____ Responds to periods, question marks, and exclamation points.
5. _____ Changes tone of voice to indicate different speakers if reading dialogue.
6. _____ Pronounces words distinctly.
7. _____ Reads words correctly.
8. _____ Does not repeat words.
9. _____ Seems to enjoy reading aloud.
10. _____ Reads at an appropriate rate. ◄

Literary Interests

An observant teacher who takes time to be a sensitive and yet critical evaluator of each child's progress is probably the best judge of the quality of a child's reaction to literature. The following questions will help the teacher in the evaluation process. Are the children

1. growing in appreciation of good literature? How do you know?
2. making good use of time in the library and in free reading of books and periodicals?
3. enjoying storytelling, reading aloud, choral reading, and creative drama?
4. getting to know themselves better through literature?
5. increasing understanding of their own and other cultures through knowledge of the contributions of their own people and people of other lands?
6. becoming sensitive to sounds, rhythms, moods, and feelings as displayed in prose and poetry?
7. maturing in awareness of the structure and forms of literature?
8. enjoying dictating stories, reading aloud to each other, exchanging books with friends?

Teachers can gain answers to these questions through spontaneous remarks by the child (for example, "Do you know any other good books about space travel?"); through directed conversation with the class (for example, "What books would you like to add to our classroom library?"); and during individual conferences, when the children have an opportunity to describe books they like and dislike.

Within every school day countless opportunities are available for obtaining information: listening to conversations between children, observing their creative activities, studying their library circulation records, conferring with parents, and the like. Time spent looking through and discussing various books in the library with a child will provide the teacher with great insight into the child's reactions.

494

Teaching
Reading in
Today's
Elementary
Schools

One excellent device for showing changes in literary taste over a period of time is a cumulative reading record, where children record each book they read, giving the author, title, kind of book, date of report, and a brief statement of how well they liked the book. Gradually, the children can tell more about what they liked and what they disliked about a particular book.

Another device is a *personal reading record,* maintained separately by (or for) each child. It classifies reading selections by topics such as poetry, fantasy, adventure or mystery, myths and folklore, animals (or more specifically, for example, horses and dogs), biography, other lands, sports, and the like. By focusing on the types of literature that the children read, teachers may encourage them to read about new topics and to expand their reading interests.

✔ Self-Check: Objective 2

Describe ways in which to assess development of literary interests. (See Self-Improvement Opportunity 9.)

Informal Assessment Procedures

Observation

It has long been recognized that observing a student's work is a good way to assess his or her achievement. The value of this way of obtaining information is evidenced by the fact that the competent teacher, after working with a class for several months, can select with remarkable accuracy the pupils who will make high scores on achievement tests.

Test scores may give teachers useful information about children's reading skills, but they provide little help in the moment-to-moment decision making that occurs throughout the school day (Johnston, 1987). Based on informal observations and hunches, teachers modify instructional strategies, clarify explanations, give individual help, use a variety of motivational techniques, adjust classroom management techniques, and provide reinforcement as needed.

Since much student assessment occurs informally, teachers need to interpret their observations with insight and accuracy. Johnston (1987) suggests several characteristics of teachers who successfully evaluate students' literacy development. Expert evaluators recognize patterns of behavior and understand how reading and writing processes develop. For instance, they notice that one child is unable to make reasonable predictions or that another uses invented spellings well. Good observers keep records, file them, and use them to understand literacy growth. Observant teachers also listen attentively and perceptively, both at scheduled conferences and during each day. Good observers evaluate as they teach, and they accept the responsibility for assessing children's needs and responding to them, instead of relying only on test data.

Informal observation of a student's work affords the teacher a valuable opportunity
to assess learning and achievement.   (© Paul Fortin/Stock, Boston)

Every day the teacher receives numerous clues related to reading performance levels. For example, as children perform in an oral reading activity,
the alert teacher can jot down notes on their ability to work with initial and
final consonants, initial and final blends, vowel sounds, syllables, compound
words, inflectional endings, prefixes and suffixes, possessives and contractions. If pupils miss words like *there, what,* and *were,* they may need more
help with difficult sight words. If they miss words like *car, hard,* and *burn,*
perhaps they need to do more work with the principle of the vowel sound
when followed by *r.* The teacher can make mental notes of how well pupils
handle picture clues, word-form clues, and various types of context clues, as
well as of how well they select meanings suitable to context. When children
read orally, the teacher has the opportunity to observe rate of reading,
phrasing, and intonation. When they read silently, the teacher can observe
reading skills through asking questions and leading discussions. To check
meaning vocabulary and level of concept development, the teacher can seek
answers to these questions:

1. Do students grasp the main and supporting ideas of a selection? Do they
   know why the main ideas are important? Do their note-taking and
   outlining indicate a grasp of how the author organizes information?
2. Can students follow precise directions given in print?
3. Can they relate ideas from various sources?

496

Teaching
Reading in
Today's
Elementary
Schools

Content area instruction offers many occasions for observing pupils at work, for detecting their grasp of special vocabularies, for checking their ability to use specialized references, and for noting their ability to adjust to different thought patterns. The teacher can think:

1. How do students attack reading tasks in social studies, mathematics, and science textbooks, or in trade books?
2. Do they know how to find information in resource materials?
3. Are they learning to read in different ways for different purposes?

To detect skill in interpretive, creative, and critical reading, the teacher can ask if students

1. look below the surface, reading between the lines and thinking as they read.
2. react actively to the material.
3. read for implied meanings, using given facts to derive fresh meanings.
4. go beyond the stated facts.
5. sense hidden meanings.
6. call sensory imagery into play and read with sensitivity and appreciation of the situation.
7. detect the author's possible bias.
8. judge and compare materials critically, evaluating the logic of the selection and recognizing propaganda techniques.

In terms of emotional response to reading, questions such as the following should be in the mind of the teacher.

1. Are the children eager to participate in reading activities and interested in finding information in books? Do they like to read orally and to listen to others, and do they enjoy choral reading of poetry or dramatization of a story? Do they use books in free-time periods?
2. What are the children's favorite books, magazines, and newspapers? What titles are they checking out from the school and public libraries?

Even though it might not be easy to record the information gathered in day-by-day observation, a certain amount of record-keeping is highly desirable. Teachers can increase the depth and accuracy of their observations by using structured checklists of basic reading skills or characteristics of literacy development. (See Example 10.5 for a sample checklist of literacy development.) To file checklists and other information on students, some teachers keep a folder for each pupil and place material in it every two or three weeks, or each time they note something special. Samples of the student's work that include teacher's explanations or supplementary notes, special notes on the student's performance, and a general statement on a student's daily work during a report period are typical. Other valuable materials for the folder include samples that illustrate a student's skill on a particular reading task.

▶ **EXAMPLE 10.5:** Literacy Observation Checklist

Child's name _____ Teacher's name _____

Place a check beside each characteristic that the child exhibits.

Characteristic	Date	Date	Date
1. Uses variety of comprehension strategies.	____	____	____
2. Expresses interest in reading and writing.	____	____	____
3. Reads voluntarily.	____	____	____
4. Applies word recognition skills effectively.	____	____	____
5. Writes coherently.	____	____	____
6. Reads aloud fluently.	____	____	____
7. Expresses ideas well orally.	____	____	____
8. Listens attentively.	____	____	____
9. Enjoys listening to stories.	____	____	____
10. Asks sensible questions.	____	____	____
11. Makes reasonable predictions.	____	____	____
12. Evaluates and monitors own work.	____	____	____
13. Works well independently.	____	____	____
14. Self-corrects errors.	____	____	____
15. Shows willingness to take risks.	____	____	____	◀

Self-Appraisal

Students who display metacognition are aware of how they learn and of their personal strengths and weaknesses in relation to specific learning tasks. They ask themselves questions in order to assess the difficulty of the assignment, the learning strategies they might use, any potential problems, and their likelihood of success. While reading or studying, their self-questioning might proceed as follows:

1. Do I understand exactly what I am supposed to do for this assignment?
2. What am I trying to learn?
3. What do I already know about this subject that will help me understand what I read?
4. What is the most efficient way for me to learn this material?
5. What parts of this chapter may give me problems?
6. What can I do so that I will understand the hard parts?
7. Now that I am finished reading, do I understand what I read?

Students who learn to monitor their reading and studying through generating their own questions are usually more successful than other students (Babbs and Moe, 1983; Baker and Brown, 1984; and Cohen, 1983).

498

Teaching
Reading in
Today's
Elementary
Schools

The self-appraisal form in Example 10.6 is designed primarily for intermediate and middle-school children. It enables them to assess their competency in various reading skills and recognize areas of strength or weakness. Teachers can use the results to understand students' perceptions of their own needs and plan appropriate instruction.

▶ **EXAMPLE 10.6:** Self-Check Exercise

Directions: Read the following sentences and put a number beside each one.

Put 1 beside the sentence if it is nearly always true.
Put 2 beside the sentence if it is sometimes true.
Put 3 beside the sentence if it is hardly ever true.

———— I understand what I read.
———— I can find the main idea of a paragraph.
———— I think about what I read and what it really means to me.
———— I can "read between the lines" and understand what the author is trying to say.
———— I think about what I already know about the subject as I read.
———— I can figure out new words by reading the rest of the sentence.
———— I can figure out new words by "sounding them out."
———— I can use a dictionary to figure out how to pronounce new words.
———— I can use a dictionary to find word meanings.
———— I know how to find information in the library.
———— I can find books I like to read in the library.
———— I can read aloud easily and with expression.
———— I know what is important to learn in my textbooks.
———— I know how to use the indexes in my books.
———— I know how to study for a test.
———— I ask myself questions as I read to make sure I understand.   ◀

Basal Reader Tests

Basal reader systems usually include tests to be used for determining how well pupils have learned the content of a specific unit of instruction. They are specific to each reader, and norms are ordinarily not supplied. Because basal reader tests help teachers determine if the children have actually learned the content of a specific unit, they can be valuable in the assessment program. They can help the teacher decide who needs corrective/remedial instruction, who can be advanced at the usual pace, and who might be somewhat accelerated.

Since these tests are generally given immediately following a unit of instruction and cover the basic objectives of that unit, they tend to be somewhat easy. They do detect the problems of children who have not achieved well in a particular unit, but often provide inadequate assessments of the very high achievers.

In addition, many basal reader programs have tests built into their workbooks. Even though these tests are limited to specific skills, they can serve some diagnostic purposes. By analyzing a child's workbook, a teacher will find more insights into the types of problems the child might have.

Graded Word Lists

The San Diego Quick Assessment is a graded word list that teachers can use to determine reading levels and identify errors in word analysis. They can apply the results to grouping pupils or to selecting appropriate reading materials. To administer this instrument, they should follow the steps below.

·1. Type each list of ten words (see Table 10.1) on individual index cards.
2. Begin with a card on a level at least two years below the student's grade level.
3. Ask the student to read the words aloud. If he or she misreads any words on the initial list, go back to easier lists until the child makes no errors.

TABLE 10.1   "San Diego Quick Assessment" Graded Word List (Partial List)

Preprimer	Primer	Grade 1	Grade 2
see	you	road	our
play	come	live	please
me	not	thank	myself
at	with	when	town
run	jump	bigger	early
go	help	how	send
and	is	always	wide
look	work	night	believe
can	are	spring	quietly
here	this	today	carefully

Grade 3	Grade 4	Grade 5	Grade 6
city	decided	scanty	bridge
middle	served	certainly	commercial
moment	amazed	develop	abolish
frightened	silent	considered	trucker
exclaimed	wrecked	discussed	apparatus
several	improved	behaved	elementary
lonely	certainly	splendid	comment
drew	entered	acquainted	necessity
since	realized	escaped	gallery
straight	interrupted	grim	relatively

Source: M. LaPray and R. Ross, "The Graded Word List: A Quick Gauge of Reading Ability." *Journal of Reading* 12 (January 1969): 305–307. Reprinted with permission of the authors and the International Reading Association.

500

Teaching
Reading in
Today's
Elementary
Schools

4. Encourage the student to attempt to read unknown words aloud so that you can determine the techniques he or she is using for word identification.
5. Have the child read lists from increasingly higher levels until he or she misses at least three words.

If the reader misses no more than one out of ten words, he is at an independent reading level. If he makes two errors on a list, he is at the instructional level; and if he makes three or more errors, reading material at this level will be too difficult for him. Although these lists are available up to the eleventh-grade level, the lists for the first six grades only are shown in Table 10.1.

To make your own graded word list inventory, compose a list of words from the glossaries of basal readers (choose about twenty words randomly from each level, preprimer through sixth reader). After you have placed the words on 3″ × 5″ cards, flash them at the rate of one card every two and a half seconds to the child. When the student becomes frustrated, present each word for about five seconds, stopping when the child misses 50 percent or more of the words from one grade level. By carefully recording the child's responses during the longer time presentation, you can get some idea of the child's word-attack skills. (Graded word lists do not produce as accurate an estimate of reading levels as teachers can obtain from an informal reading inventory, as described in the next section, because they check only word recognition, not comprehension.) Teachers can develop an informal check for sight vocabulary (word recognition within five seconds), of course, from any basic sight word list.[1]

✔ Self-Check: Objective 3
Cite procedures for administering a graded word list to determine reading levels.
(See Self-Improvement Opportunity 3.)

Informal Reading Inventory

Teachers administer informal reading inventories (IRIs) to get a general idea of a child's strengths and weaknesses in word recognition and comprehension. IRIs help teachers identify specific types of word recognition and comprehension errors so that they can use this information to plan appropriate instruction.

---

[1] Four basic sight word lists are the Dolch word list, found in Edward Dolch, *A Manual for Remedial Reading* (Champaign, Ill.: Garrard, 1945), p. 29; "Instant Words," found in Edward B. Fry, *Reading Instruction for Classroom and Clinic* (New York: McGraw-Hill, 1972), pp. 58–63; "Kucera-Francis Corpus of 220 Service Words," found in Dale D. Johnson, "The Dolch List Reexamined," *The Reading Teacher* 24 (February, 1971): 449–57; and "Sight Words for the Computer Age: An Essential Word List," found in Lois G. Dreyer, Karen R. Futtersak, and Ann E. Boehm, *The Reading Teacher* 39 (October, 1985): 12–17.

Once a child's instructional level for word recognition has been established from a word list, the teacher can use an informal reading inventory to find out the child's ability to read words in context and to use comprehension skills. An IRI can indicate a child's

1. instructional level (that is, the reading level of the material the child will use with teacher guidance).
2. independent reading level (level to be read "on his or her own").
3. frustration level (level that thwarts or baffles).
4. capacity level (potential reading level).

Four steps are involved in devising an informal reading inventory to establish a child's reading levels.

1. Selection of a standard basal series
   a. Use any series that goes from preprimer to the sixth grade or above.
   b. Choose materials that the child has not previously used.
2. Selection of passages from the basal reading series
   a. Choose a selection that makes a complete story.
   b. Find selections of about these lengths:
      preprimer–grade 1: approximately 75 words
      grade 2: 100 words
      grade 3: 125 words
      grade 4: 150 words
      grade 5: 175 words
      grade 6 and above: 200 words
   c. Choose two selections at each level; plan to use one for oral reading and one for silent reading. Take the selections from the middle of each book.
3. Questioning
   a. Develop five to ten questions for each selection at each level.
   b. Include at least one of each type of question: main idea, detail, vocabulary, sequence, and inference.
4. Construction
   a. Cut out the selections and mount them on a hard backing.
   b. Put the questions on separate cards.
   c. Have a duplicate copy of the oral reading passage for marking purposes.
   d. Make a checklist for recording types of errors, reading levels, and observations. (See Example 10.8 for a guide.)

The oral reading sequence in an informal reading inventory should begin on the level at which the child achieved 100 percent in the word recognition flash presentation. During this part, the teacher should supply words when the child hesitates for more than five seconds. Many teachers have found it helpful to use a simple system like the following for marking the oral reading errors of pupils on reading inventories.

502

Teaching
Reading in
Today's
Elementary
Schools

Error	*Marking*
(a) unknown word supplied by teacher	place TP above unknown word (teacher pronounces)
(b) word or word part mispronounced	cross out mispronunciation; indicate given pronunciation above word
(c) omitted word or words	circle omission
(d) insertion of new word	place caret (∧) and word where insertion was made
(e) reversals of word order or word parts	use reversal mark (∿) as follows: did⁀He
(f) repetitions	use wavy line, as the boy ran̰
(g) self-correction	place C beside error that was self-corrected
(h) substitution	cross out omitted word; write substituted word above it

Teachers may mark ignored punctuation marks and spontaneous corrections, but some authorities suggest that these should not be scored as errors. Mispronounced proper names and differences due to dialect should also not be counted as errors. Some teachers have found it effective to tape-record a student's oral reading and replay the tape to note errors in performance.

After the oral reading, the teacher asks questions about the selection; then the child reads the silent reading part and is asked questions about that selection. When the child falls below 90 percent in word recognition, achieves less than 50 percent in comprehension (answers fewer than 50 percent of the questions correctly), or appears frustrated, he or she should not be asked to read at a higher level. Material read silently may be reread orally and scores compared with earlier oral reading. The teacher may also time the silent reading and get some indication of word-per-minute reading rate. After the child reaches *frustration* level material, the examiner should read aloud one selection at each succeedingly higher level and ask questions about each selection until the child is unable to answer 75 percent of the questions on the material.

Material is written at a child's *independent* reading level when he or she reads it without tension, correctly pronounces ninety-nine words in a hundred (99 percent correct), and correctly responds to at least 90 percent of the questions (for example, answers nine of ten questions). The material from which the child correctly pronounces 85 percent (in grades one and two) or 95 percent (in grades three and above) of the words and correctly answers at least 75 percent of the questions is roughly at the child's *instructional* level, the level at which teaching may effectively take place.

If a student needs help on more than one word out of ten (90 percent) or responds correctly to fewer than 50 percent of the questions, the material is too advanced and at the frustration level. After the level of frustration has been reached, the teacher should read aloud higher levels of material to the child until he or she reaches the highest reading level for which the child can correctly answer 75 percent of the comprehension questions. The highest level achieved indicates the child's probable *capacity* (potential reading) level. A reading capacity level is the highest level at which a child can understand the ideas and concepts in the material that is read to him or her. For example, if a child's instructional reading level is high second grade and his or her capacity, or *potential,* level is fourth grade, that child has the ability to read better than he or she is now doing.

Various writers in the field of reading suggest using slightly different percentages for establishing a reader's independent, instructional, frustration, and capacity levels. Betts developed criteria for evaluating oral reading behaviors that have been used as standards for determining reading levels for several decades, but Powell recommended modifying Betts's criteria to give consideration to grade level placement (Allington, 1984). Powell's research revealed that older children were likely to be more accurate in their oral reading than younger ones. The list below shows how to evaluate the scores on an informal reading inventory.

Level	Word Recognition		Comprehension
Independent	99 percent or higher	and	90 percent or higher
Instructional	85 percent or higher (gr. 1–2) and 95 percent or higher (gr. 3–above)	and	75 percent or higher
Frustration	below 90 percent	or	below 50 percent
Capacity	————		75 percent or higher

The percentages of correct answers do not always give clear-cut information. For instance, if the word recognition score of a fourth grader falls between 90 and 95 percent, the reading material might be at either the frustration or the instructional level. One way to decide which level reflects the student's actual ability is to observe the types of errors he or she makes. If errors seem to occur without loss of meaning, are the result of nervousness or carelessness, or are the result of dialect differences, the score may reflect the instructional level. On the other hand, if the errors interfere with the meaning and the miscalled words bear little or no resemblance to the actual words, the reading material is probably at the student's frustration level. Another type of confusion results when the pupil's scores indicate that the reading material is at the instructional level for word recognition but at the frustration level for comprehension. Since comprehension is the ultimate goal of reading, the comprehension score is more important. But in any case, the percentages are only an estimate of a reader's abilities, and decisions about placement should also be influenced by other factors, such as the child's attitude toward reading, past performance, and determination. A good guideline to follow when a student's scores are borderline or contradictory is to give the pupil the lower-level material to ensure success.

504

Teaching
Reading in
Today's
Elementary
Schools

Teachers may make their own informal reading inventories by following the procedure suggested earlier in this section, or they may use commercially prepared inventories. Example 10.7 shows a sample reading selection with comprehension questions and scoring aid from a commercial IRI. Example 10.8 gives a summary sheet for recording a student's skill difficulties and reading levels from the same inventory. A list of sources of commercially prepared informal reading inventories follows.

Ekwall, Eldon E. *Ekwall Reading Inventory.* 2nd ed. Boston: Allyn and Bacon, 1985.

Jacobs, H. Donald, and L. W. Searfoss. *Diagnostic Reading Inventory.* 2nd ed. Dubuque, Iowa: Kendall/Hunt, 1979.

Johns, Jerry L. *Basic Reading Inventory—Preprimer to Grade Eight.* 2nd ed. Dubuque, Iowa: Kendall/Hunt, 1981.

Roe, Betty D. *Burns/Roe Informal Reading Inventory.* 2nd ed. Boston: Houghton Mifflin, 1985.

Silvaroli, Nicholas J. *Classroom Reading Inventory.* 5th ed. Dubuque, Iowa: William C. Brown, 1986.

Woods, Mary Lynn, and Alden J. Moe. *Analytical Reading Inventory.* 3rd ed. Columbus, Ohio: Charles E. Merrill, 1985.

In a review of commercial informal reading inventories, Jongsma and Jongsma (1981) made several recommendations for selection and use. The teacher should choose an inventory that corresponds as closely as possible to the instructional materials being used in the classroom and should agree with what the inventory considers to be an error. By noting the types of questions asked, the number of questions, and how scoring is handled, the teacher can examine the means of evaluating comprehension. The teacher should also give attention to the clarity of instructions for administering, scoring, and interpreting the inventory. Use of alternate forms for pre- and posttesting is questionable because forms may not actually be equivalent.

The *Group Assessment in Reading: Classroom Teacher's Handbook* by Edna Warncke and Dorothy Shipman (Prentice-Hall, 1984) is designed to replace individual reading inventories by providing a group assessment of reading ability for grades one through twelve. It gives information related to comprehension skills, study skills, reading interests, and reading levels.

Teachers should realize that the readability, or difficulty, of the text is not the only factor that affects a child's performance. According to Caldwell (1985), prior knowledge of the topic enables the child to read faster, recall and retain more information, and make more valid inferences. Readers also generally perform better with narrative text than expository text and with well-written text that has a sense of wholeness than with poorly written, isolated segments. When using IRIs to place children in groups, teachers should consider these factors. If the text is familiar and the material well written, children may appear to read at higher levels than they would normally read.

▶ **EXAMPLE 10.7:** Reading Selection and Questions from an Informal Reading Inventory

☆5 PASSAGE ———— FORM A ———— TEACHER 5☆

MOTIVATIONAL STATEMENT: Read this story to find out about a boy named Pete and a problem that he has.

"I see in the papers that the world is coming to an end," said Mr. Peters, reading the newspaper at the breakfast table. He chuckled.

Pete swallowed his bit of toast. "When?" he said.

His mother looked at his father and frowned, warningly.

"Not this afternoon," she said hastily to Pete.

Mr. Peters shrugged. "It doesn't say this afternoon," he agreed.

Pete munched his crisp cereal thoughtfully. If it wasn't this afternoon it wouldn't do him much good, he thought. For the test would be this afternoon—the test the substitute teacher had prepared for them.

Thinking about the test. Pete plopped into his seat at school with an unnecessary plunk. Miss Dingley frowned at him.

Source: Molly Cone. *Mishmash and the Substitute Teacher* (Boston, Mass. Houghton Mifflin Company, 1963)

[Note: Do not count as a miscue mispronunciation of the name Dingley. You may pronounce this word for the student if needed.]

COMPREHENSION QUESTIONS

_____ main idea

1. What would be a good title for this story? (Pete and the Test; Pete Worries About the Test)

_____ sequence

2. Name, in order, the two places Pete was in the story. (at home, at school)

SCORING AID	
WORD RECOGNITION	
%–MISCUES	
99–1	
95–6	
90–12	
85–17	
COMPREHENSION	
%–ERRORS	
100–0	
90–1	
80–2	
70–3	
60–4	
50–5	
40–6	
30–7	
20–8	
10–9	
0–10	

115 WORDS

WPM

6960

_____ inference

3. Did Mr. Peters believe what he read about the world coming to an end? (no) What did the story say that caused you to answer that way? (He chuckled after he read it.)

_____ vocabulary

4. What does the word "chuckled" mean? (laughed quietly)

_____ inference

5. Did Pete believe that the world might come to an end? (yes) What did the story say that caused you to answer that way? (He asked when it would end and decided it wouldn't help him avoid his test.)

_____ inference

6. Did Pete's mother approve of his father telling him what the newspaper said? (no) What did the story say that caused you to answer that way? (She frowned at Pete's father when he said it.)

_____ vocabulary

7. What does the word "shrugged" mean? (moved his shoulders up) [Allow students to demonstrate if they wish.]

_____ vocabulary

8. What does the word "munched" mean? (chewed with a crunching sound)

_____ detail

9. Who had prepared the test? (the substitute teacher, Miss Dingley)

_____ cause and effect/ inference

10. Why did Miss Dingley frown at Pete? (He made a noise as he plopped into his seat.)

Source: Story passage is from Molly Cone, *Mishmash and the Substitute Teacher,* Boston: Houghton Mifflin Company, 1963. In Betty D. Roe, *Burns/Roe Informal Reading Inventory,* 2nd ed. Boston: Houghton Mifflin Company, 1985. ◀

506

Teaching
Reading in
Today's
Elementary
Schools

▶ **EXAMPLE 10.8:** Summary Sheet from an Informal Reading Inventory

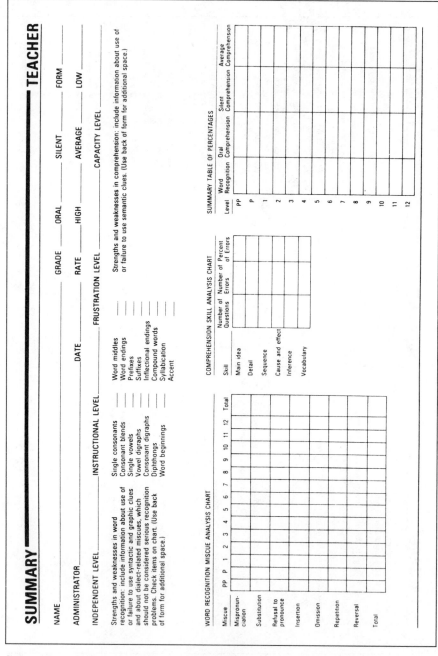

Source: Betty D. Roe, *Burns/Roe Informal Reading Inventory*, 2nd ed. Boston: Houghton Mifflin, 1985. ◀

It is important to remember that the result of an informal reading inventory is an *estimate* of a reader's abilities. The percentages achieved by the child are an important indication of levels of performance, but the teacher's observations of the child taking the test are equally important.

✔ Self-Check: Objective 4
Prepare a chart or diagram showing the procedures for constructing and interpreting an IRI.
(See Self-Improvement Opportunities 4 and 5.)

Miscue Analysis

Knowing the number of errors, or miscues, that a child makes on an IRI is not as helpful for diagnosing reading difficulties as recognizing patterns or types of miscues. Teachers should consider whether miscalled words indicate lack of knowledge about phonics or structural analysis, show inability to use context, reveal limited sight word knowledge, result from dialectal differences, or suggest some other type of difficulty. While listening to a child read, a teacher must therefore evaluate the significance of different miscues. A not very proficient reader might conceivably read "Have a good time" as "What a green toy," while a more proficient reader might read "He had a spot of dirt over his eye" as "He had a spot of dirt above his eye" (Goodman, 1970). Since different error types signify different things, educators often use the term "reading miscue analysis" to describe the interpretation of a child's oral reading performance. The child who reads "The boys are playing" as "The boys is playing" may be a speaker of a nonstandard dialect and may be using his or her decoding ability to translate the printed text to meaning. While this miscue does not interfere with meaning, many miscues do reflect problems.

Goodman and Burke have suggested a series of questions that teachers can use to identify types of miscues. The possible significance of each kind of miscue is indicated in the righthand column below.

Question	*Possible Significance*
1. Is a dialect variation involved in the miscue?	A "yes" answer may indicate that the child has gained enough proficiency in reading to use oral language competency.
2. Is a shift in intonation involved in the miscue?	A "yes" answer may suggest that the child has anticipated an unpredictable structure or is unfamiliar with the author's language structure.
3. How much does the miscue look like what was expected?	A high degree of similarity may indicate overuse of decoding in addition to lack of familiarity with the word in this context or material.

508

Teaching
Reading in
Today's
Elementary
Schools

Question	*Possible Significance*
4. How much does the miscue sound like what was expected?	High similarity may indicate overuse of decoding and lack of familiarity with the word used.
5. Is the grammatical function of the miscue the same as the grammatical function of the word in the text (e.g., noun substituted for noun)?	A "yes" answer may indicate that the child probably is reading with comprehension and is aware of the grammatical function of the substitution.
6. Is the miscue corrected?	Self-correction probably indicates that the child comprehends the reading material but anticipated an alternate structure to that of the author.
7. Does the miscue occur in a structure which is grammatically acceptable?	A "yes" answer suggests that the child is sufficiently proficient in reading to use oral language communication competency.
8. Does the miscue occur in a structure which is semantically acceptable?	A "yes" answer suggests the same possibility as 7 and indicates that the child is predicting the author's intended meaning.
9. Does the miscue result in a change of meaning?	A "yes" answer may indicate that the child is trying to read ideas in the text that are unfamiliar.

Source: Yetta M. Goodman and Carolyn L. Burke. *Reading Miscue Inventory, Manual, and Procedure for Diagnosis and Evaluation* (New York: Macmillan, 1972). Copyright © 1972 by Yetta M. Goodman and Carolyn L. Burke. Reprinted with permission.

To conduct miscue analysis, a teacher has a student read orally while the teacher marks any miscues on a copy of the selection. The marking system may be the same as recommended earlier in this chapter.

1. Choose a selection the child hasn't read, one somewhat ahead of the reader's current level.
2. Allow time for the child to do her best. Don't supply words, correct miscues, or answer requests for help. Just say, "Do the best you can."
3. Record miscues on the teacher's copy of the selection.
4. Use questions following the selection to check comprehension or ask the child to tell it in her own words.
5. In studying the child's reading record, remember that the number of miscues is less important than what they show about her reading.

In studying the miscues, the teacher should check for particular items such as:

1. Is the miscue a result of the reader's dialect? If he says *foe* for *four*, he may be simply using a familiar pronunciation that does not affect meaning.
2. Does the miscue change the meaning? If he says *dismal* for *dismiss*, the meaning is likely changed and the substitution wouldn't make sense.
3. Does the reader self-correct? If he says a word that doesn't make sense but self-corrects, he is trying to make sense of reading.
4. Is he using syntactic cues? If he says *run* for *chase*, he still shows some use of syntactic cues, but if he says *boy* for *beautiful*, he is likely losing the syntactic pattern.
5. Is he using graphic cues? Comparing the sounds and spellings of miscues and expected words in substitutions will reveal how a reader is using graphic cues. Examples of such miscues include *house* for *horse*, *running* for *run*, *is* for *it*, and *dogs* for *dog*.

An easy way to check the quantity and quality of miscues is to do the following:

Total miscues   ____
Subtract dialect miscues   ____
                        ____ Total nondialectal miscues
Subtract all corrected miscues   ____
                        ____ Total uncorrected miscues
Subtract all miscues that do
  not change meaning   ____ Miscues that do not change meaning
                        ____ Significant miscues

An extension of miscue analysis is the probe technique suggested by Barr and Sadow (1985). When teachers are uncertain about the meaning of their evaluation, they may wish to "probe," or further analyze, one or more areas (Barr and Sadow, 1985). The probe technique generally involves working with children individually to find out why they made mistakes. The teacher might question a child about an error, ask her to look at the word again, provide additional clues, and analyze her responses in order to determine why she was having difficulty. The teacher might continue working with her on other errors to further evaluate her error patterns. A teacher can use the probe technique for analyzing a child's ability to use comprehension strategies by having her reread a passage and asking her leading questions about what she reads until she is able to read it with understanding.

✔ Self-Check: Objective 5
What are nine statements you can make about the following situation? (Refer to list of nine questions regarding miscues.)
Printed sentence: At the zoo, I had my first view of a zebra.
Child reads as: At the zoo, I heard my first view of a zebra.
(See Self-Improvement Opportunities 7 and 8.)

Content Area Procedures

To make a group reading inventory of content material, have children read a passage of 1,000 to 2,000 words from their textbooks and then ask them the following types of questions (Miller, 1978):

1. vocabulary (word meaning, word recognition, synonyms/antonyms, syllabication/accent, affixes).
2. open-ended questions (or questions that do not have a single correct response, as "Would you like to have had some other ending to the passage? If so, why?" or "What other titles could you think of for this selection?" or "For what reasons did you enjoy the passage?"
3. objective questions (or questions related to main idea, significant details, following directions, literal comprehension, interpretive comprehension, critical reading, and so on).

If children can comprehend 75 percent of what they read (answer six out of eight questions), the material can be classified as suitable for instructional purposes. These students' comprehension will increase if the teacher introduces specialized vocabulary words, helps with comprehension, teaches a study method, and provides specific purposes for reading. Of course students have many different reading levels depending upon their interests and the background information that they may possess on any specific topic. Thus, teachers need to apply a group reading inventory for each specific content area.

The informal reading inventory described earlier can be modified to assess content reading skills by

1. choosing sight words that are specialized vocabulary terms from the content area (selected from glossary).
2. using oral and silent reading passages from a graded series of content textbooks.

Content books that children will study should be written on their instructional or independent levels and trade and supplementary books should be on their independent levels. To account for the wide range of reading differences in a classroom, supplementary materials of many types, such as easy textbooks, readable trade books (nonfiction and fiction), and materials especially prepared for poorer readers, are required.

✔ Self-Check: Objective 6
Explain two ways to inventory a child's ability to read content material.
(See Self-Improvement Opportunity 6.)

Cloze Procedure

The cloze procedure may be used as an alternative to the graded silent reading passages of the informal reading inventory. It can help teachers determine independent, instructional, and frustration levels for both narrative and expository material. For instructions on the cloze procedure, see Chapter 8. A commercial cloze inventory is *The De Santi Cloze Reading Inventory* by Roger De Santi (Boston: Allyn and Bacon, 1986).

Computer Procedures

Computers provide interesting and motivational alternatives to traditional testing procedures. Teachers can use them in the following ways to assess students' comprehension and word recognition skills (Johnston, 1983; Schreiner, 1985).

1. Some computer programs automatically place learners in the appropriate branches of programs regarding text, item type, and level of difficulty as determined by the child's initial item performance. In this way diagnosis is continuous because it occurs as students select their answers.
2. Computer games often require students to read and follow directions. The teacher assesses comprehension by noting the child's responses, such as the number of clues a child needs in order to get information from the text on the screen.
3. Two computer programs, "Controlled Flash" (in BASIC for the Atari and the Apple II) and "Speed Flash" (in BASIC for the Atari) offer flash presentation of words, phrases, and brief sentences. The teacher calls on individual students to read them and then evaluates students' word recognition skills.

Teachers can use computers for assessment in several additional ways. On-line testing allows students to work at terminals connected to a computer that analyzes their responses. Sometimes computers are used to scan mark-sensitive answer sheets that students have completed while working with test booklets. The computer also scores the tests, thus freeing the teacher from this task. Software is also available to help teachers modify test items and entire tests, perform test and item analysis, collect and analyze test scores and student grades, record grades for various assignments, and compute final grades (Kubiszyn and Borich, 1987).

The *Computer-Based Reading Assessment Instrument* (Blanchard, 1985) is an informal reading inventory that includes word lists, reading passages, multiple-choice questions, and probe-recall questions and answers for grades one through eight. Teachers can administer this instrument to a group of students to test silent reading comprehension without the use of computers, or they can use the computer-based version for individual testing of students' reading abilities. It is available in both Spanish and English.

Using Informal Measures with Exceptional Children

The use of informal assessment procedures is increasing in the field of special education, where such informal techniques as teacher-made tests and skill checklists are especially helpful when used in conjunction with formal measurement techniques. Teachers utilize these methods for documenting progress toward short-term objectives and annual goals, for developing and reviewing individual educational programs (IEPs), and for evaluating preplacement. They use other types of informal procedures, such as observation and interviews with children and parents, for obtaining information necessary to make decisions about classification and eligibility.

The major advantage of informal assessment is its flexibility, which allows teachers to design it for a special purpose and construct it from materials that are being used for instruction. Information from these informal tests is therefore more instructionally relevant than data from formal tests, although it has the major disadvantage of lack of technical validity and reliability. Because of this technical inadequacy, informal tests must be constructed and interpreted with great care and used along with other types of assessment (Bennett, 1982).

NORM-REFERENCED TESTS

Norm-referenced tests provide objective data about reading achievement, scholastic aptitude, areas of strengths and weaknesses, and so on. Authors of these tests sample large populations of children to determine the appropriateness of test items. They seek to verify the *validity* and *reliability* of test results so that schools can be confident that the tests measure what they are intended to measure and that results will not vary significantly if students take the same test more than once.

Before further discussion of norm-referenced testing instruments, definitions of a few terms are needed:

1. An *achievement test* measures the extent to which a person has "achieved" something, acquired certain information, or mastered certain skills.
2. A *diagnostic test* analyzes and locates specific strengths and weaknesses and sometimes suggests causes.
3. An *intelligence* or *aptitude test* measures general academic abilities or characteristics that indicate potential.
4. A *survey test* measures general achievement in a given area.

A norm-referenced achievement test is valid if it represents a balanced and adequate sampling of the instructional outcomes (knowledge, skills, and so on) that it is intended to cover. Validity is best judged by comparing the test content with the related courses of study, instructional materials, and educational goals. Evidence about validity is generally provided in a test's manual of directions. A careful inspection of the items on the test serves as

a double-check of whether or not the test actually measures what it claims
to measure. Predictive validity refers to the accuracy with which an aptitude
or readiness test indicates future learning success in some area.

Reliability refers to the degree to which a test produces consistent results.
It is usually checked by giving the same test twice to a large group of children.
If each child makes approximately the same score in both situations, the test
is considered to be reliable. On the other hand, if many children make higher
scores in one testing situation than in the other, the test has low reliability.
When measuring the level of achievement of an individual child, teachers
should use only a test of high reliability. A test of low reliability cannot be
very valid; however, high reliability does not insure high validity.

A second method of measuring reliability is to take students' scores on the
odd-numbered items and their scores on the even-numbered items and see
if they are in the same rank order (or if they have a high correlation). Still
another method is to compare one form of a test to a different but equivalent
form.

The most common ways in which results of norm-referenced tests are
expressed are grade equivalents (or grade scores), percentile ranks, and
stanines. A grade equivalent indicates the grade level, in years and months,
for which a given score was the average score in the standardization sample.
For example, if a score of 25 has the grade equivalent of 4.6, then in the
norm group, 25 was the average score of pupils in the sixth month of the
fourth grade. After the test has been standardized, if another pupil in the sixth
month of the fourth grade takes the same test and scores 25 correct, his or
her performance is "at grade level" or average for this grade placement. If he
or she gets 30 right, or a grade equivalent of 5.3, he or she has done as well
as the typical fifth grader in the third month on *that* test. Similarly, a 3.3
grade equivalent for a fourth grader means that the performance is equal to
that of the average student in the third month of the third grade on that test.

Concerned that grade equivalents were being misinterpreted and misused,
the Delegates Assembly of the International Reading Association passed a
resolution in April 1981 to abandon the use of these scores for reporting
performance. They also resolved that test authors and publishers should
eliminate grade-equivalent interpretations from their tests. This action was
taken in part because delegates felt that misuse of grade equivalents was
leading to a misunderstanding of a student's ability and that other information from norm-referenced tests was less likely to be misinterpreted.[2]

Percentile rank (PR) expresses a score in terms of its position within a set
of 100 scores. The PR indicates the percent of scores in a reference group that
is equal to or lower than the given score; therefore, a score ranked in the
fiftieth percentile is equal to or better than the scores of 50 percent of the
people in the reference group.

---

[2] See full statement of resolution in the January 1982 issue of *The Reading Teacher*, p. 464, or
the November 1981 issue of the *Journal of Reading*, p. 112.

514

Teaching
Reading in
Today's
Elementary
Schools

On a stanine scale the scores are divided into nine equal parts, with a score of five being the mean. The following interpretation for stanine scores gives information about a student's relationship to the rest of the group.

stanine 9: higher performance
stanines 7 and 8: above average
stanines 4, 5, and 6: average
stanines 2 and 3: below average
stanine 1: lower performance

Through the use of test norms—ways to express scores in relation to those of a standardization population—teachers can compare one child's score with the scores of other children of similar age and educational experience. It is also possible to determine how a child's performance on one test compares with his or her performance on other tests in a battery, and how it compares to his or her performance on the same test administered at another time. Scores from two different standardized reading tests cannot be easily compared, however, since the tests probably differ in purpose, length, and difficulty. Even the results of the same test administered on successive days may vary, depending on the reliability of the test.

When students read considerably below grade level, teachers should administer out-of-level tests, or tests designed for one grade level but given to students at another level. Students who cannot read achievement tests can only guess at answers, so their scores are not reliable. Testing these students at levels that correspond to their reading ability enables them to do their best work (Gunning, 1982; Smith et al., 1983).

Formal Tests for Beginning Readers

Teachers often administer reading readiness tests at the end of kindergarten and/or the beginning of first grade for the purpose of predicting a child's likelihood of success in reading. These tests frequently measure listening skills, letter recognition, visual-motor coordination, auditory discrimination, and visual discrimination. While reading readiness tests have certain limitations, such as limited samplings of abilities tested and possible dependence upon measures of preschool learning, they can be useful for helping a teacher decide if a child is ready for formal reading instruction.

Many basal reading programs provide teachers with readiness tests designed to measure the skills with which their own programs deal. Such tests are usually criterion-referenced rather than norm-referenced—that is, they measure achievement but do not compare a child's score with the scores of other children, as standardized readiness tests do. A list of some formal readiness tests follows.[3]

---

[3] The appendix to this chapter gives the addresses of the publishers whose tests appear in this chapter.

Clymer-Barrett Readiness Test. Rev. ed. Chapman, Brook and Kent, 1983. Measures basic skills and evaluates general background with the Readiness Survey. (grades K and beginning 1)

CTBS Readiness Test. CTB/McGraw Hill, 1977. Assesses alphabet skills, listening, language, mathematics, visual discrimination, and auditory discrimination. (grades K-0 to 1-3)

Madden, Richard, Eric F. Gardner, and Cathy S. Collins. *Stanford Early School Achievement Test (SESAT).* The Psychological Corporation, 1982. Measures the learning that a child has gathered from home and general preschool activities. (grades K to 1.9)

Moss, Margaret H. *Test of Basic Experiences 2 (TOBE 2)* CTB/McGraw Hill, 1979. Surveys conceptual development of young children in mathematics, language, science, and social studies. Useful in determining the school learning potential of children who show a language or cultural disadvantage on conventional readiness tests. (pre-K to end of grade 1)

Nurss, Joanne R., and Mary E. McGauvran. *Metropolitan Readiness Test.* Rev. ed. The Psychological Corporation, 1976. Assesses auditory memory, rhyming, visual skills, language skills, and copying. (first half of K to beginning grade 1)

Reid, D. Kim, Warne P. Hresko, and Donald D. Hammill. *The Test of Early Reading Ability (TERA).* PRO-ED, 1981. Measures performance in knowledge of alphabet, comprehension, and reading conventions. Includes prereading, readiness, and beginning reading. Useful for screening children with reading problems. (ages 3 to 7)

For a holistic or process-oriented assessment of a young child's literacy development, Clay offers an alternative to traditional readiness tests. According to Goodman's review (1981), Clay's *Concepts about Print Test: Sand* (Exeter, N.H.: Heinemann Educational Books, 1972) and *Concepts About Print Test: Stones* (Exeter, N.H.: Educational Books, 1979) can provide insight into a child's knowledge of written language. The twenty-page booklets used for administering the tests are similar to children's picture storybooks. They enable the teacher to observe how a child responds to print as the teacher reads, to discover what should be taught as the child interacts with the printed page, and to find out what aspects of language the child is learning to control.

✔ Self-Check: Objective 7
On the basis of the descriptions of reading readiness tests given above, choose the one or two that you expect would be most useful for the first-grade teacher.

Norm-Referenced Reading Survey Tests

Reading survey tests can show in a general way how well children are performing in relation to others in the same grade. Through examination of

516

Teaching
Reading in
Today's
Elementary
Schools

the scores of all the class members, the teacher can obtain an indication of the range of reading achievement in the class.

The distribution in the list below shows the reading achievement scores for one fourth-grade class. Examination of this distribution shows that four children are performing below grade level, seventeen at grade level, and seven above grade level, which implies that the teacher must make provisions for individual differences. This information helps the teacher decide how to group children of comparable achievement together. Necessary group adjustments can be made as the teacher works with the students.

Grade Score	Number of Children
7.0–7.9	1
6.0–6.9	2
5.0–5.9	4
4.0–4.9	17
3.0–3.9	3
2.0–2.9	1
	(N = 28)

Teachers should be concerned not only with a student's total achievement score but with subtest scores. Two children may have the same total score but have different reading strengths and weaknesses, as revealed in subtest scores.

	Child A	Child B
Word recognition	2.8	4.5
Word meaning	3.6	2.5
Comprehension	4.1	3.5
Reading achievement score	3.5	3.5

On first analysis, test scores indicate general areas in which students may need more help, but a more careful examination of individual test items and of children's responses to them can often supply a teacher with information about specific reading needs. Since children sometimes make the correct responses for the wrong reasons, including random guessing, the teacher may wish to go over the test items to see if the children can explain how and why they made their responses. Teachers may be able to discern patterns of error by comparing similar test items and responses.

When using norm-referenced tests for making decisions about instructional programs, teachers should also consider the student's academic potential as reported by an aptitude or intelligence test, test-taking ability or test anxiety, and current reading performance in the classroom. Intelligence test scores, despite their limitations, can be used to compare students' academic potential with their actual reading achievement. Observation of test-taking strategies may help teachers identify which students' test scores are invalid due to

Many schools regularly administer norm-referenced reading survey tests; if used properly, the subtest scores from these tests can supply a teacher with information about a reader's strengths and weaknesses.   (© Jean-Claude Lejeune)

unusual stress or failure to attend to the task. Comparing achievement test scores with classroom performance enables teachers to decide whether a child is doing as well as can be expected or should be challenged with more difficult work. By combining all of this information, teachers should be able to make reasonable instructional decisions about appropriate reading materials and programs for students (Baumann and Stevenson, 1982).

Research indicates that children who have practiced taking tests under conditions similar to those used in standardized testing situations perform better on standardized tests (Stewart and Green, 1983). Many children find the atmosphere in a formal testing situation threatening, and they are therefore unable to demonstrate their knowledge. When this happens, results are not valid indicators of the students' reading abilities. Teachers can instruct students in test-taking skills by providing practice in situations that are nearly identical with those that exist during standardized testing. Some suggestions for teaching test-taking skills include the following:

1. Discuss the nature, purpose, rules, and conditions of a formal testing situation well in advance of the actual test.
2. Practice using time limits for children to complete their work.
3. Provide practice materials that match the standardized test format. (Several teachers could work together to produce these materials, which could then be used for several years.)

518

Teaching
Reading in
Today's
Elementary
Schools

4. Establish an atmosphere of serious testing during practice sessions.
5. Avoid threatening children with the importance of doing their best because threats often create anxiety and reduce performance.
6. Discuss any problems that the children had during the practice session afterward.

Representative Norm-Referenced Reading Survey Tests

Biemiller, Andrew. *Biemiller Test of Reading Processes.* Guidance Centre, University of Toronto, 1981. Tests ability to identify letters and words quickly and to use context for facilitating word identification. (grades 2 to 6)

Brown, Virginia L., Donald L. Hammill, and J. Lee Wiederholt. *Test of Reading Comprehension (TORC).* PRO-ED, 1986. Tests knowledge of general vocabulary, syntactic similarities, paragraph reading, and sentence sequencing. (ages 6½ to 17)

MacGinitie, Walter H. *Gates-MacGinitie Reading Tests.* Riverside Publishing Co., 1978. Assesses student progress in reading comprehension and vocabulary development. (See sample Profile Sheet in Example 10.9 for an indication of the content and the recording of results.) (grades 1 to 12)

✔ Self-Check: Objective 8

Suggest three uses of norm-referenced reading survey tests.
(See Self-Improvement Opportunities 10, 11, and 12.)

Other Norm-Referenced Tests

Vision and Hearing Tests

Various screening devices are available to test children's vision and hearing. The *Keystone School Vision Screening Test* uses binocular and stereoscopic slides to check vision, and other types of visual screening tests check such capabilities as visual-motor coordination, figure-ground discrimination, spatial relations, visual memory, and visual closure. The following are examples of visual screening tests.

Allington, Richard L. *Visual Perceptual Skills Inventory.* JoMar Publications, 1981. Screens early educational difficulties and diagnoses learning disabilities. Contains four subtests: visual discrimination accuracy, visual discrimination rate, visual memory, and writing from memory. (grades K to 2)

Frostig, Marianne, in collaboration with D. Welty Lefever, John R. B. Witlesey, and Phyllis Maslow. *Marianne Frostig Developmental Test of Visual Perception.* 3rd ed. Consulting Psychologists Press, 1966. Gives seven scores, including visual-motor coordination, figure-ground discrimination, form constancy, position in space, and spatial relations. (ages 3 to 8)

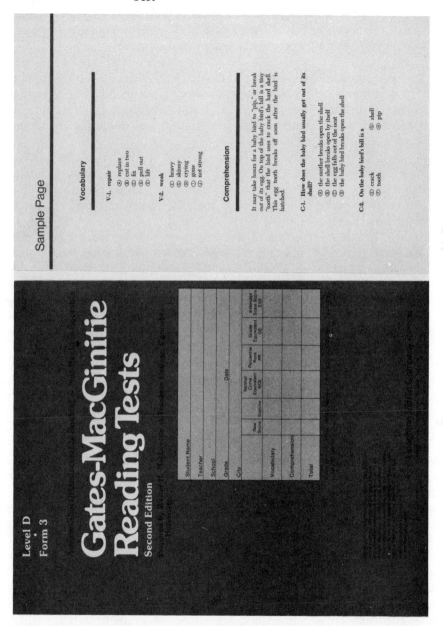

Sample Page

Vocabulary

V-1. repair
- ⓐ replace
- ⓑ cut in two
- ⓒ fix
- ⓓ pull out
- ⓔ lift

V-2. weak
- ⓐ heavy
- ⓑ skinny
- ⓒ crying
- ⓓ gone
- ⓔ not strong

Comprehension

It may take hours for a baby bird to "pip," or break out of its egg. On top of the baby bird's bill is a tiny "tooth" that the bird uses to crack the hard shell. This egg tooth breaks off soon after the bird is hatched.

C-1. How does the baby bird usually get out of its shell?
- ⓐ the mother breaks open the shell
- ⓑ the shell breaks open by itself
- ⓒ the egg falls out of the nest
- ⓓ the baby bird breaks open the shell

C-2. On the baby bird's bill is a
- ⓐ crack   ⓒ shell
- ⓑ tooth   ⓓ pip

Level D
• Form 3

Gates-MacGinitie
Reading Tests

Second Edition

Student Name
Teacher
School
Grade   Date
City

	Raw Score	Stanine	Normal Curve Equivalent NCE	Percentile Rank PR	Grade Equivalent GE	Extended Scale Score ESS
Vocabulary						
Comprehension						
Total						

520

Teaching
Reading in
Today's
Elementary
Schools

Gardner, Morrison F. *Test of Visual-Perceptual Skills (Non-Motor).* Special Child Publications, 1982. Gives comprehensive assessment of visual perception in seven areas, including visual discrimination, visual memory, visual-spatial relationships, visual form constancy, visual sequential memory, visual figure-ground, and visual closure. (ages 4 to 12)

Teachers and clinicians can use audiometers, devices for testing auditory acuity, or commercial screening tests to check students' hearing. Screening tests assess such auditory abilities as recognizing sounds, differentiating among similar sounds, and remembering sounds and sound patterns. Some examples of auditory tests follow.

Fudala, Janet B. *Tree Bee Test of Auditory Discrimination.* Academic Therapy Publications, 1978. Gives scores in eight areas: initial consonants, final consonants, vowels, memory, words, sentences, pairs, and comprehension. (ages 3 and over)

Kimmell, Geraldine M., and Jack Wahl. *Screening Test for Auditory Perception.* Academic Therapy Publications, 1981. Detects weaknesses rather than strengths. Contains six areas related to recognition, discrimination, differentiation, and retention of sounds and sound patterns. (grades 1 to 6)

Lindamood, Charles H., and Patricia C. Lindamood. *Lindamood Auditory Conceptualization Test.* Rev. ed. DLM Teaching Resources, 1979. Gives scores related to isolated sounds in sequence and sounds within a syllable pattern. (preschool and above)

Wepman, Joseph M. *Auditory Discrimination Test.* Western Psychological Services, 1973. Assesses ability to recognize differences between sounds in English speech. Administered individually and orally. (ages 5 to 8)

Achievement Tests

Most schools administer achievement tests in the spring or fall every year as a way of assessing the gains in achievement of groups of children. Most of these tests are actually batteries, or collections of tests on different subjects, and should be given under carefully controlled conditions and over the course of several days. They may be sent to the publisher for machine scoring.

Many of these achievement tests contain subtests in reading and language, which provide useful information for identifying students' general strengths and weaknesses in reading. For instance, the *Iowa Tests of Basic Skills: Primary Battery* (Chicago: Riverside Publishing Co., 1985) contains subtests in listening, word analysis, vocabulary, and reading comprehension, along with other curricular areas. Some norm-referenced achievement tests for which separate reading subtests are available are listed below.

California Achievement Test, Forms C and D. CTB/McGraw Hill, 1978. (grades K to 12.9)

Metropolitan Achievement Test. 5th ed. The Psychological Corporation, 1978. (grades K to 12.9)

Stanford Achievement Test. 7th ed. The Psychological Corporation, 1982. (grades 1.5 to 9.9)

A sample profile sheet from the *Stanford Achievement Test* appears in Example 10.10. It indicates the various subtests and scoring procedure.

▶ **EXAMPLE 10.10:** Sample Profile Sheet from a Survey Achievement Test

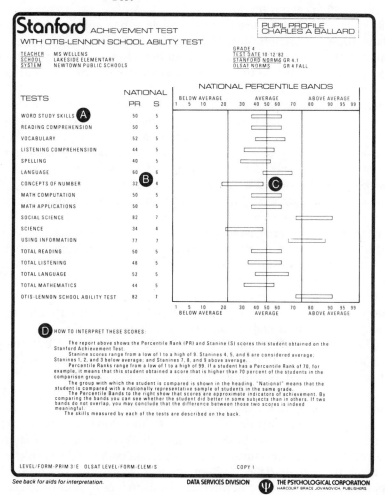

Source: *Stanford Achievement Tests:* 7th Edition. Copyright © 1982, 1983, 1984, 1986 by Harcourt Brace Jovanovich, Inc. Reproduced by permission. All rights reserved. ◀

522

Teaching
Reading in
Today's
Elementary
Schools

✔ **Self-Check: Objective 9**

What types of information can you get from norm-referenced reading and achievement tests that will help you diagnose students' needs?
(See Self-Improvement Opportunities 10, 11, and 12.)

Limitations of Norm-Referenced Reading Tests

If norm-referenced tests are properly understood and interpreted, they can assist teachers in planning reading instruction. Teachers need to understand the tests' limitations clearly, however, and they should begin by asking a series of questions about them.

Which test should I use? A test is inappropriate if the sample population used to standardize it is significantly different from the class to be tested. Test manuals should contain information about the selection and character of the sample population, such as the geographical areas and socioeconomic groups from which the sample was drawn.

What about the content? How many different skills do the test items sample? Children who have participated in a comprehensive program will not be fairly tested by tests that are narrow in scope. Most tests require only a short period of time to complete and therefore cannot possibly sample many different skills or include more than a few items covering any one skill. Thus, many tests must be viewed as gross instruments at best.

How accurate are the scores? It is doubtful that teachers should accept the results of norm-referenced tests with great confidence. They should not assume that a grade score exactly indicates an actual performance level, since a single test score on a norm-referenced reading test frequently reflects the child's frustration level rather than his or her instructional or independent level. In other words, a child who achieves a fourth-grade score on a test may be unable to perform satisfactorily in a fourth-year reader or with fourth-grade content materials. This situation is particularly true for readers at the upper and lower ends of the class distribution.

The Metropolitan Achievement Tests: 1978 Edition (MAT) (The Psychological Corporation, 1978) may be an exception to this, however. In a recent study, researchers compared cloze tests, informal reading inventories, and placement tests with the MAT to determine its validity for estimating a student's instructional reading level. They found that the MAT correlated closely with other procedures and may therefore be a useful tool (Smith and Beck, 1980).

Even if a test's norms are based on populations closely approximating the class being tested, teachers must ask if comparison with national achievement is a good way to describe class or student achievement. Consider, for example, a sixth grade class in a residential district of a well-to-do community. In such a school, the ability of pupils, the interest of parents in education, the training and skill of the teachers, and other factors that encourage achievement would be far above the national average. What is really gained by comparing the reading achievement of this class with the performance of the national sample? Certainly the performance of children in these better schools is well above the norm, but that information is not very useful. Norm-referenced tests might be improved by being based on more homogeneous and more easily described populations rather than on the extremely varied national population.

Is the test fair to minority groups and inner-city children? Test publishers have been giving increasing attention to the question of the fairness of their tests. They do not want to state questions in a way that will give certain children an unfair advantage or discourage some children so that they will not do their best. Many writers and editors from different backgrounds are involved in test-making, and questions are reviewed by members of several ethnic groups to correct unintentional, built-in biases.

✔ Self-Check: Objective 10
List four cautions to keep in mind in using norm-referenced tests.

CRITERION-REFERENCED TESTS

A criterion-referenced (or objective-referenced) test is designed to yield scores interpretable in terms of specific performance standards—for example, to indicate that a student can identify the main idea of a paragraph 90 percent of the time. Such tests do not tell the teacher anything about how a child compares with other children, but are intended to be used as guides for developing instructional prescriptions. For example, if a child cannot perform the task of identifying cause-and-effect relationships, the teacher should provide instruction in that area. Such specific applications make these tests more useful than norm-referenced tests in day-to-day decisions about instruction.

Criterion-referenced tests are usually part of an objective-based reading program that uses pretests and posttests to measure a child's mastery of skills (see Chapter 6). Such programs identify hundreds of discrete skills and arrange them in sequence. These skills become learning goals and are taught and tested. Each child must demonstrate adequate mastery of one skill before advancing to the next.

Educators have important questions, however, concerning criterion-referenced tests. How many correct answers are needed to show that the pupil has achieved an objective or performed up to standard? At what grade level should we expect a child to meet each objective? Should every pupil be expected to meet every objective? Other questions arise when a child does achieve an objective. Is it typical for a third grader to achieve this objective? Do most third graders know how to perform this task? These questions bring

524

Teaching
Reading in
Today's
Elementary
Schools

us back to comparing individuals—or to a norm-referenced interpretation of test scores.

Criterion-referenced testing has both advantages and disadvantages. It is an effective way of diagnosing a child's knowledge of reading skills, and it helps in prescribing appropriate instruction. Furthermore, students do not compete with other students but only try to achieve mastery of each criterion or objective. On the other hand, reading can become nothing more than a series of skills to be taught and tested, and skills may be taught in isolation rather than in combination. Knowledge gained in this way may be difficult for children to apply to actual reading situations.

An example of a criterion-referenced approach to reading is the *PRI Reading Systems*, which succeeds the *Prescriptive Reading Inventory*. Assessment and instructional materials provide data on each student's skill in reading to be used for placement, diagnosis and prescription, skill reinforcement, progress checks, and enrichment. Assessment materials measure the student's ability to achieve objectives that are usually identified for reading instruction in grades kindergarten through nine. Lesson plans and activities for helping students gain mastery of those skills they have not already learned are provided. An Individual Diagnostic Map from the *PRI Reading Systems* is shown in Example 10.11.

Below is a list of other commercially available criterion-referenced tests.

Chew, Alex L. *The Lollipop Test: A Diagnostic Screening Test of School Readiness.* Humanics Limited, 1981. Measures identification of colors, shapes, letters, and numbers; ability to copy shapes; and position and spatial recognition. (first half of K to grade 1 entrants)

Herbert, Charles H. *Basic Inventory of Natural Language.* CHECpoint Systems, 1979. Assesses language proficiency, including fluency, level of complexity, and average sentence length. (grades K to 12)

Pauk, Walter. *Single Skills Series.* Jamestown Publishers, 1985. Assesses student achievement in the following comprehension skills: subject matter, main idea, supporting details, conclusions, clarifying devices, and vocabulary in context. (grades 3 to 12)

Reading Yardsticks. Riverside Publishing Co., 1981. Measures students' strengths and weaknesses in reading readiness, reading, and language skills. (grades K to 8)

Woodcock, Richard W. *Woodcock Reading Mastery Tests.* Rev. ed. American Guidance Services, 1986. Comprehensive battery of individually administered tests to measure important aspects of reading ability. (grades K to 12)

✔ Self-Check: Objective 11

Differentiate between a norm-referenced and criterion-referenced test.

(See Self-Improvement Opportunity 13.)

► **EXAMPLE 10.11:** Example of Criterion-Referenced Approach

Source: Reproduced by permission of the publisher, CTB/McGraw-Hill, Del
Monte Research Park, Monterey, CA 93940. Copyright © 1980 by McGraw-Hill,
Inc. All rights reserved. Printed in the U.S.A. ◄

PROCESS-ORIENTED ASSESSMENT

For the past fifty years there have been no significant changes in reading tests
(Farr and Carey, 1986). Comprehension sections still consist of series of short
passages followed by multiple-choice questions, and the format for assessing
word recognition on both norm-referenced and criterion-referenced tests has
also remained basically the same. The tests require students to identify a

526

Teaching
Reading in
Today's
Elementary
Schools

single correct answer for each test item, and estimates of a child's reading ability are based on the number of correct answers. In the past decade major national reports, school effectiveness research, and emphasis on accountability in education have resulted in even greater attention to the measurement of small, separate skills for evaluating educational effectiveness (Valencia and Pearson, 1987).

Standardized tests serve valid purposes, and school systems will probably continue to use them. "When used intelligently as part of an overall evaluation, they are significant indicators of educational progress" (Calfee, 1987, p. 743). Researchers have begun to question their design in view of current research about instructional practices, however. For instance, is it valid to check knowledge of vocabulary by asking students to find one of several words that most closely matches an isolated key word, when readers nearly always encounter words in context? Also, is it realistic to assess reading comprehension based on answers to series of short, unrelated paragraphs, when most reading situations involve much longer passages?

Current thinking about reading comprehension as a sustained, interactive, strategic process is not being reflected in assessment. Although many publishers are changing instructional materials and many teachers are implementing procedures based on recent trends in reading comprehension, corresponding changes have not occurred in reading tests. Therefore, teachers who want their students to do well on tests are in a dilemma because tests still measure skill proficiency instead of ability to read strategically. (See Table 10.2 for contrasts between views of reading and assessment practices.)

Recently researchers have been seeking to establish more process-oriented, or holistic, ways of assessing reading ability. Process-oriented assessment views reading holistically and provides information about students' thought processes and reading strategies. Thus, instead of focusing on single correct answers, researchers are considering the entire process of reading and the strategies used. Farr and Carey (1986) have identified three ways that test developers are beginning to adapt new ideas about comprehension to their tests. In one instance, reading comprehension tests include setting purposes for reading (Metropolitan Achievement Test, 1986), and in another, analysis of incorrect responses to multiple-choice questions aids in diagnosing sources of difficulties (California Achievement Tests, 1986). An additional alternative is assessing vocabulary by asking readers to identify words embedded in text instead of words in isolation.

For statewide assessment in Illinois, researchers have experimented with concepts that encourage strategic reading of test questions (Valencia and Pearson, 1987). These concepts include choosing the best of three or four summaries of a selection, evaluating the worth of several retellings of a selection for different audiences, selecting the most useful questions to help a peer understand important ideas about a passage, identifying more than one acceptable answer to a question, and predicting the likelihood of the inclusion of certain items on a specified topic. These testing strategies take

TABLE 10.2   A Set of Contrasts Between New Views of Reading and Current Practices in Assessing Reading

New views of the reading process tell us that . . .	*Yet when we assess reading comprehension, we . . .*
Prior knowledge is an important determinant of reading comprehension.	Mask any relationship between prior knowledge and reading comprehension by using lots of short passages on lots of topics.
A complete story or text has structural and topical integrity.	Use short texts that seldom approximate the structural and topical integrity of an authentic text.
Inference is an essential part of the process of comprehending units as small as sentences.	Rely on literal comprehension test items.
The diversity in prior knowledge across individuals as well as the varied causal relations in human experiences invite many possible inferences to fit a text or question.	Use multiple choice items with only one correct answer, even when many of the responses might, under certain conditions, be plausible.
The ability to vary reading strategies to fit the text and the situation is one hallmark of an expert reader.	Seldom assess how and when students vary the strategies they use during normal reading, studying, or when the going gets tough.
The ability to synthesize information from various parts of the text and different texts is hallmark of an expert reader.	Rarely go beyond finding the main idea of a paragraph or passage.
The ability to ask good questions of text, as well as to answer them, is hallmark of an expert reader.	Seldom ask students to create or select questions about a selection they may have just read.
All aspects of a reader's experience, including habits that arise from school and home, influence reading comprehension.	Rarely view information on reading habits and attitudes as being as important as information about performance.
Reading involves the orchestration of many skills that complement one another in a variety of ways.	Use tests that fragment reading into isolated skills and report performance on each.
Skilled readers are fluent; their word identification is sufficiently automatic to allow most cognitive resources to be used for comprehension.	Rarely consider fluency as an index of skilled reading.
Learning from text involves the restructuring, application, and flexible use of knowledge in new situations.	Often ask readers to respond to the text's declarative knowledge rather than to apply it to near and far transfer tasks.

Source: Reprinted with permission of Sheila Valencia and P. David Pearson and the International Reading Association.

528

Teaching
Reading in
Today's
Elementary
Schools

into consideration the need to connect assessment procedures with current beliefs about reading instruction, including such views as the importance of prior knowledge to reading comprehension and the acceptability of more than one correct response to a reading selection.

In a similar manner, teachers can use process-oriented, or holistic, procedures in their classrooms to determine what strategies students are using when they read (Wittrock, 1987). "At the text level, these techniques include semantic networks, summaries, multiple choice cloze tests, story rewrites, cued questions, focus or attention shifting, graphic overviews, main ideas, and structured interpretations. At the sentence level, they include analogies, examples, paraphrases, similes and metaphors" (Wittrock, 1987, p. 736). Teachers can learn about students' use of various comprehension strategies by asking them questions such as: How do you know? How can you find out? What can you try next? What is the best way to predict . . . understand . . . remember . . . ? By observing and questioning, teachers can diagnose students' strengths and weaknesses in the use of effective comprehension strategies. They can then plan appropriate instruction for helping students make better use of their thought processes for reading comprehension.

✔ **Self-Check: Objective 12**
Explain how the concept of process-oriented, or holistic, assessment differs from other types of testing.

Summary

Given this myriad of tests, a teacher may well wonder what to use to assess students' knowledge and abilities. This summary may help to put assessment into a proper perspective.

Informal tests may be given at any time for a specific purpose to one or more children. These tests are usually designed to find out what a student knows about something and to determine if some students need more instruction before moving on to another skill. Most of the time informal tests are constructed by the classroom teacher, but they may also be taken from commercially prepared inventories, word lists, or other specific skill checks.

Some types of informal tests used in reading are graded word lists (which give approximate reading levels based on word recognition only), informal reading inventories (which give reading levels based on both comprehension and word recognition), and the cloze procedure (which determines how well a student can read the textbook). Graded word lists and IRIs must be given individually, but the cloze procedure may be given to an entire class at once. Teachers can also use computers in various ways to assess students' word recognition and comprehension skills.

The classroom teacher should also understand the purposes of various types of norm-referenced tests that may be part of the school program. A kindergarten or first-grade teacher may want to administer a reading readiness test to help determine if a child is ready for reading instruction. Most schools require that achievement tests be given annually to find out how much progress students have made in overall academic achievement. Reading survey tests are used to obtain general information about a student's reading level, and diagnostic reading tests are used to find specific skill deficiencies.

The teacher can construct criterion-referenced tests to determine how well a student understands a specific skill. Often these tests are part of an objective-based or systems management approach to reading and are used along with sets of skill-building materials. In addition, many basal reader series provide tests at the end of each unit to assess the student's knowledge of reading skills associated with the unit. Because these tests relate directly to the instructional materials, the teacher can tell from the results if he or she needs to reteach some skills to certain children.

Process-oriented assessment offers an alternative to informal skill-based tests and traditional standardized tests. Evaluation is based not on the number of correct responses to individual skills but on the student's ability to use skills within a whole reading selection.

The teacher's most useful assessment tool is day-to-day observation. Informal tests may be used to reinforce or supplement such observation, whereas norm-referenced tests are usually given only as mandated by the school system.

Test Yourself

True or False

_____ 1. Study skills may be assessed most effectively in situations where they are being used.

_____ 2. A check sheet for recording the kinds of miscues children make in oral reading is helpful to most teachers.

_____ 3. Results from the San Diego Quick Assessment are useful for grouping pupils or selecting appropriate reading materials.

_____ 4. The teacher must devise his or her own informal reading inventory, since none are commercially available.

_____ 5. Basal reader programs usually include tests specific to each unit or reader.

_____ 6. Material written on a child's independent reading level is less difficult than material written on his or her instructional level.

_____ 7. Selections of seventy-five words are used for each grade level in the IRI.

_____ 8. For first and second graders, word recognition at 85 percent and comprehension at 75 percent indicate the instructional level on an IRI.

_____ 9. Teachers may use the cloze procedure as an alternative to the IRI in determining narrative or content material reading levels.

530

Teaching
Reading in
Today's
Elementary
Schools

_____ 10. An IRI can be prepared for content reading material as well as for narrative (basal reader) passages.

_____ 11. Miscue analysis can help in understanding the nature of a child's reading errors.

_____ 12. Significant miscues are found in this manner: Total miscues − (dialectal miscues + corrected miscues + miscues that don't change meaning).

_____ 13. If a test has high reliability, high validity is assured.

_____ 14. Standardized reading survey tests can identify the range of performance differences within the class but cannot necessarily identify the precise achievement level of each class member.

_____ 15. Providing practice in taking standardized tests is of little or no value for children.

_____ 16. A general survey reading test does not identify the specific reading strengths or weaknesses of the reader.

_____ 17. Self-questioning is an effective tool for reading and studying.

_____ 18. Prior knowledge of a topic enables a child to read with greater ease and understanding.

_____ 19. Percentile rank (PR) refers to the percent of correct responses an examinee makes on a test.

_____ 20. A criterion-referenced assessment relates an individual's test performance to absolute standards rather than to the performance of others.

_____ 21. There are at present no computer programs for assessing reading skills.

_____ 22. There have been major changes in standardized testing in the past fifty years.

_____ 23. Process-oriented assessment focuses on small, separate skills.

Self-Improvement Opportunities

1. Prepare a structured reading checklist for one of the following: word attack skills (including contextual analysis, phonics analysis, structural analysis, dictionary usage), study skills, or comprehension skills.
2. Study a set of basal reader tests to determine how you can use them.
3. Administer the San Diego Quick Assessment to a child. Then share your findings about reading level and word-analysis errors with peers.
4. Secure a published IRI and administer it to one or more elementary school pupils. Report the results to the class.
5. Prepare an IRI using basal reading materials, administer it to a child, record the results, and share your findings with the class.
6. Prepare a group inventory, using content reading materials. Administer your group inventory to a child, record the results, and share the findings with the class.

7. Utilize the procedures suggested for a miscue analysis. Check the quantity and quality of miscues.

8. Below are some errors made by a fourth-grade student in oral reading. What kind of help do these errors suggest that this student might need?

Correct Word	Incorrect Reading
and he *hoped*	hopped
they *knew*	know
on the *map*	mape
would come *alive*	aliv
of the *few*	fun
was a *new*	now
back *home*	here

9. Discuss with a teacher and a librarian some ways to assess development of children's literary interests.
10. Secure a copy (and manual) of a norm-referenced reading survey test. Study it and report on it to your peers. Consider the purpose, range, forms, testing time, reliability, validity, strengths, and weaknesses.
11. If feasible, observe the administration of a norm-referenced reading survey test to a child or group of children.
12. If feasible, administer a norm-referenced reading survey test to a child and interpret the results.
13. Examine several criterion-referenced tests.
14. From the following list, choose which type of test is appropriate for each of the following purposes. (More than one answer could be correct.)

criterion-referenced   survey
norm-referenced   achievement
informal

a. To find out if a child has mastered a specific skill
b. To determine how much gain in general academic achievement the second-grade class in a school made during the preceding year
c. To find out how a child's reading achievement compares with that of the average child in the nation
d. To get a general idea of a student's reading ability
e. To find out what a child knows about structural analysis

Bibliography

Allington, Richard L. "Oral Reading." In *Handbook of Reading Research*, P. David Pearson, ed. New York: Longman, 1984, pp. 829–64.

532
Teaching
Reading in
Today's
Elementary
Schools

Babbs, Patricia J., and Alden J. Moe. "Metacognition: A Key for Independent Learning from Text." *The Reading Teacher* 36 (January 1983): 422–27.

Baker, Linda, and Ann L. Brown. "Metacognitive Skills and Reading." In *Handbook of Reading Research,* P. David Pearson, ed. New York: Longman, 1984, pp. 353–94.

Barr, Rebecca, and Marilyn Sadow. *Reading Diagnosis for Teachers.* Longman: New York, 1985.

Bauman, James F., and Jennifer A. Stevenson. "Using Scores from Standardized Reading Achievement Tests." *The Reading Teacher* 35 (February 1982): 528–33.

Bennett, Rand Elliot. "Cautions for the Use of Informal Measures in the Educational Assessment of Exceptional Children." *Journal of Learning Disabilities* 15 (June/July 1982): 337–39.

Blanchard, Jay S. *Computer-Based Reading Assessment Instrument.* Dubuque, Iowa: Kendall/Hunt, 1985.

Bond, Guy L., Miles A. Tinker, and Barbara B. Wasson. *Reading Difficulties: Their Diagnosis and Correction.* 4th ed. Englewood Cliffs, N.J.: Prentice-Hall, 1979, p. 62.

Boning, Richard A. *Specific Skills Series.* Rockville Center, N.Y.: Barnell Loft, 1985.

Caldwell, JoAnne. "A New Look at the Old Informal Reading Inventory." *The Reading Teacher* 39 (November 1985): 168–73.

Calfee, Robert C. "The School as a Context for Assessment of Literacy." *The Reading Teacher* 40 (April 1987): 738–43.

Cohen, Ruth. "Self-Generated Questions as an Aid to Reading Comprehension." *The Reading Teacher* 36 (April 1983): 770–75.

Durrell, Donald D., and Helen A. Murphy. "A Prereading Phonics Inventory." *The Reading Teacher* 31 (January 1978): 385–90.

Farr, Roger, and Robert F. Carey. *Reading: What Can Be Measured?* 2nd ed. Newark, Del.: International Reading Association, 1986.

Goodman, Yetta. "Test Review: Concepts About Print Test." *The Reading Teacher* 34 (January 1981): 445–48.

Goodman, Yetta. "Using Children's Reading Miscues for New Teaching Strategies." *The Reading Teacher* 23 (February 1970): 455–59.

Gunning, Thomas G. "Wrong Level Test: Wrong Information." *The Reading Teacher* 35 (May 1982): 902–905.

Hillerich, Robert L. "A Diagnostic Approach to Early Identification of Language Skills." *The Reading Teacher* 31 (January 1978): 357–64.

Johnston, Peter H. "Assessment in Reading." In *Handbook of Reading Research,* P. David Pearson, ed. New York: Longman, 1984, pp. 147–82.

Johnston, Peter H. *Reading Comprehension Assessment: A Cognitive Basis.* Newark, Del.: International Reading Association, 1983.

Johnston, Peter "Teachers as Evaluation Experts." *The Reading Teacher* 40 (April 1987): 744–48.

Jongsma, Kathleen S., and Eugene A. Jongsma. "Test Review: Commercial Informal Reading Inventories." *The Reading Teacher* 34 (March 1981): 697–705.

Kubiszyn, Tom, and Gary Borich. *Educational Testing and Measurement.* 2nd ed. Glenview, Ill.: Scott, Foresman, 1987.

Miller, Wilma. *Reading Diagnosis Kit.* West Nyack, N.Y.: Center for Applied Research in Education, 1978.

Pickert, Sarah M., and Martha L. Chase. "Story Retelling: An Informal Technique for Evaluating Children's Language." *The Reading Teacher* 31 (February 1978): 528–31.

Schreiner, Robert. "The Computer, an Electronic Flash Card." *The Reading Teacher* 39 (December 1985): 378–80.

Smith, Edwin H., et al. "Informal Reading Inventories for Content Areas: Science and Mathematics." *Elementary English* 49 (May 1972): 659–66.

Smith, Lawrence L., Jerry L. Johns, Leonore Ganschow, and Nancy Browning Masztal. "Using Grade Level vs. Out-of-Level Reading Tests with Remedial Students." *The Reading Teacher* 40 (February 1983): 550–53.

Smith, William Earl, and Michael D. Beck. "Determining Instructional Reading Level with the 1978 Metropolitan Achievement Tests." *The Reading Teacher* 34 (December 1980): 313–19.

Stewart, Oran, and Dan S. Green. "Test-Taking Skills for Standardized Tests of Reading." *The Reading Teacher* 36 (March 1983): 634–39.

Teale, William H., Elfrieda H. Hiebert, and Edward A. Chittenden. "Assessing Young Children's Literacy Development." *The Reading Teacher* 40 (April 1987): 772–77.

Valencia, Sheila, and P. David Pearson. "Reading Assessment: Time for a Change." *The Reading Teacher* 40 (April 1987): 726–33.

Wittrock, Merlin C. "Process Oriented Measures of Comprehension." *The Reading Teacher* 40 (April 1987): 734–37.

CHAPTER APPENDIX: ADDRESSES OF TEST PUBLISHERS

Academic Therapy Publications, 20 Commercial Blvd., Novato, CA 94947.

American Guidance Service, Box 99, Circle Pines, MN 55014.

Chapman, Brook & Kent, 1215 De La Vina, Suite F., P.O. Box 21008, Santa Barbara, CA 93121.

CHECpoint Systems, Inc., 1520 N. Waterman Ave., San Bernardino, CA 92404.

Consulting Psychologists Press, Inc., 577 College Ave., Palo Alto, CA 94306.

CTB/McGraw Hill, Del Monte Research Park, 2500 Garden Rd., Monterey, CA 93940.

DLM Teaching Resources, One DLM Park, P.O. Box 4000, Allen, TX 75002.

534

Teaching
Reading in
Today's
Elementary
Schools

Education Performance Associates, 600 Broad Ave., Ridgefield, NJ 07657.

Guidance Centre, University of Toronto, 1000 Yonge St., Toronto, Ontario M4W2K8, Canada.

Humanics, Limited, P.O. Box 7447, Atlanta, GA 30309.

Jamestown Publishers, P.O. Box 6743, Providence, RI 02940.

JoMar Publications, Inc., P.O. Box 9153, Schenectady, NY 12309.

Prentice-Hall, Inc., Englewood Cliffs, NJ 07632.

PRO-ED, 5341 Industrial Oaks Blvd., Austin, TX 78735.

The Psychological Corporation, 555 Academic Court, San Antonio, TX 78204.

Riverside Publishing Co., 8420 Bryn Mawr Ave., Chicago, IL 60631.

Scholastic Testing Service, Inc., 480 Meyer Rd., P.O. Box 1056, Bensenville, IL 60106.

Special Child Publications, P.O. Box 33548, Seattle, WA 98133.

Western Psychological Services, 12031 Wilshire Blvd., Los Angeles, CA 90025.

Chapter 11

Classroom Organization
and Management

Introduction

Classroom organization does not deal directly with the reading process, or with materials, methods, or approaches to teaching reading. Yet without good classroom organization and management, reading instruction may be totally ineffective. It is not enough for teachers to know what to teach; they must also know what organizational patterns and management techniques are conducive to learning.

This chapter includes various types of organizational plans and practical suggestions for forming and managing different kinds of groups. Three types of individualized instruction—learning centers, computer-assisted instruction, and seatwork—are considered, along with ways for managing independent activities. The chapter also presents recommended instructional and management techniques for the classroom based on recent research on teacher effectiveness. Madeline Hunter's model is the basis of an effective teaching plan that is included. A discussion of the influence of parents and the home environment on children's reading attitudes and achievement follows, and the chapter concludes with a presentation of the value of paraprofessionals and tutors in the school program.

Setting Objectives

When you finish reading this chapter, you should be able to

1. Name some general guidelines for organizing a classroom reading program.
2. Note some different ways that teachers might group students for reading-related purposes.
3. Explain how you might use interclass or cross-grade grouping.
4. Plan and implement some individualized reading activities.
5. Identify several criteria for teacher effectiveness in the reading program.
6. Describe a model of teacher effectiveness.
7. Name some ways in which teachers can communicate with parents.
8. Explain the roles paraprofessionals and tutors play within the reading program.

Key Vocabulary

Pay close attention to these terms when they appear in the chapter.

achievement grouping	direct instruction	heterogeneous grouping
cross-age tutoring	engaged time	homogeneous grouping
departmentalization	friendship grouping	interclass grouping

interest grouping
intraclass grouping
learning center
paraprofessional
peer tutoring

pupil pairs or
partners
research or projects
grouping

special skills or needs
grouping
student contract
teacher effectiveness
team arrangement

ORGANIZATIONAL PATTERNS

The fact that students vary a great deal in chronological age, maturity, cognitive abilities, interests, and personal experiences is no secret. In view of the obvious need to provide the most appropriate instruction for each learner, teachers must give careful consideration to plans that provide for individual differences. Students in a total reading program should participate in small-group, individualized, and whole-class activities. Many types of individualized activities are discussed in Chapter 6; other individualized plans and whole-class activities are treated later in this chapter. An extensive discussion of grouping immediately follows this section.

Some general guidelines for organization of the classroom are listed below.

1. Remember that no single classroom pattern or structuring is better than another; the local situation, the strengths of individual teachers, and the abilities of the children involved will help determine the best system for a particular school.
2. Consider many criteria in deciding upon a particular organizational plan, including results of informal and formal assessments, children's interests, your strengths and weaknesses, and specific goals of instruction.
3. Keep organizational plans flexible and alter them as you discover improvements.
4. Make low-ability groups smaller than high-ability groups so that the teacher can give more attention to the special needs of low-achieving students.
5. Provide a consistent quality of instruction for all achievement groups.
6. Organize your classroom so that it is structured and orderly, but provide a supportive emotional climate.
7. Offer opportunities for individualized learning, making sure to manage independent activities for the benefit of all students.
8. Whenever possible, provide whole-class instruction so that all students feel a sense of class unity.

✔ Self-Check: Objective 1
Cite at least six guidelines for organizing a reading classroom. Can you suggest others not stated above?
(See Self-Improvement Opportunity 1.)

Grouping

Educators have made various attempts to create organizational plans for meeting the needs of all students in the most efficient ways possible. Some schools organize classrooms homogeneously, so that children within each class are similar in achievement and ability, whereas other schools organize classrooms heterogeneously, so that children within each class vary widely in achievement and ability. Research findings indicate that homogeneously grouped students show no significant gains or losses in overall achievement, and that gains made by high-achieving students are offset by losses for students in low reading groups (Otto, Wolf, and Eldridge, 1984). Within both homogeneous and heterogeneous classes children exhibit a range of reading levels, although the spread is usually wider in heterogeneous classes. This range of differences increases with each succeeding grade as some students fall further behind and others advance more rapidly. The range of reading levels in a typical heterogeneously grouped class can be estimated by adding 1 to the grade level. For instance, at the beginning of grade 5 the midpoint would be 5.0, so the range would be 6 years (1 + 5), or from grade 2 to grade 8. The poorest readers would be 3 years below grade level and the most advanced readers would be 3 years above grade level. Similarly, in grade 4 the range would be 5 years (1 + 4), or from grade 1.5 to grade 6.5 ("Estimating Range," 1987).

In order to accommodate this wide range of levels, many teachers group children within their classrooms as a compromise between providing whole-class or totally individualized instruction. Although individualizing instruction is an ideal way to meet the needs of each student, it is impractical to deal individually with from twenty-five to thirty children all day. Furthermore, grouping children has several benefits. Students who are grouped for instructional purposes tend to spend more time on academic tasks and achieve greater gains in reading (Rosenshine and Stevens, 1984). In addition, they have greater opportunities for learning and practicing new skills under the teacher's direction, and they receive immediate feedback about their work.

Although ability or achievement is the most common basis for grouping children for reading instruction (Jongsma, 1985), this type of grouping only reduces and in no way eliminates individual differences. Students still differ in their rates of progress, in their attitudes toward reading, in their backgrounds of experience, and in their degree of motivation. Two students may have similar overall achievement scores; however, one may be weak in word recognition and strong in comprehension while the other may have the opposite problem.

Two major grouping plans have been used in heterogeneous classroom settings: intraclass (within the class) and interclass (between classes). A discussion of each major grouping plan follows.

Intraclass Group Plans

539

Classroom
Organization
and
Management

Types of Groups Dividing children into reading groups on the basis of reading level is a popular practice. This is a kind of *achievement grouping*, a method of grouping children according to the level of material they can read for instructional purposes. The teacher may divide the class into two, three, or four groups, usually using basal readers as the main fare, because the manuals and workbooks provide a careful and detailed skill-building program. Good teachers will note how difficult these materials are for each child in each group and will provide easier or harder related reading (supplementary reading, trade books, magazines, newspapers, and the like) as needed. Teachers should continuously monitor students' progress within achievement groups and consider making changes in placement when a child's progress is either substantially slower or more rapid than that of the rest of the group. It is important to keep groupings flexible.

As children show specific skill deficiencies in their achievement groups, they need *special skills* or *needs grouping*, which groups together children who need work on the same skill. Several children from each of the groups may need help with word recognition (such as recognizing certain initial consonant sounds), comprehension (such as summarizing meaning of a paragraph), or a study skill (such as graph reading). Children with a common need can work together in one or perhaps more meetings. Such special needs groups will involve different children at different times.

A teacher can assemble special skills groups when several children appear to need additional instruction and practice in a skill. For instance, five children might meet for fifteen minutes each day while the teacher explains ways of using clue words to understand sequence and then provides activities for reinforcing the skill. Children leave the group when they show mastery of the skill by scoring 80 percent or higher on a quiz. Some children may need to remain in the group longer than others, but most skills groups disband within a week.

Another type of grouping, *interest grouping* (based on shared or common interests or concerns), is recommended for certain reading activities. Children who are familiar with a topic and have a special interest in it can usually read material about it at higher levels than they normally read (Anderson et al., 1985). For example, if three or four children in a class like horse stories, the librarian, notified about this interest and the reading levels of the children, can find just the right books for them. After reading and talking, the children might prepare a discussion about the books for the entire class, or they might make a poster advertising the books they read, write a story together, or make a scrapbook. From such temporary interest groupings, more formal and long-term groups often evolve (for example, library groups, choral groups, dramatic clubs, readers' theaters, and book fair groups).

540

Teaching
Reading in
Today's
Elementary
Schools

A fourth type of grouping is based on *projects* or *research.* Such groups may grow out of a unit from another area of the curriculum, such as science or social studies. Pupils of varying ability levels work together to investigate a topic by choosing material written at appropriate levels for them and pooling their information. Their investigation usually results in a presentation to the class or the construction of something related to the topic, which might be space travel, types of mammals, community helpers, pioneer life, energy, environmental control, or something similar.

A popular form of grouping among students is *friendship grouping,* in which good friends work together for a specific purpose and within a specified time frame. Because friends understand each other, enjoy being together, and can usually cooperate well, this type of group can be particularly effective. There is a danger, however, that the primary activity may be social interaction rather than the accomplishment of the designated task. If this is the case, the teacher should disband the group until the students realize that they must *work* together, not just visit. Some purposes for friendship groups might be sharing favorite stories, responding to books through combined artwork (posters, dioramas, mobiles), and preparing a puppet show based on a story to present to the class.

Yet another type of grouping involves *pupil pairs* or *partners,* who may work cooperatively on such activities as

1. practicing sight words with picture-word cards.
2. working on dictionary skills by locating words, selecting the correct definition for the context, and so forth.
3. solving crossword puzzles based on new vocabulary words.
4. reading orally and listening to stories from basal readers or trade books.

Partners may work better on skill tasks if they have about the same degree of reading ability and if they are congenial. The directions for a paired task must be clear, the task specific, and the time limited to that needed for the task.

An intraclass grouping plan that uses all these kinds of groupings offers certain advantages. The child has the opportunity to choose or be placed in a variety of group situations, and discovers that some things are best learned in groups and others on an individual basis. Most importantly, this kind of plan provides opportunities to correlate reading with other content areas and to use the interrelationships among the language arts, since the same teacher works with the same children in all subject areas throughout the school day.

Formation of Groups Placing students in the appropriate achievement group is not an easy task. Teachers must consider several factors and may want to wait from several days to a few weeks before making group assignments. Records from the previous year usually show which basal reader was last completed by each child, and teachers can place the child in the next book in the series. They can also use achievement test scores to help them place students. If a child has transferred into the school and no records are available, the teacher will want to make an informal assessment to determine his or her reading level and group placement. Remember: a good guideline to follow when in doubt is to place a student at a level where success is virtually assured, since it is much better for the child psychologically to move *up* than to move *back*.

Other factors enter into a teacher's decision on group placement. Some children may not have read a book all summer and will need to review before moving on, whereas others may have attended summer reading programs at the library or read extensively at home and be ready to continue immediately. A student's willingness to work, attitude toward reading, and rate of progress are also important considerations.

There is no optimal group size or number of groups for a classroom. Most teachers find that three achievement groups work well in terms of classroom management and reduction of differences in reading levels, but some classes divide more logically into two or four groups. Since better readers are usually better independent workers, the high-achievement group may include a larger number of students than the low group, which should be small so that the teacher can give more attention to individual problems.

The list below shows a typical range of reading achievement levels for a beginning fourth-grade class. Table 11.1 shows how the teacher might place the children in this class into two, three, or four groups. In each case the number of children is listed with the corresponding reading level following it.

Number of Children	Reading Grade Level
2	2^1
2	2^2
3	3^1
4	3^2
9	4
3	5
2	6
1	7

The two-group plan shown in Table 11.1 provides more time for teacher-directed instruction, an advantage for effective learning, but the low group spans a wide range of achievement levels. Although the teacher could provide additional help for the lowest-level children through peer tutoring or individual help, the range is probably too wide for all children to benefit.

In the three-group plan shown in Table 11.1, the low and middle groups are small enough for the teacher to give attention to special needs within each group. Because all children in these two groups read at either the second- or third-grade level, the range of differences is manageable. Combining children who are reading at the fourth-grade level with those reading

542

**Teaching
Reading in
Today's
Elementary
Schools**

TABLE 11.1   Two-, Three-, and Four-Group Plans for a Beginning Fourth-Grade Class

Two-Group Plan			
Children	Level	Children	Level
2	2^1	9	4
2	2^2	3	5
3	3^1	2	6
4	3^2	1	7

Three-Group Plan					
Children	Level	Children	Level	Children	Level
2	2^1	3	3^1	9	4
2	2^2	4	3^2	3	5
				2	6
				1	7

Four-Group Plan							
Children	Level	Children	Level	Children	Level	Children	Level
2	2^1	3	3^1	9	4	3	5
2	2^2	4	3^2			2	6
						1	7

above grade level is a satisfactory arrangement for these children if the teacher provides additional challenging reading materials and projects for the high-achieving students.

The four-group plan shown in Table 11.1 has two disadvantages: it is difficult to schedule in a limited time period, and there is less teacher-student interaction than in the two- or three-group plans. However, this plan allows the accelerated readers to work directly with the teacher on advanced activities, such as research, story analysis, and evaluation of reading materials. There is seldom one clear-cut way to group children, and teachers should be alert to the possibilities of providing better instruction through combining groups, separating them, or moving children from one group to another.

Although achievement groups usually last all year, the number and composition of groups may change in response to the students' progress during the school year. One researcher found that teachers generally make the most changes in achievement groups during the first few weeks of school, and children in the middle group are more likely to be moved than other children (Otto, Wolf, and Eldridge, 1984).

It is a good idea to move a student if that move will facilitate learning. A teacher may have misjudged a student's placement or a student may change his or her rate of learning to read. However, before moving a pupil, the teacher should observe him or her closely and perhaps discuss the potential change with the student. A child who reads fluently, always finishes first, and knows all of the answers may be a candidate for a higher group or for an individualized approach. This student will probably be excited about advancing but must realize that the work will be more difficult; he or she might read with both the old and new groups for a period of time to avoid missing any skills and to ensure that the move is within his or her capability. Seatwork could be proportionately reduced for this period of time. On the other hand, a child who misses more than one word out of fifteen or twenty and has difficulty understanding the material should probably be moved to a lower group. This child may be disappointed initially, but will be relieved to find that the reading level is more comfortable and success is more likely to occur.

Forming achievement groups in first grade is a special problem because there are no records of any books that students might have read. A teacher at this level will probably wait longer to form groups and may experiment with temporary formations, using reading-readiness test scores, informal checklists, and observation to assign students to groups. Gradually the teacher will begin pulling together those children who seem to be ready for formal reading instruction in one group and placing those who are showing signs of interest in reading in a second group. The teacher will place children who will need many types of readiness experiences before they are ready for reading instruction in a third group.

Other than achievement groups, most groups are formed for a limited time and a specific purpose. For example, skills groups are created when the teacher recognizes that several children have a similar weakness and are disbanded as the children learn the skill. Interest groups may be formed by using an informal interest inventory (see pages 320–321) or by asking students to sign up for topics that they would like to investigate, and project or research groups may be formed by student preference or randomly by the teacher.

Group Instruction   In order to individualize instruction within achievement groups, teachers need to involve each child in group activities. The every-pupil-response technique is one way to do this because it enables each child to respond to every question at the same time without calling out (McKenzie, 1984). In this technique, sometimes referred to as signaling, students respond to either-or questions in one of the following ways:

1. Putting thumbs up for agreement, thumbs down for disagreement.
2. Raising hands for agreement, keeping hands down for disagreement.
3. Holding up the appropriate card from a pair of cards (examples: yes-no, true-false, smiley face–frowny face, short vowel–long vowel, fact-opinion.).

A variation of the every-pupil-response method is asking one child to answer a question and then asking the other children in the group to raise their hands if they agree with the answer and keep their hands down if they

544
Teaching
Reading in
Today's
Elementary
Schools

Teachers often implement a variety of grouping plans—including achievement, skills, and interest grouping—to meet a particular class's reading instruction needs. (© Sybil Shelton/Peter Arnold)

disagree. On another occasion the teacher might ask the students to read a selection silently and then point in their books to the part that answers a particular question. In each case every student responds and the teacher can see which students know the answers and which students need more help.

Although teachers should provide a consistent quality of instruction for all achievement groups, in actual practice, they often use poorer teaching strategies in low groups. They expect low-achieving students to read more orally and less silently and to read words on lists or flashcards without meaningful context. Teachers correct more of the children's oral reading mistakes and are more likely to give pronunciation rather than meaning clues for words these children do not recognize. Teachers also ask more literal questions and fewer questions that call for higher-order thinking when working with children in the low group (Anderson et al., 1985).

Students in the high group often finish the basal reader for their grade before the end of the school year, and when this happens the teacher should be ready to suggest other types of reading experiences. Individualized reading, a study of the newspaper, a unit on poetry or folklore, or a research activity is appropriate. One fifth-grade group who finished early evaluated Newbery books, first devising a checklist of criteria and then locating all of the available Newbery Award winners and runners-up. Each of the students read and evaluated several of the books, and the group then compiled the results of their evaluations.

Psychological Impact of Grouping   Even if a teacher tries to conceal the identities of the high and low groups, children are well aware of the level of each group. Many low-group students remain in the low group over the years and as a result form poor self-concepts. In classes where students are grouped tightly by perceived academic abilities, greater differences exist among students' performance levels, their perceptions of their own abilities, and their perceptions of their classmates' abilities. These classrooms further weaken low-achieving students' self-concepts, social acceptance, and social status (Rosenholtz and Simpson, 1984). Teachers should try to minimize the stigma these students feel due to their placement in the low group.

Flexible grouping provides some alternatives that help reduce the negative effects of rigid ability or achievement grouping (Unsworth, 1984). Instead of having permanent groups, teachers should create, modify, and disband groups periodically in response to observed needs. They should offer a variety of tasks and make them appropriate for the needs and interests of the students. They should also provide a clear method of coding or labeling materials so that students can locate appropriate materials independently.

Members of the low reading group should be included in whole-class reading-related activities. Some of these students may be excellent artists who can contribute to a class mural; others may love acting and can interpret a story through creative dramatics. They can also mix with members of higher achievement groups through participation in interest, project, skills, or friendship groups. These children should be seated with other class members, not segregated by reading group.

Names of groups can be labels that reinforce a slow reader's negative feelings, so teachers should avoid identifying groups by numbers or letters (1 or A for the top group, 2 or B for the middle group, and 3 or C for the low group), or by names that connote quickness or slowness. Instead they might allow children to name their own group or call a group by the title of the book that is being used.

Perhaps the most important factor in building a slow reader's self-concept is the kind of group rapport that the teacher helps to create. Children are likely to feel good about themselves if the teacher encourages them, praises their efforts, cares about them, and makes the lessons interesting. A warm, intimate atmosphere within a group will help students to feel better about reading and about themselves.

Scheduling of Groups   Reading achievement groups are generally held near the beginning of the day for about an hour and a half, and frequently this time period is used for instruction with the basal reader. A class with three achievement groups might be scheduled as shown in Table 11.2.

546

Teaching
Reading in
Today's
Elementary
Schools

TABLE 11.2 A General Plan for Grouping Within the Classroom

	Group A	Group B	Group C
10 min.	Introduction of daily reading activities by teacher		
30 min.	Teacher-directed activity	Independent work	Library reading
30 min.	Independent work	Library reading	Teacher-directed activity
30 min.	Library reading	Teacher-directed activity	Independent work
10 min.	Summary of daily reading activities by teacher		

Note: The table suggests that all groups possess the same ability to work independently. In actual classroom situations, there may be a need for more teacher-directed activities for the slower learning reading group(s).

The morning instructional period may be used for other approaches along with or instead of the basal reader. For instance, first graders might benefit from alternating basal reader instruction on Mondays, Wednesdays, and Fridays with language experience lessons on Tuesdays and Thursdays, while older students might alternate basal reader lessons with skill-group instruction. A class of students who can work well independently might engage in individualized reading every morning. The following is a variation of a group organizational plan designed for a one-hour reading session in the fifth grade where four groups are at work at the same time.

Group 1 (Low-achievement group)

The teacher starts the period with this group by helping the students compose a story for a language experience chart. After reading the chart, the pupils analyze words on the chart by applying phonics and structural analysis generalizations. The children then select books for independent reading and the teacher moves on to another group.

Group 2 (average readers)

These children have been finding information in reference books and trade books to write a group report on frogs. The teacher checks their progress, answers questions, and helps them find additional source material before moving on to the next group.

Group 3 (special skills group)

Three or four children are having difficulty with finding the main ideas. Another student who is proficient in this skill is helping them learn it by explaining it, showing examples, and helping them practice the skill on worksheets. The teacher stops by to make sure everything is going smoothly and to clarify any misunderstandings.

Group 4 (high-achievement group)

This group is reviewing sample books for the library. Each member is reading a book independently and writing a brief critique of it to be given to the librarian. The teacher checks with the students occasionally and listens to their comments about the books they are reading.

Children should not read for instructional purposes only; teachers should offer opportunities for recreational and functional reading later in the day. For a half-hour to an hour in the afternoon students might participate in whole-class or special-purpose group activities. This period should be relaxing and enjoyable so that students will realize that reading is more than skill building.

Management of Groups   No matter how good a lesson is, students will not learn much unless the teacher is able to control their behavior. Classroom management is a crucial factor in learning, especially when instruction is individualized or conducted in groups. Clear, sensible, consistent procedures can contribute to the maintenance of an orderly classroom.

The teacher must establish behavioral policies (perhaps with student input) that all students understand. At the beginning of the year these policies might be listed on a chart as part of a language experience lesson. Generally it is advisable to permit children reasonable freedom of movement and to allow them to talk quietly about task-related topics, but low voices and quiet movement should be stressed at all times. A child who breaks a pencil point, for instance, should be permitted to sharpen it without waiting to ask permission, but a teacher may want to limit the number of children at a learning center or allow only one student at a time to go to the restroom.

Children must know exactly what they are to do if they are expected to work well independently. After writing assignments for each group on the chalkboard, the teacher should spend time going over these assignments and making sure the students understand what they are asked to do. A list of things to do when they finish should also be available for students who complete their work early.

Room arrangement affects classroom management. Children should know where to find materials that they will need to use, such as workbooks, paper, scissors, and crayons, and they should know where to put completed work. Space should be provided for independent small-group work, and children should be able to move quickly and quietly to and from those areas that they use frequently.

The teacher should select carefully the best place in the room to hold basal reader groups. She should sit in a corner facing a semicircle of children who are in the group. From this vantage point the teacher can also watch the rest of the class and be aware of any problems that may be developing. If possible, she should sit by the chalkboard in order to use it for instructional purposes

548

Teaching
Reading in
Today's
Elementary
Schools

during reading groups. When children are working in other types of groups, she will move quietly from one group to another, answering questions and offering suggestions.

A good policy for teachers to follow while working with groups is to prohibit other children from interrupting, because interruptions are distracting and usually unnecessary. Appointed monitors can help solve small problems, such as identifying a word or finding a pencil, but children may consult the teacher about bigger issues if necessary while others are moving into or out of groups.

In order to maintain class control, teachers should make organizational changes slowly and gradually. Only those students who can be trusted to work well independently should be included in the initial stages if new groups are being formed or individualized reading is beginning. As more children participate in the new plan, some may not be able to handle the unstructured situation; these children may need to return to their seats and continue with traditional assignments until they can behave responsibly.

Worthwhile and interesting activities should be available for students while teachers work with groups because they can be important learning experiences. These activities are also important for maintaining good discipline, because children who are interested in their work are not apt to cause problems. Most independent activities are related to basal reader lessons, as either skill development or enrichment, but teachers should also offer a variety of interesting choices that will motivate children. Ideas may be listed on the board, placed at centers, or written on slips of paper for students to pull from an activity box. They should be changed periodically so that the class does not get bored. Students might choose from such ideas as those listed below.

Design and put up a bulletin board about your basal reader story.

See how many two-, three-, four-, or more syllable words you can find in your story.

Dramatize a story with a few other students for the rest of the class.

Read books from the class library or the school library that the teacher has checked out in advance. (The selection should be changed periodically.)

Compose a poem or short story and illustrate it on a sheet of paper that will become part of a class book.

Write a different ending for a story; write what you liked or did not like about the main character; or write another type of reaction to the story.

Fold a strip of paper (maybe three inches by twelve inches) into four sections and make a comic strip.

Look through your story to find all the descriptive words, action words, or naming words.

Make as many small words as you can from a large word that appears in your story, such as *Thanksgiving* or *spectacular*.

Write a story for the class newspaper.

Do research for a social studies or science project.

Work with a small group on a mural or diorama.

Write half a page about yourself for a class book and illustrate the rest of the page with a collage of things you like.

Arrange in sequence comic strips that have been cut into frames.

Write a story using the story starters in a commercial kit or that your teacher suggests. (Example: "I woke up in the middle of the night terrified by . . .")

Solve riddles or puzzles and create some of your own.

First graders must learn to do some things independently before they are grouped; so the teacher will need to help these youngsters develop self-control, good work habits, and social-interaction skills. In planning independent work, he or she must keep in mind the children's immaturity and limited reading ability, gradually introducing activities such as the following.

Playing a commercial or teacher-prepared game such as Lotto, alone or with a partner

Illustrating stories

Painting pictures

Cutting out pictures in magazines or catalogues of things that begin with a certain sound or objects that belong together

Modeling clay

Putting puzzles together

Engaging in dramatic play

Looking at picture books

Listening to stories at a listening station

Working with reading readiness workbooks

Using felt figures on a flannel board to retell a story

Working with word-bank cards

✔ Self-Check: Objective 2

Describe some strategies that teachers might use for managing an entire class while they are working with one reading group.
(See Self-Improvement Opportunities 2, 3, and 4.)

Interclass Grouping

Interclass grouping involves parallel scheduling of reading lessons among several sections of a grade or grades. Groups go to different rooms (or spaces within an open classroom) and are divided according to general reading level. One teacher provides instruction for one achievement group while another teacher works with another achievement level, and so on. This kind of grouping is based on the assumption that the range of skills that needs

550

Teaching
Reading in
Today's
Elementary
Schools

attention will be limited by the needs of a particular group and will be reduced for each teacher. Evidence indicates, however, that the range of skills in such situations is not appreciably lessened.

For such grouping to be homogeneous, teachers must know about many criteria. They should discover each student's achievement level, intelligence, interests, preferred learning modality, and academic motivation. Interclass grouping tends to ignore age and maturity differences, sometimes combining pupils from several grade levels, and often tends to separate reading activities from instruction in content areas.

✔ Self-Check: Objective 3
Describe several key characteristics of interclass groupings.

Other Organizational Plans

At times a teacher may find individualized or whole-class activities to be more appropriate than activities in small groups. A discussion of these other arrangements is presented below.

Individualized Learning

Teachers may wish to provide special reading activities for students in order to meet their individual needs and interests. Some may need extra practice in specific skill areas, while others may need opportunities for enrichment. Three types of individualized instruction are given here, and plans for managing independent work follow. (See also Chapter 6 for a discussion of individualization.)

Learning Centers A learning center is an area of the classroom that contains a set of materials with specific objectives, directions for meeting the objectives, provisions for various ability levels, and answers for self-checking (Harris and Hodges, 1981). The materials may be attached to a piece of masonite, hung on a pegboard, placed on shelves or in boxes, filed in kits, contained in folders or large envelopes, or displayed in some other way for children to use independently. Commercial kits and sets of materials are available for use at learning centers, but teachers often produce their own materials or collect readily available materials from various sources. Learning centers should contain attractive, varied, and interesting materials that are inviting to children. These centers supplement the basal reading program by offering extended opportunities for skill building and other reading-related tasks. Six ideas for learning centers, including suggested materials, appropriate skills to be developed, and sample activities, are shown in Example 11.1. All centers should contain necessary materials for carrying out activities and should include a comfortable place for children to work.

▶ **EXAMPLE 11.1:** Learning Centers

Telephone Directory Center
Materials: outdated telephone directories (whole books for small-town and rural areas; sections from large city directories)
Skills: alphabetizing, functional reading, following directions
Sample activities:
1. locating places (specific restaurants, doctors' offices, pet shops)
2. designing an advertisement for the yellow pages
3. identifying the steps in placing a call to Australia

Figurative Language Center
Materials: library books, old basal readers, scenic calendars
Skills: recognizing, understanding, and using figurative language
Sample activities:
1. writing a list of figurative expressions found in a story, poem, or comic strip and giving their actual meanings
2. looking at calendar pictures and writing similes that describe the scene
3. writing a story or play using many figurative expressions

Advertisements Center
Materials: magazines and cereal boxes
Skills: recognizing propaganda techniques, recognizing emotional and persuasive language
Sample activities:
1. finding and identifying examples of various propaganda techniques
2. finding appeals to buyers on cereal boxes, such as special offers, nutritional claims, recipes, and propaganda techniques
3. designing and writing advertisements with persuasive language

Travel Brochure Center
Materials: wide selection of travel brochures (available free from tourist bureaus and Chambers of Commerce)
Skills: distinguishing between fact and opinion, evaluating comparable materials, detecting misleading statements
Sample activities:
1. finding statements of fact and opinion
2. deciding which brochure has the most appeal and why
3. designing a brochure for a favorite place

Newspaper Center (primary level)
Materials: newspapers, scissors, glue, construction paper
Skills: classifying, recognizing sight words, interpreting pictures
Sample activities:
1. finding and cutting out pictures that go into certain categories, such as clothing, food, and sports

552

Teaching
Reading in
Today's
Elementary
Schools

2. finding sight words, cutting them out, and mounting them on construction paper
3. selecting a picture and writing a caption or story for it

Newspaper Center (intermediate level)
Materials: newspapers or sections of newspapers for special purposes
Skills: finding main ideas and details, making predictions, recognizing synonyms
Sample activities:

1. reading news stories without headlines, creating headlines, then matching original headlines to stories
2. reading about an ongoing local situation and predicting what will happen next based on given information
3. finding all the words that sportswriters use to mean "win" or "lose" ◄

Learning centers such as these require careful preparation and planning by the teacher. Students need to understand when they may go to the centers, how to use them, and where to place their completed work. They should be able to work independently and quietly without disturbing other children. Teachers need to provide protective coverings for frequently used materials, replenish supplies regularly, and replace center activities before children lose interest in them. Other types of centers that teachers may provide include library corners with a wide variety of reading materials and comfortable seating; computer centers; audiovisual stations with filmstrip projectors, tape recorders, and headphones; centers for puppet shows and creative drama; and writing centers with story starters and other motivating ideas.

Computer-Assisted Instruction Computer-assisted instruction (CAI) is another way that teachers can individualize learning. Although students may sometimes work in pairs or even in small groups at computer terminals, the branching and decision-making aspects of CAI make it suitable for individualized learning. (See Chapter 6 for more information on CAI.)

Most elementary school teachers believe that computers should be used primarily for tutoring basic skills, secondarily as a resource for learning about computers, and finally as a tool for doing an academic task, such as writing, solving problems, or analyzing data (Becker, 1986). Amarel (1984) also found that the most prevalent use of computers is probably for direct instruction through practice and drill in basic school subjects. Students with some knowledge of computer use and an understanding of the tasks they are to accomplish can move through increasingly difficult exercises independently. Too often, however, such drill-and-practice software allows only a limited number of response options and gives the student using the program little opportunity to think through, reconsider, or challenge prespecified answers. In order to challenge students' thinking skills, many teachers prefer to use software with gamelike formats to let students solve problems, make significant choices, restructure situations, and become actively involved in learning.

Many schools face the dilemma of how to use a limited number of computers to the best advantage. In recent years the number of computers in schools has about doubled each year (Bork, 1984), but even so, few students get sufficient exposure to computers. Becker (1984) studied computer use in elementary schools and found that only about one-eighth of the students in a typical elementary school with computers used one in any given week. Furthermore, those students who did use computers used them an average of only twenty minutes during the week, sometimes in paired or group situations. In a study involving over one thousand elementary school students, Amarel (1984) found that teachers varied in their approaches to scheduling students on terminals. Some teachers tightly controlled the use of terminals and distributed computer time uniformly among students, while other teachers allowed more aggressive students to dominate terminals, thereby limiting use by less assertive students, many of whom were girls.

A decentralized setting, such as a resource room or laboratory, may be more effective than a classroom for computer-assisted instruction intended to meet individual needs (Amarel, 1984). A number of schools are using this option to familiarize students with the computer itself and to provide experiences with programming and other computer skills. Most teachers who were questioned about the placement of a limited number of computers preferred to place them in one laboratory. Their next choice was to place half of them in the classroom and the other half in a lab, and their last choice was to place them only in classrooms (Becker, 1986).

Supervision of students using computers can be a problem for schools that have difficulty justifying the expense of a supervisor for the small number of children who may be working on computers at a single time. Currently, about two-thirds of teachers who use computers are general classroom teachers; the remainder are special education teachers, math or reading specialists, and computer specialists (Becker, 1986). The role of computer coordinator, someone who is primarily responsible for coordinating computer use within a school and is secondarily a teacher, may be emerging slowly.

When setting up computer centers, whether in the classroom or laboratory, teachers need to consider potential problems with a young child's developing vision. Some guidelines for teachers to observe in minimizing visual stress and providing comfortable conditions for working with computers are listed below (Warren and Baritot, 1986).

1. Keep keyboard, screen, and written material at an equal distance from the eyes.
2. Place screen so that it is slightly below eye level.
3. Use chairs that provide proper back support.

554

Teaching
Reading in
Today's
Elementary
Schools

4. Adjust chair height so that the user's feet are flat on the floor.
5. Adjust screen brightness and contrast for viewing comfort.
6. Eliminate glare and screen reflection.
7. Locate keyboard so that the user's wrist and lower arm are parallel to the floor.
8. Have students face an open, empty space beyond the screen, not a window or bright light source.
9. Allow students to take short breaks.

Managing computer use so that all students benefit is a challenge for the teacher. Okey and Majer (1976) experimented with having students work at computer terminals individually, in pairs, and in groups. They found no differences in academic achievement or attitude among the three organizational patterns, and they discovered that working in pairs often resulted in constructive discussions between the two students. Other possibilities for managing computer use effectively include providing opportunities for students to use computers before and after school, perhaps while waiting for buses; establishing computer centers where students can work during free time; forming computer clubs; using paraprofessionals, parent volunteers, and student tutors to supervise computer use; and scheduling specific periods of time for each child to work with the computer.

Seatwork   Teachers often ask students to do seatwork, which sometimes has been referred to negatively as "busy work," or work that serves no purpose other than to keep children busy while the teacher is otherwise occupied. Seatwork can be beneficial to children, however, if it is well planned, purposeful, related to other work that the students are doing, and carefully supervised.

Research findings indicate a number of valuable procedures for assigning and managing seatwork (Barr, 1984; Rosenshine and Stevens, 1984; Otto, Wolf, and Eldridge, 1984). In one study, teachers with higher-achieving children laid a better foundation for seatwork by initially spending more time presenting new concepts and giving clear instructions. Teachers with lower-achieving students spent less time making clear presentations so that children made more guesses and had higher error rates. In other studies both achievement and the rate of engagement, or proportion of time spent on task, for children doing seatwork increased significantly when teachers interacted with students by providing explanations and feedback. Short contacts with the teacher produced better academic performance and higher rates of engagement than long contacts, which resulted in more off-task behavior and decreased academic performance. Short contacts also enabled the teacher to monitor the work of more children in the same time span. In summary, teachers should make initial presentations of seatwork assignments carefully and should monitor students' seatwork through brief contacts.

Some guidelines for assigning seatwork follow.

1. Make sure that students understand the purpose of the seatwork. Tell them: "This will help you understand how to make inferences," or "When you finish this worksheet, you should be able to understand how to use the dictionary better."

2. Assign work that relates to the story. Some basal workbooks do not relate directly to the basal stories, so you may need to devise your own worksheets so that the children can see the connection between the story they have read and the work they are to do (Scheu, Tanner, and Au, 1986).
3. Assign work that is easy enough for the children to do without interrupting the teacher to ask for help. This is particularly important for younger children who lack the ability to work around difficult parts of the assignment (Rosenshine and Stevens, 1984).
4. Vary seatwork activities so that children don't get bored doing the same thing every day.
5. Take time to present the assignment clearly and thoroughly. Answer questions and make sure everyone understands what is to be done before letting them begin their work. Reinforce oral directions with written ones.
6. Move around the classroom when you are not with a reading group or otherwise occupied, so that you can offer assistance, encouragement, and feedback as children work.
7. Be realistic about the amount of time allotted for the seatwork. Everyone should be able to finish, and those that finish early should have choices of other activities to do until the others complete their work.

Although most teachers are likely to assign workbook pages or worksheets for at least part of the seatwork, other types of activities are also appropriate. Sentence expansion, in which the teacher gives a phrase or clause rich in visual imagery and lets students write the end of the sentence, is one useful activity. An example is "*If I met a huge bug,* I would jump on his back and smash him." The words in italics are those given by the teacher (Cudd, 1985, p. 591). Writing and illustrating expansions encourages children to use their imaginations and ponder appropriate completions for given clauses. Other seatwork activities include working with dictionaries, writing creative responses to basal reader stories, doing word puzzles and games, and working with kits or programmed materials.

Managing Individualized Work   One way to manage or keep track of individual activities is through student contracts. Students may "contract" to complete certain sequences of instruction designed to help them with their individual needs. The agreement may be formalized through the use of a contract, signed by the teacher and the child, that simply states what the pupil is to do and when the task is to be completed. A teacher can prepare and have available contracts calling for a variety of assignments and tasks, from which pupils can select those that most suit their needs, or a pupil can

556

Teaching
Reading in
Today's
Elementary
Schools

propose a contract and negotiate it with the teacher. Once agreed upon, the student should complete the contract as specified. Example 11.2 illustrates one such contract.

▶ **EXAMPLE 11.2:** Sample Pupil Contract Form

1. After listening to the librarian read aloud *The Cay* by Theodore Taylor, read one of the following to learn more about the idea of survival.
   a. *Island of the Blue Dolphins* by Scott O'Dell
   b. *Stranded* by Matt Christopher
   c. *Three Without Fear* by Robert C. Dusoe
   d. *Landslide* by Veronique Day
   e. *The Summer I Was Lost* by Philip Viereck
2. Share your research in one of these ways:
   a. Illustrate one incident in the story.
   b. Write a play dramatizing one incident.
   c. Make a model of an object that may be useful for survival.
   d. Interview an authority on the subject of some sort of survival technique and write a report.
   e. Compare the character(s) of your story with Robinson Crusoe in terms of self-reliance.

Choose one book from Number 1 and one method from Number 2 for your contract.
I plan to do 1 _____ and 2 _____. I will have this contract completed by _____.
Student's signature _____
Teacher's signature _____   ◀

A possible modification of the contract plan is called the assignment or job sheet. The teacher first identifies a definite instructional goal—for example, the mastery of a specific skill or subskill—and then organizes available material (textbooks/workbooks, and so on) to guide the learner toward that goal. Each child can proceed as fast as mastery permits. At times, children can work in pairs or teams of three to complete the assignment, which may take from three to five class periods. Example 11.3 shows a sample assignment sheet.

▶ **EXAMPLE 11.3:** Sample Job Sheet

How to Use an Encyclopedia #3 (_____ book)

Page	Directions
10	You and your partner take turns reading paragraphs to each other. Then read, answer, and check questions 1 and 2.

Page	Directions
12	You and your partner take turns reading paragraphs to each other. Then do as directed on the lower half of page 12.
13	Read, answer, and check questions on lower half of page 13.
14	Do sections 3 and 5 as directed.
18	Read and discuss this section with your partner; answer questions at bottom of page 18.
22	Write, as directed, working alone. When finished, check your work with your partner.
25	Complete blanks in the bottom right corner. Check your answers in the Teacher's Edition.

Now go to the teacher for a review discussion and check test before picking up your next assignment sheet. ◄

Teachers also need a record of the activities that students complete at learning centers. Since students do this work independently and check their own answers, teachers may not know exactly what the children are doing unless there is some way for them to keep account of their activities. One way of recording a child's work at the center is presented in Example 11.4.

► **EXAMPLE 11.4:** Sample Learning Center Record

Name _____
I worked at the _____ center or station.
Time in _____ Time out _____
How did you like the work? _____ (good, fair, poor)

Activity:

I read _____
I worked on _____
I listened to _____
I read aloud with _____
I wrote _____
I played a reading game _____
I did a worksheet on _____
I also _____ ◄

Teachers may use many strategies for managing and checking children's individualized work. They should establish policies regarding use of centers, conversations among children, visits to the library, expectations for the amount of work to be completed, procedures for recording activities, and so on. They must be sure that children understand exactly what they are to do

558
Teaching
Reading in
Today's
Elementary
Schools

before beginning their independent work and what they should do when they finish. Teachers may wish to write options for ways of using extra time on the chalkboard or on a chart. Some possibilities are given below.

1. Read your library book.
2. Write a different ending for a basal reader story.
3. Find books we can use for our social studies project.
4. Do a word puzzle from the folder.
5. Write a thank-you note to Ms. Wilbur for showing us pictures of England.
6. Practice reading your part for our play on Friday.

Teachers may post schedules or provide sign-up sheets for children to go to learning centers or work with computers. They may give pupils individual checklists for recording their activities or assignment sheets to complete and file in folders that can then be checked later. Although organizing and managing individualized instruction is not easy, it is worthwhile, because an important goal of education is to help students become good independent learners.

✔ Self-Check: Objective 4
Name three types of individualized instruction and give suggestions for implementing each plan.
(See Self-Improvement Opportunities 5 and 6.)

Whole-Class Activities

Teachers should use whole-class activities whenever possible to reduce any negative psychological effects from grouping and to develop a sense of class unity and rapport. Many reading activities are not directly related to achievement levels, so all children can participate in them together.

Among reading activities for the whole class are creative dramatics and choral reading, listening to stories read by the teacher or other students, taking part in sustained silent reading (see page 452), learning about reading study skills, going to the library, watching educational television, writing a class newspaper, creating a language experience story, watching and discussing a film or filmstrip of a story, sharing multiple copies of a student magazine or newspaper, playing word games, and sharing during a poetry hour.

Departmentalization

Under a departmentalized plan of teaching, there is a separate teacher for each subject, such as one teacher for the reading (and possibly other language arts) program, one for the social studies program, one for the science program, and so forth. A teacher may teach the same subject for five to six classes a day with one period free or devoted to giving individual help. Some correlation between reading (or language arts) and other subjects is possible

when a teacher works as part of a team with another teacher, such as the social studies teacher. In such a case, the two teachers can make use of a large block of time by teaching the two subjects back to back. Within the allotted time, many types of teaching and grouping can take place. The skills of one subject can be used to complement or develop the content of another subject. For example, since the children in social studies will need to know how to do research, the reading teacher can focus upon how to use reference materials. The major advantage of departmentalization is that the greater a teacher's understanding of a subject is, the greater the possibility for excellent instruction is, whereas the greatest disadvantage is probably that departmentalization tends to make the curriculum subject-centered rather than process- or child-centered.

Team Arrangement

A team arrangement involves combining two or three classes in one large area with a staff of several teachers. Team teaching has developed from the belief that all teachers are not equally skilled or enthusiastic in all curricular areas. While one teacher instructs the entire class or a group in an area of his particular competence, the other teachers work with other groups or individuals on other subjects. The team situation can offer a variety of activities in the best possible circumstances, making it possible to diagnose the word identification problems of a child, to group the child with other children who have the same problem, and to allow one teacher to give undivided attention to that group with no interference from the rest of the class. Meanwhile, another teacher can work with a group on a poetry unit, an activity she likes very much. Still another teacher can work with a group planning a book fair, while a fourth teacher can help some children with a particular content area reading difficulty. On other days, the teachers can work with the same children but on different problems or on the same problems with different children. Open physical arrangements in schools (three or four sections of children in a large undivided area) help to provide for this kind of teaching.

TEACHER EFFECTIVENESS

Although organizational patterns do affect student learning, a competent teacher, not a particular structure, makes the major difference. Researchers have found that "about 15 percent of the variation among children in reading achievement at the end of the school year is attributable to factors that relate to the skill and effectiveness of the teacher," but only "about 3 percent of the variation in reading achievement at the end of the first grade was attributable to the overall approach of the program" (Anderson et al., 1985, p. 85). Thus,

560

Teaching
Reading in
Today's
Elementary
Schools

the most essential ingredient of a good reading program appears to be the teacher.

Factors in Teacher Effectiveness

For many years educators have attempted to identify characteristics of effective teachers, but such qualities are often difficult to measure because of the subjective nature of interactions between teacher and pupils. Recently, research has pointed to certain factors and to models of teaching that appear to lead to improved performance by students.

According to Duffy and Roehler (1986), teachers must be instructional decision makers who organize and manage their classrooms for the benefit of students. Effective teachers:

1. focus on meaningful, purposeful reading instead of skill exercises.
2. view reading as a component of language that communicates rather than as a separate subject.
3. realize the importance of motivating children to *want* to read.
4. stress thinking and awareness instead of rote memory and single correct answers.
5. use basal readers as tools or guides and go beyond them to meet special goals and needs.
6. analyze reading assignments in basal readers and explain *how* to do the tasks.
7. realize the complexities of teaching and continually strive to develop their instructional competence by innovating and modifying their strategies.

The important point for teachers to consider as decision makers is that they must use their own professional judgment in deciding how best to teach instead of implicitly following someone else's directions.

Based on their research, Duffy and Roehler (1987) have also developed several procedures for effective instruction. When introducing a lesson, the teacher tells the students what they are to learn, when they are to use the information, and how they can learn it. Then the teacher models the learning process by reasoning aloud about the mental acts involved in reading. Guided practice follows with "responsive elaboration," an interactive process by which the teacher first assesses how well students are able to reason about and use their knowledge of reading strategies. The teacher then decides how and when to provide additional explanations to clarify students' applications of various strategies. For example, in order to determine how well a child is using mental processes when encountering an unknown word, the teacher might ask the student to think about the first thing to do and then the next, or the teacher might offer further explanations for using various strategies if the student's reasoning appears incomplete or faulty. The teacher's questioning and explanations focus on the student's thinking strategies, not on getting the correct answers.

Teacher-effectiveness research in the 1970s and 1980s has focused on measuring learning outcomes, and much attention has been given to instruction and its effect on students' learning (Rupley, Wise, and Logan, 1986). Recent studies have identified several factors related to teacher effectiveness, and five of them are discussed here: time, instruction, environment, management, and diagnosis.

Time

Academically engaged time, or the amount of time that students are actively involved in academic tasks at appropriate levels of difficulty, may be the best predictor of achievement (Harris, 1984). A study by Leinhardt, Zigmond, and Cooley had as its premise that learning occurs through engagement. "Children improve in reading in direct proportion to the amount of time they spend fruitfully engaged in reading activities at an appropriate level of difficulty" (Guthrie, 1982, p. 755). Leinhardt and others found that certain types of reading activities, or engagements, were more beneficial than others. For example, time spent in silent reading correlated positively with reading achievement, but no gains in achievement resulted from time spent in traditional oral reading or from indirect reading, including discussion and some types of workbook activities. Three teacher behaviors seemed to be most effective in gaining student attention and engagement: (1) teacher instruction, including presentations, explanations, and feedback; (2) reinforcement of student learning, such as giving praise or recognition for student efforts; and (3) "cognitive press," expressed through the teacher's support and encouragement of the student's inclination toward academic material.

Engagement rates tend to be higher when teachers spend more time pacing instruction according to the learning rates of individual students (Harris, 1984; Otto, Wolf, and Eldridge, 1984). The pace at which teachers move children through material depends on the students' ability to learn, the difficulty of the material, and the percentage of time that students are actively engaged in reading. Although effective teachers cover material at a brisk pace, they make sure that students understand the material before moving on.

In *Becoming a Nation of Readers*, Anderson et al. (1985) reported that high-ability groups cover much more text material than low-ability groups, and that there is wide variation of content coverage even within groups of similar ability at the same grade level. The amount of time teachers allocate to reading relates positively to the yearly gains students make on standardized reading test scores. In the average American elementary classroom, teachers allocate about an hour and a half per day to reading instruction, or about 30 percent of the school day.

Instruction

At one time "direct instruction" referred to a way of helping disadvantaged students learn basic skills, but many researchers now believe that direct

562

Teaching
Reading in
Today's
Elementary
Schools

instruction may be the best way to teach most subjects, including reading (Lehr, 1986). Direct instruction means that teachers control the learning that takes place by providing a structured classroom environment, setting goals, deciding what activities to use, and providing immediate feedback (Blair, 1984). Students who are taught directly by the teacher consistently perform better than those who learn for themselves or from other students (Rosenshine and Stevens, 1984). Rates of engagement also tend to be higher during teacher-directed instruction than during student-centered learning when pupils direct their own activities.

Research has identified some effective ways of performing instructional procedures, including those related to demonstration, guided practice, corrective feedback, and independent practice (Rosenshine and Stevens, 1984). Recommended ways for implementing these procedures include the following:

1. *Demonstration.* Proceed in small steps, provide many examples, and ask questions during the demonstration to monitor student understanding.
2. *Guided practice.* Ask questions frequently, use questions directly related to the material, and provide practice that enables students to achieve an 80 percent or higher rate of achievement.
3. *Corrective feedback.* Provide brief feedback for correct answers by affirming their correctness. Follow incorrect answers by asking simpler questions that give hints or by reteaching the material through explanations.
4. *Independent practice.* Interact with students during group work in order to prepare them for seatwork. Actively monitor their seatwork and supply enough independent practice so that they overlearn skills and their responses become automatic.

Skillful teachers continuously evaluate the effectiveness of their instruction by monitoring student performance and reteaching if pupils make frequent errors and seem confused.

Although most current research points toward the use of direct instruction for promoting student achievement, teachers need to be aware of potential dangers (Lehr, 1986). Too much structure and skill building denies students opportunities to think and act creatively, solve problems, and develop independence.

Environment

Effective teachers provide classroom environments that are structured and orderly. Harris (1984) reviewed research revealing the superiority of highly structured, formal programs over informal programs in promoting student achievement, developing creativity among children with high IQs, and reducing test anxiety. Indeed, some structure is desirable in most school activities, particularly those in the primary grades and for low-ability, dependent, or anxious pupils (Rupley, Wise, and Logan, 1986). Students scored lower on achievement tests when they had more freedom to choose their own activities and when they worked independently without direct supervision (Otto, Wolf, and Eldridge, 1984).

Not only do effective teachers provide structured, orderly classrooms, but they also offer supportive emotional environments for students by being friendly and accepting and by avoiding sarcasm and disapproval. They praise pupils for sincere efforts and believe that they can and will learn. When students are aware that teachers hold positive expectations for them, they are likely to do their best work.

Successful teachers also create language-rich learning environments that provide varied opportunities for children to use language (Anderson et al., 1985). Reading, writing, speaking, and listening are all important components of language programs, and teachers need to provide children with occasions for communicating ideas, learning about words, writing for many purposes, and learning new information from printed materials.

Management

Behavior control, or discipline, is also related to teacher effectiveness. Achievement scores tend to be higher when there is less disruptive behavior in the classroom (Otto, Wolf, and Eldridge, 1984), and skilled teachers know how to prevent many problems from arising and to deal quickly with those that do arise (Anderson et al., 1985). Effective teachers establish guidelines for behavior and procedures for carrying out daily routines in order to minimize confusion and time wasting. Wasted time and disturbances result in loss of attention, which in turn reduces the amount of engaged time that students spend on academic tasks. In low-ability groups children are more likely to be disruptive and to require teacher intervention, thus interfering with their concentration on reading (Otto, Wolf, and Eldridge, 1984), but classroom behavior tends to be better when reading material is relatively easy (Harris, 1984).

Classroom teachers make countless decisions daily as they manage their classrooms. Not only must they manage potential behavior problems, but they must also select appropriate materials, organize instruction, choose teaching strategies, evaluate students' work, and decide how to meet individual needs. These decisions affect students' learning and ultimate achievement (Otto, Wolf, and Eldridge, 1984).

Diagnosis

Good teachers are aware of individual learning styles, strengths and weaknesses, reading levels, and interests when providing instruction and making assignments. They observe students closely as they work for signs of problems and then provide corrective help as necessary. When teachers use the results of ongoing diagnosis as a basis for instruction, achievement scores tend to be higher. In addition, scores may be higher and attitudes more positive when

564

Teaching
Reading in
Today's
Elementary
Schools

students work on relatively easy material (Otto, Wolf, and Eldridge, 1984). Easy instructional material lets students concentrate on new words or concepts, develop fluency, and enjoy reading (Harris, 1984).

Blair (1984) claims that students placed at their instructional levels progress at rates commensurate with their ability. The likelihood for success on specific reading tasks increases for these students, but pupils who work at their frustration levels are unlikely to achieve proficiency in basic skills. When in doubt about correct placement, teachers should place children in material that is slightly easy for them, since recent research indicates that children make better progress when using easy material (Harris, 1984). Stories in basal readers vary in difficulty, however; a book at a child's instructional level may sometimes contain material that is too difficult to read comfortably.

✔ Self-Check: Objective 5

List several components of effective teaching and explain the meaning of each.

(See Self-Improvement Opportunity 7.)

The Madeline Hunter Model of Teacher Effectiveness

Madeline Hunter has developed a model based on research related to teaching and learning and on an analysis of the instructional decisions that teachers make (Weisberg, 1986). Because the only variable that teachers can control in teacher-learner interaction, according to Hunter, is their own behavior, teachers should be responsible for their instructional decisions. Her model is not a formula for decision making, but only "a vehicle for enhancing teachers' instructional decision making and their continued professional growth" (Weisberg, 1986, p. 232).

Hunter's model contains seven elements or instructional processes that affect success in learning (Hunter and Russell, 1977). Not all seven instructional processes need to be included in every lesson, however, and teachers should understand that the plan is "not a rigid formula but a set of useful elements" (Wolfe, 1987, p. 70). When teachers have a clear understanding of the purpose and application of these procedures, they are able to make intelligent decisions about if and when to include each of them. The seven elements are given below with accompanying explanations, and the model activity that follows shows how the Hunter model can be applied to a reading lesson.

1. *Anticipatory set.* The teacher prepares the students for the lesson by having them focus their attention, thereby establishing mental readiness, and by providing brief practice on previous and related learnings.
2. *The objective and its purpose.* The teacher tells the students what they should be able to do at the end of the lesson and why it is important to be able to do this, giving real-life examples.

3. *Instructional input.* The teacher decides what information the students need in order to meet the stated purpose and then presents them with this information.

4. *Modeling.* The teacher models or demonstrates what is to be learned, while giving a verbal explanation of what is happening. Such modeling helps the students understand the lesson better.

5. *Checking for understanding.* The teacher ascertains that the students possess essential information and can perform the skills needed for reaching the lesson's objective. This can be done through sampling (asking questions of the whole group and getting answers from some group members), signaled responses (getting signaled answers from all group members), or individual private responses (getting a whispered or written response from each group member).

6. *Guided practice.* The teacher monitors the children's initial work on a new learning task to make sure they understand it before allowing them to practice independently.

7. *Independent practice.* When the teacher is convinced that the children can perform the assignment reasonably well, the students continue practicing without direct teacher supervision.

The following lesson plan on teaching the main idea of a paragraph is based on Madeline Hunter's model of teacher effectiveness.

● **MODEL ACTIVITY:** *Main Idea Lesson Plan Based on the Hunter Model*

1. *Anticipatory set.* Say to the children: "Yesterday we were talking about how to find the main idea for a group of words. Let's try another example today. Look at the words on the chalkboard (apple, pear, peach, banana) and tell me the main idea." The children give the answer "fruit," and you say: "That's right. I want you to remember that the main idea includes all of the items on the list. It is the major topic for these words. Today we are going to learn more about main ideas."

2. *The objective and its purpose.* Say: "Who can tell me what a paragraph is?" Let the children respond until they give you a reasonable definition. Then say: "Today you will learn how to find the main idea of a paragraph. When you can do this, you will be able to understand what you read more easily."

3. *Instructional input.* Use teacher explanation and discussion as your means of instructional input, and use a paragraph about the usefulness of robots for your example. Tell the children: "I am going to show you how to find the main idea of a paragraph. Look at the paragraph that is written on the chalkboard. Read it to yourselves and think about what it is mostly about. Look for a topic or subject that appears in nearly every sentence. This will be part of the main idea." Pause to allow each child enough time to read the paragraph. Then ask: "What was the paragraph mostly about?" If the children say robots, then say: "Now think about what the writer is telling us about robots. Robots is the topic, but what central or major idea about robots does the writer want us to understand?" Through discussion, help them to develop the thought that robots can be used in many

566

Teaching
Reading in
Today's
Elementary
Schools

ways. Then explain that this is the main idea because it tells us the main message that the author is giving about the topic. If they do not answer correctly or cannot expand the topic into a statement of the main idea, give hints or clues that will help them find the right answer. If they continue to be confused, provide additional examples and explanations.

4. *Modeling.* Say to the children: "Now let's look at the second paragraph on the board. This time I will read it aloud for you. Then I will tell you what I am thinking as I decide what the main idea is for this paragraph." Read the paragraph aloud. Then go back and read one sentence at a time, commenting on each as follows. "This paragraph seems to be about dogs. The first sentence tells about working dogs. The second one says that dogs are pets, and the third sentence says that dogs can sometimes be used for hunting. Since all of these sentences are about dogs, the topic could be 'dogs.' Also, because the writer says that dogs can be used for working, for pets, and for hunting, I believe the main idea is that dogs have many functions. I'll read the paragraph again to make sure that I'm right." Pause. Then say: "Yes, that seems to be what the paragraph is mostly about, so 'the many functions of dogs' must be the main idea."

5. *Checking for understanding.* Say to the students: "Let's try one more example. Read the third paragraph on the board to yourselves." Let them read it.

   Sampling. Ask the students: "Class, what do you think the main idea of this paragraph is? Billy, can you tell me?" After Billy responds, ask, "How do you know?"

   Signaling. Say to the class: "How many of you agree with Billy? Show me by putting your thumbs up if you agree, putting your thumbs down if you disagree, or holding them to the side if you are not sure."

   Individual private response. Say to the students: "Write on a piece of paper what you think the main idea is for the third paragraph. I will come around and check to see if you are right."

6. *Guided practice.* Say to the class: "I am giving you a worksheet with four paragraphs on it. You are to find the main idea for each paragraph. I will be coming around to make sure you understand how to find the main idea. Let me know if you need help."

7. *Independent practice.* Say to the children: "Most of you seem to know what the main idea is for the first paragraph. Continue working on your own until you finish the worksheet." ●

The Hunter model is not without its critics. Some say that it is too simplistic and mechanistic, that it stifles thinking, and that it is too didactic (Gibboney, 1987). Other critics claim that too much instruction relies on the teacher's telling the students what to do (Glaser, 1987), and that the model is adequate for direct teaching but is not effective for the arts, discovery learning, or cooperative learning (Hunter, 1985). Furthermore, a major research study has failed to support its effectiveness. After participating in the four-year

Napa/Vacaville Follow Through Project, which was based on the Hunter model, children in the experimental group did not score higher than children in the control group in reading and mathematics (Robbins and Wolfe, 1987; Stallings, 1987).

Regardless of these criticisms, many teachers like the model. It is clear and easy to learn; it provides a sensible framework for the process of teaching; and it offers a common vocabulary for labeling teaching strategies (Freer and Dawson, 1987). Hunter claims that her model can be applied to every style of teaching and learning and that it provides "the launching pad from which creativity can soar" (Hunter, 1985, p. 58). Problems with using the model are likely to develop only when it is interpreted too rigidly and teachers feel that they must include each element in every lesson.

✔ Self-Check: Objective 6
Name as many of the seven elements in the Madeline Hunter model as you can. Try to relate them to the research you read on teacher effectiveness.
(See Self-Improvement Opportunities 7 and 8.)

Professional Development

Effective teachers continue to develop professionally in a variety of ways. They take college courses for advanced degrees and recertification; they participate in in-service activities; and they join professional organizations. Through these associations they can subscribe to publications and participate in conferences in order to learn about and apply new ideas. Some professional organizations related to the interests of elementary reading teachers are listed below, together with their addresses and major publications.

Association for Supervision and Curriculum Development, 125 N. West Street, Alexandria, VA 22314. *Educational Leadership*

International Reading Association, 800 Barksdale Road, P.O. Box 8139, Newark, DE 19714. *The Reading Teacher, Journal of Reading, Reading Research Quarterly*

National Association for the Education of Young Children, 1834 Connecticut Avenue, N.W., Washington, DC 20009. *The Young Child*

National Council of Teachers of English, 1111 Kenyon Road, Urbana, IL 61801. *Language Arts*

PARENTS

Parents and teachers should work together to create a positive learning environment for children. A child's first learning experiences occur in the home, and the home continues to provide educational opportunities that

568

Teaching
Reading in
Today's
Elementary
Schools

supplement learning activities in the classroom. Therefore, it is important for teachers to understand a child's home environment and to communicate with those responsible for the child's well-being.

In a review of research, Wigfield and Asher (1984) concluded that parents exert a strong influence on children's acquisition of reading skills and orientation to achievement. These researchers also made several observations regarding the home reading environment and implications for helping children achieve success in reading. Children's reading ability correlates positively with the availability of appropriate reading materials at home and the ways parents and children interact with each other using these materials. Parents who read to their children, take them to the library, model positive reading behaviors, and encourage their children to read increase their children's likelihood of becoming good readers. If parents provide these services for their children and have positive attitudes toward reading, their children should look upon reading as a pleasurable activity and, as a result, read more.

Home Activities

Because language usage is initiated long before children have their first encounters with school, parents are important partners in the school's endeavors. Fortunate are those children whose homes provide an outward sense of love, a feeling of security, wholesome food, adequate rest—all of which contribute to a stable environment for learning. Parents who talk with and listen to their children, who bring signs and labels to their attention, who share experiences with them, and who read to them provide a natural background for beginning reading instruction. Since not all children experience the benefits of all these activities, some parents may need assistance and information about ways to provide a good home environment for their children's success in school.

Listening and speaking with children are of paramount importance. An attentive listener encourages further conversational efforts. Conversation with parents is an important way for children to learn to be willing to let others talk in turn and to interrupt less frequently. In talking with parents, children hear sentence patterns and rhyming words, have opportunities to distinguish sounds of many types, and gain information and words. Casual conversations between parents and children may occur as children play house, build with blocks, or enjoy toys. Opportunities abound every day for talking and listening at home: weather, news, food, clothing, pictures, games, pets, furniture, and plants are all good topics for discussion between parents and children. Everyday opportunities for sharing experiences with younger children include visits to nearby parks, local shops, fire stations, and the like. Parents can easily answer children's questions and explain the meanings of new words while families are enjoying experiences together. More special trips might involve visits to a museum, zoo, bakery, dairy farm, or bottling company; longer trips provide even more talk about roads, rivers, mountains, or animals new to the children. A camping trip, for example, offers many opportunities for developing vocabulary in several areas:

Bedding: air mattresses, cots, mosquito netting, sleeping bags
Kitchen equipment: aluminum foil, charcoal, cooler, Dutch oven, grill, propane, spatula, tongs
Personal equipment and shelter: first-aid kit, ground canvas, tent, insect repellent, stakes, washbasin
Tools: ax, compass, lantern, pliers, radio, saw, screwdriver, shovel.

Communicating with Parents

It is important to maintain communication between teachers and parents. Among the traditional methods of communication are newsletters (carefully written letters and bulletins to keep the parents informed about happenings at school), school booklets (including rules and regulations and helpful information that parents need to know before and after sending their child to school), Parent-Teacher Association meetings, written reports in the form of personal letters or checklists, telephone calls, parent-teacher conferences, home visits (which give the parent and teacher a chance to discuss particular problems and acquaint the teacher with the home environment of the child), and Open House days (when the parents visit in the child's classroom—with or without the child—to familiarize themselves with the materials, schedules, and routines of the school day). For years schools have utilized these methods, in various combinations, to foster communication between school and home.

The report card is the traditional way to inform parents and children about the child's performance in school, but report cards often give incomplete information that can be misunderstood. If teachers want parents to have additional information about their children and the school program, they may arrange parent-teacher conferences.

Many schools schedule parent-teacher conferences two or three times throughout the school year, but teachers can arrange conferences whenever they are necessary. During a conference, the teacher needs to listen to the parent's concerns, share samples of the child's schoolwork, show records of achievement (test scores, for example), and offer constructive suggestions for ways that the parent and teacher can work together for the child's benefit. Parents may want to obtain ideas from the teacher for encouraging children to improve their reading skills by working with them in the home. Teachers should maintain informal records of major points discussed with parents, conclusions reached, and recommendations for the child by teacher and parents.

Parents are often interested in how homework is assigned. Most homework should be carefully planned and informal in nature, supplementing formal

570

Teaching
Reading in
Today's
Elementary
Schools

preparation in the classroom. It should be assigned only after children understand the concepts and ideas and are motivated sufficiently to do the homework unaided. Hopefully, most homework assignments will be personalized, suited to the individual, and there will be little or no regularly assigned drill-type homework for the entire class.

The fall conference or Open House is a good time to introduce parents to the reading materials used in the school and to describe the reading experiences and skills that are being emphasized in that particular year. A teacher may want to explain how the reading program is organized and the general approaches he or she uses. The teacher may also point out what (if anything) will be required of the child in terms of homework, as well as what to do when the child requests help. In an early parent meeting, the teacher also might suggest that the parents encourage supporting activities, such as reading games (homemade or commercially produced) and television logs (records of what the child watches).

In a later conference, the teacher can share children's work and test results with parents, reporting the results of norm-referenced reading tests and explaining the range of class scores, the median score of the class, and the individual student's score. These test results provide some tangible information to discuss, and this type of information is relatively free of teacher bias; therefore, it contributes to easy discussion of problems. In parent-teacher conferences, just as in discussions with students, teachers should attempt to give a true picture of test results and of their implications, pointing out any particular difficulties of the child and discussing why these difficulties exist and how the teacher is attempting to help. Interested parents may request additional ideas to use with their children for reinforcing reading skills and attitudes.

Teachers can also communicate with parents at parent-teacher meetings, through both regularly scheduled programs and informal meetings before or after a program. Some topics for parent-teacher programs might include the following:

1. What we know about how children learn to read, emphasizing individual differences and levels of development
2. Techniques for reinforcing a child's learning behaviors (providing for success, using the child's interests, values of word games, and the like)
3. Making and using homemade educational products for the child
4. Classroom observation (how to observe)
5. Use of multimedia (library, comic books, television, and so on)
6. Parent-teacher conferences (importance of home-school partnership, for instance)

Teachers also communicate with parents through letters, progress reports, and notices that they send home with children. Some basal reader series provide letters for teachers to send home periodically as children complete

Parents are important partners in the school's endeavors—by stressing the value of reading and by actually reading to and with their children, they can help build positive attitudes toward books. (© Gloria Karlson)

units of work; the school may publish brochures informing parents of school policies and special events; libraries may provide lists of recommended recreational reading suitable for various age levels; and professional societies may have helpful bulletins or pamphlets for teachers to send home. Children may write letters to their parents about a forthcoming event and practice their handwriting skills at the same time. The classroom teacher may write a personal note to a parent, especially for praising a child's performance; at the end of the school year send home a summer calendar of reading-related activities for each day; provide parents with activities to do with children that correspond to current reading objectives; or send a form letter, such as the following, that applies to a group or whole class of children.

During the past six weeks your child has been working on a folklore unit in reading class. He or she has studied the characteristics of tall tales and has attempted to write an original tall tale of his or her own after reading several examples and hearing other examples read by the teacher. Your child's story is attached to this report. You may wish to read it and discuss it with him or her. All of the children produced tall tales which indicated an understanding of this form of literature.

Some topics suitable for bulletins or letters include the following:

1. Reading to your child
2. Storytelling with your child
3. Answering your child's questions
4. Using the public library
5. Playing reading games with your child
6. Sharing poetry

General Suggestions

Following are some general suggestions to offer parents for helping their children enjoy reading.

1. Keep in touch with the school about your child's reading so that you will know how to help.
2. Help your child study and do homework by providing space, time, materials, and assistance if necessary.
3. If your child is having difficulty with reading, contact the teacher to see how you might be able to help.
4. Listen to your child read a story aloud at home and ask questions about it.
5. Encourage your child to look in books for answers to questions.
6. Read aloud to your child often.
7. Have a family reading time when everyone reads together.
8. Make library visits a family event. Check out books together and encourage your child to participate in summer reading programs or story hours.
9. Include your child in family games that promote reading skills.
10. Listen to your child tell about a favorite book or story, and ask questions about it that require thoughtful answers.
11. Buy books for birthday or holiday gifts or as surprises.
12. Be a model of good reading by showing how much you enjoy reading yourself.
13. Read interesting passages from newspapers and magazines to your child.
14. Become involved with school activities by working as a parent volunteer or attending parent-teacher meetings.
15. If possible, help your child learn to use computers at home. Provide opportunities for using word processing to compose stories, activities to promote reading skill development, and games that encourage interest in reading.

16. Encourage your child to read and use a variety of materials, including brochures on special subjects, maps and tourist information about family trips, telephone directories, and catalogues.
17. Let your child subscribe to a children's magazine and/or become a member of a children's book club.
18. Provide an opportunity for your child to write and illustrate a book.

✔ Self-Check: Objective 7
Name several ways in which parents work with the teacher for the benefit of the child.
(See Self-Improvement Opportunities 9, 10, and 11.)

PARAPROFESSIONALS AND TUTORS

Many adults work as paid or volunteer assistants or aides to the teacher by helping with individual or small-group instruction, grading workbooks or test papers, making displays, supervising computer-assisted instruction, and performing clerical tasks. These paraprofessionals need some professional training in how to relate to children positively, how to teach simple skills, and how to judge pupil progress. Under the best conditions, paraprofessionals in the reading classroom can be instructional aides as well as clerical aides. Basically, the classroom teacher is responsible for the activities the aide performs and for preparing the paraprofessional to carry out assigned activities. Teacher supervision of the aide is necessary. Some areas in which the paraprofessional may be of assistance in the classroom, assuming he or she is a capable and responsible person, are suggested below.

1. scoring teacher-made tests or worksheets
2. working with small groups or individuals on particular reading skills
3. reading to large or small groups and listening to children read individually
4. setting up and using audiovisual materials (transparencies, charts, posters, tape recorders, projectors, and so on)
5. preparing the instructional materials (word files, skills boxes, and the like)
6. arranging for guests to speak with the class
7. assisting in planning and supervising field trips
8. working with small groups in instructional games
9. assisting children in the use of reference materials
10. setting up displays and bulletin boards
11. developing and setting up learning-center activities
12. assisting in maintaining records for evaluation of pupil progress

For the most part, studies of many types of tutoring programs, including peer tutoring, tutoring by older students, and tutoring by adults, have shown

574

Teaching
Reading in
Today's
Elementary
Schools

positive results. Attitudes and achievement of both the *tutees*, those receiving tutoring, and the tutors improved (Otto, Wolf, and Eldridge, 1984).

Peer tutoring occurs when one child tutors another child, of either the same or a different age, while *cross-age tutoring* occurs only with students of different ages (Ehly and Larsen, 1984). Being a tutor and modeling teacher-like behavior boosts the confidence and self-esteem of a "problem student," and a good student benefits in a similar manner by teaching skills to other children. The tutee also profits from peer tutoring by learning in a more relaxed and informal way than is possible in the traditional classroom environment. When matching tutors with students, teachers must consider both the academic strengths and the emotional behavior of each student pair so that the two will work well together. Each tutor should receive training in planning appropriate lessons, selecting materials, following acceptable teaching procedures, and assessing the progress of the tutee.

Cooledge and Wurster (1985) describe another type of tutoring in which retirees become tutors for schoolchildren. In Arizona, the Volunteer Partners Program recruits, trains, and places retired people in public schools, where they work with individuals or small groups of children during the school year. A research study that compared differences in achievement between control and experimental groups showed that students who were tutored by the retirees made significant increases in reading achievement.

✔ Self-Check: Objective 8

Provide several examples of how paraprofessionals and tutors may be of assistance in the reading program.
(See Self-Improvement Opportunity 12.)

Summary

Orderly, efficient classroom organization is an important component of effective reading instruction. Several possibilities exist for organizing a classroom, including different ways of grouping children. The most common type of reading group is the achievement group, which is based on children's reading levels. Although achievement groups generally meet all year to provide reading skills instruction, teachers should keep membership within these groups flexible. Other types of reading-related groups include special skills or needs groups, interest groups, project or research groups, friendship groups, and pupil pairs or partners. Teachers usually create these arrangements for a limited time and a specific purpose, and they may help to alleviate negative self-concepts for low-achieving children.

In addition to forming groups, teachers may wish to individualize instruction by providing learning centers, stations for computer-assisted instruction, and independent seatwork. At times students benefit from whole-class instruction, and some schools form larger organizational patterns, including departmentalization and team arrangements. Just as there is no one best way to teach reading for all children, there is no one way to organize a class to suit the needs of every teacher or every group of children. Usually schools and teachers use a combination of plans, because each one has strengths and weaknesses.

Recent research in teacher effectiveness has provided some guidelines for reading teachers to follow. The amount of time that students are actively engaged in academic tasks correlates positively with their achievement. Students learn better with teacher-directed instruction in which teachers control the learning by setting goals, demonstrating the desired learning, guiding practice, and providing corrective feedback. A structured, orderly environment in which teachers manage behavior and allow few disruptions is likely to increase student performance. Skillful teachers carefully diagnose their students' strengths and weaknesses and then place them in reading materials at levels where they can succeed. The Madeline Hunter model of teacher effectiveness provides one framework for teachers to follow for teaching reading.

Parents strongly influence children's acquisition of reading skills and their attitudes toward achievement. Teachers should communicate with parents frequently in a variety of ways, including parent-teacher conferences, report cards, meetings, and publications. Teachers can offer suggestions to parents for helping them create supportive reading environments in the home.

Teachers can benefit from the assistance of both paraprofessionals and tutors in the classroom. Paraprofessionals, or teacher aides, can provide a variety of reading-related services, including listening to children read, grading papers, preparing instructional materials, and assisting children in locating and using reference materials. Peer tutoring, cross-age tutoring, and tutoring by adult volunteers are also effective for helping children learn to read.

Test Yourself

True or False

_____ 1. Once organizational patterns have been established, they should be consistently maintained.

_____ 2. Low reading achievement groups should have more students than high reading achievement groups.

_____ 3. A wider range of reading levels within a single classroom is more common at lower elementary grade levels than at higher elementary grade levels.

_____ 4. Every classroom should contain three reading achievement groups.

_____ 5. Achievement grouping is a method of grouping children according to the level of reading material they can read comfortably.

_____ 6. Other than achievement groups, most groups are formed for a limited time and a specific purpose.

576

Teaching
Reading in
Today's
Elementary
Schools

_____ 7. Members of the low reading achievement group should be separated from the rest of the class during other activities as well.

_____ 8. Organizational changes should be made slowly and gradually.

_____ 9. If reading skills are adequately covered during the reading instructional period, there is no need for any other type of reading during the day.

_____ 10. Classroom management is an important factor in how well students learn.

_____ 11. Even within groups based on reading achievement, there will be a diversity of abilities.

_____ 12. Specific needs grouping puts together children who need to work on the same skill.

_____ 13. Learning centers provide individualized instruction by allowing children to carry out activities independently.

_____ 14. Computer-assisted instruction can be used only with one student for each computer.

_____ 15. Most schools have specialized computer coordinators who are responsible for computer use.

_____ 16. Seatwork is only busy work that keeps children occupied while the teacher works with groups.

_____ 17. Student contracts are one way that teachers can use to manage individual activities.

_____ 18. Whole-class reading activities are most effective when introducing specific reading skills.

_____ 19. The organizational pattern of a classroom is more important than the teacher.

_____ 20. The amount of time that a student spends engaged in a learning task is directly related to achievement.

_____ 21. The more time teachers spend on reading instruction, the better their students are likely to read.

_____ 22. Student-centered learning results in higher achievement than teacher-directed learning, according to research.

_____ 23. Teachers should avoid making comments and giving feedback during guided practice sessions.

_____ 24. Placing children in books that are difficult for them to read is the best way for them to learn.

_____ 25. Classroom disruptions have little or no effect on students' achievement.

_____ 26. Freedom to choose activities and independent work yield higher achievement scores for students than structured classroom environments.

_____ 27. Madeline Hunter's model deals primarily with grouping students for instruction.

_____ 28. In reality, parents are their children's first teachers of reading.

_____ 29. In reading to their children, parents are providing a foundation for the school's reading program.

_____ 30. Sending bulletins or letters to parents is a valuable way for teachers to communicate about the school's reading program.

_____ 31. Teacher aides should do only clerical work in the classroom.

Self-Improvement Opportunities

1. Talk to at least two teachers at different grade levels to determine how they organize their classes during formal reading instruction.
2. Plan a daily reading schedule that provides for group instruction, individualized instruction, and whole-class instruction. Include time for recreational reading.
3. Using the information given below, divide a hypothetical third-grade class into reading achievement groups. In making your decisions, consider the guidelines about grouping in this chapter. Compare your grouping plan with the plans of other students in your class.

Number of Children	*Reading Grade Level*
1	1^2
3	2^1
4	2^2
8	3^1
7	3^2
1	4
2	5
1	6

4. What are some things you would do to help a child in the low reading group overcome feelings of inferiority?
5. In a small group, discuss the advantages and disadvantages of individualized plans.
6. Survey the elementary schools near your home and find out the following information about computer-assisted instruction:
   a. The number of computers for student use in relation to the number of children enrolled in the school
   b. The percentage of teachers who use computers
   c. The types of organization for computer use (classroom, computer labs, media centers, and other arrangements).
7. Rate yourself in your practicum work or classroom teaching according to the criteria for teacher effectiveness. What are your strong and weak areas?
8. Develop a lesson plan using the Madeline Hunter model. Use one of the following topics or one of your own choosing.
   a. Recognizing consonant blends
   b. Making inferences
   c. Using context clues

578

Teaching
Reading in
Today's
Elementary
Schools

d. Using an index

e. Identifying the theme of a story

9. Make a calendar of reading-related activities for children to take home at the end of the year and do during the month of June. Identify the grade level, and provide a wide variety of interesting tasks.

10. Interview the parents of a preschooler to find out if they are providing a positive environment for learning to read. Consider especially the reading materials in the home, story reading by the parents, and interactions between parents and child that promote interest in reading.

11. Prepare a letter or bulletin to parents on one of the topics suggested on page 572.

12. Talk with a paraprofessional about his or her role in the reading program. Then share your findings with members of the class.

Bibliography

Amarel, Marianne. "Classrooms and Computers as Instructional Settings." *Educational Digest* 50 (September 1984): 48–51.

Anderson, Richard C., Elfrieda H. Hiebert, Judith A. Scott, and Ian A. G. Wilkinson. *Becoming a Nation of Readers.* Washington, D.C.: National Institute of Education, 1985.

Barr, Rebecca. "Beginning Reading Instruction." In *Handbook of Reading Research,* P. David Pearson, ed. New York: Longman, 1984, pp. 545–81.

Becker, Henry Jay. "Computers in Schools Today." *American Journal of Education* 93 (November 1984): 22–39.

Becker, Henry Jay. "Our National Report Card: Preliminary Results from the New Johns Hopkins Survey." *Classroom Computer Learning* 6 (January 1986): 30–33.

Blair, Timothy R. "Teacher Effectiveness: The Know-How to Improve Student Learning." *The Reading Teacher* 38 (November 1984): 138–42.

Bork, Alfred. "Computers in Education Today—And Some Possible Futures." *Phi Delta Kappan* 66 (December 1984): 239–43.

Brophy, Jere E. "Advances in Teacher Effectiveness Research." Paper presented at the annual meeting of the American Association of Colleges for Teacher Education, Chicago, Illinois, 1979, 24 pp. [ED 170 281].

Cooledge, Nancy J., and Stanley R. Wurster. "Intergenerational Tutoring and Student Achievement." *The Reading Teacher* 39 (December 1985): 343–46.

Cudd, Evelyn. "Super Seatwork." *The Reading Teacher* 38 (February 1985): 591–92.

Dallman, Martha, et al. *The Teaching of Reading.* 6th ed. New York: Holt, Rinehart and Winston, 1982.

Duffy, Gerald G., and Laura R. Roehler. *Improving Classroom Reading Instruction.* New York: Random House, 1986.

Duffy, Gerald G., and Laura R. Roehler. "Improving Reading Instruction Through the Use of Responsive Elaboration." *The Reading Teacher* 40 (February 1987): 514–20.

Ehly, Stewart, and Stephen C. Larsen. "Peer Tutoring in the Regular Classroom." In *Readings on Reading Instruction,* Albert J. Harris and Edward R. Sipay, eds. 3rd ed. New York: Longman, 1984, pp. 187–89.

"Estimating Range of Reading Levels in a Class." *The Reading Teacher* 40 (April 1987): 830.

Freer, Mark, and Jack Dawson. "The Pudding's the Proof." *Educational Leadership* 44 (February 1987): 67–68.

Gibboney, Richard A. "A Critique of Madeline Hunter's Teaching Model from Dewey's Perspective." *Educational Leadership* 44 (February 1987): 46–50.

Glaser, Nicholas. "Thinking Students Need Thinking Teachers." Paper presented at the Colorado Council of the International Reading Association, February 1987.

Goodman, Yetta M., and Myna M. Haussler. "Literacy Environment in the Home and Community." In *Roles in Literacy Learning: A New Perspective,* Duane R. Tovey and James E. Kerber, eds. Newark, Del.: International Reading Association, 1986, pp. 26–32.

Greaney, Vincent. "Parental Influences on Reading." *The Reading Teacher* 39 (April 1986): 813–18.

Guthrie, John T. "Effective Teaching Practices." *The Reading Teacher* 35 (March 1982): 766–68.

Harris, Albert J. "The Effective Teacher of Reading, Revisited." In *Readings on Reading Instruction,* Albert J. Harris and Edward R. Sipay, eds. 3rd ed. New York: Longman, 1984, pp. 195–201.

Harris, Theodore L., and Richard E. Hodges, eds. *A Dictionary of Reading and Related Terms.* Newark, Del.: International Reading Association, 1981.

Hunter, Madeline. "What's Wrong with Madeline Hunter?" *Educational Leadership* 44 (February 1985): 57–60.

Hunter, Madeline, and Douglas Russell. "How Can I Plan More Effective Lessons?" *Instructor* 87 (September 1977): 74–75, 88.

Jongsma, Eugene. "Grouping for Instruction." *The Reading Teacher* 38 (May 1985): 918–20.

Lehr, Fran. "Direct Instruction in Reading." *The Reading Teacher* 39 (March 1986): 706–708.

McKenzie, Gary R. "Personalize Your Group Teaching." In *Readings on Reading Instruction,* Albert J. Harris and Edward R. Sipay, eds. 3rd ed. New York: Longman, 1984, pp. 177–80.

Noonan, Norma. "Parents as Partners in Reading Development." In *Readings on Reading Instruction,* Albert J. Harris and Edward R. Sipay, eds. 3rd ed. New York: Longman, 1984, pp. 410–12.

Okey, James R., and Kenneth Majer. "Individual and Small-Group

580

Teaching
Reading in
Today's
Elementary
Schools

Learning with Computer-Assisted Instruction." *A.V. Communications Review* 24 (Spring 1976): 79–86.

Otto, Wayne, Anne Wolfe, and Roger G. Eldridge. "Managing Instruction." In *Handbook of Reading Research,* P. David Pearson, ed. New York: Longman, 1984, pp. 799–828.

Robbins, Pam, and Pat Wolfe. "Reflections on a Hunter-Based Staff Development Project." *Educational Leadership* 44 (February 1987): 56–61.

Rosenholtz, Susan J., and Carl Simpson. "Classroom Organization and Student Stratification." *Elementary School Journal* 85 (September 1984): 21–37.

Rosenshine, Barak, and Robert Stevens. "Classroom Instruction in Reading." In *Handbook of Reading Research,* P. David Pearson, ed. New York: Longman, 1984, pp. 745–98.

Rupley, William H., Beth S. Wise, and John W. Logan. "Research in Effective Teaching: An Overview of Its Development." In *Effective Teaching of Reading: Research and Practice,* James V. Hoffman, ed. Newark, Del.: International Reading Association, 1986, pp. 3–36.

Scheu, Judith, Diane Tanner, and Kathryn Hu-pei Au. "Designing Seatwork to Improve Students' Reading Comprehension Ability." *The Reading Teacher* 40 (October 1986): 18–25.

Stallings, Jane. "For Whom and How Long Is the Hunter-Based Model Appropriate? A Response to Robbins and Wolfe." *Educational Leadership* 44 (February 1987): 62–63.

Unsworth, Len. "Meeting Individual Needs Through Flexible Within-Class Grouping of Pupils." *The Reading Teacher* 38 (December 1984): 298–304.

Vukelich, Carol. "Parents' Role in the Reading Process: A Review of Practical Suggestions and Ways to Communicate with Parents." *The Reading Teacher* 37 (February 1984): 472–77.

Warren, Suzanne S., and Ellen E. Baritot. "Keeping Kids Working Comfortably." *Classroom Computer Learning* 7 (September 1986): 52–54.

Weisberg, Renee. "The Madeline Hunter Model of Teacher Effectiveness." In *Effective Teaching of Reading: Research and Practice,* James V. Hoffman, ed. Newark, Del.: International Reading Association, 1986, pp. 231–57.

Wigfield, Allan, and Steven R. Asher. "Social and Motivational Influences on Reading." In *Handbook of Reading Research,* P. David Pearson, ed. New York: Longman, 1984, pp. 423–52.

Wolfe, Patricia. "What the 'Seven-Step Lesson Plan' Isn't." *Educational Leadership* 44 (February 1987): 70–71.

Chapter 12

Readers with Special Needs

Introduction

This chapter considers exceptional children, those who differ in some way from the majority of learners for whom most instructional sequences are designed. These children also need sequential, well-balanced reading programs, but these programs usually require some instructional modifications or supplements to help the children reach their full potential. The special needs, characteristics, and instructional implications of children with mild to moderate difficulties are discussed, but no attempt is made to cover children who are profoundly retarded, psychotic, autistic, aphasic, or severely impaired perceptually. These children are likely to need a special class, a special school, or a residential facility, and this chapter focuses on what the classroom teacher, not the specialist, can do.

Since many children who were formerly enrolled in special education classes are now being integrated into regular classes, teachers are responsible for working with more exceptional children than they were in the past. Educators today realize that association with children in a regular classroom may be beneficial for exceptional children, and schools are making special provisions for these children by placing them in the educational mainstream.

This chapter begins with a presentation of Public Law 94-142 and its effects on the education of handicapped children, and it then moves to a discussion of guidelines for working with students who have special needs. Next, the chapter focuses on the different types of exceptional learners—learning disabled students, slow learners, visually and hearing impaired children, those with speech impairments, behaviorally disturbed youngsters, gifted children, students with cultural and linguistic variations, and corrective and remedial readers. It concludes with suggestions for materials to use with special learners.

Setting Objectives

When you finish reading this chapter, you should be able to

1. Explain mainstreaming and its effects in a regular classroom.
2. Identify learners who are classified as exceptional and suggest several guidelines for instructing them.
3. Understand what "learning disabilities" are.
4. Explain some strategies for helping slow learners.
5. Name some desirable instructional modifications for children who have impaired vision, hearing, or speech.
6. Describe the types of problems a behaviorally disturbed or hyperactive child can cause in the classroom.
7. Understand how to adjust teaching strategies for gifted pupils.

8. Appreciate the effects of a child's culture and socioeconomic level on his or her reading achievement.
9. Discuss several important features and promising approaches to consider in a reading program for children with dialectal differences.
10. Delineate some special needs of bilingual children and ways of meeting these needs.
11. Identify underachievers.
12. Name materials that are available for working with readers who have special needs.

Key Vocabulary

Pay close attention to these terms when they appear in the chapter.

behavioral disorder	hearing impaired	PL 94-142
bidialectalism	hyperactivity	remedial reader
bilingualism	IEP	resource room
compensatory program	itinerant teacher	slow learner
corrective reader	learning disabled	specific learning
dialect	least restrictive	disabilities
ESL	environment	speech impaired
exceptional learner	mainstreaming	underacheiver
gifted	multidisciplinary team	visually impaired
handicapped	multiethnic	

HANDICAPPED CHILDREN IN THE CLASSROOM: PL 94-142

In 1975 Congress passed a law that altered the placement of handicapped students in the public schools; instead of being assigned to resource rooms, many of these children are now being mainstreamed into regular classrooms. A major reason for passage of the law was to enable handicapped students who were being neglected to receive special services. Also, under the law, these children spend time with nonhandicapped children, thus addressing the apparent ineffectiveness of teaching handicapped students in segregated classes.

PL 94-142, known as the Education for All Handicapped Children Act, states that the federal government will "assist States and localities to provide for the education of all handicapped children, and to assess and assure the effectiveness of efforts to educate handicapped children." According to this law, handicapped children are those who are mentally retarded, hard of

584

Teaching
Reading in
Today's
Elementary
Schools

hearing or deaf, speech impaired, seriously disturbed emotionally, visually handicapped, orthopedically impaired, or possessing specific learning disabilities. Students who are suspected of being handicapped are referred for appropriate testing to determine their status, and only those handicapped students who are expected to benefit from integration in a regular classroom are placed there.

A provision of PL 94-142 states that "no child between the ages of three and twenty-one can be denied a free, appropriate public education" (Hewett with Forness, 1984, p. 300). Table 12.1 gives the percentages of students receiving special education services between these ages for the school year 1983–1984. Since about 11 percent of children are handicapped in some way, each classroom teacher may have approximately three special learners.

PL 94-142 further requires that handicapped children receive the most appropriate education in the *least restrictive environment,* a concept that places children in a learning environment as close to the regular classroom as possible but in which they can still master skills and content. A series of placement levels ranging from the most to the least restrictive is as follows:

residential institution
special school
self-contained special class
resource room
itinerant teacher
regular classroom with teacher consultant

Ideally, children will advance from a more to a less restrictive environment (Kirk and Gallagher, 1983).

Severely handicapped children in a regular school may be placed in a self-contained special class, where the special teacher is responsible for most of their program. A less restrictive environment is the part-time special class, where handicapped children spend about half of the day under the direction of the special teacher. A resource room is generally a small classroom where mildly handicapped children spend a period of time on a regular basis with instruction provided by the resource room teacher. Itinerant teachers, such as speech pathologists and school psychologists, may travel from one school to another to work with children who need special help. Teacher consultants are highly trained, experienced teachers who offer help to regular teachers whose classes include exceptional children. When the least restrictive environment for an exceptional child is the regular classroom, that child is said to be *mainstreamed.*

A major provision of PL 94-142 is the development of an individualized education program (IEP) for each handicapped child who receives support through federal funding. The IEP states the child's present levels of educational performance, the projected starting date of the program, and the duration of the special services. It sets annual goals for the child's level of

TABLE 12.1 Percentage of Handicapped Students Enrolled in U.S. Public Schools, 1983–1984

Condition	Percentage
All conditions	10.98
Learning disabled	4.62
Speech impaired	2.88
Mentally retarded	1.86
Seriously emotionally disturbed	.92
Hard of hearing and deaf	.18
Orthopedically handicapped	.14
Other health impaired	.13
Visually handicapped	.07
Multihandicapped	.17
Deaf-blind	.01

Source: Valena White Plisko and Joyce D. Stern, eds., "Educating Handicapped Students," in *The Condition of Education* (Washington, D.C.: Statistical Report, National Center for Education Statistics, U.S. Department of Education, 1985), p. 182.

educational performance as well as short-term instructional objectives, which must be defined in measurable terms. The IEP also specifies educational services and special instructional media for the child.

The IEP is developed by a multidisciplinary team, sometimes called the M-team or core evaluation team, consisting of a representative (other than the child's teacher) of the local education agency (usually the school), the teacher, and one or both parents. The child and other professional personnel may be included when appropriate. The M-team for children with specific learning disabilities must also include a person qualified to give individual diagnostic exams and, when available, an appropriate learning disabilities specialist.

One format for an IEP follows:

I. Summary of assessment
    A. Areas of strengths
    B. Areas of weaknesses
    C. Approaches that have failed
    D. Learning style(s)
    E. Recommended placement, general program outline, and assignment of personnel responsibility
II. Classroom accommodations
    A. General teaching techniques
    B. Language arts modifications (and other subject matter modifications)
III. Instructional plans
    A. Long-range (yearly) objectives, along with materials, strategies, and evidence of mastery

586
**Teaching
Reading in
Today's
Elementary
Schools**

One result of PL 94-142 is that exceptional children with special needs are often integrated, or mainstreamed, into the regular classroom. (© David S. Strickler/ Monkmeyer)

III. B. Specific (1–3 months) objectives
    C. Ancillary personnel and services

In order to coordinate a special learner's reading instructional program, the classroom teacher and the resource teacher must communicate on a regular basis so that the resource teacher supplements the instruction provided in the regular classroom. Sometimes children are in "pull-out" programs in which they go to resource rooms, and sometimes they are tutored in the regular classrooms by reading specialists or aides in a "push-in" program. Bean and Eichelberger (1985), who studied both types of programs, found that in push-in programs reading specialists concentrated more on reinforcing classroom skills and less on diagnosing needs than they did in pull-out programs, but there were problems with having two teachers in one room and with implementing the program in terms of time and space. Neither program guarantees more coordination between teachers; the important issue is that teachers communicate with each other about students' strengths and weaknesses in order to provide an integrated reading program for each special learner (Allington and Shake, 1986).

Working together to plan instructional activities for exceptional children whenever possible, the resource room teacher and the classroom teacher might want to cooperate by drawing up a contract—a written agreement about specific measurable objectives, one or more activities for meeting each objective, and the date for completion (Wilhoyte, 1977). A contract helps the student focus attention on developing specific reading skills, keeping careful records, and accepting responsibility. It is based on his or her strengths and moves the child very gradually to a higher level of performance.

Under a contract, the resource teacher explains the objectives and activities to the child and writes the information on a form attached to the child's work folder. The child then takes the folder to the regular classroom in order to work independently on the activities, under the supervision of the classroom teacher. At the end of the allotted time, the child returns to the resource room for an evaluation by the resource teacher. If he or she has achieved 100 percent success in an activity, some sort of recognition is in order. Example 12.1 illustrates one possible reading contract. (See Chapter 11 for more information about contracts.)

▶ **EXAMPLE 12.1:** Reading Contract

READING CONTRACT

Larry H.
Student

Mrs. Morgan
Teacher

Objective	Activity	Date	Initials		Comments
			St.	Tch.	
To learn to read 3 new words.	Play word card game.	May 4	_LH._	_EM._	Good work!
To understand the events in a story.	Listen to a story at the listening station and tell someone about it.	May 6	_LH._	_EM._	You retold the story well.

Because regular members of the classroom play an important role in terms of offering acceptance and support to the mainstreamed child, the teacher should prepare students to receive the new class member by frankly explain-

588

Teaching
Reading in
Today's
Elementary
Schools

ing the nature of the handicap and the student's special needs. In addition, he or she might read a story about a similarly handicapped individual to help the class realize that even though the new student has special needs, his or her feelings, interests, and goals are much like their own (Rubin, 1982). It is important that the mainstreamed child be fully accepted as an integral part of the class and not just occupy space in the classroom (Hoben, 1980). After the child begins attending class, students may become actively supportive by providing necessary services, by tutoring when special help is needed, and by including the child in activities.

Cooperative learning strategies allow groups of four to eight students of varied abilities, including those who are mainstreamed, to work together on projects relating to the content areas (Maring, Furman, and Blum-Anderson, 1985). These strategies include such activities as preparing structured overviews, rewriting portions of the text in simpler language, making predictions of content based on headings and subheadings in the text, learning a task and teaching it to others, and developing relationships of concepts through a "list-group-label" activity. Being included in these groups enables mainstreamed youngsters to contribute to the activities, thereby improving their self-concepts, and to learn from their peers. The other children perceive them as part of their group and feel good about helping them learn.

Many mainstreamed children read at levels considerably below those of their classmates, which can cause feelings of inadequacy and frustration that may in turn lead to behavior problems. The teacher can do two things: enable the child to excel in some nonacademic area, and teach reading individually at the child's level (Kirk, Kliebhan, and Lerner, 1978). The special child may also have a skill or ability, such as mechanical aptitude, conscientiousness for carrying out a responsibility, dramatic talent, or athletic prowess, that he or she could develop. In teaching beginning reading to these children, teachers should follow the general guidelines and select appropriate instructional materials, such as those suggested later in this chapter.

Some strengths and weaknesses of mainstreaming have become evident (Dallmann et al., 1982). Among the strengths of the program are:

1. The plan is an attempt to provide a free education for every child in the least restrictive environment.
2. Atypical students can join with their peers in learning experiences that they might not have otherwise.
3. Parents are included in the planning and implementation of the program.
4. An individual learning program is planned for each child.

Some weaknesses are:

1. Handicapped children may experience frustration in a room where others are working at higher levels.

2. Both the handicapped child and the nonhandicapped classmates may have problems of adjustment.
3. If the special student has behavioral problems, he or she may disrupt the class.
4. Attending to the special needs of one student may be too demanding a task for the classroom teacher, who must also meet the needs of the rest of the class.

✔ Self-Check: Objective 1

Explain the impact of PL 94-142 on public schools.
What is an IEP? How is it developed and what does it include?

General Guidelines

Most of the procedures and materials already recommended in this book can be effectively used with exceptional children when teachers make reasonable adjustments for particular difficulties. The exceptional child's basic needs and goals are not so different from those of the "ordinary" child, but the means of achieving those goals and fulfilling those needs may be different. The following general practices, which apply to all learners, are crucial in teaching exceptional children.

1. *Maintain a positive attitude toward exceptional learners.* Special children require a great deal of encouragement and understanding. Show that you are interested in them: talk with them about their interests; note things they have done; be friendly and encouraging. Give each child's personal worth and mental health primary consideration, and assist each child in every way possible to develop personally and socially as well as academically.
2. *Provide opportunities for success in undertakings.* Assign tasks at or below exceptional children's ability levels to ensure reasonable success. Provide short-term goals and give immediate feedback to encourage good work. Use progress charts to make growth apparent and have children compete against their own records, not those of their classmates. Give praise for genuine efforts and successful completion of tasks. Make every effort to build self-confidence and avoid frustrating situations that may aggravate learning problems.
3. *Consider learning styles and modalities when planning instruction.* An exceptional child might be an auditory learner who readily associates sounds with symbols, or a visual learner who remembers sight words easily, or perhaps a kinesthetic-tactile learner who needs to touch, manipulate, and move in order to learn to read. Such factors as lighting, space, time of day, and temperature may also affect children's ability to learn.

590

Teaching
Reading in
Today's
Elementary
Schools

4. *Provide individualized instruction whenever possible.* De-emphasize arbitrary age-grade standards and individualize instruction so as to focus upon each child's educational needs. Provide instruction that is appropriate for the individual in a given area at a given time. Match teaching procedures to the child's needs, strengths, weaknesses, learning styles, handicaps, and interests. Consider special needs for particular handicaps, such as special equipment, seating arrangements, stimulus-reduced areas, and "time-out" sessions.

5. *Plan appropriate instructional sequences.* Provide a well-planned readiness period for each task. For example, before a lesson on using beginning sounds and context to identify an unknown word, prepare the children by using spoken context as a clue to the identification of a missing word and by helping them discriminate between the initial sounds in words. Then present one instructional item at a time with many examples and applications. At the end of each instructional sequence, evaluate the children's progress and give positive reinforcement for small improvements.

6. *Offer meaningful, balanced instructional programs.* Help the children see a reason for learning to read, and emphasize skills through actual reading, not through artificial drills. Encourage them to use different strategies for getting meaning from text, to abandon a strategy that is not working, and to think aloud while reading. Avoid the temptation to focus exclusively on decoding skills, an obvious and immediate need for many exceptional children, at the expense of comprehension skills. Keep a balance between the two.

7. *Provide materials the children are capable of using as well as ones that are of interest.* Carefully select what to use in initial instruction: concrete, manipulative materials and firsthand experiences are usually effective. Do not use reading materials with which the children have previously failed. Become familiar with various instructional strategies and learn how to adapt them to the children's learning styles, and do not overlook the effectiveness of audiovisual materials, games, high-interest, low-vocabulary books (see Example 12.2), comic books, television commercials, and other contemporary materials.

8. *Communicate with others who work with special children.* Be sure to coordinate each special learner's program with all others involved in his or her instruction, particularly the resource teacher. Discuss the child's progress and needs, and work together to provide the best possible plan, with each teacher reinforcing and supplementing the work of the other.

9. *Provide a positive classroom environment.* Help the children in the regular classroom to accept and appreciate the special qualities of mainstreamed children by including them in class activities and providing opportunities for them to make worthwhile contributions. Foster a climate of acceptance and appreciation for each child's uniqueness.

► **EXAMPLE 12.2:** Selection from High-Interest, Low-Vocabulary Book
(Grade Two Readability; Grade Four Interest Level)

591
**Readers with
Special Needs**

How Do Whales Find Each Other?

Most whales do not see well, but they have fine hearing. They can hear the sounds that other whales are making 100 miles away. They can find one another when they are 3 miles apart.

Some whales sing to each other. One kind of whale can remake its songs, changing the notes in them. When a song changes, all of the whales know the new notes. No one yet knows why the whales sing their songs or why the tune changes.

No one yet knows all the answers to all the questions about whales. People are trying to find those answers. They are also beginning to change the way they think about whales.

Source: WINGS (New Directions in Reading), by Jo M. Stanchfield and Thomas G. Gunning, p. 29. Copyright © 1986 by Houghton Mifflin Company. Used by permission. ◄

✔ Self-Check: Objective 2

Name several guidelines for working with readers who have special needs.

(See Self-Improvement Opportunity 1.)

Students with Specific Learning Disabilities

Characteristics

The most widely accepted definition of specific learning disabilities is the one included in PL 94-142: "The term 'children with specific learning disabilities' means those children who have a disorder in one or more of the basic psychological processes involved in understanding or in using language, spoken or written, which disorder may manifest itself in imperfect ability to listen, think, speak, read, write, spell, or do mathematical calculations. Such disorders include such conditions as perceptual handicaps, brain injury, minimal brain dysfunction, dyslexia, and developmental aphasia. Such term does not include children who have learning problems which are primarily the result of visual, hearing, or motor handicaps, of mental retardation, or emotional disturbance, or environmental, cultural, or economic disadvantage."

Despite this legal definition, there is a good deal of confusion about criteria for identifying those who are learning disabled. Lerner (1985, pp. 9–12) lists five elements common to most definitions of learning disabilities.

1. *Neurological dysfunction.* Learning disabilities may be related to dysfunction of the central nervous system.
2. *Uneven growth pattern.* Various mental abilities develop at different and irregular rates, with some growing as expected and others lagging behind.

592

Teaching
Reading in
Today's
Elementary
Schools

3. *Difficulty in academic and learning tasks.* The learning disabled student may have problems with speech and language, reading, arithmetic, written expression, thinking, psycho-social skills, handwriting, or motor skills.

4. *Discrepancy between achievement and potential.* A severe discrepancy exists between a student's estimated potential or ability and actual achievement level.

5. *Exclusion of other causes.* No other identifiable condition, such as a visual or an auditory impairment, is primarily the cause of the child's disability.

Identifying and labeling children as learning disabled is less important, however, than finding viable instructional strategies for increasing their ability to learn.

It is difficult to state the exact prevalence of learning disabilities because of different interpretations of definitions and varying procedures used for identification. Data show that the number of students classified as learning disabled has increased in recent years and now constitutes between 4 and 5 percent of the total school enrollment (See Table 12.1), or about 40 percent of all handicapped students who receive special services. About 72 percent of these students are boys (Lerner, 1985).

Weaknesses frequently observed among learning disabled students include

1. visual perception problems, in which the student confuses letter shapes, makes reversals, and has difficulty in identifying a figure concealed in a picture.

2. auditory perception disorders, in which the student mispronounces and misspells similar-sounding words (*aminal* for *animal*) and is unable to blend the sounds of a word in order to pronounce it.

3. fine and gross motor function disorders, exhibited through poor physical coordination, illegible handwriting, and a poor sense of directionality (cannot distinguish left from right).

4. attention disorders, manifested by a short attention span, high distractibility, hyperactivity, and impulsivity (writing answers or speaking without thinking).

5. language problems, in which students have difficulty with articulation, following oral and written directions, and expressing their thoughts accurately orally and in writing.

6. thinking disorders, involving inadequacies in memory, concept formation, judgment, and problem-solving.

Instructional Implications and Strategies

Although some learning disabled students have excellent verbal skills, many have severe communication deficits that can be observed in their oral language and reading performance. They seem to have trouble using normal language structures to speak in an organized manner, and they also appear to have trouble comprehending continuous text. When comparing learning disabled children with normal children, researchers have found delays in language development and differences in the quality of language—especially in the comprehension of logical relations, in ways of using language on tests, and in the acquisition of rules related to patterns of word formation (Wallach and Goldsmith, 1977). In an effort to help these children learn a specific word formation skill, researchers provided special instruction in recognizing suffixes, including inflectional endings of verbs. They trained learning disabled students to attend to the suffixes *-ed* and *-ing,* using paper-and-pencil exercises and oral drills. Students were praised for correct responses and given daily feedback, and errors and correct answers were recorded daily on a chart so that the children could see their progress. The researchers concluded that identifying individual errors was a good basis for instruction, a structured format for teaching a specific skill was effective, and oral reading performance improved significantly following the instruction (Henderson and Shores, 1982).

Reading improvement is the most widely recognized academic need of the learning disabled child (Gaskins, 1982). Three recent research studies have identified some teaching strategies that appear to be effective for helping various types of disabled readers increase their reading comprehension skills. In one study, children who were given a semantic map that highlighted the major events and structure of a selection before they read it scored higher on total comprehension than students who participated in a regular directed reading lesson (Sinatra, Stahl-Gemake, and Berg, 1984). In another study, middle-grade remedial students understood and remembered more of their reading as a result of self-questioning while reading expository texts, practicing recall of these texts, and learning to write text-based and reader-based questions (Hahn, 1985). Findings from the third study revealed that handicapped learners reading at upper third-grade level or above improved their understanding of stories by learning to look for causal relationships between story events (Varnhagen and Goldman, 1986).

The content and sequence of reading programs are much the same for all children, but the methods and materials vary according to the needs of each student. Some principles to observe while teaching reading skills to the learning disabled student are given below.

Respect the student. Acknowledge the child's feelings. Try to relieve his or her anxieties, and offer praise and encouragement whenever possible. Recognize special abilities and needs.

Create a structured environment. Develop a routine and provide security by having a time and a place for everything. Set clear and consistent rules with reasonable contingencies, and avoid events that distract and interfere with the instructional program.

Minimize and accept mistakes. When you make mistakes yourself, comment on them. (Example: "I tripped right over that box. Sometimes I feel so

594

Teaching
Reading in
Today's
Elementary
Schools

clumsy!") Admit that you can't remember something and look it up. Laugh at your own mistakes, help the student to laugh at his or her mistakes, and don't call attention to the student's awkward moments.

Help with language problems. When a child can't think of a word, supply it. Give directions clearly, briefly, and concisely. Make sure the child is looking directly at you. It may be advisable to have the child repeat the directions back to you.

Use varied instructional and assessment techniques. Present concepts by means of concrete objects, manipulative devices, and multimedia presentations (films, television, videotapes, recordings) to make use of the child's five senses. Provide various opportunities for practicing skills (learning-center activities, projects, worksheets), various instructional techniques (science experiments, simulation activities, role-playing), and various types of assessment (creative projects, oral reports, written tests, and presentations).

Simplify learning tasks. Let the student concentrate on achieving one task at a time. Give small amounts of learning material to him or her at one time, and repeat and reinforce each step, providing systematic instruction (Ludlow, 1982; Smith, 1981).

✔ Self-Check: Objective 3

Name some characteristics of learning disabled children. What are some ways to help these children learn?
(See Self-Improvement Opportunity 2.)

Slow Learners

Characteristics

Since PL 94-142 did not define mental retardation, each state has set its own criteria. Grossman (1983) suggests using IQ scores for rough indicators of levels of retardation as follows:

Mild retardation	IQ score from 50–55 to 70
Moderate retardation	IQ score from 35–40 to 50–55
Severe and profound retardation	IQ score below 35

In addition to considering IQ scores, most definitions today include the concept of adaptive behavior, which means that those who are retarded lack acceptable and appropriate behavior for a particular age and culture and are unable to achieve standards of personal independence and social responsibility (Henley, 1985). Adaptive behavior includes such activities as doing chores, playing games, dressing, and using money. The number of students classified as mildly retarded has declined in recent years for a variety of reasons, including concern about the overrepresentation of ethnic minorities in this group. It is possible that multiethnic students do not score as high on intelligence tests as other students because of cultural biases in these tests.

The primary characteristic of slow-learning children is that they do not learn as readily as others of the same chronological age. They are usually unable to make complicated generalizations and learn material incidentally; they need direct, systematic instruction. According to Sedlak and Sedlak (1985), mildly retarded children read less often than other children and choose material below their maturity level. They are often deficient in oral and silent reading, locating details, recognizing main ideas, using context clues, and drawing conclusions, but can usually achieve word recognition skills, knowledge of word meanings, and reading rates on a par with others of the same mental age.

Reviews of the reading characteristics of slow learners reveal several points that have implications for developing instructional programs (Buttery and Mason, 1979; Henley, 1985).

1. No one approach is superior to any other.
2. The teacher is the most significant factor in determining a child's success with reading.
3. Slow learners make more progress when they are placed in regular classrooms than when they are in special classes.
4. Slow learners are inferior to most other children in comprehension skills and in oral reading.
5. Reading comprehension is the most difficult skill for them to learn.
6. There should be a match between a student's learning style and teaching methodology.
7. It is impossible to predict the limit for any child's learning potential.
8. Children learn abstract skills best when they are reinforced with concrete experiences.
9. Task analysis should be used to break down the elements of a skill into simple steps.

Instructional Implications and Strategies

Whenever possible, slow learners should spend most of the school day in the regular classroom with teachers who recognize and know how to deal with their special needs and who are willing to try a variety of methods. Slow learners need an extended reading readiness (prereading) program, one that may last for as long as two years. Reading instruction *per se* should be introduced later, progress more slowly, and develop more gradually than is usually the case. Teachers should plan instruction with the understanding that the slow learner will stay in each stage of reading development longer than the average pupil. Slow learners will profit from using materials that do not have demanding vocabularies and from repetition. They will need a great

596
Teaching
Reading in
Today's
Elementary
Schools

deal of help in developing adequate comprehension skills. Suitable techniques for teaching slow learners are presented below.

Characteristics of Slow Learners	*Recommendations for Teaching*
1. Short attention span	1. Activities should vary, move quickly, and be completed in a short amount of time. Set short-term goals that enable students to succeed at frequent intervals.
2. Need for close supervision	2. Give instruction individually or in small groups, providing frequent project checks, reinforcement, and encouragement.
3. Concrete rather than abstract learning	3. New words should be learned through association with concrete objects or pictures, and new concepts should be experienced directly or vicariously (field trips, films, simulation, and role-playing). Learning should be by rote.
4. Low self-concept	4. Provide opportunities for child to work as part of the whole class, giving recognition for small successes and using progress charts. The environment should be non-threatening.
5. Poor language development	5. Provide opportunities for listening to stories and responding orally. Arrange time for sharing experiences and taking part in discussions.
6. High level of distractibility	6. Establish schedules and routines and minimize interruptions and distractions.
7. Short-term memory	7. Basic skills and new words should be overlearned through frequent practice. Repetition and review are necessary.

Many slow learners will be socially promoted and leave school before they can read beyond a second- or third-grade level, so teachers should provide these students with the basic functional reading skills they will need to use during their lives. (These skills are also useful for other types of disabled readers.) To teach functional or survival reading, use large assortments of product labels, old telephone books, catalogues, newspapers, magazines, order forms, movie and television schedules, cereal boxes, maps, transportation schedules, recipes, and manuals. If these resources are available, children can begin to apply the reading skills they have learned in a practical way, working with familiar materials and learning why reading is important.

Teachers can make a set of cards with imaginary situations for the children to use at a learning center where the resource materials are located. The teacher may need to pronounce some of the words on the cards and assist the children in locating appropriate materials. See suggested activities in Example 12.3.

▶ **EXAMPLE 12.3:** Imaginary Functional Situations

Your dog is sick. What number do you call for help? Where could you take your dog?

If the house is on fire, what number would you call? What are some other emergency phone numbers?

Look at several labels to find out what is dangerous about each product. Make a list of "danger" words.

You want to write a lost-and-found ad for the bicycle you lost. Write the ad and find the address of the newspaper.

Choose a magazine that you would like to order. Fill out the order form.

Follow a recipe and make something good to eat.

Your mother is coming home on the bus but you forget what time your father is supposed to meet her. Look it up in the schedule.

You want to order a game that is advertised on the back of a cereal box. Follow the directions for placing the order.

You want to watch a television special but you can't remember the time or channel. Find it in the newspaper.

Look at a menu and order a meal for yourself. Find out how much it costs.

Look through a catalogue and choose four items that you would like to have for less than $100 in all. Fill out the order blank.

You want to go to a football game in a nearby town. Find the stadium on the map and be able to give directions.

Some other ideas for working with students on survival skills are suggested below. These activities are most beneficial when students use them in purposeful and realistic situations.

1. Set up a post office. Children can write notes and address envelopes to their classmates.

598

Teaching
Reading in
Today's
Elementary
Schools

2. Obtain multiple copies of last year's telephone directories and look up the number of each student; find emergency numbers; and look through the Yellow Pages to find restaurants, a skating rink, movie theaters, and other places that are familiar to the children. Let each student make a telephone directory of these numbers.

3. Give children forms to fill out about themselves, including their names, addresses, telephone numbers, Social Security numbers, and so on.

4. Get copies of old and new drivers' manuals. Then have students match the old word signs with the new international symbols.

5. Make cards of words and phrases found in public places, such as *Wet Paint, No Trespassing, Danger, Ladies Room,* and so on. Have the children see how many terms they can recognize.

6. Obtain city maps and let students locate landmarks. Simple map-reading skills involving their own school and neighborhood should precede work with a larger map.

7. Make a collection of grocery labels and product advertisements from magazines. Then let the children pretend to go food shopping by selecting some of the labels and advertisements. They should tell the teacher and other members of the group what they "bought." Have beginning readers match pictures and words from labels that have been cut apart.

8. Have students use newspapers for locating grocery-store and other advertisements, finding the classified section and looking for items that are for sale and jobs that are available, using the index to find the comics page, reading headlines, and looking at the sports pages to find out about local athletic events.

9. Keep a collection of simple recipes that are arranged alphabetically by category in a recipe box. Obtain basic ingredients and allow the children to make something.

10. Make a game of reading television schedules. Name a popular show and let the children compete with each other to see who can find the show first.

11. Collect coupons and distribute some to each child. Encourage the children to figure out who will save the most money by using the coupons. Be sure they check expiration dates and any other conditions (such as two for the price of one).

12. Use labels from different sizes and brands of the same product and help children find which one is the most economical by comparing prices and amounts.

✔ Self-Check: Objective 4

How can you identify the slow learner in a classroom? What are some reasonable expectations for a slow learner?
(See Self-Improvement Opportunities 3 and 10.)

Visually Handicapped Children

Characteristics

A *partially sighted* child is one whose visual acuity is better than 20/200 but not better than 20/70 in the better eye with the best correction available. Educationally, the partially sighted or *visually impaired* child has difficulty but is able to learn to read print, as opposed to the blind child, who must learn to read braille.

The visual process has three main components. *Visual acuity* is clarity of vision and is seldom related to reading ability unless the child cannot see well enough to read print. *Visual skills efficiency* deals with eye focusing and tracking; problems in this area can affect reading either by creating visual fatigue or by causing the student to avoid close work. Children who have problems with *visual perceptual-motor development,* the ability to recognize and interpret visual stimuli, often fail to grasp basic concepts and have difficulty learning (Rouse and Ryan, 1984).

Teachers have many opportunities to observe symptoms of visual difficulties when students are reading. Among these symptoms are

1. squinting.
2. scowling.
3. closing or covering one eye.
4. rubbing the eyes frequently.
5. holding the book too close or too far away.
6. frequently losing the place.
7. red or inflamed eyes.
8. frequent blinking.
9. moving head excessively.
10. frequent errors when copying board work.

Alert teachers should refer a child who has these symptoms to a visual specialist.

Instructional Implications and Strategies

In general, the language of visually handicapped children is adequate and they are capable of learning to read. Several instructional ideas are proposed below.

1. Give the child many concrete objects to feel and manipulate. Provide tactile experiences accompanied by verbal explanations.
2. Permit the student to dictate many stories to an aide or into a tape recorder. Let the child read them back or listen to them.
3. Read aloud to the entire class frequently.

600

Teaching
Reading in
Today's
Elementary
Schools

4. Place commercially prepared records and cassette tapes of stories at listening stations for the child to use.
5. Seat the student close to the chalkboard or wherever there is material to be studied.
6. Encourage the child to use properly fitted glasses while reading or doing other visual activities.
7. Plan several short periods of close work alternating with active assignments rather than one extended period of continuous close work.
8. Adjust shades and lighting so there is no glare on the chalkboard.
9. Provide materials that the child can read, such as large-print books or the clearest copies of ditto sheets.

Hearing Impaired Children

Characteristics

The term *hard of hearing* or *hearing impaired* applies to those whose sense of hearing is defective but adequate for ordinary purposes, with or without a hearing aid. Three factors related to hearing impairments affect a person's development (Schulz and Turnbull, 1984). The first factor is the *nature* or type of hearing difficulty, whether it involves the frequency (pitch, or highness or lowness of sound) or the intensity (loudness of the sound). The second factor is the *degree* of impairment, or the severity of the hearing loss, and the third factor is *age of onset*. The earlier the age of onset of hearing loss, the less opportunity a child has to learn language before beginning to read.

As with visual difficulties, teachers are in an excellent position to observe telltale symptoms of auditory difficulties. Among these symptoms are

1. inattentiveness in class.
2. turning the head so that a particular ear always faces the teacher.
3. requests for repetition of directions and other verbal information.
4. frowning when trying to listen.
5. frequent rubbing of ears.
6. frequent earaches.
7. dizziness.

Children who exhibit these symptoms should be referred for auditory testing.

Instructional Implications and Strategies

A teacher who has children with auditory difficulties in her classroom should follow these directions:

1. Speak slowly, clearly, and with adequate volume.
2. Seat the child as far as possible from distracting sounds.

3. Emphasize silent reading.
4. Minimize the use of auditory channels in instruction.
5. Provide practice materials that have clearly written instructions.
6. When speaking, stand so that the child can see your lips, with light directed on your face from in front of you rather than from behind you.
7. After pronouncing a particular word, write it on the chalkboard.

Some strategies that can help the hearing impaired child learn to read are listed below (Carlsen, 1985).

1. Use a whole word approach to word recognition rather than a phonics approach because the child cannot hear sounds well.
2. Use the language experience approach to connect meaningful experiences to words.
3. Pay special attention to teaching figurative expressions, since hearing impaired children tend to be literally minded.
4. Supplement reading lessons with visual aids. Use the overhead projector, write on the chalkboard, and make pictures or charts.
5. Use easy material and limit new words and difficult sentence structures.
6. Create original storybooks by rewriting stories at easier levels or writing original stories.
7. Check comprehension frequently by asking questions about reading materials.

✔ Self-Check: Objective 5
Suggest some instructional ideas for teaching hearing impaired and visually handicapped children.
(See Self-Improvement Opportunity 2.)

Speech Impaired Children

Characteristics

Speech is considered abnormal "when it deviates so far from the speech of other people that it calls attention to itself, interferes with communication, or causes the speaker or his listener to be distressed" (Van Riper, 1978, p. 43). Such problems are considered by some authorities to be a part of the more extensive category sometimes called "communication disorders." Understanding the label, however, is significantly less important than understanding the types of speech difficulties that children might have and how they may affect the development of reading skills. This chapter highlights two of the most common speech disorders with which the classroom teacher must deal: articulation problems and stuttering problems.

1. *Articulation.* Articulatory disorders are by far the most common type of speech disorder among schoolchildren and the type with which a classroom

602

Teaching
Reading in
Today's
Elementary
Schools

teacher can accomplish the most. Such a disorder is indicated when a child persists in one or more of the following practices.

substitutes one sound for another (for example, "wittle" for "little")
omits a sound (for example, "pane" for "plane")
distorts a sound (the sounds of *s, z,* and *r* are the most commonly distorted ones).

2. *Stuttering.* Stuttering is one of the most complicated and difficult speech problems. Stuttering children may have silent periods during which they are unable to produce any sound, or they may repeat a sound, a word, or a phrase or prolong the initial sound of a word. They may also show signs of excessive muscular strain, such as blinking their eyes.

It is normal for children between the ages of two and six years to repeat a sound, a word, or a phrase forty or fifty times in every hundred words spoken. If adults do not focus undue attention on speech during this period of nonfluency, maturation will usually enable the child to overcome repetition.

Instructional Implications and Strategies

Teachers of young children with impaired speech can make considerable use of rhymes, stories, and songs in groups. They can plan more formal lessons, organized around the speech sounds that are most likely to cause difficulties, where observation indicates a need. Some of the most common error patterns can be readily identified by teachers who have trained themselves to listen. Teachers should listen for substitution of *w* for *r* and *l* (as in *wed* and *wamp*), voiceless *th* for *s* (as in *thun*), voiced *th* for *z* (as in *thebra*), *f* for the voiceless *th* (as in *fumb*), *d* for the voiced *th* and *g* (as in *dis* and *det*), *b* for *v* (as in *balentine*), *s* or *ch* for *sh* (as in *soe* or *choe*), and *t* for *k* (as in *tandy*) (Byrne, 1965). Every experience in which language is used may become an opportunity for informal speech development and improvement. For many children, a social situation in which they are encouraged to talk freely can result in increased self-confidence and independence, reflected in rapidly increasing control of speech.

It is probably wise for the classroom teacher to face the problem of stuttering in a rather indirect way. Help from parents in eliminating sources of tension is important, as is the teacher's realization that there is no such thing as "perfect speech." Many nonfluencies are accepted as normal in adult speech.

The safest suggestion to the classroom teacher with regard to helping children who stutter is a general "don't." Do not ask them to stop and start over, to slow down, to speed up, to take a breath; this may only make them more concerned about the way they are talking and may cause them to stutter more. Do not deny them the right to read and recite in class as they choose—speaking should be made a rewarding experience for students as often as possible. In fact, students should be encouraged to talk and keep on talking even if they stutter. Help them to develop confidence in their speaking ability. So far as possible, treat children as if they had no stuttering problem. Accept and react to stuttering as you would to normal speech, and help the other members of the class develop this same attitude of acceptance.

Behaviorally Disturbed Children

Characteristics

Behaviorally disturbed children exhibit unexpected or uncontrollable behavior that often has no immediately identifiable cause or reason. This behavior is most often classified as either *conduct disorder,* including aggressive behavior, or *personality problem,* which typically includes withdrawal (Quay, 1972, 1975). Usually children who exhibit these types of behavior either cannot or will not conform to school expectations (Bradley, 1978).

Children with such personality problems as shyness and depression seldom cause discipline problems in class, but they may underachieve (Romney, 1986). Shy or withdrawn children are too timid to interact with other children because they feel that they lack appropriate social skills. They may cry easily, worry excessively, and be overly sensitive. Depressed children are chronically dejected, pessimistic, and sad; they often perform poorly academically and have reading difficulties. These children need understanding, patience, encouragement, reassurance, and positive reinforcement (Gentile, Lamb, and Rivers, 1985).

Kirk and Gallagher define a child with a conduct disorder as "one who defies authority; is hostile toward authority figures (police officers, teachers, and so forth); is cruel, malicious, and assaultive, and has few guilt feelings. This category includes children who are described as hyperactive, restless, and hyperkinetic" (1983, p. 327). According to Bradley (1978), children who have serious conduct problems show intensive emotion, misbehave frequently, act compulsively, lose control of their emotions, and have poor interpersonal relationships.

Since nearly all children behave inappropriately at one time or another, the identification of children with behavioral disorders depends largely on the frequency, duration, and intensity of misbehavior. Authorities disagree about how much inappropriate behavior is required to classify a child as behaviorally disordered, so estimates of the prevalence of such children vary widely. It is generally agreed, however, that although only about 2 or 3 percent of the population needs intensive special education programs for behavior problems, at least one million school-aged children need help with these difficulties (Kirk and Gallagher, 1983).

The most disruptive of all behavior disturbances may be hyperactivity, which consists of three major characteristics: inattentiveness, impulsiveness,

604

Teaching
Reading in
Today's
Elementary
Schools

and excessive motor activity (Romney, 1986). Nine out of ten hyperactive children are boys. They may exhibit overactivity, impulsivity, distractibility, and excitability. More specifically, in the classroom hyperactive children are constantly on the move, can't focus on tasks because they are so easily distracted, don't think before they act, guess at words instead of trying to figure them out, and are easily frustrated. They may be irritable and destructive for no reason (Fairchild, 1975).

Instructional Implications and Strategies

What can teachers who have hyperactive children in their rooms do? Here are some ideas (Aukerman and Aukerman, 1981; Bradley, 1978; Fairchild, 1975).

1. *Reinforcement.* Reward good behavior even if it is just sitting still for five minutes. Use verbal reinforcers ("good work!"). If they don't work, use activity reinforcers ("When you finish you may go to the interest center"). If they don't work either, use tangible reinforcers (food, inexpensive toys). Try to ignore inappropriate behavior.
2. *Communication.* Speak clearly, precisely, slowly, and quietly. Ask students to paraphrase directions back to you. Let them know exactly what kinds of behavior are acceptable and unacceptable, and make sure that they understand the consequences for unacceptable behavior. Then be consistent in your reactions.
3. *Acceptance.* Accept the child as a person even though you cannot accept his or her behavior. Be realistic in your expectations. Show affection, make a list of good qualities, and learn about the child's interests and family. Assign work at which the student can succeed.
4. *Environment.* Keep the room environment as simple as possible and help the child to keep clutter from collecting. Use an improvised study carrel to eliminate distractions and place the child's desk or carrel near your desk.
5. *Structure.* Adhere to schedules and routines and enforce class rules. Structure can make children feel secure. As they gain control over their behavior, such structure can be reduced.
6. *Teaching methods.* Eliminate failure as much as possible. Give step-by-step directions, individualize some instruction, and make reading sessions short. Warn the child in advance that you will call on him or her during the lesson, and use contracts and progress charts. (Remember that no single method works for all children.)
7. *Outside assistance.* Get help when you see problems developing. Try a team approach, using guidance counselors, school psychologists, consultants, or social workers.

What are some characteristics of behaviorally disturbed children? What implications do these characteristics have for instructional procedures?
(See Self-Improvement Opportunity 5.)

GIFTED CHILDREN

Characteristics

Approximately 2.6 percent of public school students participated in gifted and talented programs in 1980 (Plisko and Stern, 1985). Significantly more Asian or Pacific Islander students participated than white pupils and students of other minority groups, and slightly more girls than boys were enrolled in these programs. Recognition of the importance of special educational opportunities for gifted students is growing: seventeen states have laws that require appropriate education for such children, and thirty-three have formulated guidelines for programs. Even so, federal expenditures are two hundred times greater for the handicapped than for the gifted (Lyon, 1981).

An early signal that a child is gifted or very bright may be precociously early reading. Extremely bright children frequently teach themselves to read without any formal instruction and are often able to read materials designed for beginning reading before they enter school. Studies show that approximately half the children who are gifted, as classified by intelligence tests, can read in kindergarten and that nearly all can read at the beginning of first grade.

Gifted children usually have advanced linguistic development, being above normal in their ability to use and understand vocabulary, in maturity of sentence structure, and in originality of expression. Although all normal young children learn the language of their environment without formal instruction, the bright child learns the language more rapidly.

Within the school setting, gifted children are likely to progress mentally at a rate of one and one-fourth (or more) years within one calendar year, as compared with the average child, who has one year of mental growth for each year of his or her life. However, there are both "normal" achievers and underachievers among the gifted; they do not always live up to or demonstrate their potential. Physical defects, emotional instability, and poor study habits may interfere with the recognition of the abilities of the gifted. In addition, some gifted children are nonconformists and tend to irritate a teacher, causing the teacher to consider them "brats" rather than "brains."

Although each mentally advanced child is, of course, different, some characteristics are common to most:

606

Teaching
Reading in
Today's
Elementary
Schools

1. interest in books and reading
2. a large vocabulary, with an interest in words and their meanings
3. ability to express themselves verbally in a mature style
4. enjoyment of activities usually liked best by older children
5. curiosity to know more, shown by using the dictionary, encyclopedia, and other reference sources.
6. long attention span combined with initiative and the ability to plan and set goals
7. a high level of abstract thinking
8. a creative talent with a wide range of interests.

Means for identifying the gifted vary. Typically, students in the top 5 percent of the school population are considered gifted (Lyon, 1981). A widely accepted definition introduced by the U.S. Office of Education (Marland, 1971) includes general intellectual ability, specific academic aptitude, talent in the visual and performing arts, leadership ability, and creative and productive thinking as criteria for giftedness. Students who are considered to be verbally gifted would score in the upper 3 percent among their peers in at least two of the following categories: verbal reasoning, foreign languages, reading, and creative writing (Fox and Durden, 1982).

Instructional Implications and Strategies

One strategy to use with gifted students is inquiry reading (Cassidy, 1981). In this approach good readers in grades three through six independently investigate subjects of special interest to them. During the first week they learn the procedure and each child selects one topic, identifying appropriate resources and developing contracts with deadlines for completing the task. Most of the time during the second and third weeks is spent working independently, often in the library, where students use references to take notes, or in interviews with resource people. Contracts are reviewed with the teacher and work on the culminating project is begun. In the fourth week students complete their projects and prepare and give presentations. Finally, inquiry reading projects are evaluated by the teacher and each student.

Carr (1984) identified four areas in which reading instruction for gifted children should differ from regular classroom instruction. They are as follows:

1. Since gifted children tend to learn quickly, they do not need to spend much time on skill development or drill exercises, but should move on rapidly and read at their instructional levels.
2. Because of their high level of verbal abstraction, these students are capable of understanding a wide variety of reading materials and have little need for controlled vocabulary.
3. Their ability to perceive interrelationships among the language arts

enables them to use reference materials and knowledge of story structure to write their own books.

4. Gifted students can explore complex concepts by engaging in discussions that cause them to think critically and creatively about their reading.

Keeping these points in mind, the classroom teacher should provide a wide supply of resource materials, offer opportunities for students to respond creatively to books, suggest long-term enrichment or research projects (such as in-depth investigation of the newspaper), develop a file of language puzzles and mindbenders for students to use (*Reader's Digest* is a good source), and plan many occasions for creative writing.

Simply because the gifted are capable of completing their work more rapidly than other students, they should not be expected to do more of the same kind of work if they finish their assignments early. Instead, encourage them to choose challenging and creative activities from a resource file. A dozen stimulating ideas involving reading and language are given below (Click, 1981).

1. Complete the following: If I could be a vegetable, I would be _____ because _____.

2. If a raindrop could talk, what would it say to another raindrop if it fell on a flower petal, on a teacher's umbrella, and so on?

3. Invent a new holiday. Give a reason for its existence and suggest ways to celebrate it.

4. What familiar expressions are represented by the following? When you know the answers, make up some similar puzzles on your own.[1]

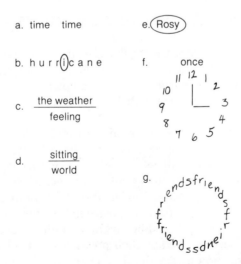

<hr>

[1] Answers: a. time after time; b. the eye of the hurricane; c. feeling under the weather; d. sitting on top of the world; e. Ring around a Rosy; f. once upon a time; g. circle of friends.

608

Teaching
Reading in
Today's
Elementary
Schools

5. Choose a political candidate to support. Write a slogan, design a campaign button, propose a budget, and develop campaign strategies.
6. Research the history of common objects, such as tin cans, buttons, or spoons.
7. Rewrite "The Twelve Days of Christmas" using more up-to-date gifts.
8. Investigate the meanings and language origins of such familiar names as Edward, Barbara, Arthur, Philip, Florence, George, Helen, Arnold, and Ethel. Decide if a name is suitable for someone you know who has that name. What name best describes you?
9. Pretend you are opening a new store to sell something unusual, such as spiders. Draw up a plan for advertising and marketing your product.
10. Put major events from your life on individual 3″ × 5″ cards and string them together in order with yarn. Illustrate the cards with photographs, drawings, or pictures from magazines. Do the same thing for the lives of famous people.
11. Write, illustrate, and bind a children's book.
12. Create your own animal by combining parts of different animals. Draw a picture of it, describe its habits and habitat, and write an adventure story about it.

✔ Self-Check: Objective 7

List several characteristics of gifted learners. What are some appropriate instructional procedures for them?
(See Self-Improvement Opportunities 3 and 11.)

CULTURAL AND LINGUISTIC VARIATIONS

America has long been known as the "melting pot" because of its assimilation of people from all parts of the world. In recent years this idea has been modified by people who believe in the "salad bowl" concept, or the rights of different ethnic groups to retain their cultural diversity within American society.

Children from some families may differ in their values, their orientation toward school, and their speech patterns from those in the American mainstream. Many speak a dialect based on their socioeconomic or ethnic background or the region of the country in which they live. Others speak English as a second language or no English at all. Both their cultural and linguistic divergencies can make a difference in how these children learn and consequently in how they should be taught, and thus educational policies in our schools have been affected by their presence and needs.

Multiethnic education means developing an understanding and appreciation of various racial and ethnic minority groups in the United States. This awareness should permeate the curriculum (Garcia, 1981). Children should be taught with consideration for their cultural heritage, their language preferences, and their lifestyles. On the other hand, too much attention to the needs of special groups may weaken the educational program, so teachers must also concentrate on teaching the skills and content that are necessary for success in American society (Thomas, 1981).

Some general guidelines for working with children of diverse ethnic origins are listed below (ASCD Multicultural Education Commission, 1977; Barnes, 1977).

1. *Learn about their culture.* Find out about their language and what things are important to them. Make home visits to learn about children's living conditions.
2. *Participate in the community.* Become involved in recreational activities and community service projects. The children and their families will appreciate your efforts and you will get to know them in out-of-school settings.
3. *Value their contributions.* Take an interest in what children bring to share. Build activities around their holiday celebrations. Listen to what they say.
4. *Share ideas with other teachers.* Observe the techniques used by teachers whom children respect. During in-service and faculty meetings, share ideas that get results.
5. *Discuss universal concerns.* Show that all kinds of people have certain things in common, such as liking ice cream and caring about their families. Use these concerns in developing lessons and units.

While these ideas are useful in any instructional situation, the following list contains practical suggestions for teaching reading to children from multiethnic backgrounds (Foerster, 1976).

1. *Choose materials carefully.* Some suitable materials include books written by the children themselves; trade books about differences in backgrounds, language, and interests; high-quality comic books; and paperback books, especially the high-interest, low-vocabulary variety.
2. *Make no assumptions.* Because of differences in background experiences, children vary in their readiness for understanding stories and concepts. Fill in gaps and clarify misunderstandings with direct or vicarious experiences.
3. *Use picture and context clues.* These clues are necessary for helping children to recognize words when their language differs from standard English in vocabulary, usage, and syntax.
4. *Let children read orally frequently.* In order to check children's pronunciation and intonation of standard English, listen to them read. You may want to use a tape recorder so that you can analyze the tapes and keep a record of linguistic changes.
5. *Plan for skill development.* Diagnose children's reading skill deficiencies and plan programs of instruction to meet individual needs.

610

Teaching
Reading in
Today's
Elementary
Schools

The following discussions deal with how children's background and specific language characteristics may affect the way they learn. They also consider strategies that teachers can use as they work with these children.

Culturally Different Students

Characteristics

Many children are from homes that differ economically, socially, and culturally from middle-class backgrounds. Although these children's cultural environments may be full and rich, they differ markedly from the school setting. Most teachers come from middle-class families and as a result have middle-class expectations regarding goals, behavior, and academic achievement. Instructional materials often deal with experiences unfamiliar to culturally different children, such as family vacations and visits to department stores. In school, children are expected to use standard English, but most culturally different children speak nonstandard dialects. Therefore, a considerable gap exists between the environment of the culturally different children and the middle-class school situation. Because of this discrepancy, many of these children have difficulty learning in school.

Often the families of culturally different children have lived in poverty for generations. Educational levels are low, and some parents may be illiterate. Parents' jobs are usually poorly paid and on unskilled or semiskilled levels, if they exist at all. Their housing is often substandard and conditions are crowded; there are no books for children to read, and there is no place to do homework. Food and clothing are often inadequate, so that children are malnourished and uncomfortable. Many families see little hope for a better life and simply struggle to survive. In addition to being frequently absent, children who come from economically deprived homes such as these are likely to have low aspirations, poor self-concepts, suspicions about school and the teacher, and poor preparation for school tasks.

Culturally different children may be found in any part of the country and may represent any ethnic heritage. Many of them are found in rural or mountainous areas, such as Appalachia, and many others are located in urban areas, such as inner-city ghettos. Migrant-worker families, found primarily in rural areas, have children with the lowest achievement rates, the highest dropout rates, and the most failures when compared with other children (Cardenas, 1976). Many of the problems of migrant children are due to lack of continuity in their school programs and to discriminatory treatment.

Many children who enter first grade from culturally different homes will not be ready for traditional reading readiness programs, since they will not know how to control their behavior and interact socially with other children, and their oral language will be inadequate for communication. They will be unfamiliar with pencils, scissors, paints, and books, and they may never have heard a story read to them.

Instructional Implications and Strategies

Teachers who work with culturally different children must first develop a positive relationship with them. Understanding their cultural heritage and learning more about it can serve as a basis for developing positive learning experiences.

During the prereadiness period, culturally different children must take part in oral language and listening activities that provide a foundation for reading and writing. Some things children can do are

1. name objects.
2. identify one object by name from several objects.
3. listen to the teacher read stories.
4. learn simple songs.
5. tell about something that happened.
6. carry on a brief conversation with another child or with the teacher.
7. point to a picture and tell what they see.
8. follow simple directions, such as "Clap your hands" and "Stamp your foot."
9. answer questions, such as "Who lives with you?" and "How did you get to school today?"
10. call other children in the class by name.

Many types of special programs have been developed to meet the needs of culturally different students. The most familiar compensatory program is Head Start, which was begun in order to give culturally different children a "head start" before entering school. Head Start was designed to enrich the background experiences of children from low-income families; although programs differ across the country, many of them focus on sensorimotor and language development.

In order to ease the adjustment between Head Start's preschool program and the traditional primary classroom, Project Follow Through was established. Also a compensatory program, Follow Through may take a variety of forms, including academic intervention models.

Information about several programs for helping migrant students is available through the ERIC Clearinghouse on Reading and Communication Skills (Reed, 1978). Most stress providing individualized instruction and helping children to become independent learners. They place curricular emphasis in the following four areas:

1. oral language programs for making the transition between language at home and at school
2. task-oriented activities for helping children solve problems
3. experience-based programs for relating home experiences to school and for expanding concepts beyond the immediate environment
4. affective programs for improving the child's self-concept.

612

Teaching
Reading in
Today's
Elementary
Schools

Basing his conclusions on extensive research, Brophy (1982) recommends several teaching strategies that should be effective with inner-city children. He points first to the importance of teacher effectiveness in producing learning gains and stresses the teacher behaviors listed below.

1. *Good teachers take the responsibility for teaching.* Teachers do not accept the failures of their students but reteach, try other methods, and believe in the ability of their students to learn.
2. *Good teachers organize and manage their classes.* Most of the available time is spent in instruction; little time is spent in transition between lessons and other nonproductive activities. Good teachers establish routines and schedules, minimize disruptions, and move instruction at a lively pace.
3. *The curriculum is geared for success.* Students should participate in a variety of meaningful activities, progressing in incremental steps and experiencing success at each level.
4. *Good teachers direct the learning process.* Teachers demonstrate skills, conduct activities, explain concepts, review materials, and actively direct students' learning experiences.
5. *Skills are taught to mastery level.* Following instruction, teachers let students practice and apply skills to the point of overlearning. Lower-level skills are learned thoroughly before higher-level skills are introduced.
6. *Teaching strategies differ at various grade levels.* In the early grades students need more individualized attention than in higher grades, but teachers must work closely with students and check their progress at all levels.
7. *Teachers need to be supportive.* Teachers offer instructional support to students by providing structured learning experiences, individualization, and continuous supervision. They also offer personal support through praise, encouragement, and appreciation of effort.

✔ Self-Check: Objective 8

What are some of the problems that culturally different children encounter as they enter school? What are some ways that teachers can help them?
(See Self-Improvement Opportunities 6 and 9.)

Dialectal Differences

Characteristics

Children who exhibit cultural differences are also likely to have linguistic differences or variations, or "dialects." A dialect may be defined as a variation of a language that is sufficiently different from the original to be considered a separate entity but not different enough to be classed as a separate language. Dialectal variations are usually associated with socioeconomic level, geographical region, or national origin. In truth, we all speak a regional dialect of some sort, and differences exist even within a regional pattern. *Idiolect* is the term referring to an individual's unique language style.

Differences in dialects occur in phonology (pronunciation), vocabulary, and grammatical construction. Each dialect is a complete and functional language system, and no dialect is superior or inferior to another for purposes of communication. However, in order to be accepted in some social classes and attain certain career goals, use of standard English is desirable. Teachers should therefore accept and respect children's dialects as part of their cultures and environments, but should make them aware of standard English as an alternative. Perhaps the most accepted view currently among linguists and educators is *bidialectalism,* which affirms both the value of home dialect and its use within the community and the value of teaching students standard English (Ovando and Collier, 1985). This means that students should be able to speak their native dialect in school some of the time without being criticized.

Dialectal differences occur in both urban and rural areas and among people of different national origins. Children from homes where a language other than English is spoken may come to school speaking a dialect that is a mixture of English and the syntactic and phonological features of the language spoken at home. Some features of four dialects are given below.

1. *Rural Appalachian.* Stewart (1969) identified speech patterns of Appalachian rural children and found such features as changed word endings (*goin', seein'*), incorrect use of the objective case of pronouns in compound subjects (*me and you, me and my sister*), addition of "n" to possessive pronouns (*his'n, her'n*), and mispronunciation of words (*duh* for *the, terry* for *very*).
2. *Black English.* Harber and Beatty (1978) reported that major differences exist between standard English and black English, but noted that the similarities exceed the differences. Phonological differences include simplification of consonant clusters (*tes* for *test*) and *th* sounds (*de* for *the, nofin'* for *nothing, brovah* for *brother*). Some syntactical differences involve linking verbs (*He goin'* for *He is going*), irregular verb forms (*Dey rided der bike [bikes]* for *They rode their bikes*), and future form (*I'm a go home* for *I will go home*).
3. *Spanish.* English-speaking children from Spanish-language backgrounds are likely to retain Spanish stress and intonation and place adjectives after instead of before verbs (*The dress blue is pretty*). Other points of difficulty might be the negative (*Jim is no here*), plurals (*The two boys are bigs*), omission of "he" (*Is fireman?*), and subject-verb agreement (*The girls runs*).
4. *Navajo.* When speaking English, Navajo children are likely to retain some of their Navajo language characteristics, such as using vowel length and nasalization to distinguish meaning. Few articles and adjectives exist in Navajo, and few nouns are changed to make the plural (*four dog*). The possessive pattern also differs (*the boy his book* for *the boy's book*) (Saville, 1970).

614

Teaching
Reading in
Today's
Elementary
Schools

Children who use dialects such as these are not using inferior language, but are simply expressing their ideas in natural speech. Reading teachers should be familiar with the principal differences in pronunciation and syntactic rules of a child's dialect in order to evaluate oral reading. Without this knowledge, teachers cannot distinguish between a child's oral misreading that results from a lack of decoding skills and oral misreading that results from dialectal differences.

There are clearly distinctions between standard English and various dialects. Since nearly all published materials are written in standard English, one might assume that children who speak nonstandard English would have difficulty learning to read because of the discrepancies between textbook language and their own dialects. Such is not the case, however, according to research cited by Mason and Au (1986), which reveals that there is little evidence to indicate that speaking a dialect in and of itself interferes with learning to read. Also, using dialect does not appear to hinder the ability to understand standard English.

Instructional Implications and Strategies

Educators have proposed several viewpoints related to teaching reading to children with dialectal variations, including the following:

1. Teach the children standard English first; then teach them to read.
2. Use materials written in nonstandard dialect or in the child's own language.
3. Use conventional reading material but accept dialect transpositions.
4. Use materials written in standard English that are culturally relevant to the target group.
5. Use the language experience approach.

The first two proposals have generally been unsuccessful. Experiments that require children who speak different dialects to learn standard English before they learn to read have usually failed, and research has not supported using materials written in the child's dialect for reading instruction (Ekwall and Shanker, 1985). The third view is supported because children who substitute their own dialect for the standard English of their texts, as long as they retain the intended meaning, are showing that they comprehend what is written but are simply translating it into more familiar language. The culturally relevant materials mentioned in the fourth position help students identify with characters and settings in stories and therefore make reading more meaningful. Both basal readers and trade books contain more stories about racially and ethnically different situations than they did formerly.

The language experience approach (see Chapter 6) offers many advantages as a method for teaching reading to students whose dialect differs considerably from standard English, but critics argue that it simply reinforces the dialect without providing contact with standard English. Gillet and Gentry (1983) proposed a variation of this approach that values children's language but also provides exposure to standard English. The teacher transcribes the children's story exactly as dictated. The process continues in the traditional way, but later the teacher writes another version of the dictated chart in standard English with conventional sentence structure, using the same format and much of the same vocabulary. The teacher presents it as another story, not a better one, and children compare the two versions. The students then revise the original chart, making their sentences longer, more elaborate, and more consistent with standard English. They then use echo reading and choral reading with this version until they can read it fluently and have acquired additional sight words.

For those who plan to teach in regions where children have divergent dialects, these classroom practices may be useful:

1. Provide an unusually rich program of development in functional oral language.
2. Relate reading to personal experiences and oral language forms that are familiar to the child.
3. Provide reading materials about characters with whom the child can identify.
4. Know the possible points of interference between the dialect of the child and the standard dialect of the school.
5. Listen to the child's language carefully to determine the nature, regularity, and predictability of such dialectal differences.
6. Base instruction (particularly phonics) on a careful analysis of the child's language. Vowel phonemes are particularly likely to vary, as are the other phonological and syntactical features previously mentioned.
7. Differentiate between oral reading errors and particular speech patterns related to different linguistic backgrounds. (See "Miscue Analysis" in Chapter 10.)
8. Accept the student's dialect but model standard English. For example, if a child says "I ain't got no pencil," you might respond with "You don't have a pencil? I'll help you find one."
9. Focus on the ideas that the children are expressing rather than on their ways of expressing them.
10. Help them see purposes for learning standard English as an alternative. Have them brainstorm occasions when they might want or need to use standard English.
11. Connect reading and writing whenever possible. Read stories to the children, let them write their own stories, and then have them read their stories to the class.
12. Provide students with opportunities for role-playing situations that call for both nonstandard and standard English.

616

Teaching
Reading in
Today's
Elementary
Schools

✔ **Self-Check: Objective 9**

Explain what dialect is. Suggest some appropriate teaching strategies for children whose dialect differs radically from standard English.
(See Self-Improvement Opportunities 7, 8, 9, and 14.)

Bilingual Children

The term *bilingualism* refers to the ability to speak or understand a language in addition to the individual's native tongue. Many people in the United States are bilingual or have non–English-language backgrounds, and their number is expected to increase from 28 million in 1976 to 39.5 million by the year 2000. Every state in the nation has non-English speakers, although some states have fewer than ten thousand and others have over a million. People with Spanish-language backgrounds make up 33 percent of all minority speakers and 60 percent of the minority school population. About 5 million school-aged children speak a language other than English or live in homes where languages other than English are spoken (Ramirez, 1985, based on data from the 1976 Survey of Income and Education conducted by the Bureau of the Census).

The Bilingual Education Act (1968) brought about the widespread use of bilingual programs to provide equal educational opportunities for students with non–English-language backgrounds (Ovando and Collier, 1985). A bilingual education program attempts to do three things: (1) continue the development of the student's primary language (L1), (2) help the student acquire a second language (L2), and (3) provide instruction in content areas by using both English (L2) and the child's native language (L1). This type of program includes historical and cultural components of both languages, so that students can develop and maintain self-esteem and pride in both cultures.

English-as-a-Second-Language (ESL) instruction is a program for teaching English to students who live in an English-speaking environment but whose native language is not English. It is an important component of bilingual programs, and ESL students make up the most rapidly expanding population in North American schools (Walters and Gunderson, 1985).

According to Hewett and Forness (1984), an ideal bilingual program uses each language half of the time by splitting the time for a subject between the two languages, teaching half the subjects in one language and half in the other, or using a combination of these two systems. Unfortunately, this goal of equal time is often not met because teachers are not proficient in a second language and students within a single school may speak several different languages. In some cases when these situations exist, itinerant resource teachers who are proficient in a second language visit the schools each week to offer instruction in the children's native languages.

Leaders in many bilingual programs feel pressured to enable students to learn enough English for school use in two or three years, even though many learners need from four to six years. Because of this pressure, many bilingual teachers reduce instruction in a child's native language and focus on instruction in English. In one study bilingual teachers used Spanish or Cantonese an average of only 8 percent of the time and used English the remainder of the time (Wong Fillmore, 1986).

Another obstacle to the implementation of bilingual education is the belief held by many educators that children with a limited knowledge of English should be "immersed" in English in order to learn the language quickly and be absorbed into American culture. These educators fail to recognize the value of students' achieving literacy in their native language. Also, students taught with such monolingual instruction have difficulty associating meaning with sounds, symbols, and structures of English. Even though they learn to communicate at a functional level after a few years, many of them never achieve English language skills at the cognitive, abstract level necessary for academic success. Consequently, they score low on achievement tests and are several years below grade level; in addition, they are retained twice as often and have twice the dropout rate of native English-speaking students (Lapp and Flood, 1986).

Characteristics

In the classroom, some bilingual students may speak very little English and others may speak English almost as well as they do their native language. Ovando and Collier (1985) have identified four types of students who might be in ESL or bilingual classes.

1. *English-dominant students with a home language other than English.* These students may need to improve their academic achievement in English-speaking schools while continuing to develop the home language skills and cultural ties that their parents wish them to maintain.
2. *Bilingual, bicultural students.* These students are generally fluent in both languages, and bilingual education only enriches their academic experiences while reinforcing the cultural and linguistic identity of their families.
3. *Limited-English-proficient (LEP) students.* LEP students are perhaps most typical of those receiving bilingual and ESL instruction. They lack sufficient English language skills to achieve in a regular classroom and need special instruction for developing linguistic and academic skills.
4. *English-speaking monolingual students with no language minority background.* Since the law requires classes to be integrated, English-speaking students who have no knowledge of other languages may also be in bilingual classes. They help socialize minority students and also benefit from exposure to a second language.

618

Teaching
Reading in
Today's
Elementary
Schools

Bilingual children may be from families of indigenous minorities, such as Native Americans; immigrants, who leave a country to settle permanently elsewhere; or refugees, who flee a country to escape from an intolerable situation. Their home backgrounds and their families' attitudes toward language, school, and culture often affect how well they learn English as a second language.

Instructional Implications and Strategies

Three categories of factors related to learning a second language are important considerations in planning instructional programs for speakers of languages other than English. These are personal factors, including age, attitudes, motivation, and psychological traits; situational aspects, including school setting, instructional approaches, and teacher characteristics; and linguistic features, particularly the differences and similarities between the first and second languages (Ramirez, 1985).

Research seems to indicate that minority students learn to read better if initial instruction is in their native language (Ovando and Collier, 1985; Lapp and Flood, 1986; Mace-Matluck, 1982), and students who can already read and write in their native tongue generally learn to read much faster in English than those who are nonliterate in the language used at home. By beginning to read in the language they understand best, students are able to develop and use strategies that are effective for learning to read. Later they can transfer these same strategies or skills to reading material written in English. In addition, the use of a child's native language for instruction is likely to build a sense of identity and self-worth and reduce feelings of hostility or ambivalence toward English. According to Thonis (1976, p. 61), *"The best predictor of success in a second language is success in the first language."*

There are certain universals or commonalities among languages that use the same alphabet, but the transfer of reading skills from one language to another does not occur automatically (Mace-Matluck, 1982; Lapp and Flood, 1986). Teachers need to identify those skills that are common to both the native language and English and then plan lessons to help students see how a particular reading skill can apply to both languages. Unless children realize that they can use the same reading strategies, they may not transfer their knowledge. Once students perceive similarities in reading processes, they can transfer not only general reading strategies and attitudes, but also such specific skills as awareness of text structure and knowledge of story grammar.

Padrón, Knight, and Waxman (1986) investigated the reading strategies used by bilingual and by monolingual English-speaking third and fifth graders and found that the bilingual students used fewer cognitive strategies, including such effective comprehension techniques as concentrating, noting and searching for important details, and self-generated questioning. While their failure to use as many strategies may have been due in part to limited

Bilingual children who are learning to read English often pose a challenge for teachers, since approaches and materials will have to be varied according to the children's special needs.   (© Elizabeth Crews)

ability in English, it may have been due also to transferring from reading in their native language to English reading before they had developed useful reading strategies. When bilingual children move too quickly into English, they tend to focus primarily on decoding rather than on developing adequate comprehension techniques.

Instruction in ESL should focus on learning languages as meaningful communication, as opposed to acquiring basic English language skills in isolation, because children learn language most easily when they understand

620

Teaching
Reading in
Today's
Elementary
Schools

it and use it in connection with things that interest them. In actual practice, however, much reading instruction stresses accuracy in skills rather than understanding and appreciation, and writing often focuses on mechanics instead of communication (Wong Fillmore, 1986). To make reading and writing more meaningful, teachers should select materials and topics that relate to the child's interests and experiences.

Many educators believe that limited-English-proficient (LEP) children need to understand and speak English before they learn to read it (Lapp and Flood, 1986; Mace-Matluck, 1982; Thonis, 1976). Although these children do not need to be completely fluent in the second language before beginning to read it, they should attain a certain level of oral proficiency. In order to learn to read successfully, a child in the middle grades should have reached a minimal level of oral proficiency that "corresponds to the mean score achieved by monolingual English-speaking first-grade students on a measure of oral proficiency. That, of course, suggests a rather complete knowledge of the basic structures of English" (Mace-Matluck, 1982, pp. 15–16).

Research thus indicates that students with limited knowledge of English need to become proficient in oral English, that they learn best by using materials related to their interests and experiences, that emphasis in reading instruction should be on comprehension, and that initial reading instruction should be in their native language. A survey of several hundred teachers who work with ESL students in British Columbia, however, revealed that in many cases teachers are not following these recommended procedures (Gunderson, 1985). Often teachers do not speak another language, so the children are mainstreamed into regular classrooms where reading instruction is conducted in a traditional manner. Most teachers provide reading instruction in English for these students immediately and place them in reading groups, generally in the lowest group. Most of them teach students phonics with flashcards and worksheets, have them read orally much of the time, and use a basal reading series designed for ESL students. Little attention is given to developing background information and vocabulary for stories. As a result of these practices, students may learn basic skills by rote, but they are unable to read with full understanding.

Even though conditions in some school systems make it difficult to implement bilingual education fully, teachers should consider the implications of research for teaching ESL students and find alternatives to traditional instruction. Many of the strategies presented for dialectal speakers hold true for students with limited English proficiency as well, and additional considerations for working with these children appear below.

If teachers must use basal readers for teaching bilingual children, they should consider the relationship between the linguistic features of the text and the child's language proficiency (Gonzales, 1981), providing instruction on linguistic structures and forms if necessary. The teacher may discuss pictures by using simple sentences, avoiding the use of phrases, clauses, or other structures that the child does not understand. She may rewrite part of the text by reducing compound and complex sentences to series of simple sentences (for instance, changing the sentence "Tim ran and played" to "Tim ran" and "Tim played"). Aukerman and Aukerman (1981) recommend, however, that teachers should speak in the natural grammatical sequences of standard English as a model for the children to follow. They also suggest teaching those phonics elements that are common to both the child's native tongue and standard English first. Errors or miscues that reflect the structure of the child's first language should not be corrected until after the child becomes a fairly proficient reader.

Associating words with concrete objects, dramatizing actions, and participating in a variety of experiences help children learn a second language. To increase vocabulary they can touch, name, label, and talk about concrete objects; and to learn prepositions they can act out phrases by placing an object *on*, *under*, or *beside* a table. Songs, games, and choral readings with motions also reinforce a child's understanding of words, as does acting out sentences ("Tina sits down") or simple stories. Direct experiences through field trips or classroom activities, along with such vicarious experiences as films and filmstrips, puppets, and pictures, enable children to learn language in meaningful ways. Philadelphia teachers working with Asian children reported success when they used manipulative objects and moved about the room while talking about what they were doing. One of these teachers used a dozen puppets and a collection of six thousand pictures to stimulate conversation. The teachers worked on the children's listening comprehension first, then on speech until the children could express themselves fluently, and finally on reading and writing skills (Loeb, 1984). Example 12.4 is a page from an ESL workbook which uses familiar expressions for oral language, reading, and writing.

The language experience approach is particularly useful for helping LEP students learn to read. Students who know very little English, however, need to acquire additional vocabulary for concepts and knowledge of oral language before dictating sentences (Moustafa and Penrose, 1985). A combination of comprehensible input, reinforcement, and language experience allows them to learn enough English to produce chart stories. *Comprehensible input* refers to the use of oral language along with concrete referents to meaning for teaching vocabulary. For example, the teacher demonstrates the meaning of *look* by pointing to an object in the room and saying "Look!" while urging the children to look in that direction. In another example the teacher asks children to identify objects in pictures. If they cannot name them, the teacher gives the answers and provides *reinforcement* by continuing the questioning until the children have internalized the answers. In the next step the teacher presents key words from the picture on word cards for children to learn, and then the children dictate sentences about the picture for the teacher to write verbatim on the chart (*language experience*). Follow-up instruction may take many forms to provide practice in reading-related skills.

Books and stories about the cultures of language-different children help them to work through their problems in adjusting to a new environment, and they also help their classmates understand how these children feel.

622

Teaching
Reading in
Today's
Elementary
Schools

▶ **EXAMPLE 12.4:** Sample Page from an ESL Book

How Are You Today?

With Your Partner

Ask and answer with your partner.

1. Are you **happy** today?
   Yes, I am.
   No, I'm not.

2. Are you **sad** today?
   Yes, I am.
   No, I'm not.

3. Are you **angry** today?
   Yes, I am.
   No, I'm not.

4. Are you **nervous** today?
   Yes, I am.
   No, I'm not.

5. Are you **tired** today?
   Yes, I am.
   No, I'm not.

6. Are you **sick** today?
   Yes, _____
   No, _____

7. Are you **hot** today?
   Yes, _____
   No, _____

8. Are you **cold** today?
   Yes, _____
   No, _____

9. Are you **hungry** today?
   Yes, _____
   No, _____

10. Are you **thirsty** today?
    Yes, _____
    No, _____

Circle Dialogue

Sit in a circle. Ask the student on your right the first question. ("Are you happy today?") That student answers and then asks the student on his or her right the same question.

Teacher: "Are you happy today?"
Student 1: "Yes, I am." *or* "No, I'm not."
       "Are you happy today?"
Student 2: "Yes, I am. *or* "No, I'm not."
Continue around the circle. Repeat with all the questions on this page.

List on the Board: What Do You Do?

Ask the class these questions. Write a list on the board of all the different answers.

1. What do you do when you are happy?
2. What do you do when you are sad?
3. What do you do when you are hot?
4. What do you do when you are tired?
5. What do you do when you are cold?
6. What do you do when you are angry?

4

Source: Tina Kasloff Carver/Sandra Douglas Fotinos, A CONVERSA-
TION BOOK: English in Everyday Life, Book I, 2/E, © 1985, p. 4. Reprinted
by permission of Prentice-Hall, Inc., Englewood Cliffs, New Jersey. ◀

Whereas some children may be able to read these books independently, in many cases the teacher will need to read them aloud to the class. In addition to stories about other lands and folktales from many countries, other good selections are those listed in Norton's *Through the Eyes of a Child* (1987), Chapter 11, "Multiethnic Literature," and in Radencich's "Books that Promote Positive Attitudes Toward Second Language Learning" (1985).

Using story grammars (see Chapter 5) to analyze story elements can help ESL students understand and create stories. Bilingual, bicultural sixth graders participated in a reading-writing project by listening to a folktale, studying its story grammar and elements, and generating ideas for writing their own folktales (Stahl-Gemake and Guastello, 1984). Divided into small groups, the students listened to each other's stories, made suggestions for improvements, and edited them. The stories were typed and the students then illustrated them and read them to younger children.

Listening to stories being read to them in either English or their native tongue can benefit LEP children. When fourth graders listened to parent volunteers read them stories in their native language, they were exposed to good role models for oral reading and to literature about their own culture. These children continued to make gains in English reading as well (Walters and Gunderson, 1985). Reading stories in English also benefits LEP children by providing them with opportunities to acquire and reinforce vocabulary, practice oral fluency, and develop a sense of story. Some guidelines for using story reading to facilitate literacy in a second language follow (Hough, Nurss, and Enright, 1986).

1. Read stories frequently to children in small groups so that they can hear many different types of stories.
2. Use verbal and nonverbal cueing strategies (pauses, exaggerated intonation, gestures, and so on).
3. Ask thought-provoking questions to promote interaction during story reading.
4. Read predictable books and encourage children to "read along."
5. Choose well-illustrated books so that the pictures provide additional clues to meaning.
6. Reread favorite stories to reinforce vocabulary, language patterns, and awareness of sequence.
7. Offer follow-up activities using different formats and materials.

✔ Self-Check: Objective 10
What are some factors to consider in working with bilingual children?
(See Self-Improvement Opportunities 7, 8, 9, 13, and 14).

CORRECTIVE AND REMEDIAL READERS: UNDERACHIEVEMENT

It is a common misconception that every child who is reading below grade level is a poor reader. From the preceding discussion of exceptionalities, it is easy to see that not all children have the same abilities, linguistic facility, or experiences. Therefore, it is unreasonable to expect all children to read at grade level, and teachers should instead be concerned that children read up to their individual potential.

Children who fail to read up to their potential are underachievers. An informal reading inventory can be administered to find a child's capacity

624

Teaching
Reading in
Today's
Elementary
Schools

level, or probable potential for reading achievement. (See Chapter 10 for information on locating capacity level.) If a child's potential exceeds her achievement level, she is an underachiever. By carefully observing a child, a teacher may suspect that the child is an underachiever if it appears that she has the ability to read better than her performance in a reading group indicates. For instance, the teacher might notice that she can read material of special interest at a much higher level of difficulty than she reads basal reader stories. In any class a few children who are determined to learn may be working above their estimated potential, while others may be working up to their potential, even if they are not reading at grade level. Some students who are reading at or above grade level may still be underachievers if they are reading below their potential.

Two terms that designate reading instruction for underachieving readers are *corrective* and *remedial*. A *corrective reader* is generally one who reads about six to eighteen months below potential; this child should receive help in skill development in the classroom from the teacher before the disparity between potential and achievement increases. A student is usually considered to be a *remedial reader* if there is a gap of approximately two or more years between expectancy and achievement levels; this student needs special help in a reading resource room from a reading specialist. Whereas reading instruction for average readers is *developmental* and proceeds normally according to a prescribed sequence, gifted readers may take part in *accelerated* reading programs. Slow learners need instruction that is *adapted* to a slower pace.

Underachievement in reading is affected by considerably different factors for each type of exceptionality. Inability to read is a common characteristic of learning disabled children who appear to have adequate mental ability for learning to read. Because of the specific nature of learning disabilities, such children will probably need to go to a resource room for additional help with reading. On the other hand, many slow learners are actually reading up to their potential even if they are not reading at grade level; they should receive instruction that is adapted to a slower pace and uses easier material. Teachers should challenge gifted children who are underachieving in terms of their potential to read more difficult materials, encouraging them to participate in accelerated programs. Visually handicapped children may be reading below their potential because they have trouble seeing clearly, but when provisions are made for accommodating reading materials to their needs, they often reach their potential through corrective or remedial instruction. Similarly, hearing and speech impaired students are often underachievers because they cannot hear or reproduce sounds accurately and thus are generally unable to profit from phonics instruction. Teachers should use alternate methods in teaching word recognition to help these children reach their potential. Because children who are behaviorally disturbed or hyperactive cannot keep their attention on the lesson, they often fail to work up to their ability. Teachers must find ways to help these children calm down before providing corrective or remedial instruction.

Children who are culturally and linguistically different also frequently underachieve in reading. These children come from environments that do not provide them with the experiences and language skills necessary for coping with a middle-class curriculum and standard English. Therefore, even though they have the ability to succeed in school, the gap between their background and the school is so great that they do not learn all that they should. In order to help these children reach their potential, teachers should use instructional strategies and materials that help them make the transition from home to school.

Children who are not handicapped and who come from middle-class homes where standard English is spoken also may be underachievers. The causes for their underachievement are varied, and there is generally no easy solution. In some homes parents are either disinterested or so concerned that they create emotional problems for their children; in others children are bothered by problems such as a new sibling, an impending divorce, or child abuse. When children come to school hungry, they cannot concentrate. Perpetual colds or headaches interfere with learning. Children who are frequently absent miss so many lessons that they do not ever learn essential skills. Their foundation in reading is so weak that it collapses at higher levels. Some children have developed negative attitudes toward reading as a result of frustrations and failure and may have such low self-concepts that they have stopped trying.

Teachers who understand the causes for underachievement are sometimes able to alleviate the situation, but at other times they can only offer understanding. In the case of vision and hearing impairments, a teacher can recommend that the parents or guardian see that the child gets professional attention. When children come to school hungry, a teacher can arrange for the cafeteria to provide them with food before school starts. If children are abused or neglected, a teacher can contact the proper authorities. Solving any one of these problems, however, seldom changes a child's reading level appreciably.

When trying to help underachievers reach their potential, classroom teachers have two major types of responsibilities. First, they should help corrective readers in the classroom by identifying specific deficiencies (see Chapter 10 on assessment) and developing plans to help these readers improve. Second, after remedial readers have been identified, classroom teachers must cooperate with the resource teacher and/or reading specialist to help plan reading instruction, arranging a time to coordinate reading programs for these children.

A teacher needs to concentrate on both developing positive attitudes and building reading skills when working with underachieving readers. Teacher behaviors and instructional procedures that are effective with these children may be found in the general guidelines near the beginning of this chapter.

Table 12.2 identifies several common reading difficulties and suggests possible remedial strategies. This list is not comprehensive, and the teacher will find that some approaches work better with some children than with

626

Teaching
Reading in
Today's
Elementary
Schools

TABLE 12.2 Common Reading Problems and Suggested Remedial Approaches

If a student . . .	*Let the student . . .*
1. makes reversals (*saw* for *was*).	a. trace a word from left to right, following the direction of an arrow at the top of a page or word card.
	b. copy a word on a typewriter or word processor.
	c. print a word, making the first letter green (go) and the last letter red (stop).
	d. do activities which require awareness of left-to-right directionality (*Simon Says*).
	e. use small squares of thin cardboard with a letter on each square and form words like those that appear on word cards.
2. reads word by word or uses incorrect phrasing.	a. read easy, familiar, and interesting material.
	b. tape-record a paragraph, listen to the tape, record it again with attention to units of meaning, and listen for improvement. Repeat this process until fluency is reached.
	c. read a paragraph silently and underline groups of words that go together.
	d. read orally with a good reader and imitate the good reader's phrasing and expression.
	e. participate in choral reading or choral speaking.
3. shows little awareness of structural analysis.	a. count the number of syllables in a spoken word by clapping, tapping a pencil, or holding up one finger for each sound.
	b. match two root words that make a compound word.
	c. create words from a flip chart that contains root words in the center, prefixes at the beginning, and suffixes at the end.
	d. underline the root words on a list of words with affixes.
	e. choose the word with the correct suffix for a sentence. (Sally _____ [walk, walks, walked, walking] a mile yesterday.)
4. lacks knowledge of sight words.	a. associate pictures with words that have concrete referents.
	b. identify names of familiar products that appear in advertisements.
	c. read words from language experience charts and student-written stories as they appear both in context and on word cards.
	d. build word banks of sight words and use them to create sentences or organize by naming or action words. (See Chapter 6 for ideas about word banks.)
	e. practice recognizing similar and confusing words, such as those beginning with *th* or *wh*, by circling differences in them on word lists and identifying them on flash cards.
5. cannot find the main idea.	a. observe the teacher modeling ways to identify main idea (what the selection is mostly about, what idea covers all important aspects of a selection, etc.)

If a student . . .	Let the student . . .
5. cannot find the main idea (*cont.*).	b. categorize objects, pictures, words, and finally sentences; name the category; and explain why items go together. c. choose an advertisement, use the product as the main idea, and select several features of the product as supporting details. d. read a paragraph that is constructed so that one sentence does not belong with the other sentences, remove the inappropriate sentence, tell why it does not belong, and state the main idea of the remaining sentences. e. write a paragraph and give it a title that tells the main idea.
6. has difficulty using context clues.	a. watch the teacher modeling ways of using semantic and syntactic context clues. b. choose the correct word from several choices to fill in the blank in a sentence and give reasons for the choice. (Jimmy played outside with his [basketball, television, potato, chair].) c. fill in blanks with appropriate words in cloze selections. (See Chapter 5 for construction of cloze passages.) d. brainstorm words that would make sense for the unknown word in a sentence and then consider phonics clues (especially beginning sound) in deciding on the word. e. underline specific types of context clues, such as definition or comparison. (See Chapter 3 for more types of context clues.)
7. cannot make inferences or draw conclusions.	a. observe the teacher modeling ways to draw inferences by thinking aloud about clues for meaning. b. look at pictures or collections of objects, find reasonable connections among them, and create stories from them. c. listen to a story and predict what will happen next. d. underline word and phrase clues that lead to making an inference. (What season is it? The *snow fell* and the *streets were icy*. It was *very cold* outside.) e. solve short mysteries. (See Donald Sobol's Encyclopedia Brown books, for example.)
8. has a limited vocabulary.	a. expand experiences by watching films and listening to stories that contain new concepts and words. b. keep a file or notebook of new words with their meanings and use some of these words in creative writing. c. play games that use word knowledge, such as *Password*. d. brainstorm with other children lists of synonyms and antonyms. e. compare figurative and literal meanings of figurative expressions. f. provide a rich environment with many varied, concrete experiences.

628

Teaching
Reading in
Today's
Elementary
Schools

others. For additional ideas, the teacher may want to consult Ekwall's *Locating and Correcting Reading Difficulties*, 4th ed. (1985) or various activity books designed for developing specific reading skills.

✔ Self-Check: Objective 11
Explain how teachers can identify underachievers and how they can help them to reach their potential.
(See Self-Improvement Opportunity 11.)

MATERIALS FOR READERS WITH SPECIAL NEEDS

Guideline 7 near the beginning of this chapter emphasizes selecting materials that exceptional children are capable of using as well as those that are of interest to them. High-interest, low-vocabulary books meet both of these requirements. These books contain especially interesting and appealing stories for slow learners, culturally different students, and poor readers; they are written at a low readability level so that these students can read them easily. A sampling of these and other materials that are especially suited to the needs of special students is found in Table 12.3; the listed materials are only a few of the many varied publications and programs that are available.

Summary

Every teacher should be aware of the needs of exceptional children, especially since the passage of the Education for All Handicapped Children Act (PL 94-142), which provides for the mainstreaming of many of these students into regular classrooms. Teachers work with other professionals in designing individualized education programs (IEPs) for handicapped children. General guidelines for working with these children include providing opportunities for success, having positive attitudes toward them, providing appropriate instruction, using suitable materials, and communicating with others who work with them.

Several types of special learners are being mainstreamed into regular classrooms. Learning disabled children usually have a significant discrepancy between achievement level and potential. Many of them have communication problems, and reading improvement is their greatest academic need. Slow learners do not learn as readily as other children, so their reading instruction should progress more slowly and offer more repetition. Students who are behaviorally disturbed may exhibit conduct disorders such as aggression or hyperactivity, or personality problems such as withdrawal or depression.

Through careful observation, teachers can usually identify children with visual, auditory, or speech impairments. Visually impaired children may

TABLE 12.3 Materials for the Exceptional Child

Program/Publisher	Levels	Audience	Components	Remarks
Story Time Alemany Press Div. of Janus Book Pub. 2501 Industrial Pkwy., W. Dept. P Hayward, CA 94545	7- to 10-year-olds	Bilingual/ESL[1] (first, second, and third years of English)	Series of readers with traditional folktales	Stories based on analysis of language used in major reading programs
High Hat Early Reading Program	Primary	Bilingual/ESL, speech impaired, remedial students	Songs, games, word cards, stories, sentence strips, posters	Structured lessons with phonics emphasis
Peabody Rebus Program[2] American Guidance Service P.O. Box 99 Circle Pines, MN 55014	Readiness, beginning reading	Remedial, bilingual/ESL	Programmed workbooks	Pictured words (rebuses) as a transition to spelled words
Multiple Skills Series	Readiness, levels 1–6	Spanish-speaking students	Booklets and manual	Skill development adapted from English edition
Profiles of Black Americans Barnell Loft 958 Church St. Baldwin, NY 11510	Intermediate	All students, especially blacks	Pupil books and teacher's manual	Art and information about black Americans with color portraits
Spiral I and Spiral II Continental Press, Inc. Elizabethtown, PA 17022	Grade 5 and up	ESL students	Video- and audio-cassettes, student workbooks	Mature, high-interest, low-vocabulary books (readability 2.0–4.9)

[1] ESL stands for English as a second language.
[2] See Example 12.5 for sample material.

TABLE 12.3 Materials for the Exceptional Child (*cont.*)

Program/Publisher	Levels	Audience	Components	Remarks
Essential Sight Words Program	Levels 1 and 2	Low-achieving, learning disabled students	Test strips, activity books, worksheets, guide	Structured presentation of frequently used words (100 at each level)
Swain Beginning Reading Program DLM Teaching Resources P.O. Box 4000 One DLM Park Allen, TX 75002	Beginning reading	Disabled readers	Lesson books, guide, word cards	Success-oriented approach; emphasis on comprehension
Reading Milestones Dormac, Inc. P.O. Box 1699 Beaverton, OR 97075	1–4	Special-needs children; deaf students	Readers, workbooks, teacher's guide	Systematic, developmental language-based reading series
Edmark Reading Program Levels 1 and 2 P.O. Box 3903 Bellevue, WA 98009	Beginning reading	Mainstreamed students	Lesson books, software, signing manual, illustrated cards	Carefully sequenced, repetitive sight word approach
Now You're Talking	Grades 5 and up	ESL students	Video- and audio-cassettes, student workbooks	Grammar-based program that focuses on communication skills
Survival Reading Educational Activities P.O. Box 392 Freeport, NY 11520	4–5	Corrective and remedial readers	Cassette tapes, guide, activity books	Reading for everyday living, basic survival words
Series of books High Noon Books 20 Commercial Blvd. Novato, CA 94947	Age 9–teens	Learning disabled, ESL, remedial students	Several series of 48-page books	Recreational reading that reinforces basic sight words

Source	Level	Audience	Materials	Description
Attention Span Series Jamestown Publishers P.O. Box 9168 Providence, RI 02940	Intermediate	Multiethnic and slow readers	Illustrated storybooks	High-interest, low-vocabulary books (readability 2–3)
Soundsalive National Textbook Co. 4255 West Touhy Ave. Lincolnwood, IL 60646	Elementary	Spanish-speaking children	Workbooks, manual, phonics cards, alphabet books	Prereading program for bilingual classes offering a phonics program
English Survival Books	Beginning to intermediate	ESL students; special learners	Sets of consumable books	Skills for understanding, speaking, reading, and writing English
The Reading Machine Opportunities for Learning 20417 Nordhoff St. Chatsworth, CA 91311	Intermediate	Slow readers	Illustrated magazines, audiocassettes, duplicating masters	Multisensory approach: high-interest, low vocabulary (readability 2–3)
Varied programs Resources for the Gifted P.O. Box 15050 Phoenix, AZ 85060	K–12	Gifted	Puzzles, kits, cards, games, activity books, computer software	Critical and creative activities for the gifted
Developmental Reading Laboratory Kit I Science Research Assoc. 155 North Wacker Drive Chicago, IL 60606	Elementary	Mainstreamed and and remedial students	Kits with booklets and cassette	High-interest, low-difficulty reading selections for individualized work
Good Books I and II Sunburst Communications 39 Washington Ave. Pleasantville, NY 10570	Grades 4–6	Gifted	Kits of paperback books, activity cards	Individualized literature programs that teach thinking skills
Reaching Their Highest Potential Zephyr Press 430 South Essex Lane Tucson, AZ 85711	All ages	Gifted	Books, task cards, kits, manuals, posters	Variety of materials on thinking skills, simulations, imagery, whole-brain learning, etc.

632

**Teaching
Reading in
Today's
Elementary
Schools**

► **EXAMPLE 12.5:** Sample Rebus Material

Source: R. W. Woodcock, *Rebus Reader Two* (Circle Pines, Minn.: American Guidance
Service, 1969), p. 16. ◄

need special classroom arrangements and large-print books, and reading
instruction for the hearing impaired should not rely on phonics. Two of the
most common speech disorders are problems with articulation and stuttering.

Gifted children can progress more rapidly than their peers and often show
advanced language development. Teachers should provide challenging tasks
for these students and help them reach their potential.

America's schools have children from a wide variety of ethnic, cultural,
and racial origins who bring with them diverse backgrounds and experiences.
Many of them speak nonstandard dialects and others are English-as-a-Second
Language (ESL) students. As a result of the Bilingual Education Act, bilingual
and ESL programs have been created to provide equal educational opportunities for these students.

Two types of underachieving readers are corrective readers who read
somewhat below their potential and remedial readers who read considerably
(about two or more years) below their potential. Teachers need to help these
students develop positive attitudes toward reading and improve their reading
skills so that they can reach their potential.

Teachers can use a wide variety of motivational materials to help different types of exceptional children learn to read. These include high-interest, low-vocabulary books; programmed materials; and audio- and videocassettes.

Test Yourself

True or False

_____ 1. The exceptional child's basic needs and goals are quite different from those of the average child.

_____ 2. The handicapped child often needs more direct, systematic instruction than the average child usually needs.

_____ 3. The language experience approach and individualized reading are generally good approaches to use with the different learner.

_____ 4. Many children who have been enrolled in special education classes are being integrated into regular classrooms.

_____ 5. The purpose of PL 94-142 is to place every exceptional child in a regular classroom.

_____ 6. The least restrictive environment enables a child to do whatever he or she pleases in the classroom.

_____ 7. Children who are being mainstreamed may have difficulty adjusting to a regular classroom.

_____ 8. IEP stands for Instant Environmental Plan.

_____ 9. A learning disabled student is one who has a low level of functioning in all areas.

_____ 10. Many learning disabled students have severe communication deficits.

_____ 11. Reading improvement is the most widely recognized academic need of the learning disabled child.

_____ 12. Slow learners are those children whose IQ scores range between 85 and 100.

_____ 13. Slow learners should be given difficult material to read so they will be challenged.

_____ 14. Functional or survival skills include correct use of the telephone as well as the ability to interpret maps and schedules.

_____ 15. Observant teachers can usually detect a child who has a visual or hearing problem.

_____ 16. Visually handicapped children need to be taught to listen and remember well.

_____ 17. Hearing impaired children should be taught to read primarily with a phonics approach.

_____ 18. Two of the most common speech disorders with which the classroom teacher deals are articulation and stuttering.

_____ 19. In order to help the hyperactive or behaviorally disordered child, the teacher should keep the room environment simple and free of clutter.

634

Teaching
Reading in
Today's
Elementary
Schools

_____ 20. Children from homes of a low socioeconomic level have no problems adapting to a middle-class school.

_____ 21. Compensatory programs are designed for gifted students.

_____ 22. Children who have cultural differences are also likely to have linguistic differences.

_____ 23. Understanding the backgrounds of multiethnic children is a good way to begin relating to them.

_____ 24. It is impossible for a gifted child to be an underachiever.

_____ 25. A corrective reader is one whose problems have been corrected.

_____ 26. For purposes of communication, some dialects are superior to others.

_____ 27. The most rapidly expanding population of special students in North America is that of the learning disabled.

_____ 28. ESL students appear to read better if they learn to read first in their native language.

Self-Improvement Opportunities

1. List the nine general guidelines given for instructing exceptional children in order of importance (in your opinion). Be prepared to justify your reasoning.

2. Go to a school office and find out how the needs of learning disabled children are met. Ask to visit a classroom where a student with a physical or sensory handicap is being mainstreamed, and observe how this child participates in class activities and how he or she is accepted by classmates.

3. Plan six activities for using the newspaper with the slow reader and six for using it with the gifted student.

4. Talk with a speech correction teacher about the role of the regular classroom teacher in helping speech impaired children.

5. Visit a classroom to see if any child appears to be hyperactive. If there is such a child, observe how the teacher works with him or her.

6. Visit a compensatory program, such as Head Start, in your community and observe how the program tries to prepare children for school.

7. Study the characteristics of the people who live in your area. How do their language patterns compare with standard English? What cultural and ethnic variations do you find? What implications do these findings have for teaching?

8. Determine which linguistically different children are in evidence in a classroom. Then compare your judgments with those of the teacher.

9. Get permission from a classroom teacher to work with a culturally or linguistically different child on a one-to-one basis for one week, and ask the teacher to help you plan an instructional program for this child.

10. Find a book you think would appeal to one type of exceptional child and plan how you would present it.

11. Visit a school and find out what provisions are made for different types of learners. Are resource rooms being used? Is there a program for the gifted? What special personnel are available to provide services?

12. If feasible, become familiar with one or more of the special materials cited near the end of this chapter. Report to the class on possible uses.

13. If possible, interview a bilingual child about how he or she learned to read. Try to discover any problems or insights about learning to read from the child's point of view. Take notes on your findings and share them in class during group discussions.

14. If the region in which you live has a large number of minority families, make an annotated bibliography of books that relate to this particular minority group's culture.

Bibliography

Adelman, Howard S., and Linda Taylor. *An Introduction to Learning Disabilities.* Glenview, Ill.: Scott, Foresman, 1986.

Alexander, Clara Franklin. "Black English Dialect and the Classroom Teacher." *The Reading Teacher* 33 (February 1980): 571–77.

Allington, Richard L., and Mary C. Shake. "Remedial Reading: Achieving Curricular Congruence in Classroom and Clinic." *The Reading Teacher* 39 (March 1986): 648–54.

The ASCD Multicultural Education Commission. "Encouraging Multicultural Education." *Educational Leadership* 34 (January 1977): 288–91.

Askov, Eunice N., and Wayne Otto. *Meeting the Challenge.* Columbus: Charles E. Merrill, 1985, Chapters 14–16.

Aukerman, Robert C., and Louise R. Aukerman. *How Do I Teach Reading?* New York: Wiley, 1981.

Bader, Lois A. "Instructional Adjustments to Vision Problems." *The Reading Teacher* 37 (March 1984): 566–69.

Barnes, Willie J. "How to Improve Teacher Behavior in Multiethnic Classrooms." *Educational Leadership* 34 (April 1977): 511–15.

Bean, Rita M., and R. Tony Eichelberger. "Changing the Role of Reading Specialists: From Pull-Out to In-Class Programs." *The Reading Teacher* 38 (March 1985): 648–53.

Behrmann, Michael M., ed. *Handbook of Microcomputers in Special Education.* San Diego: College-Hill Press, 1984.

Bradley, R. C. *The Education of Exceptional Children.* 3rd ed. Wolfe City, Tex.: University Press, 1978.

Brophy, Jere. "Successful Teaching Strategies for the Inner-City Child." *Phi Delta Kappan* 63 (April 1982): 527–30.

Buttery, Thomas J., and George E. Mason. "Reading Improvement for Mainstreamed Children Who Are Mildly Mentally Handicapped." *Reading Improvement* 16 (Winter 1979): 334–37.

636

Teaching
Reading in
Today's
Elementary
Schools

Byrne, Margaret C. *The Child Speaks: A Speech Improvement Program for Kindergarten and First Grade.* New York: Harper & Row, 1965.

Cardenas, Jose A. "Education and the Children of Migrant Farmworkers: An Overview." (October 1976). [ED 134 367].

Carlsen, Joanne M. "Between the Deaf Child and Reading: The Language Connection." *The Reading Teacher* 38 (January 1985): 424–26.

Carr, Kathryn S. "What Gifted Readers Need from Reading Instruction." *The Reading Teacher* 38 (November 1984): 144–46.

Cassidy, Jack. "Inquiry Reading for the Gifted." *The Reading Teacher* 35 (October 1981): 17–21.

Click, Aliene. "Activities for Gifted Children in Elementary School." Unpublished paper, Tennessee Technological University, 1981, 114 pp.

Cruickshank, William M. *Concepts in Learning Disabilities: Selected Writings.* Vol. 2. Syracuse, N.Y.: Syracuse University Press, 1981.

Dallman, Martha, Roger L. Rouch, Lynette V. C. Char, and John J. DeBoer. *The Teaching of Reading.* 6th ed. New York: Holt, Rinehart and Winston, 1982.

Dixon, Carol N. "Teaching Strategies for the Mexican American Child." *The Reading Teacher* 30 (November 1976): 141–43.

Ebel, Carolyn Williams. "An Update: Teaching Reading to Students of English as a Second Language." *The Reading Teacher* 33 (January 1980): 403–407.

Ekwall, Eldon E. *Locating and Correcting Reading Difficulties.* 4th ed. Columbus, Ohio: Charles E. Merrill, 1985.

Ekwall, Eldon E., and James L. Shanker. *Teaching Reading in the Elementary School.* Columbus, Ohio: Charles E. Merrill, 1985, Chapter 12.

Fairchild, Thomas N. *Managing the Hyperactive Child in the Classroom.* Austin, Tex.: Learning Concepts, 1975.

Fish, John. *Special Education: The Way Ahead.* Philadelphia: Open University Press, 1985.

Foerster, Leona M. "Teaching Reading in Our Pluralistic Classrooms." *The Reading Teacher* 30 (November 1976): 146–50.

Fox, Lynn H., and William G. Durden. *Educating Verbally Gifted Youth.* Bloomington, Ind.: Phi Delta Kappa Educational Foundation, 1982.

Garcia, Ricardo L. *Education for Cultural Pluralism: Global Roots Stew.* Bloomington, Ind.: Phi Delta Kappa Educational Foundation, 1981.

Gaskins, Irene W. "Let's End the Reading Disabilities/Learning Disabilities Debate." *Journal of Learning Disabilities* 15 (February 1982): 81–83.

Gentile, Lance M., Patrice Lamb, and Cynda O. Rivers. "A Neurologist's Views of Reading Difficulty: Implications for Remedial Instruction." *The Reading Teacher* 39 (November 1985): 174–82.

Gillet, Jean Wallace, and J. Richard Gentry. "Bridges Between Nonstandard and Standard English with Extensions of Dictated Stories." *The Reading Teacher* 36 (January 1983): 360–65.

Gonzales, Phillip C. "Beginning English Reading for ESL Students." *The Reading Teacher* 35 (November 1981): 154–62.

Grossman, H., ed. *Manual on Terminology and Classification in Mental Retardation.* Washington, D.C.: American Association on Mental Deficiency, 1983.

Gunderson, Lee. "L2 Reading Instruction in ESL and Mainstream Classrooms." In *Issues in Literacy: A Research Perspective,* Thirty-Fourth Yearbook of the National Reading Conference. Jerome A. Niles, ed., and Rosary V. Lalik, assoc. ed. Rochester, N.Y.: National Reading Conference, 1985, pp. 65–69.

Hahn, Amos L. "Teaching Remedial Students to be Strategic Readers and Better Comprehenders." *The Reading Teacher* 39 (October 1985): 72–77.

Harber, Jean, and Jane N. Beatty. *Reading and Black English Speaking Child.* Newark, Del.: International Reading Association, 1978, pp. 46–47.

Harris, Albert J. "An Overview of Reading Disabilities and Learning Disabilities in the U.S." *The Reading Teacher* 33 (January 1980): 420–25.

Harris, Albert J., and Edward R. Sipay. *How to Increase Reading Ability.* 7th ed. New York: Longman, 1980.

Henderson, Anne J., and Richard E. Shores. "How Learning Disabled Students' Failure to Attend to Suffixes Affects Their Oral Reading Performance." *Journal of Learning Disabilities* 15 (March 1982): 178–82.

Henley, Martin. *Teaching Mildly Retarded Children in the Regular Classroom.* Bloomington, Ind.: Phi Delta Kappa Educational Foundation, 1985.

Hewett, Frank M., with Steven R. Forness. *Education of Exceptional Learners.* 3rd ed. Boston: Allyn and Bacon, 1984.

Hoben, Mollie. "Toward Integration in the Mainstream." *Exceptional Children* 47 (October 1980): 100–105.

Hough, Ruth A., Joanne R. Nurss, and D. Scott Enright. "Story Reading with Limited English Speaking Children in the Regular Classroom." *The Reading Teacher* 39 (February 1986): 510–14.

Kirk, Samuel A., and James J. Gallagher. *Educating Exceptional Children.* Boston: Houghton Mifflin, 1983.

Kirk, Samuel A., Joanne Marie Kliebhan, and Janet W. Lerner. *Teaching Reading to Slow and Disabled Learners.* Boston: Houghton Mifflin, 1978.

Lapp, Diane, and James Flood. *Teaching Students to Read.* New York: Macmillan, 1986, Chapters 13 and 14.

Lerner, Janet. *Learning Disabilities.* 4th ed. Boston: Houghton Mifflin, 1985.

Levine, Daniel U. "Successful Approaches to Improving Academic Achievement in Inner-City Elementary Schools." *Phi Delta Kappan* 63 (April 1982): 523–26.

Loeb, Vernon. "In Schools Here, Asians Find Success." *Philadelphia Inquirer* (March 16, 1984): 1-A, 16-A.

Ludlow, Barbara L. *Teaching the Learning Disabled.* Bloomington, Ind.: Phi Delta Kappa Educational Foundation, 1982.

Lyon, Harry C., Jr. "Our Most Neglected Natural Resource." *Today's Education* 70 (February–March 1981): 18 E.

638

Teaching
Reading in
Today's
Elementary
Schools

Mace-Matluck, Betty J. "Literacy Instruction in Bilingual Settings: A Synthesis of Current Research." Los Alamitos, Calif.: National Center for Bilingual Research, 1982. [ED 222 079]

Maring, Gerald H., Gail Chase Furman, and Judy Blum-Anderson. "Five Cooperative Learning Strategies for Mainstreamed Youngsters in Content Area Classrooms." *The Reading Teacher* 39 (December 1985): 310–13.

Marland, Sidney. *Education of the Gifted and Talented: Report to Congress of the United States by the U.S. Commissioner of Education.* (Washington, D.C.: U.S. Office of Education, 1971).

Mason, Jana M., and Kathryn H. Au. *Reading Instruction for Today.* Glenview, Ill.: Scott, Foresman, 1986, Chapter 9.

McGuinness, Diane. *When Children Don't Learn.* New York: Basic Books, 1985.

Moustafa, Margaret, and Joyce Penrose. "Comprehensible Input PLUS the Language Experience Approach: Reading Instruction for Limited English Speaking Students." *The Reading Teacher* 38 (March 1985): 640–47.

Norton, Donna. *Through the Eyes of a Child.* 2nd ed. Columbus, Ohio: Charles E. Merrill, 1987, Chapter 11.

Ovando, Carlos J., and Virginia P. Collier. *Bilingual and ESL Classrooms.* New York: McGraw-Hill, 1985.

Padek, Nancy D. "The Language and Educational Needs of Children Who Speak Black English." *The Reading Teacher* 35 (November 1981): 144–51.

Padrón, Yolanda N., Stephanie L. Knight, and Hersholt C. Waxman. "Analyzing Bilingual and Monolingual Students' Perceptions of Their Reading Strategies." *The Reading Teacher* 39 (January 1986): 430–33.

Plisko, Valena White, and Joyce D. Stern, eds. "Educating Handicapped Students." *The Condition of Education.* Washington, D.C.: Statistical Report, National Center for Education Statistics, U.S. Department of Education, 1985, pp. 177–99.

Quay, H. C. "Classification in the Treatment of Delinquency and Antisocial Behavior." In *Issues of the Classification of Children,* N. Hobbs, ed., Vol. 1, San Francisco: Jossey-Bass, 1975.

Quay, H. C. "Patterns of Aggression, Withdrawal and Immaturity." In *Psychopathological Disorders of Childhood,* H. C. Quay and J. S. Werry, eds. New York: Wiley, 1972.

Radencich, Marguerite C. "Books That Promote Positive Attitudes Toward Second Language Learning." *The Reading Teacher* 38 (February 1985): 528–30.

Ramirez, Arnulfo G. *Bilingualism Through Schooling: Cross-Cultural Education for Minority and Majority Students.* Albany: State University of New York Press, 1985.

Reed, Linda. "ERIC/RCS The Migrant Child in the Elementary Classroom." *The Reading Teacher* 31 (March 1978): 730–33.

Romney, David M. *Dealing with Abnormal Behavior in the Classroom.* Bloomington, Ind.: Phi Delta Kappa Educational Foundation, 1986.

Rouse, Michael W., and Julie B. Ryan. "Teacher's Guide to Vision Problems." *The Reading Teacher* 38 (December 1984): 306–307.

Rubin, Dorothy. *A Practical Approach to Teaching Reading.* New York: Holt, Rinehart and Winston, 1982.

Saville, Muriel R. "Providing for Mobile Populations in Bilingual and Migrant Education Programs." In *Reading for the Disadvantaged: Problems of Linguistically Different Learners,* Thomas D. Horn, ed. Newark, Del.: International Reading Association, 1970, pp. 115–34.

Schulz, Jane B., and Ann P. Turnbull. *Mainstreaming Handicapped Students.* 2nd ed. Boston: Allyn and Bacon, 1984, Chapter 6.

Sedlak, Robert A., and Denise M. Sedlak. *Teaching the Educable Mentally Retarded.* Albany: State University of New York Press, 1985.

Sinatra, Richard C., Josephine Stahl-Gemake, and David N. Berg. "Improving Reading Comprehension of Disabled Readers Through Semantic Mapping." *The Reading Teacher* 38 (October 1984): 22–29.

Simpson-Tyson, Audrey K. "Are Native American First Graders Ready to Read?" *The Reading Teacher* 31 (April 1978): 798–801.

Smith, Sally L. "Plain Talk About Children with Learning Disabilities." *Today's Education* 70 (February–March 1981): 46 E–52 E.

Stahl-Gemake, Josephine, and Francine Guastello. "Using Story Grammar with Students of English as a Foreign Language to Compose Original Fairy and Folktales." *The Reading Teacher* 38 (November 1984): 213–16.

Stewart, William A. *Appalachian Advance* 4 (September 1969): 12.

Thomas, M. Donald. *Pluralism Gone Mad.* Bloomington, Ind.: Phi Delta Kappa Educational Foundation, 1981.

Thonis, Eleanor Wall. *Literacy for America's Spanish Speaking Children.* Newark, Del.: International Reading Association, 1976.

Van Riper, C. *Speech Correction: Principles and Methods.* 6th ed. Englewood Cliffs, N.J.: Prentice-Hall, 1978.

Varnhagen, Connie K., and Susan R. Goldman. "Improving Comprehension: Causal Relations Instruction for Learning Handicapped Learners." *The Reading Teacher* 39 (May 1986): 896–904.

Wallach, G. P., and S. C. Goldsmith. "Language-based Learning Disabilities: Reading Is Language Too!" *Journal of Learning Disabilities* 10 (March 1977): 178–83.

Walters, Ken, and Lee Gunderson. "Effects of Parent Volunteers Reading First Language (L1) Books to ESL Students." *The Reading Teacher* 39 (October 1985): 66–69.

Wilhoyte, Cheryl H. "Contracting: A Bridge Between the Classroom and Resource Room." *The Reading Teacher* 30 (January 1977): 376–78.

Wong Fillmore, Lily. "Research Currents: Equity or Excellence?" *Language Arts* 63 (September 1986): 474–81.

Glossary

Achievement grouping   Placing pupils into various groups on the basis of achievement.

Achievement test   Measures the extent to which a person has assimilated a body of information.

Affective   Relating to attitudes, interests, values, appreciations, and opinions.

Analogies   Comparisons of two similar relationships, stated in the form of the following example: *Author* is to *book* as *artist* is to *painting.*

Analytic approach to phonics instruction   Teaching the sounds of letters in already known words. Sight words are taught first; letter sounds second.

Anaphora   Use of a word as a substitute for another word or group of words.

Anticipation guides   Sets of declarative statements related to materials about to be read that are designed to stimulate thinking and discussion.

Antiphonal   Characterized by choral reading or speaking performed by two alternating groups.

Antonyms   A pair of words that have opposite meanings.

Appositive   A word or a phrase placed beside another word or phrase as an added explanation.

Aptitude test   Measures general academic abilities and other features that indicate an ability to learn or develop proficiency in some area.

Arrays   Freeform outlines, composed of key words and phrases from a story arranged in a way that shows their relationships.

Articulation   Formation of speech sounds that involves producing words.

Assessment   Procedure of evaluating.

Auditory acuity   Sharpness of hearing.

Auditory discrimination   The ability to differentiate among sounds.

Auditory memory   The ability to recall information or stimuli that one has heard.

Auditory perception   The way the brain comprehends information it receives by sound.

Auditory sense   Sense of hearing.

Author's chair   A chair in which children sit when they read their own books or trade books to an audience.

Bandwagon technique   An approach that utilizes the urge to do what others are doing. The impression is given that everyone else is participating in a particular activity.

Bar graphs   Graphs that use vertical or horizontal bars to compare quantities.

Basal reader series   Coordinated, graded set of textbooks, teacher's guides, and supplementary materials.

Behavioral disorder   Disruptive conduct that is likely to interfere with social adjustment and learning.

Bidialectalism   Ability to communicate in more than one dialect of a language.

Bilingualism   Ability to speak or understand another language in addition to one's native tongue.

Book-recording device   A way of keeping track of the number and type of books that students read.

Bottom-up models   Models that depict reading as being initiated by examination of the printed symbols, with little input being required from the reader.

Caldecott Award   An annual award for excellence in illustration.

Card stacking   Telling only one side of a story by ignoring information favorable to the opposing point of view.

Categorization   Classification into related groups.

Cause-and-effect pattern   A writing pattern organized around causes and their effects.

Characterization   The way persons come to life through words of the author.

Choral reading   Dramatic reading of poetry in a group.

Chronological order pattern   A writing pattern based on time order.

Cinquain   A simple five-line poem.

Circle or pie graphs   Graphs that show relationships of individual parts to a whole circle.

Classification pattern   A writing pattern in which information is ordered under common headings and subheadings.

Cloze procedure   Method of estimating reading difficulty by omitting every nth (usually fifth) word in a reading passage and observing the number of correct words a reader can supply; an instructional technique in which words or other structures are deleted from a passage by the teacher, with blanks left in their places for students to fill in by using the surrounding context.

Cognitive development   The acquisition of knowledge.

Comparison/contrast pattern   A writing pattern organized around likenesses and differences.

Compensatory program   An educational program to enrich the experiences of children from low-income families.

Computer-assisted instruction   Instruction that makes use of a computer to administer a programmed instructional sequence.

Computer-managed instruction   Use of the computer for such tasks as record-keeping, diagnosis, and prescription of individualized assignments.

Concept-text-application approach   A way to organize lessons to help elementary school students understand expository text.

Concept/vocabulary development   The acquisition of words and their meanings.

Concrete experiences   Direct experiences, involving all senses.

Concrete-operational period   Piaget's third stage of cognitive development (approximately ages seven to eleven).

Connotations   The feelings and shades of meaning that a word tends to evoke.

Conservation of substance   The concept that a change may occur in a system without changing the fundamental characteristics of that system.

Content area textbooks   Textbooks in areas of information, such as literature, social studies, science, and mathematics.

Corrective reader   A reader who reads about six to eighteen months below potential.

Creative dramatics   Acting out stories spontaneously, without a script.

Creative reading   Reading beyond the lines.

Criterion-referenced test   Test designed to yield measurements interpretable in terms of specific performance standards.

Critical reading   Reading for evaluation.

Cross-age tutoring   Tutoring between those of different ages.

Culturally different   Pertaining to those who come from homes that differ economically, socially, and culturally from middle-class backgrounds.

Decentration   The ability to consider more than one aspect of a situation at a time.

Denotations   Dictionary definitions.

Departmentalization   Instructional systems in which there is a different teacher for each major subject area.

Derivatives   Words formed by adding prefixes and suffixes to root words.

Diagnostic test   A test that helps to locate specific skill strengths and weaknesses.

Dialect   Regional or social modifications of a language; distinguishing features may include pronunciation, vocabulary, and syntax.

Dialectal miscue   Miscalled word due to dialect.

Diorama   A three-dimensional scene.

Direct instruction   Teacher control of learning environment through structured lessons, goal setting, choice of activities, and feedback.

Directed inquiry activity   A technique based upon the directed reading-thinking activity, in which predictions related to who, what, when, where, how, and why questions are made after previewing, but before reading, the content material, in order to set reading purposes.

Directed reading activity   A strategy in which detailed lesson plans are followed to teach the reading of stories.

Directed reading-thinking activity   A general plan for directing the reading of content area reading selections or basal reader stories and for encouraging children to think as they read, to predict, and to check their predictions.

Directionality   Reading from left to right and top to bottom.

Dramatic play   Simulating real experiences.

Echoic verse   Lines repeated after a reader.

Eclectic approaches   Approaches that combine desirable aspects of a number of different major approaches.

Ellipsis   The omission of a word or group of words that are to be "understood" by the reader.

Emergent literacy   A developing awareness of the interrelatedness of oral and written language.

Engaged time   Amount of time students are actively involved in academic tasks at appropriate levels of difficulty.

ESL (English as a second language)   A program for teaching English language skills to those whose native language is not English.

Etymology   The origin and history of words.

Euphemism   The substitution of a less offensive word or phrase for an unpleasant term or expression.

Exceptional child   One who deviates from the normal child to such an extent that he or she cannot derive maximum benefit from regular classroom instruction; additional or different curriculum instruction or setting is required.

Expectation outline   A categorized list of questions that children expect to be answered by a selection.

Experience charts   Written accounts of interesting activities developed cooperatively by the teacher and a pupil or class.

Experiential background   Fund of total experiences that aid a reader in finding meaning in printed symbols.

Explanation of a process pattern   A writing pattern in which processes are described, frequently involving illustrations, such as pictures, charts, or diagrams, which are designed to clarify the textual material.

Expository style   A precise, factual writing style.

Expository text   A text written in a precise, factual writing style.

Fable   A brief moral tale in which animals or inanimate objects speak.

Figurative language   Nonliteral language.

Fixations   Stops made by the eyes during reading in order to take in words and phrases and to react to them.

Flexibility of reading habits   Ability to adjust reading habits to fit the materials and purposes for reading.

Formal (standardized) test   Testing instrument based on extensive normative data and for which reliability and validity can be verified.

Format   The size, shape, design of pages, illustrations, typography, paper, and binding of a publication.

Friendship grouping   Allowing friends to work together for a specific purpose and within a specified time frame.

Frustration level   A level of reading difficulty with which a reader is unable to cope; when reading material is on this level, the reader usually recognizes 90 percent or less of the words he or she reads or comprehends 50 percent or less of what he or she reads.

Genre   A distinctive type or category of literary composition.

Gifted (intellectually)   Possessing high intellectual development, a mental age that is above the norm, and consequently a high IQ score.

Glittering generalities   Using vague phrases to influence a point of view without providing necessary specifics.

Grade equivalent scores   Test scores expressed in terms of grade level, comparing a student's score with average achievement of the population used to standardize the test (a score of 6.4 represents achievement equal to that of an average child in the fourth month of the sixth school year).

Graded word list   List of words from successive reading levels, as preprimer, primer, Grade 1, and so on.

Grapheme   A written symbol that represents a phoneme.

Graphic cue   Clue provided by the written form of the word.

Guide words   Words used in dictionaries, encyclopedias, and other reference books to aid users in finding entries. The first guide word names the first entry on the page; the second guide word names the final entry on the page.

Guided reading procedure   A method designed to help readers improve organizational skills, comprehension, and recall.

Haiku   A three-line Japanese poem.

Handicapped   One who is mentally retarded, hard of hearing or deaf, speech impaired, seriously disturbed emotionally, visually handicapped, orthopedically impaired, or possessing specific learning disabilities.

Hearing impaired   One whose sense of hearing is defective but functional for ordinary purposes.

Heterogeneous   Different or unlike.

Holistic assessment   A process-oriented approach for evaluating a student's abilities to integrate separate skills into an entire selection.

Homogeneous   Similar or like.

Homographs   Words that have identical spellings but sound different and have different meanings.

Homophones   Pairs or groups of words that are spelled differently but are pronounced alike.

Hyperactivity   High level of activity characterized by impulsivity, distractibility, and excitability.

Hyperbole   An extreme exaggeration.

Idiom   A group of words that, taken as a whole, has a meaning different from that of the sum of the meanings of the individual words.

IEP (Individual Education Program)   A written account of objectives, strategies, curriculum modifications, and classroom accommodations for a student with learning problems.

Improvisation   Acting without a script.

Independent level   A level of reading difficulty low enough that the reader can progress without noticeable hindrance; the reader can ordinarily recognize at least 98 percent of the words and comprehend at least 90 percent of what he or she reads.

Individualized reading approach   An approach to reading instruction that is characterized by pupils' self-selection of reading materials and self-pacing and by pupil-teacher conferences.

Inflectional endings   Endings that when added to nouns change the number, case, or gender; when added to verbs change the tense or person; and when added to adjectives change the degree.

Informal assessment   Nonstandardized measurement.

Informal reading inventory   An informal instrument designed to help the teacher determine a child's independent, instructional, frustration, and capacity levels.

Informal drama   Spontaneous and unrehearsed acting.

InQuest   Investigative Questioning, a comprehension strategy that combines student questioning with creative drama.

Insertions   Words that do not appear in the printed passage but are inserted by the reader.

Instructional level   A level of difficulty low enough that the reader can learn as he reads; the reader can ordinarily recognize at least 95 percent of the words in a selection and comprehend at least 75 percent of what he reads.

Instructions for experiment pattern   A writing pattern containing step-by-step procedures to be followed.

Interactive processing   Processing in which one uses both information supplied by the text and information from one's own prior world knowledge and background of experiences to interpret the text.

Interactive theories   Theories that depict reading as a combination of reader-based and text-based processing.

Interclass grouping   Forming groups from a number of classrooms.

Interest grouping   Placing pupils into various groups on the basis of common interests or friendships.

Interest inventory   Device used to assess a person's preferences in various areas.

Interpretive reading   Reading between the lines.

Intraclass grouping   Grouping within a classroom.

Invented spellings   Unconventional spellings resulting from children's attempts to associate sounds with letters.

Irregularly spelled words   Words not spelled the way they sound.

Itinerant teacher   A teacher who travels from one school to another to work with children who need special help.

"Job sheet"   Assignment sheet designed for individuals or groups.

Juncture   Pauses in the flow of speech (marking the ends of phrases, clauses, or sentences).

Kinesthetic   Having to do with body movements.

Kinesthetic-tactile approach   A method of using whole body movements and the sense of touch for learning.

Kinesthetic method   A motor approach to learning to read based on tracing letter shapes in words.

Knowledge-based processing   Bringing one's prior world knowledge and background of experiences to the interpretation of the text.

K-W-L Teaching Model   A teaching model for expository text; stands for What I *Know*, What I *Want* to Learn, What I *Learned*.

Language arts   Listening, speaking, reading, and writing skills.

Language experience approach   An approach in which reading and the other language arts are interrelated in the instructional program and the experiences of children are used as the basis for reading materials.

Language experience story   A story composed by a child or a group of children and recorded by them or the teacher.

Language facility   Listening comprehension, speaking ability, reading skill, and writing ability.

Learning center   An area containing several independent learning activities based on a theme.

Least restrictive environment　A setting in which a child can master skills and content; it resembles the regular classroom as closely as possible.

Legend (of a map)　The map's key to symbols used.

Line-a-child　Reading or saying one or two lines individually in a choral selection.

Line graphs　Graphs that show changes in amounts by connecting points representing the amounts with line segments.

Linguistics　The scientific study of human speech.

Linguists　Scientists who study human speech.

Literal comprehension　Understanding ideas that are directly stated.

Mainstreaming　Integrating handicapped or exceptional children into the general reading program of the classroom.

Metacognition　A person's knowledge of the functioning of his or her own mind and his or her conscious efforts to monitor or control this functioning.

Metacognitive strategies　Techniques for thinking about and monitoring one's own thought processes.

Metalinguistic awareness　The ability to think about language and manipulate it objectively.

Metaphor　A direct comparison not using the word *like* or *as*.

Metaphoric language　Nonliteral language.

Minimally contrasting spelling patterns　Words that vary in spellings by only a single letter.

Miscue　An unexpected oral reading response (error).

Modality　A sensory system for receiving and processing information (visual, auditory, kinesthetic, tactile).

Morphemes　The smallest units of meaning in a language.

Motivation　Incentive to act.

Multidisciplinary team　A group of people who construct an IEP for a handicapped student.

Multiethnic　Pertaining to various racial and ethnic minority groups.

Name calling　Using derogatory labels to create a negative reaction without providing evidence to support such an impression.

Newbery Award　An annual award for the most distinguished contribution to American literature for children.

Nonrestrictive clauses　Appositive clauses; clauses that do not restrict the information in the main clause but add information.

Norm-referenced test　Test designed to yield results interpretable in terms of a norm, the average or mean results of a sample population.

Objective-based approach　An approach in which instruction is offered to each child based upon needs discovered from the administration of criterion-referenced tests over specified objectives.

Oral reading strategy   A technique in which the teacher reads material to the students and has them restate it in their own words.

Paired-associate learning   Learning in which a stimulus is presented along with a desired response.

Pantomime   Dramatizing through movement without using words.

Paraprofessional   A teacher's aide or other adult with some professional training who works in the classroom to assist the teacher.

Peer tutoring   One student helping another student learn.

Percentile rank   Test score expressed in terms of its position within a set of 100 scores.

Perception   The interpretation of sensory impressions.

Performance sampling   Examples of children's work collected periodically for later analysis.

Personification   Giving the attributes of a person to an inanimate object or abstract idea.

Phoneme   The smallest unit of sound in a language.

Phonemic segmentation   The process of separating the sounds within words.

Phonics   The association of speech sounds with printed symbols.

Picture graphs   Graphs that express quantities with pictures.

Pitch   Highness or lowness of sound.

PL 94-142   The Education of All Handicapped Children Act, which provides federal assistance for the education of handicapped students.

Plain folks talk   Relating a person or proposed program to the common people in order to gain their support.

Plot   The plan of a story.

Potential reading level   An estimate of a person's anticipated reading achievement level based upon intelligence or listening comprehension.

Predictable books   Books that use repetition, rhythmic language patterns, and familiar concepts.

Preoperational period   Piaget's second stage of cognitive development, extending from age two to age seven.

Prereading guided reading procedure   A procedure in which children tell what they know about a topic and then read to check the information.

Process-oriented assessment   Measures a student's use of thought processes and reading strategies.

Programmed instruction   A method of presenting instructional material in which small, sequential steps, active involvement of the learner, immediate reinforcement, and self-pacing are emphasized.

Project or research grouping   Placing students of varying ability levels together so that they may investigate a topic.

Propaganda techniques   Techniques of writing used to influence people's thinking and actions, including bandwagon technique, card stacking, glittering generalities, name calling, plain folks talk, testimonials, and transfer techniques.

Psycholinguistic theories   Theories based on research in the two disciplines of psychology and linguistics.

Pupil pairs   Partners who work cooperatively on activities.

Question-only strategy   A technique in which the students question the teacher about the topic of study and try to learn all they can in that way before reading the material on that topic.

Readability   An objective measure of the difficulty of written material.

Reader's theater   Reading aloud from scripts in a dramatic style.

Reading checklist   Listing of significant reading behaviors and a convenient form for recording results of teacher observation.

Reading rate   Speed of reading, often reported in words per minute.

Reading readiness   The level of preparedness for formal reading instruction.

Reading readiness test   A test for predicting a child's readiness to begin formal reading instruction.

Reading/study skills   Techniques designed to enhance comprehension and retention of written material.

Realistic story   A story that could have happened to real people.

Rebus   A device in which pictures are used in place of words.

Reciprocal teaching   A technique to develop comprehension and metacognition in which the teacher and students take turns being "teacher." They predict, generate questions, summarize, and clarify ideas.

Reconciled Reading Lesson   A plan to use the parts of the DRA in a way that fits well into the framework of schema theory.

Recreational reading period   A time for motivating/stimulating voluntary reading interests and appreciation.

ReFlex Action   An approach for developing flexible readers.

Refrain   A phrase or verse recurring regularly in a poem.

Regressions   Eye movements back to a previously read word or phrase for the purpose of rereading.

Reinforcement   Something done to strengthen a response.

Relative clauses   Clauses that refer to an antecedent (may be restrictive or nonrestrictive).

Reliability   The degree to which a test gives consistent results.

Remedial reader   A reader whose reading achievement is two or more years behind reading expectancy.

Resource room   A classroom where mildly handicapped children spend a period of time on a regular basis, with instruction provided by the resource-room teacher.

Restrictive clauses   Clauses that restrict the information in the main clause by adding information.

Reversals   Changing the position or orientation of letters, parts of a word, or words.

Reversibility   The ability to reverse an operation to produce what was there initially.

SAVOR Procedure   A procedure based upon the semantic feature analysis technique, but focusing on reinforcement of essential content area vocabulary.

Scale (of a map)   The part of a map showing the relationship of a given distance on a map to the same distance on the earth.

Schema   A pre-existing knowledge structure developed about a thing, place, or idea.

Selection aids   References that identify and evaluate publications.

Self-concept   An individual's preception of himself or herself as a person, his or her abilities, appearance, performance, and so on.

Self-contained special class   A class for severely handicapped children in a regular school.

Semantic cues (or **clues**)   Meaning clues.

Semantic feature analysis   A technique in which the presence or absence of particular features in the meaning of a word is indicated through symbols on a chart, allowing comparisons of word meanings.

Semantic maps   Graphic representations of relationships among words and phrases in written material.

Semantic webbing   Making a graphic representation of relationships in written material through use of a core question, strands (answers), strand supports (facts and inferences from the story), and strand ties (relationships of the strands to each other).

Sensory handicap   Hearing and/or visual impairment.

Sequence   The order in which the events in a story occur.

Setting   The time and place of a story.

Sight words   Words that are recognized immediately, without having to resort to analysis.

Simile   A comparison using *like* or *as*.

Slow learner   One whose intellectual development is low normal or below normal.

Special skills (needs) grouping   Placing pupils into various groups on the basis of skills deficiencies.

Specific learning disability   A developmental disorder exhibited by imperfect ability to learn certain skills.

Speech impaired   Those whose speech deviates sufficiently from normal speech to interfere with satisfactory oral communication.

SQRQCQ   A study method consisting of six steps: Survey, Question, Read, Question, Compute, Question.

SQ3R   A study method consisting of five steps: Survey, Question, Read, Recite, Review.

Stanine scale   A ranking of test scores on a scale of one through nine.

Story grammar   A set of rules that define story structures.

Story mapping   Making graphic representations of stories that make clear the specific relationships of story elements.

Stress   Degree of emphasis placed on a syllable or sound.

Structural analysis   Analysis of words by identifying prefixes, suffixes, root words, inflectional endings, contractions, word combinations forming compound words, and syllabication.

Student contract   Negotiated agreement about what the pupil is to do and when the task is to be completed.

Study guides   Duplicated sheets prepared by the teacher and distributed to the children to help guide reading in content fields and alleviate those difficulties that interfere with understanding.

Stuttering   A type of speech impairment characterized by hesitation, sound prolongations, and/or repetition.

Style   An author's mode of expressing thoughts in words.

Subskill theories   Theories that depict reading as a set of subskills that children must master and integrate.

Survey test   Measures general achievement in a given area.

Sustained Silent Reading (SSR)   A program for setting aside a certain period of time daily for silent reading.

Synonyms   Groups of words that have the same, or very similar, meanings.

Syntactic cues (or **clues**)   Clues derived from the word order in sentences.

Syntax   The rules for combining words to form grammatical sentences.

Synthetic approach to phonics instruction   Teaching pupils to blend together individual known letter sounds in order to decode written words. Letter sounds are taught first; sight words second.

Tactile   Related to the sense of touch.

Teacher effectiveness   Factors related to instructional decision making that result in improved student performance.

Team arrangement   Two or more classes combined with a staff of several teachers.

Testimonial technique   Using a highly popular or respected person to endorse a product or proposal.

Text-based processing   Trying to extract the information that resides in the text.

Theme   The main idea that the writer wishes to convey to the reader.

Theory   A set of assumptions or principles designed to explain phenomena.

Top-down models   Models that see reading as beginning with the generation of hypotheses or predictions about the material by the reader.

Topic sentence   A sentence that sets forth the central thought of the paragraph in which it occurs.

Topical order pattern   A writing pattern organized around central themes or topics.

Trade book   A book for sale to the general public.

Transfer technique   Associating a respected organization or symbol with a particular person, project, or idea.

Underachiever   One who reads below potential reading achievement.

Unison   Combination of voices doing choral reading/speaking together.

VAK (Visual-auditory-kinesthetic) method   A reading program that incorporates visual, auditory, and kinesthetic experiences.

Validity   The extent to which a test represents a balanced and adequate sampling of the instructional outcomes it is intended to cover.

Variants   Words formed by adding inflectional endings to root words.

Vicarious experiences   Indirect experiences, not involving all five senses.

Visual acuity   Sharpness of vision.
Visual discrimination   Ability to differentiate between different shapes.
Visual memory   The ability to recall what one has seen.
Visual perception   The brain's processing and understanding of visual stimuli.
Visualization   Picturing events, places, and people described by the author.
Visually impaired   Those who are partially sighted but able to read print.
VLP   An approach to prereading activities involving vocabulary, oral language, and prediction.

Word bank   A collection of sight words that have been mastered by an individual pupil, usually recorded on index cards.
Word configuration   Word shape.
Word webs   Graphic representations of the relationships among words that are constructed by connecting the related terms with lines.
Word Wonder   A procedure in which children predict words that will appear in their reading material and read to check their predictions.
Wordless picture books   Picture books without words.

Appendix: Answers to "Test Yourself"

Chapter 1   True-False

1. F	9. T	17. F	25. T
2. T	10. F	18. T	26. T
3. T	11. F	19. F	27. T
4. F	12. T	20. F	28. T
5. F	13. F	21. T	29. T
6. F	14. T	22. F	30. T
7. T	15. T	23. F	31. F
8. T	16. F	24. T	32. T

Chapter 2   True-False

1. F	8. T	15. F	22. T
2. F	9. T	16. T	23. T
3. T	10. F	17. F	24. T
4. F	11. F	18. T	25. F
5. T	12. F	19. T	26. F
6. F	13. F	20. T	27. T
7. T	14. F	21. F	28. F

Chapter 3   True-False

1. F	10. T	19. T	28. T
2. F	11. T	20. F	29. T
3. T	12. F	21. F	30. F
4. F	13. T	22. T	31. T
5. T	14. T	23. T	32. T
6. T	15. T	24. T	33. T
7. F	16. T	25. T	34. T
8. T	17. T	26. F	35. T
9. F	18. F	27. F	36. F

Chapter 3 Multiple-Choice

1. a	5. c	9. b	12. c
2. c	6. a	10. b	13. b
3. a	7. c	11. a	14. a
4. b	8. b		

Chapter 4 True-False

1. F	9. T	16. T	23. T
2. T	10. F	17. F	24. F
3. F	11. T	18. T	25. T
4. F	12. F	19. T	26. T
5. T	13. T	20. T	27. F
6. T	14. T	21. T	28. T
7. T	15. T	22. F	29. F
8. T			

Chapter 5 True-False

1. T	11. T	21. F	31. T
2. T	12. F	22. T	32. T
3. F	13. T	23. T	33. F
4. T	14. F	24. F	34. T
5. T	15. T	25. F	35. T
6. T	16. F	26. T	36. F
7. F	17. T	27. F	37. F
8. T	18. F	28. T	38. T
9. T	19. T	29. F	39. T
10. T	20. T	30. T	40. F

Chapter 6 True-False

1. T	8. T	14. T	20. T
2. F	9. F	15. T	21. F
3. F	10. T	16. F	22. T
4. T	11. T	17. T	23. F
5. T	12. T	18. F	24. T
6. F	13. T	19. F	25. F
7. T			

Chapter 7   True-False

1. F	9. T	16. F	23. F
2. T	10. T	17. T	24. T
3. T	11. T	18. T	25. F
4. T	12. T	19. F	26. T
5. F	13. F	20. T	27. T
6. T	14. T	21. T	28. F
7. F	15. F	22. T	29. T
8. F			

Chapter 8   True-False

1. F	8. F	15. T	21. T
2. T	9. F	16. F	22. F
3. T	10. T	17. T	23. T
4. F	11. T	18. F	24. T
5. F	12. F	19. T	25. T
6. T	13. T	20. T	26. T
7. F	14. T		

Chapter 9   True-False

1. T	7. F	13. F	19. F
2. F	8. F	14. T	20. F
3. F	9. T	15. F	21. F
4. T	10. T	16. T	22. F
5. T	11. F	17. T	23. F
6. F	12. F	18. T	24. T

Chapter 10   True-False

1. T	7. F	13. F	19. F
2. T	8. T	14. T	20. T
3. T	9. T	15. F	21. F
4. F	10. T	16. T	22. F
5. T	11. T	17. T	23. F
6. T	12. T	18. T	

Chapter 11   True-False

1. F	9. F	17. T	25. F
2. F	10. T	18. F	26. F
3. F	11. T	19. F	27. F
4. F	12. T	20. T	28. T
5. T	13. T	21. T	29. T
6. T	14. F	22. F	30. T
7. F	15. F	23. F	31. F
8. T	16. F	24. F	

Chapter 12   True-False

1. F	8. F	15. T	22. T
2. T	9. F	16. T	23. T
3. T	10. T	17. F	24. F
4. T	11. T	18. T	25. F
5. F	12. F	19. T	26. F
6. F	13. F	20. F	27. F
7. T	14. T	21. F	28. T

Index

Student Response Form

Many of the changes made in the fourth edition of *Teaching Reading in Today's Elementary Schools* were based on feedback and evaluations of the earlier editions. Please help us respond to the interests and needs of future readers by completing the questionnaire below and returning it to: College Marketing, Houghton Mifflin Company, One Beacon Street, Boston, MA 02108.

1. Please tell us your overall impressions of the text.

	Excellent	Good	Adequate	Poor
a. Was it written in a clear and understandable style?	____	____	____	____
b. Were difficult concepts well explained?	____	____	____	____
c. How would you rate the frequent use of illustrative Examples?	____	____	____	____
d. How comprehensive was the coverage of major issues and topics?	____	____	____	____
e. How does this book compare to other texts you have used?	____	____	____	____
f. How would you rate the activities?	____	____	____	____
g. How would you rate the study aids at the beginning and end of each chapter?	____	____	____	____

2. Please comment on or cite examples that illustrate any of your above ratings. _____

_____

_____

3. Were there any topics that should have been included or covered more fully? _____

_____

_____

SR-2

Teaching
Reading in
Today's
Elementary
Schools

4. Which chapters or features did you particularly like? _____

_____

_____

5. Which chapters or features did you dislike? _____

_____

_____

6. Which chapters taught you the most? _____

_____

_____

7. What changes would you like to see in the next edition of this book?

_____

_____

_____

8. Is this a book you would like to keep for your classroom teaching
experience? _____ Why or why not? _____

_____

_____

9. Please tell us something about your background. Are you studying to be
an elementary school classroom teacher or a reading specialist? Are you
inservice or preservice? Are you an undergraduate or a graduate student?

_____

_____

_____